CNVR LEARNING RESOURCE CENTER

3 4022 02705 8746

P9-CSS-317

Max R. Traurig
Learning Resources Center Library
750 Chase Parkway, Waterbury, CT 06708

OLD BULLION BENTON

Senator from the New West

Portrait by Matthew Harris Jouett (circa 1825)
The Cleveland Museum of Art, gift of Mrs. Otto Miller

OLD BULLION BENTON · Senator from the New West

Thomas Hart Benton
1782–1858

by WILLIAM NISBET CHAMBERS

AN ATLANTIC MONTHLY PRESS BOOK
Boston · LITTLE, BROWN AND COMPANY · Toronto

COPYRIGHT, ©, 1956, BY WILLIAM N. CHAMBERS

ALL RIGHTS RESERVED. NO PART OF THIS BOOK IN EXCESS OF FIVE
HUNDRED WORDS MAY BE REPRODUCED IN ANY FORM WITHOUT
PERMISSION IN WRITING FROM THE PUBLISHER

LIBRARY OF CONGRESS CATALOG CARD NO. 56-9067

FIRST EDITION

ATLANTIC—LITTLE, BROWN BOOKS
ARE PUBLISHED BY
LITTLE, BROWN AND COMPANY
IN ASSOCIATION WITH
THE ATLANTIC MONTHLY PRESS

*Published simultaneously in Canada
by Little, Brown & Company (Canada) Limited*

PRINTED IN THE UNITED STATES OF AMERICA

TO

my mother
LUCY MATTHEWS CHAMBERS

and my wife
SUSAN ROSS CHAMBERS

The lives of useful and eminent men should be written, not for the dead, but for the living. They should display not a vain panegyric, but a detail of circumstance which would lead the living to the same line of conduct and the same honorable result.

—THOMAS HART BENTON
1818

"What are the facts? Give us the *facts!*"

—THOMAS HART BENTON
In conversation, 1844

Contents

PART IV

THE ORDEAL

PART V

LONG AND BITTER WAR

The Public and the Private Man

ONE "GLORIOUS FOURTH" in the 1840's, Thomas Benton was scheduled to speak at Hannibal, Missouri. Before the event, young Tom Sawyer (or, perhaps, young Sam Clemens) was filled with anticipations concerning this "greatest man in the world (as Tom supposed)." But he was disappointed when it turned out that the famous Senator Benton "was not twenty-five feet high, nor even anywhere in the neighborhood of it!"

The boy in Hannibal was not the only person of his time who envisaged Benton of Missouri as larger than life. The fame Thomas Hart Benton commanded in his day was immense. His name was a "household word," as contemporaries put it — and as he himself put it, with a dashing egotism which grew to match or exceed his very substantial abilities and influence. As lawyer, soldier, editor, political leader, and publicist, Benton was a large man. As a Senator from the New West for three decades, he was a powerful force in the nation's destiny. From the ominous Missouri controversy of 1820, through the stormy battles he fought against the "monster" Bank of the United States in the 1830's, to the alarms of civil war in the 1840's and 1850's, he was always at or near the center of the arena in every major national political conflict. His contemporaries saw him as the equal, even the superior, of his great senatorial adversaries, Clay, Calhoun, and Webster.

It is an odd turn of fate that a man of such stature should be so little known to our generation, for Benton epitomizes his age. In both his private life and in his long public career, he represents many of the salient qualities of his time. Beyond this, his story offers a triple interest for our own day — first, because he was a unique, robustious, always interesting, controversial person; again, because his career in context makes a revealing case study not only in the politics of his era, but in American democratic politics in general; and finally, because what he stood for is a part of the democratic heritage on which we may draw as we face the problems of today. Perhaps Benton has been so nearly forgotten in part because Jackson has been taken as the symbol of the faith in and practice of popular democracy Benton also espoused. Again, the loss of many of Benton's private papers in a fire shortly before his death has imposed on the biographer the task of combing innumerable scattered collections, if he would reconstruct Benton's life story in the round. Certainly, however, Benton deserves his place in the American tradition.

In the first instance, Benton's claim to a place as representative man rests on the sheer scope of his life and public career. He was born in the North Carolina hills in 1782; he spent his young manhood on the Tennessee frontier; emigrating to St. Louis in 1815, he became the editor of the second newspaper established west of the Mississippi. He was Andrew Jackson's friend and efficient Congressional leader, and a key organizer of the mass movement and political party that gathered around Jackson's name. He was instrumental in the 1840's in extending the American domain to the Pacific. He remained active until the day before his death in 1858. His last important work was a book-length excoriation of the proslavery Dred Scott decision, in which he set forth many of the ideas Abraham Lincoln was to symbolize. His useful, dynamic, electric life spans the decades from the father of American democracy, Jefferson, to the man who toiled to preserve the nation on Jefferson's principles, Lincoln. Thus Benton's seventy-six years embrace much of the seed-time of American democratic politics.

In another sense, also, Benton stands forth as a symbol of his times. More than any other leader except Jackson, he was the distinctive advocate and representative of the democratic movement of his age. In the senatorial cockpit his colleagues Clay, Calhoun, and Webster all served some narrow, limited class or interest-group combination — whether Northern and Eastern commerce, manufacturing, and capital, or Southern plantation slaveholders. In Benton, however, the mass of the nation's freeholding farmers, together with urban small traders and workingmen, found their great champion, an able exponent of their interests. His early, untiring advocacy of large measures, from free lands for settlers or gold-and-silver currency in the interest of plain farmers, to populating the Far West with free men instead of slaves, won him passionate devotion — and also the affectionate sobriquet "Old Bullion," which became a symbol for democratic, agrarian doctrines and action. Despite some confusions and contradictions, Old Bullion Benton became in his maturity the most consistent, persuasive national spokesman for the emergent popular democracy of the day. As such, he stood out from the ranks of lesser politicians, including some who served as President, like his friends Van Buren, Polk, and Buchanan. He believed deeply in "the capacity of the people for self-government"; believed deeply that democracy must serve as an instrument of popular well-being. As politician, publicist, and legislator, he labored to realize these principles in practice.

The age of Jackson, like the eras dominated by Lincoln thirty years later and by Franklin Roosevelt a hundred years later, marks one of the most exciting and consequential stages in the development of American politics. But the movement-and-party that Jackson led, like the movements Lincoln and Roosevelt championed later, was riven by internal conflicts, contradictions, and confusions; thus the character of the democratic upsurge in the age of Jackson, and its significance for the American political tradition and for the understanding of American politics, have been subject to continuing debate. In perspective, Old Bullion Benton stands out not only as *a* key leader in the Jackson movement, but as *the* dominant exponent of a distinctive faction, congeries of groups, and set of doctrines within that larger movement. It follows that we can achieve no adequate appreciation of the Jackson era and its long-range significance unless we understand the part Thomas Benton played in the portentous events of his times.

As a personality also, Benton was a near-epitome of important aspects of his period. He was a man of great muscular energy, physical bulk, and pugnacity, a man with an immense personal drive, a constant striving for high achievement. In his maturity, this drive was realized in a strong sense of public duty, and a leadership so firm and courageous that he sacrificed his cherished place in the Senate rather than sacrifice his principles. He had a trigger-touchy sense of personal honor, which involved him in fights and pistol duels; in an early quarrel in Tennessee he and his brother nearly killed his later chief, Andrew Jackson, and another angry duel in Missouri ended in the death of Benton's youthful antagonist. He had a showy pride in his own wide-ranging, self-acquired learning, which often prompted him to play schoolmaster in the Senate or in print. He was a powerful, polemical speaker and rhetorician in the free grand style of the day, and yet he was known as a man who insistently demanded the facts, facts, facts, concerning any issue; often he carried a point in debate by the panoramic array of evidence he had worked up in long days and nights of advance preparation. His intellect was sharp, strongly directed to practical consequences, and enriched by a curiosity which ranged far beyond political questions. He was indefatigable, and his sense of public duty never allowed him to retire. More than once, in his sixties and seventies, he undertook arduous speaking tours of a thousand miles or more in the blazing Missouri summer, traveling by horseback or carriage over dusty, rutted roads. Propped in bed, he triumphed over the racking pain of his final illness to finish a demanding literary task he had set himself.

In public, Benton was austere, and little given to the amiable arts with which most politicians cultivate their constituents. Yet, this street lion was a house lamb. At home, with his gracious Virginia-born wife, his daughters, sons, nephews, and nieces, or his circle of intimate friends, he was easy, charming, affectionate, delightful, courtly. His daughters in particular were handsome, or accomplished, or both — one of them became famous as the wife of the explorer-politician-soldier, John Charles Frémont. Friends, and political enemies too, were invariably impressed with Benton's familial devotion, with his easy grace as a brilliant conversationalist who listened as well as talked, and with his warmth and tact as a host.

When he was seventy-four, and engaged in a last, uphill political fight, Old Bullion Benton made an open-air speech to a huge crowd in the bailiwick of his chief political foe. The event was etched vividly in the memory of a contemporary, who recalled Benton as he stood, "his majestic form . . . attired in a handsome tailor-made suit of broadcloth" — "his eyes sparkled at every angle and his face was all aglow with dazzling brilliancy" — "the sun was hot that day, but those Missourians stood with bared heads for two hours, listening and shouting for Benton." Such attention and admiration was often Benton's measure throughout his long career. But his strong, unyielding political convictions, and some of the prickly, unyielding traits of his personality, brought him bitter enemies as well as devoted disciples. He was damned as a demagogue, charged with inveterate self-seeking and self-aggrandizement, even with dishonesty, scorned as a humbug, and castigated as an overbearing egomaniac.

The story of the forming of this complex, contradictory figure is fascinating. As a representative man in both his public and private character, he was the product of the early-American, Western culture in which he grew and developed. But particularly, he was the product of a special family background, and a special early experience — at sixteen, he embroiled himself in a searing incident which plunged him into disgrace, and gave him an overreaching need to prove himself to the world. His character as a man and a convinced democrat was formed in the rough school of the New West, and in the hurly-burly of national politics. These are the outlines. But Benton's motivations, personal character, and public influence cannot be understood except in the details of his own experience, of his private and public life.

To reconstruct the man whole, to describe and analyze the panorama of political conflict in which he made his mark, and to present the popular democratic faith he represented, is the purpose of this portrait in American politics.

WILLIAM NISBET CHAMBERS

Washington University
Saint Louis, Missouri

PART I

Making the Man

O you youths, Western youths,
So impatient, full of action, full of manly pride and
friendship,
Plain I see you Western youths, see you tramping with
the foremost,
Pioneers! O Pioneers!

— WALT WHITMAN

CHAPTER 1

Mainsprings

1782 - 1799

IT WAS MARCH, 1782, in the Piedmont region of North Carolina. The cobblestones which Lord Cornwallis had placed in the streets of Hillsborough so that his artillery would not bog down had been there only a year. About three miles west of the town on the right bank of a pell-mell hill stream called the Enoe River, a young lawyer named Jesse Benton and his wife Ann lived on their modest family plantation. In that month which usually brings a touch of spring and bright flowers to the foothill country, their third child and first son was born.[1] They christened him Thomas Hart Benton, after his mother's uncle.

The boy was born in turbulent times. It was not quite six years since Thomas Jefferson had written his Declaration of Independence, and the peace which ended the American Revolution was still a year in the future. Some five years would pass before men like James Madison and Alexander Hamilton gathered in Philadelphia to write a new Constitution for the new nation.

That same year, 1782, saw the birth of four others who were to be deeply involved in the Piedmont child's future. These were the children who later became the affable Martin Van Buren, "Red Fox" of politics and eighth President; the iron-willed and steel-sharp John C. Calhoun, defender of the Southern slave system; the granite-hewed Daniel Webster, able, self-important exponent of American capitalism; and the phlegmatic Lewis Cass, soldier, senator, and presidential candidate. With these and other leaders, like Andrew Jackson and Henry Clay, Thomas Hart Benton the man was to work and spar for decades, in the center of the American political arena.

By the time Thomas Benton was born, his family was well established on the Piedmont slope. Long before the Revolutionary war his forebears had settled in the hilly country with its deep-green pine forests, red-clay banks, and black bottom-land. His ancestors had come, not from the old, aristocratic Tidewater estates to the East, but from central Virginia to the North. They had been part of a current of vigorous English and Scotch-Irish settlers who had poured into the upcountry in the middle 1700's, and who, through their own individual efforts, had made themselves gentry in the region.

The founder of the family fortunes was the infant's grandfather, Samuel Benton. He began his great rise in 1752, when he was appointed colonial Justice of the Peace for Granville County, a huge area covering most of what was then central North Carolina. This was the first step in a long, passionate pursuit of political jobbery which soon led to other offices, including a seat in the Provincial Assembly. Each job gave Samuel Benton certain perquisites and patronage, and a chance to arrange deals on the side. Thus, despite some early reverses like a stay in jail for debt, the magistrate soon appeared also as a landed proprietor — Samuel Benton, *Esquire*. He secured for himself a large plantation in the western part of Granville County, which he called Oxford,* and also acquired a large competence in slaves and money, and a fine library which gave him a reputation as a cultivated man. As early as the 1760's he was a leading member of the local squirearchy and a favorite of the Royal Governor, as well as chief of the courthouse ring, political czar of the Granville region.

In 1764, Samuel Benton brought off a great coup. With a little log-rolling he got a measure passed in the Assembly to divide Granville County and build a new county seat in the section in which he lived. A commission, headed by Samuel Benton, selected as the site of the new town a plot on Samuel Benton's plantation, Oxford. Thus he inflated the value of his land, and guaranteed himself sales to the county and to the people who were bound to settle at the new court town. The rise of the squire of Oxford did not go unchallenged. An angry, aggrieved common folk resented the deals their betters arranged among themselves. Soon a movement of protest called the "Regulation" swept the central counties, and the status Samuel Benton had achieved was marked by the fact that

* His neighbors believed that Samuel Benton had been educated at Oxford, England, and the name he gave his plantation lent weight to this idea. But investigation of the records at Oxford fail to reveal any Samuel Benton matriculating there, though a Joseph Benton and a Thomas Benton, sons of Samuel Benton of Kings Norton, County Worcester, England, did attend the University *c.* 1720 (Letters from William Reaves, Oxford, July 22, 1948, and from C. H. Paterson, Assistant Registrar, Oxford, May 29, 1948). Anyone is welcome to speculate that Samuel, of North Carolina, was the grandson of Samuel, of Kings Norton, but I have been unable to discover any records concerning the Benton lineage earlier than the 1750's.

the "Regulators" made him a prime target. When Samuel had been made an assemblyman, he was expected to be "a poor man's Burgess," but it had turned out that all his acts had been "for that dear self of his!" As a county official, for entering a bond, "the work of one long minute," Samuel charged whatever fee he pleased, and then added insult by offering his victim a chance to pay by a month's labor on Oxford plantation.

This was the grandfather of Thomas Benton — "Gent.," shrewd, unscrupulous, predacious, but sure, self-made, cultivated, and successful.[2]

The family tradition was carried on by Samuel Benton's oldest son, Jesse Benton. When Samuel died in 1770, his will made Jesse executor, though it left the bulk of the land and slaves to Samuel, Jr., for the widow's and the family's use; meanwhile, Jesse received a special bequest of ten pounds to buy him that mark of a gentleman, a sword. He also acquired after his father's death the place of Register for Granville County, which he worked, presumably, for what it was worth.

It was Jesse who brought the Benton line to Hillsborough, in Orange County. There he was remembered as a practicing lawyer who labored steadily at his profession, made money at it, and took pride in it. There also he began speculating in land. His chief interest was in the area then ranged by hunting Indians, across the mountains in the far-western part of the province which was later to be called Tennessee. His first venture was as a partner in a concern called the Tranyslvania Company. Into this concern Jesse put what cash and talents he had, joining with local enterprisers like Richard Henderson and Thomas Hart, and a traveler and trail blazer named Daniel Boone. In 1775 Jesse and some other Transylvanians set out toward Sycamore Shoals in the wild mountain country, where in March they held a parley with O-con-os-to-ta, chief warrior and first representative of the Cherokee Nation. The necessary ceremonies were observed, Lawyer Benton read a legal paper to the feathered and painted Indians, and the Transylvania Company had purchased for some trade goods and two thousand pounds an empire of fertile western lands. The tract included the whole of the Cumberland River Valley in what later became Tennessee, and about two thirds of what later became Kentucky. Later, the Cumberland claim was voided and the company was given other — and lesser — lands instead, but the "Watauga Purchase" started the Transylvania enterprise on its road to success. On his own, Jesse also acquired other properties across the mountains.

Meanwhile, Jesse Benton had a full life in the Piedmont. He had his law practice to keep him busy, and he had a library which, like his father's, was known as one of the finest in the region. According to family tradition, he was a reserved, scholarly man, distinctly conservative in his thinking, who cherished his volumes of Greek, Roman, French and Spanish writers, ranging through Homer and Cervantes and Shakespeare to Madame de Sévigné. At some time in the middle or late 1770's, Jesse Benton married Ann Gooch, niece of his friend Thomas Hart, and by the end of the decade the couple had two daughters living, whom they named Margaret or "Peggy," and Mary or "Polly."

Gradually Jesse's life fell into a pattern set by property, position, and family. Certainly as a man of enterprise he did well for himself at home as well as in the West, acquiring land and chattels which he managed in a business-like way with a painstaking grasp of detail. His pride was the family plantation of one hundred and seventy-four acres on the Enoe River about three miles from town, but he also held more than a thousand acres in other parts of the new state, ten Negro slaves, and a quantity of cattle. He valued the whole estate at nine thousand, four hundred and seventy pounds, specie. As befitted a man of his position, he was elected to the State Assembly, where he put in a month's term in the 1781 session, taking the creditor's side in disputes precipitated by a currency inflation. For his services, routine and undistinguished, he was paid the impressive-sounding sum of twenty-nine hundred pounds — in debased paper currency.*

This was the father of Thomas Hart Benton — an exemplar of the spirit of Enterprise like grandfather Samuel, reserved, conservative, cultivated, always devoted to his family and concerned for their place and future.[3]

On his mother's side too Thomas Benton was descended from a family of consequence in the Piedmont. The most prominent member of this line was Thomas Hart, born in Virginia of a family that dated its American residence back to 1690; a delegate to the first North Carolina revolutionary convention in 1774, and a colonel in the Patriot army, he had business interests so extensive that when he left North Carolina to live in

---

* The story has been widely circulated that Jesse Benton was the first of his line in America, and that he came over from England with Governor Tryon in 1765 and was his private secretary. Apparently this legend had its origins with Jesse's granddaughter and namesake, Jessie Benton Frémont, in "Biographical Sketch," 1, and it is repeated in Meigs, *Life of Thomas Hart Benton,* 13-16, and in biographical dictionaries and encyclopedias.

Maryland and later in Kentucky he found it necessary to appoint Jesse Benton his agent. The mother of Thomas Benton also came from Virginia — Hanover County. According to family tradition Ann Gooch was a lovely, brown-haired, bright-eyed girl who was a good companion to Jesse Benton, who called her not by the formal name Ann, but "Nancy." When she was a child Ann Gooch's parents died, and she was reared thereafter by her mother's brother, Thomas Hart, whose ward she was when she was married.[4]

[2]

THE CHILD THOMAS HART BENTON was born on March 14, 1782, when his mother was about twenty-four. As he grew, a blue-eyed, fair-skinned infant, he was always closest to his young mother, who took special pride in him as her first son — but she was aided in tending him by Milley, a Negro girl of twelve who was in training as a house slave, and little Thomas's older sisters, Peggy and Polly, were there to pet him and teach him his first words.

Before Thomas was a year old, he was moved with his family across the Enoe River to a larger plantation. This two-hundred-and-fifteen-acre plot, called Hartford or Hart's Mill, had beside the rushing, rock-choked stream a grist mill, fulling mill, and oil mill, all of which could be worked commercially; Jesse bought the place from Thomas Hart on an installment basis. The plantation house was a frame building surrounded by oaks, with a path running from it to a spring at the rear. Beyond was an orchard and the then fertile fields, all surrounded by the ubiquitous dark border of the pines, which reached to the hilltops on all sides.

As young Thomas grew, his father kept steadily at the business of shoring-up the family fortune. It was not all progress, and in the year following Thomas's birth there was not enough water to raise good crops or to run the mills commercially. During this "most fatal hard year," Jesse was happy with an Orange County clerkship he had acquired — he thought this "the best Mill I own," for it brought in a steady return of a hundred and fifty pounds specie annually. But the year passed, Jesse managed to add to his property, and while Thomas was still a young boy, his father paid taxes on the largest single landholding and slaveholding listed in the Hillsborough district. Meanwhile, he continued to pile acre on acre in the region beyond the mountains. He launched vast speculations in the Green River area of what was later central Kentucky, and along the Powell Valley in the mountains just east of Cumberland Gap, as well as on the Chickasaw Bluffs of the Mississippi, on the Cumberland River, and on the headwaters of the Obion River near the Mississippi, all in the Tennessee district. Much of this property was in inchoate or uncertain claims, but in claims it totaled more than thirty thousand acres, or the equivalent of a township nearly seven miles on each side — an imperial patrimony indeed for the family at Hartford!

In the spring of 1786, when Thomas was four, his father marked the family's prosperity by building a new manor house on "the pleasantest and most beautiful situation in Orange," as Jesse Benton wrote Thomas Hart. Around the new home he put in a twenty-acre farm, and he rented the old house and stables to a tavern keeper and planned to rent his plantation tan yard before fall.

In such fortunate circumstances, little Thomas could settle into the routine of a boy's existence. He had to learn to accept the fact that his father was away from home a good deal, for Jesse Benton's practice carried him around the court circuit in Orange County and beyond. But as the years passed, younger brothers and sisters helped fill the house — Jesse, Jr., little Nancy, young Samuel, young Nathaniel, and little Susannah. All the children, Jesse Benton remarked, were blessed with a good share of natural understanding. The two elder girls had been taught to sew, and under Nancy's guidance the brothers and sisters grew into a close, happy, loyal family group.

Years later, Thomas Benton remembered instances that punctuated the easy flow of his boyhood life. Once a young South Carolina lawyer named Andrew Jackson visited at Hartford, and stayed all night — he was then a tall, slender, graceful youth with handsome steel-blue eyes, who affected a broadcloth coat and a ruffled shirt. When he was about six, Thomas watched grimmer visitors who came to see his father. He never forgot these nameless veterans of the Revolution who had been induced to sell their land bounties to speculators for next to nothing during the hard times, and who now asked Lawyer Benton how they might get them back. The sight of the plain, defrauded men who came to see his father, sometimes ragged, desperate men with worn wives and hungry children, deeply impressed young Thomas.

Misfortune of another kind threatened the Benton family. Gradually Jesse Benton's health grew poor and gave way to consumption, and he worried more and more that the estate he had tried to build would not after all provide for Nancy and Thomas and the rest. To finance his investments, he had gone heavily in debt. "The thought which frequently intrudes upon me," he lamented, "of the uncertainty of a Man's Days, and leaving a Family incapable of settling an incumbered estate, carries with it a melancholy idea." Still he persisted in his speculations. When Thomas was four Jesse made what he thought "a Capital stroke," managing to enter and pay for, in his own name, nearly twenty thousand acres on the Cumberland River in the Tennessee district, part of the area purchased from the Indians by the Transylvania Company. When Thomas was seven, Jesse made a final effort to secure his claim to the Chickasaw Bluff lands on the Mississippi, in the area where Memphis was later built. He sent out a surveyor, who returned a few months later to report that he had run the boundaries and established his employer's rights. At home Jesse sought a new fuller for his mill — "Mr. Jones has become a Drunkard and the People suspect him of stealing their Cloth" — and he sought "some good Tanner" to come and "rent my Tan-Yard." Despite his ill health and his fears, the enterprising Jesse's standing as a man of property seemed to rest on increasingly firm foundations.*

His effort to establish title to his Chickasaw claims was Jesse Benton's last great attempt to provide for his heirs. Before the cold winter of 1790–1791 was out, he was dead, dead of the consumption that had haunted him in his last years.[5] The young widow was left to provide for the eight-year-old Thomas and for seven other minor sons and daughters as best she might.

In his will, Jesse sought to secure the family's present and future. He left Nancy a plantation on McGowen's Creek called Meadow Place to live on, the three house slaves Jack, Milley, and Rose, the horses, cattle,

---

* About this time, 1788, the big topic of conversation around Hillsborough was the new Constitution adopted at Philadelphia. The opinions Jesse Benton expressed toward the controversy reflected his status in the community. He noted with concern that the citizens of the Piedmont were generally against it; all, that is, except a few who "understood" the business of government, and these would have a hard time getting into the state convention which was called to act on the document. It was the old problem again, those who had and those who had not. Surely, Jesse Benton thought, the have-nots would never permit the new plan to be adopted, for fear it might cut them off from means of cheating their creditors with fraudulent paper currency, and "such-like dishonorable advantages" (Jesse Benton to Thomas Hart, Hartford, June 29, 1788, Thomas J. Clay Papers, LofC). A state convention in August, 1788, did withhold ratification, pending the addition of a Bill of Rights to the Constitution. After Congress had submitted a Bill of Rights as amendments, a second North Carolina convention was called for November, 1789, and Jesse's brother, Samuel Benton, Jr., was elected a delegate from the Hillsborough area. He voted with the 194 to 77 majority for ratification.

sheep, hogs, and fowls, all the house and kitchen furniture, the still, wagon, gear, and all the plantation utensils, and all the meat, corn, wheat and forage on hand, as well as a hundred pounds in current money. He left the children the other slaves and most of the huge western landholdings, with all to be divided into equal lots whenever one of the youngsters came of age or one of them married; and they were to receive an education at the expense of the estate and be taught the English language as perfectly as might be found possible. But the estate was not clear. Jesse had to provide that his executors Nancy Benton, Alfred Moore, William Waters, and Absalom Tatum might dispose of his lawbooks, the plantation and mills at Hartford, and such other lands as they might select, to pay his many debts. At the same time he enjoined them to advance whatever was necessary to secure his western land speculations.

Only thirty-two when she was made a widow, Nancy Benton was deeply afflicted by her husband's death. She became despondent and fell ill under her heavy sorrow. But illness or no illness, she was determined to keep her children in comfort.* At once she resolved to stay in the family home at Hartford, despite the injunction of Jesse's will. The problem of Jesse's debts was a large one, and Nancy went about solving it in businesslike fashion. She put herself in bond to her uncle Thomas Hart to pay the more pressing creditors in the neighborhood; she rented the mills at Hartford; and she sought a purchaser who could pay good hard cash for some of Jesse Benton's holdings in the Piedmont. Finally, she put herself in bond again to Thomas Hart, who agreed to buy a large part of Jesse Benton's estate when it was put up for public sale, and to hold it in trust for the family. Four years after her husband's death, by the time Thomas was twelve, the mistress of Hartford could pride herself on holding and paying taxes on a really secure estate which embraced one thousand, one hundred and forty acres of land and six slaves.[6]

The next eight years in Thomas Benton's life remained graphic in his

* A good deal of twaddle has been written about the economic standing of Thomas Benton's family before and after his father's death. One biographer, with a romantic notion of the alleged equalitarian character of the Piedmont in 1780-1790, placed the Bentons "on the frontier, where caste was, and is, almost unknown," and thereby assumed that the Bentons were poor like everyone else (Theodore Roosevelt, *Thomas H. Benton,* 21). Another actually feared that after Jesse's death his family faced "grinding poverty" (Meigs, *Benton,* 17). Neither of these writers went to tax records, wills, or other documents to find out what the structure of society at the time and place was, and what the Bentons' place was in it.

memory. Decades later he recalled the events of this epoch, and as his own children grew, he told them many of the things that had happened during these formative, adolescent years.*

One shattering experience was transmitted with particular vividness through the long corridor of time. During the illness that followed her husband's death, Nancy Benton was confined to her room, and her children were not allowed in the room for some months. Finally they were taken in. When Thomas saw his mother — so his daughter in future years remembered the story — he was struck with awe and terror, for there, in place of the gay, brown-haired companion he had known, was a white-faced, white-haired woman who seemed already old. Hesitating, the children went toward her. As they stood by her, she took Thomas's hand in hers, and placing it on the hand of his baby sister, told the eight-year-old boy that he was the eldest son and must learn somehow to take his father's place and help her care for the others. When the children left the room, Thomas broke away from the rest and burst from the house, running to a grove of trees nearby; there, with cries and tears, he made war on himself, trying to accept the ghost he had seen as his plump, bright, affectionate mother. His placid, happy life was demolished. For a whole week Thomas was restless and moody. The next Sunday, a chaplain who was a friend of the family took Thomas by the hand and led him again to the grove of trees. Here he read the boy a verse from a Greek text of the Sermon on the Mount — "Blessed are they that mourn: for they shall be comforted." They remained in the grove until the chaplain was sure Thomas understood the words he read, until the passionate young boy was able to reconcile himself to what had happened. But never again could Thomas feel the old, complacent security of his first years on the Enoe's banks.

The years that followed — Thomas remembered afterward — were

* The narrative of this period is based on memoirs. Unfortunately, not much contemporary evidence is available concerning Thomas Benton's earliest years, and in order to give anything like an adequate account it is necessary to reconstruct a good deal from reminiscences. The memoirs have not been used uncritically, but have been checked against one another, against such documents as are available, and against developments which may be inferred from these documents. Stories which do not stand this testing have been rejected. Recollections which are Thomas Benton's own have an added probability about them, for comparing his memoirs with the record when possible shows that he had a phenomenal memory. Many reminiscences of Jessie Benton Frémont are stories her father told her and she set down, probably with considerable exaggeration, which has been allowed for as much as possible.

dominated by his strong-willed mother. As soon as she was able, she started Thomas on a training designed to make him a man of cultivation and a lawyer — like his father. When Thomas was barely ten — a tall, vigorous boy — his mother set him to work on the folio editions of the British State Trials in the family library. She read the narrative portions to him, and then encouraged him to go on and pick up all he could. His mother also led him to the Scriptures, to Plutarch's *Lives,* to history in general, and to British history in particular. At an age when other youngsters adventured with Robin Hood and Robinson Crusoe, he was struggling with law folios, the Bible, the stories of ancient heroes, and world events. From such precocious reading, the boy took an early, childish dislike of Sir Edward Coke for his treatment of Sir Walter Raleigh, which made him unable in later years to quote the great jurist. Again, he mourned at the fate of Lord William Russell, Algernon Sidney, and Lady Alice Lisle, and he was much older before he realized that they belonged to another country and to another century.* How Thomas loathed King Charles, how deeply he grieved at the fate of those carried off at the royal behest to the dungeon or to the scaffold, there to be half-hanged and cut down half-alive, with the belly ripped open and the bowels torn out! It was strong stuff for a lad, and young Thomas early absorbed from his reading an old-Whig intellectual passion for liberty and hatred of tyranny.

A genuinely pious woman, Nancy cultivated the moral and religious education of her children too, leading them to the path of righteousness and the Episcopal Church of which she was a communicant. Stressing the minor as well as the major virtues, his mother warned Thomas against tobacco, and he never touched it; she asked him not to game with cards, and he never gamed; she admonished him against drinking, and he never took hard liquor in his life.

When he was in his teens, his mother managed to send Thomas to a private school in Hillsborough. This was an academy kept by Richard Stanford, a New England immigrant, who later served in Congress. Going

---

* All involved in activity against Charles II and James II immediately preceding the Glorious Revolution of 1688. Lord William Russell (1639-1683) was accused of treason, convicted in a trial of doubtful legality, and executed; Algernon Sidney (1622-1683), lieutenant of Oliver Cromwell, and author of *Discourses Concerning Government* (1681), was charged with treason, imprisoned in the Tower without trial, finally convicted by a packed jury, and beheaded; Lady Alice Lisle (1614-1685) was accused of harboring traitors and sentenced to be burned, but her sentence was commuted to beheading.

to school broadened Thomas's physical horizon — riding the three miles to Hillsborough, he could stable his horse and wander about the streets of the little town.

While he was still a student, about sixteen, young Thomas experienced his first adventure in politics. In the last days of George Washington's Presidency, the old General had recalled James Monroe from his post as minister to France, in circumstances which reflected on the minister's honor. Soon after his return, Monroe had published a hundred-page pamphlet attacking Washington as a deserter from the republican cause. A copy of this pamphlet found its way to Hillsborough, where Thomas read it. He immediately became incensed at Washington and sympathetic to Monroe — surely, Thomas thought, with precocious and doubtful wisdom, Washington had sold himself to the British King! He went into every company he found, declaiming with the fury of a miniature sans-culotte against the base ingratitude of the ex-President, and extolling the dismissed minister.

As the years went by, Thomas learned not only from books. In the rolling, pine-forested Piedmont there were hills to climb and rivers like the nearby Enoe for fishing or wading or swimming. As they grew up, each of the Benton brothers, Thomas, Jesse, Nathaniel, and Samuel, was given his own dog to train, though for a long time they had to share one gray horse among them.[7]

Under all these influences, Thomas's character took form. His father's death and the sight of his mother afterwards had demolished his early secure world. His mother had constantly urged him to take his father's place in the family's life — thereby very probably planting in Thomas the seeds of an ambition to win supreme favor in her eyes by becoming a greater figure than his father had been. A boy already endowed with a strong will, a sharp mind, and developing physical strength, he must under his mother's tutelage have acquired additional impulse or drive, and a heightened sensitivity, which portended some extraordinary result.

[3]

SHORTLY AFTER CHRISTMAS in the year 1798, when he was sixteen, young Thomas Benton set out from Hillsborough to the town of Chapel Hill twelve miles to the south. He was going to college, at the University of North Carolina.*

* The story has been widely reprinted that Thomas Benton studied law under the famous St. George Tucker, Revolutionary soldier, professor of law at the Col-

The boy could look forward to his college experience. The university, which had opened four years before, already had a reputation which had drawn to it the sons of the aristocratic Tidewater as well as a few fortunate youths from the Piedmont. The inviting campus, with its sweet-gums adding a touch of russet and gold to the forest green, was a center of pride to educated North Carolinians. When Thomas arrived, he was placed in the yellow-brick East Building. This two-story structure, with its small porches at either door, contained the dormitory quarters in which students lived four to a room, sleeping on beds rented from townsfolk. Thomas was settled with Fleming Saunders, William Cherry of Tidewater Bertie County, and Marmaduke Baker. There were only two-score students at the college. The curriculum had a strong classical bias — Latin introduction, Virgil's *Eclogues,* the Greek Testament, Telemachus, Cicero; and later, algebra; astronomy; De Lolme on the English constitution; Horace; trigonometry; Millot's *Elements of History,* Paley's *Moral Philosophy,* and Blair's *Lectures.* A dozen men matriculated with Thomas Benton in January, 1799, but of this dozen, only three were to graduate. The diet in the dining room was no more generous than that of the classroom — breakfast and dinner were minimal, and supper was limited to "the necessary quantity of bread or biscuit," with coffee, tea, or milk.[8]

In his second month at the university, Thomas was elected to an organization called the Philanthropic Society. Every student joined one of two societies: the "Phi" or Philanthropic Society, or the "Di" or Dialectical Society. These were literary clubs with regular Thursday-night meetings which gave the members opportunities for reading aloud, declamation, and the delivery of original compositions. These groups were largely responsible for college discipline, and to be dropped from the Phi or the Di was tantamount to being expelled.

Thomas kept apart from some other aspects of student life. He did not run about and spend his money in the town the way his roommates did,

lege of William and Mary in Virginia after 1800, and a judge in Virginia after 1803. Just when Thomas might have fitted this interlude into his life it is hard to say, and in any case an inquiry to officials at the College elicits the reply that his name does not appear on their books and that there is not even a local tradition to the effect that he studied there — and, "tradition through the centuries has usually laid claim to the education of every prominent man who stepped in the city limits of Williamsburg" (Letter from Robert L. Bidwell, Williamsburg, April 6, 1948). Apparently just another example of the improbable apocrypha that gather about any great name.

and they thought the Hillsborough boy extremely parsimonious. He did make friends, however — for example, a small, retiring boy named John Duncan Toomer, who remembered the rangy Thomas as a kind companion and protector. He also recalled that Thomas was not receiving money from home so liberally as he might have wished.[9]

Soon Thomas's routine was broken by a student brawl. There was a grammar school on the same grounds with the college, and one day he undertook to reprimand a grammar boy named John Lytle for conduct he thought unbecoming a small child. For this, the boy's older brother called Benton a "damned rascal." The high-spirited, muscular scion of Hillsborough and Hartford challenged Archibald Lytle to a fight. When Archibald refused because it was against the rules, Thomas taunted him and called on him to be a man and take his whipping. An argument followed in which Lytle called Thomas a liar, whereupon Benton drew a pistol. Immediately Archibald rushed off, and quickly returned with a loaded weapon of his own, but by the time he got back a professor had taken away Thomas's gun. Later the sixteen-year-old Benton assured his teachers that he had really not intended to *kill* Lytle — only to *wound* him under the shoulder.[10]

Early in March, young Thomas let himself in for a more serious scrape. One night when he was alone in his room, he went to his trunk, took out his key, opened the chest, and picked up a purse Fleming Saunders had asked him to keep safe. From this Thomas Benton took nine dollars. Toward the end of the week, Saunders asked for his purse; looking inside, he cried that he was sure some of his money was missing. Straight-faced, Benton expressed surprise. Nothing came of the matter, the other roommates ascribing it to bad memory on Saunders's part. Soon, however, William Cherry complained that his pocketbook with eight dollars in it had been taken from his coat during the night, and a little later Marmaduke Baker missed eighteen dollars and a shilling. By this time, Thomas Benton's companions were thoroughly suspicious. In his wallet Cherry had had a new Federal one-dollar note which he thought was the only one of its kind in the college, and now Saunders and Baker went to the merchants and tavern keepers in town and asked them to watch for this bill. A clerk in Scott's Store reported that he had seen the note in Benton's possession, and that the boy from Hillsborough refused to part with it even for specie. Meanwhile the roommates noticed that Thomas stayed up later than they did, and that he always tied on his neck-handkerchief carefully before he went to bed as if he was hiding something there. Certain that Benton was the thief, they went to President Caldwell with their story, and with President Caldwell they arranged a trap.

That night, March 16, Saunders stayed awake until almost midnight. When he was sure Benton was asleep, he got up, searched Benton's purse, and found William Cherry's bill there.

The next morning, Saunders suggested that the roommates all have breakfast in the country. The group walked out into the pine woods, with Thomas staying ahead of the rest until finally the others called him back and told him their suspicions, insisting that they be allowed to search him. At first, Thomas refused, but he was finally forced to agree. When Cherry's bill was found in his pocket, Thomas confessed to taking Cherry's money. He had intended to replace it, he said, and at first he insisted that he had not taken more. Pressed, he admitted to the other thefts.

Just three days after his seventeenth birthday, Thomas was exposed as a petty sneak thief.* It was the end of his career at Chapel Hill. On March 19, 1799, he was expelled by a unanimous vote from the Philanthropic Society, and thereby from the university itself.[11]

The episode illuminates much of Thomas Benton's future character and career. If it had been only one incident, if only he could have lived the last few weeks over, if only he could have replaced the money he had taken, if only it had not been so easy, if one theft had not so readily led to another! But the facts were there, and Thomas was swamped in the sea of humiliation. Out of this sea there emerged, apparently, new drives to prove himself and to vindicate his honor in his mother's eyes and in the

---

* The facts of this lamentable story have remained obscure for 150 years, despite innumerable rumors and traditions. The leading history of North Carolina and the semi-official history of the university credit Benton's expulsion to a "youthful prank," and put the stories of his misconduct down to political passions. These writers, and earlier biographers of Benton, either did not have access to the Faculty Records at Chapel Hill or did not use them. One biographer says that a trick was played on young Thomas, some money being hidden in his cravat by some cousins with whom he was staying, and then "discovered"; and this story, told on the authority of Thomas's cousin Rebecca Hart, is said to have given rise to the reports that followed Benton in later life that he had stolen money in his youth (Meigs, *Benton,* 53). This account sounds tailored to cover up the facts. There can be little doubt that Thomas did steal the money, for though his roommates may have disliked him and the Faculty Records contain only their testimony and that of one other student, to put the whole thing down as a hoax requires too many improbable assumptions and too much credulity in general.

eyes of the whole world. These drives were to render him, in the long future, compulsively touchy about his honor, extraordinarily proud of the learning he was forced to acquire on his own, and inordinately determined to achieve a station in life.

There was nothing for young Thomas to do but pack and leave for home. A Chapel Hill legend has it that he was speeded on his way by a large crowd of students who stood in the yard and jeered at him. According to this tradition, young Benton turned on his tormentors as he mounted his horse, and cried, "I am leaving here now, but damn you, you will hear from me again!" [12] This tale is probably no more than allegorically true, but if it is accepted it can certainly be said that for the rest of his life Thomas Benton exerted himself mightily to keep his word.

Expulsion was not the end of his disgrace. A day or two after he reached Hartford, on March 21, he was called to the door of the manor house to find waiting for him in the yard his former roommates Saunders and Baker, accompanied by another Chapel Hill student named Thomas King. Immediately King asked Thomas Benton if he had stolen some money from him also. He had missed some, and had not known whom to suspect until he had heard of Benton's confessing the other thefts. Accused again, Benton admitted that he had had a key made which fitted the lock to King's trunk, and that he had used this to open the chest and take the money.[13]

To be sent down in disgrace before his university career was three months old — to be shamed by his roommates — to have to come home to the family seat of the proud Benton line, there to face his brothers and sisters, and above all his moralistic, pious mother, and confess his errors in a scene which must have had terrifying overtones — and then to be shamed again in his yard — at last, young Benton's measure of ignominy and bitterness must have been full.

CHAPTER 2

Border Advocate

1800 - 1812

FOR NEARLY TWO YEARS, Thomas Benton and his family remained at Hillsborough. But as the seasons came and went, the Widow Benton thought more and more of taking her children beyond the big mountains, and settling them in the Cumberland River Valley in the new state of Tennessee; and about the time Thomas was turning nineteen, she, her eight children, and the slaves joined the great tide of emigrants that was moving ever west.*

The most-traveled route to the Cumberland settlements was a tedious trek. The emigrants poured along wagon trails through the Blue Ridge and down the muddy, rushing French Broad River to what was called White's Fork or Knoxville, where the Piedmont "goers" joined fellow adventurers from Virginia, South Carolina, Georgia, and Pennsylvania, and even from New England. Some were rich, and some were poor, for the frontier attracted aristocratic planters and slaveowners as well as poor yeoman farmers and ne'er-do-wells. Here were great wagons and farm carts piled high with possessions, and gentlemen riding blooded mares. Here too were crude sledges on hickory runners, or whole families too poor to own a horse, who walked through the dust and carried their possessions on their backs. This main-traveled road was, presumably, the road the Benton family took — until they came to Nashboro or Nashville on the sea-green Cumberland River. From this village they worked south across the pleasant rolling hills of the region, across the Little Harpeth River, and down between the sharp ridges of a long green valley. There they claimed a homestead of two thousand, five hundred and sixty acres on the Leiper's Fork of the West Harpeth River — all the family

---

* The exact date of the Bentons' exodus is uncertain. The family friend John Umstead places them still in Hillsborough in August, 1800, with Nancy thinking of moving, while the Tax Book, Williamson County, Tennessee, shows no Bentons for 1800 and a payment of the family lands in 1801. Taxes were assessed at the spring session of the County Court. It seems probable that the Bentons moved when winter lifted in 1801.

could prove of a plot of twenty thousand acres Jesse Benton had entered.[1]

[2]

THE WIDOW BENTON'S PLACE, as the few neighbors soon called it, was twenty-five miles south of Nashville. It was the outside settlement bordering the hunting grounds of the powerful Cherokee, Chickasaw, Choctaw, and Seminole Indians to the south. Their great trail, the Natchez Trace, ran within a few hundred paces of the homestead, and over it the red men came in time of war for plunder and in time of peace for trade. It was a precarious situation for the widowed Nancy and the nineteen-year-old Thomas, with children under age and only a few slaves. They soon put up a house, partly of wood and partly of stone, all resting on twenty-foot yellow-poplar sills which in turn rested on an L-shaped stone foundation. The stone basement story was dug several feet into the ground — like so many pioneer dwellings, the house was part home and part miniature fort.* From the wide veranda Nancy, Thomas, and the others could look over a handsome prospect. The house was on a rise about a quarter of a mile above Leiper's Fork, with the green valley below it and a slope reaching to the rounded hilltops of Duck Ridge behind. Beyond the creek in front lay another line of hills. Between these two low ranges the good, sparsely settled bottom lands of the valley ran almost ten miles east — to Franklin, frontier outpost and county seat. Seeking security from the Indians in neighbors, the family decided to try to develop a small colony by granting leases to settlers for seven years without price, with moderate rents thereafter. The little community was first called Benton Town and later Hillsboro; and before long it could claim a log school-and-meetinghouse, and a mill.[2]

Meanwhile, the Bentons cleared their land for crops — corn and cotton, mostly. A sharp new demand for cotton for export at New Orleans had quickly boosted the price until it was selling for fifteen cents a pound. The yield was good the first year and by fall the Bentons had a harvest of three or four hundred pounds to the acre. Young Thomas rode to

---

* The house is no longer standing. It existed, rebuilt and modified, until about 1915, when it was torn down and a new frame building was put up on the old foundation; one souvenir-hunter of the region, Kossuth R. Plummer, had some pieces of the yellow-poplar sills made into canes as mementoes. The homestead is on what is now a side road, some distance from the present village of Leiper's Fork.

Nashville to sell the crop, only to discover that the port of New Orleans
had been closed by the Spanish governor of Louisiana, and the cotton
could not be marketed. The next year they planted cotton again, and one
fine moonlight night young Thomas and his three brothers went with the
head Negroes to the fields to look at the crop. There it lay, white and
beautiful — the promise of a successful yield and a comfortable year. In
the morning when Thomas came out of the house, he noticed a chill in
the air. The cotton was blackened and ruined with frost. Once, when he
had just finished tilling a field of corn, Thomas had dropped the plow
into a fence corner and remarked to his brothers that there must be an
easier way of making a living. Now he vowed that he would turn to a
pursuit in which his labors could determine the result.[3]

But homesteading had its pleasures as well as its disappointments. A
young man on the frontier who liked to ride and to shoot, as Thomas did,
could practically live on a horse, with a gun; and Thomas — maturing
as a six-foot-tall, muscular, solidly built stalwart — developed a love of
horseback riding. He could also participate in frontier games, bear hunting, deer driving, throwing the tomahawk, jumping, boxing, wrestling,
horse racing. At neighbors' houses he could listen to impromptu concerts
on the violin, the bugle, or the fife and drum, or occasionally attend a
"frolic" at one of the settlements.

Another diversion was "winning" beef at shooting matches, and
Thomas was long remembered for his skill at this sport. Nearly every Saturday afternoon in fair weather a farmer with a steer to kill would bring
him in. The young men paid shares to meet the farmer's price and, with
the steer thus "put up," began a long round of target shooting in which
the man with the best scores got the choice quarters. There were five
"quarters" — the two fore parts, the two hind parts, and a sort of booby
prize consisting of the hide and tallow. Thomas seldom came home with
the fifth quarter.[4]

[3]

THE HALF-DOZEN YEARS after his arrival in Tennessee were years of
growth for Thomas Benton, years of finding himself as a man.

Traveling to Nashville in the fall of 1801, young Thomas got a glimpse
of the Cumberland bench and bar. He stopped at the new courthouse to
watch the proceedings of the augustly entitled Superior Court of Law
and Equity for the District of Mero of the State of Tennessee. Despite the

fact that he was only nineteen, he was called from the back of the room for jury duty in one case. He agreed with his fellow jurors that Andrew Greer, Jr., should have three hundred and fifty dollars' damages from Pleasant Emmeson, who had forced the plaintiff's slave Cato to ride a wild horse which had thrown Cato and killed him. One of the judges was Andrew Jackson, who had visited the Bentons in Hillsborough; he had come to Tennessee about 1790, and was already a legend in the new state. Watching him, Thomas was sure that he was a frontiersman worth emulating, though, in charging a jury, Judge Jackson used some poor grammar which grated on the better-educated Benton's ear.[5]

Life in Tennessee was rude compared with the graces of Hillsborough, but the Bentons' background and their holdings in slaves and lands made them "quality." Of the two hundred and fifty freeholders in Williamson County, fewer than a score had as much land or as many slaves as the Bentons had. As a gentleman of at least some leisure, Thomas found time to read in the books of his father's fine library. A serious-minded, inquiring youth, he considered history and geography light reading; when he studied, he turned to civil and common law, and the procedures of law usually pondered by law students. If he was never to have a university degree, he was determined to *know* as much as most university men, or more.[6]

In the summer of 1803, news reached the Cumberland that the United States had purchased the vast territory called Louisiana from Napoleon of France. This was a boon to the Tennessee settlers, dependent, as Thomas had learned to his sorrow, on the whim of foreign governors in New Orleans for the chance to sell their crops. In a practical application of the ideals of Thomas Jefferson, the young Republic had acquired millions of acres into which new waves of freeholders or yeomen farmers could spill, and Thomas Benton always thought of the event as second only to the great Revolution itself.

In 1804 Thomas left the farm to teach school, and to teach himself more about the law as he did so. The school was at Duck River, an isolated spot about forty miles west of Leiper's Fork. There for the winter, Thomas was determined to have books, even if he put himself in debt for them. He had made friends with John Hardeman and Nicholas Perkins Hardeman, general store proprietors; the latter was also the first clerk of the Williamson County court. In December Benton wrote the Hardemans from his school: "Those books I spoke of when with you, I request you will now send me. They are: Millot's General History;

Legar's Fred on William; Cooke's Voyages; Goldsmith's Natural History;
Gay's Fables and Sheridan's dictionary." But the schoolteacher needed
more prosaic items too — "Further, I want you to send me an almanac,
not a last year's one, a pen knife, best double bladed, a comb to
straighten out my hair with, a pair of black cotton stockings, half a dozen
quires of common writing paper, and one pair of strong coarse shoes, any
size." He wanted all this on tick. Putting it in somewhat high-flown language, he asked for his account — "a knowledge of it will interest me in
the regulation of my financial concern"; though he knew very well that
he was "more thine than mine own." [7]

The next year, teacher Benton was back in Nashville at the Mero
Court, but this time he was no mere hanger-on. In August, 1805, he
claimed, a man named Jim Clendennin had stopped him on the road,
poked a pistol at his ribs, and taken from him forty Spanish milled dollars. In November, Clendennin was brought to trial, and his accuser
went to Nashville as a witness — but the prosecutor failed to convince
the jurors beyond a reasonable doubt, and Jim Clendennin went free. [8]

As the years passed, the country went on growing. Where pioneers
had hunted and trapped, trading furs for liquor and flintlocks, settled
farmers or yeomen were now swapping their crops of cotton and tobacco
for hardware, drygoods, and home furnishings. Soon, brick and stone
buildings began to appear, and even window glass. At the same time
more and more taverns opened — the newly established *Impartial Review and Cumberland Repository* called them, in 1806, "places where
men sell madness by the bottle." The madness-mills were not for young
Benton. While men about him, indulging the most common vice of the
frontier, sank their fortunes and dissolved their talents in whisky, he held
to his mother's precept and his own resolution of abstinence.

By 1806, when he was twenty-four, Thomas was ready to venture into
law practice. His mother's aspirations and his own ambitions — that he
should be a lawyer like his father — were about to be realized. To get a
license he simply appeared before the judges of the Superior Court of
Mero, headed by Hugh L. White, who certified him as an attorney permitted to practice in any court in the state. On July 15, 1806, he came
before the court of Williamson County, showed his license, took the
oaths, and was admitted to the Williamson bar — and waited for cases.
In a growing community, in which land titles were doubtful, the ups and
downs of fortune uncertain, and most men's standing insecure, contentious settlers often fought in the streets, and brought to law issue after

issue involving only a few dollars or a few acres. At first, however, few
of these cases went to Benton, for people would not trust a neophyte until he had proved himself. A young lawyer therefore had to work at his
own expense, or appear to hang without employment on the rear of the
bar. Fortunately Thomas had influential friends — such leaders as
Thomas Hardeman and others helped him. He set up an office in a little
brick building near the new Franklin courthouse, and gradually he won
clients — though some people recalled that his manner was unformed,
while others thought his full, forceful voice harsh and untuned. His earliest concerns were, apparently, with the barest routine business — co-
signing bonds, aiding in property sales, and the like.[9] In addition, there
was the lawyers' "circuit" to ride. The Williamson court held its quarter
sessions in January, April, July, and October, and soon he was also ranging east to Rutherford County, and south to Maury County.

On these journeys Thomas met other ambitious young lawyers, men
who had the world before them and nothing but their exertions to depend
on. All of them spent long leisure hours reading — history, poetry, elocu-
tion, biography. They went through books like beavers through the brush,
and were specially interested in the ennobling speeches of living and
dead statesmen. One item in particular sank deep into young Benton's
memory — Lord Chatham's resounding panegyric on the founders of the
American Republic, that encomium which became to early-day Americans a sort of gospel. Young Thomas also read Jean Jacques Rousseau,
spokesman of rationalist democratic thought, of belief in the natural
rights of man.[10]

At home, Benton soon found himself in contact with major events.
A coxcomb from New York named Aaron Burr, who had been Vice-
President and had killed Alexander Hamilton in a duel, visited Nashville, stopped with Andrew Jackson, and went on to Kentucky. Could it
be, as some said, that he had come to seek recruits for a plot to divide
the Union and establish a separate western republic? Moved by such rumors, a public meeting was got up at Franklin, two days after Christmas
in 1806, with Major William Neely acting as chairman and attorney
Thomas H. Benton serving as secretary. Speeches, applause, and finally
resolutions — the local citizens surely lived under the freest government
in the world, and would defend "that government by whose fostering care
they have so rapidly grown and prospered," and, therefore, *Resolved,*
"that the General Government sustains the most endearing relations with
this section of the Union." Again — "that Thomas Jefferson ought to

be rewarded with the affections of a grateful people, for his distinguished services." Thus was Aaron Burr summarily disposed of.

Meanwhile, the boom in the Cumberland continued, and prices went up and up. By the end of 1806, wholesale at Nashville, beef was three dollars a hundredweight and pork the same, and whisky seventy-five cents a gallon; while the next year, with as many as two hundred persons a day migrating into the state, bacon went from eight cents to twelve and a half cents a pound, and corn soared from a dollar a barrel to as much as five dollars. The boom and the immigration, bringing new contentions over land titles and small debts, portended a gradually increasing law business for Thomas Benton. He traveled from court to court mixing with the crowds of merchants, farmers and artisans. His darting mind gathered facts, impressions, ideas, and day after day he worked what he observed into a pattern of beliefs he could call his own, a pattern close to Western ways, sentiments, and hopes.[11]

When he had been at the bar about a year, one cause took young Benton to Nashville as an attorney. In the May term, 1807, he appeared before the Mero court to request admission to practice before this body — according to the Minute Book, "Thomas H. Benton Gentleman licensed to practice the law in the several Courts within this State took the oath to support the Constitution of the United States, the Constitution of the State of Tennessee, and the oath of an Attorney at Law he is therefore admitted to practice as an attorney in this Court." He then proceeded to argue and win an action for his friends John Hardeman and Nicholas Perkins Hardeman, involving a debt of $80.97 with damages of $6.33 and costs of $8.57½. Thomas Benton, "Gentleman," kept his connections at Nashville,* and for about two years joined in practice with a lawyer named O. B. Hayes, a land-law pleader whose briefs were noted for their erudite citations of previous decisions. His law practice finally

---

* In a memoir Jessie Benton said that her father took a case in Nashville more sensational than Hardemans *vs.* Maury. This involved a Negro slave girl charged with murdering a white baby she had been given to wet-nurse; according to Jessie, Benton argued that she had done this because her own child had been taken from her, and only after she had been hit over the head by her mistress when she demanded to know where her own child was. By pleading these circumstances, the story goes on, Benton was able to save the girl from a death sentence. While Benton may have taken a case for a Negro slave girl, the story as Jessie Frémont weaves it is improbable, in view of the fact that it was told years after by a woman steeped in antislavery sentiments, and has the general ring of the "horror tale" current at the time (cf. Frémont, "Senator Thomas H. Benton," 244). My own investigations of the court records failed to turn up the case.

brought Benton to a personal meeting with former Judge Andrew Jackson, at a frontier town to the south. The Judge, now retired, was just back from a trip through the Indian country, and when he removed his overcoat, Benton noticed on the white lining of the sleeve a tiny crawling insect. He brushed it to the ground, and put his heel on it; Jackson smiled and thanked him, and soon a conversation was under way during which the older man asked the younger's name and parentage. He recalled staying at the Benton home in North Carolina, and invited Thomas to visit him at the Hermitage north of Nashville. Before long Benton found himself a protégé of Nashville's distinguished citizen, a chance which was to provide important access to men of position and influence.[12] Though he was no leader at the bar yet, Thomas, ripening with an ambition typical of the Western spirit, was certainly on the way up.

At home, the younger members of the family looked upon their elder brother as a sort of stepfather. He was gentle and affectionate, and he enjoyed tuning the guitar for his sisters and playing and singing with them. But the happy companionship was soon broken. When Thomas was just establishing himself at the bar, his sister Peggy died of consumption. Soon after, his sister Nancy was put to bed, weakened with fever and torn with coughing. In January, 1807, Thomas drew a will for her in which she named him executor, and before spring came, she too was dead. The family buried her beside Peggy, in the small graveyard on the slope near the plantation house.[13]

There was other family business to attend to, less melancholy but harassing enough. Shortly before Thomas was admitted to practice, one Patrick Campbell had haled Nancy Benton to court in Nashville in a breach of covenant suit which grew out of some of Jesse Benton's land enterprises in 1783, in which Jesse had made surety for another speculator. A verdict of $4000 damages was awarded against the Widow Benton and against Thomas Benton and his brothers Jesse Jr., Nathaniel and Samuel, and sisters Polly and Susannah. In 1807 Thomas Hart, now living at Lexington, Kentucky, brought suit for $1493 against the heirs, "to be levied on the real and per'. estate which was of sd. Jesse Benton, dec'd." This was part of the sum the widow had bound herself to pay her uncle; she had faithfully met most of the debt, but had never been able to pay it off in full. This suit was also decided against the family, and a sheriff's sale of the family's entire plantation of Leiper's Fork was ordered. But Thomas and his mother were able to arrange a settlement out of court with Patrick Campbell, and they managed somehow to satisfy Thomas Hart. They did not go bankrupt, although their previously augmenting holdings were cut by half — to one thousand, two hundred and eighty acres and five slaves.

Despite these difficulties, Thomas always maintained his regard for Thomas Hart, and always used the middle initial "H" when he signed his name. He took pride in the fact that his great-uncle had been "a patron of Daniel Boone in settling Kentucky," and thought him "the foremost of the *social* founders of the State," eschewing politics "to head the utilitarian progress" there.[14] In April, 1799, a short time after Thomas was expelled from Chapel Hill, Uncle Hart's daughter Lucretia Hart had married at Lexington a dashing, popular young man named Henry Clay. In the years to come, cousinly connections with Henry Clay were to play an important part in Thomas Benton's career. All in all, the aspiring young man at Leiper's Fork could count himself lucky that he had such an uncle to give him his name.

[4]

AS HE WORKED AT THE LAW, Benton let his eyes wander off to farther horizons. The impulses that moved him were probably many. He wanted to live up to his mother's ambitions for him, and perhaps still to vindicate himself from his disgrace at the University of North Carolina. In a half-dozen years in the state, he had become convinced that some things were wrong in Tennessee, and he wanted to be the man to put them right. He was ambitious, and he was by 1808 a taxpaying freeholder in his own right. In short, he had both the motivation and the position to embark on a public career.

His early background had given Thomas a Federalist bias, but after a few years in the West he had conceived an abiding admiration for Jefferson. Furthermore, Tennessee had voted for the Democratic-Republican leader every presidential year since its admission in 1796, and no man could rise high in politics there unless he adhered to the Jeffersonian standard. Thus, Thomas Benton entered the political arena as a proper Jeffersonian. This did not mean that he took a radical position and classed men politically either as aristocrats who did not or democrats who did believe in rule by the common people, as Jefferson and some of his more doctrinaire disciples had done. There were significant distinctions in property, position, and power in the Cumberland, with most of the best lands taken up by wealthy investors or lesser gentlefolk like the

Benton family. Driven by the spirit of Enterprise, such leaders were building a society which was by no means wholly equalitarian, and in which popular democracy based on broad popular participation was still in the future.[15] On the other hand, opportunity and relative freedom of upward movement still prevailed, and the dogma of equalitarianism was strong in the frontier culture. As long as the growing community provided opportunities for humble men to become wealthy or comfortable, the Cumberland saw no reason to class people as sheep or goats according to whether they were rich or poor.* Young Thomas was compassionate, sympathetic to people less fortunate than himself, imbued through his mother's teaching and his own reading with old-Whig ideals of liberty and justice, and possessed of a logical, imaginative, efficient mind. Thus he began his public career as a reformer, a people's advocate. In keeping with the spirit of the Cumberland society, however, his advocacy was directed not to radical goals, but to greater equality of opportunity; specifically, to greater equality before the law.

In his practice, young Benton had observed that Tennessee legal procedures were burdensome to common folk. On court days he heard farmers, merchants, mechanics, and even lawyers themselves complaining at the delays, expenses, and uncertainties they faced. He carried a notebook, and wrote down the criticisms he heard; what he learned "from the unlettered orders of society, plain farming men," he then mulled over, as he sat his horse on long rides from court to court or waited in his office for clients. The whole judicial system, he concluded, was awry, and he expressed and elaborated this conclusion in a series of articles for the *Impartial Review and Cumberland Repository* at Nashville, entitled "Sir John Oldcastle's Remarks on the Judiciary of the State of Tennessee." Beginning in February, 1808, and running through July, these articles showed the young writer's self-conscious erudition in their repeated references to authorities like Blackstone, John Randolph,

* Interesting problems of analysis are involved here. A widely accepted picture of the West of the early 1800's, derived largely from Frederick Jackson Turner and the great Turner-*verein* of historians, is one of a thoroughly equalitarian and belligerently democratic society. But an inquiry into the records and a reading of works like those of Thomas Perkins Abernethy raise serious doubts about all this, for the distinctions of upper class and lower class clearly existed in some form in the Western society of Tennessee once it got beyond the trapper stage, though of course there was also great upward mobility. The present analysis is based on an inquiry into the records and into the general background as revealed in the press and contemporaneous writings, with due regard to the seminal ideas of both Turner and Abernethy.

Swift, St. George Tucker, and Hume. But they were throughout shaped in a popular, reforming interest; they were throughout designed as an appeal to the plain men of the region.*

At the outset, Benton attacked the Tennessee law's delay. Cases dragged on for years, and then were lost over some trifling error in the way an attorney had drawn them up — "justice is perpetually suspended on points and quibbles." The answer — a new system, "founded in common sense and the principles of natural justice." Probing deeper, SIR JOHN went on to examine the County Courts. Charged with administering county affairs from roads and taxes to arranging for the maintenance of bastards, and also with dispensing justice and interpreting law, they were generally composed of magistrates without legal knowledge. Any wily lawyer could gull them, and case after case was appealed by dissatisfied clients. Thus the County Courts were "so many little systems of attraction for collecting suits to feed the great vortex of the district courts," thereby increasing the expense of legal action by piling costs on costs. Even the Superior Courts were far from ideal. The traveling judges of these appeals courts, having only a few days at each place of sitting, could "just take a peep at the business that is collected for them" — and in such delays, costs again piled up. This system, OLDCASTLE exclaimed, *"is an oppression upon the people . . . [for] is not the speedy administration of justice a constitutional right belonging to every citizen?"* Moreover, people often had to travel a hundred miles across poor roads to Superior Court sittings, and then wait for their cases. "Justice should be brought home to every man," Benton wrote at his worktable, "and the centre of his own county is the place where he has a right to demand it." Of course, "rich folks may not feel this oppression, but to farming men it is a serious calamity."

There was an even greater weakness. Cases argued under common or

---

* The name Oldcastle was something Thomas dredged from his reading of English history. The original Sir John, born in the 1300's, was a leader in the Lollard movement, inspired by Wycliff, an important popular, anti-hierarchical, church reform movement. For his opinions, Sir John was convicted of heresy and hanged in 1417. Though Sir John was the prototype of Shakespeare's Falstaff, "my old lad of the castle," the stage character was little like the actual person. The authorship of the Oldcastle articles is readily established, though Benton's name does not appear in connection with them. Not only is the style and approach Bentonian, but Benton years later stated, in answer to a friend's request, that he had written them (recollection of John M. Lea, in Meigs, *Benton,* 56). In addition they fit the pattern Benton was to follow soon after as the chief architect of the Tennessee judiciary reform act.

statute *law* were handled entirely separately from cases argued under the freer principles of *equity,* though the same dispute might legitimately be brought under either or both headings, and thus lawyers often prepared two suits for the same case. Farmers and yeomen were often told: "Sir, you must lose your suit in a court of law, but I can gain it for you in a court of Equity!" The double system added further to the expense and trouble of litigation. A bill of injunction — money; a copy — more money; *"replication — more money";* rejoinder — more money; *"sur-rejoinder — more money";* a rebutter — more money; and finally, *"a sur-rebutter — more, more, more money."* A poor man with small concerns was bound to lose more than he could ever gain. The pattern of Roman jurisprudence should be applied to Tennessee, SIR JOHN declared, with "law and Equity administered together by the same tribunal, and at the same moment." [16]

The self-confident Franklin lawyer was not the first to cry out for court reform. The year before, the respected Hugh L. White had headed a committee in the Tennessee Senate to weigh the matter, but nothing had come of this inquiry.[17] Now, Benton's vigorous propaganda fired widespread controversy, and soon the issue was argued in courtrooms, in taverns, and in the streets. In the *Impartial Review* JUNIUS and MR. Z—— attacked SIR JOHN bitterly, but BRUTUS defended him in two letters, as did FARMER in five; and another self-styled husbandman who liked Latin and called himself AGRICOLA wrote four letters to praise SIR JOHN. On the other hand PERICLES, remarking on the reformer's "insolence," thought the whole thing a bid for public office. Young Benton let the storm blow — he probably enjoyed the hullabaloo he had set off, and the fact that as his identity became known he became a public figure. In the conflict of interests he had stirred, much of the wealth and much of the officialdom of the state opposed him, as did many established lawyers. But he had directed his propaganda to the interests of plain farmers and tradesmen, and he was sure he had most of them on his side.

Through May and June, 1808, SIR JOHN proposed and argued for a "New System" based on four main reforms:

> First, a single Supreme Court to sit alternately at Nashville and Knoxville, with power of supervision and correction over lower courts, but no original jurisdiction.
> Second, six judicial circuits with a court of one judge in each to hold three sessions a year in each of the counties out of which the district

was composed, with law and equity administered together in these courts.

Third, the county magistrates to be divested of power over law jurisdiction, and left to manage county affairs.

Fourth, the summary jurisdiction of the magistrates in minor matters to remain, with appeal to the circuit courts.[18]

The OLDCASTLE articles marked Thomas Benton's first major appearance as a propagandist and rhetorician. Throughout life he was to be a prolific "word-man," with a gaudy and expansive style clothing a factual and argumentative content, all of which became as much a part of his character as his driving personality, alert mind, and massive presence.

The law-reform articles certainly helped the twenty-six-year-old Benton toward a public career — as they also aided his law practice. From a struggling neophyte he became one of the successful attorneys of the region, and from 1808 through 1812 his name appeared in an increasingly large number of actions in the court minute books.

A pattern ran through several cases he took. For Charles Boils, he won a suit requiring Constable William Alexander to pay him money due and not yet tendered; for Charles Wright, he got a verdict requiring Constable Joel T. Rivers to make payment of a debt he had collected for Wright and not delivered; and for Isaac Crow, he won another case against Constable Rivers of the same sort. The critic of court abuses in the Nashville press was also the gadfly of court officers in practice.

But, having once aimed himself, Thomas Benton did not deviate from the political trajectory. He wrote a new series of articles about the Presidential election of 1808, signed this time simply OLDCASTLE, in which he made it clear that he was no extremist.* There were several contenders for the Presidency — Secretary of State James Madison, Governor Clinton of New York, James Monroe. To Benton it was clear that only Mr. Madison's election would insure a continuation of Mr. Jefferson's policy — George Clinton was too old, and Monroe was the man of a "little knot of protestors, the opposition band of republicans, Johnny Randolph & Co., the candidate of factious radicals." OLDCASTLE particularly deplored Monroe's affection for France and his antagonism to George

---

* The authorship of this series of articles is not so readily established as that of the SIR JOHN essays. Once again, the style is Bentonian, and a careful search reveals no internal evidence which would contradict authorship by Benton. In addition, one incident is related which places the author as of Benton's age, and general place of origin. All this, together with the signature, seems to establish OLDCASTLE as SIR JOHN OLDCASTLE, *alias* Thomas Benton.

Washington — why, the man had even kept Tom Paine in his house when Paine was writing his scurrilous letter to the President! Though he had sympathized with Monroe's attack on Washington in 1798, that was years ago and he knew better now.[19]

Meanwhile, at home Thomas learned a new lesson about the economic and social foundations of Jeffersonian politics. The great immigration of 1806 had carried with it at once a horde of speculators who crowded in to buy up the best plots of land for resale, and also a new wave of settlers who hoped to find a new yeoman's Arcadia in the new West. One of these Thomas Benton long remembered — "Granny" White, sixty-year-old widow from the Tidewater of North Carolina. Driven from the seaboard by poverty, with two orphaned grandchildren bound to her, she had no claim to land of her own in Tennessee. A kindly Irish freeholder gave her a fifty-acre plot on two facing hills — Benton never forgot the way the pumpkins Granny White raised had to be propped with sticks to keep them from rolling down the incline, or that part of one of the hills had to be torn away to make room for a house. But with only this advantage, Granny White and her children advanced themselves to well-being — money, slaves, horses, cattle, and new fields extending into the valley below. Here, Thomas Benton proclaimed later after he had had a chance to digest the allegory, was the true system. Cheap land for those who wanted to settle on it would provide a chance for small independent freeholders to make their way in the nation. Nor did this system have to be limited to farming. Throughout the country, handicraft producers, mixing their own labor with their own raw materials in their houses and in small shops, fabricated shoes, cotton and linen cloth, hosiery, lace, iron nails, and a host of other items — and near Benton's home small owners were operating cotton gins and warehouses along the Cumberland River, while the creeks were dotted with mills where processors who did their own work ground out flour. This small-commodity-producers system, as a subordinate partner to farming on the Granny White model, was everywhere. Over the years, his observations and his reading made the moral clear to Benton: Give the people land and opportunity, and they could build in the great Western expanse an Arcadia of happy, self-respecting, republican freeholders.[20]

A year after his appearance as SIR JOHN, Thomas Benton was a candidate for the State Senate of Tennessee from a wide district composed of Williamson, Rutherford, Maury, and Bedford counties. At that time, in the Cumberland, established party and campaign machinery was

Max R. Traurig
Learning Resources Center Library
750 Chase Parkway, Waterbury, CT 06708

practically nonexistent, and election to office depended overwhelmingly on the personal appeal of the candidate. Young Benton had a reputation as a lawyer throughout the region, his reform articles had given him renown and won the popular imagination, and he was elected. In September he made the two-hundred-mile trip east to the state capital at Knoxville, and when the Eighth Assembly convened on September 18, 1809, he was one of twelve senators to answer the roll call.

Though he was only twenty-seven, he quickly became a leader among these twelve men. The second day of the session he was named to a committee of five to consult with the House on changes in the state judicial system, and some two months later a comprehensive court bill reported by the committee won passage in both chambers. This measure set up a new Supreme Court of Errors and Appeals; abolished the Superior Courts and substituted five circuit courts which were to sit at stated times in each county seat in the circuit; and provided for appeals from the County Courts to the Circuit and Supreme Courts. It also placed broad original jurisdiction over matters of law *and* equity in the Circuit Courts. This "New System" was put quickly into operation, with its success apparently assured by the appointment of the respected Hugh L. White as one of the Supreme Court judges. At least some of the delay, uncertainty, and expense that SIR JOHN OLDCASTLE had condemned in Tennessee justice now belonged to the past. This was no small accomplishment for a young man, only three years at the bar, as yet a neophyte in political propaganda, and in his first term as a legislator. Still, Benton was not entirely satisfied. He thought the so-called Supreme Court was too loaded with other duties to perform successfully its proper functions as final arbiter of the law, and he feared other weaknesses. But, though he fought doggedly and alone for further improvements, he was able to accomplish only some further clarification of procedures — for example, that land litigation must take place in the county where the disputed freehold lay.

In addition to all this, Benton served on the committee on lands. Here he was at the center of an arena in which the fortunes of disciples of Enterprise might be made or broken, in which the hopes of modest settlers in the new Arcadia might be realized or destroyed. In an overwhelmingly agricultural society, land questions proved fertile ground for conflict of interests in politics as well as in law. A major land issue in the session of 1809 involved a petition from some old settlers in East Tennessee. The yeomen in the hilly country south of the Holston and

Max R. Traurig
Learning Resources Center Library
Chase Parkway, Waterbury CT 06708

French Broad rivers near the North Carolina line asked the Assembly to grant them certificates of pre-emption — that is, the option or first right to buy the land on which they had settled years before — even though they held no warrants or titles to the property. Some settlers came to Knoxville, determined to save their homes. Toward Thomas Benton, he remembered later, these roughly-dressed folk were at first diffident, for they were suspicious of lawyers and people of "quality," but they discovered he was sympathetic to the problems of farmers and would espouse their interests. The requested pre-emption law was passed, with Benton voting Yea. Meanwhile, Benton also submitted a quantity of pleas from settlers in his own district asking for recognition of their claims. Furthermore, he knew that many settlers had built houses and cleared fields on lands to which they had some title, only to find that other men had better interfering titles. He therefore proposed and got passed legislation to assure such settlers the chance to hold the land they had, or to acquire from the state another equal plot.

Still, Benton was not so free as some of his colleagues wanted to be in land matters. He kept to a middle course — pulled, probably, to the left by his admiration of Jefferson, Granny White, and the freeholding system, and pulled, probably, to the right by the cautioning influences of his early legalistic precepts, training, and reading. Perhaps what decided the matter was his background as a member of a family of middling gentry, not wealthy investors, but not poor farmers either. When a bill was brought in to allow persons settling on granted lands which they believed vacant to recover from the legal owners the value of the improvements they put on the land, Benton offered a lawyer's argument against it. *First,* the sacredness of contract denied the legislature power to authorize settlement on lands already granted. *Second,* under the trespass laws a squatter was liable for damages for what he might consider improvements and the owner not, and it was absurd to grant recovery under one law for acts liable to damage under another. *Third,* it was impolitic to encourage settlement on granted lands. The bill passed the Senate eight to four, though it never became a law.

As a legislator, Benton extended his humanitarian feelings to slaves as well as to settlers. On the second day of the session, he brought in a resolution for a committee to inquire into ways to assure slaves a fairer trial in cases in which their lives were at stake. In addition, he asked that the committee be authorized to examine the laws concerning the emancipation of slaves and the regulation of free Negroes. He was named chairman of a committee of three to study the problem, but no legislation resulted.*

Throughout the session, Benton had the legislator's usual host of local and special-interest errands to run. He submitted a divorce plea; introduced and nursed into law a bill setting up a new county out of part of Bedford, which was called Lincoln; and got measures carried permitting the county of Williamson to build a jail, and incorporating a water supply company for the town of Franklin. In addition, he acted on the usual round of routine committees, and his colleagues also named him alone as the Committee on Engrossed Bills, responsible for putting all measures passed into final and legal form. This job gave him many long evenings of labor, but it was the sort of precise, semiliterary work he loved. While he was in the Assembly, he also undertook at least one case of job-getting for a friend. He thought himself the "patron" of a young man named Alfred Balch who lived in the Cumberland area, and he was able to secure the post of Solicitor General of Tennessee for this protégé.

At last, the session adjourned.[21] When the *per diem* was summed up, Senator Benton received two hundred and seven dollars and fifty cents plus four hundred miles' travel expenses, for a labor of sixty-seven days. In that labor the man who began his public career as SIR JOHN OLD-CASTLE had shown that he was one whose actions were as vigorous and effective as his words. As he set out on the long journey through the woods to his home he could stand a little straighter, hold his broad shoulders a little squarer, throw his large head back a little further. He was Senator Benton, sir, author of the new Tennessee court system, father of Lincoln county, the man who engrossed the bills so they'd be legal, sir, and a proved hand at legislative policy and routine. When he reached home, he could tell his mother and his brothers and sisters all about it — his mother would be proud of him.

---

* Years afterward, Benton thought that the legislature had passed the slave law he wanted — "he was the author of a humane law, giving to slaves the same full benefit of jury trial which was the right of white men under the same accusation" (Benton, "Auto-Biographical Sketch," iii). But this time the records do not confirm Benton's often reliable memory. There is no indication that his committee succeeded in carrying any measure (*Senate Journal, passim*), and the laws passed by the session do not include one granting jury trials to slaves (*Acts of 1809, passim*).

[5]

BACK AT LEIPER'S FORK, Thomas could ride in the woods, hunt, read, or enjoy the company of his family in the chill winter evenings at home. Most of his attention, however, was devoted to an increasingly prosperous law business. As a man of reputation, he was now sought out by litigants, and he handled case after case and won judgment after judgment, though his cases were often suits over small sums. As he rode the court circuit, he still carried a notebook, with a light green paper cover and unruled sheets. In it he made regular entries in his fine, clear hand. Sometimes, the entries had nothing to do with the law — in January, 1811, he reminded himself to write once a month to Dr. Watkins asking him to return the copy of Rousseau's *Confessions* the physician had borrowed four years before. But mostly it was business, and the causes of action Lawyer Benton listed in his notebook were ramified — slander, trover, divorce, suits of equity, land conveyances, trespass, ejectment, assault and battery, all were grist for his legal mill.[22]

Land causes were the bulk of his business, most of them involving work outside of the courtroom. He had to advise clients concerning entries and titles, and he made a study, in the diligent, thoroughgoing way that characterized him, of the principles of Tennessee land regulations. Many land entries then were established without real surveys. An entry, to stand up, Benton noted in his book, should set forth the place where the land was situated, the nearest water courses, the nearest mountains, any remarkable places hard by, and the natural boundaries and other items that might divide it from other lands. The Franklin lawyer's clients would never lose their homesteads through *his* carelessness! From the fall of 1810 to the middle of 1812, Benton was active in more than forty-five cases at law.[23] If he was not exactly a match for the elegant pleaders of Nashville, who handled causes involving thousands of dollars, he was at least a leader at the bar in his own region south of the Cumberland River.

One matter in which Benton was of counsel grew out of a bloody feud. On a chilly October afternoon in 1810, in front of Bedford courthouse at Shelbyville, a man named Patton Anderson was approached by Jonathan Magness and his sons Perry and David. There were long-standing bitter feelings between the Magnesses and Anderson. Soon the conversation exploded into a quarrel, and Anderson pulled a dirk from his pantaloons — but his friends rushed up and dragged him away. The Magnesses stood about for a while, in close conversation among themselves, and occasionally curses were tossed back and forth between Anderson and his enemies, while the crowd in the square gawked and waited for something to happen. The wait was not long — after a few minutes, Perry Magness walked over and calmly shot Patton Anderson through the heart. The dead man had had a quick temper, and had tended lately to a sporting life which put him in the company of knaves, and to a habit of drinking which increased his passions. Nonetheless, he had also had important friends, including Andrew Jackson, who swore vengeance against the Magnesses. "Old Magness" and his sons were apprehended and brought to trial in Bedford County, but when they objected that they could not get a fair trial there the case was shifted to Williamson County, at the Franklin courthouse. There brilliant counsel contended the issue — the revered John Haywood, the recently elected United States Senator Jenkins Whiteside, and, in a very junior capacity for the prosecution, Thomas Benton, Esquire, of Franklin. Chief attorney for the Magnesses was Felix Grundy, a rising young man who was unsurpassed as a jury-swaying defense counsel. According to the later recollections of one observer at the trial, the nimble Grundy trapped Jackson into a damaging statement on the witness stand.

"Sir," the fiery, imperious master of the Hermitage is reported as saying, "my friend, Patton Anderson, was the *natural enemy of scoundrels.*"

When Felix Grundy made much of this in his summation to the jury, this account goes on, Andrew Jackson resented it and called Benton to one side.

"That is not fair play," he complained. "When you come to sum up for the prosecution, I want you to skin Grundy alive on that point."

"I'm afraid, General," Benton replied, "that he has got us down, on that point — flat on our backs. I reckon we had better let it alone."

However this may have been, Felix Grundy's efforts were effective. After a difficult trial in which forty-two witnesses were called and every point was contested, the jury finally brought in a verdict of manslaughter; Perry Magness was sentenced to an eleven-month prison term and to be branded. The next May, Jonathan Magness, accused of pressing his son to shoot Patton Anderson, was found not guilty. The case stirred bitter feelings, and for many years "Old Magness" was known to the citizens of the Cumberland as the fiercest foe Thomas Benton had.

Young Benton's part in the pleadings was a minor one. But as junior counsel, he had to precede his elders in the summation, and he outdid himself. When he had finished, Andrew Jackson complimented him heartily — though Benton later suspected that Jackson found his efforts better than they were simply because they lay on the side of his feelings. What had been an acquaintanceship now ripened into an intimacy, and what had been an occasional visit to the Hermitage now became a matter of regular stops of a friend with a friend.[24] The young man from Leiper's Fork had been adopted by the kingmaker of Middle Tennessee.

Perhaps because he was so occupied with the law, or perhaps because he had accomplished his court reform, Thomas Benton did not seek re-election to the Senate. He stayed on the side lines, and saw Colonel Newton Cannon defeat his old friend John Hardeman for the post.

[6]

MEANWHILE, THE BENTON PLANTATION prospered, and so did the family. In March, 1810, Thomas advertised in a new Nashville paper, the *Democratic Clarion,* that he and his brothers and sisters would petition the court of Maury County for a division of thirty-two hundred acres left them by their Uncle Thomas Hart, who had died at Lexington. That same year, the prosperous family sent Susannah to a boarding school for young ladies at Franklin. Here "Brother THB" visited her one Sunday in October; he, who enjoyed good conversation so much, was pleased to find that his once taciturn sister was developing a fondness for talking. It was a gay place, everyone was as merry as a cricket, and Susannah loved it — though she regretted that she had disappointed Thomas by failing to win the class prize.[25]

The next year, Thomas — by now a fine-looking, fair-skinned, blue-eyed young man — affirmed his position as head of the family by paying the taxes not only on the land but also on the six slaves. Now, too, Jesse and Samuel were of age, and Nathaniel was near twenty, and all were able to help support the family.[26] At last, their mother's hopes for her children seemed fulfilled.

But before another year was out, the budding Susannah was dead, and of all Thomas's sisters only Mary was left. The schoolgirl died as her father and sisters had, from consumption, and she was buried with Peggy and little Nancy in the filling cemetery on the hillside. For years, one of the landmarks in the valley was the "Grave of the Three Sisters" on the Widow Benton's place.

Sometime later Thomas himself was besieged with fever, a hacking cough, a prodding thirst — the signs of consumption. He could not sleep nights, and he had no energy days; he had to drive himself with all his will to tend to his practice and to family business. In his weakness and despair he felt a need for stimulants. His code denied him hard liquor, but he allowed himself wine, and soon he developed a fixed habit of taking wine with his meals and during the day to relieve his constant thirst. But this only seemed to make his fevers worse; and one day, riding through a wooded field alone, he determined to drink only water. But nothing he could do seemed to conquer his illness, though from time to time his fevers abated and he felt his strong, ready self again.[27]

In the midst of these vicissitudes,* the family finally proceeded to divide Jesse Benton's estate among his children. The will was brought to the court of Williamson County, which appointed seven commissioners to arrange the property and the slaves into equal lots for the children. Each had a plot of land, with Thomas getting two hundred and sixteen acres marked out by imaginary lines running from a beech to "a sugar tree sapling" to a certain buckeye to a red elm and so on, bordering in part on Leiper's Fork itself. Each also was given a portion in slaves. In this division Thomas drew Old Tom and his wife Dorcas, valued at one cent, with a compensating payment for one hundred and fifty-nine dollars and ninety-nine cents from his brother Nathaniel, who had drawn the younger and more valuable Judith. In this roundabout manner, the shares were equalized.

It was unpleasant business for a family, Thomas thought. Years later he remarked that there was no greater curse to children than to leave them to arrange the questions of family property in law.[28]

* Unfortunately, the only evidence concerning Thomas Benton's illness in this period is from memoirs; it is therefore impossible to date the illness exactly, weigh its seriousness, or offer any more details. That Benton was afflicted during his residence in Tennessee seems beyond doubt. An illness in this period is referred to not only in the memoirs cited, but in correspondence in later years; and he was to suffer minor recurrences of his trouble throughout his life.

CHAPTER 3

Thwarted Warrior

1812 - 1815

IN THE NASHVILLE PAPER, Benton might have read an advertisement:

For sale in the Clarion office, price 75 cents the single, 50 cents by the dozen, *The Military Instructor,* Containing all Steuben's regulations for the decepline of an army, that can apply to the militia.

Such was the mood of the times. What men in the West saw as a train of abuses and insults heaped on the young Republic by a Tory government in England had convinced these men that their local militias might soon have to prove their "decepline." In Congress the man of the hour was the young, engaging, forceful Representative from Kentucky, Henry Clay — the man who had married Thomas's cousin, Lucretia Hart. As Speaker of the House, young Clay led a group of martial spirits including Felix Grundy of Tennessee, recently elected to Congress, John C. Calhoun of South Carolina, and William Crawford of Georgia. These men were scored as "War Hawks" by John Randolph of Virginia — but their clamor resounded throughout the nation. In Tennessee, the call was taken up by Benton, who wanted to be in on the great events he expected would soon occur.

At the end of January, 1812, he sent a letter to his friend Andrew Jackson, Major General of the Tennessee Militia. "In the event that a volunteer force should be raised," he wrote, "there is no question, I fancy, but that you will command the division which goes from this state; and as I have always been resolved to quit the gown for the sword, whenever the sword was to be used, I mean, on some terms or other, to be in that corps." The young man could raise troops from the counties in which he had practiced, but he thought a more eligible situation would be aide to the Major General — "the natural inclination which all young men feel, or ought to feel, to advance themselves in the world, has induced me to say to you, that if you should lack an officer of this kind, and should be able to find none better than myself, that I should deem myself honored by your approbation." The self-consciously elegant sentences rolled on. If he were appointed and went on an expedition, young Benton would "make an experiment of my capacity to use the pen as well as the sword," by keeping a journal of the expedition and memorable transactions. "You Sir, who feel a generous wish to see young men come forward by their own intrinsic strength, will not smile at this presumption. . . . I think with Tacitus, that every man should aim at doing something worthy of being written, or at writing something worthy of being done." [1]

A bill to raise volunteers had passed the House thirteen days before Thomas Benton mailed his letter, and it passed the Senate the day after he wrote. But the news did not reach the restless border lawyer until a raw day in February, when the mail arrived at his law office. Immediately, he drew up a plan to put three volunteer regiments in the field. He then saddled his horse and rode thirty miles to the Hermitage to see Jackson, charging through rain, hail, sleet, and wind, along poor roads deep in mud mixed with ice. The Major General was struck with the plan, and prepared to act upon its proposals. But things did not go so quickly — in the capital Felix Grundy fretted that the chief of the army, old Henry Dearborn, was doing nothing, and all official Washington seemed to have the slows; while in Tennessee, the ambitious Benton had to content himself with lesser glory. On April 29, 1812, he was commissioned captain of a volunteer infantry company. His brother Nathaniel Benton was his ensign. [2]

In this capacity Thomas found himself concerned, not with war against England, but with raids by Indians. The red men — spurred on by England, according to prevailing opinion in the Southwest — carried out foray after foray against the white settlements. In May, for example, four Indians came into a lonely house in McSwine's Bottom south of Franklin, took a nine-day-old child from the lap of a woman who was sitting in the parlor, threw it against the wall and killed it, shot the woman, scalped her, jabbed arrows into her body, and then went on to kill other members of the family. Young Benton, by this time promoted to major, was ordered to Nashville to give his advice on ways of catching these marauders, but though troops were sent promptly into the forest they flushed no Indians. By June, 1812, however, war was declared, and by Independence Day the great news reached the Cumberland. In Franklin for the annual July 4 celebration, Benton could read in the Nashville paper:

WAR. By the mail last night we received the declaration of war
against Great Britain . . .

> *A day, an hour of virtuous liberty*
> *Is worth an eternity in bondage.*

The crowd at the July Fourth meeting cheered the routine toasts, the
repeated volleys fired by a company of light infantry, and the martial
music. Among the volunteer toasts was one by Thomas Benton
— "The War against England: Honor and life to its friends; confusion to
its enemies." [3]

In the midst of the exultation, Thomas planned action to suit his resolution. With British agents stirring the red men to attack, the war against
the Indians was now a part of the war with England; thus Benton was
proud to be able to report to Jackson that Captain Mason's company had
met and defeated a troop of Creeks. He was "glad he has got some
blood: it will keep the war alive." But a full-scale expedition against the
Creeks was necessary — and in the square at Franklin and on the roads
Thomas talked with people and persuaded them to join such an expedition. Yet the summer wore on, and there was no action. The militia
drilled, and waited, and Thomas feared that there would never be an
end to marking time. Thoroughly impatient, he wrote Henry Clay that
he was resolved to go to Washington himself when Congress convened.
The chief theater of war was on the Canadian border — where, in August, General Hull had surrendered Detroit without a battle. Perhaps
some new Federal troops would be raised to go to the northern front,
Thomas thought, and if they were, he wanted to be among them. [4]

At last, the word was given to mobilize in Tennessee, and Thomas
Benton was again in a spin of activity. The volunteers were called on to
go down the Mississippi to reinforce the Southwest troops, and perhaps
defend New Orleans from a possible British attack. "Every man of the
western country turns his eyes intuitively upon the mouth of the Mississippi," General Jackson proclaimed to his citizen-soldiers in mid-
November, 1812; "he there beholds the only outlet by which his produce can reach the markets of foreign or the Atlantic States: Blocked
up, all the fruits of his industry rots upon his hand — open and he carries on a trade with all the nations of the earth." As Jackson's right arm
in raising troops in the Franklin area, Benton made speech after speech,
dashing from muster ground to muster ground, waving the General's
proclamation, ardently striving to stimulate the courage and patriotism of

the community. His abilities were soon marked by Benton's comrades. On a cold Saturday late in November, 1812, the ninety men who were to be officers in the Tennessee Volunteers met in Nashville. There the proposed division of 1500 men was separated into one regiment of cavalry and two regiments of infantry, and the council elected field officers, naming Thomas Benton Colonel of the Second Regiment, Infantry. Thus honored, the young commander soon provided himself with a gorgeous uniform. The enlisted men might appear, according to General Jackson's orders, in blue or butternut or brown, homespun or not, with hunting shirts or coats, and white pantaloons and vests to be worn on parade; but the field officers must wear the uniform of their grade as prescribed by the regular army. Years later, friends were to recall Colonel Benton, tall, handsome, and erect, mounted on an elegant horse.[5]

The division was called to muster on December 10 — a bitter cold day, truly the first day of winter, with a heavy snowfall which began in the morning and drove violently with the wind until night. Despite the weather, companies poured into Nashville in shoals until 1800 men had reported, and the next day another two hundred volunteers arrived. Soon after the muster, Thomas Benton had another job — Andrew Jackson announced that he would perform the duty of "first Aid," in addition to acting as "colonel commandant" of his regiment.

While the division made ready, Young Benton had a unique opportunity to indulge his sense of the dramatic. An unfortunate private, one Oliver Bush, deserted his company. Desertion was a grave danger to a militia corps, and when Bush was convicted General Jackson determined to make a bitter example of this first case. At three in the afternoon of December 14, the two infantry regiments were drawn up along a front to a quarter of a mile. Oliver Bush, surrounded by bayonets which pointed at his back, his breast, and his sides, was conducted to the head of the line, followed by the music of the fife and drum. The guard halted the prisoner, the music stopped, and then the Officer of the Day on horseback — Thomas Benton — advanced, stopped before the first company, and spoke.

"Soldiers," he boomed, "I am commanded by the General, to superintend the execution of the sentence which a court-martial has pronounced upon Oliver Bush. Oliver Bush, a private in Captain Wallis's company of volunteers, has been convicted of the crime of desertion. By this crime, the most infamous which a volunteer could commit, he has rendered himself unworthy of associating with the voluntary defenders of their country. The court-martial have sentenced him to be expelled from the camp of the volunteers; and have forbid him ever again to enter it. The officers, noncommissioned officers, and privates of the volunteer corps are forbid ever again to associate with him; his crime having brought a disgrace upon their name which can only be wiped off by driving him eternally from their presence. In expelling him from the camp, in turning him loose, exposed to the scorn of his fellow citizens, which will pursue him wherever he goes, the court-martial has pronounced, upon Oliver Bush, the severest sentence which it was in their power to inflict."

When he had finished, the music began again. The guard marched the prisoner to the next company, and the Colonel repeated his excoriation, and so on, through twenty-two companies. Then Oliver Bush was driven straight off at quick-step, the rogue's march playing at his rear; about a mile and a half from camp, he was turned loose by the guard, his coat wrong side out, to face the hoots of the people wherever he went.

In addition to executing the sentence against Bush, Benton wrote out the whole story and gave it to the Nashville press.[6] As aide-de-camp, he acted as a sort of public relations officer, and this job was in the line of duty. But as he wrote he revealed between the lines that he relished his part before the troops on the parade ground, and his part at his desk.

[2]

BY THE BEGINNING OF 1813, the division was on its way to drive the Imperial troops of England from the Mississippi delta if they should attempt a landing there. On January 8, Colonel Benton received orders from Jackson to superintend the embarkation of the First Regiment, Infantry, down the Cumberland River, and to march his own troops overland. At half-past twelve, noon, the signal was given to slip the cables, and the flatboats wheeled into the sea-green, icy Cumberland. Looking on, Benton observed that every face was animated with joy. At one o'clock, the Second Regiment set out over the difficult roads, with Colonel Benton marching on foot at the head of his seven hundred men. He summarily impressed all the private boats he could find along the way, so his men too might be afloat before they left the Harpeth region.[7]

At four in the morning Thomas turned back to Nashville. There he joined Colonel Anderson, who was setting out to take command of his regiment at Fort Massac on the Ohio, and at midnight the two colonels left Nashville by boat. Now Thomas began the journal which a year before he had vowed he would write. The installments, which he sent to the *Clarion* at Nashville, demonstrated a strong predilection for dramatization, melodramatization, and self-dramatization; a growing self-esteem; and a literary bent which expressed itself in the cadences of a rolling, Gibbonesque, if sometimes diffuse prose style.* The night of his second departure from Nashville was "intensely cold," he wrote in his journal —

> . . . but still, and nothing was heard to interrupt the silence that reigned save the hollow murmuring of the water which broke upon the rocky shore. . . . Col. Anderson placed himself at the helm; the other officers stood by him. No one said he was afraid; but the question of Caesar to the pilot, *Quid times?* repeatedly and involuntarily occurred. Finally, recollecting that they were fatalists, they gave the boat to the stream, surrendered themselves to their destiny, and went below to the cabin.— Having floated two hours, they came to for the balance of the night.

Two days later, on the autumnlike morning of January 12, the fatalists caught up with the boats of General Jackson.

At Clarksville, sixty-seven miles downstream from Nashville, Benton stopped to wait for his regiment. The division was short of flour, and General Jackson commanded his aide to secure some from merchants who were hoarding it. The impetuous Benton "sent out the bayonet," and soon "this weapon had produced him 70 barrels of flour," at eight dollars a barrel. But Thomas's regiment lost ten days for want of boats, all because the quartermaster had left them in the hands of businessmen who wanted to get their inventories to market. The angry Benton calculated that the delay would cost the United States twenty thousand dollars, and asked, Should not a commanding general have control over all his officers, including his quartermaster? "As things stand at present," he complained in his Journal, "if an army is stopped on its march for want of bread, or stuck in the mud for want of transportation, all that

---

* The authorship of this Journal is readily established. It contains internal evidence, in references to the feelings and emotions of Colonel Benton, as well as details of his doings, which could have been known only by him. Further, it was the basis of an attack in the papers on Benton, in the outcome of which Benton assumed the responsibility of authorship (cf. the *Clarion*, February 23, May 5, 1813). Finally, the style of the Journal, if immature and arty, is still early Bentonian. The Journal has not been used before by any Benton biographer, and so far as I have found, not by any other scholar. The compiler of Jackson's correspondence noted that Thomas Benton intended to write a journal, but appears not to have known whether he ever did, and in any case not to have seen a copy (Bassett, *Correspondence,* I, 256).

the general can do is to send a complaint to the president, perhaps a thousand miles off; the delinquent commissary, or Quarter Master, at the same time sends his counter-affidavit." Meanwhile, "the season for action passes entirely away."

By January 23 boats had been found, and the expedition went on into Kentucky. Finally, at dark on January 26, the regiment reached Smithland, a little town at the confluence of the Cumberland and the Ohio; there the big river was a mass of crushing, grinding ice floes, and local old-timers advised against entering the stream. "It rested with Col. Benton . . . to decide. He had never before felt the responsibility of command; and his anxiety became painful as he reflected that upon a word which he was to speak, it *might* depend whether a multitude of fine men should perish in the ice, or live to see their friends again." Finally, he gave the word to go ahead, after securing long poles spiked with iron to keep off the sheets of ice. "The order," Benton noted, "was obeyed with perfect alacrity" [8] — and so the regiment was on its way to a planned rendezvous with General Jackson at Natchez.

Progress down the Mississippi was swift. By the evening of February 13, 1813, Colonel Benton and his regiment arrived at Natchez, a little village perched above the brown immensity of the lower Mississippi. They had traveled some two thousand miles in thirty-six tedious days and nights, and they were at last within striking distance of their goal. Making camp, the volunteers waited for orders . . . and waited . . . and waited. It was a wearisome time, devoted to routine garrison tasks. Then word came from the War Department. On February 5, Secretary John Armstrong had written Jackson, but the orders did not reach him until March 15. That afternoon, Benton received a message to come to the General's tent. There, the ramrod-thin commander, stiff with rage, showed him the secretary's note — the British were no longer expected at New Orleans that winter, and General Jackson would disband his troops where he was, dismissing them from public service. Meanwhile, he would accept the thanks of the President of the United States! With the full agreement of his aide-de-camp, Jackson determined not to obey the order to turn his men loose in the wilderness five hundred miles from their homes. He would lead his volunteers as a body back to Nashville and discharge them there — if he had to pay the transportation costs himself! [9]

In a few days, the division was on the weary road home. Slowly the troops crawled north, along the Natchez Trace, through the Choctaw nation, past Thomas Benton's home at Leiper's Fork, balked, thwarted, the fine chance at glory on which they had so much counted, all gone. Still, the trip was not a complete loss to Benton. On the journey he realized the immensity and possible importance of the great West beyond the Mississippi. The vast flowing river and the black land beyond inspired in him a vision which helped him break away still further from his seaboard background, escape from his lawyer's shell of precedent and safe usage. On the journey, too, his illness left him. Enthusiasm and forgetfulness in larger pursuits, exercise, sleep in the open air, simple and regular food, sunshine, bathing and drying in the sun — all these things helped him back to vigorous health.[10]

In Nashville, Thomas, at a dinner with a group of fellow officers at Clayton Talbot's tavern, spoke of the solicitude Jackson had shown for his men, and of his magnanimity in refusing to discharge them into the wilderness at Natchez. The young Colonel himself came in for his portion of praise, too. According to the *Clarion,* "he shared every fatigue with the most common soldier, and in no case shunned the mire his men had to wade through. In camp his police was admired by all — we hope he may have an opportunity of signalizing himself in the field." [11]

Despite these encomiums, the expedition had an unpleasant aftermath. Its source was in the remarks Benton had made in his journal about quartermasters. When Major William B. Lewis read these strictures, his blood rose — *he* was the Deputy Quartermaster of the volunteer troops, and he was sure the remarks were aimed at him. He proceeded to write the most insulting letter he could devise in reply, identifying the author of the journal and roasting his literary excesses — "Most inimitable Journalist! — 'He mounts his stilts, and at every step, kicks out a star!' " Again, what was this *"Quid times"* business when the boat left Nashville? "It is true, *I suppose,"* the Major wrote with juvenile sarcastic emphasis, "that no one *said* he was *afraid,* but, why turn *pale:* Why *tremble?"*

When Thomas saw Major Lewis's letter, he was in a passion. The afternoon he arrived in Nashville, April 22, at four o'clock exactly, tired and dusty from the journey as he must have been, he wrote a reply. "Words are not to be employed," he fumed; "I shall neither give nor take explanations: my mind is made up, and you must fight me, sir. . . . I lay before you the pistol, the sword, and the dagger: take which you like." There was no time to waste, for he planned to leave the state, he declared as he dispatched his messenger, Ensign Lyttleton Johnston — the meeting should be in Kentucky in two or three days, or at sunup if

Lewis wanted it in Tennessee. The nimble Major sidestepped. He couldn't fight, he wrote, because he was too busy disposing of public property left over from the expedition; when this business was done, he would indulge the Colonel in his propensity.

Such dodging would not do for Thomas Benton. Within the hour, he sat down at his table in the cantonment near Nashville to answer — the Major was as much in the public service when he penned his insults as he was now, and, "in a word you must fight me, sir, or you must flinch openly. I give you until the rising of the sun on Tuesday morning." When Major Lewis once again regretted that he just couldn't say when he might fight, the impatient Benton decided that Lewis was "a cockaded and gold-laced coward." He rode to the printer's in Nashville, had all the correspondence set up and run off, and distributed it as a handbill. This nettled Major Lewis, who now tried a few defiant drumbeats of his own: he *would* meet the Colonel, *sometime* — and hadn't Thomas Benton in publishing his leaflet taken an easy, safe way out of the situation? If Lewis really thought he could get away with this, he did not know Thomas Benton. Writing at his candle about nine o'clock that night, Benton snapped back a note — he would postpone his trip if Lewis would name the day, the hour, and the place; it might be any day soon, any hour, any place. *Now,* what would the Major do? The Major, very simply, declined once more to be definite.

This was Benton's first experience, or near-experience, with what was known as the "field of honor." He now gave the whole of the Benton-Lewis correspondence to his friend the Nashville editor, self-importantly apologizing to the PEOPLE OF THE STATE OF TENNESSEE for staying to settle a personal quarrel when the Republic was attacked, but his *honor* had required it — and, he might have added, his general self-esteem, aggressiveness, and literary pride. Now he was leaving to seek an active, *honorable* place in the war. He could not resist a final melodramatic flourish — "if the chances of war prevent me from returning, suffer me not to be lied out of your friendship by men without honor, without shame, without public character." [12] Though it was all a bit absurd, Benton had nonetheless bested his adversary without loading a pistol.

[3]

THE YOUNG COLONEL was on his way to Washington in pursuit of a new military career with some action in it. Before he left, he rode by the

Hermitage to get a letter of introduction to the Secretary of War from Major General Jackson, who praised him warmly — "his uniform good conduct, his industry and attention to the dicipline and police of his regiment, speak more for his fitness than words, and a personal acquaintance with Colo. Benton will soon decide on the capacity of his mind." The General's drafts for money to pay the expenses of bringing his division back from Natchez had been refused payment by the auditors at New Orleans, and in Washington Benton planned to present Jackson's case again to the Federal government.[13]

On May 10 he left Nashville, and at last on May 26 he was at the capital. Certainly the town, with its muddy streets, unfinished buildings and provincial ways, could not compare with New York or Philadelphia; but to Benton, who had never seen a larger place, it might have been another London. He got his first glimpse of Congress in action in the as yet domeless Capitol. Everything seemed very slow, and political intrigue hung over every maneuver. He also visited some of the executive offices, and noticed how the War Department machinery creaked along. Finally, he chatted at the Executive Mansion with mild little President Madison, who asked carefully after General Jackson's health. After almost twenty days of delay, Benton managed to convince Secretary of War Armstrong that there must be some place for a willing young man in the war, and that Tennessee would gladly put more men in the field. And he proved himself a successful lobbyist for Jackson's claims — only, however, by working out himself a scheme for payment which he managed to get the Secretary to adopt.* He wrote triumphantly to his mentor, saying that he hoped to be on his way home in a few days, his business finished and a new career before him. By June 18, his new appointment was confirmed in the Senate. Under the newly commissioned Colonel John Williams of East Tennessee, he was to serve as Lieutenant Colonel of the Thirty-ninth Infantry Regiment, Regular Army — a regiment whose flesh would be recruited in Tennessee. One of his ensigns was to be a young man named Sam Houston — an immigrant from

---

* Remembering and recounting this incident many years later, Benton said that he had to threaten the Administration with the loss of the political support of the state of Tennessee, in order to get the War Department to honor Jackson's claims ([Benton], *Addresses on the Sword,* 38). This sounds like frontier exaggeration, for no reference to any such threat appears in the letter the Colonel wrote Andrew Jackson from Washington at the time. Nonetheless, the story is repeated and apparently given its face value in a chief biography of Thomas Benton (Meigs, *Benton,* 71-72), and the earliest biographer also summarized this account and appeared to accept it as accurate (Roosevelt, *Benton,* 29).

western Virginia, known for his six-feet-two-inch height, which seemed huge at the time. For his services, Lieutenant Colonel Thomas H. Benton, USA, would receive $1543.08 a year, while his privates would get $96.00 each for the same period.[14]

In Washington, Benton had another chance to watch the course of national politics. He might, for example, have marked a new Representative from New Hampshire who had established himself back home with a scathing oratorical attack on President Madison for precipitating an "unnecessary" war — a man born in the same year as Thomas Benton, named Daniel Webster. In Congress, Webster continued to harass the Administration, suggesting nullification by the states of Federal laws and hinting at disunion. He submitted a set of resolutions designed to embarrass the Administration, which were debated while Benton was in the capital, and which passed the day before he left. In addition, Thomas could observe the harassments inflicted on the government by the state of the currency. The first Bank of the United States had been refused a recharter, and no substitute had been devised for its notes. The currency was a muddle of foreign coins, fractional silver, and copper supplemented by uncertain, depreciating, excessive note issues from the incredibly proliferating state banks. As Benton recalled it later, the treasury was generally about empty and the public credit impaired, while the Federalists who had originally proposed the national Bank cried "We told you so" and flaunted the difficulties of their political enemies.[15]

Moved, perhaps, by such developments, the newly appointed officer wrote his cousin-in-law Henry Clay a long, confiding letter. "I am now a soldier for the war," he declared, "and have an unbounded desire to make some figure in it. My younger brothers have also entered: they will do something, or they will perish." He was afraid that the enemy would prolong the conflict, to divide the Union and to pull down those who were then in power — and the Federalists from New England would encourage this. He wanted to tell the *honest* Federalists, of which there were some in Tennessee, what he had seen — "they will be filled with horror," he thought, "for they have no idea of treason and of civil war." [16]

[4]

BACK IN THE CUMBERLAND, Thomas heard startling, disturbing news. His younger brother Jesse — one of those who "will do something," or "will perish" — told Thomas that he very nearly *had* perished. He had agreed to serve as Ensign Lyttleton Johnston's second, in a challenge to Major William Carroll, thereby returning the favor Ensign Johnston had done Thomas in his affair with Major Lewis. When Carroll refused to honor Johnston's challenge, Jesse Benton tartly suggested to Carroll that he himself might stand in Johnston's place. If the Major would not meet the Ensign, surely he would not refuse Jesse Benton of Benton Town.

To Billy Carroll, this was all a great weariness. He called on Jackson, who tried to dissuade Jesse Benton by insisting that he, Jesse, had no quarrel with Carroll. But young Jesse, with all his brother's impetuousness but apparently little of Thomas's judgment or style, would have none of such pacifications. The duel was set, and Jackson, ever warm-blooded, always a man of intense personal attachments, resolved a conflict of loyalties in this instance in favor of his old friend Billy Carroll, and agreed to act as his second in arranging the meeting with Jesse Benton. The men fought on June 14. Both were wounded, young Jesse dangerously. At the fire, frightened, he pulled his trigger, turned his back to Carroll, and quickly assumed a low squatting position — and Carroll's ball lodged in the very widest part of Jesse Benton's frame.[17]

When Thomas Benton heard all this, he exploded. Perhaps Jesse had no quarrel with Billy Carroll, perhaps poor Jesse had played the poltroon by making a bull's-eye of the seat of his pants, but family feeling required Thomas to take Jesse's side. Embroiled indirectly in the storm of Andrew Jackson's hot emotions and conflicting loyalties, he was particularly incensed at his old mentor. Why, on the very day the General had been superintending the shooting of his brother, Thomas Benton was in the War Department in Washington pleading the General's case! Though he picked no quarrels and stayed at Franklin, keeping himself remarkably close, rumors reached the Hermitage that Thomas had been making ill-natured remarks against Andrew Jackson. Now the General sent an ominous note — Did Benton speak disrespectfully of him? And did he threaten to challenge him to a duel? Taking a grip on himself, Thomas sat down to compose a reply. What he had said was, *one,* that it was poor business for a man of Jackson's age to conduct a duel between two young men; and, *two,* that Jackson had meanly drawn the challenge from brother Jesse; and, *three,* "that if you could not have prevented a duel you ought at least to have conducted it in the usual mode, and on terms equal to both parties"; and, *four,* that Jackson had on the contrary conducted it in "a savage, unequal, unfair, and base manner."

He had not challenged Jackson, but "the terror of your pistols is not to seal my lips." When Benton folded his letter, he knew that his friendship with Jackson was ended. But he was no man's toady; he must uphold his place, prove his honor, vindicate his growing self-esteem and pride. In reply, Jackson offered a homily — men of *honor* did not "quarrel and brawl like the fish woman." [18]

So the matter rested throughout the hot days of August. But on September 4, Thomas and Jesse went to Nashville on business, and put up at Clayton Talbot's tavern, an inn they knew Jackson did not frequent. The town gossips rushed to the Hermitage to tell the news. Soon, Jackson and his oak-tall friend Colonel John Coffee arrived and took rooms at the Nashville Inn. They walked to the post office, and then went out of their way to pass the hotel where the Bentons were, where they saw Jesse step from the pavement into the hotel. Promptly Jackson and Coffee followed Jesse inside, and there in the hall near the back portico of Talbot's the General came face to face with Thomas Benton.

"Now defend yourself, you damned rascal!" Jackson cried.

The words were a fuse which set off a paroxysm of gunfire, pushing, pulling, wrestling, fist-fighting, shoving, gouging, stabbing, and jabbing. The General drew a pistol from under his coat, and strode toward Thomas. Promptly, Jesse aimed and fired on Jackson from a sort of ambush in the barroom next to the passage, while Jackson shot at Thomas, and Thomas drew his gun and fired twice at the General in return. In the crash of pistols, Jackson toppled to the floor, blood spurting from his left arm, while the muzzle blast of his weapon seared a hole in Thomas's coat-sleeve. The towering Colonel Coffee now charged through the smoke. He blazed away at Thomas, but his ball slashed harmlessly past the young man's head into the wall. By this time, three other men were in the battle. The struggling, weaving figures lunged through the hall and into the barroom. Disarmed, Thomas found John Coffee and Alexander Donelson rushing him with drawn daggers, while Jesse was attacked by Charles Hammond with a dagger and by the gigantic Stockley Hays with a sword cane. Retreating backwards down the hall, Thomas received five slight knife-wounds. In the barroom, Hammond and Hays got Jesse on his back and stabbed at him while he tried to parry the blades with his bare hands. He was saved only when another warrior, James Sumner, rushed in and helped drive off his attackers. In the struggle, Jesse clapped a pistol to the body of Stockley Hays to blow him through, but the gun missed fire. The melee now came to a farcical peak. Fending off the daggers and clubbed pistols of Coffee and Donelson, the bulky, dignified Thomas managed to fall backwards down a flight of stairs at the rear of the hotel.

This bit of slapstick ended the engagement, and now Jackson was discovered lying, bleeding, in the back doorway. The man who had advised his junior officer against brawling like the fishwoman had precipitated a fray in which he had nearly lost his own life. He was carried from Talbot's to the Nashville Inn, where he soaked two mattresses through with his blood, while the Nashville physicians took turns trying to save him. Meanwhile, Thomas and Jesse strutted in front of Talbot's, denouncing Jackson as an assassin and a defeated assassin at that, defying him to come out and renew the battle. Finally, Thomas took to the public square a sword of Jackson's he had found, and ceremoniously broke it in two in front to the watching crowd[19] — a symbolic conclusion for the affray.*

From his position as a rising star Thomas Benton was suddenly reduced to the place of a pariah. Soon after the brawl, he wrote: "I am literally in hell here," the meanest wretches under heaven to contend with, liars, affidavit makers, and shameless puppies — "the scalping-knife of Tecumpsy is mercy compared with the affidavits of these villains." Nothing but a decisive duel could save him, "for it is a settled plan to turn out puppy after puppy to bully me, and when I have got into a scrape, to have me killed somehow in the scuffle." He saw no alternative but to kill or be killed, for he would not "crouch" to Jackson. Within two weeks, he thought his decisive duel was at hand, when Billy Carroll published a statement of his position. Thomas Benton interpreted this as

---

* The account given here of the brawl with Andrew Jackson is based chiefly on Thomas Benton's circular in which he sets forth the story in his characteristic fashion, with each item numbered, 1, 2, 3, 4, 5, 6, 7, 8. In addition other authorities have been used to fill out the picture. The story of the affair which appears in most published works follows Parton, who says that he had his account of the business orally from an old friend of the parties who in turn got it directly from Colonel Coffee — when, Parton does not say. Now, Thomas Benton's account appeared six days after the event, and therefore seems better evidence than an oral reminiscence, told and retold and finally put in print in 1860, and Parton himself reprints Benton's circular with the note that his account is, perhaps, as true as Colonel Coffee's. Of course, the brawl was something not even witnesses could have described uniformly and with complete accuracy, and certainly the descriptions of participants can give only partial and biased pictures. The only solution, and the one attempted here, seems to be that of giving a reconstruction, carefully built from a comparison and dovetailing of all accounts into the one chiefly followed.

a challenge to himself, and wrote Carroll: "The challenge which you addressed to me in your publication of yesterday is accepted." But Major Carroll disappointed the aggressive young man — he challenged no one, he replied, though he would meet Benton if Benton challenged him.[20]

No fight took place to drain off the ill-feeling, and the feuding parties went on being angry at each other for weeks, months, and years to come.*

[5]

ON SEPTEMBER 14, 1813, the *Clarion* printed a notice: *The Officers attached to the 39th U. S. Regt. of Infantry, are required forthwith to repair to Nashville* — JOHN WILLIAMS, COL. COMMANDANT. The *Clarion* call brought Benton again to Nashville, and brought new visions of glory to his head. When finally the new regiment was formed and trained, he hoped, he and Colonel Williams might lead it into the heart of the fighting on the Canadian border.

But events again brought disappointment and frustration instead. While Benton was helping organize the Thirty-ninth, news came from Fort Mims, far south near Mobile Bay in Mississippi Territory, of new depredations by Creek warriors, spurred again by the British. Promptly Andrew Jackson, physically weakened as he was, called for "retaliatory vengeance," ordered his volunteers to rendezvous, and by November the militia had met and defeated the Creeks under Chief Red Eagle. Had Benton remained in the volunteers, he might have gone on these avenging adventures. As it was, he faced the prosaic task of training a new command, while victories and honor were going to Billy Carroll, John Coffee, and other "puppies of the Genl. [Jackson]." Young Benton

---

* The story has been widely circulated that Thomas Benton was scared out of Tennessee by General Jackson and his "puppies," or that he left the area immediately because of the fight. One biography of Jackson suggests this (Parton, *Jackson,* I, 396), and another says: "Friends of Jackson vowed to even the score. 'I'm literally in hell here,' Tom Benton wrote and left town" (James, *Jackson,* 154). But a man who will not crouch, and who vows to kill or be killed, and looks for a duel to settle the score himself, does not sound like one who is ready to be scared out of town. And the fact is that "Tom" (nowhere in any contemporary account or record that I have seen does the usage "Tom" appear) did not leave town — he was in and near Nashville on September 12, on November 22, and until at least the middle of December, 1813. That Thomas Benton *two years later* when the war was over, removed to Missouri because he felt his opportunities in Tennessee were curtailed or eliminated because he was on the outs with Jackson, is possible. But the evidence available leaves even this proposition only a conjecture.

would give half his earthly goods to be with his friend Colonel Anderson on the Canadian border, "upon a theatre which affords scope for action." Waiting was torture.[21]

The weeks stretched out into months, and 1813 gave way to 1814, before the Thirty-ninth was ready to march. But at last it was ordered south to join General Jackson, and to reinforce a militia that was meeting reverses and melting away, despite some new victories over the Indians. By the beginning of February, reinforced by dependable if green regular troops, Jackson planned a final drive against the Indians — and now, in the field with his regiment, Thomas Benton could hope again for a day of glory. But once again, he was doomed to disappointment. The decisive battle was fought at Tohopeka on the Tallapoosa River about 150 miles south of the Tennessee border, but Benton was not there. At the last minute, he had been ordered to leave his regiment and return to Tennessee, on recruiting duty. The hostilities now shifted south, and by July, 1814, Benton was in the field again — with the Thirty-ninth at Mount Vernon north of Mobile Bay, in command of the Regiment *vice* Colonel Williams, who had gone to Washington. Here Benton learned that the Indians were scattered along the Escambia River as far as Pensacola in Spanish West Florida. Is there anything, he wrote General Thomas Flournoy, in command at New Orleans, to forbid the Thirty-ninth going to Pensacola to bayonet the villains? Without waiting for an answer, he set out three days later for the Escambia. Once again, his hopes of action rose, and soon looked beyond the point of guerrilla raids. Why not go on to *occupy* the Indians' headquarters at Pensacola, and thereby win a base from which troops could constantly scour the Escambia and keep it clear of Indians? What if Pensacola was a Spanish town, in Spanish territory? But a third time Thomas's hopes were balked, for on July 13, after getting his troops across the Alabama River fifty miles above Pensacola, he was taken very ill and was obliged to return to Fort Stoddert. Near Pensacola, the expedition under the command of Colonel George Nixon *did* meet the Indians and fight gallantly — but Benton wasn't there.

Meanwhile, the Indian wars were brought to a close. In June Jackson was given command of the entire Southwest Military District, and ordered to deal with the Creeks. On August 9, he called a council with the Indians and presented them with a take-it-or-fight treaty by which the United States acquired practically all of the Creek lands and the warriors were left beaten and helpless.[22]

By mid-August Benton was recovered and in active command of his regiment again. In September he was ordered by Jackson to Montgomery's Redoubt, near old Fort Mims on the Alabama River above Mobile Bay, where he was to watch the British, who had made their headquarters at Pensacola. Before long he sent what he thought was exciting news to General Jackson. From a man named Boyles, who wandered between American and Spanish territory, he had learned that ships were setting out from Pensacola for Mobile Point, with a miscellaneous cargo of British, Indians, escaped Negro slaves, American deserters, and "refuse Spaniards." In reply, the Headquarters Staff warned the anxious Benton not to fall into a British trap — perhaps Boyles had been sent by the English to divert American attention from Pensacola. This chilly communiqué did not slow the Colonel, who went on sending what information he had, while the Staff plied him with additional smug cautions about border adventurers and possible "faints" to draw American attention away from Pensacola. Then, the British *did* strike at Fort Boyer at the mouth of Mobile Bay, in an attack that was barely repulsed.[23] Apparently headquarters had been wrong, and the border spy and Benton right. Apparently it was no "faint" the English had in mind, but a genuine thrust into American territory.

Meanwhile ominous word came from across the Atlantic — "Wellington's army to America! . . . Bonaparte dethroned. Peace in Europe; English coming to swallow U.S." It now seemed that the decisive battle might really be expected — and from New Orleans General Jackson received a frantic cry for help. Sure that any British force would set out overland from Pensacola, the General promptly called for volunteers from Louisiana and planned a full-scale attack against this favorite target. The great movement would require Benton's troops. GATHER YOUR REGIMENT, a command from headquarters read, AND BRING THEM TO THE BAY OF PERDIDO, just west of Pensacola. By September 22, Benton had mobilized all his detachments at the Bay, battle again seemed imminent, and another time the sniff of action thrilled his nostrils. But the assault was delayed, and Benton found himself back at Fort Montgomery, where he soon had to worry about the depleting strength of his regiment as men took their discharges when their year of service was up.[24]

In the last week of October, Jackson formed his force again for the attack on Pensacola. Once again the supreme moment seemed to be at hand. At just this moment, however, Benton and six of his fellow officers were ordered back to Tennessee. When they heard the news, they protested to the Adjutant General — "finding ourselves unexpectedly ordered upon the recruiting service at a moment when active operations were about to commence, unwilling to be seen creeping home at such a period, desirous of being employed in some way . . . we respectfully request that we may be permitted to serve in the rank of the file . . . now under the command of Major Blue in the service of the United States." The answer at General Jackson's headquarters was — No. The commander. applauded the patriotic ardor the protest breathed, but he had to give places which might win laurels to those who had served with him in the winter campaign. Recruiting it was, and once again the young Colonel's martial career was blighted before it had blossomed.[25]

Even this did not hold Benton for long. He was tenacious as well as mettlesome, and he determined a last time that he *would,* somehow, get into the fighting on the major front. He would go to the North, to the Canadian border, alone, if he could not go with his outfit. He got Colonel Williams to order him to Washington, and once again he made the long trip over the mountains. As he traveled, in December 1814 and January 1815, troops under Andrew Jackson fought the long-expected battle with the British around New Orleans — and the struggle ended in a triumph which established General Jackson's reputation throughout the land. But once again Benton, seeking service, was absent when his fellow Tennesseans marched down the glory road! *

* According to one authority, Thomas Benton acquired about this time a quadroon girl as a mistress — a girl who later married the son of the co-founder of Memphis and went there to live (James, *Jackson,* 306). He offers no documentation, and my own researches around Nashville and Franklin failed to unearth anything more positive. In response to a request, James placed the story in a memoir about the city of Memphis (Letter from Marquis James, Rye, New York, August 15, 1948); a survey of a dozen or more volumes finally resulted in discovery of the story (James D. Davis, *The History of the City of Memphis . . . Also, the "Old Times Papers"* [Memphis, 1873], 73). Though it is repeated in recent histories of Memphis, clearly following Davis's account, the tale seems improbable. He says that Benton picked up "Mary" in New Orleans, when he was there commanding a regiment under General Jackson, and that he brought her back and kept her (presumably in Tennessee) for two or three years, after which he turned her over to the man who married her. The fact that Benton was not at New Orleans with Jackson, but in Washington, and the fact that he moved to St. Louis in the late summer or fall of 1815, makes it hard to understand when or how he acquired the girl, or how he could have kept her in Tennessee two or three years. Finally, the whole thing seems out of character for Benton. It must be noted that Davis went to Memphis only in 1824; thus, though he may well have found a "Mary" there as

In Washington — still blackened and scarred by the fires the British had set in August — Benton prepared a memorandum for the Adjutant General. He was there, he noted on January 23, *first,* to settle his accounts, *second,* to request employment for his regiment in the North, and *third,* to request northern service for himself if the request for the regiment could not be granted. And then he waited . . . and waited . . . and waited. At last, he was rewarded with an order to proceed to Canada. But before he left Washington word came — "GLORIOUS NEWS! *Orleans saved and peace concluded. . . . Who would not be an American? Long live the republic! All hail! last asylum of oppressed humanity!"* The treaty had been signed at Ghent on December 24, 1814, even before the glorious victory Jackson had won at New Orleans.[26]

As late as March, 1815, Thomas Benton still signed himself "Lieutenant Colonel, 39th Infantry," but the war was over, and for a last time he had missed his chance.

[6]

ON THE LONG ROAD from Washington in the spring of 1815, Thomas paused at Smithfield, in the western part of Virginia, to visit an acquaintance — Colonel James Preston. Perhaps it was their mutual connection with the Hart family that brought Thomas Benton and James Preston together; in any case, the two men became friends. The Prestons lived in a large frame mansion house, painted white, which had a long veranda running under the four dormer windows of the second floor, a spacious parlor with a tall mantel, and a fine library filled with volumes of ancient classics, the English poets, and early-day scientific works. Thomas long remembered the mansion, with its view of the peaks of the colorful, misty Blue Ridge, as "a temple dedicated to Felicity" — and a spot where he received a most gratifying hospitality.

The Prestons were an unusual clan, and the young man's friendship with them was an important element in his life — another link with men of position and influence. One of the five brothers, Thomas Preston, served as co-editor with Thomas Ritchie of the leading Virginia newspaper, the Democratic-Republican *Enquirer,* of Richmond; one of the seven sisters, Laetitia, married John Floyd, a Governor of Virginia; another brother, Francis Preston, was the friend of Benton's second cousin

wife of the son of the co-founder, the Benton part of the tale he must have had at second or third hand.

Nathaniel Hart; Susan Preston married this same Nathaniel Hart; and James Preston himself was to serve as Governor of Virginia too. Through Colonel Preston, Thomas met Colonel James McDowell, who had married James Preston's sister Sarah. Eighty-odd miles northeast of Smithfield, past the wonderful stone Natural Bridge, near Lexington, James and Sarah McDowell lived with their three children, Susan, Elizabeth, and James Jr., on a modest but charming plantation called Cherry Grove. There the rangy, six-foot-two, vigorous, intelligent Colonel McDowell played warm host.[27]

Very soon Thomas's interest focused on James McDowell's daughter, Elizabeth. A bright, brown-haired girl, she was approaching twenty-one in the spring of 1815. The thirty-three-year-old Thomas found her radiant, captivating, gracious in manner, full of intellect and energy, and also, as he put it later, of exalted moral tone. She was of a family equal to any in America, he thought, and he was sure she would make a wife and mother of education and accomplishments, with regard for every social duty — and he admired her womanly devotion to her church, the Presbyterian old school. Moved by all these qualities, he quickly proposed, but Elizabeth rejected him.[28] Nonetheless, he never forgot her, and as the years went by he showed that he was as determined in love as he had been in war.*

Meanwhile, Benton faced a major decision. He had resigned the commission which had brought so much fatigue and so little glory, and received an honorable discharge dated June 15, 1815. What next? Should he, defying Andrew Jackson's "puppies," return to Tennessee and take up his old life, or should he find new fields for his ambition? Perhaps in the newer frontier he had seen briefly, perhaps in the broad, sparsely settled Missouri Territory, a man determined to come forward by his own intrinsic strength might realize a new destiny. Talking with Colonel Preston at Smithfield, his thoughts must have turned increasingly to this idea. He decided to set out for the new West and make a new life for himself there.

---

* This account is necessarily reconstructed from earlier and later documents and memoirs, for no contemporary documents I have seen reveal just when Thomas Benton met and proposed to Elizabeth McDowell. It is highly probable, however, that it was in the middle of 1815. The description given here of Elizabeth's appearance and character is also based on later documents and memoirs — but these are consistent, if somewhat general, on this point. If the Benton family private papers — letters, for example, from Thomas to Elizabeth — had not been so largely lost, the matter could be established with greater assurance.

PART II

Education of a Democrat

That land alone is truly rich,
And in all things the tippy,
Where eating goes to highest pitch,
As on the Mississippi.

Republican can best be got,
'Twill be with me a maxim,
Where plenty bubbles in the pot;
No tyrants there can tax him.

— *Missouri Republican*, 1826

CHAPTER 4

New Fortunes

1815 - 1817

O
N A SUNDAY EVENING in the early fall of 1815, Benton stood on the flat Illinois bank of the Mississippi River and looked west at the wooded hills of Missouri. He was waiting for a boat to carry him across the wide stream to his home-to-be, St. Louis. He was, as he said later, "an adventurer ready to begin on a new theatre," where he was determined to lay "some foundation of character and fortune." Though he had only four hundred dollars in his pocket, he had other assets. He was thirty-three, large, muscular, physically tough; he was intellectually capable; he was temperamentally as aggressive as a Missouri bobcat and as determined as a storybook hero; he had proved in Tennessee that he had the stuff of success in him. The Missouri wilderness welcomed such men.

As he crossed the Mississippi, with its strong current seeming in places to boil up from the bottom, the Tennessean could survey his future home town. Its whitewashed wood-and-mud or stone buildings rose from the bank to the summit of a bluff, giving the whole village the appearance of an amphitheater, surrounded by an undulating open area which was half prairie and half shrubbery. Only three streets deep from the shore, the town ran raggedly along the bank for almost twenty squares. Here Thomas must make new friends, learn the French language, which was widely used in the area, and revise his law reading[1] — but the task did not awe him.*

* Various writers give various dates for Benton's arrival in St. Louis. A later Missouri friend says that he moved to the village in 1813 (Bay, *Reminiscences of the Bench and Bar of Missouri*, 5); his daughter Jessie gives the date 1817 (Frémont, "Biographical Sketch," 8); one of his senatorial successors, George Graham Vest, author of the famous Eulogy on the Dog, declares in *Proceedings in Congress Upon the Acceptance of the Statutes of Thomas H. Benton and Francis P. Blair*, 79, that the Colonel first settled in Ste. Genevieve and after a few years moved to St. Louis; only Billon, *Annals of St. Louis* (St. Louis, 1886-1888), II, 162, offers the date 1815-1816. The matter can be definitely established from two documents — Benton signed the list of attorneys in St. Louis in October, 1815

Once on the Missouri side, Benton sought a place to stay. As he was asking directions in the street, he was approached by "a most respectable old gentleman," who invited him to his own imposing home. This white-haired patrician, Thomas's first friend in St. Louis, was Charles Gratiot. He was a French settler who had come to St. Louis in 1777 as a merchant, and married Victoire Chouteau, sister of the Auguste Chouteau who with Pierre Laclede had founded the village in 1764. A successful investor, fur magnate, and land agent, Gratiot had been President of the town Board of Trustees, and his daughters had married other prominent French settlers: Jean P. Cabanné, Silvestre Labadie, and Pierre Chouteau, *fils*. In short, he was a man of affairs and influence, a leader in the town's elite of property, position, and power. His house was a mansion for the time. Its façade was crossed by a wide gallery, while at the back there was a courtyard with a barn and a separate kitchen. Here the rich and powerful of the town stopped in to call, and such leaders as William Clark of the Lewis and Clark expedition, now Governor of Missouri Territory, visited regularly. Here Thomas Benton occupied one of the seven rooms in the living quarters above the basement floor. Certainly few promising immigrants had so helpful an entree. "How precious are the rites of hospitality!" Thomas wrote. "It has been my happiness everywhere to meet with good people."

His new home was a situation well suited to a man of Benton's particular temperament and character. In St. Louis, as in the "new West" in 1815 generally, the fluid state of society provided a field in which an immigrant with ability and address could quickly command respect. Undoubtedly Gratiot and his associates saw in Benton a promising agent for their manifold interests, and a promising addition to their circle. In untamed, growing Missouri, men took themselves and their prospects seriously and often humorlessly; they placed nearly supreme value on ambition, on achievement, on striving; they saw personal drive and self-reliance as leading virtues. As a man of talents, and of commanding and even magnetic personality and manner, Benton was soon to win intense business, professional, and later political loyalties — as he was also to reap a harvest of bitter hostilities and rivalries. These loyalties often ripened into personal friendships, and the warmer side of Benton's personality which emerged in intimate relationships brought him friend-

---

(Roll of Attorneys, Circuit Court for the City of St. Louis), and in November, 1815, he wrote James McDowell that he was settled in St. Louis.

ships outside of his professional orbit too. Typically such loyalties —
with respect serving as the original foundation for friendship and regard,
often combined with an intense eighteenth-century devotion to "honor"
— could link men together with strong and durable bands — though in
a conflict of loyalties or a conflict over "honor," the bands might break as
they had between Benton and Jackson in 1813, and a fierce quarrel
might ensue. His early disgrace at Chapel Hill, and his coming of age
in the frontier culture of Tennessee, had produced in Benton a fierce
aggressiveness tempered with sentiment which was almost an epitome
of the personality of the time and age, but exaggerated. Over the years
Benton's character was to change, to develop and mellow. But what he
was at thirty-three marked him for success, and esteem, and friendship on the new Missouri frontier.

His enthusiasm for his new home increased as time passed. He was
sure that Missouri had a great future, for the flow of immigrants was
immense; this would "soon entitle this Territory to a place" as a state,
and its position and resources would "make it the most powerful of all
the western states," he wrote James McDowell back in Virginia. If the
rejected suitor thought of the brown-haired Elizabeth, he did not mention her.[2]

[2]

PROMPTLY AFTER HIS ARRIVAL in St. Louis, Benton's "profession of the
law," as he put it, was "ardently recommenced." On October 2, 1815,
he went to the courthouse in St. Louis, paid his fee, and enrolled as an
attorney privileged to practice at the local bar.* He set up an office in a
small room on the south side of Laurel Street, near Second, whence he
could walk from the Gratiot house. In addition, there were the cir-
cuits to ride through remote counties, following the northern Circuit
Court up the Missouri River into the fertile, black lands, and the southern Circuit Court from Ste. Genevieve down the Mississippi into the
cotton country.

The courts were centers of the frontier community life. In them
Thomas met territorial leaders who were judges, like the unbending,

---

* This same date saw the registration of another attorney, a young man named
Henry S. Geyer — who, more than thirty-five years later, was to run against and
defeat Thomas Benton for the post in the United States Senate he had by then held
for thirty years.

cantankerous John B. C. Lucas, and the genial, widely popular David Barton. Court week in the remote towns was also a favorite time to settle grievances outside the legal arena, and judges frequently adjourned the legal proceedings so that all might go out to watch the fights. There was nevertheless plenty of legal business to attend to. The early French and Spanish settlers had brought a system of Latin civil law with them, while the later immigration from the seaboard states had introduced the English common law. Jurisprudence in 1815 was thus an uncertain thing, with few local precedents and fewer books of reference. Courage, understanding of general principles, and resourcefulness, characteristics Benton had in force, were the main stock of the effective pleader. Fees were small, but people went to law about small things. For securing a "final judgment" in a case, Benton could demand a minimum of five dollars, while for "making out a *praecipe* and filing a declaration if the suit is ended before judgment is obtained," the legal minimum was three dollars.[3]

Of the less than two dozen men at the territorial bar, Benton soon chose one as a model. This was Edward Hempstead, a former territorial delegate to the national Congress, the chief lawyer in St. Louis, with a reputation as a man of strong sense and a great special pleader. He had developed a sharp, fierce, barking manner of courtroom oratory, which awed juries and was aped by Benton and other young men until it became a sort of legacy to the whole bar.[4] Soon Thomas became a protégé of Hempstead, and a fast friend to his brothers.

On his own, Benton developed a specialty — land claims and titles. The old Spanish Government in the area had granted concessions totaling more than a million and a half *arpents*,* but only a baker's dozen of the titles were complete. Few settlers had found the time or money for surveys and for journeys to New Orleans to have their grants validated by the Governor-General. Under American rule, more than five thousand old Spanish claims had been investigated, but a land commission headed by Judge John B. C. Lucas had rejected as many claims as it had approved. Under later regulations, validation required direct action of Congress on specific claims, which meant that a land-claim attorney had to be lobbyist as well as lawyer. Stoutly maintaining that the old titles should not be rejected merely because they were technically

---

* The *arpent* was an old French measure the value of which varied with locality. The *arpent de Paris,* about .84 acre, was the one used in the land grants in the Missouri area.

weak, Benton soon had many claims under his care. This put him, in Missouri, as it had in Tennessee, at the center of a great conflict of interests. In one group, he found old, early-arrived French families, determined to hold their all-embracing ancient titles. In the other group, he saw ambitious, more recently arrived enterprisers and speculators (like Judge Lucas himself), determined to clear the way for buying low and selling high.

His land practice earned Thomas a reputation in some quarters as a lackey for the local French aristocracy. Claims to huge areas *were* held by men like Auguste and Pierre Chouteau, "Don Moises Austin," and Charles Gratiot, and at least some of these vast grants were given under circumstances suggesting fraud. But there were hundreds of small holders involved too, both French *petits paysans* and American small farmers. Looking at the *Registres d'Arpentage,* Benton could count about 140 great concessions, surveyed, but more than 860 family plots, surveyed, of 800 *arpents* or less. In addition, there were hundreds or thousands of unsurveyed small family claims.[5]

As a result of his land-title work, Benton gloried in one case involving a semiaugust personage. This was the matter of Sieur Etienne Bogliolo, late of Genoa, Sardinia, but now of New Madrid, Missouri — the locals called it New *Mád*-rid — over lands claimed by the Sieur Bogliolo and one Joseph Michel. A partnership between the two men had terminated at Michel's death, whereupon Bogliolo sought to have Michel's heirs enjoined in chancery from disposing of the disputed acres — and Lawyer Benton was successful in securing the injunction. When he advertised it to the Territory, he put the matter with a flourish which converted a simple legal notice into a piece of florid literature.[6]

But his work was not all matters of *arpentage.* He also had an extensive trial practice in the St. Louis court, which often handled fifteen cases in a day. Once, his trial practice involved Benton in a quarrel with the favorite son of Judge Lucas, young Charles Lucas. At the Circuit Court in St. Louis, in October, 1816, Thomas and Charles found themselves counsel for opposing clients. Young Lucas was a sturdy antagonist. Just ten years Benton's junior, he had an extensive practice, and was a member of the territorial legislature. He was industrious, sober, plain-mannered, quiet, prudent, and he loathed brawlers — probably he seemed to the rugged Benton a little prim. The time came for final pleas to the jury. In gaudy, dogmatic style, Benton asserted that since the evidence *was* as he had presented it, the jury *must* decide

as he asked. Immediately Lucas was up to correct his antagonist —
there was no such evidence.

"I contradict you, sir," Benton cried, his eyes flashing.

"I contradict *you,* sir," responded Charles Lucas.

"If you deny that, you deny the truth," Benton barked, thrusting his
huge head at Lucas.

"If you assert that, you assert what is not true," was the firm answer.

The jury found for Lucas's client. Within a month, the ultrasensitive
Benton demanded satisfaction for the insult to his ultrasensitive honor.
Query by Lucas: What kind of satisfaction? Reply by Benton: A duel,
sir, with whatever weapons you choose, sir. But Lucas would not be
called to account privately for his actions at the bar in behalf of a client. He wrote Benton this, and that was the end of it [7] — though the
ill-feeling persisted.

Meanwhile, Benton went on with his work, and his practice grew.
The perambulating Presbyterian missionary, Timothy Flint, noted before long that Benton was "supreme at the bar," though Flint was a
little concerned about Benton's flamboyant courtroom style — "he is
acute, labored, florid, rather sophomorical." Nonetheless, he was certainly "a man of strong sense," and well endowed with the passion and
industry that commanded so much respect on the frontier — "there
flashes 'strange fire' from his eye, and all that he does 'smells of the
lamp.' " [8]

As a lawyer, Thomas Benton had an excellent opportunity to observe
the town and Territory he had made his home. St. Louis must have
seemed to him a different world from the one he had known in Tennessee. The village still exhibited a culture which was as much French
as American. French was spoken on every side, and in the narrow,
unpaved streets pedestrians had to dodge out of the way of little French
carts drawn by ponies. Surrounding the increasing number of stone or
brick homes of the well-to-do were meaner dwellings built in the French
manner of logs or planks driven vertically into the ground and daubed
with mud. A local show place was the dwelling of the man who had
helped found St. Louis when he was thirteen — Auguste Chouteau. His
home and its outbuildings took up a whole square at the center of town,
between the Rue de la Tour and the Rue de la Place. Inside a visitor
could admire the polished walnut floors and the train of servants the
aging *Français* kept around him.

Though the town was small, it was the scene of a vigorous life and the center of the expanding, new "Far West." When Benton arrived, it had only about two thousand inhabitants and some three hundred slaves. But it had boasted since 1808 of the first newspaper west of the Mississippi, the weekly *Missouri Gazette,* edited by Joseph Charless. The *Gazette* reflected the local culture, not only in its editorial columns, but in its ads announcing "Negroes for Sale," its plugs for "Lee's Genuine PATENT MEDICINES for FAMILIES," its discreet physicians' "cards." Beyond the town was its tributary area, which Thomas Benton saw as he rode circuit, a near-wilderness dotted here and there with clearings and houses. Its great resources were lead, furs, and land — the rich, black earth of the valleys, supporting good crops of wheat, of maize or corn, of rye, of oats. The inhabitants Benton came to know were varied. They included the lead miners in the Potosi region southwest; the "backwoodsmen," half-trappers and half-farmers, a little rough in manners and speech, living on pork, venison, game fowl, and corn bread, and wearing clothes made from deerskins and bearskins; and finally the yeomen farmers. More and more settlers were pouring into the region, poor, plain men on foot or horseback, and wagon trains of well-to-do plantation families. Watching a homestead-seeking crowd at a Federal land auction one day, Benton was once again convinced that the Territory must soon be a state.[9] In the "Far West" beyond Missouri were the fur-trapping and trading areas — reaches of lucrative enterprise which sent men from the outfitting post of St. Louis deep into the forests and mountains. Filled with a heady, typically American enthusiasm for expansion and development, Benton was determined to grow with the new West and play a big part in Missouri's untold future.

Meanwhile, he made friends in his new home. His chief intimate was another attorney his own age, Luke Lawless, a Dubliner born who had served a turn in the British navy, and then become a colonel in Napoleon's army. There was Robert Wash, from Virginia, a college graduate, also a lawyer, and a huntsman who always kept a pack of hounds. There was Jeremiah Connor, auctioneer, businessman, real-estate operator, who was St. Louis's third sheriff, and one of those who helped organize an Erin Benevolent Society in the town. Finally there were two more Virginians, Major Joshua Pilcher and Dr. Bernard Farrar — certainly Thomas had enough Virginia friends in St. Louis to intensify an already developing affection for the Old Dominion. Pilcher, eight years younger than Benton, had come to St. Louis during the War of

1812 and had gone into merchandising. Farrar, whose family had crossed from England in 1621, had come to St. Louis as one of its first physicians. Through men like Wash and Farrar, through his host Charles Gratiot, through the James McDowell family, the Colonel had an entree to the home of William Clark, the explorer Governor, himself from Virginia and married to a kinswoman of the McDowells.[10] Soon Thomas could count the Governor also as a friend.

One of Benton's friendships brought him to another contact with the field of honor. Before he had been in Missouri a year he was asked by Edward Hempstead's brother Thomas to act as his second in a challenge to Judge David Barton's brother Joshua. The Colonel and Joshua Barton's second, Edward Bates, drew up the papers, and on August 10, 1816, the principals and seconds went to a barren island in the Mississippi River to try the issue. After each duelist had fired without effect, they agreed that they were satisfied and could be reconciled, and Benton and Bates prepared another statement to this effect.[11] Presumably everyone was thus much happier than he had been. But later Benton's part in the affair was remembered and held against him by Joshua Barton's intimates and allies.

Soon Thomas felt well enough established to bring his mother to St. Louis. Of all the loyalties of the time and place, that of the family as a close-knit unit was strongest. Early in 1817, Benton went to Leiper's Fork to fetch his mother and his sister Mary; by May the family was re-united in St. Louis; the partnership of mother and son was resumed. The Virginia-born Nancy Benton, nearing sixty, seemed strangely out of place in the pushing, brawling, half-French, half-American village, with its streets masses of mud when it rained or tracks of dust when it was dry. But she was happy to make a new home for Thomas, who now bought a house for himself and his enlarged family. It was a large frame building in a distinctly American style, built by Jerry Connor on the northwest corner of Laurel and Rue de l'Eglise, in a new subdivision which was later called Washington Avenue. Before long nephews and nieces, the sons and daughters of Samuel Benton, congregated about the rising scion of the Benton line, and Thomas found himself with a large establishment to provide for. It was not easy. Prices had gone up with the influx of settlers — at the new Market House, poor beef was netting six cents a pound, fresh pork five cents, eggs twelve-and-a-half cents per dozen, and cornmeal the outrageous price of a half dollar a bushel![12]

Meanwhile, Thomas's life was marred by grief. In April, 1817, he noted, "My first friend in the place, Mr. Gratiot, is just dead of a paralytic stroke." Four months later, in August, Edward Hempstead was thrown from his horse and killed. Thomas was shaken at his idol's death, stayed up with his friend's body all night, and attended the funeral at Stephen Hempstead's plantation. "The lives of useful and eminent men," he wrote in a memoir of Edward Hempstead, "should be written, not for the dead, but for the living. They should display not a vain panegyric, but a detail of circumstance which would lead the living to the same line of conduct and the same honorable result." In August also Thomas's sister Mary died at the age of thirty-seven.[13] Now none of the four girls, Margaret, Little Nancy, Susannah, and Mary, remained, and the Widow Benton had left only Thomas and his brothers Jesse, Samuel, and Nathaniel.

At the age of thirty-five, not quite two years a resident of Missouri, Thomas Benton was a leader at the bar, a man about town with friends who had achieved or were rising to position and influence, and a householder.

It was only proper that such a man should have his portrait painted, and this Benton did shortly after his mother had arrived in St. Louis. The painting, a bust on a large canvas, showed an elegant man of the times. Set on broad, bulky shoulders, his head was massive and his face full, with a fair, high-pink complexion and smooth skin. His wavy hair was worn long at the back and at the temples, with one lock falling almost to his right eye. A very high forehead made an impressive setting for his gray-blue, close-set eyes. His long, full nose, slightly beaked, reached toward a thin-lipped mouth and a prominent, fleshy chin. At his neck, he wore white stiff linen with silver studs and a black stock and cravat knotted in a bow, and his thick shoulders were covered by a black button-around coat. His patrician countenance was already serious, almost stern, yet with an underlying suggestion of pleasantness and readiness to smile. His intensity, dogged, aggressive resolution, and curiosity, were marked in his eyes, nose, mouth, and chin.[14]

If any of the belles of St. Louis thought this fine-looking man eligible for marriage, none caught him. Presumably his heart was still set on the comely, accomplished Elizabeth McDowell far to the east, in Virginia.

[3]

FROM THE BEGINNING OF HIS residence in Missouri, Benton probably looked forward to a public and political career. At the place and time lawyers took to politics as readily as settlers did to land; and certainly Benton's contacts and eminence at the bar could be expected, in due time, to assure him a place or even a headstart in the political racing. But even so fortunate a man had to establish himself fully before he could step onto the uncertain track of office seeking.

Though politics in Territorial Missouri was often merely a matter of personal rivalry, definite groups had begun to form. Nearly every man claimed to be a Democratic-Republican, and the citizens elected only the members of the Territorial legislature and their delegate-without-vote to Congress, while other officials were appointed. Thus, national party divisions were largely absent. But beneath the surface of single-party allegiance there were alignments of property, position, and power, of interest groups and political factions, and there were issues at stake. One group, called the "little junto" by Editor Charless, was dominated by old-French business leaders and holders of huge *arpentages* under Spanish land grants, men like Auguste Chouteau and his innumerable connections, such as Gratiot and the fur magnate Bernard Pratte; this group had been led in politics by Governor Clark, Edward Hempstead, John Scott of Ste. Genevieve, and some others. An "anti-junto" group was composed largely of American settlers who had come to St. Louis since the Louisiana Purchase, new enterprisers like the land-octopus William Russell and the speculator-Delegate Rufus Easton; the political spokesmen for this group were Judge Lucas, his son Charles Lucas, and to some extent the popular David Barton and Editor Charless himself. His interest in land-title cases and his associations and friendships led Benton to the "junto" side.

As he went deeper into politics, he found himself more and more at odds with the potent Jean Baptiste Charles Lucas. Though he had been born in France, in 1758, Judge Lucas did not run with the French and Créole leaders. In France he had imbibed republican ideas, which led him in 1784 to emigrate to the United States and become John B. C. Lucas; settling near Pittsburgh, he became in 1803 a member of Congress. After the Louisiana Purchase, Thomas Jefferson appointed him Territorial Judge and Land Commissioner in the new area. In St.

Louis he began speculating in town lots and undertook numerous business ventures. Thus, circumstances threw his interests with the later American settlers rather than with the old French. A passionate, intense, self-willed man, Lucas was to find his life curiously intertwined with that of Benton for a number of years.

Neither the "junto" nor the "anti-junto" was close to the masses of plain people. Politics was still dominated by gentlemen of substantial property, and common men played little part on their own in the political sweepstakes. Both groups operated in the spirit of Enterprise, of developing the new country and making it pay off, though the "anti-junto" made a noisy to-do about the alleged aristocratic connections of the "junto." Generally, the "junto" faction demanded a generous recognition of the old Spanish land-grant claims, without emphasis on technicalities, while the opposition faction supported the strict policy set by Lucas as Land Commissioner. The controlling conflict of interests was, Who was to get the major share of Missouri's virgin lands? [15]

By 1817 Benton had begun to seek his place in this political picture. A visitor to the Gratiot home noted that the young man was already "ascending the political ladder"; the first step was apparently an appointment by Governor William Clark to the newly established Board of Trustees for Schools in St. Louis, to sit with the Governor, Auguste Chouteau, and two others. At the first meeting in April, Benton was chosen secretary pro tem. The minutes, in his clear, fast-marching hand, tell of the earliest attempt to set up a school system in the town — a resolution to investigate landholdings available for school purposes. Soon also, Benton began to write articles for the local press. In May, 1817, a new paper appeared in St. Louis, the *Western Emigrant,* presumably a "junto" press to match the "anti-junto" *Missouri Gazette.* With his Tennessee journalistic experiences behind him, Benton became a regular contributor.[16] It was a small thing, but it must have helped give him a reputation as a man of political promise.

In the summer of 1817 rumor had it that Benton might be a candidate for Delegate to Congress. In the end he did not run, though his advocacy of an easy land policy played a part in the campaign. The "junto"-faction candidate, John Scott, won over Rufus Easton in an election which brought out less than 4500 votes.

[4]

THIS ELECTION SET OFF a dramatic series of events. When Benton approached the voting clerks on August 4, his old enemy Charles Lucas challenged his right to vote and asked if he had paid his taxes — whereupon Benton, impeached again, granted the young man a withering look and turned majestically to the election judges.

"Gentlemen," he said, according to later reports, "if *you* have any questions to ask, I am prepared to answer, but I do not propose to answer charges made by any puppy who may happen to run across my path!"

To Lucas, this was abusive talk. Certainly the word "puppy," a favorite of Benton's, was a term likely to grate on an ambitious and successful youth of twenty-five, but Thomas refused to recant and went about his business, leaving his barb to rankle in Lucas's sensitive mind.

On August 11 Lucas wrote a letter. He began formally, "Thomas H. Benton, Esq., Sir," noted that the Colonel had called him "Puppy," and went on to demand "that satisfaction which is due from one gentleman to another for such an indignity." The challenge reached Benton at a distressing time. He had just sat through the night with the body of Edward Hempstead and had returned to his office to refresh himself before going to the funeral when, about eight in the morning, Joshua Barton arrived with Lucas's note.

"Sir," he replied immediately, "I accept; but I must now go and bury a dead friend; that is my first duty, after that is discharged I will fight, tonight, if possible; if not, tomorrow morning at daybreak. I accept your challenge, sir."

The articles were drawn up that day. Benton and Lucas were to face one another at six in the morning, on an island in the Mississippi, with smoothbore pistols not exceeding eleven inches in length. They were to stand thirty feet apart. Each was to be asked if he was ready, and when the command was given either might present and fire; if either man fired before the signal, the other's second was to shoot him down immediately. The terms were signed by Luke Lawless for Benton and by Joshua Barton for Lucas.

The sun rose the next morning about five o'clock. All the preparations had been made, the boats were ready, the pistols secured. The grim parties rowed quietly from the bank. It must have been a lonely, silent scene, the sandy island with its scrubby growth, the only sound the voices of the men and the swish of the current and lapping of the waves at the shore. Lucas was "cool and collected," and Benton's well-steeled nerves were calm as the seconds paced off the distance and the principals took their places. After each man had stated that he was ready, the command was given — "Fire!"

Two reports broke the morning quiet. The steady Benton aimed well, and his bullet went through Lucas's neck to the left of his windpipe, while the younger man barely nicked his six-foot, bulky target. Blood poured from Lucas's wound, and his surgeon, Dr. Garrit Quarles, refused to allow another fire. When Lawless asked Lucas if he was satisfied, he said that he was and that he would not ask for another meeting. This was recounted to Benton, who declared loudly and energetically that he was not satisfied. Young Lucas then agreed to fight again as soon as his wound permitted, and was helped to his boat by his friends — and there he fainted.

The Colonel's wound was a slight contusion below his right knee. This was nothing for his surgeon, Bernard Farrar, to worry about, for the ball had not even cut Benton's pantaloons. But it was a source of wry amusement for Judge Lucas, who noted that when his son's enemy went to his office he let out, "though involuntarily," a few "symptoms of momentary lameness."

Gossip about the duel soon divided gentlemen and ladies into pro-Benton and pro-Lucas factions. In Judge Lucas's view, Benton in saying he was not satisfied "demands eagerly the remainder of Mr. Lucas's blood"; this made the matter no longer "an affair of honor" but "merely and simply an affair of blood and extermination." Meanwhile Thomas's friends argued with him that his too sensitive regard for "honor" would look like vengeance, and they urged him to withdraw his demand. Before the month was out Lawless wrote Charles Lucas that Benton now authorized him to say that he no longer insisted on a second meeting. But gossip still ran in the streets and in the coffeeshops. Some believed that old Judge Lucas, always sensitive, vindictive, and bitter, was put out at his son for avoiding a second encounter.* Others

---

* In a long-after-the-fact account, Amadée Soulard tells of a conversation between Lucas, *père,* and his son Charles in a vacant lot outside Planters House. According to this account, the old man walked about gesturing nervously, while young Charles was hesitant and followed his father with an air of weakness. Finally, Judge Lucas's voice rose: "You must fight him again! You must fight him again, I say! The Lucas honor requires it!" Soulard goes on to report that

had it that both old Lucas and young Lucas looked upon Benton as a desperado who had fled Tennessee to escape trial for a crime. The rumors reached Thomas Benton's ears sooner or later. With the fact of his fall from rectitude at the University of North Carolina always at hand to haunt him and sharpen his sense of "honor," he could not stand for such reports running through the town. Thus pricked, he dispatched a new challenge. He had yielded to "a feeling of generosity in my own bosom," he wrote, and had deferred to the judgment of others when he released Lucas from his promise of a second meeting. But in view of the reports filling the country, this feeling would have to be set aside. The challenge must be sent, "to bring these calumnies to an end, and to give you an opportunity of justifying the great expectation which has been excited." This message was dated September 23. Young Lucas was out of town attending court, and when he returned three days later he made one more attempt to patch things up in a conference with Lawless, insisting that he, Charles Lucas, had nothing to do with the rumors in the town. With this, Lawless went back to Benton. No, sir, it would not do, sir — nothing but a written declaration would satisfy him, and Lucas's oral assurances were inadmissible.[17]

At last, Lucas accepted — "I shall give you an opportunity of gratifying your wishes and the wishes of your news carriers," he wrote — though he was sure that the "calumnies" had been "fabricated" by Benton's friends and not by his own. The meeting was arranged for six in the morning, September 27, with terms substantially the same as those of the first meeting, except that the distance was cut to ten feet. After the command to fire, three seconds were to be counted off and the parties must fire within that time.

The fateful day broke hot and close. Even on the island in the river, the air lay still and the sun beat down oppressively on the principals, seconds, and surgeons — Benton, Lawless, Dr. Farrar; Lucas, Joshua Barton, a second second named Eli Clemson, and Dr. Quarles. As a friend of Lawless reported this witness's memory of the event later, Benton was particularly disturbed by the warmth of the day. While the pistols were being made ready, he removed his coat and rolled up his

Charles, after a pause, replied: "Well, then, my dear father . . . Well, then, I will be guided by you once more. If the Lucas honor, whatever it is, requires it, I will fight him again!" ("The Bloody Island Cross Mark," *Globe Democrat,* June 25, 1899.) This account sounds somewhat improbable and overdramatic, and though Soulard states that it was based on his father's contemporaneous journal, it is hardly possible to credit this interview without supporting evidence.

shirt sleeves, revealing a red flannel undershirt, and went to a basin of water to bathe his arms.

"Gentlemen, are you ready?" called Colonel Clemson.

"Don't you *see* I'm not ready?" snapped Thomas Benton.

He dried himself, stepped to his place, and took his pistol from his second. The red of his undershirt flashed in the sun.

"Now I am ready," he called.

The drawing of lots had given Eli Clemson the duty of ordering the fire. Forgetting first to give the word "Fire!" he began to count, "One . . . two . . . three." Startled, Benton looked toward Clemson, and the suspicious Lawless moved his hand toward his pistol, while young Lucas raised his gun. Quickly, Benton lifted his own weapon and fired like a flash of lightning. Both men fired so nearly together that the seconds and surgeons heard only a single report. Benton was untouched, but his ball passed through young Lucas's left arm and into his heart. He fell to the ground, and Benton promptly stepped toward him; but Lucas turned his head away.

"Colonel Benton," he murmured, "you have persecuted me and murdered me! I cannot forgive you."

Finally, however, Lucas turned toward Benton —

"I can forgive you — I do forgive you," he sighed, and a minute later he was dead. For the rest of his life, Thomas was unable to forget the anguish he felt when he saw young Lucas fall, the pain he experienced when young Lucas died.

On the day of the affair, the *Gazette* carried a mournful article.

> The infernal practice of duelling [Editor Charless wrote] has taken off, this morning, one of the first characters of our country, Charles Lucas, Esq., Attorney at Law . . .
>
> *Tale bearers this is thy work!*
> *Innocent blood lies at thy doors!*

Meanwhile, old Judge Lucas insisted that Benton was "a great proficient in the art of shooting men down," and filled the pages of the *Gazette* with expressions of "horror [at] the demand *of the adept duellist* (Mr. Benton) for a second meeting." In the Benton-Lucas quarrel, intense personal, family, professional, and political loyalties had clashed. Ever *difficile* and a bitter hater, old Lucas now developed a long-lasting, near-paranoid obsession with his son's "murderer," and at every opportunity poured out a stream of bitterness against Thomas

Benton. Nor did he lack friends — long letters hounding Benton appeared in the hospitable pages of the pro-Lucas *Gazette,* with one correspondent signing himself magnificently "A Friend to Man." Three weeks after the duel, Judge Lucas could exult that at "two considerable meetings" in St. Charles County "it had been agreed that none of the members of the meeting should employ Benton as attorney," while "at Potosi B. was pretty well countenanced during the last term of the court." Three months after the duel, Judge Lucas was writing to Billy Carroll in Tennessee, to ask three questions — "What kind of a reputation Thomas H. Benton enjoyed when he was a student in North Carolina? . . . What is his general reputation in the State of Tennessee? . . . What was understood to be the cause of Benton leaving Tennessee?" Again, Judge Lucas informed Secretary of State John Quincy Adams that Benton had "relentlessly pursued Charles Lucas. . . . The real motives were that he foresaw that the fair character and promising talents of Charles Lucas would stand in the way of his ambitious views." The dead man's father never gave up the pursuit. Three years after the affair, the *Gazette* called the Colonel "a man crimsoned with the blood of one of our most promising young citizens," and the sandbar on which the men fought was soon known locally as "Bloody Island."

In the face of this furious storm, Benton held his peace. He had been pigheaded, perhaps, and all his touchy pride and hot temper and muscular pugnacity had shown themselves at their worst in the affair, making him appear bloodthirsty indeed. But he had other sensibilities and was deeply distressed at the event. After the duel he tried to live a somewhat more pacific life, and if the duel was mentioned in his presence, he grew somber and refused to talk of it. Shortly before he died, he summed it up in a sketch of his life. "A duel at St. Louis ended fatally," he wrote of himself, "at which Col. Benton has not been heard to speak except among intimate friends, and to tell of the pang which went through his heart when he saw the young man fall . . . As proof of the manner in which he look[ed] upon all these scenes, and his desire to bury all remembrance of them forever," he had had all his papers relating to the matter burned. He hoped no future curiosity or industry would bring to light what he wished had never happened.[18]

[5]

IN ADDITION TO HIS OTHER DOINGS, Benton was increasingly active as a businessman — particularly in those areas which so absorbed men of Enterprise in the new West: land speculation and banking.

Compared to those of his grandfather and father, Thomas's land ventures were modest. At the beginning he limited himself to the purchase of town lots on the rising St. Louis market, buying small parcels until he had by the fall of 1817 pyramided his holdings to a value of three thousand dollars or a little more. Perhaps to raise cash for such ventures, he tried to sell out his lands in Tennessee. He went in the spring of 1818 to Leiper's Fork and sold to his brother Jesse the two hundred and sixteen acres of the family plot he still held there. At the same time, he looked into his father's old claim to lands on the Chickasaw Bluffs above the Mississippi — a treaty was in prospect with the Chickasaw Indians which would remove them from the property. But the Benton claim had to yield to a stronger one held by Andrew Jackson. Not long after the Indian treaty was signed, Thomas saw the city of Memphis grow on the property he had had to waive!

In the spring of 1819, Benton joined with a dozen other men to advertise a new "Town of Osage," at the junction of the Missouri and Osage rivers. Declaring that this town would be the center of the future state of Missouri, its promoters projected streets a mile along each stream, with great connecting avenues and many public squares. When Benton saw his name in an announcement of the Osage project in the *Gazette,* he wrote a letter ordering Editor Charless to "expunge" his name, "and never to insert it in your paper again, except for the purposes of scandal and defamation." [19] As with so many other grand ventures in the new West, nothing important came of the Osage project.

His law work and business activities brought Benton into contact with banking. In Missouri as in the nation, credit and money for exchange were short and uncertain. The immense fur business, the lead mining industry, the ordinary trade of the towns, and the transactions of farmers all depended largely on barter and a bewildering mixture of foreign coins and paper money, issued by an equally bewildering variety of local banks and other firms. Almost superhuman skill was required to distinguish between sound banknotes, counterfeits, and notes issued by "rag barons" who never intended to redeem in specie. Money that was "good" in one locality might be valueless a few miles away. The number of note-issuing state banks jumped from 88 to 246 between 1811 and 1816, while their note circulation was extended from forty-five million dollars to a hundred million between 1812 and 1817 — sizable amounts for the time. Largely moved by the great capitalists in New York and Philadelphia, men like John Jacob Astor and Stephen Girard who feared for the future of business in general and their investments in particular, Congress in 1816 had chartered a second Bank of the United States. This semipublic corporation was expected to supply credit and a sound national currency, and at the same time to regulate local bank-note issues by refusing to accept unsound paper in payment of government accounts — so the political leaders in the movement like Clay and Calhoun argued.[20] These benefits, however, took some time to materialize, particularly in the new West, where the money-muddle persisted.

In Missouri, two years before Benton had come to the Territory, the legislature had taken steps of its own. Responding to a petition from Auguste Chouteau and other St. Louis businessmen, it had chartered a corporation, to be known as the Bank of St. Louis, which began business at the end of 1816. This bank extended credit by issuing its own bank notes to borrowers.* Before long, it began granting excessive loans on real estate operations; though this was a boon to the new-come American speculators, it led to bank-note issues beyond the margin of safety. The cashier, John B. Smith, was the key figure in this activity. Meanwhile, Benton had become a stockholder in the Bank of St. Louis, and as an attorney he was authorized to act as agent for other stockholders. In this capacity, he was allied with his friend Joshua Pilcher, the field leader of a conservative, minority-stockholder bloc apparently associated with Auguste Chouteau, which condemned the bank's management for overlending and for failing to redeem its notes in specie. In a directors' meeting, Pilcher succeeded in having John B. Smith removed for "malversation."

---

* Before the Civil War, most bank loans were made not through the modern practice of establishing a credit or deposit in the borrower's name, but by issuing notes on the bank to the borrower, and such notes circulating made up the bulk of the paper money of the day. Each bank engraved its notes in its own design, in accord with a common form, as the following:

The President, directors, and company of the BANK OF ST. LOUIS promise to pay $5.00 to ―― or Bearer on demand.

Saint Louis, Mo. Territory   *June 18, 1817*
       S. HAMMOND, *Pres.*   JOHN B. SMITH, *Cash.*

Despite this victory, the minority bloc remained dissatisfied with the bank's policies. On February 11, 1818, what the bank's officers called "a tumultuous assemblage" gathered in the street outside the bank building. After a while, Pilcher, Benton, and another minority leader named Elias Rector led the crowd into the bank and proceeded to hold an informal stockholders' meeting. A resolution authorized the leaders to demand the keys from the bank officers. This accomplished, Pilcher, Benton, and Rector ordered everyone outdoors, padlocked the building, and strode away with their flock to Pilcher's "counting room." There a committee was set up to see that the bank did not open until the minority won an agreement which they thought would protect their interests. On February 16, the committee of safety, which included Benton, returned the keys to the bank's officers. Despite an announcement that business would begin again on February 23, nothing happened, and the minority issued a statement of protest signed by fifteen men, including Thomas Benton for "self" and three others. The failure of the bank to pay notes in cash and the failure to reopen, they proclaimed, was likely "materially to injure the interest of the stockholders."

In the midst of the fray, the rebels were hauled into court. On February 13, a Grand Jury reported indictments against Pilcher, Benton, Rector, *et al.,* for highhandedly marching in and taking possession of the bank building and bank assets. The men were not convicted, but all were required to post bonds to keep the peace toward the bank's president Eli Clemson and the new cashier Theophilus Smith. Benton's bond of one thousand dollars was secured by his friends Dr. Farrar and Robert Wash, and he himself went surety for Elias Rector.

The Bank of St. Louis finally opened its doors. In a little more than a year, however, it failed, a victim of speculation, paper money expansion, mismanagement, and the ravages of internal dissension. In the huggermugger Benton had learned something about frontier banking problems and practices. Western men were not agreed on the pros and cons of paper issues. To many budding capitalists, anxious for easy credit to launch profitable speculations, large paper issues seemed a boon; but to more conservative businessmen, and to many small farmers concerned with a steady return on their labor, excessive issues were a bane. In his experiences with the Bank of St. Louis, Benton had met these issues in a very practical way[21] — issues which in turbulent years to come were to hold the center of the national political arena and engross his attention.

Meanwhile, the expansion swept on, and the progress of the territory filled Benton with enthusiasm. The first steamboat had chuffed up the Mississippi in 1817, and by 1819 Thomas could write James Preston that the river was "enlivened with commerce." Immigrants poured in "with a force and steadiness which should announce to the old states that the power of this continent is gravitating to the borders of the Mississippi" — in short, to Missouri. Land prices zoomed, with town lots that had sold in 1815 for thirty dollars an acre now commanding two thousand an acre — "if I had brought with me twenty or thirty thousand dollars," Benton exclaimed, "I should have been worth today from a quarter to half a million." Look, the budding disciple of Enterprise cried, "look back to what we were thirty years ago; see what we are today; tell us what we must be in 1830." Surely, men of hope and ambition should "plant themselves betimes on the waters of the West." [22]

CHAPTER 5

The *Enquirer* Man

1818 - 1820

DESPITE HIS DUEL with Lucas, and the antic quarrel over the Bank of St. Louis, Benton retained the loyalties of his friends and of a substantial faction of the village's leaders. He gave attention to politics, and within three years of his encounter with Lucas his persistence, commanding ability, and flair enabled him to win a place as one of the Territory's important political leaders.

In the beginning, his energies were often devoted to modest projects. In the early months of 1818, for example, he was concerned about his friend, Governor Clark, who had been absent from St. Louis on family matters — "some wretches have spread it abroad that the Governor was unpopular" in the Territory. When the explorer returned to town, Benton did what he could to counter the canard — he called a group together in his office, and with them arranged a testimonial dinner to his patron and ally. Later in 1818 he wrote Ninian Edwards, Governor of the Illinois Territory, about a matter of patronage — "Our mutual friend, Gen. Bissell, wishes to command in this department . . . Mr. Scott [the Delegate to Congress from Missouri] will speak with the Secretary of War, and your voice would doubtless have its weight if joined to his." [1] Patronage was ever the cement of politics, and Benton apparently believed that he who would help himself must first help others.

Before the year was out, he himself was one of twelve candidates for a place on the five-man Board of Trustees of St. Louis. The election took place in January, 1819, and when the count was announced Benton found himself last.

It was an inauspicious beginning, but running for petty office was not the only way into public affairs. In August, 1818, Sergeant Hall, proprietor-editor of the *Western Emigrant,* sold out; he was succeeded as proprietor by Isaac Henry, formerly of Nashville, and as editor by Thomas Benton. They changed the name of the paper to the *St. Louis*

Enquirer, and made it a vigorous, zestful competitor to the longer established *Gazette.* Throwing himself enthusiastically into his new job, Benton worked diligently in the little shop on Main Street, opposite Manuel's Corner and adjoining the post office — a spot at about present First and Chestnut streets. At the beginning, the *Enquirer* published each Wednesday. Subscription rates were four dollars at the end of the year, or three dollars in advance, and the publishers announced that "whoever will guarantee the payment of ten papers, shall receive the eleventh gratis." Advertising brought one dollar for twelve lines. With a format similiar to the four-page *Gazette,* the rival paper was larger, had wider columns, and contained more editorial matter and less advertising.

His new job gave wide compass for Benton's probing mind and vigorous prose, and for his interest in politics too. A new era was at hand in which politics was becoming more and more a matter of mass participation, and effective power or influence was to depend on the combination of large numbers of like-minded men. Newspapers were coming to the fore not simply as purveyors of information and entertainment, but as molders of mass public opinion, as partisan instruments through which scattered individuals realized some sense of identification as adherents of a group, as beacons of political leadership. Editors were emerging more and more as key leaders in politics. "Newspapers are the school of public instruction," Editor Benton wrote in his large but didactic way — "they are in America what the Forum was in Greece and Rome, with the advantage of speaking to a *nation* instead of an *assembly;* and when conducted with talent and directed to objects of public utility, they are justly deemed the most powerful *lever* which can be applied to the human mind." [2] Even when he dealt with great public issues, Benton crowded his pages with schoolmasterish historical and philological references — the man who had not finished at the University of North Carolina was apparently determined to prove the intellectual prowess he had developed on his own. Always, however, he was an effective propagandist.

The *Enquirer* expanded and increased its influence, and its editor's prestige rose. In the summer of 1819, for example, Benton participated in a grand dinner tendered to the officers of Colonel Atkinson and Major Long's military and scientific expedition, which was about to ascend the Missouri River to the Yellowstone. As he walked the two short blocks from his home to the imposing red-brick Mansion House hotel, he must have taken a just pride in the affair — he was to be a vice-president assisting the president, General Rector, and the other vice-presidents, Auguste Chouteau and Major Christy. He was also sought out by visitors who wanted information. When Dr. Lewis C. Beck came to St. Louis to gather materials for his compendium of information about the New West, he called at the back room of the *Enquirer* to see what he could learn from the editor. He was specially pleased at the history Benton gave him of *l'année du coup* — the year 1780, when the little French post was attacked by Indians urged on by the British.[3]

In June, 1819, Henry and Benton, assisted now by a practical printer named Charles Keemle who served them as shop foreman, announced that in September they would issue the *Enquirer* two times a week. The venerable *Gazette* was unable to follow suit.

[2]

IN EDITORIAL ARTICLE after article, Thomas Benton probed great issues of the day, exhibiting his tendency to mix soaring ideas and heavy erudition.

One series of articles dealt with the future of the West. Drawing on the experience of the Lewis and Clark expedition and on what he had learned from talking with fur-trade leaders and common *voyageurs,* Benton envisioned a future in which immigrants would spill into the untouched lands of the great Pacific Northwest, or what was then called the "Oregon country." At the same time he saw a day when Americans would fill the plains of the then Spanish province of Texas. As Benton thought about these matters, negotiations were going forward with Great Britain over conflicting claims to the Oregon country, and with Spain over conflicting claims to Texas. In October, 1818, a convention was signed which provided for ten years joint British-American occupation of the Northwest area — an agreement the *Enquirer* condemned vigorously. Meanwhile, insisting that the Louisiana Purchase made Texas, up to the edge of the Rio Grande watershed, American property, the doughty Western editor called a warning to the Eastern-bred statesmen at Washington — "the magnificent valley of the Mississippi" was *ours,* including Texas, and "woe to the statesman that undertakes to surrender one drop of its water, one inch of its soil." But in February, 1819, a treaty was signed by Secretary of State John Quincy

Adams and the Spanish Minister Luis de Onis, by which the United States acquired Florida but yielded Texas. Again, the *Enquirer* denounced this treaty and John Quincy Adams bitterly. In his wrath at the Oregon and Texas agreements, Benton proclaimed a principle which served as a keynote for his whole series of articles on the subject and for much of his life. *"It is time,"* he wrote portentously, *"that western men had some share in the destinies of this Republic."*

On his own, he now urged his fellow Westerners to think about ways to settle the Oregon country. The national government should encourage and protect the fur trade there, and encourage settlers to emigrate to the Northwest — the climate was temperate, the soil "rich and highly susceptible to cultivation," and the region would sustain a rich economy of *"furs* and *bread."* In time, Benton argued further, the "Asiatic commerce" of the country could be funneled along the Lewis and Clark route, up the Missouri and down the Columbia, and thence on to Japan, China, India, and the Pacific islands; and settlers could also travel this route. It would run hard by the (then) far northern provinces of the Spanish colony, Mexico, which were believed to be fabulously rich in gold and silver, and an expanded trade along the route could help supply the Mississippi valley with vitally needed hard money, gold and silver coin, specie. If Spanish hostility to foreign traders blocked this scheme, "an efficient aid," the expansive editor serenely explained, "would be given to the Mexicans, and their independence would be established" — it was as simple as that! The existing sea route to Asia required immense investments in each voyage, and thus "all that useful class of traders 'whose enterprise is greater than their capital,' " were cut off; but along the overland route, "small capitalists" would have a chance. Thus future Oregon settlers might advance themselves by gathering a modest capital and investing it in the new trade. One thing more remained to round out the picture, Benton argued — a powerful force to open the new country and serve as a core for its development, which might be supplied by "the operations of an [*sic*] American Fur Company, headed by men of enterprise," and protected by Federal military posts along the route. Such a concern would "sap at its foundation the solid pillar of British wealth and power [in America], and give the Republic her day of pre-eminence among the nations of the earth." [4]

The Oregon articles covered a wide social and political, as well as geographical, range. On the one hand Benton expressed the aspirations of many farmers, small fur trappers, small traders, and *voyageurs,* the dream of Arcadia; on the other hand he bespoke the interests of the business and commercial groups in St. Louis, the allurements of Enterprise. There was, of course, already "an" American Fur Company — incorporated in 1808 under John Jacob Astor of New York, *the* American Fur Company had sought unsuccessfully to establish its power over the Oregon domain, and as an aspiring monopoly it had in 1818 reached a business agreement with the St. Louis firms that had been controlled by Auguste Chouteau, Charles Gratiot, and their associates. The American Fur Company part of Thomas Benton's vision must certainly have pleased the old-French, established fur magnates and their powerful group in St. Louis. At the same time, his "lever" must have had an effect on the minds of many yeomen, self-employed tradesmen, and petty merchants who, in the fluid society of the West, could hope someday to become capitalists of considerable substance — as well as on the minds of modest would-be settlers hungry for fertile farmlands. In short, Benton was engaged in a feat of political Roman-riding, astride the steeds of Enterprise and Arcadia at the same time.

At the *Gazette,* Joseph Charless sneered at his rival's large vision and gaudy rhetoric. "What a prodigy this editor is," he cried, "who can alone see better into the interests of the nation, from the point he occupies, near or at the mouth of the Missouri River, than . . . Mr. Adams." [5]

Undeterred, the *Enquirer* editor went on proclaiming his views — on banks and banking, for example. The zeal to purchase lands for resale was a fever in the West, and more and more large acreages were bought on credit at inflated prices, while merchants laid in immense stores from suppliers in the East, also largely on credit and at inflated prices. Credit for such speculations was supplied, in notes, by the ever-expanding state-chartered banks. Through 1818 the nation's leading, business-minded weekly, *Niles Register,* ran several articles which aptly described the country's developing financial structure as a "paper system." Riding the boom, a few men who had easy access to bank paper money were able to establish local monopolies, while plain farmers and working men found that zooming prices decreased the real value of their produce and labor. Thus, the *Niles Register* article complained, *"speculation* is seated in the parlor, but *labor* is refused *repose* on the dung hill" — while an ominous threat developed that a "rag nobility" of financiers might establish itself in a business contraction by foreclosing on the nation's mortgaged lands and property. These articles were picked up by the *Gazette,* but Benton at the *Enquirer* determined to go further and point an accusing editorial finger at *particular* unsound banks and practices. Thus . . .

> The Farmers and Mechanics Bank, at Cincinnati — issuing notes on "empty boxes."
> The Bank of Georgetown, in Kentucky — its one-dollar bills were being cleverly altered to one-hundred-dollar notes!
> The Edwardsville Bank, nearby in Illinois — "insolvent according to its own showing" despite the fact that it had had twenty thousand dollars of (somebody's) specie on hand, "all arranged, like a china-work shop, to catch [the] eye." (The political leader Ninian Edwards was interested in this bank, and Benton's attacks on it were to play a part in a later antagonism between the two men.)
> The Farmers and Mechanics Bank, at Cincinnati, again — it has "exploded."

And so on, through bank after bank in the West and South — the long list revealed how widespread the speculative, paper-money mania had become.

Toward the new Bank of the United States, the *Enquirer* was ambivalent. The big Bank, under its first president, William Jones, had joined in the fever of paper flux. Not until the 1820's under the capable, domineering Nicholas Biddle did the big Bank begin to perform efficiently its functions of handling public moneys and restraining local bank issues. Throughout its early days of mismanagement, the *Enquirer* criticized the Bank of the United States but did not oppose it as such. In 1818-1819 the Maryland legislature imposed on the Bank's branch in Baltimore a tax so heavy that it would make operations there impossible. The issue was settled when the Supreme Court, through Chief Justice John Marshall, held the tax unconstitutional. This decision comes "very opportunely," Benton wrote in the *Enquirer,* "to give confidence to the public authorities to *oppose* [similar] resolutions to plunder the branch banks in Kentucky and Ohio." The decision in McCulloch *vs.* Maryland, plus the selection of the respected, cautious Langdon Cheves as the Bank's second president, indicated that "the institution may now be considered permanent and national." [6] All told, the *Enquirer* failed to indicate any formed opposition to the corporation Benton was to fight unrelentingly in later years.

The passage of time brought Benton another matter to consider in his paper. The spring and summer of 1819 had seen the collapse of the great speculative boom and the beginning of a severe contraction throughout most of the country, though Missouri managed to escape for some time. In this contraction or depression, unsound banks failed and left their note holders with worthless or nearly worthless paper. The "explosion of so many banks," the *Enquirer* noted, was not necessarily *all* bad, for it was producing "a sensible fall" in the prices of "most of the necessaries of life"; but the collapse of the boom entailed an uneven adjustment, and hardship and privation were settling on the Eastern states. In St. Louis, however, people still asked how one could say "hard times" — when on the streets one saw ladies elegantly dressed with Leghorn bonnets and gold watches on chains, and dandies with narrow corset-coats and wide pantaloons — when so many went about in *"tip-toptissime"* style?

In Missouri, meanwhile, the currency question remained. The shortage of sound money, the difficulty of finding business capital sufficient to the needs of the population, still plagued the West. What was the answer? If paper-money issues were rejected, what was to be offered in their place to meet the money needs of the yeoman and the enterpriser? Increasingly, Thomas Benton was looking toward a hard-money currency as the solution. He hoped that silver and gold might flow in from Mexico, and suggested that copper from the region of Lake Superior and the Falls of St. Anthony might serve as a basis for small notes. In any case, he soon looked upon a specie-based system as a *desideratum,* with "the hard" serving at least as a firm foundation for notes and also as much as possible as a currency. The *Enquirer* carried an item:

> *Banish paper and you introduce gold and silver.*
>
> *Where gold and silver is the standard, the price of everything is reasonable, and a dollar stands for a dollar.*[7]

His place at the *Enquirer* also gave Thomas Benton a platform from which he could offer over-all political leadership. In June, 1819, he proposed a thirteen-point program for Missouri.

His first point was "The change of the Territorial for the State form of Government." In November, 1818, the territorial legislature had petitioned Congress for recognition as a state — but nothing had been done. To Benton, statehood was a matter of right, and he called upon the Federal lawmakers to act promptly.

The next issue was "The adjustment of the land titles derived from the late Spanish Government in Upper Louisiana," particularly the unsurveyed concessions which had not been confirmed by the American authorities. This point would certainly please the "junto," but Benton knew that it would also appeal to many small holders and yeomen too.

As items three and four, Benton listed two demands tailored to the interests of the fur-trading group. The *Enquirer* urged better "protection of the Missouri frontier," through more military outposts, and it asked bluntly for the "protection of the Missouri Fur traders." This could be accomplished, *one,* by building forts at the Falls of St. Anthony on the Mississippi and at the Mandan villages on the Missouri, *two,* by abolishing the Federally operated trading posts in the Indian areas, the so-called "Indian factories," and *three,* by "the incorporation of an American Fur Company" — incorporation by the *national* Congress.

Next, Thomas Benton focused on two Missouri natural resources, salt and lead. Salt was an essential to farmers in feeding stock and curing meat, and they had to pay high prices for imported salt; thus —point five — "the principal salt springs [should be] granted to the people, and the inferior ones sold out as private property." Throughout his public life, Benton argued the issue of cheap salt for farmers. A related issue — plank six — was "working the lead mines," then like the salt springs under Federal government control, with limited leases granted to operators. All the mines should be put in the hands of individual enterprisers in *"freehold title,"* in order to get them worked as fully as possible. Here, in the arguments for yielding the salt works and lead mines to private operation, were solid economic reasons to buttress the *Enquirer's* demand for statehood.

Next, Thomas Benton outlined a system of transportation improvements for the entire West. He had traveled Western roads, and knew their muddy, time-consuming, twisting character; thus, he called for national government action to build:

7. *A national road to Washington City.*
8. *Post road to New Orleans . . .* [to facilitate] the success of mercantile operations.
9. *Post routes throughout the territory.*
10. *Post route between St. Louis and Louisville, by way of Vincennes.*

Finally, point eleven, the national government should establish St. Louis as an official port of entry, with its own customs house, and build:

12. *A canal between Lake Michigan and the River Illinois.*
13. *A canal to unite the Mississippi with the Lake Superior.*[8]

This essay revealed that Benton was still Roman-riding, with one foot on the horse of the St. Louis commercial groups, and another on the horse of the small farmers who worked family plots in the countryside. Furthermore, he was not exactly consistent in his conception of the role of the national government. He asked the government to step *in* to certain areas, like the protection of the fur trade and road building, and *out* of other areas, like the operation of the Indian "factories," the salt springs, and the lead mines. But a central interest pervaded the whole-program — the speediest possible development of Missouri on a free-holding and private-enterprise basis.

Before the year was out, Thomas Benton's paper paid a fulsome tribute to the role of the small farmers in this process. "Of all the descriptions of citizens," the *Enquirer* opined, "none are formed by the habits of their life, to become so useful to their country, as those who own and cultivate the soil. They are the chosen of God . . . It should be the object of a good government to increase, by all possible means, the members of this useful class of its citizens." To effect this "the refuse lands of the Republic," the *Enquirer* proposed, should be made "the subject of donation to such as will cultivate them," and a new land policy should be built about the interests of the actual settlers.[9]

[3]

ZEALOUS AS HE WAS in applying his newspaper "lever" to public opinion, Benton still found time for the law, for business affairs, and for his home. No wonder the man who had once faced the debilitations of consumption thanked Heaven for "health to perform my office"!

As a lawyer, his reputation was spreading. It was he, for example, who was chosen by the Philadelphia write-publishers Mathew and Henry Carey to take a suit against his rival editor, Joseph Charless. It was he who was chosen by Ninian Edwards, now Senator from Illinois, as attorney in another case. By August, 1819, Benton found it advisable to take a law partner, and he announced that he and Robert P. Farris would act as colleagues as *attorneys,* though "the business of *Counsellors at Law* will remain distinct." In the language of the time, this meant that Benton would be released from the routine of keeping office, while as a trial lawyer he would travel to any part of Missouri or Illinois to plead civil or criminal cases. Meanwhile he persisted in mild flyers in St. Louis town lots, generally realizing petty profits or petty losses in

small transactions, though one tract of four hundred *arpents* in St. Louis
county, which he purchased with his brother Samuel in October, 1819,
carried a price of three thousand dollars.[10]

While he inveighed against unsound banking in the *Enquirer,* Benton
involved himself personally in another banking venture which he hoped
would be sound — the Bank of Missouri. Sponsored in 1817 by Auguste
Chouteau and other fur-trade leaders to replace the speculative, falter-
ing Bank of St. Louis, the Bank of Missouri cleaved at the beginning to
conservative policies, and proudly kept up specie payments on its notes
— though in part its prosperity reflected the fact that it was the Far
Western depository for United States government funds. Though Benton
held only a small amount of stock in the Bank of Missouri, he was a
large depositor and he was becoming more prominent in the business
community, and on May 1, 1820, the other stockholders elected him
to the Board of Directors of the corporation. His relations with the
Bank of Missouri brought him cash dividends, but they also brought him
pain. His enemies could charge that his activities in the Bank of St.
Louis farce had been dictated by a developing interest in its rival, and
they pointed to this interest as new evidence that he was a mere lackey
for the Chouteau-"junto" group. His foes could also claim that his attacks on unsound banks and banking in the *Enquirer* were merely the
result of narrow self-interest in the Bank of Missouri. Benton like many
other directors borrowed from the bank, and the debt was to haunt
him and harass him in the future.[11]

In his dual role as editor and banker, Benton became involved in a
new personal quarrel. In July, 1819, a speculator and note broker
named Richard Venables published an advertisement in the *Enquirer*
offering to pay a premium of 1 per cent above the market price for notes
issued by the Bank of Missouri. When Venables later boggled at making
good on this offer, Benton roasted him in an editorial. Immediately
Venables turned to the *Gazette* to lambaste the ungrateful Benton — "I
feel it a duty due my character to drag [him] before the public, who no
doubt must see Colonel Benton in *this instance* in no other point of
view, than as the hireling tool of the Missouri Bank."

The day the *Gazette* came out with this statement, Venables walked
by the *Enquirer* office several times. Finally, as he paused in the dusty
street before the building, Isaac Henry went to the door and ordered
Venables away. The touchy Venables drew a pistol and pointed it at
Henry, who dived into the shop to get a weapon of his own. Benton

was working in the back room, and when he heard his partner run into
the office, he went to a gallery which surrounded the building to see
what was going on. When he saw the situation, he called to Henry:
"Don't shoot the damned assassin." At this, Venables turned his pistol
toward Benton and cursed him. Cool as always in such situations,
Thomas Benton, unarmed, vaulted over the gallery railing into the street
and picked up a stone as large as his own large head. He advanced
on Venables, who turned tail and ran into a doorway across the street.
The Colonel let fly with the large stone and several smaller ones, which
left dents in the wooden door behind the note broker but did not hit
him. By this time a crowd had gathered to watch the sport, and some
of them disarmed Venables. Cornered, Venables rushed his muscular
enemy, locked his arms about Benton's neck, dragged him in his fine
suit to the ground, and beat him with his fist. Men in the crowd quickly
pulled Venables off and sent him packing, and Benton returned to his
office to take up the writing he had left at his work table. Four days
later, Venables published a long account of the fracas, in which he indulged a sort of pettish whine about the whole undignified business.
Perhaps he resented the fact that he had not been honored with a challenge to a duel! In any case, he was determined to "tear the mask"
from Thomas Benton, "and drag him naked before the public," in all
his "hideous and contemptible deformity" — but verbally, and thus
safely.[12]

Despite his public pugnacity and alleged "deformity," Thomas was a
devoted homemaker. About his new house he planted a number of the
thorny-branched, dark-barked locust trees which were typical of the village, and which gave a stately air to the grounds. In May, 1819, for
eleven hundred dollars "in hand," he acquired from Jeremiah Connor
the final equity in the house and the 150 by 180 foot lot on which it
stood — but he was soon forced to mortgage the whole as security for
a two-thousand-dollar loan from John Mullanphy, at 10 per cent annual
interest. He was never able wholly to retire this loan, and he was finally
to lose his home.[13]

[4]

PERSISTING IN POLITICS, Benton found himself involved in a major national controversy as well as in petty local affairs. In February, 1819,

when the House of Representatives at Washington was considering a petition from Missouri for statehood, James Tallmadge of New York had moved an amendment to a statehood bill to prohibit further introduction of slaves into the area, and to free all slave children in Missouri when they reached the age of twenty-five. Thus embroiled, Congress adjourned without acting on Missouri's petition. The national conflict over restricting the spread of slavery resulted in the formation of "violent parties" or factions in Missouri, and Thomas Benton soon assumed militant, belligerent leadership on the proslavery side. It is not surprising that he took the position he did — he was the son of a slaveholding family in a slaveholding community, and he was a petty slaveholder himself.

His side was certainly the popular one in Missouri. Thousands of immigrants had brought slaves with them from Southern states, and by 1820 the slave population of the Territory exceeded ten thousand. In addition, many citizens not deeply interested in slaveholding themselves could see no reason why an area whose future depended on immigration should shut out potential settlers simply because they owned Negroes. Throughout the spring of 1819 the *Enquirer* blasted away at restrictionists actual and alleged, lumping them with the bitter foes of the Democratic-Republican creed, damning them as the "disorganizers or emissaries of King and Clinton [arch-Federalists in New York], the busy spirits of anarchy!" In addition, the *Enquirer* printed several letters charging the *Gazette* and John B. C. Lucas with restrictionism. Though the charges were greatly exaggerated and genuine restrictionists were so few as to be negligible in Missouri itself, the issue made effective propaganda and furthered Benton's push for leadership.[14] It was an issue on which he could appeal not only to particular interest group demands, but to the local patriotism of Missourians in general.

In May, Benton carried the attack directly to the people in a great mass meeting in St. Louis. As chief speaker, he proclaimed that Missouri must "make a fair and regular stand against the encroachment of Congress upon the Sovereignty of the States." Anyway, slavery was not the genuine issue — the important question was *freedom* versus *coercion*. "When the abolition of slavery," he thundered, "should be the order of the day throughout the Republic," then perhaps "the people of Missouri would go *voluntarily* as far . . . as any other portion of the Union"; but until that time, "no process of reasoning can make it right that they should be *forced* to the surrender of their slaves." In his orderly way, he then introduced six resolutions — *first,* Congress had no control over a state constitution beyond requiring a republican form of government; *second,* to prohibit slavery was "contrary to the rights of the State"; *third,* the delay in Congress was an insult to Missouri; *fourth,* Missouri's *right* to statehood depended solely on the Louisiana Purchase treaty and the Constitution; *fifth,* the people had a right to form a state government, and a second rebuff by Congress would make it expedient to exercise that right; *sixth,* if Congress rejected a constitution thus adopted it would be the same as an attempt to rule Missouri out of the Union. After it had been read, Benton's miniature Declaration of Independence was adopted by a unanimous shout of "Aye."

During June and July, agitation reached a crescendo. At a dinner at the Mansion House, Thomas Benton and other leaders paraded the great issue again, with a dramatic toast: "THE FUTURE STATE OF MIS-SOURI: *Equal in sovereignty to the original states, or — nothing!*" In this sentiment, greeted by *"repeated cheering — music, Bonaparte's march — reiterated discharges of artillery,"* slavery was not mentioned as such — it was all a matter of rights, sovereignty, equality.[15]

The emergence of the slavery issue produced a modification of political lines. The old "junto" and "anti-junto" groups increasingly merged into newer alignments formed on the statehood-slavery agitation. In the re-alignment, Thomas Benton found himself increasingly friendly with David Barton, who despite an excessive fondness for whisky was able, powerful, and popular. With Joseph Charless and John B. C. Lucas emerging as leaders on the other side, the opposing armies were assembled and in the next year the great political battles of Missouri were fought out on these lines.[16]

Meanwhile, Benton was also occupied with side-skirmishes — an election campaign, running for office himself, offering political advice and playing political manager, and a newspaper feud.

The election, scheduled for August, was for the post of territorial delegate in Congress. The contest soon settled down to a race between the incumbent John Scott, still condemned by the *Gazette* as the tool of the old "junto," and Samuel Hammond, who had been president of the Bank of St. Louis in its final agonies. The *Enquirer* supported Scott, and charged that Hammond, who was a receiver at the Territorial land office, was in arrears in the monies he handled. When the *Gazette* publicly asked Isaac Henry where the *Enquirer* had got such information, the answer was, from Colonel Benton, who had it from John Scott, who had it from the recorder at the land office, Alexander McNair. The *Gazette* thereupon accused Benton and Scott of "conspiring to ruin an innocent individual, & *of procuring under false pretense* [government financial] statements." In reply, the *Enquirer* printed an exchange of letters. Exhibit A — Benton to McNair, noting reports that he, Benton, had conspired to secure statements from the land office dishonorably, and asking if this was true. Exhibit B — McNair to Benton, stating that he had furnished the information upon formal request and that there was nothing dishonorable in this, since the land office was after all a public one. Whether it was the *Enquirer's* exposé that did it, or something else, John Scott was elected.

Four months later, Benton himself sought public office again, as a Trustee for St. Louis, and this time he was named to the position he had failed to win a year before — a position in which he dealt with small matters like authorizing ferries across the Mississippi or the control of mad dogs.[17]

Meanwhile, he kept his eyes on broader ranges of issues and men. In January, 1820, he wrote a long letter to John Scott in Washington. He, Benton, was just home after a ten-day trip from Nashville, "a horrid ride through the rain and mud of Ten. and Ken. and the snow and ice of the 'free State' [Illinois]." He had Scott's letter, and would suggest that the Delegate come out at once on the road question, proposing a great highway eighty feet wide from Washington, and also a Post Road from Missouri to New Orleans — "if you do not succeed first trial, still the people at home will be pleased." In addition, Scott might work toward a national measure to extend the time hard-pressed settlers had to pay for public lands. Before long, Scott might have added support at Washington, for the Arkansas Territory was sending a man Thomas Benton knew as their Delegate, James Bates — "you will be natural supporters of each other, and you will therefore see the propriety of giving him a frank and cordial reception." As to Missouri, "D. B. [David Barton] has had only one frolic [drinking escapade] since I went to Ten."; because he was "honest and capable . . . the frolics which have happened, will be nothing if not repeated." He thought Barton would be pleased with a good judicial appointment and that he should have it.[18] Already Thomas Benton assumed the authority to give oracular advice and dispose of the personalities of politics.

The Colonel's work at the *Enquirer,* and the cross-currents of personalities and politics, brought a constantly intensifying war of words

with Joseph Charless at the *Gazette.* Again and again the older editor
scored "the *Enquirer* man, bent-on mischief," while Benton in turn ridiculed "Old Charley" and accused him of writing his own letters-to-the-
editor for popular effect. The peak was reached during the August election campaign, when the *Enquirer* accused the *Gazette* of making up a
hundred lies against John Scott, and the *Gazette* challenged Benton to
produce a bill of particulars. He promptly massed an actual "List of One
Hundred Lies fabricated by the old communications maker," consisting
of quotes numbered 1, 2, 3, 4, 5, and so on up to 100! At last "the
Enquirer man" came to an open break, writing in October, 1819, another of his curt letters — "Mr. Joseph Charless will discontinue my
subscription to his newspaper. Thomas H. Benton." [19] The rising leader
apparently felt a need to make quite clear his hostility toward his rival.

In the arena of larger issues, the statehood-slavery controversy was
nearing a compromise in Congress. At the end of 1819, the part of Massachusetts known as Maine applied for admission as a state, and a
middle-of-the-road proposal was finally worked out by Senator J. B.
Thomas of Illinois — the First Missouri Compromise. By this compromise, Maine was to be admitted as a free state, and Missouri was to be
admitted without restriction while the rest of Louisiana Territory above
latitude 36°30' was closed to slavery. On March 6, 1820, President
Monroe signed the Missouri bill, after being unanimously assured by his
cabinet of the constitutionality of a measure prohibiting slavery in Federal territory. In the *Enquirer* Thomas Benton exulted: "The agony is
over and Missouri is born into the Union; not a seven-months baby but
a man child!"

With the issue apparently settled in Congress a convention was called
to write a state constitution. For a time Benton considered seeking election as a delegate, but his hopes were apparently dashed when a caucus
met in St. Louis, proposed an anti-restrictionist slate for the county, and
left his name off the list. Ten days later he received a letter signed by
138 St. Louisans, including such prominent and influential men as Auguste Chouteau, David Barton, members of the Gratiot family, Alexander McNair, and the fur-trading magnate Manuel Lisa, who urged
him not to feel bound by the anti-restriction meeting. He replied flatly
that he would not run, and would support the slate. He did not want to
waste votes and divide the anti-restriction support — and he was busy
with his work at the courthouse, where the Circuit Court was in session.
All this touched Joseph Charless's risibilities. He jibed at his rival:

"The modest Colonel thinks it his duty to prevent a large waste of votes. . . . Truly, we hardly believed he knew his own merits so well, as to feel that all votes given for him would be wasted." An antislavery caucus, chaired by the old enemy of caucuses and juntos, Joseph Charless, adopted a resolution opposing bringing any more slaves into Missouri, and named a slate headed by Benton's bitter enemy John B. C. Lucas. Thus, the battle was joined. But when the election returns were in, they showed an anti-restrictionist triumph throughout the Territory.[20]

The convention met, and began framing a constitution. The sessions were held in the block-square, three-story Mansion House in St. Louis, two blocks from Thomas Benton's home, and he probably found it no trouble to circulate among the delegates and invite them to his house. Meanwhile, in his paper, he urged the delegates to study the *Federalist* and, more specifically, to adopt a clause prohibiting emancipation of slaves without their owner's consent, as a way to prevent later "foreign interference in our affairs." By July 9, the convention under chairman David Barton produced a charter which not only prohibited emancipation without an owner's consent, but also barred free Negroes from the state. The new body politic had at last a frame of government. The pro-slavery, anti-restrictionist interest had triumphed, and Missouri was apparently launched on her course as a slaveholding state in the Federal union.[21]

[5]

WITH MISSOURI ON THE ROAD to statehood, the great question was, Who would fill the new positions statehood brought with it? By the end of June, Joseph Charless thought he knew at least the plans of the transformed "junto," which he claimed now centered among a few St. Louis lawyer-delegates at the Convention. The *Gazette* carried an article:

> THE CAUCUS . . . have met and met again, and determined upon what shall be done in Missouri, and whom the people shall elect to office. . . . For Governor — William Clark. For U. S. Senators — Mr. Benton and Mr. Jones. For Superior Judges — Mr. Barton, Mr. Harper and Mr. Cook.

Though he would, perhaps, have preferred not to have had it announced in this way, Benton was in fact a candidate. As such, he was not happy at being tagged as the protégé of the "junto." In a series of letters in the *Enquirer,* he launched a furious if indirect attack on the "Caucus" story, crying out that the *Gazette's* purpose was defamation — "Six individuals to be lied out of the way. . . . What a wholesale villainy!" Finally, the *Enquirer* struck out in verse. Alas, poor Joseph Charless — a jingle in Benton's paper lamented —

> *Spleen to mankind his canker'd heart posses't,*
> *And much he hated all, but most the best;*
> *'The Enquirer Man' his everlasting theme,*
> *And filthy scandal his delight supreme. . . .*
> POPE, JR.

For a time, it looked as though the question of who was to be Senator would resolve itself into just another newspaper feud. But soon all factions concentrated on the serious business of crying up favorite candidates for the several offices subject to popular vote — with due attention to candidates for the State Assembly, for national Senators then were elected not by the people but by the state legislatures. Benton promptly plumped for his old friends William Clark, for Governor, and John Scott, for Congressman. In the issue preceding the election, he gave plenty of space to appeals by candidates for the state legislature, men who might have the disposition of the national senatorships in their hands.[22]

At the end of August, 1820, the voters went to the polls. The result of this popular decision was somewhat dismaying to Thomas Benton and his factional allies. Though John Scott was elected Representative without opposition, Alexander McNair swamped William Clark for the governorship. As to the Assembly, Benton would have to make the best of a "doubtful" situation — he was on friendly terms with the gentleman from Jefferson; he considered two members from St. Charles County for him and one against him; Major Berry was going to Boon's Lick to see what he could do with the members there; State Senator-elect McGirk of St. Louis was serving as an emissary to Montgomery; and so on. Finally, Benton wrote Scott, David Barton has "great zeal for me."

The issue was still in doubt when the two houses convened in the middle of September, 1820. The session was held in St. Louis, at the new Missouri Hotel, a stone, semi-Georgian building with two high-roomed floors at front and three stories at the back, and a low flight of steps at the side entrance on which members could gather to discuss issues and candidates.

As the Assembly organized, Scott bombarded state political leaders with letters urging Benton's election. From a sickbed at Ste. Genevieve he wrote Nathaniel Cook, another senatorial hopeful: "D. Barton should be satisfied to take a place on the bench. You ought to place Benton on your ticket for the Senate, and induce McNair to lend his aid. . . . Benton must not be sacrificed. He has done all things for the party within the power of man — expences were no object to him." If Benton failed in his bid for the Senate, he should have a judgeship — "but sacrificed he must not, *nor shall be*. . . . Clark was beaten. You were defeated in the election [for Superior Judge]. Benton now to be neglected will be three of the principal men overturned. This will not do." The next day John Scott wrote "D. Barton," cursing the sickness that kept him, Scott, from the election battle. "For God's sake," he pleaded, "exert yourself for Benton as well as yourself. . . . Can you not make M'Nair act right in regard to Benton? He ought not to wield the executive arm now against him. . . . We must act so as to save our friends." Soon, it became clear that in the race for the Senate seats there were three front runners. These were the popular "D. Barton"; John B. C. Lucas, who never allowed himself to forget or forgive the death of his son; and "the *Enquirer* man," Thomas Benton. Both Senators were to be chosen together, on Monday, October 2. The anti-Benton members were unable to unite on a candidate, and three days before the election a partisan could write: "Benton gains ground daily with the members, & we have great hopes that we shall not again be defeated, the most influential and honest class of society here are using their endeavors to get Benton Elected." As to Barton, his election was "shure." [23]

The next day — or so one of Benton's political enemies recalled it afterwards — the Benton forces made an informal canvass. Of the fifty-two members, Benton could apparently count on twenty-six, or one less than a majority, and thus the problem was how to add one more man to the ranks of his supporters in the Assembly. The solution — as his foes later reported it — was a conference at the Auguste Chouteau mansion. On hand were Chouteau himself, Jean P. Cabanné, Pierre Chouteau, and Sylvestre Labadie — and Assemblyman Marie Philippe Leduc, who had sworn he would lose his right arm before he would vote for Benton. This *Français* legislator had some large Spanish land grants among his holdings, and the argument centered on this point. Was it not clear that, as a Senator, old Lucas would be as hostile to the Spanish titles as he had been as a Commissioner? Was it not equally obvious that, as a Senator, young Benton would be as vigorous in their support as he had been as a lawyer, land-lobbyist, and budding politician? Was not Representative Leduc's path apparent? The argument ran intermittently throughout the night, but as morning dawned over the Mississippi, the old *Français* agreed, and assured his exhorters that he would vote for Benton.* Thus, at this critical point in his life's career, the young man who admired Thomas Jefferson's yeoman's Arcadia, but who had meanwhile found it possible by Roman-riding to maintain the favor of St. Louis's old-French aristocracy of Enterprise, was saved by the influential leaders of this very group.

Finally, the decisive hour came, October 2, at three in the afternoon. The legislators, both Senators and Representatives, gathered in the House "chamber" at the Missouri Hotel, and waited anxiously to cast their votes. Everyone knew that the future careers of two old personal and political enemies were at stake — would it be Thomas Benton, or would it be John B. C. Lucas? Each member was to vote for two of the candidates, and the two men receiving the highest votes were to be declared elected, if each had twenty-seven votes or more.

At the last minute Representative Daniel Ralls was brought into the chamber — so ill his physicians had despaired of his life. He was unable even to sit up in bed, and when the time came four stout Negroes had to carry him and his bed into the hall, but he was determined to cast a tally for his friend Benton. "If I should faint in the house," he instructed his bearers, "recover me there, and by no means take me out before I have given my vote." Old Judge Lucas declared that he heard Daniel Ralls "muttering and speaking all the while as if he had not the use of his senses" [24] — but then the Judge was not exactly an unbiased witness.

The nominations were made, and finally the roll was called. A son of Daniel Boone, Representative Jesse B. Boone of Montgomery County, put Thomas Benton's name in nomination. The members spoke their

---

* This story depends on one memoir (Darby, *Recollections,* 30-32). This writer was a long-time political foe of Benton, and his full account is certainly somewhat exaggerated. Still, the best over-all study of the election credits the story in the main (Squires, "A New View of the Election of Barton and Benton," 28-45), though a later writer discounts it (McCandless, *Benton, His Source of Political Strength,* 32). The essentials of the story are offered here with this warning, because other evidence indicates the major part the land claimants played in Benton's early political career, and because it at least epitomizes the role of these prominent and influential men in Benton's political ascent. Despite some errors, and dubious interpretations based on apparent bias, the over-all factual kernel of Darby's report of the election is in the main in accord with contemporaneous evidence.

choices. The names echoed in the chamber — Barton and Benton; Barton and Lucas; Benton and Elliott; Lucas and Jones; and, from two Assemblymen, Benton and Lucas! When the name of Daniel Ralls was called, he was too weak to raise his head, but he cast his vote as he had intended — *Barton and Benton*. Soon after, he died, and the *Enquirer* wrote:

> *When rack'd by disease in his litter he lay,*
> *He was borne in that litter the tribute to pay*
> *To his friend, his loved Country, while Senate beheld*
> *The last moments of Chatham by Ralls parallel'd.*

In the Assembly, the roll call was completed, and Thomas Benton had exactly the number necessary to elect: David Barton 34, Thomas Benton 27, John B. C. Lucas 16, Henry Elliott 11, Nathanial Cook 8, and John Rice Jones 8. Although Benton had been tagged as the candidate of the little St. Louis "junto," he had won votes from every county but four and could claim a more widely distributed vote than Barton himself. Nonetheless it was a close thing, with his alliance with established interest groups and his association with superior factional organization apparently decisive. His vote was composed overwhelmingly of Assemblymen from the St. Louis area and the older-settled, richer counties along the Missouri River, and he had failed to attract votes from representatives of the counties on the lower Mississippi River and the advancing frontier to the West. In short, he had little assurance of mass popular support, of a lasting power base — an ill-omen for the future.[25]

Still, he had won. At thirty-eight, the mid-point of his life, five years to the day after he was admitted to the St. Louis bar, Thomas Benton was launched on a national political career.

CHAPTER 6

Decision

1820 - 1825

THE SENATORS-DESIGNATE, Thomas Benton and David Barton, set out for Washington scarcely a week after their election. Traveling mostly on horseback, they took the long overland route through country that was often wilderness, stopping briefly at Lexington, Kentucky, to visit with Henry Clay. Benton was short on ready cash, but he carried with him a draft for a hundred and fifty dollars on his Kentucky cousin-in-law, signed by a Missouri friend. This would give him the money he would need to establish himself in the national capital.

The journey was instructive for Benton. Years later, he recalled the trip — "one long ride amidst the crashings and explosions of banks." Everywhere, it was the same — "No employment for industry — no demand for labor — no sale for the product of the farm — no sound of the hammer, but that of the auctioneer, knocking down property. . . . DISTRESS, the universal cry of the people: RELIEF, the universal demand thundered at the doors of all legislatures, State and federal." Some three million people, a third of the population, were directly distressed, and in Eastern cities soup kitchens had appeared to feed the hungry. In the West and South, property that had been mortgaged to the Bank of the United States was taken in foreclosure. Sentiment against the big Bank and its loan-contraction policy was rolling up like the waters of an Ohio River flood.[1]

But the trip had its pleasant side, too. On the way Thomas stopped at Cherry Grove, near Lexington, Virginia, to see Elizabeth McDowell again. She was now twenty-six. Her bright, brown-haired beauty, combined with intelligence, gracious manner, and what the men of the day called "moral feeling," seemed more irresistible than ever to Thomas. Again he proposed marriage to her — and this time she accepted him.[2]

By mid-November, 1820, Benton was in Washington. There he heard fears expressed that the depression was creating a spreading rift between those who lived by labor and those who lived by speculation on the labor of others. Men like the perceptive John Calhoun of South Carolina, and even the cold, cautious John Quincy Adams, were talking ominously of a general disaffection with the traditional course of politics, an unrest likely to be seized by any new leader.

In Washington, Benton settled at Brown's Hotel on Pennsylvania Avenue. That year there were many other legislators at Brown's "Indian Queen," including David Barton, John Scott, Benton's former colonel in the Thirty-ninth Regiment, John Williams, now a Senator from Tennessee, and John Floyd, from Virginia, an uncle of Elizabeth McDowell. The Washington that Benton had known in 1815 had not changed much. All about were brickyards, making bricks for the unfinished Capitol building. The streets were muddy. Common pastures were filled with cows owned by the residents of the city. Such conditions reflected the fact that Washington was the capital of a nation still in childhood, with its population just under ten million. But to Benton's flamboyant imagination the place might have seemed a new Rome, and he a tribune in the Forum, and his colleagues potential Gracchi or Ciceros.

It was a great moment for Benton, probably the greatest so far in his life.

Congress convened on December 13, but both Benton and Barton were denied full membership until Missouri was formally accepted as a state. They were granted the right to attend sessions, and to receive pay of eight dollars *per diem* and eight dollars per twenty miles travel allowance. The sessions were a curious combination of the sedate and the ludicrous. The Senate's members were crowded into a semicircular, domed room in the north end of the Capitol, with mottled-gray marble columns at the front, a great eagle over the Vice-President's dais, and a rail or bar making a half-circle at the rear. The Senate was dignified, courtly, and a little out of the center of things. In the House, in the larger south chamber, informality prevailed and oratory attracted a flow of visitors. Fashionable ladies made up "Capitol parties," and, coiffed and jeweled, went to the House in mobs when a speech by a favorite was announced. Once, when Henry Clay was speaking, a lady found the galleries so crowded it was impossible to join her party. An amiable member came to the distressed lady's rescue, taking her to a seat on the floor of the House itself.

Even in Washington, Benton was pursued by his old, vengeful enemy

John B. C. Lucas, who wrote letters designed to poison the minds of the newcomer's colleagues against him. The Colonel's election was tainted with fraud, Lucas wrote Congressman Robert Moore; and he was "blood-thirsty, bold, and desperate," though at times he could "put on an appearance of suavity, borrow a language sentimental and exalted." In a letter to Secretary John Quincy Adams, the old judge charged again that Benton had shot down Charles Lucas because he foresaw that young Lucas "would stand in the way of his ambitious views." [3]

While the Senators-elect waited for their seats, Benton occupied himself as best he could. Early in January, 1821, he went before the United States Supreme Court as co-counsel with Senator John Henry Eaton of Tennessee, in the case of Lessee of George Walker *vs*. Ann W. Turner, on appeal from the lower court in West Tennessee. It was accepted practice at that time for Congressmen to handle Supreme Court business on the side. Throughout the winter, often in collaboration with Barton and Scott, Benton busied himself with representing Missouri interests in land claims or Indian affairs before executive agencies — his debut in the role of Congressman-as-errand-boy for local interests, which every member found it necessary from time to time to play. Meanwhile, he gave attention to further preparation for his career. He thought he ought to know Spanish, and so with a master proceeded to learn the language and study much of its literature. Still, he had some time for pleasure, and for making new acquaintances. At a dinner at the home of the Secretary of the Navy, the ambitious Delaware politician and Congressman Louis McLane met "the renowned Col. Benton" and marked him as "a man of no ordinary scale" — "intelligent and improved [educated] in a very great degree . . . a strong, manly genius of no common cast . . . will or I am mistaken make a figure in Washington." The Colonel's old Tennessee commander, Senator Williams, noted that Benton was much admired by everyone in Washington except the minions of Andrew Jackson. [4]

In the early months of 1821, Benton spoke out again on the Missouri admission question — which had reached another dead end. The clause in the Missouri constitution barring free Negroes from entering the state was bitterly attacked by northern Congressmen, as a violation of the Federal Constitution's guarantee that the citizens of any state were entitled to the privileges and immunities of citizens in any of the several states. While the issue approached a new deadlock in Congress, Benton rushed off an article to the *Enquirer* in which he trumpeted that the question was no longer one of *admission,* but of *exclusion.* There must be no backing down:

> What shall Missouri do, if rejected? Fall back into the territorial grade? we hope not. Set up for herself? we hope not. The former would be to succumb to the Catilines of the north; the latter would be to promote their views.

Missouri must stand firm!

The deadlock was resolved in the second Missouri Compromise. A resolution submitted by Clay, requiring the Missouri legislature to pledge itself against any enactment which would conflict with the guarantees of the Federal Constitution, was adopted, and at last Missouri was to be admitted. On March 3, Congress adjourned.

Though he could not participate, Benton was nonetheless impressed with his first session of Congress. Talent, close attention to business, honesty — these qualities pervaded the "whole list" of members, he thought, and he felt that he was among masters whose pupil he must long remain before he could hope to become a teacher. On face-to-face acquaintance, he even came to admire the character and finished manners of some old-Federalist members, like Rufus King of New York.[5]

[2]

AS SOON AS HE COULD after adjournment, Benton hurried to Lexington, in Virginia. At last Elizabeth McDowell would be his — "in six days from this 14th Day of March, which will be Tuesday the 20th . . . your friend *Benedict* will cease to belong to the order of bachelors," he wrote a friend in St. Louis.

He waited for the wedding at Cherry Grove, the McDowell estate — where he and Elizabeth were to spend much of their time after marriage. It was a delightful place, with the modest, long frame house set between two great trees, with stone kitchens and slave cabins to the rear. The front door admitted him to an entrance hall with a narrow enclosed staircase leading to the second floor at the rear, and doors opening into parlors on each side. Each of the parlors possessed frame mantels surrounding brick fireplaces. The parlor walls were decorated with painted wainscoting rising to a height of about two feet, and with mouldings at the top edged with hand-carved, square-toothed "dental" work. The whole place possessed a quiet, elegant, but modest charm. The grounds, fields, and orchards, about ten miles north of Lexington, merged with the sharply rolling country which ran to the Blue Ridge to the north and east, and the Alleghenies to the west. At Cherry Grove, Thomas could enjoy the kind of home life he sought for himself. There both men and women were expected to show intellectual and artistic sensibilities, and to help make rich the life of the home. Thomas was particularly taken with Elizabeth's mother, Sarah Preston McDowell, who could play beautifully on an old mandolin-like English guitar.

Finally March 20, the *"great day,"* came. In the evening, the Presbyterian clergyman Henry Ruffner united Thomas and Elizabeth in marriage. Early the next month, they set out for Missouri, stopping a day with Governor Preston at Smithfield, and another day with Elizabeth's uncle Congressman John Floyd. Then they went on toward the West.

By the latter part of May, Thomas and his bride were in St. Louis. Marriage had brought Elizabeth far from her early circle of friends and comforts, but Thomas admired the way she faced the change. The St. Louis to which Elizabeth came was still a rough town, its streets unpaved — though a third of the 650 dwellings were now made of limestone quarried from the riverbank or of bricks made from clay. The town boasted a population of 5600, white and black. But at Laurel Street, with her own servant Sarah to make her comfortable, and Thomas's mother's slaves to wait on her, the buoyant Elizabeth found her new life pleasant. She wrote her mother that she was in good health and spirits, and urged her brother to come and settle in Missouri. Meanwhile, Elizabeth proved herself a good wife. She was able to share Thomas's large ideas, as his mother had done, and it came as second nature to her to make a well-ordered home. Her influence over Thomas must have been great. After his marriage he became a calmer man and lived a quieter life. He also became a regular churchgoer, and later in Washington he took a pew in the Presbyterian church.[6]

In 1821 Missouri was hit by the national depression. Immigration had stopped, with the result that land prices fell; farmers with good crops were almost without markets; and overstocked merchants were in debt. The paper-money boom also collapsed, and everywhere cash was short. Newspapers reported bankruptcy sales and tax sales; the people Benton might meet on streets, in coffee shops, in parlors, and in offices lamented the "hard times." There was a mounting demand for some sort

of "relief." A special session of the legislature adopted a "stay law" giving a man whose land was sold for debt a legal right to redeem it. The
Assembly also set up a state loan office, which lent debtors certificates
or "promises to pay" on the credit of the state. Neither of these acts was
in effect for long, but at the depths of the deflation, when Benton returned from the East, they were major issues in Missouri. Men like
Pierre Chouteau, Marie P. Leduc, and Dr. Bernard Farrar stood as
"relief" candidates for the legislature, or acted as commissioners for the
St. Louis branch of the loan office — though many small farmers and
small property holders participated too. The appearance of such old-
French leaders in the "Relief Party" led to the charge that it was not
the small "honest debtors," but the "big bankrupts" and "spendthrifts"
who put across the loan office to save themselves. Though Benton did
not take much part in the controversy, he gave at least indirect support
to the relief movement — thus drawing again the charge that he was
acting in the interest of his powerful friends.

The hard times and relief agitation taught Benton and many other
Missourians an economic lesson. This was that abiding prosperity came
not from land speculation and paper-money speculation, but from culti-
vating the soil, and working the lead and iron mines. Aided by the development of new markets for farm products and new channels of commerce, prosperity slowly returned. One stimulant was a developing trade
with far-off Santa Fe — available to Missouri enterprisers after 1821,
when Mexico revolted against Spain and established itself as an independent republic.

A victim of the panic was the Bank of Missouri — Thomas Benton,
depositor, stockholder, and director. In mid-August the bank found it
impossible to continue specie payments, and suspended operations, its
chief outstanding obligation being a debt to the United States government of $152,343, the sum of government deposits and interest thereon.
At first Benton did not fear any significant loss in the collapse. Later he
found that the suspension placed him under a new burden of debt. This
indebtedness became a favorite weapon of attack for his political enemies, when the United States secured a judgment of seven thousand and
seventy-six dollars against him as a director of the bank.[7]

Meanwhile, Benton occupied himself with business and law. To raise
some ready cash he mortgaged a 300 *arpent* town lot against a loan of
$3000, handled some business affairs in St. Louis for Henry Clay, and

undertook several cases in the courts — traveling in the dog-days of the scorching Missouri August to Cape Girardeau to spend two weeks at the court sessions there. Despite financial difficulties, he and Elizabeth were happy together, with Elizabeth feeling "exceedingly well" in St. Louis, and Thomas and Elizabeth both looking forward to an invitation from Clay to stay with him at Lexington when they had the opportunity.[8]

Nor was the public news that summer all bad. In June, the Missouri legislature passed a "solemn public act" meeting the conditions Congress had set for statehood, and in August, President Monroe formally proclaimed Missouri's admission as a state. Thus Benton and Barton were assured their seats in the Senate.

By mid-October Thomas and Elizabeth were on their way East. They stopped over for a week in Kentucky with Clay, and went on by stagecoach through the mountains, where they were delayed four days by an "indisposition" of Mrs. Benton — who was pregnant. They then proceeded at the good rate of twenty miles a day to Cherry Grove, where Elizabeth stayed while Thomas hurried on to Washington for the Congressional session.[9]

[3]

THE SEAT BENTON was given in December, 1821, was the one he was to occupy for the rest of his service. It was in the third or last row, the seventh desk left of the center aisle as he faced the Vice-President's dais. At this desk, the Missourian could listen to his colleague's speeches, or write letters (as he often did), or rise to join in the formal debates. When he wanted to stretch his legs he could walk to the little rotunda outside, with its gray stone Corinthian colonnade, its small ornate dome and skylight above, and its "well" to the floor below. When committees were chosen, Benton was named to Public Lands and Indian Affairs — committees of particular interest to a man from the new West.

Thus established, Benton waited. In mid-December he wrote James Preston that "nothing essential" was going on — oh, yes, "the Captain General of all the Floridas [Andrew Jackson, who had been given military command over the territory] has resigned," and was "bestowing his inconsiderate and intemperate abuse upon his old friend the President." But Thomas had news about his family. He planned to visit Cherry Grove at Christmas, and again in February, for "my dear Elizabeth ex-

pects to be a mother at that time." On February 12, 1822, Thomas's
first child was born — a daughter, who was promptly baptized Elizabeth
after her mother.[10]

Over the years in Washington, Benton came to know the men who
governed the new Republic. The President was James Monroe, the tall,
raw-boned Virginian whose aspirations Benton, as OLDCASTLE, had condemned in 1808. At the State Department the short, plump John
Quincy Adams presided, a New Englander and former Federalist —
composed, circumspect, cautious, reserved, grave. At the Treasury was
William H. Crawford, a massive Georgian, "in stature, 'a head and
shoulders' above the common race of men," Benton described him later
in his memoirs — "justly proportioned, open countenance, manly features, ready and impressive conversation, frank and cordial manners."
At the War Department the tall, spare, deep-eyed, erect John C.
Calhoun, of South Carolina, just Benton's age, stood as a nationalist
defender of protective tariffs and of "internal improvements," like roads
and canals. All these leaders were nominally Democratic-Republicans.
But, except for the President, each was identified with some section, interest group, or doctrine which he sought to serve, and each leader
worked to build a faction or party-within-a-party around his own ambitions. Behind the façade of party unity and good feelings, each man engaged in elaborate political infighting. Still, the established place these
men held seemed threatened by no one outside their group — unless it
was the magnetic Congressman, the rising star of the West, Henry Clay.

For the long future, however, other men were to have greater influence over Benton. The Congress he entered consisted of 48 Senators representing twenty-four states, and 187 Representatives. He
was quick to learn from any man who would teach. Before he had been
in the Senate two years, he arranged to take his meals at one of the
famous Capitol Hill "messes," Dawson's Number Two, the particular favorite of Southern, old-Republican members. There the Missouri newcomer met Nathaniel Macon, the aged Senator from North Carolina
who had served with Jesse Benton in the State Assembly of 1781, and
John Randolph, the veteran Representative from Virginia. The upright
Macon, a symbol of Revolutionary days in his navy-blue suits cut simply in the old fashion, appeared to Thomas to be the ideal Democratic-
Republican statesman. He assumed nothing for himself. Once praised
for a committee report actually written by another, he promptly expressed his own approval of the document and named the author. Politi-

cally, Macon revered Jefferson, advocated strict constitutionalism as a means of protecting plain men against the designs of too-powerful government serving special interests, saw the origin of wealth in labor and sweat, and opposed the paper-banking system. Boyish, beardless, flamboyant, Randolph was touched by genius and could be gay and witty, but he also suffered from chronic ill health, occasional dementia, and the agonies of sleepless nights. Years later Thomas was to recall that when he and Randolph stayed at the same rooming house, Randolph "at all hours of the night was accustomed to tap at my door very softly." Being "very wakeful" himself, Benton usually admitted the visitor, and the two men would sit and talk for hours in the dark. Despite an erratic extremism, Randolph had been a great Republican champion, a dogged opponent to speculative, boom-and-bust paper-money banking, and a master of acid if intemperate political invective. An aristocratic republican, he sometimes aimed his invective at what he called the reign of "KING NUMBERS," or majority rule. With Macon, Randolph, and lesser habitues of Dawson's Number Two, Benton became an admiring friend. In turn his dinner companions remarked on his studious demeanor, noting that his "lamp never went out till one or two o'clock." His new friendships became so close that partisans in Missouri accused Benton of becoming John Randolph's "puppet" — though "pupil" would have been more accurate.[11]

During Benton's first Senate term, newer leaders also emerged to contend with the old, cabinet-based elite. Two of these were also just Thomas Benton's age — Martin Van Buren, in the Senate from New York, short, smiling, and tactful, an adept political broker and leader of the "Albany Regency" or New York state party organization; and Daniel Webster, back in the House from Massachusetts after a long absence, jet-haired, mastiff-mouthed, heavy-browed, and pompous, with an imposing legal and oratorical ability.

Never one to play retiring neophyte, Benton charged promptly into the legislative struggle. Through 1822, 1823, and 1824, in the Seventeenth and Eighteenth Congresses, he introduced bill after bill, and at the same time began the process of finding his place in the complex conflict of particular and local interests which underlay the variegated politics of the day. At first, attentive to his Missouri constituency, he too essayed the role of political broker and sought to pay political debts to the particular interest groups that had been influential in his election, expecting thereby (presumably) to strengthen his power-base in Mis-

souri for the future. This involved him in three major interests — the
Spanish land titles, the fur trade, and Missouri's lead mines.

On the land title matter, Benton scored a significant success. He
raised the issue first in February, 1822. The next month he proposed a
bill to authorize the Federal District Court in Missouri to dispose of the
claims, and to settle them on the basis of Spanish or French legal procedures rather than English or American. Though he urged adoption of
the bill in a long, carefully prepared, erudite, exhaustive, and logical
speech, and got it through the Senate, it was tabled in the House. Persistently, and having tilled the Congressional ground some more, he
raised the matter again in the session of 1823-1824. In January, 1824,
he could write his friend Bernard Pratte, the St. Louis claim-holder and
fur magnate, that he could assure him not only of his willingness "to
oblige . . . my individual friends," but also that appropriate bills were
actually *progressing* in both Senate and House. By May, a bill referring
the old Spanish claims to the District Court was adopted. Though Benton could not claim full credit, he had been instrumental in winning a
disposition of the matter that satisfied the old-French *seigneurs* in St.
Louis — and some *petits paysans* in the countryside too.

Next Benton turned to matters of critical interest to the fur trade
leaders. Since the administration of George Washington, who had first
suggested the system, the national government had operated what were
called "factories," actually trading-posts, in the Indian territories. For
some time spokesmen of the fur trade, particularly agents of the American Fur Company like Ramsay Crooks, had lobbied against these public "factories," and urged that the Indian trade be opened up entirely to
licensed private business. Staying like Benton at Brown's Hotel, Crooks
had discussed the issue with the Missourian at length. In March, 1822,
a bill was introduced to abolish the government trading-posts, and Benton promptly rallied to its support with a long speech in which he cited
price lists and recited poetry, analyzed the balance sheets of the "factories" to buttress a contention that they were a financial burden on
government, and quoted statements from Crooks and others. Over all he
condemned the government trading-post system as a public monopoly,
shot through with corruption, and serving to bar private enterprise from
a legitimate area of operation. Allied with him in this battle Benton
found another rising leader just his age — the one-time soldier and explorer Lewis Cass, now governor of the fur-rich Michigan Territory. By

May, 1822, the bill to abolish the "factory" system had passed both Senate and House, and Ramsay Crooks could write gratefully to Thomas Benton, "You deserve the unqualified thanks of the community for destroying the pious monster." A few months later the American Fur Company expressed its gratitude more concretely by employing Sentor Benton as an attorney. The ethics of this legislative action, loose by later standards, were in keeping with the pattern of special-interest political brokerage which dominated the decade.

Finally, Benton pressed for private operation of the government-owned Missouri lead mines. In April, 1822, he submitted a resolution requesting information from the executive concerning the government's lead mine leases — Were the leases making money for the government? Who held the leases, and under what terms? Were they granted in private contract, or by public auction? These inquiries were soon followed by arguments for private ownership. This campaign brought Benton into conflict with Secretary of War Calhoun, who was responsible for administering the leasing policy, and who saw Benton's efforts as part of a long-matured "plan of attack" against President Monroe's administration. In January, 1823, Benton took the next step, offering a bill to abolish the government leasing system and offer the mines for sale as freehold property at public auction. The bill failed — but once again Benton had labored to strike a blow for the budding tycoons of his home state.[12]

His land-grant, fur-trade, and lead-mine campaigns were an index of Benton's position at the beginning of his Congressional career. The formally organized, membership associations that later characterized American interest-group political activity scarcely existed in the 1820's, and men with goals to realize in politics looked to business leaders, lawyers, editors, party leaders, and legislators as their *direct* spokesmen. In Missouri, Benton had proved himself a capable actor in the first four roles, and in his first years in the Senate he proved himself adept as a legislative representative of special interests too. He fought well for the spirit of Enterprise, and for particular enterprises. He had learned at least the elements of legislative strategy and maneuver in the Senate, and his floor speeches, though still pedestrian, exhibited a detailed and near-exhaustive grasp of information as well as skillful reasoning and argumentation, and were thereby cogent and effective. Still, he had concerned himself only with relatively minor issues of par-

ticular interest to Missouri businessmen. It was not until his second
session in the Senate that the broader vision that he had exhibited as
"the *Enquirer* man" began to reveal itself.

In early February, 1823, Benton called the attention of his colleagues to the Oregon country. The 1818 agreement for joint
American-British occupation of the huge northwest region would expire
in 1828, and the impetuous Missourian thought it none too soon to
act to buttress American claims to the country. He offered a resolution
to inquire into the "expediency" of measures "to take and retain
[American] possession of the territories," and committed himself in
another fact-crammed speech to a policy of strengthening the American
title with *de facto* control as a way to bilk the British. This belligerent,
expansive contention was bound to please the American Fur Company
agents like Ramsay Crooks, with whom Benton had discussed the matter, and likely to please also the Missouri fur magnates and perhaps
some yeomen and merchants with an eye to the future. But the issue
also involved the eventual Western development of the nation as a
whole. Though he won no action in 1823, and was condemned again
for trying "to excite the prejudices of the Western people" against the
Virginia-Massachusetts administration of Monroe and Adams, Benton
was to persist in his Oregon occupation campaign. Before long, he and
Elizabeth's uncle, Representative John Floyd of Virginia, became known
as the leading protagonists of American control in the Northwest area.

Actually, Benton was not always so clearly and persistently expansive. In 1825, perhaps as a concession to moderate Eastern opinion
that had been shared by Jefferson himself, he agreed that such a distant
land as Oregon might never be part of the United States, whose Western
border might lie along the Rocky Mountain ridge — there, he
trumpeted, "the statue of the fabled god, Terminus, should be raised
upon its highest peak, never to be thrown down." Still, the American
stake in Oregon should be established, so that a separate republic
might organize itself there, tied to the United States by culture and
interest.[13] Later, however, Benton swung back to the view that Oregon
should be a potential integral part of the United States itself.

Two other measures that Benton introduced in the session of 1823-
1824 marked a significant break with his whole previous Senate
course. These sweeping proposals, one political and the other economic,
indicated the political road he was to follow for the rest of his life.

The first was a plan to amend the Constitution to change the manner

of election of the President and Vice-President. What Benton urged —
the idea was not original with him, but he made himself its peculiar
champion — was the abolition of indirect election through the electoral
college, and its replacement by a direct vote of the people:

> *First,* by dividing each state into electoral districts, with each person
> in such districts qualified to vote for Representatives in Congress being
> also entitled to vote, "in his proper person," for President and for Vice-
> President.
>
> *Second,* by providing that the candidate for each office winning a
> majority in any district would thereby receive one vote, and that the
> candidates who received majorities of such votes would be declared
> elected, with a proviso that if no candidates for President or Vice-
> President received majorities, the election would go to the Federal
> Congress.

In January, 1824, Benton advocated his plan in a speech which
took parts of three days to deliver. In his argument he reviewed the
constitutional convention of 1787 and the highlights of the *Federalist*
papers of Madison, Hamilton, and Jay, and went on to discuss in some
detail the electoral systems in various states, pointing out that by 1824
eighteen states had adopted election of presidential electors by the
people, while only six persisted in the old practice of choosing electors
through the legislature. But "the people can vote for a President as
easily as they can for an elector" — why then should they have to act
through intermediaries? In the enlightened era of 1824 any genuine
democrat must accept the maxim that *the people should rule* — why
then should not citizens be allowed to go to the polls and announce,
I vote for Thomas Jefferson to be President? The existing electoral
system was contrary to the genius of democracy — why must a citizen's
vote be filtered and filtered again through the hands of agents and
political managers? Historically, intermediate electors had been the
"favorite institution of aristocratic republics," but *direct popular votes*
had been the "favorite institution of democratic republics." And so on at
length, in a style that was to become increasingly characteristic. It
was too long and too full, circular in its excessive amplification, cumber-
some; yet it was emphatic, dramatic, and effective, and contained a
new fire that depended not only on oratory but on the popular democratic spirit of its content. In short, the speech revealed the beginning
of a new rhetorical and propaganda style to match the beginning of a
new political course.

Heroic as it was, the three-day oration nearly cost Benton his life. On the third night he was taken violently ill with a fit of coughing, the result of an inflamation of the lungs, apparently a recurrence of the consumption he thought he had conquered. While his wife and friends anxiously waited, physicians despaired of his life; but Benton's rugged, powerful body threw off the attack. He found thereafter, however, that he must rest his voice before long addresses, and he was often disturbed by flecks of blood in his throat after a major speech.[14]

Though the Senate voted to postpone the subject, Benton's electoral reform proposal was a landmark in his career. Offered when national politics were effectively controlled by the Washington clique, or established elite of political brokers and managers, such a popular democratic measure was bound to seem radical. Undaunted by defeat, Benton was to press it again and again. Democracy, he insisted, should mean what the Greek roots of the work suggested — *demos krateo,* as he rendered it, the *demos krateo* principle, the people to govern, the majority to rule.* Expressive of growing opinion nationally and in Missouri against the capital coterie, his proposal was the harbinger of a trend in American politics.

The second great measure Benton offered was a plan to reform the national land policy. In effect, it would have established a broader economic foundation for a broader political democracy. In Missouri he had observed and resolved eventually to "make war" on "two repulsive features" in the system of public land sales. These were, first, sales to the highest bidder, and second, donations to no one, which meant that, auctions aside, the price of all lands good or bad was the same, one dollar and twenty-five cents per acre. In April, 1824, Benton submitted a "graduation-donation" bill to provide —

> *First,* that any lands of the United States offered at public sale, and remaining unsold at the end of five years' time, should be again offered at public sale, at a reduced or *"graduated"* price not to be less than fifty cents an acre.
> *Second,* that any bona-fide settler on any quarter-section of land thus offered and not sold, "upon inhabiting and cultivating the same for three successive years," should be entitled to receive the plot as a Federal *donation.*

* Democratic, presumably, not in the derogatory sense of Plato or Aristotle, but perhaps in the sense of Pericles as reported by Thucydides — "our constitution is named a democracy, because it is in the hands not of the few but of the many."

In a brief argument for his bill, Benton declared that he knew it could not pass after being introduced so late in the session, but he hoped "to turn the minds of the Senators to the changes contemplated." The public lands had previously been sold to supply public revenue, in particular to pay off the Revolutionary debt bondholds. Now, Benton insisted, the government must look upon the public lands not as a source of *revenue,* but as a means for promoting the interests of the people. In particular, of course, he was concerned for the interests of plain men who might swell the ranks of freeholding farmers.

Over the years, Benton's reiterated land proposal was bound to have a broad popular appeal and to make bitter enemies. It touched a fundamental conflict of interests of the time. It seemed to offer to farmers and the sons of farmers an extension of the freeholding system, in easily acquired lands. In addition, Western merchants could see in it a means to populate and build up their section and its trade. Finally, such a proposal seemed to many urban workingmen and reformers to offer a chance at a new life. Actually, few established wage earners could go West and take up farming — but many young men in the cities and on the older farms of the East could, and this might reduce competition for jobs in the cities and thus have a favorable effect on wages. On the other hand, many leaders in the East saw in his proposal a menace to the East's supremacy in population and political power. Manufacturers generally opposed a liberal land policy because they *feared* it would do what workingmen *hoped* it would.[15] Finally, conservatives opposed the plan as a threat to the nation's financial soundness, and to established land values.

Though Benton's record in 1822, 1823, and 1824 was mixed, it showed a significant trend. He had begun by playing political broker for the established Missouri interest groups who had been instrumental in his election. But he had emerged in 1824 as a political advocate, pressing measures in the interests of larger groupings in the population, measures which embraced an enlarging conception of democracy and the "general welfare." In doing so, he identified himself with a radical reaffirmation of the democratic spirit of Jefferson, as he had it from Macon and Randolph — though perhaps none of these older, Eastern leaders could have gone all the way with him. Again, in doing so, he also began a break with his colleague Barton, who was to oppose both his electoral and land reform plans. In all probability, Benton was keenly aware that his emergence as a reformer would give him a new political appeal in Missouri, enable him to lay the foundations of a new power base among the state's small farmers and small traders. He was learning, finding himself, developing, and time and dramatic events to come were to confirm his nascent commitment.

After he had finished his massive oration for direct popular presidential elections, Benton had it printed in pamphlet form. This act, which began a practice he was to follow throughout the rest of his career, was symbolic — as a legislator-pamphleteer, he would broadcast his popular democratic arguments in a grand attempt to influence mass public opinion, to build a mass following to support him in his new course.

[4]

AS AN EDITOR, in 1819, Benton had proclaimed: "It is time that western men had some share in the destinies of this Republic." As an emerging national leader, he sought to give effect to this maxim by throwing himself into the long, involved maneuvering that was to culminate in the presidential election of 1824.

At the beginning, four obvious front runners dominated the presidential racing. Three of these were cabinet members looking to a continuation of the tradition of cabinet succession to the Presidency — Adams, Crawford, and Calhoun. The fourth was Henry Clay of Kentucky, the then-recognized leading spokesman for Western interests, and Benton's favorite. A warm, magnetic, convivial leader who loved to drink whisky and gamble, "Harry of the West" could be willful and impetuous, but he had also proved himself an adroit politician and a master of compromise. He, like Benton, had condemned the Adams-Onis treaty of 1819 as throwing away Texas, and he, like Benton, proposed grandiose schemes to develop the West. In addition, he had made himself the symbol of opposition to cabinet succession and to the Congressional-caucus system that had hand-picked presidential candidates in the past. Among Missouri leaders he had the support not only of his cousin-in-law Benton, but of Barton, too, and many Missouri citizens who had emigrated from Kentucky still looked upon Clay as a favorite son. With all the other candidates coming from the Atlantic states, he was the obvious choice for Western men.

As early as March, 1822, Benton essayed his first effort in the presidential contest — a small, West-oriented propaganda maneuver, aimed at stigmatizing Adams for favoring a proposal to permit navigation rights to Great Britain on the Mississippi River, a proposal Clay had opposed. Later that same year, Benton spoke out more energetically. After the adjournment of Congress in May, he went to Cherry Grove to spend some time with Elizabeth and their daughter Eliza, and then proceeded with his family to St. Louis — where politics quickly claimed his attention. It appeared that Clay was to have a Western rival. In July, 1822, a Nashville paper had proclaimed: "GREAT RACING!!! . . . Why not *Tennessee* put in her stud? and if so, let it be called *Old Hickory*" — and it soon appeared that Andrew Jackson was indeed a candidate. The Clay men in Missouri decided to get a resolution through the state legislature declaring for "Harry of the West"; and as a rising leader Benton used his influence to secure favorable action. One citizen later alleged that, in his enthusiasm, Benton maintained that if the doughty Jackson became president, any man who opposed him would have to "guard his house with BULL-DOGS and BLOOD-HOUNDS." When the Missouri legislature convened at St. Charles, the temporary capital, Benton was there to support the pro-Clay resolution,[16] which passed without important opposition.

By November, 1822, Thomas and his family were back in Washington — where they were surrounded by presidential gossip. On the road east, their carriage had overturned and pitched violently on its broad side down a rocky hill, but though Thomas had suffered a cut four inches long on his head, the others were unhurt. In the capital, the family took up residence at Mrs. Clarke's boardinghouse on F Street, North, within easy walking distance of the Capitol. It was a residence better suited than Jesse Brown's convivial "Indian Queen" to a young couple and child. Soon after they were settled, Thomas and Elizabeth began a round of calls with a visit to James Monroe at the Executive Mansion — and noted that everywhere they went the election was the great topic. Most observers, Thomas remarked, gave Crawford and Clay "the best chance," with Adams a poor third.[17]

Through the next several months, however, the field shifted somewhat. Although Crawford suffered a stroke which nearly incapacitated him, he stayed in the race — and his continued presence on the track made Benton's position more difficult. Many of the friends Benton was making at Dawson's mess, like Macon and Randolph, supported their fellow Southerner, as did James Monroe and Thomas Jefferson himself, and Crawford also enjoyed the support of the powerful "Richmond Junto" of Virginia planters and politicians headed by Thomas Ritchie, editor of the *Enquirer* at Richmond. Finally, Martin Van Buren of the "Albany Regency" emerged as Crawford's effective campaign manager. Despite these influences, Benton managed to remain faithful to Clay. Meanwhile, Adams built increasing support, particularly among established merchants, manufacturers, and financial leaders in the Northeast. A discouraged Calhoun dropped out of the presidential racing, to make a bid for the Vice-Presidency.

In the summer of 1823, after the adjournment of Congress, Benton went to Tennessee on business — and again estimated the presidential racing. From Nashville in July, he wrote Clay that he had "been entirely through the State from one end to the other," and could report that popular sentiment there strongly favored Jackson, with Clay, Adams, and Crawford following in that order — *but,* "Jackson out of the way, the State will go for you, and there is hardly anyone who thinks he has any chance," nationally. Still, the Jackson men were putting up a good fight. Later in 1823 they were able to elect Jackson to the Senate, over Benton's friend John Williams, in a strategem calculated to bring Jackson once again into national political notice.[18]

One result of this manuever was a personal though not political reconciliation between Benton and Jackson. When Congress convened again in December, 1823, and committees were named, Benton was made chairman of Indian Affairs, and removed from Public Lands and switched to Military Affairs — committee posts he was to hold for years to come. The chairman of Military Affairs was Jackson, who was also given a seat next to Benton on the Senate floor.

"Colonel," Jackson said one day, "we are on the same committee; I will give you notice when it is necessary to attend."

"General," Benton replied civilly, "make the time to suit yourself; it will be convenient for me to attend at any time."

After these formalities, the two old foes found themselves doing committee business as any other Senators might. Next, they were asking after one another's wives. Finally, Jackson left his card at Thomas and Elizabeth's lodgings at Mrs. Clarke's, and Benton returned the call. As guests at a dinner given by President Monroe, the General and the Colonel bowed to one another and shook hands as friends, and Benton introduced Elizabeth to the man he had tried to kill scarcely ten years before. Then, amazed at it all, Thomas commented — "Well, how many changes in this life!"

This was not the only reconciliation Jackson effected in Washington.

Men who had expected Old Hickory to appear as a wild man with tomahawk and scalping knife were finding him grave, well-mannered, and mild — in short, altogether *presidential* in his bearing.[19] Still, Benton saw no reason to desert Henry Clay in the election contest.

Throughout the election maneuvering, Clay had become identified with a specific program for national development, which was carefully tailored to a broad range of interests. In Congress in 1824, several specific bills were brought forward which were to test Benton's allegiance to this program. The program — the "American System" as it was often called — was an amalgam of three items:

> *The Protective Tariff* — to "present motives to the capital and labor of our country to employ themselves in fabrication at home . . . the manufacturing system."
>
> *"Internal Improvements"* — "a comprehensive system of roads and canals, the effect of which would be to draw the different parts of the country more closely together" — in order to assure a wide, easily accessible market to the developing home manufactures. This program to be undertaken by the Federal government, out of "surplus revenue"; for the private "capitalist" would not or could not do it — he "might not be re-imbursed three per centum annually upon it."
>
> *The National Bank* — to assure "a general medium [of exchange]" — if not specie, at least in national paper on which manufacturers and traders might depend — "although its value, in comparison with specie, may fluctuate, it will afford an uniform standard."

This "American System," as Clay proclaimed it, polarized economic and doctrinal conflict in politics. It appealed strongly to established manufacturers in the East, to speculators, incipient capitalists, and men of Enterprise everywhere, and to men of the West who wanted their section built up. But it roused opposition from planters in the South, and from politically conscious plain farmers everywhere, who saw tariffs adding to the cost of what they had to buy, and saw internal improvements adding to the tax burden — there was in fact no "surplus revenue." Again, the whole scheme seemed to presage a transition to an urban, manufacturing and commercial, capitalist nation on the model suggested by Alexander Hamilton, which would mark the extinction of the agrarian and small producers' Arcadia that Jefferson had envisioned. Finally, members of the republican "Old School," like Macon and Randolph, feared the "American System" as a cloak for business monopolies and overextension of the power of the national government.[20]

In this conflict, Benton stood undecided. He had been caught up in the spirit of Enterprise. He had urged in the *Enquirer* a system of roads, canals, and ports for the West consistent with Clay's internal improvements plans. Though he had not had to express himself fully on tariffs or the Bank, he had spoken sympathetically of the latter. On the other hand, he had persisted in his admiration for the yeoman's Arcadia typified by the history of Granny White. He was beginning to come under the influence of men like Macon and Randolph, and in 1824 he was to introduce his public lands or graduation-donation proposal. Subject again to such cross-influences, his course remained unclear.

The first "American System" test measure to come before Benton and his colleagues in 1824 had to do with internal improvements. It was a bill providing for *national* government surveys in the several *states* for roads and canals. Concerned lest the old, populous states hog the benefits, Benton called for safeguards "to apply the fund nationally, to make roads and canals where the national interest requires them, without regard to population" — in short, in the West. In addition he expressed concern for the prerogatives of the states, and urged that the state governments be consulted before roads were run through state lands. Despite these caveats, Benton joined the majority of Yeas when the bill finally came to a vote.

In addition he spoke out vigorously for internal improvements he considered truly *national* — which meant, perhaps, *Western.* He defended a proposal to improve navigation on the Ohio and Mississippi Rivers with what he himself called great "force and animation." Indeed, he spoke so vehemently that the kindly, polished old-Federalist from New York, Rufus King, advised him to proceed more calmly. After the debate, Thomas reported in a letter to his wife, then in Virginia, King "came and sat down in a chair by me, and took hold of my hand and said he would speak to me as a father — that I had great powers, and that he felt a sincere pleasure in seeing me advance and rise in the world, and that he would take the liberty of warning me against an effect of my temperament when heated by opposition; that under these circumstances I took on an authoritative manner, and a look and tone of defiance, which sat ill upon the older members; and [he] advised me to moderate my manner." Though Benton vowed he would try to follow King's advice as to manner, he remained for some time a proponent of national or Western internal improvements in substance.

The second "American System" test measure Benton had to consider in 1824 was a tariff bill. Under protective duties established in 1816 domestic manufacturing had thrived, reaping profits that ran well ahead of agriculture and sometimes reached an annual total of 25 per cent on investment. Now manufacturing interest groups pressed for a new tariff bill, which would carry further the process Benton condemned as making "protection the object of the law, and revenue the incident" instead of vice versa, as he would have liked it. The Senate voted item by item, which opened the way to almost unrestricted bloc trading or logrolling. Though he rejected the *system* of high protection, Benton voted on roll call after roll call in favor of high duties on commodities produced in the West (hemp, cotton cloth, twist, yarn and thread, wool, cotton bagging, blankets), and against protection on manufactured articles the West had to buy (iron, silk, manufactured wool products, worsted goods . . . and frying pans). On final passage, he was able to vote Yea with the majority. The total effect of the new tariff was an average duty nearly twice the 1816 level.[21]

The supporters of Henry Clay could claim the "American System" votes of 1824 as a partial vindication of their candidate. More significantly, the votes indicated the disorganized state to which political parties had fallen in the era of "good feeling." They also indicated the extent to which Senators and Representatives patterned their behavior to the demands of dominant classes, special-interest groups, and factions in their various sections and constituencies. For example, Jackson and Van Buren both voted for the tariff, while the great nationalist-to-be Webster carefully tested business sentiment in his district and found it still anti-tariff, and thereupon voted Nay. Coming as they did in the same session in which he offered his agrarian land-reform proposal, Benton's votes showed that he had not entirely foresworn political Roman-riding. At the same time, his remarks in debate revealed him as a questionable ally for Clay in the "American System" cause, as a cause.

When the session adjourned in May, 1824, Benton stayed on briefly in Washington to participate in one more presidential maneuver. Fearful of the possible outcome of a four-way race to the post, Van Buren had worked out a plan — Clay to *withdraw* in favor of Crawford, who would take Clay as his vice-presidential running mate and later presidential *successor*. Noting that Benton was an "ardent friend" of Clay as well as "a young Senator of much promise," the wily Van Buren persuaded Benton that a Crawford-Clay ticket was bound to succeed, and got Benton to press the matter on Clay with all his "usual earnestness," but Clay declined.[22]

[5]

BUSY AS HE WAS with politics, Benton's large spirit and inquiring mind found other outlets too — as it was to do throughout his life.

Early in his Senate term, for example, he was elected to the grandly titled American Academy of Language and Belles Lettres. His letter of acceptance was equally grand — "An enlightened age owes it to itself and to posterity to make great exertions to perfect and preserve its language and science; nor can we admit that too much can be done upon these subjects when we look back to the point from which learning declined eighteen centuries ago, and reflect upon the long night of darkness which afterwards overhung the human intellect." He would accept a place in the Academy. On another occasion, Benton corresponded with one of the leading students of the West, Henry Schoolcraft. Yes, he wrote the scholar, he *had* seen and wondered about the " *'prints'* of human feet" on the limestone river bank at St. Louis, "but I do not think them 'impressions,' but the work of hands." His reasons — first, the hardness of the rock; second, the want of other "tracks" leading to and from those observed; third, the "difficulty of supposing a change so instantaneous and *apropos*" in the material, as would be required to take the "impressions" and then fix them. Of course, Benton noted in his precise, schoolmasterish way, his archeological theory faced objections too — and the problem remained unresolved.[23]

Meanwhile, he faced the more immediate problem of providing for an enlarging family circle. He thought himself always "full of business and short on cash," as his expenses continued to mount. It was not easy, providing for Elizabeth, whose upbringing had accustomed her to some luxury, and for Eliza, and for the family slaves. In addition, Thomas's niece Sarah, who was living with his mother at the Laurel Street house in St. Louis, was becoming a greater expense — "she attends the balls and plays in company with the best people of this place," his mother wrote him, and Thomas had promised to bring Sarah to Washington for a season, which would mean more expense still. The senatorial salaries of the day were not adequate to such responsibilities, and Thomas was regularly engaged in efforts to supplement his income.

It was for this purpose that he journeyed to Tennessee in the spring and summer of 1823. Back in the Cumberland, he met with his brothers Jesse, Samuel, and Nathaniel, and worked out an agreement which was signed in late June, by which he acquired title to certain family lands which he might sell as his own. While he was in Nashville, he also took a law case for a rugged adventurer named John Smith T, a man of many quarrels which had grown out of his rare persistence in freezing onto old Spanish land claims for mining properties. (The "T" in his name was not an initial — he simply thought there were too many plain John Smiths and added the letter for distinction.) The case Benton took, involving a Spanish grant to land near Ste. Genevieve in Missouri, was in the Supreme Court of Tennessee on appeal, having been dragged through the lower courts since 1814. Drawing on his Missouri background in such matters, Benton offered an expert, involved, technical argument. But after further delays and a rehearing in which Benton did not participate, the court found against Smith T, though it accepted much of Benton's general argument. He apparently thought his brief of such general interest, or so cogent, that he had it published as a pamphlet.

Meanwhile, Benton's fortunes in St. Louis suffered further reverses. Over the summer of 1823, six of his town lots were listed for sale for taxes, and he lost another lot and house in a lawsuit when another claimant contested Benton's old Spanish title. Fortunately Samuel sent some money to Nancy Benton for the Laurel Street household, and though she could get only ninety cents on the dollar for the North Carolina bank notes, this tided her over a lean time. Meanwhile, returning to Washington by way of Cherry Grove without going to St. Louis at all, Thomas busied himself with two cases in the Supreme Court.[24] Throughout his career, he was to act as counsel in occasional cases in the high court.

After the adjournment of Congress in May, 1824, Benton hurried again to Cherry Grove. There, Elizabeth and little Eliza were staying with the McDowells — and there, on May 31, 1824, a second child was born to Thomas and Elizabeth, a daughter they christened Jessie Ann after her grandfather Jesse Benton and her grandmother Ann Gooch. This infant was to grow up a sprightly, accomplished, and beautiful young lady, and became her father's close companion.

A few weeks after Jessie's birth, Thomas set out for the West — canvassing along the road for Clay. It was late July before he reached St. Louis. There he found that his brother Nathaniel had had some success selling out lands for him in Tennessee, but also that he had lost some of his remaining properties in St. Louis to speculators — and once again, he found his mother and his household on Laurel Street short of cash. This did not seem so important to Nancy as the fact that her son, two years absent, had in St. Louis "good Friends and Great ones" who looked forward to his return.[25]

Not everyone was Benton's "good Friend." One evening, at a ball at Planter's House in St. Louis, he was noticed by John B. C. Lucas, who walked with his son James deliberately across the ballroom floor, to come face to face with the "murderer." The judge stood for a moment — so later reports had it — and then turned to James.

"It is a con-so-la-shion, my son," he intoned in a voice loud enough for all to hear, "that whoever knows Meester Colonel Thomas H. Benton knows him to be a rascail — eh, my boy?"

The tall, bulky Colonel simply stalked away from the short, slight Judge Lucas without answering.[26] It was surely wiser for a man in his position to ignore the old *Français,* and his abiding malice, than to be provoked into resuming a quarrel that might develop into a duel-for-duel blood feud.

The incident marked a growing moderation and self-control in Benton's character. His early childhood experiences, and his expulsion from the University of North Carolina, had apparently given him an intense compulsion to prove his worth to the world. Always able, always capable of close friendship with a few intimates, generally gracious, he had nonetheless seemed too aggressive, touchy about his honor, and prickly, to suit many men. But now, the world was accepting him as somebody — the Missouri legislature had named him to the Senate, Elizabeth McDowell had married him, men and women in Washington and St. Louis gave him respect and affection. Calmer and more secure, Benton could refrain from an angry answer to Lucas, and yet feel that his "honor" was intact.

[6]

IN MISSOURI, through the summer and fall of 1824, Benton was engrossed again in presidential electioneering. To counter a rising support for Jackson, he stumped nearly every part of the state for Clay, proclaiming that his old General was unfit, ungovernable, and despotic, while Clay was pre-eminently qualified. By fall, he was so busy that he had to decline an invitation to a public dinner in his honor in St. Louis — he was about to leave for the upper part of the state, "on a visit of duty and inclination to my more distant constituents." All told, he traveled more than eight hundred miles in Missouri in an effort to elect Clay and defeat Jackson.[27]

When the voters of Missouri went to the polls to choose electors, they gave the Clay slate 2042 tallies, while Jackson netted 1166, Adams 218, and Crawford none. Soon, news came of the voting elsewhere. For the first time, the bulk of the presidential electors — in eighteen out of twenty-four states — were named not by the legislatures but by popular vote, and the result was the greatest political shock in years. Nationally, tickets for Jackson polled a total of 152,901 votes, while electoral slates for established leaders ran well behind — for Adams, 114,023, for Crawford, 46,979, and for Clay, 47,217. A count of electoral votes showed Jackson 99, Adams 84, Crawford 41, and Clay 37. No candidate had a majority, and the House of Representatives would have to select a President from among the highest three.

At first, the established politicos found it difficult to explain this result. To be sure, Jackson was an impressive figure — tall, slender, gracefully erect, with a long, thin face set off with small, clear blue eyes, a straight, Grecian nose, prominent cheekbones, and a lantern jaw, all topped by gray hair which stood as erect as his person. He seemed to many the personification of massive strength. But political popularity was not built by appearance alone. The shrewd New York manager, Martin Van Buren, thought Jackson's strength with the masses in 1824 due to three things — his military character was admired; he had a reputation for integrity in all things which was taken as a portent of faithful service to popular interests in government; and he was known as the enemy of the old Congressional caucus system of choosing presidential candidates. Despite equivocations on many issues, he was taken as a symbol of a rising popular democracy, as a new Moses to replace old leaders who were popularly identified with the distresses of economic depression, as a man "from the bosom of the people." Vaguely felt as this new popular democracy was, the fact that Jackson had become its symbol was portentous.

The effective choice in the House would be between Adams and Jackson — between "the trained scholar and statesman," and the emerging leader from the new West, "rather lank in look, but fire in his eye" — as one observer saw the contestants.[28] This situation presaged the end of political Roman-riding for Thomas Benton. He had to decide.

In Missouri, meanwhile, he had been active in another political contest. As early as 1822, an antagonism had developed between Benton and Barton, an antagonism which apparently had its roots in recriminations over the election maneuvering of 1820. In 1823, the breach was widened further when David and Joshua Barton charged that William, Rector was using his post as public land surveyor for Missouri, Illinois, and Arkansas to feather his relatives' nests. The surveyor was one of Benton's personal friends, and Benton quickly came to his defense—thereby drawing the charge that he had descended from "the high dignity of a Senator" to become counsellor for an officeholder. The hostility between Benton and Barton was intensified by the fact that, in the Senate, they had taken opposing positions on Benton's electoral reform and graduation-donation proposals. With Barton's four-year Senate term about to expire, a "Benton party" and a "Barton party" emerged in the state, with Benton working actively to prevent Barton's re-election. As he traveled the state, he labored to stir public opinion against Barton, and sought to influence the members-elect to the State Assembly that would choose the Senator from Missouri. As part of his campaign, his enemies complained, he wrote and distributed "huge handbills," urging the defeat of his former ally. A major charge in the anti-Barton barrage, though Benton himself apparently did not indulge in it, was that Barton spent so much time with the wine, whisky, and brandy bottles that he was incapable of giving proper attention to public business. When the Assembly met at St. Charles in November, 1824, Benton, Governor McNair, and others buttonholed members and sought an anti-Barton candidate — settling finally on Benton's old friend, the former explorer William Clark. Before the decision came, Benton had to leave for Washington. Nine days after he had left, the Assembly voted overwhelmingly to return David Barton to the Senate.

Gleefully, anti-Benton men hailed this triumph over "the most outrageous Slander circulated against [Barton] by his enemies Rectors, Benton, Govn'r McNair and others." The "aspiring political *genius*," as one partisan sarcastically dubbed Benton, had failed in his attempt to play political manager.[29]

[7]

UNDAUNTED AND PERSISTENT, Benton turned to new matters. Soon after Congress covened in December, 1824, he presented a petition from "sundry inhabitants" of his state which cited a considerable trade going on between Missouri and the Mexican provinces around Santa Fe — cottons and other goods out, gold, silver, furs, and mules in return — but noted that the commerce was threatened with extinction by hostile Indian tribes. To meet this danger, the petitioners requested national government aid. They asked, first, for treaties with the Indians to secure the right of unmolested passage along a designated route, and second, for a military post where the route intersected with the Arkansas River. After reading the petition, Benton asked that it be sent to his own committee — Indian Affairs.

This accomplished, he left Washington for a short visit with his family at Cherry Grove. Nine days later, he left again for the capital, stopping at Monticello, the home of Thomas Jefferson, near Charlottesville. Here he spent Christmas Eve with the aged hero of democracy. The individual must manage badly, Benton remarked later, who could find himself in the presence of that great man, and retire from it without taking with him some item of utility to the human race. On this occasion, Jefferson told Benton of an old map he remembered, at that time, he thought, in the Library of Congress, which might have some bearing on the Missourian's interest in the trade route to Santa Fe. In addition, they discussed politics. The younger man remarked that Clay had told him that he intended to throw his strength to Adams, a fact of great importance that was not yet generally known. Surely, Benton continued, this meant that Adams would be elected —

"And if he is elected, I believe that, from the necessity of the case, he would have to make up a *broad-bottomed* [coalition, or broadly-based] cabinet — How do you think it would do?"

Promptly, Jefferson replied: "Not at all — [it] would never succeed — [it] would ruin all engaged in it."

Back in Washington, Benton turned again to the Santa Fe trade issue. Two days after the New Year, 1825, he presented a long letter from Augustus Storrs of Missouri, answering twenty-two questions addressed to him by Senator Benton. These dealt in detail with a vast congeries of items — the extent of the trade, the route usually followed, and so on.

This exhaustive document, given national circulation by Hezekiah Niles in the *Register,* was picked up by local papers and attracted widespread attention. When Jared Sparks, Harvard prodigy and editor of the *North American Review,* asked for the document, Benton could comply only by sending him his own personal copy.

Having thus prepared the way, Benton finally presented a bill designed to satisfy the "sundry inhabitants" of Missouri. The measure was in three sections — *first,* to authorize commissioners to mark a road from Missouri to the Mexican border and to treat with the Indians for peaceful passage; *second,* to authorize the President to arrange with Mexican authorities for the United States to mark the road in the wild Mexican territory to the border of New Mexico (about 150 miles beyond the Arkansas); and *third,* to appropriate a total of thirty thousand dollars for these purposes. On January 25, the Missourian began debate on the measure with a careful, scholarly, but — for him — unusually brief speech. In peroration, he mentioned his Christmas Eve conversation with Jefferson. He showed the Senate the map the ex-President had recalled, which revealed a precedent for one nation marking a road in another nation's territory — "with this triumphant precedent, I leave the fate of the bill to the wisdom and to the justice of the Senate." The Senate responded by a handsome vote of 30 to 12,[30] and, soon after, the bill passed the House. It was signed by President Monroe as one of his last official acts.

Once again, Benton had labored to serve the interests of diverse groups. The trade bill was bound to please the commercial leaders and fur magnates of St. Louis, but it also held out the promise of new opportunities for small traders, and a promise of service to Missouri's yeomen, because an expanded Santa Fe trade would assure a flow of specie into an area previously harassed by a lack of hard money.

Meanwhile, Washington was an arena for complicated, last-try maneuvering in the presidential contest. Largely under the impact of the four-way canvass, old patterns of compromise and political infighting under the cloak of seeming party unity were breaking up. Established business-interest groups and leaders, particularly in the East, were pinning their hopes on Adams, and they were joined now by many budding capitalists in the West, ready to follow their defeated leader Clay to Adams. On the other hand, many of the nation's yeomen and small producers looked increasingly to Jackson as their leader. But Old Hickory also had the support of some elements of the business classes, enterprisers and would-be enterprisers who felt that the established mercantile groups stood in their way; and he also found favor with many planters in the South. (Many issues, of course, were not clearly drawn, and there were groupings within these main groupings, based on local or personal considerations.) Faced with such a situation, what was Benton to do? He was determined not to follow Clay to the support of Adams — he had no love and little respect for the New Englander, and the people of the West had made it clear that Adams, considered by some an "aristocratic" candidate, was not their man. Benton was sympathetic to the candidacy of Crawford, and in late January, 1825, some Crawford leaders counted him "warmly" in their cause; but apparently he soon realized that Crawford could not command sufficient support to make himself a serious contender in the House. Seemingly there was only one course to follow — come out for his old enemy, Jackson.

It was a decision of far-reaching consequences. It entailed a break with Clay, a strain in Benton's relations with the Missouri nabobs and politicos who would follow Clay to the Adams standard, and the practical end of political Roman-riding. On the other hand, the decision was consistent with the position Benton had taken in his electoral and land-reform proposals, and with the *"demos krateo"* principle. He had now fully identified himself with the nascent popular-democratic spirit abroad in the nation. Practically, the decision at once enabled and required him to look to the growing strength of the pro-Jackson democratic movement in Missouri as his power base for the future. Sarcastically, David Barton commented — "of all the unnatural coalitions (not to say the most insincere) is that of our Senator Pomposo, of imperial port and mien, with the General!" [31] But Benton held to the commitment he had made.

One of his colleagues was also making up his mind. Under the unit rule giving each state one vote in the presidential election in the House, Missouri's strength would be wielded by John Scott, Benton's long-time friend and political ally. During the 1824 canvass, Scott had declared that if the election came to the House he would vote the wishes of his state — where the popular vote had shown that Jackson was, next to Clay, a runaway favorite. But in Washington other influences intervened — a continuing attachment to Clay, and perhaps to his program, and suggestions by Adams that he might satisfy Scott on certain patronage and personal matters. Early in 1825, Scott decided to vote for Adams.

On February 5, Scott notified Benton of *his* portentous decision — and received a stinging rebuke in answer. Benton was astounded at this decision, he wrote — "so inconsistent with your previous conversations, so repugnant to your printed pledges, so amazing to your constituents, so fatal to yourself." The vote Scott planned to give was not his own, but that of *the people of Missouri,* who were against Adams — and "I, in their name," Benton trumpeted, "do solemnly protest against your intention, and deny your moral power thus to bestow your vote." The nine-year association between the two men must be dissolved, and dissolved in a way which meant everlasting separation. The day of the voting would be "the day for your self-immolation; if you have an enemy, he may go and feed his eyes on the scene"; your "former friend" would shun the "afflicting spectacle." Thus, dramatically, did Benton excommunicate Scott. Thus did he cut himself off, utterly and finally, from another of his influential old associates in Missouri politics.[32]

The break was consummated on February 9, when Scott cast his vote for Adams, in an election giving Adams thirteen states, Jackson seven states, and Crawford four states.

After the election, Henry Clay was appointed Secretary of State. Thus, he was in the position of heir-apparent to the Presidency, but before long it was clear that the appointment would work to his detriment. It was cited and cited again by "Jackson men" as evidence that Adams and Clay had made a "corrupt bargain," whereby Adams would appoint Clay Secretary of State in payment for the latter's support in the election in the House. This charge Benton did not believe. He told his friends that Clay had informed him in the first half of December, 1824, that he intended to vote for Adams as the man best suited for the job. This "voluntary and faithful testimony" elicited a letter of thanks from the Secretary to the Senator in 1827, whereupon Benton repeated his disbelief of the charge in a public letter.[33] Still, Benton and Clay had come to an irrevocable parting of the political ways.

The election marked a political setback for Benton. On his first day in office, Adams determined that, despite the recommendations of Senator Poinsett and the inclinations of President Monroe, he would never appoint Benton as Minister to Mexico — or to any other position, presumably. For the four years of the Adams regime, Benton realized, he would be without influence on the executive. He would exercise, as he put it, no more effect there than "God and his Grace [the Duke of Ormond]" had at the Court of Charles II — in short, none at all. Back in Missouri, the *Republican* attacked "the recent adhesion of Col. Benton to the fortunes of Gen. Jackson" as a plan by Benton to buoy up "his own sinking fortunes." But Benton had made his decision, and would abide by its consequences. He was convinced that the election of Adams was "a violation of the *demos krateo* principle,"* and that all those involved would finally be "signally rebuked" by the *demos,* by the people. Before the year was out, Benton's expectation was proving itself in Missouri at least. The news aroused anger and resentment even among those who had not been "Jackson men," but who feared an "aristocratic government" by a President who was not the people's choice. In such fertile soil, a full-scale movement for Jackson in 1828 began to sink stronger and deeper roots, while "Adams men" like Barton and Scott began to lose influence. In short, as Benton analyzed it, the election in the House "re-established parties upon the basis of principle," making political democracy a key issue. It "drew anew party lines, then almost obliterated under the fusion of parties," and the efforts of leaders to "make personal parties" for themselves.[34]

Thus, Benton was still unbowed. A man of his driving personality and broad views would not give in to defeat, and he was to emerge as one of the leaders of the new national democratic movement, and to triumph in Missouri.

* Discussing these events, M. Ostrogorski, with his usual irony, notes the proclamation of the *"demos krateo* principle" by Thomas Benton — "who had learnt his Greek in the Far West" (M. Ostrogorski, *Democracy and the Organization of Political Parties,* II, 45).

CHAPTER 7

Opposition

1825 - 1828

B Y APRIL, 1825, Thomas, Elizabeth, and their daughters were back
in St. Louis. They came overland this time only as far as the Ohio
River, where they boarded one of the increasingly popular steamboats
for the long but pleasant trip down the Ohio and up the Mississippi to
their home. Members of Congress were allowed eight dollars for each
twenty miles of travel by the most usual route. On this occasion Benton
calculated his mileage by the meanders of the rivers, submitting a
bill for $3,302.40 for *per diem* and mileage to Barton's overland-
calculated $1,683.20 *per diem* and travel. Benton's enemies were later
to make much of this contrast.

At the end of April, Benton helped welcome a distinguished visitor
to the town. The old Revolutionary hero, General Lafayette, was making a tour of the nation whose independence he had helped establish.
When he reached St. Louis aboard the steamer *Natchez* Benton was one
of a committee of distinguished citizens who received him. Through the
din of cannon firing and the hurrahs of an immense crowd, the committee conducted the Marquis from the Market Street landing to the Pierre
Chouteau mansion, which was opened to all comers. At a dinner later,
Benton was called upon to speak briefly. He noted proudly that there
were present representatives of four Western states, none of which had
existed when General Lafayette had helped found the Republic.

Politically, Benton was subjected to periodic abuse and ridicule during
his stay in Missouri. Throughout the summer and fall of 1825, his old
enemy the *Republican* mocked "Senator *Lungs*," and damned him in-
discriminately for his views, his alleged determination to climb "higher
on ambition's ladder," and his burgeoning egotism. Fortunately, "Senator *Lungs*" had a new defender. The *Enquirer* had fallen on hard
times, but in 1825 a new paper called the *Missouri Advocate* moved
to St. Louis from St. Charles, absorbed the *Enquirer,* and emerged as a
stout defender of Benton and his works, including his electoral reform

and graduation-donation proposals. Soon, John B. C. Lucas had it that Benton was "the occult Editor" of the *Advocate* — a charge that paper denied, though it hailed Benton as "a man of the first talents, and the most able writer west of the Allegheny mountains." Meanwhile, evidence mounted that the plain farmers who were the majority of Missouri's citizens supported Benton in his new course. The trend of public opinion was confirmed when the governor died, and a special election was called to choose a successor. In the election, Benton became identified as the sponsor of John Miller, who ran as a "Jackson-man," and Barton in turn sponsored David Todd, who was billed as an "Adams-man." Miller was a strong winner in a field of four — and thereafter the state patronage was used to strengthen the Jackson party in Missouri.[1]

Ever buoyant, Thomas was apparently unaffected by the attacks he sustained. He took some law cases in St. Louis and outstate to improve the family finances, dealt with some minor political and patronage matters, and enjoyed the summer and fall in Missouri with his family. His pleasure was marred by another financial difficulty — his one-time friend John Mullanphy foreclosed the mortgage on the Laurel Street house, leaving the Bentons there as tenants, though with the right to claim the property on full payment of the debt. Still, in July, 1825, writing to John Randolph to congratulate him on his elevation to the Senate, Benton could add: "I have the pleasure to say that, thus far, the banks of the Mississippi have proved as favorable to our healths as the summit of the Allegheny." [2]

[2]

AT THE END OF 1825, the first session of Congress under President Adams convened. In the session of 1825-1826, and in later sessions in 1826-1827 and 1827-1828, Benton stepped forward as a major opposition leader, both by advocating his own proposals and by attacking proposals the President submitted.

His first effort was a revival and revision of his plan for the popular election of Presidents and Vice-Presidents. At Benton's instance, a committee was named to study the matter, and he was made chairman. By January, 1826, the committee reported a proposed amendment embracing all of Benton's old plan, with the additional provision that in a presidential election where no candidate had a majority, a run-off election was to be held between the two leading contenders. This scheme, Benton argued, would avoid the great objections to the election that had brought Adams to the Presidency. In a three- or four-way race, it would provide in effect "a *nomination* by the people," and then the final choice of the President by the people instead of by the House of Representatives. Thus, Benton proclaimed, the triumph of "the democratic principle — the *demos krateo* — the majority to govern," would be assured. It was a timely proposal, but it soon became apparent that it could not gather the necessary two-thirds vote in the pro-Adams Senate.[3]

With greater hope of success, Benton pressed his plan to reduce prices on, and provide donations of, the public lands. In May, 1826, in January, 1827, and in April, 1828, he spoke out for the proposal, in its original or in revised forms. In a steadily strengthening forensic style, he argued the issue in the interest of the nation's "freeholders," whom he praised as "the natural supporters of a free government." He contrasted the graduation-donation policy with the Administration position, which was emerging as the old one of holding the public lands for maximum revenue. Over the years, he linked the land reform issue to other great problems of the day — the public debt, the tariff or taxes, the banking system, and the development of capital concentrations in the East. The lands were originally to have been "*disposed* of" to pay the public debt, but instead had been "hugged up in the arms" of government, he declared. By speedier sales under his plan, "the public debt [might] be paid off in five years." This in turn would permit a reduction of tariff duties "upon *comforts* and *necessaries*," he continued — thereby relieving "the people . . . from the annual levy of twelve or fifteen millions of taxes," which was his estimate of the burden of the new tariff duties. This would aid consumers in the agricultural South and West, where the tariff-tax load fell most heavily — though the proceeds were mostly spent in the East, where "commerce collects her accumulated treasures," and where "multiplied banks diffuse an abundant paper currency" on this foundation. Land reform would thus, in its effect, strike at the existing process of accumulation and aggrandizement for merchant and banking capitalists in one section at the expense of the general population, he summed up. When he had finished, he had offered an antithesis at every point to the Administration, or American System, idea of national economic policy. Meanwhile, salting his more bookish arguments with accounts of travels among the frontiersmen, he reiterated his demand for land reform so that government might work *"for* the poor," instead of "against them."

Again and again during the land debates, Benton ran afoul of his colleague Barton. When Benton hammered and jabbed at the Administration, Barton leaped to his feet to defend that Administration from such "extraordinary and unnecessary denunciations," and to deny stoutly that the West was disaffected from the Adams-Clay standard. Before long a New York journalist noted that the two gentlemen from Missouri, so different politically and personally, "never converse or associate either in public or in private."

In his electoral reform and land reform campaigns, Benton revealed his developing skill at applying a "lever" to public opinion. He was now fighting, all-out, for a political economy of popular, majority-rule democracy, based on a population of small farmers, small producers, and small traders. Appropriately, he carried this fight to the mass of the population, in a propaganda style which he was to utilize throughout his career. His speeches were widely reprinted in the press; and in 1826 and again in 1828 he issued fat pamphlet editions of his graduation-donation arguments, buttressed with appendices stigmatizing Adams and Secretary of the Treasury Rush as the great "new antagonist[s]" to land policy reform. His insistence and colorful pleading caught attention. His appeal was accurately directed at the pre-existing interests and attitudes of millions of freeholders, sons of freeholders, and would-be freeholders in a land-hungry population. He always concluded with specific proposals for action. He made a strong though not impregnable factual, historical-statistical, and logical case. At the same time, he took care that he would be understood by the public at which he aimed, and he made effective use of such propaganda devices as simplification into black-and-white contrasts, argument to the authority of the Jeffersonian-democratic tradition, a plain-folks appeal, and untiring repetition. By early 1828 he could inform his Missouri political ally, the Reverend Finis Ewing, that action favoring his graduation-donation proposal had been taken by the legislatures or governors in six frontier states and territories in the South and West. While a "personal opposition" in Missouri had kept the Assembly there from acting, Benton had a petition signed by four thousand Missouri citizens urging his bill. Alas, Adams lamented in his diary, Benton's campaign for his land proposals had stimulated all the people of the Western country to madness!

In April, 1828, the land issue came to a showdown vote in the Senate. It followed long debate, during which Barton attributed the excitement for the bill in the West to Benton's desire for "personal and political advancement." (The tension between Barton and Benton had reached such "great heat" that once when Barton rose to speak Martin Van Buren led Elizabeth Benton from her place behind the bar of the Senate, to spare her from hearing the expected attack on her husband.) The debate concluded with a leviathan, three-day speech by Benton — an effort which brought blood from his lungs again, much to the concern of his friends. When the roll was called, members from the commercial, manufacturing and slaveholding sections to the East presented a nearly solid front of Nays, while every Senator from the South and West, where farmers and small producers were the bulk of the population, voted Yea — with the exception of Barton. But the bill lost — Nays 25, Yeas 21.[4]

Meanwhile, Benton joined in more direct assaults on the Administration. Though Jackson had retired from the Senate, his forces remained active in Washington. The Jackson leaders trained their fire on President Adams, and on his supporters like Clay and Webster. Though he did not play so prominent a role as better-established leaders like Vice-President Calhoun, Martin Van Buren, or John Randolph, Benton participated effectively in this program of "blowing up" the Administration.

One issue came up toward the end of December, 1825. Inspired by a suggestion from the South American revolutionary Simon Bolivar, Adams proposed to send delegates to "a Congress of American nations to be assembled at Panama to deliberate upon the objects of peculiar concernment to this hemisphere." In secret sessions of the Senate in February and March, 1826, the opposition stepped forward. For his part, Benton fired off a long speech, printed in pamphlet form so the attack might be spread throughout the country. He offered a piebald medley of arguments, including the Southern one that attendance would require United States delegates to join with Negro representatives, and proposed "amendments" which would have effectually precluded participation. The plan was nonetheless finally adopted [5] — though nothing came of it, for, thanks to the delays in Congress, the American delegate arrived after the Panama meeting had adjourned.

Domestically, the opposition charged that the Administration's power to let contracts to publish the laws was being used to give it, as Macon argued, "a monstrous influence with the editors of newspapers," while the Executive was also accused of misusing its appointive power to win friends and influence votes. A committee was appointed to investigate this situation, and Vice-President Calhoun named Benton chairman. In May, 1826, Benton presented a slashing, argumentative, partisan report, which urged "the expediency of reducing the patronage of the executive." He offered six separate bills toward this end. The country, he charged dramatically, was tending toward the time when "the principle of public action will be open and avowed, *the President wants My vote, and I want HIS patronage; I will VOTE as he wishes, and he will GIVE me the office I wish for.*" Nothing came of this hullabaloo, beyond an order to print six thousand copies of Benton's report, the largest printing that had up to that time been given any document.

Opposition, whether on elections or land policy, on Panama or patronage, suited Benton's driving, bulldog temperament. And the opposition was effective. The mid-term Congressional elections of 1826 brought an anti-Adams majority to both Senate and House, and the only gain the Administration could claim was the elevation of Webster to the Senate. The political trend was shifting. As it shifted, a new generation of leaders was coming to the fore, in which the maturing Benton was to become increasingly important in carrying the Jacksonian banner.

In the new Congress, Benton pressed another alternative to the American System. After consulting with Vice-President Calhoun, and with Senators Macon and Tazewell, he prepared and offered a resolution calling for a committee inquiry into the Administration's fiscal policy, particularly to see if the national debt and thereby customs-duty taxes might not be reduced more quickly. Arguing for his resolution in March, 1828, he insisted that more of the Treasury's funds should be applied regularly to debt reduction. There was always a large sum on hand, "constituting a standing deposit" in the Bank of the United States, "certainly yield[ing] a handsome profit to that institution," but at the expense of a continuing burden of taxes on plain men, producers and consumers. It was time to reject the Hamiltonian doctrine, which he charged the Administration had adopted, "that a public debt [is] a public blessing." The motion for an inquiry was agreed to — but again no practical consequences ensued.[6]

The session of 1827-1828 also saw a revival of the protective tariff issue itself — and here Benton's opposition to the Administration was not so consistent. In 1826 and 1827, what Calhoun called "a great excitement" had been "got up in Boston by the Capitalists," looking toward increased tariffs on woolen products. This had led to "a general convention of the manufacturing interest" at Harrisburg, in Pennsylvania, looking toward greater over-all protection. This movement had been pushed in the House with the encouragement of key Administration figures — but the matter was taken away from them by the partisans of Jackson. His business-minded supporters in New York and Pennsylvania were interested in protection for certain raw materials and commodities, like Pennsylvania's surplus grain and the products Pennsylvania's innumerable distilleries made from it. Under the aegis of Van Buren and Calhoun, leaders from the Middle States effected a combination with Jackson leaders from the South, strongly opposed to any tariff increase. This alliance pared away the duties desired by the New England "Capitalists," and placed extremely high duties on raw materials — all with the hope of driving the Administration and New England forces to oppose and so (possibly) defeat the bill. Thus, the Jackson leaders hoped to win support among pro-tariff men in the Middle States, hold support among anti-tariff men in the South — *and* discredit the Administration.

The bill, however, passed the House, and came to the Senate in May, 1828. As item after item was worked over, Benton applied the touchstone he had found in 1824. Stifling a rising general antagonism to high protection, he looked after the interests of his section. He plumped for protective duties on such products as lead, furs, and indigo — all to spread the benefits "of the American system . . . to show that the country south [and west] of the Potomac is included in the bill for some other purpose besides that of oppression." And so on, through item after item. However, Administration leaders and some New England members managed to get some of the duties favoring manufactures back into the bill, and with their support it passed. With his eyes on his Missouri constituency and partisan advantage, Benton spoke "with repugnance and misgiving" a calculated "Yea," along with other Jackson men from the Middle States and the West. Webster, noting the rise of manufacturing in Massachusetts, reversed his 1824 position and also voted Aye. Bloc trading, complicated by problems of party advantage, had produced curious combinations indeed. By such political brokerage, "a majority [was] made up," as Benton put it later, "to pass a measure which they [did] not approve." [7]

Despite his vote, Benton did not suffer all this without a savage blast. This tariff, he remarked, came to him "under new and revolting aus-

pices, as the antagonist to my graduation bill." The Administration policies, high tariffs and high land prices, were twins — "keep the lands out
of the reach of the poor . . . and then they become an excess, in the
language of [Benjamin] Franklin, who cannot get land"; at which point
"they become proper material for the use of the manufacturer," people
who "must hire themselves out, and hire for small wages." All this
Benton put in an appendix to the land-speeches pamphlet he sent out
among the people. Four years later, in another tariff argument in the
Senate, Benton recapitulated his views on the tariff bills of 1824 and
1828. He was "a friend to domestic industry," he declared, and had
"voted for the tariff of 1824 with the approbation of my judgment,"
but "for that of 1828 with repugnance and misgiving." He could never
approve such a "high rate of protection."

The perennial problem of Federal expenditures for internal improvements also engaged Benton's attention in 1828. In January, he
announced himself for a bill to complete work on a section of the National or Cumberland Road — a work begun, he noted, under a Federal-
state compact which eliminated the need to debate Federal powers. In
April, he urged that the big road go on to the capital of Missouri. Slowly
he was evolving a compromise position which was to prove typical of
the Jackson party. This was, simply, to reject Federal expenditures
for *local* improvements, as forcing the whole population to subsidize
particular interests, but to accept national spending for projects of truly
national scope. National projects, yes; pork for special, local interests,
no — and the West must participate fully in any program.

When Congress adjourned in May, 1828, Benton was content to wait
until "the ensuing presidential election" should put into power a new
Administration, under which both the tariff and internal improvements
policies might be properly "regulated." Some other members of the
Jackson coalition were not willing to wait, however. In South Carolina
men muttered of a "tariff of abominations," and political spokesmen led
on the quiet by Calhoun prepared an "Exposition" condemning the new
tariff as grossly unfair to the Southern, exporting, consuming population
and their interests. The Constitution, this protest proclaimed, was a
"social compact" which gave the Federal government only certain limited powers beyond which it must not go; if it did, the *states* had a
"bounden duty to expose and *resist* all encroachments upon the true
spirit" of the compact. This doctrine portended future conflicts in which
Benton was to be deeply involved.

The drift of politics had already drawn Benton into new personal conflicts. One of these grew out of his ripening intimacy with John Randolph. On the first of April, 1826, Randolph suddenly appeared at Benton's lodgings — he was staying again at Brown's Hotel, for Elizabeth and the children were spending the season at Cherry Grove. Was Benton, Randolph asked without explanation, related to Lucretia Clay? The question, it developed, was prompted by a prospective duel. In the Senate, Randolph had tongue-lashed the alliance of Adams and Henry Clay as "the coalition of Blifil and Black George — the combination, unheard of until then, of the Puritan with the blackleg." This ill-tempered invective had drawn a challenge from Clay. Randolph wanted Benton to act as his second, but he witheld his request when Benton informed him that he was indeed a blood-relation to Lucretia Clay. Once Thomas might have offered fiery encouragement. Now, affected perhaps by Elizabeth Benton's gentle influence, he offered his services as peacemaker. For a week Thomas and some others "laboured" to effect an adjustment, but in vain. At the duel, Benton was present only "for the purpose of interposing mediation at the first practicable moment," as he put it. The parties met near Little Falls Bridge on the Virginia bank of the Potomac beyond Georgetown. They exchanged a round with no effect, whereupon Thomas drew his friend aside, and renewed "more pressingly than ever, [his] importunities to agree to some accommodation"; but Randolph refused, and returned to a second fire. This time, however, he discharged his pistol in the air, while Clay put a hole in Randolph's long coat. Thereupon, Senator, Secretary of State, seconds, and guests returned to Washington, full of honorable satisfaction — "it was," Benton remarked later, "about the last high-toned duel that I have witnessed." For his services, Benton acquired a family seal and motto, which John Randolph found in the Herald's Office on a trip to London. The seal was, appropriately, a *Lion Rampant,* and the motto, *Factis non Verbis;* which Randolph suggested, appropriately, might well have been amended by changing the *non* to *et.*[8]

The duel dramatized the fact that the political breach between Benton and Clay had become a personal estrangement as well. This fact was noted, and regretted, by an old friend of the two, James Brown of Louisiana, who had married Benton's cousin, Clay's sister-in-law, Ann Hart. Though they had corresponded faithfully in the past, Brown complained that he heard from Benton no longer, and went on to lament that party spirit was "carried so far as to interrupt the harmony of society and lessen the bonds of kindred association." He was particularly sorry that Benton had "thought it necessary to prove his friendship to Jackson by renouncing it for any of his old friends," Brown wrote to Clay, "but more especially to you." [9] The list of "renunciations" was growing. Now Clay himself, and his friends and kin, were set aside by Benton. Moving toward larger leadership, he was impetuous, imperious, politics-absorbed, and, apparently, quite sure of himself.

[3]

IN MISSOURI IN 1826, Benton's assurance was to be tested. His Senate term was expiring, and he faced a contest for re-election in the Assembly that would be chosen in August, 1826, and would convene in the late fall.

During his absence in Washington, Benton's Missouri enemies had been busy organizing an opposition. Their fortress, of course, was the *Republican,* which kept up a drumfire of attack and abuse, rhetoric and ridicule, largely in the form of communications from readers. In February, for example, A FARMER argued that Benton was illegally elected, "at this day a spurious Senator," and ridiculed him as taking credit for all important measures in Congress. A FRIEND TO MISSOURI charged him with thinking of nothing but "popularity hunting projects." In May, one AMOS JONSTING contributed a plain-folks burlesque — "as grate men is scace at washinten and the curnil the biggist man among them i wil voat for him for hes a mity frendly man to poar men for he shuk hands with me last summer jist as ef he had a knowd me." But AMOS was not without his doubts — "sum of the peopel in thees parts laff at him and say tush man when tha hear enny boddy cal him a grait man." In June, the *Republican* predicted the "curnil's" political downfall. Meanwhile the *Advocate* defended Benton — with editorial polemic, its own communications (one of which charged that A FARMER was really John B. C. Lucas), and accounts of meetings endorsing the Senator.

Early in July, the target of this barrage arrived in St. Louis, with Elizabeth and their daughters. Despite the attacks on him, Benton was in high spirits and confident of success.

The pro-Adams publicists were out of step with the mass of the people. Ordinary citizens looked toward the promise of a fuller democracy which the Jackson movement seemed to offer. Taking advantage of the state of public opinion, the Benton partisans labored to get candidates for the Assembly to pledge themselves to vote for Benton for Senator, proclaiming that such a *"test"* was "the Right of Instruction," the *demos krateo* principle, "in *practice.*" Such pledged candidates offered themselves in most of the state's thirty counties: an indication of the extent to which Benton had built a broad popular power base. When the voters went to the polls on Monday, August 7, they retired the previously invincible John Scott from Congress. He was replaced by Edward Bates — who had declared himself a follower of Jefferson, who supported Adams while differing from him on some issues, and who announced blandly that he belonged "to no party!" Still, the voters had removed the man who had given Missouri's vote to Adams. In addition, they elected a number of Benton-pledged Assembly candidates.

The battle was not over, however. The Adams men exulted at the number of Assemblymen-elect either opposed to Benton or not pledged to him, and set out to undermine what strength he had by another, far-flung propaganda barrage. It was led by a doughty warrior who called himself Curtius, and who under the title "Torch Light" contributed to the *Republican* eight separate attacks on Benton and all his works. The articles were later gathered into a pamphlet for distribution among the people. The "Torch Light" essays concerned themselves first with Benton's opposition to Adams. It was a plot to thwart plans for the protection of domestic manufactures and construction of roads and canals — apparently Benton had become the captive of John Randolph, the anti-American System's "present supreme director" of the opposition. As to his switch to Jackson — Benton, Curtius declared, "never wavered [in his hatred for Jackson] . . . until after the electors were chosen, and the result of the Presidential election, so far as it depended on them, was known — when suddenly the hostile chiefs became reconciled." This was not accurate — the Colonel and the General were reconciled personally well before the election — but it was probably good propaganda. This out of the way, the "Torch Light" was turned on Benton's record in Congress. Thus: "Mr. Clay is the advocate of internal improvement, and Col. Benton voted against the bill for repairing the great Western avenue, the Cumberland road. . . . Mr. Clay is friendly to the protection of domestic manufactures; and Mr. Benton has announced his intention of voting for a reduction of the Tariff, now but a short time in operation, and passed by the aid of his vote." Finally, there was the matter of Benton's travel to and from

Washington. The allowance was for the most usual route; but, CURTIUS charged, Benton, along with some other Western members, took this to mean "crooked navigable *river.*" And this meant a difference between eight hundred miles and fifteen hundred miles. Admittedly, the travel allowance was inadequate, but Barton didn't charge by the river distance, and Benton did.

From February through November the *Republican,* a four-page, five-column weekly, managed to print no less than sixty-seven full columns of vituperation of Thomas Benton.* The literary peak was reached in mid-August, in a near-column of doggerel which had Benton, significantly, concluding —

> *That land alone is truly rich,*
> *And in all things the tippy,*
> *Where eating goes to highest pitch,*
> *As on the Mississippi.*

> *Republican can best be got,*
> *'Twill be with me a maxim,*
> *Where plenty bubbles in the pot;*
> *No tyrants there can tax him. . . .*[10]

In the face of this attack, Benton fought back — by distributing broadcast his pamphlet reprint of his land speech. Even John B. C. Lucas had to admit that circulation of what he estimated as some five thousand copies of this document had "excite[d] the liveliest interest among farmers," and had "produced a considerable effect in [Benton's] favor." In Washington, Adams studied reports from the West, and lamented — "Benton has made himself amazingly popular by the resolution he offered for graduating and reducing the price of the lands . . . I have no doubt that he will be re-elected." [11]

---

* It is interesting to speculate on the authors of the innumerable *Republican* attacks on Benton in the year 1826. It is always possible that the current editor followed the procedure of "the old communications maker," and wrote at least some of his "letters to the editor." Some of the items make use of phrases apparently original with Barton, which suggests the possibility that the other Senator wrote some of the attacks. In a letter to Adams, Lucas said that he had written three newspaper articles bringing "most serious charges" against his old foe. On November 9, 1826, the *Republican* picked up an item referring to the CURTIUS articles as having been written by Judge Lucas, only to deny this, and then to declare that the Judge *had* written the series signed A FARMER. On February 1, 1827, the *Republican* noted that the "Torch Light" Essays had been widely reprinted, and that Barton had been named as their author, but denied that this was so.

Nonetheless, Benton suffered a setback during the campaign. The *Advocate* began running occasional communications criticizing him — though it usually balanced them with editorial praise. In late September, the *Advocate* editor found himself faced with a sudden demand for payment in cash of a note Benton had held against the old *Enquirer*. When the editor, Stephen W. Foreman, was unable to meet the demand, some of his printing materials were attached and "knocked off" at a forced sale to A. L. Magenis — a local lawyer who often acted as Thomas Benton's confidential agent. For the time being, the *Advocate* survived these harassments — to appear as an all-out anti-Benton paper, its columns now full of attacks like Lucas's FARMER letters and others.[12] Once again, Benton was without newspaper support in St. Louis — a consequence, apparently, of an imperious demand for total approval.

Meanwhile, Benton canvassed the election situation. In early September he wrote his ally Finis Ewing that, among the Assemblymen-elect, "every engine of intrigue will be put in motion, and every lie told that can make a *personal* or political enemy." But by early October, Benton was on the way to the East with his family — confident of the outcome.[13]

The Assembly met toward the end of November, 1826, at the new capital near the center of the state — Jefferson City. One of the members, an ally of Benton's, William Carr Lane of St. Louis, noted that Finis Ewing, General Thomas Smith, Alphonso Wetmore, and others were on hand electioneering for the Colonel, though there seemed no doubt of the outcome: "He will be elected — The voice of the people demands it — Who dares disobey?" Or, as one citizen put it: "Benton, right or wrong, is the people's man." But the opposition did "dare" a last, frantic attempt to effect a reversal of fortune — by bringing charges of "malpractice" against Benton, and then arguing that the election should be *postponed* until the legislature had had a chance to "investigate." At this, the *Republican* solemnly assured the Assemblymen that sentiment in many counties had now turned anti-Benton. In St. Louis, an opposition petition proclaimed that the Colonel was "unfit for the office he now fills." But a pro-Benton counterpetition affirmed "confidence in the integrity and ability of Col. Benton . . . it is . . . the wish of the great majority of the voters of this county that he should be re-elected."

In the end, all the desperate stratagems failed. Finally the day came, and on December 29, 1826, at three in the afternoon, the members of the State Senate filed one after one into the House Chamber and took seats. When nominations were declared open, only two names were offered, Thomas H. Benton and one Joseph C. Brown, a near-unknown. The opposition *was* largely *"personal,"* and no important figure offered himself against the popular leader of the new, pro-Jackson democracy. The roll call gave Benton forty votes, to Brown's thirteen.[14] Benton had been vindicated in his great decision to reject the course of Henry Clay and espouse the popular democratic movement.

[4]

THE MIDDLE YEARS OF THE 1820's saw Thomas and Elizabeth Benton settle into a pleasant routine of marriage, home, and children. Their home life centered increasingly around the McDowell estate, Cherry Grove. There, between sessions, Thomas could enjoy a rest from business, and time with Elizabeth and his daughters, surrounded by the beauties of the Blue Ridge summer or fall. Frequently also Thomas left Elizabeth and the children in Virginia for all or part of the sessions of Congress, while he stayed at Brown's Hotel or one of the capital messes.

In mid-March, 1826, he interrupted his attendance in the Senate to hurry to Elizabeth's side at Cherry Grove, where his third daughter was born. She was named Sarah, after Elizabeth's aunt, Sarah Preston. Two years later, Thomas was looking forward to a fourth child. From Washington in April, 1828, he wrote a friend that Elizabeth was "occupied in her rooms with three children on their legs, *and No. 4 on the Stocks."* Five months later, however, in the midst of a political tour through Missouri, he heard from Elizabeth and Mrs. McDowell in Virginia "the painful intelligence of a *still born* child," and "the perilous condition" of the mother. This "distressing news" brought him, as quickly as he could get away, from Missouri to Cherry Grove. There, he found Elizabeth recovering.

He suffered new financial reverses too. The Administration undertook to collect sums due the United States from the old Bank of Missouri — and in February, 1827, in St. Louis, the trustees of the defunct bank secured a judgment against Benton for seven thousand seventy-six dollars and fourteen cents, his share, presumably, of the bank's obligations. In lieu of cash payment, the trustees settled for a remaining equity Benton held in the lot and home on Laurel Street, which they then sold to John Mullanphy.[15]

Meanwhile, Benton was more and more noted by observers in the capital. One journalist recalled him as "a large, heavily framed man with black curly hair and whiskers, prominent features and a stentorian voice." He wore a "high black silk neck-stock and double-breasted frock coat . . . varying with the season the materials of which his pantaloons were made, but never the fashion in which they were cut." His energy in debate was apparent — "he would rush forward with blind fury upon every obstacle, like the huge wild buffaloes then ranging the prairies of his adopted state." Still, he was "not a popular speaker," and when he took the floor the gallery would clear, "while many Senators devoted themselves to their correspondence." But in "private life Colonel Benton was gentleness and domestic affection personified." [16] Thus the senior Senator from Missouri, aged forty-five years, in the last months of his first term.

A portrait of about this time by "the Kentucky Rembrandt," Matthew Jouett, also showed him as a striking figure. In it a strong, sharp face marked by a thin, craglike, inquiring nose, and by lips drawn close in self-possessed determination, looked steadily out from beneath masses of dark, wavy hair rising above a high forehead, and falling fully behind the ears. This rugged darkness was brilliantly set off by the white collar and white, bow-tied, flowing stock, above a black coat which covered strong, massive shoulders.[17]

As his fame increased, the college society that had expelled young Benton in 1799 reconsidered its action. Perhaps viewing his re-election as a vote of confidence and mark of success, the Philanthropic Society, or Phi, at the University of North Carolina, voted on May 9, 1827, to readmit him to membership.[18] The former Hillsborough lad had traveled a long road from the pines of Chapel Hill to the dignity of the Senate chamber, and now, twenty-eight years later, at least part of his disgrace was removed.

[5]

THE OPPOSITION to Adams reached its peak in 1828. In that year Jackson ran again for the Presidency, and in that year many Congressional contests turned on the issue of support for Jackson or support for Adams. After a visit with his family at Cherry Grove, Benton went on in July, 1828, to Missouri, where he put in the summer and fall electioneering.

Well before his arrival, the Administration partisans in Missouri had launched an effort to make Benton himself a campaign issue. In February, for example, the *Republican* had gleefully reprinted an item from a London paper entitled "American Manners," which reproduced Benton's account of September, 1813, of the brawl he and Jesse Benton had had with Jackson. The English journal, noting that Jackson was now running with Benton's support, pointed to the fracas as "giving an extraordinary idea of the *savageness of the South Western states.*" In February also, and again in the fall, the Administration party brought forward the question of Benton's position on the charge of a "corrupt bargain" between Adams and Clay. They noted that Benton had published a letter contradicting the accusation that Adams had agreed to make Clay Secretary of State in return for the latter's support. But, the *Republican* declared, *despite this letter* he had broadcast the story, in his visits to upper Missouri in the summer of 1827. To be sure, some "Benton men" had made affidavits that the Senator had always branded the charge false, but there was "good reason to believe" that he had in fact retailed it in Missouri — "Oh! honesty, honesty! and art thou but a *name?* where hast thou fled, what cavern is thy abode?" A citizen who claimed to have witnessed Benton's duplicity signed a statement on the matter. He had gone into Mack's Tavern at St. Charles, where he heard Benton speaking of intrigue and corruption between Adams and Clay. When he asked Benton if he really believed this, the answer was — "Believe it! I am bound to believe it — I may say I know it — no man in his common senses, at the public scene of action, as I was, could believe otherwise." In the face of these attacks on his veracity, Benton rested on his letter.* But the Administration spokesmen insisted on characterizing him as a "wily" political manager or boss, who "has not scrupled to avail himself of the use of every weapon calculated to effect the ruin of his political opponents." [19]

Meanwhile, the electoral canvass developed on a broader scale. The weight of wealth, established influence, and officialdom was on the side of the Administration, but the Jackson men found an answer to this alignment of property, position, and power. This answer depended on

---

* The truth in this matter is difficult to determine. The evidence the *Republican* offered was, at bottom, of the "good-reason-to-believe" variety, and the *Republican* would probably not have scrupled to build up such charges out of very little or nothing. Both sides seem to have had sworn affidavits or formal statements. In this situation, where there are apparently no impartial witnesses available, and the only evidence at hand comes from partisan sources and is contradictory, the truth remains in doubt.

applying a "lever" to public opinion, and on mobilizing the voters through organization. Handbills, newspapers, and innumerable personal contacts were utilized, and in addition mass meetings were organized, often on county court or militia muster days when crowds were available. The keynote was Jackson's personal character, as a *symbol* of democracy. At Fayette in the center of the state, for example, a meeting toasted "the cause of General Jackson, a cause of principle, the cause of a majority against the minority." Organizationally, the Jackson men labored to build a mass electoral mechanism. Local rallies endorsed candidates for local and state offices, and sent representatives and resolutions to county or district assemblies. A state meeting proclaimed the party candidates for President and for Vice-President (John Calhoun), chose a slate of electors, and named a state committee to carry on the campaign. Back at the base of the pyramid, meanwhile, executive committees were established in many election districts, and "Committees of Correspondence" in key counties. The organization actually achieved was spotty, but a beginning was made. These developments in Missouri reflected developments in the nation, which were to go further in future years. A new era was at hand, an era in which suffrage was extended in state after state to all white, adult males. This expansion of voting rights, coupled with the rising democratic spirit, presented new opportunities to leaders willing and able to build a mass following, willing and able to organize an effective popular majority. Over the years this electoral machinery developed into the present pattern of party leadership and organization.

Despite such developments, Benton found the party in Missouri split over the Congressional election, "employed in attacks upon each other, to the utter neglect of the common enemy." The split was over men. Both William Carr Lane and Spencer Pettis were candidates on the "Jackson ticket" for Congress. The two submitted their cases to the "umpirage" of Thomas Benton, who, on July 24, declared that, "in obedience to the only legitimate principle of action in a republican government, — *that the will of the majority ought to prevail,*" he had found that Spencer Pettis united the greater popular support. The next day, Lane withdrew. The Senator-umpire followed his decision with a handbill carrying his "Declaration" for Spencer Pettis, and a broadside attacking the pro-Adams incumbent, Edward Bates. Dismayed, the *Republican* howled at the PROCLAMATION OF THE DICTATOR — for "what else is this caucusing umpirage of Benton but *dictation* to the Jackson party?" But Benton's decision was carried forward in the counties by "well drilled" party *"warriors"* (as Bates called them), while Pettis traveled the counties proclaiming reiterated endorsements of Benton's graduation-donation reforms. In consequence, the August voting gave Pettis a smashing victory[20] — and thereby presented Benton with a staunch Congressional ally.

From this canvass, Benton turned quickly to another political problem. He wrote the Kentucky editor, Amos Kendall, to urge him to establish a newspaper in St. Louis. The *Advocate* had expired, and the thriving town thus had only one newspaper, "and that a mere mud-machine," Benton maintained, though it enabled its owners "to live in fine brick houses." He hoped Amos Kendall would come, *"first,* to make money, which I am sure that an imperial sheet, twice a week for the town, once a week for the country," could do; *"secondly,* to maintain the ascendency of the political principles which you espouse." [21] But Kendall did not take up the offer. Finally Benton's old *Enquirer* foreman, Charles Keemle, who had also been associated with the *Advocate* in its pro-Benton phase, set up a new pro-Benton press in St. Louis.

Through the fall, both parties in Missouri labored vigorously in the presidential campaign. At meeting after meeting around the state, Benton spoke out for Jackson. In September, for example, he went to Fayette on the Missouri River to the West, to deliver an address an hour-and-a-half long, in which he scored the Administration and predicted that Jackson would roll up an "immense majority" in Missouri. In counterattack, the Adams party fired another blast at Benton — in particular, a grandly entitled pamphlet, *Edward Bates Against Thomas Benton.* Throughout his life, Bates charged, Benton had shown "a stoical disregard of the future infamy attendant upon his acts, provided his present ends can be accomplished." Bates would not "touch upon the *indiscretions* which clouded the prospects of [Benton's] early manhood." Perhaps in charity his "juvenile error" ought to be left "to slumber in oblivion, in the classic shades of Chapel Hill." But he did assert that as a recruiting officer in the War of 1812, Benton had defaulted in his accounts; that as a director of the Bank of Missouri had borrowed an unknown sum, and owed the government seven thousand, seventy-six dollars and fourteen cents; and that he had "grossly defrauded the treasury" by drawing excessive mileage.[22] But, as in 1826, such last-minute vilifications were of no avail.* The voters of Missouri gave the Jackson electors 8372 tallies to 3407 for Adams.

Meanwhile, throughout the nation the Jacksonians were building a powerful movement. In ostensible retirement in Tennessee, Andrew Jackson served as the center of a far-flung, if loose, organization, maintaining contacts with such pivotal leaders as Van Buren in New York, Calhoun and Robert Hayne in South Carolina, and a self-styled "efficient friend" named James Buchanan in Pennsylvania. The Jackson coalition encompassed groups whose interests were sometimes in concord, sometimes in conflict; but they all shared one purpose — to oust Adams and Clay. The movement appealed to the yeoman class, and to slaveholding planters; to some businessmen who favored the Bank of the United States, and to other men of Enterprise who opposed the Bank as the citadel of an established, monopoly-inclined, conservative business oligarchy; to men variously opposed, favorable, or neutral to Federal internal improvements and the protective tariff; and to reforming, self-styled workingmen's associations and to many individual workingmen in Philadelphia and other seaboard cities. Out of this patchwork of classes, interest groups, and factions, the Jacksonian politicians labored to construct a majority. Given such diverse foundations, it is not surprising that the campaign for Jackson was a maelstrom of slogan, symbol, and shout, rather than a campaign based on explicit declaration of policies. Still, the new party was aided by a popular ground swell which had been running throughout the 1820's. The unrest and dissatisfaction produced by the depression of 1819, a widespread feeling that the Administration was the agent of an entrenched few and that it had failed to meet the problems of the many, an inchoate but pervasive feeling that the nation had somehow got off the democratic course Jefferson had charted — all these elements provided a fertile field for Jacksonian propaganda and organization. By 1828, thousands of plain men saw Jackson as the Moses who would lead the way to a new era of

* There was, however, *some* basis for all of Bates's specific charges. The "juvenile error" at Chapel was a fact. In 1828, a judgment for four hundred and thirty-nine dollars was found against Thomas Benton in relation to his accounts as a colonel in the War of 1812, though no charge of fraud was made; the claim was settled by the forced sale of a town lot in St. Louis which Benton owned (Original and General Records, St. Louis, P, 73-75). The facts of Benton's relations with the Bank of Missouri, and of his mileage claims, have already been recounted. Whether the last three items were scandalous, as Bates charged, and whether *any* of the charges had *any* relevance to the presidential contest, is doubtful.

government for the many. The election of 1825, as Benton noted, had begun the realignment of parties around the issue of oligarchy-versus-democracy, and the canvass of 1828 continued the process.[23] As a practical political leader, Benton understood the diversity of the special-interest groups ranged around his candidate, and advised Jackson to avoid *"particular* confession" on thorny questions like internal improvements and the tariff. But as an advocate, Benton also understood the importance of the popular-democratic base his party possessed. He saw to it that copies of his land speech pamphlet were widely distributed — the issue would "operate well" in Ohio, Indiana, Illinois, Louisiana, and other states where "this subject of the lands, and A[dams's] & R[ush's] opposition to my Bill, go home to the houses, hearts and bosoms of the people." [24] On this issue, and others, like his presidential election reform plan and his debt retirement proposals, Benton at least offered some definite, popular democratic policies to go with popular-democratic slogans.

The voting gave a decisive victory to the Jackson coalition. With twenty-two out of the twenty-four states choosing electors by popular ballot, Jackson won 647,276 votes to Adams's 508,064, with the electoral tally standing at 178 to 83. The crucial decision Benton had made in 1825 was fully vindicated. While Adams carried his own New England, the Jackson party broke even in the Middle Atlantic section, and carried the South Atlantic, the Northwest, and the Southwest.

What sort of person was this President-elect? To the fastidious French traveler, Alexis, Comte de Tocqueville, he was "a man of violent temper and very moderate [mediocre] talents," clearly not "qualified to govern a free people," always opposed by "the majority of the enlightened classes of the Union." (He was elected "solely" by the "inconceivable influence" of "military glory.") Years later, with the advantage of hindsight, Benton tried to refute de Tocqueville's charges one by one. As to temper — Jackson had "a good temper, kind and hospitable to everybody, and a feeling of protection in it for the whole human race, and especially the weaker and humbler part of it." As to his talents and fitness to govern, let his record during his presidency speak! As to his opposition — "a majority of those classes which Mons. de Tocqueville would chiefly see in the cities, and along the highways — bankers, brokers, jobbers, contractors, politicians, and speculators — were certainly against him, and he as certainly against them." But — "the mass of the intelligence of the country was with him!" [25]

Looking back on the election, Adams attributed much of Jackson's success in the West to Benton's land-reform proposals. His bitterness toward the Missourian knew no bounds. Why, Adams asked himself, had Benton brought forth his land proposals "as a substitute for the American System of Mr. Clay?" His caustic answer was — "to supplant [Clay] as the leading statesman of the West." [26]

While Benton was hardly the leading statesman of the West, he had gone a long way in his years of opposition since 1825. He was to go still further in the years immediately ahead.

PART III

Democracy's Advocate

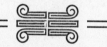

How can we call those systems just
Which bid the few, the proud, the first
Possess all earthly good . . . ?

PHILIP FRENEAU, 1793

CHAPTER 8

The Breeze Blows

1829 - 1830

A S THE NATIONAL CAPITAL awaited the arrival of Andrew Jackson,
Daniel Webster mused gloomily:

> *Nobody knows what he will do when he does come . . .*
> *My opinion is*
> *That when he comes he will bring a breeze with him.*
> *Which way it will blow, I cannot tell. . . .*
> *My* FEAR *is stronger than my* HOPE.

Certainly, no one could be sure precisely what policies the new
political movement would bring with it. But the next dozen years were
to confirm Webster's deepest fears — as they were to confirm Benton's
highest hopes.

In mid-February, the President-elect entered Washington — quietly,
avoiding a formal reception. The capital was growing up a little. There
were still miles of dirt roads, and miry lanes, and ruts and holes; but the
Executive Mansion was now flanked at four corners by imposing State,
Treasury, War, and Navy Buildings. The Capitol was inspiring on its
hill, with its terraces, lawns, and shrubbery well kept; the classic, intimate Senate chamber was charming; and visitors also sought the col-
umned House chamber, and the little Supreme Court room in the
basement. Most Congressmen lived — like Benton — at boardinghouses
or hotels; but by now certain places, such as John Gadsby's National,
offered first-rate hospitality.[1]

Staying at the National while he awaited his inauguration, Jackson
made up his cabinet. Some observers like Duff Green, editor of the
Telegraph (the special organ of John Calhoun, and pro tem the new
Administration's organ too) thought Thomas Benton a likely selection
for one of the places. Finally, however, the President decided on
Martin Van Buren for Secretary of State and filled the other posts with
undistinguished partisans from Pennsylvania, Ohio, Tennessee, North
Carolina, and Georgia — no one from Virginia or South Carolina! Im-

mediately there were cries of distress from the particular friends of Vice-President Calhoun. They had wanted the Treasury for a strong anti-tariff man, and it had gone to a business-Jacksonian from tariff-minded Pennsylvania, Samuel D. Ingham. The Calhoun men also thought the cabinet lineup entirely too favorable to a potential rival — Secretary Van Buren.[2]

At last, the time came for the inauguration. Tall, thin, erect, his narrow face clearly lined with wrinkles, his white hair combed straight back, Jackson was a commanding and dramatic-looking man. A somber expression had settled upon him since the death of his beloved Rachel after the election. To take the oath, he stood at the East Portico of the Capitol, and looked out on a crowd of nearly twenty thousand people who moved about without distinction of rank — silent, orderly, and tranquil. The aging, old-Federalist Chief Justice, John Marshall, gave the oath of office to the stormy son of the West. The new President turned and bowed to the people — "yes," one observer remarked, "to the people in all their majesty." He then spoke his brief inaugural address, and the ceremony was over. It was followed by a party at the Executive Mansion, where the press was so great that barrels of orange punch were taken into the yard to draw off the crowd. Meanwhile, like many other Jacksonians, Thomas and Elizabeth Benton were entertaining at their lodgings, Dawson's Number Two. "Here was a perfect levee," cried one of their hundred "rejoicing" guests — "wine and cake was handed in profusion."

The scenes at the inauguration were signs that the old, quasi-aristocratic republicanism was giving way to a new, *hoi polloi* democracy. The Kentucky editor, Amos Kendall, soon to have an office in the Treasury, wrote to his paper: "It was a proud day for the *people* — General Jackson is *their own* president." But the New England Federalist, Mr. Justice Story, sniffed — there were "the highest and most polished down to the most vulgar and gross. . . . The reign of *King Mob* seemed triumphant." In short, it was a victory for what Benton called the *demos krateo* principle — though the shadow of the political manager lay always in the background.[3] And the question remained, Which way would the breeze blow?

[2]

AFTER THE INAUGURATION, Thomas, Elizabeth, and their daughters left Washington for the far Southwest. For three weeks in April, they visited with Elizabeth's relative, Colonel J. T. Preston, in New Orleans. In May they left for St. Louis, making the trip up the broad Mississippi in twelve days, through the lucky accident of meeting an upper-river steamer at the mouth of the Ohio, where they changed boats without touching land. Their New Orleans "sojourn" had been delightful, Thomas and Elizabeth assured Colonel Preston by letter — "one of the most agreeable periods that we have passed since our marriage." For their part, "the little children [were] full of remembrances of yourself and your kind lady." [4]

The vacation from politics was all too brief. The new Administration was undertaking its first reform. During the long one-party domination, officeholders in the Federal government had become almost a favored caste, looking upon themselves as the *owners* of their jobs, with little sense of responsibility to the populace. Many of them had been active against the upstart Andrew Jackson in the election of 1828. There were many instances of corruption and incompetence in office. Echoing Administration views, the *Telegraph* in Washington called for a thorough cleansing of "the Augean Stable" of the government service. The *Telegraph* in turn was echoed by party papers throughout the land — including the new paper set up in St. Louis by Charles Keemle with Thomas Benton's support, the *Beacon*. "The people," Keemle declared, "expect and demand of General Jackson the *reform of all abuses.*"

The changes in office did not find Benton idle, though he never became an all-out patronage-monger. In March, 1829, he had had to write to Colonel Hamilton of Laurel Hill, Louisiana, that he could not support Mr. Haralson for Federal Attorney in New Orleans, since — as Benton had learned when he had proposed Colonel Preston for that office — the post had already been given to John Slidell! And in May, Benton wrote Secretary of War John Eaton to recommend John F. A. Sanford as Indian Agent on the Missouri River — "I think I can say that his promotion may be solicited on grounds of public advantage." (This gentleman was closely associated with the American Fur Company, and when he was later fired from the job Benton proposed him for, he became an official of the company. Still later, Sanford was to attain notoriety as the defendant in a law case involving a slave he owned, named Dred Scott.) Again, in March, 1830, Benton was concerned with a removal and appointment which involved charges of incompetence.

The President wrote characteristically to Secretary of the Treasury Ingham, regretting that "the Mr. Findly *removed*" as Register for the Land Office in central Missouri was the brother of a hero of the War of 1812 and current pro-Jackson Congressman from Ohio; unfortunately, "Mr. Findley *is incompetant from intemperance to discharge the duties of the office.*" Both Senator Benton and Representative Pettis had "coincided" in asking that the place be given to Benton's political ally, Finis Ewing, and this was done.[5]

The enemies of the Administration made much of its "proscriptions." In Congress and in the partisan press, huge exaggerations echoed — and these were soon given the stamp of authority by Alexis de Tocqueville. This again aroused the ire of Thomas Benton, who later quoted the Frenchman: "I am not aware that General Jackson allowed a single removable functionary employed in the public service to retain his place beyond the first year which succeeded his election." The facts, Benton lectured Tocqueville, would not sustain this interpretation. *First,* there were whole classes left untouched — judges, commissioners, and the like. *Second,* removals during the period specified numbered only "about six hundred and ninety," and only 491 of many thousand Deputy Postmasters were removed — in short, "the government archives contradict Mons. de Tocqueville." *Third,* after "a revolution of parties" removals were inevitable, especially when "by engaging in the election" officials "became combatant." *Fourth,* the President was following the path of Thomas Jefferson, who had told the Missourian at Christmas, 1824, that he (Jefferson) had not made as many removals as he should have. In fact, Jackson did not originate the spoils system, which was well established in New York and Pennsylvania, or carry it to the extremes of " 'sweeping' removals" it later reached. The removals he made often were for incompetence, corruption, or other good cause, and during his whole Administration only about one tenth to one fifth of the officeholders were removed.[6]

In St. Louis in 1829, Benton took up another issue. In the heat of the Missouri July, he penned two long articles for the *Beacon,* signed AMERICANUS, in which he argued again the problem of the Texas region. Renewing the charge that Adams in 1819 had thrown away an area equal to all of New York, New Jersey, Pennsylvania, Maryland, Virginia, Ohio, and Kentucky, he urged that the "lost" expanses be regained for the United States, by *purchase* from Mexico. The articles, filled with characteristic enumerations up to "Twelfthly," and spiced with invective, were part of a larger design. To his old Tennessee friend and army comrade Sam Houston (now an Indian trader at Fort Gibson, Arkansas Territory), Benton wrote enclosing "two No's on our South Western boundary, of which I am the author, and which I want as extensively republished as possible." "This subject, and the public lands," he noted, "are the two *levers* to move public sentiment in the West. If you have ulterior views your *tongue* and *pen* should dwell incessantly upon these two great topics." * He wrote another friend at Natchez urging that the essays be "extensively republished on the lower Missi." [7] The AMERICANUS articles were widely noted. Through September and October, the *Beacon* picked up comments about them from "Jackson Republican presses" in Alabama, Massachusetts, Pennsylvania, and Kentucky. Benton's personal influence with Thomas Ritchie of the august Richmond *Enquirer* was credited with getting the essays published in full in that paper.

Encouraged, Benton turned out another series of nine articles, signed LA SALLE. Here he elaborated his theme and in passing raised another issue, the slavery question. The agricultural South and West, he charged, had a common enemy. It was the Northern, "Federal" party, "which discouraged the settlement of the West by refusing . . . to vote for equitable prices for the public lands . . . and in every question in the South West between the white people and the negroes or Indians[,] regularly, officially, impertinently, and wickedly, takes part with the Indians and negroes against their white fellow citizens and fellow Christians." Northern politicians had revealed, in a series of incidents "all tending to one point," a sinister purpose — *"the abolition of slavery, under the clause of the Declaration of Independence, which asserts the natural equality of all men."* This matter had little to do with Texas, but much to do with conflicting social-sectional interests, and possible new sectional alignments in politics.

While Benton wrote, Jackson had quietly instructed his Secretary of State to undertake (in secret) negotiations for a new Southwest boundary. To help the Mexicans see the wisdom of this plan, Van Buren was

---

* Probably the Senator used the term "ulterior" in a sense common to the time, and close to the Latin roots, meaning lying beyond that which is immediately present; future, further. One should not read into the term its modern emotive connotations of deceit, self-seeking, or scheming. It is interesting to note that Sam Houston, who had left Tennessee when his newly-wed bride deserted him, was widely suspected of planning some filibustering activities in Texas. Actually, his interest in the Mexican state at that time was slight and incidental.

authorized to offer the sum of five million dollars. As "the first and earliest advocate for the recovery of Texas," Benton recalled later, he was "a little consulted" and knew "what was intended." Thus, the AMERICANUS and LA SALLE articles appeared as the work of a one-man propaganda engine to support his chief. Nothing was to come of it for the time, however, though efforts to secure part of Texas continued for several years.[8]

Even as he turned out the Texas articles, Benton was busy with other, lesser matters. *Item:* A proposal to Father van Quickenhorne of the Roman Catholic hierarchy in St. Louis that he (Benton) might petition Congress to give a proposed Catholic college in St. Louis a grant of 48,000 acres of land. The priest agreed to the plan, and the politician pressed it, but without results. *Item:* A chance to return a favor to the Hardeman family, the kin of John Hardeman who years before in Tennessee had given young Benton a chance to study law by giving him books on credit. He would now gladly help the family on their land claims, and that without fee. . . . And so on through summer and fall: the little routine of the man of politics.

Meanwhile, on November 11, 1829, Elizabeth Benton gave birth to her first son, who was christened John Randolph Benton after his father's friend, Randolph of Roanoke.[9]

[3]

THE CONGRESSIONAL SESSION OF 1829-1830, the first under Jackson, gave some indication of the way the breeze would blow. It began with a long, dramatic debate — which underscored the alliance of South and West Benton had suggested, provided an exposition of prevailing winds of political doctrine, and ultimately required from Benton a reassessment of some of his ideas.

The debate was touched off in the Senate when Samuel A. Foot of Connecticut offered a resolution. It was to inquire into "the expediency of limiting for a certain period the sales of the public lands" to tracts that had already been offered for sale. This proposal pricked Benton at a sensitive point, and he began the attack on it. An early pragmatist, he weighed the "practical effect" of the resolution and concluded that it "would be to check emigration to the Western States." It would limit settlement, it would block off the West as an asylum for oppressed people. It was all, he suspected, part of a systematic effort to build manufactures at the expense of agriculture, Enterprise at the expense of Arcadia, by keeping people in the East "to work in the manufactories." The aspirations of yeomen, he maintained, and the "growth and settlement of the *West*," had been consistently opposed by the great mercantile, shipping, and (now) manufacturing groups of the *Northeast,* and as consistently favored by the agricultural groups of the *South,* or South Atlantic section. Later, Robert Hayne of South Carolina joined the discussion. Though he sought to bring the talk back to land policy, he echoed Benton's note of alliance between West and South.

Thus, the debate took in more and more ground. Beginning with a question of inquiry into land policy, it spread to include the issue of other clashing interests between classes and groups, and the issue of sectional antagonism and alignments. Still, the matter might have dropped but for the efforts of the next speaker, Daniel Webster — who chose to answer, not the Westerner (Benton) but the Southerner (Hayne). Defending "the always reproached East," he postulated a sharp division between North and South, referred to the *tariff* as the underlying cause of contention, and finally made an indirect reference to *nullification* — the idea "that it is time to calculate the value of the Union." All this was by design. Hoping to blight the proposal for a South-West alliance before it bore fruit, Webster ignored Benton and attacked Hayne because the latter was the more vulnerable, particularly on the issue of nullification — the claimed right, argued in the South Carolina tariff protest of 1828, of a state to declare void a Federal government law.*

The war of words began to draw a crowd. A Representative from New York watched the proceedings, and wrote sketches of the warriors. He began with Benton:

> . . . Fine portly figure — rather aldermanic — neither tall nor short — sandy hair — large whiskers — a narrow, retiring forehead — a grey eye, that can glance like lightning — full face — regular features — a mouth well formed — tongue quick and voluble — altogether a handsome and a great man. His delivery is very accurate and distinct — his

---

* Rereading the account of the debate five years later, John Quincy Adams questioned the wisdom of this strategy. In staking everything on his answer to Hayne, Webster had "rather affectedly avoided noticing Benton, who was the great and real assailant." In Adams's opinion, an answer should have been given to both the Westerner and the Southerner, an answer "exposing the profligate combination between nullification and the robbery of the public lands, which urged the joint attack" (Adams, *Memoirs,* IX, 236).

words flow sensibly and fluently — always in a soft, winning tone —
except when his indignation is excited, for then the very d---l himself
(my readers will pardon the expression) could not speak and look more
terrible.

Next, Hayne —

. . . Full, round face without whiskers — light brown hair, which he
wears in the *exquisite* style . . . features not large but regular, and not
so manly as Mr. Benton's — wide mouth — glib tongue.

Finally, Webster —

. . . Large head, covered with long, black hair, which is combed back,
and on one side stands erect, owing to his habit of rubbing it up while
he is engaged in debate — very large and very prominent forehead . . .
black, scowling brows — wide mouth — pale face . . . figure of the
middle size . . . not a particle of Mr. Benton's fiery indignation.

The eloquence of Benton resembled "the broad-side of a ship of the
line," that of Webster "the murderous report of a rifle."

Through most of January, the debate raged between Webster and
Hayne. At the end of January and beginning of February, however,
the "ship of the line" counterattacked and ranged for three more days
over a sea of subjects. Many of these Benton mentioned only because
Webster had injected them into the talk.

> *First Day* — The politics of the Louisiana Purchase; the Resolutions
> of the Massachusetts Legislature in June, 1803, calling the Purchase un-
> Constitutional; and the Missouri Question of 1820. *Documentation* in
> full throughout. Why, the Colonel exclaimed, "the State of Missouri was
> kept out of the Union one whole year," and Senator Benton from his
> seat, because of the hostility of "these characters," the North-Eastern
> *quondam* friends of the Negro — *"Les Amis des Noirs."*
>
> *Second Day* — A disquisition on slavery, showing that it had dis-
> appeared in certain areas not as a result of *moral* condemnation (the
> Bible did not condemn it) but of *economic* calculation; and an attack
> on New Englanders for their quasi-dis-Unionist attitude during the days
> of the War of 1812, the Hartford Convention, and the Five-Striped
> Flag. Again, *documentation.*
>
> *Third Day* — An attack on the doctrine that the Supreme Court had
> authority to declare *state* laws un-Constitutional; condemnation of such
> doctrines as a threat to States Rights, and possibly a threat to the exist-
> ence of slavery; a long, detailed, unfavorable analysis of the claim that
> the North was the West's "friend" on *tariffs,* and *internal improvements.*
> *Documentation* — facts, contrasts in parallel columns, figures, votes in
> Congress.

This speech — John Randolph remarked that its delivery consumed one more day than the French Revolution of 1830 — was made into a thirty-page pamphlet by the *Telegraph,* and was widely reprinted in the press. The *Beacon* in St. Louis thought it would be well received by "the great majority." Its distribution helped solidify public opinion and draw party lines.

The great debate, however, had reached its peak in a contest between Webster and Hayne. This involved the nature of the Constitution, and rival doctrines of sovereignty. Hayne defended the extreme state rights doctrine — "it is the right of a state to judge of the violations of the constitution on the part of the Federal Government, and to protect her citizens from the operation of un-constitutional laws." Webster offered by contrast a doctrine of Union based on a single sovereign people who had established a *national* state — "the supremacy of the constitution and laws of the United States is declared. The people so will it." The exchange was concluded when "the godlike Daniel" intoned a peroration that was to become famous — "Liberty *and* Union, now and forever, one and inseparable!" For the moment, Benton had no doubts as to where his sympathies lay in this doctrinal skirmish. He complimented Hayne on his noble effort "to vindicate himself, his State, and the South," and castigated Webster as a naughty pupil who "occupied the floor two days," without taking "notice of facts so highly authenticated" as those Benton had presented.[10] Later, however, he stopped to reconsider the issues, and despite a personal friendship for Hayne, he finally adopted views close to those of Webster.

In February, 1830, meanwhile, Benton found himself suddenly made the subject of discussion. His colleague David Barton unleashed a two-day, three-hour speech, which wandered over innumerable topics but repeatedly turned back to slap at Thomas Benton.

In the beginning, Barton spoke of the recent "Saturnalia in the Senate." The "author of this party warfare" was "a minor chieftain of the party, of not much renown." No true son of the West, he had come to Missouri uninvited, complaining "of having been driven by tyranny and persecution." Thus "the Percy" (Henry Clay) found him, "and nourished and medicined him — put on his own collar and inscription at large, with a special ☞ pointing to the words 'cousin to Percy's wife' " — and without this, Benton would not have reached "his present rank." Having been succored, the adder coiled and became "the assailant of our characters and our motives"; having "thought it a fruit-bearing species," the men of the West "nourished it, and it grew; when, lo! it proved a political *bohon upas,* and blighted and desolated all for miles around its stem."* The enemy thus characterized in mixed metaphor, Barton went on to condemn Benton's "new-born zeal against the American System," induced, presumably, by his friendship for Randolph. He dwelt on this "wooing, billing, and cooing . . . towards the *outré* nymph, the river Roanoke" (Randolph), and offered a suggestion — "let the lovers marry." The *Beacon* in St. Louis called this " 'hurly-burly' harangue" one of the "most vituperative and vulgar tirades ever uttered in a deliberative assembly." [11] Benton, not so touchy-tempered as he had once been, refrained from public answer or violent response.

Beyond the Senate, an epilogue to the great debate was played out. A grand dinner to commemorate the birthday of Thomas Jefferson was arranged for April 13 at Jesse Brown's Indian Queen hotel, with Benton and Hayne acting as the leading organizers of the affair.

The festivities were surely a strain on the eating-drinking-sitting capacities of the celebrants; for the doings ran well past midnight, and there were "together *one hundred and four* toasts!!!" As chairman of the committee on regular toasts, Benton must have enjoyed himself. His own offering was to "NATHANIEL MACON: . . . *he has been the friend of me and mine through four generations.*" But other expressions were not so innocuous. The extremists of the South took advantage of the occasion to speak of "unequal taxation" (the tariff), and to observe that "there is no treason in resisting oppression." One gentleman from Georgia compared the Federal government with the tyrannies of Tiberius, Augustus, and Trajan. This flaunting of nullification sentiments did not sit well with Andrew Jackson; and toward the end of the evening he proposed a dramatic volunteer toast which was to become historic: "OUR FEDERAL UNION: *It must be preserved.*" These simple words were followed by a volunteer from Vice-President Calhoun: "THE UNION: *Next to our liberty most dear; may we all remember that it can only be preserved by respecting the rights of the states and distributing equally the benefit and burden of the union.*" As Benton noted later,

---

* The *bohon upas,* or *bohun upas* — a tall tree of Java known for its acrid, milky, virulently poisonous juice, used by natives as a source of poison for tipping arrows. Toward the end of the 1700's a Dutch surgeon who had observed the plant spread the marvelous story that its exhalations were fatal to all other life, that birds flying over the tree fell dead, and that each *bohun upas* was thus surrounded by a desert. All this was not quite so, but the term came to serve as a figure of speech for a morally pernicious influence.

this sentiment touched "the tender parts" of the new issue: "liberty *before* union — *only* to be preserved — *State rights* — inequality of *burthens* and *benefits*." When Webster had reached his "Liberty *and* Union" peroration in the great debate, it had sounded strained to Benton. But he was finally to conclude that the words of Calhoun served to justify it.

At the moment, however, these issues were not so clear to Benton or many others. Immediate reaction was concerned with the party purpose of the dinner. The anti-Jackson press portrayed Benton as "the chief cook . . . it seemed as if the whole affair rested on his broad shoulders," and a Philadelphia paper referred to the "Jeffersonian (alias Bentonian)" public dinner — the purpose, presumably, to weld stronger the party alliance of *South* and *West*. A year later, however, the pro-Jackson press offered another interpretation. The whole thing was a "nullifying dinner," gotten up by Calhoun's friends "under the *pretense* of commemorating the principles of the patriot Jefferson,"[12] with the hope that the patriot Jackson would lend it sanction.*

In the midst of such political posturings, the members of Congress were considering some more specific issues. In February, 1830, Benton rose in his place to offer a bill "to provide for the abolition of unnecessary [tariff] duties," in order "to relieve the people from sixteen millions of taxes." This tariff-reduction bill showed that he at least wanted to give substance to his proposal for a West-South alliance. It provided that for ten years after January, 1832, the United States should seek agreements with other powers for mutual or reciprocal reduction or abolition of duties, on a list of products which ranged from coffee and cocoa to lace and bombazine, but did not touch articles manufactured in the United States. In short, Benton was seeking a compromise between the tariff-minded New York and Pennsylvania wing, and the anti-tariff South Carolina and Virginia wing, of the Administration party, while at the same time serving the interest of yeomen-consumers. The bill was condemned by protectionists as a proposal to pull down the tariff pillar of the American System "by degrees," but it could never

* In his account of the Jefferson Day dinner, Benton practically skips by his own important organizing role, stressing the Union–dis-Union aspects of the business and suggesting that the initiators or leaders planned it as a nullification sounding-board (Benton, *View*, I, 148-149). Reinforcing this interpretation years later, Van Buren reported that he heard the President say "Our Union," and that the word "Federal" was inserted for the record only at the anxious request of Senator Hayne (Fitzpatrick: *Autobiography of Martin Van Buren*, 415.)

satisfy gentlemen from the South. In early March, Benton himself withdrew his bill. Later, the Administration carried a bill to reduce duties on coffee, tea, cocoa, and salt — but these steps were still too short to satisfy the South Carolina-Virginia-Calhoun faction.[13]

Meanwhile, Benton once more submitted to the Senate a revised version of his perennial bill to reduce the prices of the public lands. In a brief, businesslike debate, Benton led off with an unusually brief, businesslike speech, and Senator Hayne ably seconded Benton's advocacy. After attempts by Foot and Webster to have the issue held up for a year's "study" were beaten back, the measure — somewhat amended — was brought to a vote and, on May 7, 1830, *passed,* 24 to 22. The result was a triumph for the fledgling West-South alliance. Votes *for* the measure were cast by all members from the West but one, and by all members from the South but two, while the bulk of the votes *against* the bill came from Northern members. It was a great moment for Benton, who promptly wrote the *Beacon* in St. Louis, telling them the news and expressing hopes that the bill would pass in the House. But these hopes were thwarted. The House tabled the bill.[14]

Also in May, 1830, Congress dealt with another pillar of the American System. This was the matter of internal improvements, represented by a bill to subsidize a road from Maysville, Kentucky, to Lexington, Kentucky. The matter was a poser for Benton. In his Gargantuan oration on the Foot Resolution, he had argued that the internal improvements had been "a fraud upon the West," with money going for petty, local schemes, mostly in the North and East. As a proponent of a West-South alliance, he was sensitive to the fact that Southern opinion generally opposed internal improvements. But the Maysville bill was a *Western,* though petty, local project, and there was no doubt that such proposals still commanded support in the West. In his " 'hurly-burly' harangue," Barton had particularly attacked Benton's growing coolness toward internal improvements — and there was an election coming in which Barton might be replaced if care were taken not to give his faction any ammunition. When the Maysville Road bill came to a vote, Benton was recorded with the Yeas — giving the decision, apparently, to sectional and electoral considerations.*

* This vote was partly offset when Benton voted against a bill to subsidize another, newfangled venture — a railroad company called the Baltimore and Ohio, which was striking out for the West and which in 1830 purchased its first American-built, boiler-on-a-flat-car locomotive, the "Tom Thumb." The bill was defeated.

From the Executive Mansion, Jackson returned a stinging veto. Any works the Federal government subsidized should be "of a general, not local, national, not State," character, he declared. He added an argument Benton himself had espoused — without "unusual diversion" of the public funds, the *debt* could be paid off in two years, and this would permit *tariff reductions*. All this would serve the working masses of the nation — existing fiscal policy bore most "severely upon the laboring and less prosperous classes of the community," because payments on the *debt* required continued *tariffs,* and the tariffs were "imposed on the necessaries of life." Here was another indication of the way the breeze was blowing. To the *political* democracy that had characterized the Jackson movement, the President was beginning to add doctrines of *economic* democracy. Years later, Benton cited the Maysville Road veto as "a killing blow" to the over-all "system" of internal improvements.[15] Jackson's act apparently produced a greater firmness in Benton's attitudes toward national expenditures for local projects. Still, with his approval, expenditures for genuinely national works like the Cumberland Road and certain river-and-harbor projects actually increased in years to come.

Near the end of the session, Benton turned to a more pleasant matter — the nomination of John Randolph as Minister to Russia. Assuring his friend that "your candle is yet too bright to be hid under a bushel," Benton predicted a favorable outcome — and the nomination was confirmed.[16]

On the last day of May, 1830, Congress adjourned. During its course the breeze had blown, intermittently, perhaps, but steadily enough to show that its direction was contrary to that of the prevailing winds of the last several years. Meanwhile, Calhoun worried — "the times are perilous . . . All the great interests of the country are coming into conflict, and I must say . . . that those to whom the vessel of state is entrusted seem either ignorant or indifferent about the danger." [17] In the blowing of the breeze, the Jacksonian warship was beginning to come apart at the seams.

[4]

BY MID-JUNE, Benton was in Missouri. He returned to a state that, after a decade of rapid growth, had reached a population of one hundred and forty thousand, though St. Louis was still a town of barely five thousand inhabitants. His family had stayed in Missouri through the session, so that the children might continue uninterrupted with their studies. Eliza and Jessie Ann, eight and six, were at a French school with French-descended children, where they carried on their games and amusements in the French language.[18]

At home, Benton faced another battle. Technically it involved the election in which Senator Barton would be returned or replaced, but the campaign focused so much on Benton as a symbolic issue that it sometimes seemed that *he* was the candidate. The *Beacon* appealed to the "democratic party" (thereby using the label the Jackson men would carry in the future) to replace Barton with a true Jackson-Benton man — "one who will consider the voice of the *majority* as the rule of his conduct." The opposition labored to make an issue of the Maysville Road veto; thereby, the *Beacon* charged, undervaluing "the intelligence and equity of the people," who would support the President "against partial and local expenditures of public money for internal improvements." The opposition also complained that their candidates for the Assembly that would elect the Senator were "abused, villified & even blackguarded by Benton's tools." On the other hand, Charles Keemle at the *Beacon* complained of a new form of pressure on him. About twenty business houses and individuals ordered him to cancel their advertisements and subscriptions. The letters were written "evidently in unison and concert," the *Beacon* alleged, evidencing a "combination" to eliminate the only St. Louis rival of that paper (the *Republican*) which had "poured . . . abuse . . . on Col. Benton for FOURTEEN *years*." In defense, the *Beacon* could only appeal to the "People of Missouri" for support.

On the first Monday and Tuesday in August, these people went to the polls. Around St. Louis, the business capital of the state, a pro-Barton slate triumphed. But in the farming areas, candidates who were expected to support what Keemle had called a "firm, unwavering democrat" for the Senate were returned. At the Laurel Street house, Benton analyzed the returns in detail, decided that Barton had no chance, and wrote his outstate ally Finis Ewing to suggest that the place go to their friend John Miller — the unusually capable, widely popular governor. But there was a scramble for the honor, now available after ten years, and the list of hopefuls was long.

Meanwhile, the pro-Jackson press attacked Barton. His bouts with the bottle were thoroughly talked over, and this was offered as explanation of his propensity to fly "at Col. Benton like a dog every time he rises" in the Senate, thus forcing his colleague to "engage in a blackguard quarrel," or to "go out, the latter of which he always does." By October, however, the Jackson or Benton men began to suspect that Barton's iniquity was not the important point. The *Beacon* feared that the only recourse for the opposition was to *"make a* BARGAIN *with some turn-coat, and* BARTER *with him for the* CLOAK *of his name."* Their "hatred" of Benton was such that they would support anyone who would "counteract and defeat his measures." Noting that "the belief here is that D.B. is given up," Benton urged the pro-Jackson Assemblymen *and candidates* to "ascertain the strongest," and then *"unite* upon him . . . sacrificing all private or particular feelings." Soon after, the two symbols around whom the fight revolved left Missouri. Their departure was noted by the *Beacon* in a way that in itself seemed symbolic —

Col. THOMAS H. BENTON left home on Saturday last [November 6], for Washington City.

Judge BARTON departed here the Wednesday previous [November 3].[19]

Early in December, the Assembly balloted. The results — Alexander Buckner 35, John Miller 26, William Ashley 2 — were hailed with joy by the *Beacon,* which observed that Barton's chances had been so hopeless that his friends did not dare to put him in nomination. But before long some doubts were raised. The national newsmagazine, *Niles Register,* described Buckner as favorable to tariffs, and to internal improvements, and opposed to "proscription" of officeholders; and then noted that *all* the anti-Administration Assemblymen, plus five others, had voted for him. Perhaps, Hezekiah Niles surmised, pledges *not* to vote for Barton would explain all. In fact, the new "Democratic" party had been bilked. Taking advantage of confusions of policy in the party, and of weaknesses in organization, the anti-Jackson leaders had seized upon the "cloak" of Buckner's name to rally anti-Jacksonians and quasi-Jacksonians who had pledged *against* Barton but *for* no one, as well as whole-Jacksonians who thought Buckner was one of them. Rumor reported that Edward Bates had arranged the scheme at a caucus shortly before the election, and four months afterwards the ex-Congressman was bragging that his party would "Bucknerize" the Jackson-Benton forces in another election. The State Senator from Ste. Genevieve, Lewis F. Linn, remarked that *he* might have had the place, "if I had not *disdained* to be elected by my political Opponents." [20]

The breeze had blown Barton out of the Senate, after half a dozen years as a gadfly to Thomas Benton — but that gentlemen could not say he was satisfied with the replacement.

CHAPTER 9

The "Monster"

1831 - 1835

A S THE CLERK READ the measured sentences of Jackson's annual message of December, 1830, Benton listened intently. The President called upon Congress to consider, before the charter of the Bank of the United States expired in 1836, a substitute for that institution which would perform its *public* functions without placing in *private* hands a dangerous dominion over "the hopes, fears, or interests of large masses of the community." The words marked the beginning of a new phase in Thomas Benton's life. By speaking out boldly on this and related issues, he was to ascend to a peak in his career as a political leader, and as advocate, propagandist, and rhetorician.

The Bank issue was not new. In his first message to Congress, in 1829, the President had questioned "both the constitutionality and expediency" of the B. U. S., as it was often called. In response to this hint, Benton had promptly sent Jackson a note enclosing part of a letter from John Randolph, proposing that the customs houses and land offices become branches of a sort of public bank, thus securing the transfer of public moneys without private aid. The President had endorsed the letter on the back — "a substitute for the U. S. Bank — to be filed — the general ideas are good — A. J." [1] But nothing had come of the matter that session, except a Congressional inquiry that heard testimony from the Bank's chief Nicholas Biddle, and endorsed the institution. In the session of 1830-1831, however, Benton determined to force the matter. Laboring days and nights at Dawson's Number Two, where he was staying, he prepared a long drum-roll of a speech, which was to be one of the most important of his life. In February, he mounted the first battle of the long Bank war with a blunt resolution — "That the charter of the Bank of the United States ought not to be renewed."

At last, all the lessons Benton had learned about finance, from personal experience and from such seers as Macon and Randolph, were to be put in practice. The demise of the Bank he saw as only an essential first step in a comprehensive financial system he was beginning to evolve. In his long speech, he summed up his objections to the Bank under three main headings.

First, it was an institution "too great and too powerful to be tolerated in a Government of free and equal laws." Such a "money power," if perpetuated, would inevitably draw to itself "too much of the political power of this Union." The Bank's power rested on its charter rights to issue notes, to own property, to handle Federal government receipts, and to use "undrawn balances" of the public moneys. This power was exercised by a small directorate, "none of these elected by the people, or responsible to them"—rather, convinced that they were *not* so responsible! This directorate threatened to become "the sole *authority* . . . to which [all] must, of necessity apply, for every loan which their exigencies may demand." Thus, in accord with the Biblical maxim, "the rich ruleth the poor, and the borrower is the servant of the lender," a concentration of wealth threatened the future of the American Republic. Here was a perennial *political* problem — conflict between oligarchic economic power and the aspirations of equalitarian political democracy.

Second, Benton feared certain other "dangerous and pernicious" *effects* of "a great moneyed power." These were "to make the rich richer, and the poor poorer; to multiply nabobs and paupers." The tendency of institutions like the B. U. S. was "unfavorable to small capitalists," because "it is the principle of money to eschew the needy and unfortunate." It was "injurious to the laboring classes," because — through speculation, based on bank-note credit — the price of land or other property they might hope to buy was "raised to the paper maximum," while "wages remain at the silver minimum." Also by spawning "profuse issues," and then precipitating "sudden contractions" in the amount of bank notes or paper currency available, a great Bank could stir waves of economic expansion and contraction, and during the contraction acquire property from those unable to repay loans, in this way transferring millions "to the Neptunes who preside over the flux and reflux of paper." Thus, in its *economic* aspects, the bank-and-paper system encouraged accumulation for "great capitalists" on the one hand, and threatened impoverishment for the masses of the people on the other. For evidence, the orator cited the history of the Bank of England. Throughout Benton's attacks on the B. U. S., the Bank of England was

to crop up periodically like King Charles's head in the thoughts of
David Copperfield's friend Mister Dick.

Well warmed to his subject, Benton rumbled on with his *thirdly*. The
B. U. S. was objectionable, he declaimed, "on account of the exclusive
privileges" it gave to the stockholders. Among the most important was
the power the great Bank had over state banks — Nicholas Biddle himself had declared that "there are very few [state] banks which might
not have been destroyed by an exertion of the power of the [national]
bank," though none had ever been injured.* This, to Benton, was
"proof enough!" — for those who were unwilling to see "a moneyed
oligarchy established in this land." Furthermore, though "republics
want freeholders, not landlords and tenants," Benton saw the B. U. S.
emerging more and more as a landlord over tenants. He knew "towns,
yea, cities, and could name them" (he might have named Cincinnati,
for example) "in which this bank already appears as a dominant and
engrossing proprietor." Finally, the Bank's position was bulwarked by
the fact that it was a limited-liability corporation. This form of organization, which was to become integral to large-scale capitalism, Benton
attacked as "unjust." If the Bank failed, its stockholders might still
"live in splendor upon the princely estates acquired with its notes,"
while the "industrious classes" would be "unable to receive a shilling
for them." Here were some of the *social* aspects of the issue, with the
Bank pilloried as an actual or potential rallying point for an aristocracy
of wealth.

In concluding, Benton alluded to one more question. When re-charter
of the first national bank had been refused in 1811, the Jeffersonians of
the day had made "a fatal error." They had failed to provide a *national
substitute* for the national bank's currency, and had fallen back upon
the inadequate support of local banks. Now, in 1831, Benton was
determined that this error should not be repeated. In his opinion, "the

---

* It is likely that Biddle was trying to express, if somewhat gaily and boastfully,
the caution with which he thought the B. U. S. had exercised its public regulatory
powers, based on its role of presenting State bank notes to their issuers for payment, after these notes had been received and deposited by the Federal government. An abuse of this power was of course possible, and the Bank president was
apparently indulging himself in a moment of pride because he had not abused
the power (Cf. Hammond, "Jackson, Biddle and the B. U. S.," 4). Of course, all
this left untouched the question which agitated Benton — the fact that this public,
regulatory power was held by a private, nonresponsible corporation.

hard money mentioned and intended in the constitution," would serve. "Gold and silver is the best currency for a republic; it suits the men of middle property and the working people" — rural yeomen and urban laborers, presumably — "best." If he were "going to establish a working man's party, it should be on the basis of hard money; a hard money party against a paper party." [2]

When Benton finished, Webster was promptly on his feet to ask for a vote on Benton's request to introduce the resolution against the B. U. S. — denied, 23 to 20. But no matter — the Missourian's speech was one "to be read by the people — the masses — the millions; and was conceived and delivered for that purpose; and was read by them." Evaluating both his senatorial and his national audience well, Benton knew that he had little chance to change at the moment the views of his colleagues, but a large opportunity to influence as yet inchoate public opinion on the subject. The issue was made, and made dramatically.[3]

In particular, the speech was carried to the people and to local Jackson presses by a new Washington paper called the *Globe*. During the summer, the President had decided that he could no longer depend on the *Telegraph,* loyal more to Calhoun than to Jackson, and he had brought from Kentucky an editor named Francis P. Blair to establish a new organ. A skeleton-skinny, mild-mannered individual, with a round bump or dome at the back of his head where (it was said) he carried his brains, Editor Blair was not a rugged frontiersman personally, but he was a warrior with scalping-knife polemic in print. Like Benton, he was ready to use his scalping-knife on the Bank.[4] In the decades to come, the slender, unimposing Blair and the massive, aggressive Benton became firm friends.

In his speech of February, 1831, Benton had carefully avoided certain aspects of the Bank issue. He had barely touched on the *public* functions of the B. U. S., as a government depository, and as a means of restraining excessive state bank note issues by demanding specie payments on state bank paper received. In addition, he had ignored the faults of the state banks themselves. But in New York, in Philadelphia, and particularly in the go-ahead West, the Jackson coalition depended in part on new-come men of Enterprise, including local bankers. Such men opposed the B. U. S. but not the paper system — they were "Democrats *by trade,*" as one partisan put it, rather than "Democrats *in principle,*" like Benton. Feeling as yet too weak "to encounter all the banks of all the States at once," as well as the big Bank, Benton avoided the state bank issue — a tack he hoped would be temporary. The speech did, however, mark a new advance in the development of popular democracy. To many self-styled followers of Jefferson, "democracy" had come to mean only *political* equality, and perhaps in operation little more than hurrahs for "people's candidates" as against "aristocrats." In 1830 and 1831, however, the question of relative *economic* and *social* equality was brought to the fore again. The Maysville Road veto had checked one phase of the American System of preference and profit. Now, in the attack on the B. U. S., another step had been taken.

The massive speech was praised by Benton's old mentor, Nathaniel Macon. "You deserve the thanks of every man who lives by the sweat of his face," Macon wrote from North Carolina — though his Old Republican honesty made him add, "I observe some bad grammar: you must pardon my freedom." [5] Despite bad grammar, the lines of combat in a great conflict of interests that would dominate the decade, had been marked out. The first battle of the Bank war had been joined.

[2]

WHEN THE SHORT SESSION adjourned in March, Benton went on to Cherry Grove to join Elizabeth and his family. By mid-April, they were all on their way to Missouri.

During Benton's absence from Washington, events occurred which were to have a far-reaching effect on his political future. The developing conflict between Jackson and Calhoun had been sharpened by the Case of the Tavern Keeper's Daughter and the Case of the Seminole War Letters. The first involved the young, pretty wife of Secretary of War Eaton, Peggy O'Neale, whose pre-marital chastity a number of Washington ladies doubted. True to his sentimental inclinations, Jackson championed Peggy's cause, while Floride Calhoun emerged as the leader of the battalions bent on snubbing that young lady. The second dragged up the Indian wars in Florida in 1818. Correspondence was published which revealed that Calhoun (as Secretary of War in 1818) had sharply disapproved of Jackson's conduct of the Florida campaigns. These developments further divided the Jackson coalition — a division dependent fundamentally not on the question of Peggy's virtue or the scars of old wars, but on the fact that leaders representing incompatible groups and advocating incompatible doctrines could no longer live together in the same political house. Finally, Van Buren brought the domestic squabbles to an issue. As he and Jackson took one of their frequent horseback rides together along the Tennallytown Road, he offered a modest proposal. The entire cabinet should resign, freeing the President to appoint a new one. During the spring and early summer, this scheme was carried out.

The *coup* was gratifying to Benton. It brought Calhoun, the *Telegraph,* and other previously covert enemies out openly against the Administration — and soon the *Telegraph* was operating on the strength of a loan from the B. U. S. The shift also gave Benton an opportunity to advance as a political leader. He seized it so effectively that he soon "took first rank in the Senate," as the "champion of the Administration." [6]

Paradoxically, Benton was almost equally pleased by a sequel to the cabinet shuffle. Soon after Van Buren had stepped down as Secretary of State, Jackson nominated him as Minister to England. When the nomination finally reached the floor of the Senate in Januray, 1832, there ensued a series of "set speeches," as Benton saw them, aimed at "killing off" his friend Van Buren "in the public mind." One of the leaders in the parade was Henry Clay, back in Congress as a Senator from Kentucky; and he was joined by Daniel Webster. Twice a tie was contrived to bring Vice-President Calhoun on record, and both times he voted against the Administration. The divided state of the Senate, and the final break-away of the Calhoun faction, was clear. After the vote, there was jubilation among the anti-Van Burenites.

As Benton remembered it later, he heard Calhoun exclaim to a doubting friend:

"It will kill him, sir, kill him dead. He will never kick, sir, never kick."

But Benton thought differently. "You have broken a minister," he said exultantly to the pro-Calhoun Senator Moore of Alabama, who sat near him, "and elected a Vice-President."

Soon after the voting, Benton wrote Van Buren a letter in which he weighed his friend's prospects. The rejection by a jealous combination would win him sympathy, and the New Yorker should look ahead — "as for myself, when I find myself on the bridge of Lodi, I neither stop to parley, nor turn back . . . Forward, is the word." * Why should not

* During the Italian campaign in the spring of 1796, the French Revolutionary Armies under Napoleon faced the Austrians, with fourteen big guns, across the

Van Buren set out definitely for the Vice-Presidency, on a ticket with Andrew Jackson? If he would take a clear, firm position on "a few cardinal principles of the old democratic school," he would be distinctly "worth contending for." The whole "dynasty of '98 (federalists)" was against Van Buren. If he was "not against them, the people, and myself, as one of the people, can see nothing between you and them worth contending for." But if he *was* against them, that was another matter, the plain-spoken Benton concluded. He wanted "to see the right principles prevail, and friends instead of foes in power." [7]

Meanwhile, in Missouri, Benton had been concerned with another divisive political battle, in which the result was less gratifying. His friend Pettis was a candidate to succeed himself in Congress. As the campaign progressed, with Benton's battle-worn enemy David Barton brought forward as the opposition nominee, young Pettis was attacked in a series of anonymous newspaper letters. Pettis was, the letter-writer proclaimed vituperatively in shifting metaphor, "a mere dish of skimmed milk . . . a sort of political Harlequin . . . a garrulous old lady." For a time, Spencer Pettis kept his peace, but finally in a public letter of his own he named his traducer as Thomas Biddle — brother to Nicholas Biddle of the B. U. S., and himself a director of the St. Louis branch of the Bank and compatriot of older leaders in the established St. Louis business community. Furthermore, Pettis declared, Thomas Biddle was "not only a federalist, but an overbearing *aristocrat,* [and a] *miserable poltroon"* to boot. At the time Pettis's letter was published, in July, 1831, he was staying at the City Hotel in St. Louis. Feeling unwell and finding the "musquitoes" troublesome at night, he left his room and went to sleep on the rear, upper porch of the hotel. There he was awakened about daybreak "by several blows" — with a stick and a fist. His assailant was Biddle. A great scuffle ensued, with Biddle brandishing a pistol and Pettis defending himself with a sword-cane. Gradually the two men fought their way down the stairs of the hotel, and were finally separated on the lower porch. Soon Benton was involved in the brawl. The noise and cries of "murder" from Pettis carried readily to the Benton residence across the open lot above the

---

Adda River, near Lodi. After some preliminary actions, Napoleon ordered his infantrymen to cross the 750-foot-long bridge. The column moved forward, about thirty men broad, but was soon checked by the devastating fire from the guns of the superior Austrian forces. At this point Napoleon himself came forward, rallied his soldiers, and thus effected the astonishing crossing. Afterwards, Napoleon referred to Lodi as the decisive turning point in his career.

hotel, where they woke Elizabeth Benton. She promptly roused her husband, who dressed and went to the hotel. There he confronted the illness-enfeebled Pettis, bruised, bleeding, and shaken, who announced his intention to challenge Biddle to a duel immediately. He was dissuaded by Benton, who argued that death in a duel would, at such a late date, almost certainly result in the election of Barton. *After* the election — then, sir, he might avenge his honor! *

Early in August, the citizens voted — and gave Pettis a smashing victory. He promptly challenged Biddle, and on Friday, August 26, late in the afternoon, the two men met on the same Bloody Island where Benton and Lucas had fought. The distance was fixed at *five feet* — due to the nearsightedness of Biddle. In the fire, both men were severely wounded. They were quickly brought to the shore, where immense crowds were waiting. When Pettis was brought in, Benton went to him to comfort him. During the night and the next day, he was often with Pettis at Andrew Burt's boardinghouse, and he was at his bedside when the young man died Saturday afternoon. For thirty days Benton and other friends wore crape on their left arms, "as a tribute of respect." On Monday morning Thomas Biddle also died.

In a letter to Lewis Cass, the new Secretary of War, Benton commented: "A U. S. Bk. Director has been interfering in our election; the consequence is the death of the Director & of the Representative." [8]

A successor had to be chosen for Pettis, and two men presented themselves for the nod. One was William H. Ashley, who had been one of the great magnates of the Western fur trade, and who was in 1831 a well-to-do leader in the St. Louis business community, a director of the local branch of the B. U. S., and openly for recharter. The other was Robert W. Wells. Promptly, Senator Buckner supported Ashley, while Senator Benton endorsed Wells. In mid-October, Benton and Wells appeared together at a huge meeting at the St. Louis Court House, where Benton spoke for an hour and a quarter, drawing the battle lines with "the Bank on one side, the people on the other." In particular, he attacked the "branch drafts," which were issued by local B. U. S. offices

---

* This account of Benton's interview with Pettis depends entirely upon the statements of Edward Dobyns, written out some time after the fact. It is accepted here, first, because it is wholly consistent with contemporaneous evidence from a number of sources (cf. *St. Louis Beacon,* 1831, July 28; September 1; October 1); and second, because Dobyns, who was in a position to know, scores unusually high when his memoirs are checked against the record on other points.

instead of regular central-office notes — thus, Benton cried, the branch banks were flooding the nation with an unsound, inflationary, and (allegedly) illegal currency! In his turn Wells condemned Ashley for favoring recharter, and scored the enemies of the Administration for trying to break it by dividing it on the Bank issue. Soon it became clear that Wells was to be "Bucknerized." The anti-Jackson leaders (who were beginning to call themselves "National Republicans") labored to add an *"undivided anti-Jackson vote"* to Ashley's "Democratic" vote. Ashley won a narrow victory over Wells, a victory that was cinched by a two-to-one plurality in mercantile St. Louis. Disgusted, Benton growled — "the old Adams party here are delirious with joy . . . they now boast openly that they will dissolve organization of the Jackson party by running Jackson men against Jackson measures." And, Benton thought, they would succeed, "unless we drop *men* and take *principles* for our guide."

Through the raw, gray days of approaching winter, Benton and his family stayed on in St. Louis. On the eve of leaving for the East, in November, he wrote a parting testament:

> *Of the "New Party,"* or combination of Clay men and pro-Bank Jacksonians: "They will use their Jackson men for candidates at the August elections, and put in for nothing on the Adams and Clay side til the Senatorial election."
>
> *Of the Bank:* "The B. U. S. is the turning point. That *political engine* of the old federal monarchical party, will draw the lines between parties again." As to his own situation — "the Bank intends to have me instructed if it cannot defeat me . . . I understand that Bank candidates will be put up for the general assembly in every county." Every pro-Bank former Jackson man belonged to the "New Party," while all the Adams-Clay pro-Bank stalwarts belonged to it.
>
> *Of the 1832 Congressional Election:* "If W[ells] will be in the field next August, he ought to begin to act at once, and write essays to guide public opinion, and make speeches to advance himself." The master even suggested the proper timing — "Essays should begin *now,* speeches in April." [9]

[3]

IN CONGRESS, and in the political arena outside of Congress, the year 1832 saw new, momentous battles in the Bank war. Disturbed by the attacks on the Bank in the President's message and Benton's massive

onslaught of February, 1831, and urged on by Henry Clay,* Nicholas
Biddle decided to press immediately for a renewal of the charter. He
thereby precipitated the second battle of the Bank war. Immediately,
Benton stepped forward to lead the opposition.

His first major attack was a resolution declaring the "branch drafts"
illegal, and calling for their suppression. This resolution was the occasion
for a long polemic, soon issued in pamphlet form, in which Benton
labored to link the Bank to sectional alignments. The branch drafts, he
argued, facilitated a steady flow of specie from the *West* and *South* to
the *East* — an "ABDUCTION OF . . . GOLD AND SILVER," in which "the
hard money of the *country,*" on which no interest was paid, was siphoned
to the East, while the "paper money of a *company,* for which bank interest is exacted," took its place in the South and West. Excessive, pyramided paper credits were encouraging an orgy of borrowing and expansion in these sections. But someday, payment of the principal would have
to be asked, and in this contraction forced sales might provide "the foundation for the titles and estates of [a] future nobility," Benton cried
melodramatically — "Marquis of Nashville! Count of St. Louis! Prince
of New Orleans!" Before such lords, "the next generation of American
farmers must 'crook the pregnant hinges of the knee!' " — unless the
branch drafts were outlawed, the Bank itself finally discontinued.

It was a shotgun attack, longer on rhetoric and Shakespeare than on
economic analysis. In oversimplifying for propaganda effect, Benton
ignored other factors related to the flow of specie to the East, factors
rooted in the course of trade; and he also ignored certain practical
justifications for the use of branch drafts. The long, dramatic speech
was followed by a brief, prosaic debate, in which Benton's attack was
successfully fended off by Webster, by Alexander Buckner, and others.[10]

Meanwhile, Biddle was marshaling his forces. He could count on
Clay, Webster, and the old Adams men or National Republicans practi-
cally in force. He could also depend on three members of Jackson's new
Cabinet, including Lewis Cass, and on a number of Democratic mem-

---

* Once Clay had bitterly opposed a national bank as "a splendid association of
favored individuals." But the financial difficulties brought on by the War of 1812,
and his subsequent recognition of the concern of manufacturers for an easy access
to business capital, had led him to change his mind. By the 1820's he was one of
the Bank's most "useful and valuable" political attorneys — "your remuneration,
liberal as it was designed to be, has been amply earned," Biddle once wrote
him (Langdon Cheves to Clay, February 23, 1821, and Nicholas Biddle to Clay,
March 11, 1825, Clay Papers). Through the 1820's and 1830's, Clay and Biddle
acted as close political allies.

bers of Congress who declared themselves simultaneously loyal to Jackson *and* the Bank. With the Administration party thus divided, Biddle brought his friend Thomas Cadwalader to Washington to act as a "lobby-agent," "lobby-member," or "lobby-ist," as the jargon of the day variously had it. Soon, Benton noted, Cadwalader was meeting separately with a National Republican caucus, and a smaller Democratic, pro-Bank caucus. Nothing was to be left to chance, and the intense, arrogant, but nimble Nicholas Biddle was sure that unity and organization in the Bank forces would win the day.*

The anti-Bank leaders like Benton conceded, in fact, that the bill for recharter would pass both houses. Their only hope was — a presidential veto. Therefore, Benton and other leaders undertook a long-range strategy, rallying their followers in Congress "to attack incessantly, assail at all points, display the evil of the [Bank], rouse the *people*" — and thereby "prepare them to sustain the veto." Innumerable inquiries and amendments were prepared for the Senate, and a full-scale investigation was planned for the House. In keeping with this strategy, the *Globe* and satellite party presses worked to rouse public opinion. They carried the anti-Bank speeches of Benton and others in column after long column of six-point, and advertised pamphlet reprints of Benton's anti-Bank addresses.

As the emerging Jackson leader in Congress, Benton arranged in some detail the move for an investigation in the House. He gave a member from Georgia, A. S. Clayton, a memorandum of charges against the Bank. It was a brief outline, which Benton had expected Clayton to elaborate; but he had not done so, and had only the Senator's notes when he was unexpectedly called on to justify his motion. While he spoke, he rolled the narrow slip of paper Benton had given him around his finger, as on a cylinder, to prevent the Senator's handwriting from being seen. Suddenly, the Bank party was on the defensive. Should it resist an investigation, and appear to have something to hide? Or accept an investigation, and wait while the issue was paraded again be-

* The term "lobby-agent" appeared in the American language as early as 1829, and by 1832 this term and the shorter form "lobbyist" were in common use in Washington. National, organized, permanent, professionally led interest group associations like the NAM, the American Bankers Association, or farm and labor groups, as sponsors of professional lobbyists, were still half a century or more in the future — but the work of Biddle and Cadwalader, relying on the pre-existing national organization of the B. U. S. itself, was a foreshadowing of processes to come. The Bank possessed what was probably the strongest, most national, most cohesive organization of the day.

fore the public? The Bank forces finally agreed, against Biddle's
desires, to a committee of inquiry. The committee Benton had spawned
came out with a majority blast against the Bank, as well as a minority
report favorable to it.[11]

In May, the bill for recharter was called up in the Senate. A two-
week debate ensued, during which Benton harried the Bank armies,
driving them back with sudden sorties wherever he could — while Clay
and Webster advanced the bill inexorably toward passage. At the end
of May, Benton launched a speech in which he sought first to place
the Bank forces on the defensive, and then to create a diversion. Why
such haste, he asked, when other issues (like reducing the prices
of the public lands or modifying the tariff) had been brought up first?
The democratic principle, he argued, required that the Congressional
decision be postponed. The sitting Congress was based on the census of
1820, and did not represent the actual distribution of population; the
next would be based on the census of 1830 — as between the two, "in
the West alone, a million of people lose their voice in the decision!"
Furthermore, the presidential election was due in four months, and
Jackson and Clay had been named as rival candidates — let the people
decide the issue, by choosing between anti-Bank and pro-Bank champions. But if action there must be, he would offer an alternative to the
single, monopoly Bank, an alternative consistent with "*the diffusion
of wealth and power*" which was appropriate to *republics*. The proposal: *three* banks; no exclusive privileges; each stockholder liable to
the amount of his stock for failure of the bank to redeem notes in
specie; no notes for less than twenty dollars to be issued, received, or
paid. The diversion was not taken up — but Benton had made his
point.

In June, the Senate considered amendments — with Benton and his
allies seizing every opportunity for harassment and dramatization. One
abortive proposal, to give the states power to tax branch banks, evoked
new heights of rhetoric from Benton. It was the branch banks, he
declared, that served as tentacles to bring increasing wealth to the
central Bank — thus, "all the flourishing cities of the West" were, or
would soon be, "in the jaws of the monster! a lump of butter in the
mouth of a dog! one gulp, one swallow, and all is gone!" On his own,
Benton offered no less than four amendments, with long speeches explaining and advocating each. Time, and more time, consumed . . .
Sessions grew longer, most of a week was used up, Senators grew wearier

and their tempers shorter. Bank leaders like Clay and Webster grew angrier. Meantime Benton hammered at the issue, attacking again and again in the face of certain defeat, dramatizing his objections to the B. U. S. in specific legislative proposals. At the end, in a final attempt at delay, he moved to refer the completed bill to the *Administration,* for "consideration and report" — after all, the pro-Bank argument rested on the assumption that the Bank was necessary for the financial operation of the government. On this point, as on all others, Benton was voted down — but once again, he had made his point.

At last, the time came for final debate and decision. Late in the afternoon of Friday, June 8, the indefatigable Benton began a long speech, the early part of which he interrupted to permit a motion to adjourn. The time consumed by a roll call he utilized "by going out, and taking a slight dinner," thereby fortifying himself to go on, while other Senators, less favored alphabetically, had to wait in the chamber. Thus strengthened, he continued his speech for another three-quarters of an hour — when the Senate adjourned for another day. The next morning, Saturday, June 9, he picked up where he had left off, drumming away with old arguments, blasting at the Bank as part of the old American System, at "those twin monsters, the bank and an ultra tariff." It was time, he cried, for men of the West to come forward and save their section "from the grasp of a foreign power" — the Monster. . . . Here Benton looked about him, abruptly terminated his discourse, and sat down. Immediately his old friend, Felix Grundy, now in the Senate from Tennessee, rose to move indefinite postponement. On a snap roll call, this motion was lost by the relatively narrow margin of 24 to 20. Friends of the Bank suspected "a *ruse de guerre.*" Reporting the event, H. Niles's *Register* noted that several pro-Bank Senators were absent, having inferred that "as Colonel Benton had commenced his tirade only the day before," he would surely "not complete his orbit before Tuesday." Apparently, Benton *had* counted on his reputation as a marathon orator to take the Bank forces unaware, and he had almost turned the trick.

At the next meeting of the Senate, on June 11, 1832, recharter was finally brought to a vote and passed, 28 to 20. The roll call reflected the dominance of the forces of Enterprise and capitalism in New England, and in the Middle Atlantic region; a strong opposition to the Bank in the planting and agricultural South; and a divided opinion in the Northwest and Southwest, where Enterprise and Arcadia contended.

This division was epitomized in the vote of the gentlemen from Missouri — Benton, Nay; Buckner, Yea. The bill readily passed the House on July 3, with William Ashley of Missouri voting for recharter. After the triumph, a smiling Nicholas Biddle mingled with members on the floor, who crowded to shake hands with him. Later, he responded with an elaborate party at his lodgings. Looking forward, Biddle wrote to Cadwalader, "Now for the President." The second battle was over.[12]

Now for the President — but there Biddle was not so successful. Ill, wearied by the blazing Washington July, haggard, "Old Hickory" was as resolute as ever — "The bank, Mr. Van Buren," that gentleman recalled Andrew Jackson saying during a midnight visit, "is trying to kill me, *but I will kill it!*" By July 10, a stinging veto message had been sent to the Senate — and the third battle of the Bank war was launched. After announcing that in *his* opinion, the Bank was unconstitutional, Jackson went on to denounce it on social, economic, and political grounds, in terms that echoed Benton's strictures. Too often, he declared, "the rich and powerful . . . bend the acts of government to their selfish purposes." When government undertook, by law, "to make the rich richer and the potent more powerful," then "the humble members of society — the farmers, mechanics, and laborers," had a right to complain. *He* would not be a party to making the wealthy "richer by act of Congress." [13]

To the Bank forces, the message was a red flag. "It has all the fury of a chained panther," Biddle cried. "It is really a manifesto of anarchy," he went on, "such as Marat or Robespierre might have issued to the mob of the Faubourg St. Antoine." These sentiments were echoed in the Senate in a less literary but more pompous way by Webster and Clay. The Bank orators had refrained from extended speeches before the veto, but they indulged in them now, appealing broadly to such symbols of stability and rectitude as law, the Constitution, order, and government. Most of the nation's press, including such influential family organs as the *Saturday Evening Post,* also cried out against the veto.

In the Senate, Benton answered the giants of opposition, and there was now a note of triumph in his voice. Why, he asked, in the jabbing, repetitive, rhetorical style he was developing, *why* "this *post facto — post mortem* — this posthumous — debate?" It was, he answered bluntly, "not for the Senate, nor the President, nor to alter the fate of the bank bill," but for the crowded galleries, for the electorate. It was "to rouse the officers of the bank . . . to bring out its stream of corrupting influence, by inspiring hope, and to embody all its recruits at the polls" — to bring disrespect on Jackson and defeat him in the coming election. This verbal appeal, Benton feared, was a prelude to power of a more material sort. The Monster threatened to call in its loans and bring about a contraction on the 1819 model, in which "even the growing crops, quite up to Boon's Lick [the Missouri frontier]" would lose value — thus effecting "a turn of the screw upon the borrowers — to make them all cry out and join in the clamors and petitions for a renewed charter!" This asserted, Benton twitted the National Republican leaders as subservient twins — Clay and Webster, "the duplicate Senators." Finally, he had a word for certain Democrats, for "the Jackson bank men, present and absent." It was possible, he allowed, to be for *a* bank and for the General, but not "for *this* bank, and for Jackson." The B. U. S. was "now the open, as it has long been the secret, enemy of Jackson." Lines were drawn, and men must choose.

In rebuttal, Clay launched some jibes of his own at Benton. Concerning alleged appeals to the crowded galleries — "No member knows better than the honorable gentleman that, when some other [members] rise, the galleries are quickly emptied, with whatever else the chamber may then be filled." As to decorum in debate — "I cannot allow the member from Missouri to instruct me in etiquette and courtesy . . . go with the member from Missouri and his Indian blankets to Boon's Lick, to be taught the rules and practice of politeness." Concerning attacks on the chief magistrate — "I never had any personal rencontre with the President; I never complained of the President beating a brother of mine after he was prostrated and lying apparently lifeless." In conclusion, Clay reminded Benton of the reports that Benton had said, in 1824, that if Jackson became President, legislators would have to carry firearms. Here Clay paused, looked fiercely at Benton, and asked: "Can the Senator throw his eyes on me — will he look in my face and assert that he never used language similar to that imputed to him?" After a pause, Benton stood, pointed his finger at Clay, and said "he could — he could." Three times the Kentuckian asked the question, and elicited each time the self-conscious, measured response — whereupon Clay sat down. Still on his feet, Benton added: "I look, sir, and repeat that it is an atrocious calumny; and I will pin it to him who repeats it here"; this done, "it would stick, stick, stick there, and there he wished it to remain." At this, Clay rose and resumed the inquisition, declaring that he himself had heard from Benton "the very words" — but he was greeted by the sound of his antagonist's bull voice intoning "False! False! False!" Clay then cried: "I fling back the charge of atrocious calumny!"

Calls of "Order, order" from several gentlemen . . . Hurly-burly, during which Littleton Tazewell, in the chair, George Poindexter, who had been presiding, Clay, and Benton were all on their feet. Finally, another acrid exchange . . .

> SENATOR BENTON: "I apologize to the Senate for the manner in which I have spoken; but not to the Senator from Kentucky."
> SENATOR CLAY: "To the Senate I also offer an apology. To the Senator from Missouri, none." [14]

With this huggermugger over, the Senate proceeded to a vote. The bill failed of the two-thirds majority necessary to pass it over the President's veto. Jackson, Benton, and their allies had won the third battle in the great Bank War. Three days later an exhausted Senate adjourned as the pro-Jackson press carried the issue to the people. The *Globe* praised Benton's defense of the veto and his bearding of Clay and Webster as "a total discomfiture to the grand electioneering attack . . . a rout . . . a carnage." The editor of *Paul Pry,* the rambunctious, gossipy, feminist Anne Royall, who had watched the encounter with Clay, remarked that Benton's words had "rolled in torrents, mingled with thunder and lightning, transfixing the listeners to their seats." Indeed, "Mr. Clay was no more in Mr. Benton's hands than a kid in the paws of a lion." [15]

Still, Benton was not satisfied. He looked forward to an over-all reform of the national financial system, in which paper money as a whole, whether issued by the big Bank or by state-chartered banks as well, would be replaced by a hard-money currency. Others, including Jackson himself, would go down the road he advocated — but the time was not yet.

Immediately after adjournment, Benton set out for Missouri. There, he, Elizabeth, and the children spent the summer and fall of 1832 together at the Laurel Street house, while Thomas threw himself into the election campaigns that constituted a fourth battle in the Bank war.

A strong opposition to Benton had been building in Missouri. It included not only men of large, long-established wealth like the heir of the Chouteau dynasty, Pierre Chouteau, Jr., but also such quondam Jackson men as Representative Ashley, William Carr Lane, and now Charles

Keemle of the *Beacon*. The Bank was the decisive issue. Over the Bank, its alleged indispensability to "the commercial community" in the West, and the veto, the *Beacon* had swung around to a flat opposition to Benton, thereby leaving him once again without newspaper support in St. Louis. In Missouri, as in the nation as a whole, the Democratic party was dividing into factional groups — conservative Democrats, identified with Enterprise, but anxious to make business opportunities more open to newcomers, and radical Democrats, loyal to the standard of Arcadia. In Missouri, old-line National Republicans and new conservative Democrats joined in the hope of unseating Benton when he came up for re-election in the fall. Since 1831, this "New Party" had been organizing a slate of Assembly candidates who would be, as one participant put it, "particularly and positively anti-Benton." For their part, Benton and his allies emphasized their anti-Bank, agrarian, and popular democratic views. Their power base was increasingly among the mass of the small farmers of the state, and to the yeoman who "lived by the sweat of his face" (as Nathaniel Macon put it) they directed their appeals.

The voting at the beginning of August produced a mixed result. Pro-Benton candidates for Governor and Lieutenant Governor won handily over National Republicans; but with both men running as Democrats again, the pro-Bank Ashley nosed out the pro-Benton Wells again for Congress. The mercantile, mining, plantation-slave, and rich-farming counties went for Ashley, while yeomen-dominated counties generally fell to Wells. The returns for the Assembly elections were slow in coming in. Near the end of August, Benton wrote to governor-elect Daniel Dunklin — "We are still without exact returns. . . . I should be glad to have your opinion as to the members. . . . All that money & intrigue can do, will be done, to put me down." By September, Benton's "calculations" indicated a majority for him — but still, opposition continued.

In particular, Benton noted, the forces of the big Bank fought him. Soon after the branch in St. Louis had been established in 1829, it had gone "to work to gain men and presses, to govern the politics of the State," as he put it later, with the aim of keeping him from re-election. To political leaders in Missouri, "myriads of bank documents were sent," until the state was deluged with such favors. In the summer of 1832, the branch-Bank forces were in the field against him in every town, "its directors traversing the State," and after the elections going to the homes of the Assemblymen to try to influence them. A review of his speech on the Veto Message was circulated, and, he charged, "SEVENTY-FIVE THOUSAND copies of that review was paid for by the Bank of the United States!" The theme of all these attacks was that Senator Benton was a "very unfit person" to represent the state. Meanwhile, the *Republican* poured out its usual spate of abuse on Benton — and the *Beacon* was not far behind.

When the Assembly met at the end of November, however, he scored a smashing victory. The balloting gave Benton 46 votes, the National Republican selection, Abraham J. Williams (a well-to-do Boone County merchant, tobacco warehouseman and drygoods dealer who had once served briefly as Missouri's Governor) 12 votes, and William Ashley 4 and David Barton 2.[16] The voting in the Assembly, like voting in the Ashley-Wells race, reflected the developing divisions in the population — mercantile, mining, plantation-slave, and rich-farming counties, anti-Benton; and yeoman-dominated counties, pro-Benton.*

* A detailed analysis is revealing. In the popular voting for Representative, pro-Ashley majorities marched west from St. Louis along the Missouri River, taking in St. Charles, Montgomery, Callaway, and Boone Counties — areas of rich lands, large and prosperous farms, most of them with considerable slave populations; three of the four of them involved in mercantile activities stimulated by their location on the Boon's Lick immigrant trail to the West; and one of them, Callaway, a center of Missouri-mule raising, a profitable industry which exported its mobile products well out of the state. Farther west, on the River, Ashley won Clay County — centered around the town of Liberty, then the chief outfitting and trading center for travelers and commerce going west and along the Santa Fe Trail; an area dominated by a strong oligarchy of merchants and planters. South of St. Louis, pro-Ashley votes were recorded in Washington, St. Francis, Ste. Genevieve, and Perry Counties — the first three centers of the leadmining industry, the third still an important trading center, and the fourth in this orbit and perhaps influenced by the fact that it lay in the same State-Senatorial district as the second and third. On the Mississippi farther south, New Madrid and Scott Counties went for Ashley — the county seat of New Madrid was a river port, and both counties boasted flat, rich, bottom lands planted in that commercial crop, cotton; but some special conditions must be assumed to explain the fact that Ashley got 377 votes in these counties while Wells got only 10. Finally, north of St. Louis, on the Mississippi, Pike County, another rich-land area with interests in trade north into the Iowa Territory, showed a close pro-Ashley vote. Three other counties bordering on the Missouri — Howard, Cooper, and Chariton — went for Wells, and these counties showed considerable plantation-slave-agriculture development; but in 1832, the last two ran back into hilly, small-farming country, and Howard was headquarters for an influential political clique which, out of statewide considerations, still favored Thomas Benton and his faction. In yeomen-populated counties like Jefferson, Franklin, Gasconade, Cole, and Jackson, Wells won smashing majorities. In the Assembly voting for Senator, a nearly identical pattern can be discerned — though Benton picked up a few votes from counties Wells had lost. Votes for Williams, the National Republican nominee, came en-

In the nation, meanwhile, the Presidential canvass was running its course. The candidates had been nominated by a new procedure which was to become standard in the American political system, national party conventions. A state meeting at Jefferson City had named Benton to serve as a delegate to the Democratic convention, but he opposed the idea of nominating conventions except in emergencies, and stayed away. (In any case, the battle over re-chartering the Bank was at its height when the convention met.) The choice of Clay and Jackson as party champions, with Van Buren as Jackson's running mate, made the election turn on the great national conflict of interests, on fundamental policy questions — the American System in general, and the B. U. S. in particular.

Confident of a Jackson victory nationally, Benton expected Missouri to give Old Hickory "a majority of two to one." Even the *Beacon* announced that it would support Jackson, despite its disagreement with him on internal improvements and the Bank — but perhaps the *Beacon* was losing its influence, for by the end of 1832 its light had flickered out. In any case, the vote in Missouri gave the Jackson electors 8904, the Clay electors 4760 — "a majority of two to one." Nationally, the popular margin was not so great, though the electoral vote was overwhelming — for Jackson, 700,000 popular and 219 electoral votes, for Clay 550,000 popular and 49 electoral votes. Though Van Buren fell behind Old Hickory in his race for Vice-President, he still won easily. It was another triumph, with the Jackson party strongly increasing its pluralities over 1828.[17]

The results reflected Jackson's strength with the mass of the people. Despite party factionalism, despite the opposition of interest groups that had built up during his first term, despite the efforts and influence of the Bank, despite the magnetic appeal of Clay's personality, the "Old Hero" swept every section except New England. Like Benton, his power base lay chiefly in small-farming areas. Unlike Benton, however, Jackson could claim increasingly significant support in the cities, in the East, among the increasingly active workingmen's groups. The Bank issue, with which Jackson had become identified, appealed strongly to these reform groups,

---

tirely from areas where mercantile or mining interests were important, while the plantation-agriculture and prosperous-farming representatives gave their anti-Benton votes to lesser candidates. Delegations from small-farming counties like Jefferson, Franklin, Gasconade, Cole, Jackson, and so on, were unanimously pro-Benton.

among which antagonism to paper money was intense. This was particularly the case in New York City; and even in mercantile, manufacturing, and conservative Boston, Jackson ran surprisingly well in the poorer wards where workingmen lived. The outlook of the workingmen's associations, like that of their leaders, was middle class, focusing on monopoly as a threat to opportunity, and on a concern for status — but this was sufficient foundation for anti-Bank, pro-Jackson opinion. The new popular democracy, with Jackson as its symbol, stood as a strong, national movement.

The fourth battle in the Bank war had ended in glorious victory for the Jackson men. "It was a question of systems and measures," Benton noted later, "tried in the persons of men who stood out boldly and unequivocally . . . on the issue." [18] So it was — but in the future, remembering that speaking "boldly and unequivocally" had brought defeat, the anti-Jackson forces were to adopt less candid tactics.

[4]

THROUGH 1832 AND 1833, while the Bank war ran its course, other issues had boiled up into a dramatic climax. These were the tariff, the price of the public lands, and the public debt.

The issues took shape in complex Congressional maneuvering. In his message of December, 1831, Jackson noted that the national debt might be paid off within a year, and that tariff duties might thus be reduced to the level needed to supply revenue for the ordinary operations of government. In mid-March, 1832, Benton rose in the Senate to endorse tariff reduction. He condemned the "present high rate of protection," as an undue aid to manufacturing (in the East), at the expense of the farmer (in the West, and throughout the nation) and the planter (in the South). The issue was referred to the Committee on Manufactures, headed by Clay. To this routine reference an amendment was added, instructing the committee to consider also "the propriety of reducing the prices of the public lands," the other great source of national revenue. Thus, Benton and his cohorts hoped, tariff reduction and land price reduction might be linked as twin measures — which might be carried together by the alliance of South and West Benton and Senator Hayne had sought to promote. But the wily Clay avoided the trap. In mid-April, ignoring the tariff for the moment, he brought in a report rejecting the proposal to reduce the land prices. He proposed instead to distribute the proceeds of the land sales among the several states, for state internal improvements and other purposes. This distribution scheme would have maintained the land prices and created vested interests in the states against Benton's perennial price-reduction proposals. It would also have strengthened the high tariff argument by making tariffs the sole source of national government revenue.

Immediately, Benton lashed out. The distribution scheme was the old restrictive land policy in new guise, he cried, favoring "the principle of money — money — money," instead of the human value of "an increase of man — free man." More maneuvering, through May, June, and July, 1832, brought another personal encounter between Benton and Clay, in which Clay roundly condemned Benton for championing "visionary plans for squandering the public domain." In July, Benton moved to amend Clay's bill to strike out its distribution features and insert provisions to reduce the land prices. The amendment was lost, in roll calls which revealed most members from the older states of the South voting against price reduction — an ill omen for the fledgling South-and-West alliance. The distribution bill passed the Senate, but the Administration forces were able to get it tabled in the House.

The tariff issue was not settled so readily. In mid-July, 1832, under Clay's adroit supervision, a bill was passed which offered only minor reductions in protective duties. On this bill, Benton and other members from the West broke in turn with the South to vote affirmatively. This new legislation provoked a new defiance in South Carolina. Under the leadership of Calhoun and Hayne, during the Congressional recess, resistance was organized. A state convention proclaimed an ordinance "nullifying" the tariffs of 1828 and 1832. It declared boldly that any attempt to enforce the tariff laws would cause South Carolina to secede from the Union and set up for herself. Thus joined, the issue came before Congress in the session of 1832-1833 — while Calhoun resigned as Vice-President to take a seat in the Senate, the better to fight the tariff battle from the floor. More maneuvering, with Henry Clay emerging in his old role as "Great Pacificator" or compromiser again, produced a new bill. It retained the principle of protection, while effecting a gradual reduction of duties over the years until, in 1842, all duties would stand at a uniform 20 per cent. During the maneuvering and debate, in which an Administration tariff-reduction bill was sidetracked to let Clay's bill by, Benton was unusually inactive and silent. He could see, presumably, that the alliance of South and West he and Hayne had sponsored was doomed; and he found it necessary to re-assess his views concerning the South as represented by Calhoun, Hayne, and their doctrine of state rights in the form of nullification. Meanwhile, it became apparent that the proposal of the erstwhile ultra-protectionist Clay was favored by the nullifiers. Indeed, Clay and Calhoun had conferred and agreed, and a new anti-Jackson alliance of their factions was in the making. With such support, the "Great Pacificator's" tariff passed both houses and became law. Calhoun was listed among the Yeas, while Benton found himself joining with the protectionist and Unionist Webster among the Nays.[19] Thus, the tariff controversy as such was removed from the legislative arena for ten years.

But a related issue still agitated Congress. This was a measure to provide the President with means of coercion to carry out the tariff laws in the face of nullification in South Carolina. Not only to nullifiers, but to many state-rights Jeffersonians as well, the Administration's "Force Bill" seemed to reflect dangerous, Hamiltonian doctrines of "consolidation" and Federal domination. Adhering to Jackson, but still influenced by the long tutelage of such state-rights advocates as Macon and Randolph, Benton was of two minds on the issue — and presumably for this reason did not speak up in the Senate. Privately he confided to Nathaniel Beverly Tucker, a friend of Calhoun's, that he could not concur in some of the doctrines that lay behind the Force Bill. But because the President was "the *only* barrier against the B. U. S.," and "the *best* hope for the reduction of the revenues," he could not "see the policy which should induce *me* to express opinions," or enter the field for state rights, which were "in the Caudine Forks, led there by the madness of S[outh] C[arolina] nullification." On the other hand, he wrote to Martin Van Buren (whose vice-presidential term had not yet begun) urging that gentleman to bring his diplomatic self to Washington to seek an accommodation. The Force Bill contained more, Benton thought, "than the exigency requires, and enables the opposition, upon that *more,* to agitate the whole South, and perhaps unite it . . . the *militia force* part of the bill is what I consider *superfluous.*" Nothing came of this, however, and in late February, 1833, the Force Bill passed the Senate — with Benton, Calhoun, Clay, and several others abstaining.[20] It also passed the House, and was signed by the President. Acceptance of the compromise tariff of 1833 in South Carolina, however, made it unnecessary to carry it into action.

Meanwhile, in the session of 1832-1833, the land and distribution bills came up again. In his message of December, 1832, the President endorsed Benton's long campaign for lower land prices, in the interest of "elevating every cultivator of the soil to the noble and independent rank of a freeholder." Encouraged, Benton, in a full-dress speech which was made into a pamphlet, advocated a new price-reduction bill as an alternative to Clay's distribution plan — which he condemned now as a new part of "the American System," a "junior brother" to high tariffs, internal improvements, and the B. U. S. But Clay had, in advance, made support for a revived distribution bill part of his tariff compromise. Thus, the Benton-Administration bill to reduce land prices was defeated. Soon after, near the end of the session, Clay's distribution bill was passed by both houses. But the President proceeded to kill it with a pocket veto.[21]

Apparently, the new factional alignment had produced a presidential-legislative stalemate. Again, in a later session, and again with Jackson's support, Benton was to press his graduation-donation plan — and again he was to see it lose. Once more also, he was to advocate his old proposal for a constitutional amendment to provide for the popular election of President and Vice-President — and once more, though Jackson in his annual messages repeatedly urged such a measure as demanded by "the first principle of our system, that the majority is to govern," Benton was to suffer defeat. The clear popular majority that had elected Jackson and other Democrats in 1832 was not reflected in a united, effective party majority for an Administration program in Congress. The interest group and factional coalition Clay had forged dominated in the legislative struggle.

[5]

IN 1832, BENTON was fifty. Mature, established, formed, his work in the Bank war had brought him enlarged national prominence. Long before the days of officially designated floor leaders, he was accepted as the head of the Administration forces in the Senate, or (as a pinochle-minded friend put it) "the right bower of General Jackson's administration." In this brilliant stage of his career, he was much commented on, so that gradually a composite portrait of him was taking shape in the national consciousness.

As a personality: "Of commanding talent, untiring application, industry unequalled, and energy unmatched," according to a friendly journalist, "with an honesty of intention and purpose such as seldom man can justly lay claim to."

As a publicist: He knew well how to translate the ideas of great political thinkers into a dialect which the multitude could understand: "they read his words and comprehended their meaning."

As orator, through the eyes of a hostile journalist: "Imagine the gallant Colonel, who weighs 200 pounds, to thunder [his speeches] in a roaring voice — with uplifted arm — and a terrible dash of newspapers and documents on his table. . . . Colonel Benton has read a good deal; but his mind is like a baggage wagon, full of all kinds of lumber. . . . His imagination is a sort of Cyclops' great sledge hammer, heavy, weighty, crushing, iron-wrought." But a friendly journalist found his style "trenchant and elevated," and his "facts generally impregnable."

As an egotist: "Naturally vain and satisfied of his own superiority." The "flattering attentions" often paid to him by the public and in the pro-Jackson press, one contemporary observed, "were well calculated to increase his confidence in his own powers."

As a believer: "A sincere Christian."

As a target: Second only to the President, according to Roger Taney, as an object of abuse in "anonymous publicity," spawned by the B. U. S., "containing the grossest and coarsest libels."

As a husband: Married to a gentlewoman who sometimes surprised fashionable society by her scruples, for example, not receiving visitors on the Sabbath. Once Nathaniel Macon named her with Martha Washington as among the few ladies he had known not altered by residence at the capital.

As a parent: A loving father who enjoyed the companionship of his children, and who in turn was loved by them with a warmth often lacking in the formal households of the day.[22]

As the "right bower" of the Administration, Benton grew increasingly close to Jackson personally. By the time the Bank war had reached its peak in the spring of 1832, they could joke about old quarrels. For some time the bullet that had been lodged in Jackson's arm in his brawl with Jesse and Thomas Benton in 1813 had been disturbing the old man, and physicians decided it should be removed. The President bared his arm and took a strong grip on his walking stick. An incision was made, and in a few minutes the offending piece of lead was taken from his flesh. A tale circulated in Washington that Francis Blair, of the

Globe, secured the bullet and offered it to Benton, who declined it, remarking that "twenty years' peaceable possession" gave Jackson title
to it under common law.

"Only nineteen years," Blair amended.

"Oh, well," Benton replied, "in consideration of the extra care he had
taken of it — keeping it constantly about his person, and so on — I'll
waive the odd year!"

The friendship between Benton and Jackson was marked by the affection the President expressed for Benton's daughter Jessie Ann. Fair, gay,
almost nine when Jackson was inaugurated for his second term in March,
1833, Jessie Ann went more and more with her father to visit the
stern-visaged but friendly "Old Hero" at the Executive Mansion. She
knew she must not fidget, even when Jackson kept his hand on her
head during the political talk and absently twisted his fingers a little
too tightly in her curls.[23]

Meanwhile, Thomas himself was happily absorbed with his family. He
watched Elizabeth's always precarious health carefully, and was pleased
when the chance of getting the "ladies cabin entirely to ourselves" on a
river boat to St. Louis brought a marked improvement in his wife's
health and spirits. He was pleased when, in June, 1831, Elizabeth was
safely delivered of her fifth child, a second son, who was christened
James McDowell Benton after the master of Cherry Grove, his maternal
grandfather; and pleased again when, not quite two years later, a fourth
daughter was born, who was named Susan, a name common to both the
Benton and McDowell families. He enjoyed the notes his elder daughters
scrawled on a letter he wrote from St. Louis to Elizabeth's mother at
Cherry Grove. (From Eliza, then nine: "We went to a french school
yesterday and took little sarah with us. Mr. Levaring sais that we have
improved." From Jessie Ann, then seven: "i want to see you very bad
and i wish you would come here.") Nor was Thomas's interest confined to his immediate family. Busy as he was with the Bank war in the
early months of 1832, he readily agreed to undertake a regular correspondence with his "dear favorite niece" in Virginia, Sally Campbell
Preston McDowell. "I do it most joyfully," he wrote the precocious,
effervescent child, "and will expect often to hear."[24] The august Thomas
and the sprightly Sally developed a warm affection which was finally
tried by tragedy.

Torn between the excitements of politics and the pleasures of home
life, Thomas thought of retiring from the Senate. His personal (finan-

cial) interest and the growing state of his family prompted this inclination, he wrote Finis Ewing in the fall of 1831, "and if I can get enough of
the Graduation Bill passed this winter as will accomplish my great object, I shall then be for claiming my discharge." On the eve of the
second battle of the Bank war, early in 1832, he wrote Lieutenant
Governor Dunklin in Missouri: "My seat here has but few attractions
for me. *I am ready to retire.*" [25] Apparently, however, the protracted
Bank war determined him to stay at his post. As he became engrossed
in issue after issue, he never did retire.

At the end of 1832, Benton's new prominence was marked by the
Philanthropic Society at the University of North Carolina. The "Phi" requested a contribution, and Benton replied that it would "give me great
pleasure to contribute, according to my means . . . say about $20." He
wished "the young gentlemen of the Society every prosperity." [26] The
man who was reported to have cried, "I am leaving here now, but damn
you, you will hear from me again!" was sought after by the very organization that had presided at his downfall.*

The next year Benton lost a dear friend — John Randolph. Though
Benton knew Randolph's faults as well as his virtues, his affection for
the "political meteor" of his day never wavered, and he was deeply
distressed by Randolph's death. The owner of an "immense" estate,
estimated by the press at nearly a million dollars, Randolph had written
several wills and codicils, in one of which he bequeathed Benton a tract
of 600 acres on the Little Roanoke and a brace of fancy pistols. After
long litigation, however, in which Benton was a witness, an earlier will
was validated by which Randolph left the bulk of his property to his
kin, while manumitting and providing for his Negro slaves. At his death,
Randolph also left a paper with the caption, "A List of My Principal
Friends." Among the first was the name of Thomas Benton.[27]

[6]

FROM MARCH THROUGH NOVEMBER, 1833, Benton enjoyed a brief
respite from active politics — though he attended carefully to the political events that went on about him. These months he spent with his

---

* The facts here contrast sharply with campus tradition at Chapel Hill. According to this tale Benton, solicited, wrote that he had the letter from the "Phi" in
front of him as he sat in his bathroom — and that immediately after reading it,
he had it behind him.

family — at Cherry Grove; in a long spring visit to New Orleans, where, at a grand dinner in his honor, he spoke enthusiastically of the charm of the city, its people, its buildings and streets, its levee, and the magnificent steamboats on the river; at St. Louis; and again at Cherry Grove.

In St. Louis, Benton was a guest at a July 4 celebration at Jefferson Barracks. To a toast in his honor by one of the officers of the post, he responded fulsomely: "THE OFFICERS OF THE AMERICAN ARMY: *They have proved that citizen and soldier are not incompatible, and that arms and letters may be united.*"

During the Benton family's stay in Missouri, a cholera epidemic swept the state. Raging through almost helpless towns and counties until it finally disappeared, the disease carried off the two young children of Benton's friend Luke Lawless in St. Louis, and also struck down Senator Alexander Buckner at his Cape Girardeau County home. The Benton family escaped unharmed — and, ironically, Benton profited politically from the epidemic. To fill Buckner's place in the Senate, Governor Dunklin named Lewis Linn of Ste. Genevieve. He was "an 'original' Jacksonian," as the *Republican* put it, and he had praised his personal and political friend Benton as the only Missourian "whose splendid talents, unwavering purpose of Soul, and expanded views entitled him to the Character of a great Man," who would probably be *President* one day. At last, the cholera and an appointment had given Benton what elections had failed to provide — a strong home-state ally in the Senate.

Another summer political development was not so favorable to Benton. Under the census of 1830, Missouri was entitled to a second Representative, and three men carrying the Jackson banner announced for the place. It was suggested that Benton play umpire as he had done in 1828, and decide between the two leading Democrats, George Strother and George Shannon. But Strother huffily declined to submit to umpirage. Thus, Benton remarked, the issue was "put beyond calculation" — "this election may have the effect of inducing the Jackson party to take effective measures, and that without the consent of volunteer candidates, to concentrate the vote of the party hereafter." The need remained, in Benton's view, for stronger formal and effective party machinery to promote party action and party discipline. The immediate result of the lack of such organization was a narrow victory for the National Republican candidate, one John Bull.[28]

At Cherry Grove again for the late summer and fall, Benton heard momentous news from Washington. The B. U. S. charter still had three years to run, and Jackson feared that the Bank and its political allies might use those years to reverse the decision of 1832. To counter this threat, he undertook a simple protective maneuver — *removing the government deposits from the Bank.* When Louis McLane and then William J. Duane at the Treasury balked at carrying out this decision, Jackson removed *them* to make way for Roger B. Taney as a Secretary who was willing. The order went out in September, 1833 — and the lines were drawn for the fifth battle in the Bank war. When Benton heard of Jackson's new order, he was deeply stirred — it was a master stroke, "high and daring, and requiring as much nerve as any enterprise of arms." [29]

The new battle in the Bank war was fought out in the Congress of 1833-1834. As the warriors gathered at the capital in November and December, the visiting Irish actor Tyrone Power met and described some of them with impartial, friendly respect.* The President, Jackson, on horseback: "A fine, soldierly, well preserved old gentleman, with a pale wrinkled countenance, and a keen clear eye, restless and searching." The newly elected Vice-President, Van Buren, presiding attentively over the Senate: "Cool, courteous; with a tone quiet but persuasive, a voice low-pitched but singularly effective." The opposition leader, Clay: An impression "all in Mr. Clay's favor," and "confirmatory of the *bonhommie* and playful humor ascribed to him." But the capital was still a village, with streets "all but impassable," even though the avenue from the Capitol to the Executive Mansion "had recently been redeemed from the mud according to the plans of M'Adam [macadamized]." [30]

As Jackson had feared, Biddle began to fight back, launching both economic and political counterattacks. The Bank made sharp reductions in loans, discounts, and note circulation, until even Hezekiah Niles had to admit in his pro-Bank *Register* that he had "never seen or felt anything like the present [financial] pressure." Some curtailment could be justified on the grounds that the B. U. S. had to wind up its affairs. But Benton and other Jackson leaders accused Biddle and the Bank of deliberately fomenting a panic-producing contraction for political and propaganda effect — "the pressure was made to fall upon the business community . . . so as to throw as many laboring people as possible out

---

* This Tyrone Power (1797-1841), who specialized in comedy, had a grandson named Tyrone Power (1869-1931) who lived in the United States and specialized in heroic roles as leading man to Julia Marlowe and Mrs. Fiske, and a great-grandson named Tyrone Power (1914-   ), who won popularity in moving pictures.

of employment." Privately, Biddle remarked that "nothing but the evidence of suffering abroad will produce any effect in Congress." Soon "distress memorials" began to flood the Senate. Benton noted sarcastically that consideration of these pre-planned, prefabricated "lugubrious document[s]" became "a regular morning service." The "services" generally concluded with demands for restoration of the deposits or recharter of the Bank. At the same time, delegations of businessmen from New York, Philadelphia, Boston, came to plead with the President. The steely old man adopted a stock reply, designed to turn the onus on the Bank and its chieftain. "Go to Nicholas Biddle," Jackson reiterated — "we have no money here, gentlemen; Biddle has all the money." In the Senate, Benton declared that as in mythology the frightful appearance of Pan could "scare an army out of its senses," so these frightful memorials were designed to scare Congress. After Pan, "Panic" might well be "the name of this Congress."

Pressing to the attack, Clay injected a new issue into the controversy. He offered a resolution condemning the President's removal of the deposits as an unwarranted use of executive authority, in a way "dangerous to the liberties of the people." In a dramatic, three-day speech, he cried out against this alleged "concentration of all power in the hands of one man," the President. Thus Clay sought to divert the issue from *economic* policy to *political* liberty, by raising the new slogan of *"executive despotism."* In this effort, Clay was joined by Calhoun, still smarting from the tariff and Force Bill controversies — and another band was forged in the developing anti-Jackson coalition. The Clay-Calhoun attack was met by Benton, who undertook in a *four*-day speech to justify Jackson's action and restore the Bank as the great threat to the "property and liberty of the American people." By March, 1834, Clay was able to win acceptance of an amended version of his resolution of censure. Pressing to the advantage, he offered another resolution calling for the return of the deposits to the B. U. S., and again he was able to push it through despite vigorous opposition from Benton and other anti-Bank stalwarts. In the House, however, the Jackson leader James K. Polk was able to carry a counterresolution to legalize the deposit of government funds in various state banks. This stalemate left the disposition of the deposits effectively to the President's discretion.[31] The Senate's censure resolution still stood, however. Meanwhile, with redoubled fury, the anti-Jackson press trumpeted the cry of "executive despotism" throughout the land.

In June, 1834, the "Panic" session took a curious turn. Seeking always to dramatize the "distress," Clay had won adoption of another resolution calling on the Treasury for a report on the nation's finances. In mid-June Roger Taney submitted the report. His investigations had revealed (perhaps a little to his own surprise) that the nation as a whole was relatively prosperous. Before the report was submitted, Taney called Benton to his office, and the two men made plans to dramatize *this* point as Clay had hoped to dramatize *his* point. When the reading of the report was begun, and as soon as its drift was clear, Webster hastily moved to dispense with the reading and refer the matter to his Committee on Finance. At this, Benton rose magisterially to demand that the report be read through. When this was done, he launched into a long, hammering, prepared speech. He proclaimed that the "alarm operators" had dug a pit for Taney, only to fall into that pit themselves. There had been some *"commercial* distress," he agreed, brought about by "the screw and pressure operations of the Bank," but the general level of economic activity was high. Now "the game [was] up," for Taney's report "had expelled forever the ghost of alarm from the chamber." The Taney-Benton dramatization was hailed by the pro-Jackson press. The Maine *Journal* thought the Senator "in himself a host . . . as formidable as the Macedonian phalanx," while the *Pennsylvanian* called his speech "the requiem of panic-ism." A New York partisan printed a broadside containing key passages from the address, adorned with a border like a fancy picture frame — the document was "worthy of a place on the walls [!] of our homes." A grandiose title was supplied, "Mr. Benton's Wind-Up of the Bank." [32] The fifth battle in the Bank war had ended in another, and practically final, victory for the anti-Bank forces.*

Still, the triumph was only partial. The leaders of the popular democratic movement, like Jackson and Benton, had taken no effective measures to institutionalize the doctrine of majority rule, to give it effect in party and governmental structure. Through the years the "Democrats *in principle,"* like Jackson and Benton, found their energies more and more used up in bitter struggles between the organs of government — Congress against President, Senate against House, and so on. [33] This conflict was symbolized in June, 1834, when Jackson nominated Roger Taney,

* By fall the financial panic itself had come to an end. Even the dogged Nicholas Biddle could not prolong the "pressure" indefinitely, particularly when he found himself losing the support of key leaders in the business communities of New York, Boston, and other cities. In September, the Bank embarked once again on a policy of *expansion,* greatly extending its credit in various forms.

who had been serving under a recess appointment, for a regular appointment as Secretary of the Treasury. Despite Jackson's prestige and Benton's efforts, the Senate rejected the nomination. The post went by default to the mild, noncontroversial Levi Woodbury.

During the "panic" battles Benton had launched a counterattack of his own. He feared note-issuing *state* banks as much as he feared the note-issuing *national* Bank, and he saw the deposit of the government funds in the state banks as only "a halfway house" on the road to a sound financial system. This, in Benton's view, would be a system founded on a universal, specie, gold and silver currency — in short, *hard money*. This was the system he had suggested in his first great attack on the B. U. S. in February, 1831; and in 1834 he moved to give it effect. In a probing, carefully organized, two-day speech, he outlined the hard-money doctrine. He maintained that the Constitution provided for specie currency only. He called for action by both the national and the state governments to make gold and silver "the common currency of the people." He was willing to accept "large bank notes and bills of exchange," on a sound specie foundation, for large commercial transactions, but "the bank note circulation below twenty dollars ought to be suppressed." He argued that the value set on gold by law was too low, and that in consequence the "yeomanry of this America" had been deprived of a gold currency for twenty years. He urged a revaluation of gold, as another way to "keep down small notes" — for "the farmer, the artisan, the market man, the day laborer," would refuse bank paper if they could get "guineas, eagles, half-eagles, doubloons, and half joes." Under the paper system, "if a bank stops payment, the holders of the small notes, who are usually the working part of the community, are the last to find it out, and the first to suffer." By the "restoration of the gold currency," these "evils of a small paper circulation" could be avoided.

Once again, Benton had stood forth as the advocate of a bold new program. Once again, he had aimed his appeals at the nation's farmers, workingmen, masses. The hard-money slogan was to be a rallying cry for radical Democrats in the nation and in the states for years to come. The President approved, Taney approved, and Blair in the *Globe* publicized Benton's argument and praised it fulsomely as "the most important speech on the currency which has ever been pronounced in Congress." State-banking, business-minded "Democrats *by trade*" felt differently, of course, and they were soon to raise a powerful opposition.

The immediate consequence of Benton's advocacy was legislation to revalue gold. The old law had required that a silver dollar weigh fifteen times as much as a gold dollar, while by Benton's proposal the ratio was fixed at sixteen to one. This new ratio established a practical bimetallic standard for years to come. In the Senate, this mild measure won broad support, including Calhoun, and even Daniel Webster, while in the House James K. Polk was able to drive the legislation to easy passage.

The effects of the coinage legislation of June, 1834, were quickly felt. During the summer, the *Globe* was able to announce that "Dr. Benton's yellow lozenges," in the shape of five-dollar pieces, had made their appearance at the Philadelphia mint — "they are about the size of twenty-five cent pieces, but a *leetle yallerer.*" The President himself declared that the "gold bill" had done more for the nation's economy, "by rousing the people to a sense of their own prosperity," than all other legislation since the Constitution — Benton, and Polk, deserved "golden medals" for their work. In fact, Benton's sponsorship of hard money was soon to win him a nickname he would wear proudly in years to come — "Old Bullion." But friends of the paper system, hoping to bring the gold system into disrepute, distributed burlesques in brass or copper, "with grotesque figures," Benton noted, "and ludicrous inscriptions — the 'whole hog' and the 'better currency.' " To match the name "Old Bullion," the sobriquet "Gold Humbug" was created. But "the instinctive feeling of the masses!" — as Benton saw it — finally carried the day for the new currency.[34]

In the Senate meanwhile, Benton had launched another counterattack — this time at the "executive despotism" cry. On the last day of the session, he introduced a proposal to "expunge" from the record Clay's resolution censuring Jackson for removing the deposits. In the next several years, this "Expunging Resolution" was to be the focus of the continuing conflict between Jackson and anti-Jackson partisans.

At the end of June, 1834, the "Panic" session adjourned. As a result of his work during the session, Benton's prestige had risen even further. Across the Union, Democratic papers praised him as "the lion of the West," or "the Ajax Telemon of the Constitution" — "May he be the President of the United States." In Richmond, Virginia, the sober, influential *Enquirer* declared that one might admire "the fascinating eloquence of Clay, the profound logic of Webster, the brilliant imagination and metaphysical graces of Calhoun," but for "clear comprehension," for "efficient and triumphant reasoning," Benton stood above all. However much Webster might "curl his lip at Benton as he speaks," Old Bullion "had gallantly born away the palms of victory from the allied champions of the opposition."

During July, Benton's rising stature was marked at Philadelphia and at Baltimore. On Independence Day, he was an honor guest at Democratic rallies in the Pennsylvania city. At an elaborate noonday dinner at McArran's Gardens, an overflow crowd seated at tables under trees festooned with flags cheered a toast to "the faithful, the fearless, the generous, and the indefatigable Senator." That evening at Southwark Hall Benton was again lauded — "He has routed the whole host of paper money manufacturers, and rescued the golden coin of our fathers from the grasp of the speculator." Near the end of the month, at Baltimore, he was orator of the day at a dinner of more than 1500 people at the Columbian Gardens to honor Maryland's native son, Roger Taney. In the midst of Benton's speech praising Taney and defending the specie currency, lightning flashed, the wind carried away the awnings over the tables and blew trees down, and gusts of rain began to sweep through the gardens. It was fortunate that this was not "a BANK PAPER meeting," Benton remarked, "for such might have been DISSOLVED," whereas "the METALLIC party" was "not likely to melt under a shower." By the time Benton had finished his remarks, however, the guests were forced to retire to nearby taverns.

The fall brought a final mark of respect. A Democratic convention in Mississippi, looking toward the elections of 1836, unanimously nominated Van Buren for President and Benton for Vice-President. In a long letter to the convention officers, Benton declined the honor. He praised his friend Van Buren, and predicted that victory could be won in 1836 by *unity* of "the productive, and burthen-bearing classes," which he listed as "planters, farmers, laborers, mechanics (with a slight infusion from the commercial and professional interests)." But this admirably "disinterested" letter, as the *Globe* called it, did not remove Benton's name from speculation. Rumor soon had it that he was in any case in line for the Presidency, as part of a program of the inner Jackson circle — "Andrew Jackson, eight years; Martin Van Buren, eight years; Thomas H. Benton, eight years." [35]

Whoever the candidates in 1836 were to be, they would face a vigorous opposition. By the fall of 1834, the anti-Jackson coalition had

reached the stage where it raised a new party banner, inscribed "Whig."
Looking upon the President as "King Andrew," his enemies took the
party name the, adversaries of the English autocrats had used. Pro-
tariff, Henry Clay National Republicans in the North, and some dissident Democrats, joined somehow with anti-tariff, state rights, and even
John Calhoun nullifiers in the South, to constitute this new Whig party.
The cohesive element in the combination was opposition to Jackson, expressed in the slogan "executive despotism." [36]

Unconcerned for the moment with such events, Thomas spent the
summer and fall in the East with his family. Much of the time they
stayed at Cherry Grove, but an illness Elizabeth and some of the
children suffered led Thomas to take the whole family to the White
Sulphur Springs in far western Virginia for parts of August and September. At the mountain resort, they enjoyed a peaceful interlude together.[37]

[7]

IN THE SHORT SESSION OF 1834-1835, Benton became entangled in
another personal encounter — this time not with Clay, but with Calhoun.

The precipitating issue was the role of the executive again. As Benton
in 1826 had attacked Adams for misuse of the executive's patronage
powers, Calhoun now attacked Jackson on the same grounds. Now Benton not only defended the Administration, but insisted vehemently that
Calhoun had misrepresented the situation in the interest of factional, or
Whig-partisan, politics.* The encounter occasioned widespread comment.
The deaf, spinsterish, waspish English traveler, Harriet Martineau, had
already marked Benton as "a temporary people's man, remarkable
chiefly for his pomposity" — "swelling amidst his piles of papers and
books," he looked "like a being designed by nature to be a good-
humored barber[!], but forced by fate to make himself into a mock-
heroic senator." Now Miss Martineau noted that the "fantastic senator"
had made a personal attack on the noble Calhoun, "which would have
been insufferable if it had not been too absurdly worded to be easily

---

* The year before, Hezekiah Niles had noted in his *Register* (May 10, 1834,
173) that "several of the newspapers are *wickedly* republishing Mr. *Benton's*
famous speech" of 1826, on the "powers, patronage, privileges" of the executive.
The *Register* referred its readers to the speech in its files for "a hearty and long
laugh."

made anything of [*sic*]." The New York merchant, speculator, and Whig politico, Philip Hone, in Washington at the time, recorded that "the fiercest tiger in the den" of Democracy, Benton, had "insulted" Calhoun. Rumor said Calhoun would challenge Benton — "but it cannot be . . . I would as soon think of challenging one of the hyenas of the zoological institution for snapping at me as I passed." [38] There was, of course, no duel, and the episode ended in words.

The Democracy, meantime, was jubilant at another triumph. In his message to Congress, Jackson announced that at last the public debt was paid. For the first time in its history, the Republic was free of debt and debt-charges — though it was not for long. Here was another blow to the American System. Hamilton, and his disciples like Clay and Webster, had seen the debt as a binding tie in the marriage of wealth and government, while Jefferson, and his disciples like Jackson and Benton, had made abolition of the debt a cardinal policy. On January 8, 1835, the anniversary of Jackson's military victory at New Orleans twenty years before, a banquet was held at Brown's Hotel to celebrate the extinction of the debt — with Thomas Benton "President-of-the-Day." When the cloth was removed, Benton made a brief, exulting speech, which was followed by innumerable toasts.[39] All told, it was a magnificent occasion for the Jackson men.

CHAPTER 10

Old Bullion

1835 - 1837

TO CONSERVATIVE JACKSON MEN, victory over the Bank of the United States was a consummation. To Benton and other radicals, it was only a beginning. Ever courageous, and increasingly consistent in the application of his agrarian doctrine, Benton insisted that the fight be carried on — to the total overthrow of the small-bank-note, paper system, to the total triumph of the gold-and-silver, sound-money cause. Here was a new war declared, and it brought a new division in Democratic ranks.

As he traveled west via New Orleans in the spring of 1835, Old Bullion could ponder omens of the new party split. In New York Governor Marcy, drawn by marriage more and more into the business community, shied from the hard-money program. Old Tennessee friends of Jackson's, like Speaker John Bell and the former president of the Bank of Tennessee Hugh Lawson White, broke the traces. In state after state, men began to line up as "Hards" or "Softs" on the currency question. The Hards were increasingly led by agrarian partisans, while the Softs were chiefly "Democrats by trade" whose concern had always been to enlarge economic and business opportunity. In addition, the reformist, self-styled workingmen's associations in several Eastern cities swung solidly behind the hard-money policies. In New York City, the labor-Democratic-hard-money movement got the name "Locofoco" — which became a general symbol for Democratic radicalism.* The labor reformers argued that wage earners were regularly cheated by receiving wages in paper issues

---

* The origin of the term "Locofoco" is interesting. At a meeting in October, 1835, which one account called a "GRAND ROW — AT TAMMANY HALL, NEW YORK" (*Niles Weekly Register,* XLIX [November 7, 1835], 163), the conservatives or Tammany "regulars" tried to quell a radical "revolt" by turning off the gas lights in the hall. But the radicals were prepared. Having brought supplies of the new-fangled friction or "locofoco" matches with them, they supplied their own illumination — lighting up candles, or sperm-lights, which they had cached behind a transparency of Andrew Jackson in the hall. Like the term "Quaker," the label "Locofoco" was originally applied sarcastically, and then worn proudly.

— depreciating, counterfeit, or worthless as they often were. A specie currency was the way out.[1]

The political situation was further complicated by a divide-and-conquer strategy the Whigs were developing. In the coming presidential election, several candidates were to be sent into the arena — Daniel Webster to appeal to New England voters; the Hero of Tippecanoe, old William Henry Harrison, to appeal to the Clay men, and to the masses in the West; and Hugh L. White to appeal to disgruntled Democrats, and to the Southwest. A Democratic convention, meanwhile, had nominated Martin Van Buren to run against the Whig field.

On his way West, Benton warned against the new Whig strategy. In a public letter declining an invitation to a proposed meeting in his honor at Louisville, he declared that the B. U. S., thwarted in Congress, was still acting an "efficient and dangerous part in our politics." It and its allies worked "to bring the next presidential election into the House of Representatives." From Louisville, Thomas and his family went downriver to New Orleans. He liked the city, and he was apparently still interested in the possibility of settling at the delta — "my professional prospects here," he wrote a Missouri friend, "are as flattering as I could reasonably ask." His several-weeks stay was punctuated with pronouncements on public affairs, including a statement of what he saw as the great issues before the country— "the small bank-note currency, which is not yet put down . . . the gold and silver currency, which is not yet sufficiently established . . . the expunging resolution, which is not yet carried" . . . the graduation-donation issue — and the threat that the presidential election might again be thrown into "the intriguing and bargaining forum of the House." [2]

Meanwhile Benton was the subject of a new rumor. Gossip had it that Jackson would appoint him Chief Justice of the Supreme Court, whenever the aging, ailing John Marshall should retire or die. To his friend Van Buren, Benton expressed himself earthily concerning Whig rumors to this effect — "these fellows are no more able to comprehend me than old hack lawyers, according to Burke, are able to comprehend the policy of an empire, and that was no more than a rabbit, which breeds twelve times a year, could comprehend the gestation of an elephant, which carries two years. . . . Dying for small honors themselves, they cannot understand that I can refuse all, even the Chief Justiceship." His favorite for Chief Justice was Roger Taney.[3] When John Marshall did die a month later, Taney got the place.

In late June, Thomas and his family went on to St. Louis. There Benton broke his custom, to accept an invitation to a grand public dinner in his honor, held at the National Hotel in mid-July. He seized the occasion for an expansive speech which served at once as a keynote and as propaganda for the agrarian radicalism he had espoused. At the outset, he summarized the Bank war, and the character of the anti-Jackson coalition. Now, he trumpeted, the war must be carried on against the *state* banks, against *all* "chartered monopolies and exclusive privileges." Under "the paper system," and the interest payments and other charges it exacted, the productive classes were "taxed" some twenty million dollars a year. The answer? — "the GOLD CURRENCY," which would be "the pride and glory of Jackson's administration." In this war, despite the going confusion of parties, factions, and candidates, there were fundamentally and effectively "but two parties; there never has been but two parties; all the rest are modifications of these two." The foundation of parties was "in the radical question, whether PEOPLE, or PROPERTY, shall govern"; whether there should be democracy, "a government by the people — *demos* (the people), *krateo,* to govern," or aristocracy, "a government of the rich — *aristoi* (property, or the rich), *krateo,* to govern." In the coming presidential election, the issue would be "literally and truly a question between PEOPLE and PROPERTY! between MEN on the one side and MONEY on the other!" While he spoke to the diners at the National Hotel, Benton aimed his broadside at a national audience. He had selected his issue with attention to the predispositions of his public, presented it with dramatic simplicity, and driven it home with hammering repetition. The speech was reprinted in full by a pro-Benton paper that had been established in St. Louis that spring, the *Missouri Argus,* and picked up by *Niles Register* and other national publications.[4]

In Missouri, meanwhile, the divided Democrats faced another Congressional election. Three candidates claimed the Jackson label for the two places to be filled — the incumbent William Ashley, Albert G. Harrison, and George F. Strother. In issue after issue of the *Argus,* the editor, Abel Rathbone Corbin, attacked Representative Ashley. Was he not "for White, and against Van Buren?" — had he not opposed the "noble" Benton's graduation plan? — had he not voted against the gold bill? But victory went to Ashley and Harrison, and once again Missouri's delegation would be divided.

The Saturday before the election, August 1, saw an acrimonious quarrel between Benton and Strother. About five in the afternoon, Benton

and his friend Editor Corbin were sitting on the porch of Benton's Laurel
Street home, when they saw George Strother and William Millburn com-
ing up the street. Benton rose, walked to the end of the porch, and said:
  "Good evening, *Major Millburn.*"
  At this, both Millburn *and* Strother bowed to Thomas Benton, who
called to Strother in a torrent of rage:
  "Don't bow to me, sir; you damned traitor, don't bow to me. Gentle-
men" — to Corbin and Millburn — "take notice that I order him never
to bow to me again . . . You damned traitor, go home . . . Major
Millburn, walk in."
  In the house, Benton regained his composure almost in a minute —
but he declared that he would not vote for Strother, who could not be
in Washington a single night before he would be in communication with
Calhoun, with the pro-Calhoun editor Duff Green, and with Clay.
  The result of this interview was a challenge, which Benton loftily
declined — whereupon Strother proclaimed his intention to shoot the
Senator on sight! The matter was gleefully publicized by the opposition press — Hezekiah Niles, for example, remarked without tears that
one or both of the antagonists might be killed.[5]
  Meanwhile, death did strike other members of the Benton family. For
weeks Thomas and Elizabeth had watched little McDowell Benton suffer
a protracted illness, and finally on August 3 — the day Colonel Strother
wrote his challenge — the boy died, aged four years and two months.
Six weeks later Elizabeth's father James McDowell died at Cherry
Grove in Virginia. The tall, handsome, gracious planter, about whose
home so much of Thomas Benton's and Elizabeth McDowell's life had
centered, was no more. He left no will, and his estate (which included
twenty-seven slaves and a library of twelve hundred books) had to be
settled by his heirs.[6]
  In early November, 1835, Thomas, Elizabeth, and their children left
St. Louis for Washington. At town after town on the way, from Cincinnati to Pittsburgh and Harrisburg and Philadelphia, Old Bullion was
greeted with fanfare and invitations to public dinners. Always he declined, always in long manifesto-letters in which he reiterated the new
issues of the day as he saw them. From Pittsburgh to Philadelphia,
the Bentons went by way of the new Pennsylvania canal system. Along
it they traveled wide-eyed, passing through a tunnel twenty-nine hundred feet long, and crossing five mountain ridges by inclined plane.
The Colonel was amazed by the "magnificent works, which permit us

to go day and night without loss of sleep or rest — which enable us to
ascend mountains without fatigue — pass rocks without a jolt — go
through where we cannot go *over*." Ever admiring of progress, Benton
perhaps did not realize that the Pennsylvania canal system was a portent
of the technological genius that was to remake America, taking it far
from the agrarian society he praised as he traveled.

At Washington he took rooms, this time at Dawson's Number One
on Capitol Hill. There a newly elected Congressman from Maine who
was to become Benton's fast friend, John Fairfield, saw Old Bullion
early in December — and, Fairfield wrote his wife, "would have been
right glad to become his messmate," but the house was old and "cracky,"
and the furniture in keeping, and the fastidious Fairfield "couldn't go
that." [7]

[2]

AS A LEGISLATOR, and as an advocate before the bar, of national public
opinion, Benton fought through the first half of 1836 for his hard-
money program. He knew that both national and state action would be
necessary to give it effect.

Taking the lead for national action, Benton offered a "Specie Resolution" in the Senate. This provided simply that after a certain date, "nothing but gold and silver coin ought to be received [by the Treasury]
in payment for public lands." In the two-and-a-half years since the government deposits had been removed from the B. U. S., a speculative land
boom had developed. As the Federal monies were placed with state
banks, the number of these banks increased until, in 1836, more than
seven hundred such concerns were operating — a disproportionate share
of them in the West. The multiplying banks in turn multiplied their
note circulation, against which speculators borrowed to purchase ever-
larger quantities of land — and again, this activity was particularly rife
in the West. From 1833 to 1836, the total of Federal land sales increased
five times, from about five million to more than twenty-five million dollars. The phrase, "doing a land office business," became a symbol of the
day. In every section, the price of commodities rose. The get-ahead, ambitious, speculating impulse that characterized so many capitalists and
proto-capitalist farmers was driving more and more Americans to adventures in land or trade. As a Western man, Benton could "inform the
Senate" how it was that sales of the public lands had "run up" so —

"speculators went to banks, borrowed five, ten, twenty, fifty thousand dollars in paper, in small notes"; then, "loaded with paper," these speculators "would outbid settlers and cultivators, who had no undue accommodations from banks." Requiring specie payments for the lands "would stop the flood of paper" into the public-land states, and help "the settler and cultivator who wished to purchase land," by relieving him from the competition of "fictitious and borrowed capital." In Congress, Benton won little support. Only a few friends and firm radicals like Lewis Linn of Missouri and Silas Wright of New York stood by the hard-money advocate. Opposition was led by the redoubtable Webster, whose attack on the "visionary project" may have been decisive in defeating it.[8]

Undaunted, Old Bullion counterattacked on another front. Developing a comprehensive economic and social argument, he advocated a Fabian program for the realization of a total hard-money system. A stable currency would provide a stable economy, hostile to speculation and restrictive to large Enterprise, but favorable to "farmers, laborers, and market people" who bore the "burthens and losses of the paper system" — in brief, to Arcadia. This agrarian alternative to the American System could be realized by regulating the receipt of bank notes by *any* national government agency —

> Of less than $20, none after March 3, 1837,
> Of less than $50, none after March 3, 1838,
> Of less than $100, none after March 3, 1839,
> Of less than $500, none after March 3, 1840,
> Of less than $1000, none after March 3, 1842,
> And no paper at all after March 3, 1942!

Again, no legislation was forthcoming. But on the cover of a pamphlet reprint of Benton's speech advocating his hard-money program, Jackson wrote: "This to be carefully preserved — it is the true principle . . . by which . . . the labours of the people can be protected from the curse of a paper currency." [9] In concrete, dramatic terms, the issue had been posed.

After Congress adjourned, Benton pressed the question again. He proposed that Jackson should establish by executive order what Congress had refused to establish by legislation — that nothing but specie should be received in payment for the public lands. The President, Benton recalled, "summoned his cabinet — laid the case before them — heard the majority of adverse opinions — and directed the order to issue." During the cabinet meeting, Benton was in an outer office, and the President's secretary Andrew Jackson Donelson came to him and asked him to draw a draft of the order, which was "carried back to the council — put into official form — signed — issued." The document became famous as Jackson's "specie circular" or "specie order." * This order, Benton remembered, "made an immediate sensation." The President's bold, solitary action was reminiscent of his decision to remove the deposits from the B. U. S., and once again the "Congress was considered insulted, the cabinet defied, the banks disgraced," while "disappointed speculators raged." The order also brought a factional show-down on the hard-money question. Conservatives like Senator Tallmadge of New York, and Senator Rives and Thomas Ritchie of the *Enquirer* in Virginia, cried out against "Benton and Co." and the "Gold Humbug," and stepped forth as leaders of a definite paper-money, state-banking faction in the Democratic party.[10]

A combination of conservative Democrats and Whigs pressed, in the Congressional session of 1836-1837, a bill to rescind the specie order. It was passed, despite a plea from Old Bullion, who foretold a "revulsion" or depression like that of 1819 unless the speculative boom were checked, and offered a self-conscious, melodramatic peroration — "I am one of those who promised gold, not paper. I promised the currency of the constitution, not the currency of corporations. I did not join in putting down the Bank of the United States, to put up a wilderness of local banks. . . . I did not strike Caesar to make Antony master of Rome." But the radicals still had their champion in the Executive Mansion. The unyielding Jackson gave the bill a pocket veto, and thereby saved the specie order.

Meanwhile, in 1836, Benton had been busy as an advocate of state action for the hard-money program. In January, for example, he wrote to a Democratic convention in Ohio, condemning the increasing tendency for state legislatures to charter banking corporations. If all paper money under twenty dollars were suppressed — "I had far rather say one hundred, but . . . the public mind is not yet sufficiently matured for complete remedies" — the gold and silver currency might be built up in the next two years until it reached one hundred million. The state legislatures could accomplish the suppression of small notes, by *taxing*

* It was officially signed by Levi Woodbury, the Secretary of the Treasury. The effective date for the prohibition on the receipt of paper money was August 15, 1836.

the issues of such paper. Benton also wrote the Cincinnati editor Moses Dawson, urging him to fight to see that these principles were "applied," and he called Dawson's attention to his hard money proclamations in the Senate. They were "intended for a signal to the Democracy of the country," and should "be followed up." In February, Benton dispatched a similar signal to "the Democracy of Pennsylvania," in which he linked old battles with new issues. The charterless B. U. S. had turned to the legislature of Pennsylvania in a desperate effort to stay alive. That assembly had obligingly granted state incorporation under the grandiose if somewhat contradictory name, the Bank of the United States of Pennsylvania. With this in mind, Benton offered a "sentiment" to be read at a Pennsylvania party rally: "THE DEMOCRACY OF THE UNION: *May it have courage and constancy to fight out the battles with the Bank of the United States under all the shapes and forms which the hydra and Protean monster may assume.*" The Jeffersonian, state-rights tradition which the Jacksonian agrarians had inherited placed narrow limits on the scope of national government action. In consequence, Benton and other radicals had to turn to an also desperate struggle for hard-money action in the several states.

This was Old Bullion — "the noble, heroic old Tom, the veteran democrat and probable successor to Mr. Van Buren," as John Fairfield described him.[11] As a mere legislator, meanwhile, Benton was confronted in 1836 with an ominous re-appearance of the endemic conflict over slavery in two new aspects.

The first concerned what were called "incendiary publications," and a demand for their suppression. A rising antislavery movement, spurred on by men like William Lloyd Garrison in his aggressive *Liberator,* was taking the campaign to the South. Papers, pamphlets, and pictures were sent through the mails, urging abolition of slavery or slave insurrection. This issue was seized upon by the ever-ready planter-partisan, John Calhoun, who proposed a bill forbidding postmasters to deliver such matter in areas where state law made it illegal. Though he regretted that the mails had been "made a pack-horse for the abolitionists," Benton was unwilling to give such broad authority to ten thousand individual postmasters, even for the "suppression of so great an evil." * He was

* Later, Benton described to the Senate one product of "the abolition mint" he had received — an engraving, showing "a large and spreading tree of liberty, beneath whose ample shade a slave-owner was at one time luxuriously reposing,

among a majority which voted Nay when a revised version of the bill was finally brought to a roll call.

Antislavery groups had also bombarded Congress with petitions for abolition of slavery in the District of Columbia. Usually these petitions had been referred to a committee, where they were forgotten. When a petition was received from the Society of Friends at Lancaster, Pennsylvania, in 1836, however, Calhoun decided to turn passive resistance to positive opposition. He proposed that Congress refuse even to receive such "offensive" petitions. In the debate on this proposal, Benton offered his views on the developing controversy. Many antislavery men, he was sure, were benevolently concerned "to ameliorate the condition of one part of the human race." Others he saw only as "incendiaries and agitators." He had watched "the black question, like a portentous cloud . . . gathering and darkening," and he "trembled, not for the South, but for the Union." Here, he feared, he saw the fatal work of dissolution about to begin. He hoped and believed, however, that the good sense of "the great body of the people" would put an end to agitation, and assure "the harmony and indivisibility" of the Union. As for the immediate issue, Congress should follow the old practice of receiving the petitions without acting on them. When the matter was brought to a vote, Benton joined with a majority of Yeas for receiving. Later, the prayer of the petitions for abolition in the Federal district was rejected, with Benton again voting with the majority.

In perspective, the mid-1830's marked a new phase in Benton's thinking on the slavery issue. He had tended to look, as he put it later, "to the North as the point of danger from the slavery agitation." Now, however, he began to look "to the South for that danger" — though he was always "equally opposed to [agitation] in either quarter." [12] In the next two decades he was to become increasingly resistant to slavery and Southern demands. Always, however, his first concern was preservation of the Union against disruptive agitation.

Though he had failed to carry any of the hard-money measures he had advocated in Congress, Benton was again marked as a leading member. A Whig Representative from Massachusetts, Amos Adams Lawrence, found him an effective debater — his "manners on the floor while

---

with slaves fanning him; at another carried forth in a palanquin, to view the half-naked laborers in the cotton-field, whom drivers, with whips, were scourging to the task."

speaking, and at other times," the merchant-politician reported, "are those of a gentleman; he never reads without applying a double glass to his eye in a very genteel way." Even an anti-Jackson man who observed Benton in action noted that he spoke "with ease, grace, and elegance . . . he is fairly entitled to a place among the first rate orators . . . far more powerful in every way, than a great many people are willing to allow." On the other hand, Webster damned Benton for a propensity to "wear us all out" by "endless" speeches. Often a lion in the Senate, Benton could be a lamb in the drawing room. During the session of 1835-1836 he went to a dinner at the home of John Forsyth, the Secretary of State; Senators Hill (New Hampshire) and Niles (Connecticut) were also guests. At leavetaking time, Hill said good night to his host and went straight for the door, taking no notice of the circle of ladies at the fireside in the drawing room. But Benton paid his addresses to all the ladies, bowing gracefully to each. After him was Niles, small, awkward, and self-conscious, who first tried to emulate the Missourian, and then found himself seized with panic. Pulling a bandanna handkerchief from his pocket, he gave a loud blast on his nose, and shot out of the door in retreat. Meanwhile Benton, stately, unruffled, completed his round, said good night finally to his host, and departed. No wonder an observer thought the rugged fighter in politics *"an old courtier"* in private life.[13]

This gentler side of Benton's personality was particularly remarked by Elizabeth Benton's niece. The pretty, sprightly, teen-aged Sally Mc-Dowell spent the winter with the Benton family in their lodgings at Dawson's, on Capitol Hill. There Sally learned to love "Uncle Benton," who introduced her to the great and near-great of the capital. Once at the Executive Mansion, she wrote her mother, she was presented to "the royal family" and others "as [the Colonel's] *niece* — and of course from that circumstance [she] received the compliments of all." Sadly, Sally noted that politics made Uncle William and Aunt Penelope Preston act coldly toward the Benton family, and the Prestons' daughter was so mean to Eliza and Jessie Benton that "Aunt Benton" had to forbid her to see them. Despite the pressure of work, "Uncle Benton" had found time to get a new French teacher, and he was also trying to get a guitar teacher for the girls and a dancing master to replace one who had left. In short, "Uncle Benton" was a dear. But Sally also had a chance to observe her uncle at work, and in July, 1836, she reported that he was busy on one of his "great" schemes to stop paper money.

Though the cabinet was against him, the President was favorable and his scheme would prevail — his "very heart and soul seems set upon it," Sally noted, "and you know how determined he is when he takes a notion in his head; he will carry it out at all hazards except that of *justice* and *honor.*" This, of course, was just what "Uncle Benton" did — the "scheme" was the specie order.

Later, Sally went with Thomas's daughters Eliza and Jessie Ann to Miss English's Female Seminary at Georgetown. There they enjoyed the orderly classrooms, the fancy-handled two-pronged forks, the beautiful gardens of the suburb, and what intellectual fare there was. To Sally as the oldest, Thomas wrote advice for all three, urging on the girls "the necessity of doing three things in carrying on your studies, *to wit: first,* to look for every word in the dictionary, the *exact* meaning of which is not known to you; *secondly,* to search for every place on the maps which is mentioned in your studies; *third,* to observe the chronology of all events." When the girls came down to Washington on days off from their school, Thomas and Elizabeth continued to introduce them about — and the sprightly Sally continued to charm the men. In particular, she attracted a man twenty years her senior with whom her life was to become tragically linked, Representative Francis Thomas of Maryland. She became so friendly with Senator Lewis Linn that a jealous Mrs. Linn accused Sally of carrying on "a serious flirtation." For the moment Sally, perhaps indiscreet but certainly innocent, seemed youthfully oblivious to any threat to her gay, headlong existence. Meanwhile, she continued to be charmed with "Uncle Benton's" kindness, "so entirely voluntary," and wanted to "do everything to please him." [14]

Beyond the family circle, Old Bullion's reputation as a public man was developing into a tradition. Years later a St. Louis chronicler reported that " 'Tom' Benton, it [was] said, could sit at his desk," after studying an issue, and write a speech, "without change or erasure, throwing the numbered pages to the floor; and without another glance at the writing would the next day, or the day after, deliver his speech verbatim, crammed with figures and blazing with invective." [15] This legend exaggerated Benton's "mental powers," but it caught the spirit of his character.

[3]

THE FALL AND WINTER of 1836 and 1837 brought new triumphs to Benton and the radical Democrats, though they did not mark any significant progress in the hard-money program.

The first triumphs were registered in the local and national elections of 1836. In Missouri, a complete ticket pledged to support "the matchless BENTON," as the *Argus* called him, was returned — headed by Lilburn Boggs for governor, and Albert Harrison and Benton's old friend John Miller for Congress. The anti-Benton Representative, Ashley, had made a try for the governorship — and this was the practical end of his curious political career, for twenty months later he was dead. The Assembly chosen in August later re-elected Lewis Linn to the Senate unanimously. Thus Benton was assured of a united, favorable Congressional delegation. There was, however, one difficulty. The only state in the Union without a bank was Missouri, where commerce was thus dependent on a still limited supply of specie and on the often unsound notes of "foreign" banks. Demands that Missouri charter a bank became an election issue. In his campaign, Lilburn Boggs had endorsed the proposal for a state bank, albeit a specie-paying bank, issuing no note under twenty dollars, and carefully regulated by the state.[16]

Nationally, the Whigs elaborated and applied their strategy of divide and conquer in the Presidential race. In 1832, Clay had run on a straightforward, pro-B. U. S., American System platform, and had been soundly beaten. In 1836, Webster, William Henry Harrison, and Hugh Lawson White resorted to personal and sectional appeals, mingled with platitudes. The year before, Nicholas Biddle had proposed that his favorite, "Old Tippecanoe," "say not one single word about his principles or his creed — let him say nothing." By and large, Harrison realized this ideal, even when he made a barnstorming tour through Virginia and the Middle Atlantic states. The election result had some scares in it. Van Buren's vote in both the Southwestern and Northwestern sections was less than that of his combined opposition, and if the Whigs had been able to carry New York, or Pennsylvania, or Virginia, the choice *would* have been thrown into the House of Representatives. As it was, however, the electoral tally gave Martin Van Buren a comfortable majority.[17]

Through all of the election excitements, Benton remained in Virginia with his family — part of the time at Cherry Grove, and later at the western Virginia resort, Warm Springs. When Congress convened again in December, however, he was ready to lead the Democratic forces to their final triumph of the season.

This was a symbolic victory for the Jackson men over the old Whig charges of executive despotism. Once again, Benton introduced his Expunging Resolution. Black lines must be drawn around the text of Henry Clay's resolution of censure, and the words "Expunged by order of the Senate" written across the offending passage. "Solitary and alone, and amidst the jeers and taunts of my opponents, I put this ball in motion," Benton declaimed. But "the people ha[d] taken it up, and rolled it forward," in instructions from legislatures to Senators, and in the Presidential and Congressional elections. In mid-January, 1837, the issue was brought to a head. Expecting that the critical sitting would last well into the night, and knowing (from his military experience) how difficult it was to keep men at their posts "when tired and hungry," Benton arranged to have a supply of cold hams, turkeys, rounds of beef, pickles, wines, and hot coffee available in a committee room. The debate did last into the night. As "the great chandelier was lit up, splendidly illuminating the chamber," while "the lobbies and galleries filled to their utmost capacity," Benton noted, the scene became "grand and impressive." The expungers were confident of victory, but when they went to the refreshment-filled committee room it was in groups of four or six, always leaving enough "on watch" in the Senate chamber. Finally, Webster rose to speak. "We solemnly PROTEST," he cried, "against this whole proceeding." But he knew the resolution was to pass, and having protested, no more was possible. When Webster sat down, no one else rose; "there was," Benton remembered, "a pause, a dead silence, and an intense feeling." The silence was finally broken by cries of "Question! Question!" from several members. Then, as the hand of the clock moved from nine to ten, the roll call was finally taken. The vote was 24 to 19 for the resolution, in a strict party division.

Immediately, Benton was on his feet to demand that the order be carried out. While many members left the chamber, the Secretary opened the Journal to the resolution of March, 1834. The dramatic black lines were drawn about the text, and the legend was written across its face. At last, two years and seven months after Benton had introduced his original resolution at the end of the "Panic" session, the symbolic deed was done.*

Comment on the event spread through the land. To a friend Clay wrote — "the Senate is no longer a place for a decent man: yesterday Benton's expunging resolution passed." Under the heading, N. TOM O'LOGICAL STUDIES, a New York printer issued a cartoon broadside, THE GREAT TUMBLE BUG OF MISSOURI, BENT-ON ROLLING HIS BALL. This showed an insect with the Missourian's face, laboriously backwards-pushing uphill a huge ball labeled "Expunging Resolution," with the line underneath, *solitary and alone* — and so on. Other partisans repeated the *solitary and alone* line until it became a household phrase. In Baltimore, jubilant Democrats fired salutes to the Senators who had voted for the resolution — twenty-five for Benton, five each for each of the others.

The whole business served to bring Jackson and Benton closer together. The Senator sent the President the pen that had been used in the expunging. Jackson returned his thanks, and promised that after his death the pen would be given back to Benton as a token of his "regard" for "your talents." The pen was taken to the Old Hero by Randolph Benton, aged seven, and Jackson's letter added his "blessing on the dear little boy." Soon after, Jackson gave a grand dinner to the leading expungers and their wives. Being ill, he only met the company, and then retired to his sickroom, after seating Benton in the chair of honor.[18]

Though Benton had won his fight in behalf of Jackson as symbol and leader, he was unable to make progress in the hard-money program. The Senate that passed the Expunging Resolution was the same Senate that voted overwhelmingly to rescind the specie order. In addition, while Benton was able to get Senate approval for a bill to limit land sales to small acreages and to actual settlers, as a further brake to inflation, his measure failed in the House and never became law. In the

---

* The story of the "expunging" given here is reconstructed from various sources, avoiding probable apocrypha. One contemporary journalist, writing in 1858, recalled that Benton's foes had come to the gallery for the final scene *armed with pistols* ("The Late Thomas H. Benton," 63 cf. Notes, 6) while a later writer has Lewis Linn bringing pistols to protect his friend and colleagues from possible assault, and also has Elizabeth Benton, "seriously alarmed," taking her place by her husband's side on the floor (Bowers, *Party Battles*, 470). Neither writer gives documentation for this item, and I have not been able to find any confirmation for it in reliable evidence.

face of the speculative expansion, the hard-money "ball" was a hard one to roll.

Sure that the boom must be followed by a bust, Benton warned the President-elect of impending collapse. One day in February, 1837, as he recalled it later, he invited Van Buren into a committee room in the Capitol, and there expressed the opinion that "we were on the eve of an explosion." He had planned to elaborate, but Van Buren brought the interview to a sudden end:

"Your friends," he said, "think you a little exalted in the head on that subject."

The two men left the room together, with Old Bullion miffed and saying to himself, *You will soon feel the thunderbolt.*

He did not press the matter. He knew that Van Buren's regard for him, "both personal and political," had not weakened — Van Buren was even then pressing him to take a cabinet position. But he was hurt, and felt that he could not insist where his opinion was not valued.[19]

In fact, the "thunderbolt" was but a few months in the future.

[4]

THE FIRST PART OF MARCH, 1837, was bright and balmy, as if to honor Andrew Jackson as he prepared to retire from the Presidency. His last official act was to send a Chargé d'Affaires to the Republic of Texas — the new nation that had declared itself independent of Mexico, and whose president was Jackson's and Benton's old subordinate in the Tennessee volunteers, Sam Houston.

As a parting legacy to his countrymen, Jackson prepared a "Farewell Address." In it, he reviewed the progress of his Administration, in particular the Bank war, attacked "the paper system," and spoke out firmly for "a circulating medium of gold and silver," in the interest of "the planter, the farmer, the mechanic, and the laborer" — words that must have seemed golden indeed to Benton. He also alluded to the threatening controversy over slavery, to "systematic efforts publicly made to sow the seeds of discord between different parts of the United States," and called in George Washington's name for a rededication to sectional compromise and the preservation of the Union, for "harmony and concord" — sentiments that Benton was to echo again and again in stormy years to come. Ironically, Jackson's last act as President was ominous for his last counsel as President. Before long, a raging controversy over Texas was to bring slavery conflict and sectional animosity to the forefront of politics, and call men to new battle stations.

The inaugural itself, on March 4, was gala. Crowds lined Pennsylvania Avenue and cheered as Jackson and Van Buren rode together in a carriage drawn by a pair of the Tennesseean's gray horses. At the ceremonies, at the eastern portico of the Capitol, the crowd stood silently. Looking down from a side window, Benton interpreted the silence as the stillness of "reverence and affection." For once, "the rising was eclipsed by the setting sun," for "it was evident that the great ex-President" was the object of the people's homage. Under such circumstances did Van Buren take the oath of office before Chief Justice Taney, and begin his mentor's "third term." Meanwhile, Richard M. Johnson of Kentucky, who had been chosen Vice-President by the Senate after the electoral vote failed to give any candidate a majority, was also installed in office. The administration of Andrew Jackson was over.[20]

At an end, also, was a bit of Benton's influence and prestige. Under Jackson, Benton had played the part of unofficial but effective Administration leader in the Senate. Under Van Buren, though Benton was to remain a major leader, the place of Administration spokesman was to be occupied more and more by the incisive, capable, radical Senator from New York, the President's particular friend Silas Wright. This was no source of distress to Benton, who greatly admired Wright — the simple, kindly, laborious Silas, a farmer and village lawyer, was indeed (as Benton saw him) another Cincinnatus or Nathaniel Macon, as he worked between sessions on his thirty-acre New York freehold.[21] In any case, there were more days of triumph to come, and they held work and glory enough for both Benton and Wright.

Two days after the inauguration, Jackson left Washington, by railway, from the new depot on Pennsylvania Avenue. Before he left, he and Benton had a friendly chat, alluding together for the first time to the bloody quarrel of 1813 that might have brought death to both men before fame touched them.[22] For three decades, the lives of Benton and Jackson had been fatefully interwoven — first almost as father and son, then as violent personal enemies, again as amiable acquaintances, and finally as political cohorts and faithful friends. The Nashville brawl lay in the limbo of the past, and by 1837 both men had lost all rancor.

CHAPTER 11

The Bulwark

1837 - 1841

THE MISSOURI APRIL, like the Washington March, was balmy and pleasant. After an absence of a year and a half, the Bentons were settled again at the Laurel Street house in St. Louis, which his mother and various nieces and nephews had continued to occupy during his absences. There Thomas could enjoy the quiet spring days with his family and renew old friendships in the town. He had scraped together enough cash to retire the mortgage on the Laurel Street property — though John O'Fallon refused to acknowledge the right to redeem, and a seven-year lawsuit ensued.[1] Through their stay in 1837, meanwhile, the Bentons continued to live in the house.

The private idyll was shattered by a public event: the "thunderbolt" that Benton had predicted struck. The banks of New York City suspended specie payments on May 10, 1837, and a full-scale economic depression soon raged. Prices and wages dropped disastrously; unemployment, suffering, and distress spread through the cities; debtors were unable to pay their creditors; business firms failed; hungry men cried for "Work! . . . Work!" The collapse, portentous for Benton and the whole popular democratic movement, was the product of a diverse combination of conditions. These included the unsound character of the business boom itself, based on the dizzy pyramiding of paper credits — the effect of the destruction of the B. U. S. as a fiscal agent in removing an important brake on credit expansion — the inflationary consequences of depositing the Federal funds in the state banks — the deflationary effects of the specie order of 1836 — and finally, crop failures, requiring an unusual export of specie to meet the unfavorable balance of foreign trade. The situation had been aggravated by the failure of important foreign business houses, like Baring Brothers in England.[2]

Immediately, partisans sought to fix blame for the collapse and to propose remedies. Men like Benton and Jackson suspected a plot to recharter the B. U. S. Opponents of the Administration pointed accusingly to the specie order, demanded its repeal, and abused Benton and other hard-money men. In a speech in New York, Webster had earlier ridiculed the order as having been prepared by "a member of Congress," who had "stood 'solitary' and 'alone' [a laugh]" for it. Now burlesque notes with grotesque caricatures of the friends of hard money were issued, with legends like THE GOLD HUMBUG EXPLODED. One cartoon issued in New York spread itself in glorious color over a sheet nearly two feet wide and a foot and a half high. This self-called SHIN PLASTER showed the "Expunger" and Jackson chasing a butterfly labeled GOLD HUMBUG over the edge of a cliff, while the ex-President cried, "By the eternal!! I'll have it, Benton!" Under the drawing were the words, *I Promise to pay Thomas H. Benton, or bearer,* FIFTY CENTS, *in Counterfeit Caricatures,* and the signature (ADV'T) of the publisher. Of this masterpiece, the *Argus* in St. Louis noted that Jackson was shown mounted on a hog, and Benton on an ass — in order, "we suppose, to picture the manner in which these two gentlemen have rode *the Whig party:* very emblematical!" Laboring to contain the Whig attack, radical partisans expostulated that only "Benton and Benton's much ridiculed 'humbuggery'" had kept the nation from plunging deeper into the "vortex" of expansion, and consequent contraction.

The panic raised a question — what would the new President do? Would he rescind the specie order? Would he retreat from the hard-money standard and accept some new version of a national bank? From the Hermitage, Jackson called on Van Buren to be "steady, firm, and unwavouring . . . your Senate will again resound with Benton's voice . . . no temporizing or you are gone." [3] Van Buren called a special session of Congress, but gave no hint as to what he would propose.

In St. Louis, meanwhile, Benton noted that Missouri was still enjoying prosperity. Hard money had "given us solid, permanent, and *diffused* wealth, with happiness and tranquillity" — the epitome of the Jeffersonian dream.* In fact, the economy of the state *was* sound, in significant

---

* The *Argus* noted another aspect of this dream in an item which called attention to the *political* democracy the new republic had achieved, and adumbrated a notion that was to become part of the mythology of American politics. Under the heading, THE POOREST BOY MAY BE PRESIDENT, this article noted the poor-boy origins of both Jackson and Van Buren, and remarked that the latter was "the son of a farmer, who was obliged to till the soil with his own hands [what, no plow?], for means of support." Thus, the Presidency was "within the reach of the humblest urchin that roams the streets of our villages . . . *Liberty and Equality* is the glorious motto of our republic" (*Argus,* June 9, 1837). A man who was in 1837 a "humble" storekeeper, odd-job man, and state legislator (Whig) in neighboring Illinois, Abraham Lincoln, later became the standard symbol of this idea.

part as a result of Old Bullion's influence. There were no "wildcat" banks; trade along the Santa Fe Trail brought in a steady flow of specie; there had been no state-financed internal improvements mania, as in other states; there had been no over-extended speculative boom; with a steady stream of immigration, population increased; both farm income and city wages were steady and higher than they were in the East; and yet the cost of living remained comparatively low. In short, Missouri was almost the model of an Arcadian, hard-money commonwealth.

In the midst of this prosperity, the Bank of the State of Missouri began business. On the very day banks elsewhere closed their doors, the Missouri bank opened its doors. Though Benton had opposed chartering the bank in the first place, his influence had helped make it a strict specie-paying, "Discount and Deposite" institution. It began by issuing no notes under twenty dollars, and followed a policy of giving preference to small, nonspeculative loans. Symbolically, Old Bullion's picture was printed on many of the new bank's notes. Untouched by enthusiasm for large-risk credits, the bank became known as the "Gibraltar of the West," one of the soundest concerns in the nation.[4]

Encouraged by Missouri's economic health in the midst of sickness, Benton wrote reassuringly to Van Buren. He had never felt in "better spirit for a contest," and he, like Jackson, was against all "compromises and capitulations."[5]

[2]

THE CONTEST WAS JOINED in Congress, in the special session in the fall of 1837, and in the regular session in the winter of 1837-1838. Throughout the long debates, Benton's voice "resounded" again and again in dogged defense of the agrarian, hard-money position.

At the beginning, Van Buren sounded a call to advance. Insisting that it was not the function of government to offer "specific aid" and "special favors" in the crisis, he flatly rejected the idea of rechartering the B. U. S. in any form, and announced that he would not revoke the specie order. Instead, he proposed another step in the hard-money system. This was a new "Sub-Treasury" or "Independent Treasury," in which the government itself would keep its own funds. This proposal to "divorce" government from banking crystallized the developing realignment of interest groups, political parties, and factions. With the conflict over the B. U. S. spent or quiescent, the hard-money and Independent

Treasury issues became the polarizing storm center of a new conflict of interests, a new contest of Enterprise and Arcadia. Business and state-banking spokesmen, particularly the Whigs, clamored against this quint-essence of "Bentonian-Jacksonism," as an application of the evil text, "Perish commerce — perish credit." Men like Rives and Ritchie of Virginia, and Marcy and Tallmadge of New York, condemned the "rot of radicalism," and Rives, Tallmadge, and other conservative Democrats set up a new press in Washington, the *Madisonian,* as their organ. On the other hand, John Calhoun and his allies swung back to the main body of the Democrats. Shrewd and single-minded in his devotion to the plantation interest, Calhoun had become convinced that Whig nationalism, devotion to industrial and financial capitalism, and demands for a new national bank, were more dangerous enemies at the moment than Democratic radicalism. Meanwhile, Van Buren stood fast for his Independent Treasury, and drew closer to the Locofoco, hard-money forces. More and more, radicals like Benton entrenched themselves at positions of control in the Democratic fortress.[6]

In 1837, and again in 1838, an Independent Treasury bill was introduced by Silas Wright. On both occasions, the fight for the bill was led by Wright, Benton, *and Calhoun* — who was in consequence stigmatized by a former Calhounite as now raising "hosannas to Bentonian humbuggery." The opposition was led by Clay and Webster, and the new "duplicate Senators," Tallmadge and Rives. In mid-March, 1838, Benton mounted a major argument for a revised, enlarged version of the Independent Treasury bill. In this long, discursive, exhaustive oration, he discussed everything from the attitude of Jackson toward *the* Bank and banks, to the present state of parties and factions, before he turned to the bill at hand. That bill was now founded, as a result of an addition proposed by Calhoun, on *"two* principles" — "1. The exclusion of all *banks* from the use and custody of the public moneys," and "2. The [eventual] exclusion of all *bank notes* from the receipts and expenditures of the Federal treasury." Pushing on, Benton recalled his arrival in the Senate, during an "explosion of the paper system," and his early associations with Macon and Randolph, and his early reading, which had convinced him that the government had been "formed by hard money men," and that it should depend on "gold and silver coin." The Independent Treasury bill would aid toward this end, and would make the government master of its own money. The "error of Mr. Madison's administration," in turning to state banks after the expiration of the first Bank, had "ruined the currency in 1814 and 1819," and the *repetition* of the error had "ruined" the currency again in 1837. That error must now be corrected. Entering the Senate in the midst of this speech, Francis Blair found Benton "lashing at Clay," expressing himself in "striking words and determined manner." In his *Globe,* Blair devoted twenty columns of close type to reprinting the address, and Benton himself wrote Jackson that the speech was coming out in pamphlet form — "our friends believe it must have considerable effect." The pamphlet was offered through the *Globe* "at cost." The Vice-President franked copies in bundles for the faithful. The President sent out copies too, and his correspondents assured him that Benton's "conclusive argument" would certainly produce "the happiest results" in public opinion. Though the bill passed the Senate in both 1837 and 1838, it died in the House; and the great "contest" was laid over to another Congress.[7]

During the two sessions, Benton addressed himself to another crisis-oriented question. This was an Administration plan to meet the failing finances of government by borrowing, through the issue of "Treasury Notes." Opposed to even this degree of paper financing, Old Bullion argued with Van Buren that the Treasury Note proposal would further divide the party and give the opposition "a club to beat us with." In 1837, he swallowed his scruples and went along with party, President, and Silas Wright for the issue; but in 1838 he quietly abstained from voting. As the depression and government deficit persisted, Benton scolded Van Buren for making the Treasury Notes an *"habitual* resort," and again and again expressed his disapproval.[8]

As Benton saw it, the government finances could be shored up by another device, which was meritorious in itself. Before the special session, he had suggested to Van Buren that the government might raise new revenues by reducing the prices of the public lands for settlers. In December, 1837, the President commended the graduation policy to Congress. By so doing, Benton declared in a public letter to the *Argus,* Van Buren had "infused new life into the bosoms of the [Western] delegations." Members of these delegations spent two weeks in conferences hammering out a plan, which they brought before the Senate in April, 1838. Personally, Benton regretted a compromise by which stages in price reduction had been cut from four in previous plans to two: a dollar an acre for lands five years in the market, seventy-five cents an acre for lands ten years unsold. Still, "to the farmers and cultivators of the soil, the passage of the bill [was] eminently due." The banker, who "produces nothing," dealing in old handkerchiefs made "into silk paper," cut "into little slips," and sprinkled over "with figures for dollars," commanded "the first cares and labors of the [state] legislative bodies." In contrast, "the agricultural class . . . [could] scarcely conciliate a majority for a pre-emption law, or a graduation law." In the interest of "the productive classes of the United States, the laborers of all kinds as well as the agriculturalists," the graduation bill *must* pass. Pass it did, in the Senate, despite opposition from the inevitable Clay and from old-state Democrats like Buchanan and Calhoun. But the matter was allowed to die in the House, and once again the graduation principle was lost.

Meanwhile, Benton was busy trying to "conciliate a majority for a pre-emption law." Debate raged on a bill to extend and enlarge the right of pre-emption (or first purchase) to actual settlers on the public lands. Noting that he had voted as a Senator in Tennessee in 1809 to grant pre-emption to occupants on the French Broad and the Holston, and praising pre-emptioners everywhere as "hardy pioneers," Benton fought for the measure. His great antagonist in several days of debate was, again, Clay. But a bill was finally passed in both chambers, extending pre-emption for a limited time.[9]

In the special session of 1837, Benton turned to another matter almost as dear to him as hard money and land policy. In the Territory of Florida, tensions between white settlers and Seminole Indians had broken into effective war, and troops were needed to carry on the battle. This situation reminded Benton of the hostilities in Tennessee in 1812, and the thwarted warrior of that day was apparently anxious to participate vicariously in the new campaigns. He proposed (privately) to the Administration that a regiment of volunteers could be had immediately in Missouri under Colonel Richard Gentry, "who was expressing to me, before I left home, the pleasure he would have in leading his 1000 to Florida." The proposal was taken up, and Benton wrote Gentry that a War Department order was going out that day "for the march of 600 of your volunteers."

Even before Congress adjourned in October, 1837, Benton left for Missouri. After a flying trip of "ten days & *nights* traveling in the stage," he reached St. Louis on October 24 — in time to see Colonel Gentry's regiment depart. The volunteers had marched from Columbia (the commander's seven-year-old son, Thomas Benton Gentry, riding with his father for a mile or so) to Jefferson Barracks, south of St. Louis. There Benton addressed the troops, taking (publicly) responsibility for suggesting that a call be made on them, and watched the regiment embark down the Mississippi. After he had seen the troops on their way, he dispatched an indignant message which connected the movement of the volunteers with the hard-money issue. He urged Secretary of War Poinsett to take up with Secretary of the Treasury Woodbury the question of the kind of money used in payments to troops. The paymaster in St. Louis was handing out "drafts upon broken banks," and the volunteers had received some "2000 in this kind of trash" for their clothing! If such rag payments continued, Benton cried in a similar admonitory letter to Van Buren the same day, the friends of hard money would "lose ground." [10]

The Florida expedition brought Richard Gentry to his death. On Christmas Day, 1837, at the Battle of Okeechobee, he was mortally wounded. The report General Zachary Taylor later submitted concerning the battle was immediately attacked as doing grave injustice to the Missouri troops. Back in Washington for the Congressional session, Benton denounced it in the Senate. He was, he declared, "under peculiar obligations to see that justice was done to these volunteers," because they were from his state, because their commander had been his good personal friend for twenty years, and because he had sent them on their way to Florida. More practically, Benton tried to do what he could for the commander's widow. In March, 1838, he was able to report her appointment as Postmistress at Columbia, and add that a pension for her was in process.[11]

Also in 1837-1838, Benton had to mourn the death of his mother and of a mentor. In January, 1838, at the St. Louis home of Joshua Brant (who had married Thomas's niece Sarah), Nancy Benton died after a long illness, in her eightieth year. A few months before, at his North Carolina farm, Nathaniel Macon had died.

To his mother, and to Macon also, Benton owed much. As he noted somewhat egotistically later, Nancy Benton had "lived to see the fruits of her pious and liberal cares" — all her boys grown as men of "character," and one of them "taking his place among the historic men of the country for which she had begun so early to train him." In his will, Nathaniel Macon left to "my friend," Thomas Benton, a pocket knife once given him by "my friend," John Randolph.[12] But as a prophet of Arcadia, Macon had left a larger legacy — the dream of an agrarian,

democratic commonwealth, a dream for which Benton fought valiantly
even as the aged Macon died.

[3]

THE DISTRESS OF 1837 imposed a severe test upon "Democrats in
principle," and Benton in particular met it well. His determined defense
of the hard-money program, his courage in the face of adversity and
attack, his willingness "to fight it out without flinching, or compromis-
ing, or calculating [political] consequences," as he put it — all this
brought him increased respect as the bulwark of the radical Democratic
forces. Although Van Buren was president, and Wright chief leader in
the Senate, it was Old Bullion who caught the imagination of the masses,
who won nation-wide popular support.

This popularity was marked by persistent talk, across the nation, of
Benton for president. In editorials, in toasts at public meetings, in
speeches, he was praised as "the next President," as "the successor of
Martin Van Buren," as the favorite of "the great body of the working
people" — for 1840, or 1844. In manifestoes to the sachems of Tammany Hall in New York, to Democratic committees at Louisville and
elsewhere, and to the nation in general through the press, Benton
scouted these proposals. He urged that the re-election of Van Buren in
1840 be made "a matter of *form,* and not of *contest.*" Declaring that he
had seen the nation often injured by rivalries for the Presidency, he
called for "a truce from this turmoil." Still, the talk went on. Visiting
Washington in the spring of 1838, Thomas's niece Sarah Benton Brant
became convinced that Uncle Thomas *would* "be our President one of
these days," though "he does not seem to dream of it yet and does not
like his friends to talk about it" — certainly, "he has the good of the
people more at heart than any of the leading politicians I know." [13] If
not in 1840, then perhaps in 1844 . . .

In fact, Benton's leadership was distinctive. There was much of the
political broker, of the crowd-representative, in the "Little Magician,"
Van Buren, and in other radical Democrats. But Old Bullion had
become overwhelmingly the proposer of great measures, the crowd-
compeller. No disciple of Hamilton's doctrines, he was yet an exemplar
of Hamilton's maxim: "Wise men ought to walk at the head of affairs
and produce the event." Aware that effectiveness as a politician was
necessary to effectiveness as a statesman, Benton understood the signifi-

cance of favors, patronage, organization, and compromise in building a successful political movement. But he saw such procedures as means to the realization of program and policy, and not as ends in themselves. Physically, temperamentally, and by conviction, he was cut out to play the part of advocate. These characteristics were noted by his fellow partisans in the first of a series of sketches of Democratic leaders, which appeared late in 1837 in the initial issue of a new quarterly grandly titled *United States Magazine and Democratic Review*. As a man, Benton was "robust, of florid complexion, and powerful frame, capable of enduring great fatigue, both mental and physical, under which but few other men could bear up." As a leader, he was spokesman for the "ploughman and planter of the land," who, guided by "the single polar star of democratic principle," always went "fearlessly forward," always laboring to get "public opinion to come up with him." Of such were "the men that work great revolutions and reforms." * Looking upon his Senate seat as the place of greatest use for an advocate of the hard-money program, he was above "the attractions of *office.*"

His muscular energy, burgeoning egotism, and imperious style, coupled with his tendency to push "fearlessly forward," made Benton increasingly tactless and driving in personal relations. His colleague and confidant Lewis Linn warned Silas Wright that Old Bullion "must be handled more delicately than he handles his friends sometimes"; and the Virginia conservative Henry A. Wise damned him flatly in the House as "the Big Bully Bottom, Tom Benton."

Still, the bulwark of the radical Democracy was an appealing figure.

---

* The role of popular democratic leader was not always easy, Benton knew, and near the end of the 1830's he offered a mordant comment on the relative political participation of different classes and interest groups in the population. The "merchants and money dealers and manufacturers," he noted, were "always on the watch," quick to "meet and cry out for the smallest pressure on their interest," but yeomen farmers were too often prevented by their "dispersed condition and . . . daily labors" from "combining and acting together" effectively. At any threat to the interests of "the mercantile classes . . . the whole fraternity would be in commotion; meetings, petitions, resolutions would issue from every town and village; hundreds of presses would resound with their daily complaints." There was, alas, something in Sir Robert Walpole's estimate of "the two classes . . . comparing the farmers to sheep, which might be sheared to the quick without a bleat, and the merchants to the devil shearing the hogs, all cry and no wool" (Benton to [Corbin], September 16, 1839, Corbin Papers, Copy in MoHS). There was, of course, still more to the question of differential advantage in the political arena than Benton noted here — but what he saw convinced him that only vigorous leadership and mass action could redress the balance.

One observer in the Senate galleries found Benton a fascinating if "august" orator, whose "erect and commanding person seemed a fitting socket for his resolute will." Another "Looker On" offered a fuller portrait. Benton seemed "to dress with particular neatness and care, to use in a style of apparent dandyism the eyeglass which hangs upon his bosom in fetters of gold, to be almost perpetually engaged in writing or in the examination of the heaps of documents and papers piled upon his desk." But withal, he was "a finely attired, pleasant-seeming gentleman." At fifty-six, he appeared "to be yet in the vigor of health and manhood." [14]

His great prominence made Benton's bid for re-election in 1838 a new test for the radical Democracy. Here was the unyielding, outstanding advocate of the hard-money cause, up for the Senate again in the wake of the national depression! Much appeared to hang on the outcome — "the battle," as Webster noted portentously, "must be fought in Missouri." The Benton men in Missouri were happy to accept the battle in these terms. Damning "paper trash" as

> *Whiggery — Whiggery rank,*
> *Such as pleases Whig and Bank . . .*

Democratic publicists praised hard-money "yellow jackets" as

> *Jackson's — Benton's plan,*
> *Such as charms the honest man.*

The *Republican,* under a new, thirty-year-old, vigorous editor, A. B. Chambers, plumped boldly for "A NEW NATIONAL BANK," cursed Benton's "mint drops" as "humbugs," and sang, significantly —

> *Now Biddle's notes were clever things*
> *They gave to Enterprize her springs*
> *'Til Loco Focos snapt the strings. . . .*

A Whig circular bemoaned the democratic "despotism, not of a single tyrant, but of a thousand," and urged Missourians to "drive from the councils of the nation the most dangerous man who has ever yet held a place in them" — Benton, of course. Democrats responded with a warm defense of "this rule of the *majority of the* PEOPLE — this dominion of King NUMBERS, in which the vote of the humblest and poorest yeoman counts as well as the proudest and wealthiest aristocrat." Here in epitome was nearly all of the symbolism and rhetoric of the national

political struggle.* As to "that dangerous man," the *Argus* assured the
Whigs that "BENTON and DEMOCRACY" would once again win with the
voters —

> *They'll elect him, they'll elect him, and then if they can,*
> *They'll a President make of "that dangerous man."*

Propaganda was buttressed by leadership, personal contact, and organization. Though Benton himself stayed in the East until late October,
local lieutenants worked effectively. These included old friends like
Magenis and Millburn, newer recruits like Francis P. Blair's son
Montgomery Blair, who had recently settled in St. Louis as Benton's
protégé in law and politics, and the *Argus* editor, Corbin. Throughout the state, rally followed rally, particularly in Whig-inclined St.
Louis, where "MECHANICKS AND WORKING MEN" were called on to
demonstrate and unite against the "wicked speculating Bank rulers and
Artistocratic Nabobs." Slates of Assembly candidates, firmly pledged to
"the re-election of THOMAS H. BENTON," were carefully devised.[15]

The voting, which ran through three days in early August, produced
a total Democratic triumph. The *Argus* proclaimed that Benton's re-
election by the Assembly was beyond doubt — he will "remain in the
Senate until the PEOPLE CALL HIM TO THE PRESIDENCY." The *Republican*
noted, however, that the Whigs had won "in all the old and more
densely populated counties, where trade and business have assumed
something of a regular channel" (fifteen counties), and they had. The
Democrats again swept the farming, yeomen-settled, poorer regions
(forty-four counties). When the Assembly voted in November, there
was no doubt as to the outcome. One Whig member, James S. Rollins,
later famous as "the father of the University of Missouri," even complained that a Whig colleague, "drunk as *a bitch,*" had deserted to *"old
Tom Benton by God"* — "when he is drunk he is a *loco-foco,* & when
sober a Whig."

The vote was 75 for "old Tom Benton," to 48 for Abiel Leonard, of

* The *Republican* picked up a business-minded comment on the election from
the Springfield, Illinois, *Journal.* The dominance of Old Bullion in Missouri had
given the state a reputation that sapped "the confidence of capitalists abroad in her
institutions," this paper opined. While other states could get loans to finance banks
and internal improvements, "keen-eyed capitalists [had] but little confidence in a
state which is subjected to the control of such an individual" (*Missouri Republican,*
September 4, 1838). To this, the small farmer, small producer, agrarian Democrats could only answer: *Amen.*

Howard County, who had been nominated by the desperate Whigs without his knowledge or consent.[16]

In late October, Benton arrived in St. Louis, "in excellent health . . . and fine spirits." He settled at Joshua Brant's house, on Washington Avenue, where, the *Argus* announced, he "would be pleased to see and converse with his friends." With his mother's death, and the lawsuit over the Laurel Street property, Benton began a practice of staying at Brant's house when he was in town.

The chance to enjoy his personal triumph in the election was not all that had brought Benton to Missouri. He was more concerned with advancing the hard-money cause in the state. He spent a month working for that cause as a party leader, advocating it before the bar of public opinion, and lobbying for it behind the bar of the legislature. The mercantile group in St. Louis maintained a steady demand for a freer currency to conduct and expand their business. Certain concerns there had begun issuing commercial paper that passed as the practical equivalent of bank notes, while brokers had sprung up to deal in notes from Illinois and other "free banking" states. Now, in St. Louis and in visits to neighboring counties, Old Bullion lashed out at this new danger. There were "houses in St. Louis which should have this inscription over their doors: *'Paper money importing and hard money exporting ware-houses'* "; and they should be summarily suppressed. In Jefferson City, Benton visited with Assemblymen and tried unsuccessfully to get Governor Lilburn Boggs (or so the *Republican* charged) to take a stronger hard-money line. Returning to St. Louis, he dispatched a manifesto to his fellow Democrats in the Assembly. He warned that "several corporations" in St. Louis were "exercising banking privileges in defiance of the constitution," and called bluntly for legislation to stamp out this new "deluge of pestilential paper money." Business spokesmen condemned this *"Message* from Senator Benton to the Legislature," as a virtual *"letter of instructions."* No action was forthcoming at the moment, but Benton was to return, and successfully, to the battle.[17]

Through the winter of 1838-1839, Benton was in Washington, for the short, "lame-duck" session of Congress. It was an uneventful session, in which he essayed his Old Bullion role again in relation to certain minor issues, but without significant results. He also dealt with an important item of patronage. His old friend William Clark, Superintendent of Indian Affairs in Missouri, had died, and Benton proposed that it would be "for the public service" to name another old friend,

Joshua Pilcher, to the post.[18] In March, 1839, the appointment was made.*

Meanwhile, Benton had an opportunity to enjoy pleasant times with his family. They were all in Washington for the Christmas holidays of 1838, much to Elizabeth's satisfaction. On a fine New Year's Day, 1839, "all the world" attended a levee at the Executive Mansion. In the drawing room the diplomats "in full costume remained several hours (contrary to custom)," and Thomas presented his older daughters and their school-ma'am, Miss English, to the genial, urbane Martin Van Buren. The girls seemed "on fairy ground" at the brilliant scene. Afterwards the Bentons had several friends, including Dr. Linn, to dinner in their lodgings at Dawson's Number One. The family were all well, except "poor little Ran who looks thin pale & feeble & has had several attacks of sore throat." A tonsil operation was planned for spring. After the adjournment in March, 1839, Benton stayed in Washington. Elizabeth and the children (all, including Ran, by this time in good health), planned to spend the summer at Georgetown, so the girls could continue at Miss English's school. Thomas intended to tour Missouri. He would go "all over the state," he informed Andrew Jackson, "to see the faithful people who have stood so nobly by *us* and by their country" — and, incidentally, to advocate the hard-money program.[19]

The tour began in May, with Benton's arrival by steamboat at Cape Girardeau, in southeast Missouri. At "the Cape," and the next day at Jackson, the county seat, Old Bullion was "incessantly engaged" with visitors at his hotels. Though it was a busy season for farmers, many left their fields to talk with him. Declining public dinners and public meetings, but writing out his views on banking, hard money, the Independent Treasury, land policy, and other issues, Benton set a pattern

---

* In urging Pilcher's appointment, Benton was working in harmony with the "public service" — Pilcher proved himself an unusually capable officer. But, in addition, Benton was aiding an old friend, and working in harmony with the interests of the American Fur Company and its St. Louis associates like Pierre Chouteau, Jr. and Jean P. Cabanné — who had specifically suggested that the *"Tout Puissant"* Benton might secure Pilcher's appointment. No longer the ally he had once been of the old-French nabobs of the St. Louis business group, Benton still never broke entirely with the great fur-trading concerns. They represented a powerful interest group in Missouri politics, and also a sound, productive industry which was playing a key part in taming the Far West, as contrasted with the quick-gain, speculative enterprises the radical Democrats condemned. In office, Pilcher maintained his personal and political friendship with Benton — "a first rate Bentonian wireworker," as one Whig partisan in Missouri described him. He was removed in the change of administrations in 1841, and died in 1843.

he was to follow throughout his tour — "a free and easy intercourse with all who will do me the honor to call on me." Impressed with the number who responded in Cape Girardeau county, he remarked that before "the revival of democracy" with Andrew Jackson, "the body of the people paid but little attention to political subjects," but now public interest was awakened and political information widely "diffused." In St. Louis, the *Argus* commented that the Whigs regarded the tour "with terror." They had portrayed Benton as a "demon." Now many people who knew him only from such reports would see him face to face, hear him expound his program, and observe "his courteous manners and frank nature."

From Jackson, Benton went west and north through the lead belt in Madison, St. Francis, and Washington counties. Traveling always on horseback, he then swung toward Springfield on the far southwest frontier. When news reached that town on May 30 that the Senator would be there next day, a number of citizens prepared to ride out to meet him on the road and escort him to the town. At Springfield, Benton penned another long manifesto letter, reviewing his currency arguments, and going on to praise Jackson's policy of removing Indians from the national domain, observing that the Springfield area of Missouri was "the last to be settled, because longest encumbered by an Indian population." Next, he turned his horse north to the county that was named after him. At Warsaw, the county seat, on June 7, he remarked that the region was "almost entirely covered by pre-emptioners" — the settlers Whigs contemptuously dubbed "squatters." But he noted that the "respectability, industry, and wealth" of these yeomen had been "visible to him in their farms and improvements, and in the hospitable reception" which they offered when he stopped with them. From Warsaw, he went on to visits in the latter half of June at Liberty, in Clay County, and at the Falls of the Platte, Weston, and other villages — all in the frontier "Platte Country," the northwest corner of the state that had been added to Missouri by special act of Congress in 1836. At Weston, "the most western town in the state of Missouri," and thus in the nation, he exclaimed at "the sound of the hammer and the axe," as the business of conquering the wilderness went forward.

On Independence Day, Benton made a special stop at Fayette, in mid-Missouri. There he attended a "non-partisan" public dinner to celebrate the day, and listened to somewhat partisan toasts in his praise, by men like the party leader Dr. John J. Lowry and Mayor H. H. Hughes.

One toast was offered by a Robert Hancock — "I am a pre-emptioner, and I am proud to see here today the pre-emptioner's friend, Thomas H. Benton."

From Fayette, Benton moved rapidly northeast to Paris, the county seat of Monroe, and thence to Bowling Green in Pike County on the Mississippi. There, many citizens who were in this county seat for the court sessions were very agreeably surprised by his visit. Talking with him, "listening to his varied and interesting conversation," and to "his exposition of national policy," one man after another saw that he was by no means the demagogue he had been painted. Winding up his hegira, the Senator stopped at Troy, in Lincoln, the county immediately south of Pike. There on July 16 he dispatched another long letter, stressing action to outlaw bank notes under twenty dollars in Missouri. He regretted the shortness of his stay, but "the advance of the season, and the approach of the summer heat," required him to end "an excursion which has already extended to eleven hundred miles of riding." On Wednesday evening, July 17, Benton reached St. Louis. "In fine health," the *Argus* reported, and "highly gratified by his intercourse with the People," he settled at Colonel Brant's. Considering the roads of the time, and the heat of the June-July sun in Missouri, the tour was an achievement, demonstrating that at fifty-seven Benton retained his old rugged strength. He had been well received everywhere, winning an especially "cordial welcome" from farmers.

At St. Louis, Benton produced a final manifesto. "Multitudes," he wrote, "are attracted to our State by the fame of its natural advantages, others by its happy exemption, thus far, from the evils which afflict some other states" — the paper system, mounting state debts, "grand improvements in new countries," and unsound banking. He was pleased that St. Louis had taken "the first place among the cities of the West next after New Orleans!" But he warned that her growth had been "upon the solid rock of hard money," and that she was "now making the experiment of floating upon an ocean of paper," and that a "storm" might be expected in that "ocean." In the past the radical Democrats had been chiefly occupied with *national* policy, but "hereafter the policy of the *State* [would be] entitled to absorbing attention." [20]

These caveats were to the point. The illegal note-issuing business in St. Louis had increased, and tattered paper of every description flooded the town. These developments were given an added impetus that fall when the cautious Bank of Missouri announced that it would receive for deposit only its own notes, notes on specie-paying banks, or specie. It thus barred the Illinois bank notes on which many business houses in St. Louis depended. Insurance companies, the St. Louis Gas Light Company (chartered in 1839), and other concerns spewed out paper. The conflict between the "Hards" and the "Softs" intensified, with Old Bullion and the outstate farmers acting as the backbone of the Hards, and the rapidly expanding mercantile and business interest groups of the state, particularly in St. Louis, supplying recruits for the Softs. This question was linked to a new aspect of state-sponsored internal improvements. Among the "grand improvements in new countries" that capitalists of the day found particularly enticing, were railroad projects, often local, such as the Iron Mountain Railroad in Missouri. In 1839, Benton took a strong stand that "such roads were not at present desirable in any part of the West." The *Argus* particularly praised him for his opposition to proposals for Federal land grants for railroad projects — "the gull trap . . . to capture several hundred thousand acres of the public domain." Contemporaries recalled his strictures on railroad plans as a revival of the obsolete "American System" idea. They also noted his pleasure in comparing debt-ridden, bank-paper, Whig Illinois with debt-free, hard-money, Democratic Missouri.[21]

Once again, Benton had played the role of bulwark for the agrarian, hard-money program, had thrown his vast energy and great personal influence into the uphill fight for that program. In the sphere of state action, as in the sphere of national action, he had proved his determination to "fight it out without flinching," to labor to get "public opinion to come up with him," to act as advocate of "great . . . reforms." With the battle-lines thus drawn in his home state, Benton left by stagecoach for the East.

[4]

EARLY IN AUGUST, 1839, Thomas rejoined Elizabeth and the children at Georgetown. Replying to a testimonial letter from a local Democratic committee, he remarked on how much his family had enjoyed their sojourn "in your quiet, healthy, and agreeable town." He would not (of course) accept a public dinner, but would be happy to receive friends in his rooms at the Union Hotel, tomorrow evening, "at any time from dark until midnight."

Regretfully, Benton declined an invitation to spend a week with

James Buchanan at Lancaster, Pennsylvania. The two men were becoming increasingly friendly, apparently mostly on Buchanan's initiative. Benton wrote Buchanan that he and Elizabeth would like someday to send young Randolph for a visit, so that, among Senator Buchanan's German constituents, the boy might "learn their widespreading and useful language." The Bentons did spend September and October in the Blue Ridge region of Virginia. For three weeks they stopped at a resort called Alum Springs, "which is famous," Thomas wrote his friend Magenis in St. Louis, "for curing *totter worm*," with which some of the children were afflicted.[22]

In mid-October, Benton heard news of a new "thunderbolt," or financial crisis. The Bank of the United States of Pennsylvania suspended specie payments and closed its doors for a second time, and most of the banks of the nation (except those of New York and New England) had to follow suit. At last, Benton commented dourly in a letter to Jackson, the "monster of iniquity" had "shut up." [23] In fact the B. U. S. as such, though not the idea of a national bank, was doomed. By 1842 it had gone down amidst recriminations and charges of malfeasance, and when Nicholas Biddle died in 1844 he died in disgrace.

Returning to Washington at the end of October, the Benton family settled for the first time in a private dwelling. They rented a house and grounds at 2 C Street, between "3d and 4½ Streets," at the foot of Capitol Hill to the northwest. It was a good building with spacious rooms and thick walls. The family improved the grounds to the rear, training ivy and scarlet-trumpet creeper to cover the garden walls and stable. The Senator kept his work to an "office" or study-library he fitted out on the third floor, and in the drawing room or at the table joined in the family give-and-take in which all members down to the youngest were expected to participate. While Thomas and Elizabeth each had what Jessie later recalled as "settlements" on either side of the drawing-room fireplace, the four sisters — Eliza, Jessie Ann, Sarah, and Susan — adopted the square dining room table for their lamp, workbaskets, and portfolios. Sometimes Jessie would play Beethoven or the contemporary Rossini on the piano for guests — some of whom enjoyed the music, while others, like the prim Buchanan, were only put out by the "interruption" to the talk. Rest, happiness, and courtesy were the household rules, and a sulky face or sullen action would lead to "banishment" of the offender. Thus, the C Street house quickly became known for its hospitality. A Washington journalist marked it as "one of the most agreeable" homes in the capital, particularly because of the Bentons' "accomplished and graceful daughters." A Virginia friend recalled the girls' skill in languages, declaring that at the Bentons' table a diplomat from France, Germany, Italy, Spain, or Russia might at any time "hear the Misses Benton addressing him in his own tongue."

A caller at the Bentons' new home that December was Francis Thomas of Maryland. Speaking of his visit in a letter to Sally McDowell, Elizabeth Benton remarked that rumor had it that Sally (aged nineteen) would marry Francis (aged forty-one). "Heaven forbid," Elizabeth exclaimed, "that such an event should ever happen." [24]

Austere in public, Benton was affectionate and gentle with his "accomplished and graceful daughters." Once, Jessie Ann recalled, one of them had trouble tuning a guitar. Then her father, looking up from his "settlement" in the drawing room, asked that the instrument be brought to him. "I often tuned their guitar for my sisters," he said, "and sang with them." Even the crusty John Quincy Adams noted this parental tenderness. Visiting the Senate one day, he sat next to Benton, and remarked that his old foe had one of his daughters with him, "most of the time on his knee." (It was Susan, the youngest, though Adams did not know this.) The ex-President wrote in his diary that Benton's "affectionate fondness for his children almost disarms me." [25] "Almost" . . . but with Adams, that much was an accomplishment!

While the Bentons were settling themselves at their new dwelling, a new Congress was laboring to organize itself. Despite the developing depression, the Democrats had managed to maintain their formal majority in both houses. Even so, there was a protracted contest over the Speakership of the House. In this contest, Benton and Calhoun (both nominally Democrats) served as opposing leaders in a complex maneuvering. An Administration caucus selected John W. Jones of Virginia for the Speakership. But on six successive ballots Jones was unable to secure a majority, because a bloc of Congressmen influenced by Calhoun threw their votes to lesser candidates. Then an agreement was made by Administration leaders and the Calhoun faction to support Dixon H. Lewis of Alabama. But on four more ballots Lewis was unable to secure a majority, because a number of Congressmen followed Benton's advice that *they* throw away *their* votes rather than support a Calhoun man! Finally, an eleventh ballot showed a majority for Robert

M. T. Hunter of Virginia, a nominal *Whig* who was not Calhoun's choice
even though he was a Calhoun man. Thus Benton had what he
wanted — a "clean defeat," rather than victory secured by "capitulation" to the Southerner's bloc.[26] With this huggermugger finally settled,
Congress was ready to listen to Van Buren's message, in which he advocated again his Independent Treasury plan.

In January, 1840, the Independent Treasury bill was brought to the
floor in the Senate. The debate was brief. The issue had been thoroughly discussed at previous sessions; it was obvious that the bill would
pass. In his remarks on the measure, Benton recalled his prophetic
words in his anti-Bank speech of February 2, 1831 — "gold and
silver is the best currency for a republic; it suits the men of middle
property and the working people best; and, if I was going to establish a
working man's party, it would be on the basis of hard money; a hard
money party against a paper party." He then reviewed the various parts
of the hard-money system as he had envisioned it, and trumpeted in
peroration that when Congress satisfied "the demand of an immense majority of the American people for the instant and total divorce of Bank
and State," then "the financial map which I spread before me ten years
ago [will see] the last of its objects on the point of consummation." How
far public opinion, and political brokers who tried to march in careful
step with public opinion, had "come up" with Old Bullion was shown
in the speeches and votes of Robert J. Walker of Mississippi and James
Buchanan. In 1837 Walker had condemned "the wild, visionary, ruin-
ous and impracticable schemes of the Senator from Missouri," but now
he praised Benton as one of "the original Loco Focos and hard money
men of the Union." On January 23, 1840, the Independent Treasury
bill passed the Senate, and in June it passed the House also. The
"DIVORCE [was] DECREED," as Benton put it. A wind-up of the work
Jackson and Benton had begun, and Van Buren and Wright carried on,
it was the peak of triumph for what the *Argus* called "the *genuine,* radical Democracy."

The act provided for sub-treasuries to keep the Federal funds, thus
removing them from the vaults of state banks. It also stipulated that
after June, 1843, all Federal revenues should be received *only* in gold
or silver coin. Thus, Benton declared, a full-fledged "HARD MONEY GOV-
ERNMENT" was in prospect.[27]

As unproductive talk continued in Congress, Van Buren effected the
second great measure of his tenure. By executive order, on March 31,

he reduced the working day on all Federal public works to a standard ten hours, instead of the sunrise-to-sunset schedule that had been operative in many public and most private jobs. The effect of the order inevitably extended beyond the government works, and it was a milestone in the long struggle of workingmen for a shorter labor day. The order satisfied another major demand of the urban workingmen's groups with which the radical Democrats had become allied.

As the session drew to a close, Benton gave some thought to the vice-presidential nomination for the coming election. In a private letter to Jackson, he noted that the incumbent Richard M. Johnson had fallen "far behind the strength of his party" in 1836, and doubted that he should be renominated. He, Benton, had been proposed for the place, but had firmly rejected the suggestion. He thought that James K. Polk of Tennessee was "the proper person for the democracy to support," but he also believed that in the circumstances no one should be nominated by the forthcoming party convention. He had discussed the matter with Wright and other friends, and all were agreed that it would be best to use "the names of the most popular candidates in different states." [28] When the Democratic convention met in May, it unanimously proposed Van Buren for re-election, and left the number two spot open.

[5]

IN THE SUMMER OF 1840, Thomas went with his family to Chesapeake Bay, "for the benefit of the salt water and salt air for the children." There, while the presidential fight warmed up, the Bentons stayed until late August.

The election campaign was unprecedented, fantastic, and portentous. The developing convention device gave such new-school Whig leaders as Thurlow Weed the chance to put aside the policy-committed Henry Clay, and nominate William Henry Harrison, who was committed to little or nothing, and who had proved a vote-getter in 1836. As Benton summed it up later — *"availability,* to use their own jargon, was the only ability which these managers asked." The vice-presidential nomination went to the state-rights ex-Democrat John Tyler, of Virginia. The Whigs were thus prepared for battle with a combination made up of old National Republicans; of dissident Democrats; of many advocates of state banking, rallying to the leadership of men like Tallmadge and Rives, who were now openly acting as Whigs; of remnants of the demagogic Anti-Mason party; and finally of plantation state-righters. Harrison, the amiable relic of the War of 1812, was counted on to rouse the pioneer, Western voters, as Old Hickory had roused them in 1828. The Whigs offered no platform, and throughout the campaign they saw to it that "Old Tippecanoe" Harrison made no statements more definite than platitudes about the evils of Locofocoism. This opened the way to a *"hurrah"* campaign, unlimited.* In state after state the Whigs sang:

> *Farewell, dear Van,*
> *You're not our man,*
> *To guide the ship,*
> *We'll try old Tip. . . .*

> *For Tippecanoe and Tyler too — Tippecanoe and Tyler too;*
> *And with them we'll beat little Van, Van, Van,*
> *Van is a used-up man;*
> *And with them we'll beat little Van. . . .*

"Old Tip" was sedulously portrayed as a homespun man of the people. His Virginia-aristocratic origins and his spacious Ohio house ignored, he was repeatedly linked with log cabins, coonskins, and hard cider. While torches flared, drums and fifes blared, and partisans paraded, the "plain folks" theme was labored by speaker after speaker. One of these was Honest Abe Lincoln, the railsplitter and Whig politico, who reported that "Old Tip's" nomination was taking "first rate" in Illinois. The technique of the smear and namecalling was also developed: Van Buren was vilified as a dandy who had made the Executive Mansion a Frenchified palace — a *champagne* drinker! In short, the Whigs had

---

* In his description of the 1840 canvass, Ostrogorski emphasizes that it was the convention device, and the tendency of parties to become "amalgam[s] of numerous factions" without principle, which enabled managers like Seward and Weed to determine the nominee. Thus — "the national convention . . . supplied the politician with the means of carrying out their design — to get it said, in the name of the people, who doted on Clay, that they did not want Clay." With leaders who stood for something "put on one side, the Organization stepped into their shoes as a joint-stock company takes the place of the private individuals who have founded the firm." Behind this new "democratic formalism" of the allegedly *"vox populi"* convention, the organization managers ruled (Ostrogorski, *Political Parties,* II, 72, 76, 77). When the ever-ambitious Webster expressed his doubts to Weed concerning the nomination of Harrison, the New York manager snapped — "Question is, who will poll the most votes" (Cleaves, *Old Tippecanoe,* 315).

rejected old-Federalist slogans of stability, and appropriated many of the propaganda symbols of *hoi polloi* democracy.[29]

Some of the Whig antics had Benton as a target. In memory of his boast, "Solitary and alone, I set this ball in motion," two huge balls, twelve and fifteen feet in diameter, were propelled across Ohio to the capital, Columbus —

> *With heart and soul*
> *This ball we roll;*
> *May times improve*
> *As on we move.*

> *This Democratic ball*
> *Set rolling first by Benton*
> *Is on another track*
> *From that it first was sent on.*

In Missouri the campaign broke out into vituperation — and violence. At Whig "jollifications" (hard cider for men *and* boys), the *Argus* charged, bacchanalian songs were punctuated with chants of "Tom Benton and the Devil." In St. Louis in June, political passions produced the brutal murder on Market Street of one of Benton's friends who had recently taken over as proprietor of the *Argus,* Andrew Jackson Davis — an event which brought Abel Corbin back to the editorial helm. Nationally, a piercing note which must have retarded the women's suffrage cause by decades was struck by one Lucy Kenney. The very title of an election pamphlet she published was a stump speech in seven different type faces: A HISTORY OF THE PRESENT CABINET. *Benton in Ambush for the next Presidency . . . Gather all your strength, and oused [sic] the Cossacks, draw their teeth in time, unless they should devour you.* An Exposition of Martin Van Buren's REIGN.

When Jessie Ann Benton read such partisan attacks on her father, she would look up from her chair at the man himself. Though he was described as a "florid, aggressive demagogue," she would find before her a "calm, powerful, fair face — serene as Jove's — and with eyelids of unwinking calm." She would note her father's "most aristocratic white hands, so well shaped and small, and so untiring!" She would then remember how gentle and patient he could be, and wonder at the spleen politics provoked.[30]

At the end of June, Benton offered his own "exposition" of the Whig campaign. With his Congressional colleagues Linn, John Jameson, and Miller, he prepared a long public letter to the people of Missouri, where it was printed in the party press and distributed in pamphlet form. The Whig propaganda was described as "an insult" to the electorate. If parties generally adopted the Whig practice of no commitments on program, "the privilege of voting [would become] an empty farce." Similar arguments were put forth, though more reflectively, in the *Democratic Review*. In their desperation, the Whig "managers and leaders" had "at last learned from defeat the very art of victory. We have taught them how to conquer us!" — by a popular appeal based on "the dazzle of a military title," plus the cry of *hard times*. Surely "there is no demagogism so low as that of an aristocratic party which courts the suffrage of a democracy it at heart despises!" Echoing Benton vigorously, the *Democratic Review* denounced the empty, hurrah campaign as "nothing short of High Treason" to the spirit of democracy.[31]

The Democrats conducted a generally sober, program-oriented canvass. They did parlay into national prominence the symbol "O. K.," as an abbreviation for "Old Kinderhook," a nickname for the President after his New York home, Kinderhook. But by and large they pointed to the record, reaffirmed their old program, hammered at old issues.

Toward the end of August, Benton left his family and traveled West, reaching St. Louis on September 21 aboard the steamboat *Valley Forge*. The town and state he returned to were growing up. Under the impact of immigration, the population of Missouri had jumped from 140,455 in 1830 to 383,702 in 1840, while the population of St. Louis had risen from less than five thousand to 16,469. The Democrats had swept the August elections, with the "Log Cabin party" failing utterly to carry the log cabin counties; but Benton still urged his Democratic followers to "work as hard as if all depended on us" in the presidential campaign. In St. Louis, the radical Democrats were finding new sources of strength to tap. Gradually industry was developing in the city, creating a new population of wage earners who were organizing labor unions — small, independent groups of bricklayers, blacksmiths, boatmen, carpenters, draymen, machinists, painters, saddlers, shoemakers, stonemasons, tailors, and others. Though the unions disclaimed "connections with either political party" and strove to organize a Mechanics and Workingmen's Party, many workingmen and finally the movement as a whole found itself in practical alliance with the forces of Benton and the Missouri "Locofocos." The stripling labor-political movement died out in the mid-1840's, but it operated for a while in the radical Democrats' favor.[32]

In Missouri, Benton was much sought after as a political orator. In long public letters reviewing the real issues as he saw them, he declined invitations to speak at ward meetings in St. Louis, and town meetings at Hillsborough and elsewhere. He did, however, write a long prefatory letter for a party pamphlet, which reprinted in fifty-five close-set pages the letters he had addressed to his constituents the previous summer. At the beginning of October, he went by stage to Jefferson City to attend a Democratic convention. The thousand participants gathered at noon, October 8, and marched in procession to the Capitol building, Benton and Congressmen-elect John C. Edwards and John Miller walking among the leaders. At the State Capitol, Dr. Lowry of Fayette introduced Benton, who proceeded to deliver an address more than two hours long. He jabbed at the Whigs for their contempt in addressing a campaign to "the ignorant multitude," and for singing "the cuckoo song of change! change! change!" The *Republican* complained that Benton set his teeth hard whenever he mentioned "St. Louis, Banks, or Merchants," and argued that he was in general "a demagogue" (!). Two weeks later Benton made another long speech to a Democratic meeting at Palmyra, in Marion County, a Whig stronghold to the northeast.[33]

At last, the November day of reckoning came. The voters were aided in the election by printed party "tickets," carrying the names of party candidates and party electors, by which the citizens could cast their votes — forerunners of the official ballots of later years. These new-fangled tickets were generally offered by the party printeries. In St. Louis, for example, the *Republican* advertised at the end of October that Whig tickets were available at their office for both Missouri and Illinois.

When the votes were counted, they added up to disaster for the Democrats. Nationally, the popular count for "Tippecanoe-and-Tyler-too" was 1,275,016, that for Martin Van Buren 1,129,102; but the Whigs carried 234 electoral votes to the Democrats' 60 electoral votes. Even in Missouri, where "Old Kinderhook" won over "Old Tippecanoe," his margin fell four thousand short of the ten thousand Benton had set as a goal. The Democratic vote was larger than in any previous election. But ballyhoo and buncombe had brought out an even larger vote for the Whig slate. The days of triumph were over for Old Bullion and his fellow spirits. The thunderbolt of economic crisis, and the

thunderbolt of electoral defeat, had struck the radical Democratic movement, which never recaptured its momentum. The "Log Cabin and
Hard Cider Campaign" was a portent for future politics. Never again
was a conservative party like the Whigs to fight a major, national election with the same candor that had characterized Henry Clay when he
chose the Bank of the United States as an issue in 1832. From bitter
experience, the conservatives had learned that in a democratic political
system such candor could not serve them half so well as hurrah, and
the appeal of an attractive candidate.

In the mind of one leading Democratic intellectual, the result provoked
profound pessimism. Looking back at the 1830's, in 1843, Orestes
Brownson noted that the politics of the period had moved around "the
direct issue, as Mr. BENTON expressed it, between MAN and MONEY."
The contest had been "between the interests of associated or corporate
wealth, or more strictly perhaps of business, on the one hand, and
the interests of labor (agricultural, mechanical, &c), on the other."
But on this issue, the Democrats had lost. Thus, Brownson declared,
he saw "that if we make up the issue, as Mr. Benton has put it, between
MAN and MONEY, we necessarily bring about a horizontal division of
the parties, in which the party of Money will always carry the day."
The solution, for Brownson: reject the majority-rule-democratic position
typified by Benton, and accept a minority-protection position close to
that of Calhoun.[34]

For Benton, personally, the election may also have been a portent.
Rumor persisted that there had for some time been a definite program
for the Democratic succession — "Andrew Jackson, eight years; Martin
Van Buren, eight years; Thomas H. Benton, eight years." Now, the
chain was broken.

Undaunted by defeat, Benton went stoically about his political business in Missouri. Soon after the election he traveled to Jefferson City,
where he spent a week in mid-November talking with members of the
convening legislature, playing party leader and advocate-as-lobbyist
again. Noting that his hotel room was "crowded from nine in the morning until eleven at night," the *Argus* reported that he spoke out freely on
national and state issues, insisting in particular that the Democracy
should concentrate at once on Van Buren for re-election in 1844. To
suggestions concerning his own possible presidential future, he responded by referring to a motto he had coined some years before —
"self-denial: everything for the CAUSE, nothing for MEN." The Whigs

fumed. One Assemblyman complained that "the great *Ballroller*" had held "a gran caucus with his sycophants," in which he "gave them their positive orders," particularly in relation to currency legislation. Another reported that Benton had ordered a "rotten borough system," by establishing new counties to maximize Democratic strength in future legislatures. The "sycophants" were unable to carry any important currency measures that session. They did, however, create fifteen new counties, bringing the state's total to seventy-seven.[35]

In late November, at St. Louis, Benton boarded the steamboat *Dolphin* for the East.

[6]

THE LAST SESSION OF CONGRESS under Van Buren was due to convene on December 7, 1840; but for the first few days there was no quorum because, as Benton remarked, "a terrible fall of snow for three days has blocked up the roads, and stopped travellers."

While he waited Benton tried to rally his party after its defeat. He wrote to Moses Dawson, editor of the Cincinnati *Advertiser,* to congratulate him for proposing Van Buren for renomination in 1844, and to Abel Corbin of the *Argus* to urge him to "put up Mr. Van Buren's name." If Missouri did not take a lead in this matter, "both the State and myself will lose the brightest honor that ever awaited us . . . Put up the name." On December 15, Corbin "put up the name" at his masthead, and he kept it there in succeeding issues. He knew, Benton said, that he was early in his strategy of urging Van Buren "against the world." But, as he told Dawson in a private note, "it is my fate to begin things early" — witness the Bank war, the Expunging Resolution, the gold bill, the Independent Treasury. Clearly, Thomas Benton's ego had suffered no deflation in the election defeat.[36]

Meanwhile, Congress had set to work. Promptly, Benton introduced a bill for permanent pre-emption, "in favor of the hardy and industrious settlers upon our public lands — *the log-cabin men.*" The "Log Cabin bill" was a masterstroke of irony-in-action, designed to expose the discrepancy between Whig slogans and Whig practice. The matter was debated through January, 1841, with the opposition led by Henry Clay, and finally, early in February, the bill was passed. The House, however, failed to act on the measure, thereby giving Democrats the opportunity to cry that the Whigs really preferred the (presidential) "palace" to the "log cabin." Persistently, Benton offered another measure, for a Federal tax on bank notes. He had in mind, he said candidly, *two* objectives — revenue ("it is time to make the banks pay, and let salt go free"), and "to effect the gradual suppression of [small] notes." To secure the latter objective, he proposed "an annual progressive increase" in the tax on notes under twenty dollars, until it reached 12 per cent per year. Here again, Old Bullion was showing his tendency "to begin things early," though the idea was not wholly original.* But nothing came of the matter[37] — in fact, no important legislation came of the entire session.

In February, 1841, Harrison arrived in Washington to await his inauguration. On February 13, Van Buren (urbane even in defeat) gave an informal dinner at the Executive Mansion for the President-elect, a dinner at which most of the guests were Democrats. During the meal, Old Tippecanoe spoke across the table to Old Bullion — "Benton, I beg you not to be harpooning me in the Senate; if you dislike anything in my administration, put it into Clay or Webster, but don't harpoon me." The Senator (also urbane even in defeat, and personally friendly to Harrison in any case), bowed in jovial acquiescence.

Nineteen days later, the "Old Hero" of the Whigs took the oath of office. The "third term" was over, the Administration of Martin Van Buren was done. "No president," Benton remarked, "ever had a more difficult time." [38]

---

* A 10 per cent tax on the notes of state banks was the device used by Congress under Lincoln in 1865 to destroy the state-bank-note circulation of the time and develop the new national banking system, which had made disappointing headway against the state banks since its establishment in 1863. One effect of this tax was to speed the trend away from notes and to deposits as the chief way of creating bank credit; of course this way was the *only* credit-creating recourse of the state banks after 1865.

PART IV

The Ordeal

But my *narves it kind o' grates,*
Wen I see the overreachin'
O' them nigger-drivin' States. . . .

Ez fer war, I call it murder. . . .

— JAMES RUSSELL LOWELL, 1846

CHAPTER 12

The "Dictator"

1841 - 1843

EARLY IN APRIL, 1841, Thomas Benton and his family watched a solemn procession pass through the street below them. They stood in the workroom of the lodgings a young lieutenant in the Army Engineers had in a private house on Capitol Hill. The procession they watched was the funeral cortege of William Henry Harrison. Exactly a month after his inauguration, the old man had died of a surfeit of officeseekers — though his physicians had another diagnosis of the immediate cause.

The lieutenant-host was a recent acquaintance of the Senator's — an ambitious young man named John Charles Frémont. One of a team of mapmakers, he had first met Benton in an official or "duty" visit to that gentleman. Soon afterwards, he had seen the sixteen-year-old Jessie Ann Benton at a concert at Miss English's school in Georgetown, "just then in the bloom of her girlish beauty," he recalled later, and full of "bright talk." After this meeting, Lieutenant Frémont, twenty-eight, handsome, raven-haired, and intense, became a frequent visitor at the Benton home.[1] When he invited the Bentons to his lodgings, he was as much interested in seeing Jessie Ann as he was in complimenting an influential statesman.

Official Washington, meanwhile, was more concerned with what the new President would do. Succeeding to office, "Tyler Too" kept Harrison's cabinet, including Webster as Secretary of State and many Clay men, and waited for a special session of Congress "Old Tippecanoe" had called for May 31.

The new Congress contained 52 Senators and 221 Representatives to act for the growing nation. They came from twenty-six states, from Maine in the Northeast to newly-admitted Michigan and Arkansas in the Northwest and Southwest. Beyond the Western border lay the Texas area, the Northwest or Oregon country, and the outlying provinces of Mexico. The census of 1840 had shown a total population of

17,069,453, a jump of more than four million since 1830. But vast spans of the Western and Southwestern states (including Missouri) still showed fewer than six inhabitants per square mile — officially "frontier." Less than a tenth of the population lived in the forty-four "cities" of eight thousand or larger, though the Northern, industrializing, urbanizing sections were fast gaining in population over the Southern, plantation-dominated, slaveholding section. Total national income was only about a billion and a half dollars a year, and national government expenditures ran about twenty-five million dollars a year.

At the beginning of June, the Whig-dominated Congress received Tyler's message. But Henry Clay, whose nationalist ideas were far from those of the Virginia state-righter in the White House, determined to match the formal leadership of the President with an effective Congressional, premier-like leadership of his own. On June 7, he offered for the Senate a programmatic resolution — Benton, in opposition again for the first time in twelve years, thought it "virtually" another message. Its salient points were the "repeal of the Sub-Treasury," the "incorporation of a bank," a new tariff (to replace the Compromise of 1833 which was about to expire), and a new plan to distribute the proceeds of the public lands sales. It was this alternative "message" that won attention.[2]

The repeal of the Independent Treasury act, and its hard-money provisions, was rushed through Congress and signed by the President — and thus the great achievement of the "third term" was erased.

The establishment of a national bank was not carried so readily. In June, Clay offered a bill to incorporate in the District of Columbia a new "Fiscal Bank of the United States." A hybrid when it was submitted, this measure was further mangled by attempts among the Whig factions to make it conform at once to the *national* views of Clay men and the *state-rights* views of Tyler men. In addition, it was beaten and buffeted by the Democrats, who followed a strategy later described by Benton — "sudden, short, and pungent speeches, directed against the vulnerable parts" of the measure; and amendments, nearly forty in all, "always commendably calculated to expose an evil, and present a remedy." The object — delay, and an appeal to public opinion through the *Globe* and other Democratic organs, which carried the speeches "fresh and hot, to the people," as Benton put it. While Clay raged at such harassment, it was August before a bill of any sort could be sent to the President — who kept the bill ten days, and then returned it with his veto. The objection was promptly sustained in the Senate, amidst dismay and disgust among Whigs, and jubilation among Democrats. When the veto message was read, it was greeted by hisses (or *a* hiss) from the gallery, which brought Benton to his feet to denounce the "ruffians." He was not mollified until one of the offenders (or *the* offender) had been apprehended and forced to apologize. Ex-President Adams sniffed that "the doughty knight of the stuffed cravat" (an oblique reference to stories concerning Benton's fall from grace in his college days) had made "a ridiculous scene."

The Clay men in Congress went to work again, and devised a new hybrid to be called "the Fiscal Corporation of the United States." In debate on the bill in late August and early September, Benton ridiculed this "Corporosity" — "Heavens, what a name! . . . too long! too long! and fraudulent besides. It will never do. People cannot go through all that . . . Some say a name is nothing — that a rose by any other name would smell as sweet. So it will; and a thorn by any other name would stick as deep. And so of these fiscals, whether to be called banks or corporations . . . but a short name they must have." The "Corporosity" was passed; but once again, it was returned with a veto, and once again the veto was sustained.[3] At last, the national bank proposal was dead, and it was never successfully revived. With the Independent Treasury destroyed, and no national bank to take its place, the Federal funds were again deposited in the state banks.

On the third item of his program, tariff revision, Clay was only moderately successful. All that could be achieved at the moment was a slight revision upward within the framework of the compromise legislation of 1833 — a proposal that brought Nay votes from both Benton and Calhoun.

The fourth proposal Clay offered was a new model of his old scheme to distribute the proceeds of public land sales. To secure its passage, the bill was "richly freighted," as Benton recalled, "with inducements to conciliate every interest" — including a pre-emption clause for "the log-cabin men" or settlers! This clause gave any adult male or family head the right to settle on one hundred and sixty acres of public land, and later buy the plot at the minimum government price, free from competitive bids. These concessions did not keep Benton from attacking the distribution part of the measure, as detrimental to the hope of lower land prices. The hodge-podge bill passed, but with a proviso linking the distribution plan with the tariff duties. The result was that distribution never went into operation. Ironically, Clay had sired an act which granted distribution in name only, and pre-emption in practice.[4]

Two days before the special session adjourned in mid-September, 1841, Tyler's Cabinet blew up. He had never been "Tyler Too" on the main economic, social, and political policies desired by the interest groups that dominated the Whig coalition; and during the summer he had asserted (in the *Madisonian,* which was becoming an Administration mouthpiece) the independence of the Executive under the Constitution. The Whigs in Congress had read him out of the party, and every member of the Cabinet resigned, except Webster. Unable to return to the ranks of a Democracy dominated by "the reign of *locofocoism*" under Van Buren, Benton, and Wright, Tyler hoped to build a third party for himself. A legislative stalemate, and now a party stalemate, produced a virtual interregnum — which was to persist until a new issue exploded on the scene at the end of Tyler's term.

All this brought no tears to Benton's eyes. He had always trusted "the *'sober second thought of the people'* " (the phrase was Van Buren's), and "the 'Hundred Days' " of the special session had already seen "the foeman fly." [5]

[2]

IN THE MIDST OF THESE DEVELOPMENTS, Benton was concerned with a number of personal and business matters.

In June, 1841, his favorite niece, the twenty-year-old Sally McDowell, was married to the fortyish Francis Thomas, Congressman from Maryland, at the McDowell's residence in Virginia. Out of this union there was to come nothing but pain and bitterness, in which Sally's "Uncle Benton" was soon involved.

Meanwhile Benton's seventeen-year-old daughter, Jessie, had fallen in love with the handsome, impetuous Lieutenant Frémont. He in turn adored the effervescent Jessie Ann, with her appealingly beautiful oval face, brown hair, and bright brown eyes. Seeing the two constantly together during John Charles Frémont's frequent visits to the C Street home, Thomas and Elizabeth took alarm. Their daughter was too young, and Frémont too low on the long ladder of Army advancement, for the pair to plan marriage. They must wait, as Thomas had waited for Elizabeth twenty-five years before. A year's "probation" was agreed on. Frémont was sent West in charge of a surveying party, and Elizabeth whisked Jessie off to Lexington for the Thomas-McDowell ceremony. Apparently Thomas and Elizabeth did not understand what Jessie Ann later called "that *besoin d'aimer* that made loving and being loved necessary to me" — or perhaps they understood it only too well, and proceeded accordingly. All this opposition was of no use, however, for Jessie and John Charles had tenacity to match Benton's. On October 19, some time after Jessie had returned from Virginia and Frémont from the West, they were married clandestinely in a parlor of Gadsby's Hotel in Washington. They lived apart until some time in November, with Jessie Ann staying with her parents. Finally, in the library of the C Street house, they revealed their secret to Benton and thereafter made their residence together in the Benton home.[6] Over the years Benton, Frémont, and Jessie were to work together on a series of projects for the development of the great Far West.*

Also during the fall, Elizabeth's mother, Sarah Preston McDowell, died. She left the family to settle the distribution of her personal effects — a distasteful task Thomas, Elizabeth, and the others determined to carry through without recourse to "legal proceedings." For example, Elizabeth was willing to be accommodating, but she did want her house slave Sarah to have the bed "Mama" had given her.

In mid-October, Thomas and Elizabeth undertook to buy the C Street house. This they were able to do only by a piece of complicated financing, including a loan of two thousand dollars advanced by Elizabeth's brother James McDowell, but the family felt great joy in acquiring the

---

* The story of Jessie Ann and Frémont, romantic enough in its facts, has become surrounded with apocrypha. Many of the legends were propagated by Jessie herself (capable, intelligent, charming, but an incorrigible romance-writer in her old age), and by her descendants, while others are the products of memoir-writers and (apparently) of attempts to glamorize the pair when John Charles ran for President in 1856. One story, which a memoirist maintains he had from Benton in 1856, reports that Frémont asked James Buchanan how a man could steal a girl under age and marry her without committing a crime; when the answer was to let the girl steal the man, Jessie Ann "mounted her sorrell horse and quietly rode over [to] the Frémont home and John C. Frémont also mounted the horse behind her and she went to the parson's" (Oliphant, "Recollections of Thomas H. Benton," *Missouri Historical Review,* XIV [April-July, 1920], 434). One of the Frémont granddaughters says that Benton ordered Frémont out of the house when told of the marriage, commanding Jessie Ann to stay, and that Jessie silenced her father by clutching her husband's arm and quoting Ruth — "Whither thou goest, I will go; and where thou lodgest, I will lodge" (Recounted in Nevins, *Frémont,* 71). And so on . . . and some of these wonderful stories may even be true. In this account, I have resisted temptation and tried to offer as accurate a report as the sparse available information allows.

title to their home. The completion of the arrangements made it possible for Thomas to leave Washington in mid-October for Kentucky, to look into some parts of the McDowell estate he and Elizabeth had inherited near Versailles, Woodford County, in the center of the state. There, in November, he fell ill, abandoned his original plan to go on to Missouri, and decided to stay in Kentucky until it was time to return to Washington and Congressional business.[7]

The session of 1841-1842 was the longest the Republic had seen, and yet the factional or party stalemate made it aimless, leaderless, and unproductive. It dealt with only two items of importance — while many members, including Benton, gave more attention to presidential politicking than to legislative labors.

The first question of the session was another try at tariff revision. To effect the parturition of a law, it took nine torturous months and resorts to what Benton later called "contrivances, ridiculous inventions, absurd circumlocutions." The problem again was the leadership and counter-leadership of Clay and of President Tyler, who vetoed two measures he didn't like. "Such," commented Benton mordantly to Van Buren, "is the result of attempting to carry on the government by a president without a party." During the debates, Benton took particular occasion to defend the tariff of 1828 from Calhoun's attack on it as a tariff of "abominations," and to reaffirm his (old Jacksonian) belief in a tariff "giving *incidental* protection to home industry." He was anxious, he told Van Buren, to draw a clear line of separation between the Van Buren and Calhoun wings of the Democratic party, in order to head off a developing movement to present Calhoun as "our champion, leader, & *candidate*" — for 1844. But when a bill was finally brought to a vote in August, 1842, it contained too many outright high-protective features to please Benton, and he joined Calhoun in voting against it. Tyler, seeking revenue, managed to approve it. The roll call clearly reflected the strength of interest groups and sectional alignments, and the impotence of party.

The second important item of the session was a proposed new treaty. Since 1783, the boundary between Maine and the British provinces to the north had been uncertain. As Secretary of State, Webster negotiated a treaty with a special British envoy, Lord Ashburton, which was submitted to the Senate for ratification in August, 1842. Promptly Benton attacked the agreement, ranging over the whole history of the affair in an immense, hours-long speech. In particular, he condemned the treaty for what it failed to settle — *the status of the Oregon country in the Far West.* The Convention of 1818 for joint American-British occupation had enabled the British to take *de facto* possession of the right bank of the Columbia, and of the whole fur trade. Meanwhile, "our citizens are beginning to go there" — and yet this matter was left un-resolved in the Webster-Ashburton negotiations! But Benton's oratory was of no use: the treaty was ratified.[8]

Meanwhile, Benton had seen an antagonist of years withdraw from the senatorial cockpit. Weary, ill, disgusted with events, Henry Clay had determined to resign, and on March 31, 1842, he offered a crowded chamber and gallery an emotional, self-exculpating, tear-marked "fare-well" address. It was, Benton jibed, "a true theatrical performance," for soon, he predicted, the orator would "enter the arena," to bring himself forward as the "logical" Whig candidate for 1844. A few days after Clay's resignation, the Russian Minister Baron Bodisco gave a dinner for forty, honoring Lord Ashburton. Sitting side by side among the distinguished, all-male company, Benton and Silas Wright looked at the mercurial Clay "completely miserable" opposite them, "his face clouded, his tongue silent, and his air abstract and desolate." Alas, "poor Clay," Benton commented in a letter to Van Buren, he "lingers here, and seems loth to quit the stage." [9]

At home in Washington, Benton was occupied with other matters. He kept up his correspondence, personal and political, and he practiced some law, arguing a case before the Supreme Court against John J. Crittenden of Kentucky. And . . . he was as always marked by ob-servers in Washington. *By a military man who frequently visited the capital:* No one in Congress "so completely filled my idea of a Roman Senator . . . I admired the ponderous majesty of his presence, and listened with admiration to his surcharged arguments." *By a hostile journalist who wrote "Hurry-Graphs" of national celebrities:* "A carica-ture likeness of Louis Phillippe [the "Bourgeois" King of France] — the same rotundity, the same pear-shaped head . . . His lower features are drilled into imperturbable suavity, while the eye, that undrillable tale-teller, twinkles of inward slyness . . . He wears an ample blue cloak, and a broad-brimmed hat with a high crown." *By a journalist, summing up general repute:* Next to Rufus Choate and Edward Everett (Dartmouth and Harvard), the most finished classics student to serve in Congress, with prodigious knowledge of Roman, English, French, and American political history — "in the minutiae of its details," as well as the "vastness of its comprehension."

Others remarked on Benton's appearance, and even more his habits. The acerbities of politics mellowed by the years, Senator Preston of South Carolina (a kinsman by marriage, but no friend) recalled Benton as inclined to corpulency, not handsome, but to be "remarked in any crowd as a fine-looking *gentleman.*" His Washington routine made him known as the most laborious man of his time — a late dinner — a short nap — perhaps lessons with the younger children until ten — occasionally to some private party with Elizabeth — back by midnight — sleep until *four* AM, when he arose — work in his study for two hours — an early walk — breakfast — and then out of the house for the day's business! In a similar recollection of her father's regimen, Jessie Benton Frémont remembered that he would light his own fire in the third floor study when he rose, and pull a white flannel gown over his underclothes before he sat down to work. This toilsome routine apparently affected Benton's health in 1842. He suffered a lung ailment similar to the one that had prostrated him in 1824, and even he admitted that he felt "uneasy." Friends like Wright thought he was "feeble for him." But as April came Silas observed that Thomas was "mending," and Thomas himself noted in mid-April that he felt "as sound as ever." He thought, though, that "a *campagné* at the Vir[ginia] springs would do good." [10]

Throughout the winter and spring of 1841-1842 Benton had watched the President-making maneuvers. The Tyler Administration bumbled on, "adrift in an eddy," as Benton put it, and various leaders and factions hoped to end the drift in 1844. At the *Globe,* Blair insisted that the overriding issue was a return to power of the old radical Democratic group, under its old Van Buren-Benton-Wright leadership. Condemning an abortive "design to join the democracy to Tyler," Benton recalled his initiative in the movement to have Van Buren renominated — "I saw the course of things as clearly then as I see them now." Everywhere, Van Buren maintained his relations with the old radical Democracy — in New York with the Locofocos, for example, or in Virginia, where James McDowell was an important leader in Van Buren's cause. Everywhere, too, it was assumed that he would be the nominee — although, thinking Benton "the most prominent leader" of his party after the disaster of 1840, several Democrats in politically critical

Pennsylvania and elsewhere proposed Benton as a candidate. But he "most positively" rejected all such suggestions, and asked his would-be sponsors to support Van Buren.[11]

Not everyone, however, was so retiring. A boom was begun for Lewis Cass, soon to return from diplomatic post. The fat, phlegmatic Michigander became a regular caller at the Benton residence, and Benton was pleased to find Cass in entire agreement with him on the Webster-Ashburton treaty. In addition, what Benton called the "intrigue" for Calhoun developed, while Calhoun's friends warned him that the election of Van Buren, and "the succession of Mr. Benton," were the darkest clouds in his future. Meanwhile, Benton's friend James Buchanan emerged as a "favorite son" candidate — complaining, however, that he could not count on *unanimous* support in Pennsylvania, as Benton could count on "such a support from the Democracy of Missouri in case he were a candidate." In the West, finally, movements were launched for the former Vice-President, Johnson of Kentucky.[12]

From February through July, Van Buren made a long trip through the South and West. His ostensible purpose was to visit Old Hickory at the Hermitage. But he also hoped to counter Calhoun's efforts to destroy his influence in the South. As Van Buren traveled, Benton bombarded him with letters. He urged the New Yorker to go up the Missouri River as far as Booneville and Fayette, into "the most magnificent agricultural country upon the face of the earth — an upland Egypt." He also urged a journey through Illinois and the Territories of Iowa and Wisconsin to the Falls of St. Anthony on the Mississippi River — "it will be a sensation if you visit these remote parts." He proposed a return route by way of Erie, Pennsylvania, and Pittsburgh — "you see I chalk out a good circuit for you," a circuit the traveler did not quite achieve. He declared that the spontaneous enthusiasm for Van Buren in the "Great West" — "no machinery, or secret springs, have been set in motion" — showed that "it is not gunpowder popularity alone which can excite [the people's] enthusiasm." [13]

[3]

THOUGH THE NATIONAL GOVERNMENT was at a stalemate, Benton saw hope for the radical Democratic program in his home state. Soon after the aimless session of Congress adjourned at the end of August, 1842, he left (without his family) for Missouri, to play hard-money advocate and local party leader again. In the process, he became embroiled in a new hurly-burly of factional fighting.

Traveling down the Ohio on his way west, Benton suffered a comic mishap. At Cincinnati he left his steamboat to make a visit in Kentucky. The boat rounded to before dawn to land Benton, who in the darkness stepped off for the ground. The craft was not in far enough, and he dropped (cloak, baggage, and all) into the water. Drenched but unharmed, he soon resumed his journey to St. Louis, where he arrived on October 16. Meanwhile, two of his kin were completing a longer trip. In June, Frémont had set out in command of an expedition through the Far West, into the Rocky Mountain country around South Pass. With him were Benton's son Randolph Benton, aged twelve, and Joshua Brant's son Henry Brant, eighteen. The boys, however, were left at Fort Platte in July, before the expedition went on into the dangerous upper Missouri River country. Young Randolph, Lieutenant Frémont recalled, "had been the life of the camp, and the *petit garçon* was much regretted by the men, to whom his buoyant spirits had afforded great amusement." Back in Missouri by early October, the explorer stopped off briefly at St. Louis on his way to Washington.[14]

Throughout his stay in Missouri, Benton's time was devoted to politics. In April, 1842, the Democrats had elected a majority of the city council in St. Louis, and the Mayor — Benton's young protégé Montgomery Blair. In August, 1842, they had elected (at large) all of the *five* Congressmen the state was entitled to under the new census, all of them pro-Benton. Still, all was not well from Old Bullion's point of view. In the spring of 1841, Abel Corbin at the *Argus* had started to backslide from the hard-money gospel, toward the heretical "Soft" financial opinions of the St. Louis commercial groups. Soon he was attacking the outstate Democratic leaders at Fayette, in the center of the state, as the "Fayette junto." The attack was aimed particularly at Benton's friend, Dr. John J. Lowry, president of the Fayette branch of the Bank of Missouri, and was brazenly conducted in the name of "Col. Benton himself." But the Colonel ("measures, not men") was not deceived, and he determined that "another press or an exchange of editors" was in order, as he put it to Governor Reynolds. He consulted with the veteran, fiftyish Shadrach Penn of the Louisville (Kentucky) *Advertiser,* and with V. P. Van Antwerp, of Iowa Territory, with that end in view. In October, 1841, the *Argus* was sold to Penn, who replaced it two months later with a new journal called the *Missouri Reporter.*

In 1842, meanwhile, the situation had been further complicated when
the chill of hard times finally reached Missouri, accompanied by a
currency shortage, falling prices and wages, and sheriff's sales. Cries
for "relief" were heard, and to many "relief" meant *easy money.* The
conflict between Softs and Hards sharpened, taking more and more the
form of an antagonism between St. Louis and outstate factions.

With characteristic energy and decision, Benton projected his influence into this situation. Stopping only briefly in St. Louis, he went on to
Jefferson City. There he essayed once again the role of lobbyist and
active party leader in behalf of his currency program, closeting himself
at length with Governor Reynolds and with legislators. Publicly, he
warned again that "a base currency afflicts the state," which the "Federalists" sought to perpetuate in order to drive the people to a new
national bank. He cried: "I began the war against this Bank almost
'solitary and alone' twelve years ago (for I had but few backers, but
among them JACKSON and VAN BUREN), and have lived to see the
institution in dust and infamy, and its foremost champion [Daniel
Webster] referring to it as 'an obsolete idea.'" This broad composition
drew angry comment from the *Republican.* It was, Editor Chambers
cracked, "a specimen of bombast and egotism which could hardly be
excelled . . . the pronouns *I* and *me* are the most conspicuous words in
the letter, and it is evident the writer thinks himself the Hercules of the
day." [15]

Back in St. Louis, Benton faced a new flare-up of factionalism. The
Reporter, the paper he had midwifed the year before, had taken up a
devious course of supporting Soft policies and partisans in St. Louis,
while avoiding an open breach with the Hards. Now, on November 1,
1842, the *Reporter* carried an angry editorial. No man, it declared,
should be allowed "to dictate to a party" — "men of the same party
[might] often differ," and no one should be permitted to act as "an
arrogant and arbitrary [party] *dictator."* This doctrine was of course
anathema to Benton and his fellow radicals, who labored for a militant,
responsible party to serve a programmatic democracy. The day Shadrach
Penn published this "Private Judgment" editorial, Benton wrote Governor Reynolds, noting that the *Reporter* had gone on "til it came to the
point of openly attacking me: I say openly, for the two or three columns
against the dictator had as well been against me by name." A few days
later, however, the breach was apparently patched. The "dictator" had
stopped his subscription — "this brought things to a *head,* and now all

seems to be orthodox." [16] Actually this was too sanguine. In trying, turbulent years to come, as Benton persisted in the role of policy advocate,
the *dictator* cry and the doctrine of "private judgment" within the party
were used against him again and again.*

Meanwhile, Benton busied himself again with the currency legislation
he wanted passed in the Assembly. On the eve of his departure, in
mid-November, he wrote a parting political testament to Governor
Reynolds — he had sent to Assemblymen W. G. Minor (of Cole)
and G. W. Huston (of Lincoln) "sketches of two bills a little more
matured, but of the same structure with the skeletons I gave you." Ten
days later the legislature met. Early in the session it re-elected, all but
unanimously, Benton's old friend Lewis Linn to the Senate, and then
turned to financial policy. Bills giving flesh to the "skeletons" Old
Bullion had prepared were introduced, and passed, under the effective
party leadership of Minor, Huston, and other lieutenants, including
Claiborne Fox Jackson of the powerful Fayette group of politicians. The
new laws prohibited, with severe penalties, the passing by any corporation, moneylender, or broker of bank notes smaller than ten dollars;
outlawed dealings in the notes of non-specie-paying banks and in other
"shinplasters"; and prohibited banking and note-issue operations by any
corporate body other than the Bank of Missouri. These measures
were at once assailed as outrageous bills of "pains and penalties" by
conservative Democrats (including Shadrach Penn in his *Reporter*), and
by Whigs. But they marked a final triumph for Old Bullion and his
radical Democratic allies.

In his years-long crusade for hard-money action in Missouri, Benton
had shown his ability to play politics on two levels. He had operated on
the doctrinal level of *program* — cleaving to the majority-rule principle,
laboring to get "public opinion to come up with him," persisting without
retreat. He had also operated on the pragmatic level of *organization,* of
strategy and tactic — outmaneuvering men like Penn, and allying himself with the Fayette group. His skill as both advocate and organizer
was typical of successful movers and shakers.

Still, the factional opposition persisted. Glumly, but perceptively,
Benton summarized the situation in Missouri. "Our majority is *too*

* While Benton had acquired new enemies like Shadrach Penn, he lost one old
one in 1842. On August 29 in that year, his confirmed, unforgiving, malevolent,
personal foe of twenty-five years, John B. C. Lucas, died. One of the legacies the
old patriarch left his family was a tradition of undying hostility toward the "murderer" of Charles Lucas.

large," he wrote a friend; "we shall be much stronger when the number is reduced, and when two or three newspapers shall *openly* act with the enemy which are now secretly doing it." [17] With the Democratic party clearly ascendant, diverse interest groups were contending for control within its organization.

[4]

IN WASHINGTON, where party stalemate and continuing lack of effective presidential leadership produced another ineffectual session of Congress, Benton was absorbed in family affairs. In particular, he was concerned about his wife's health. Often ill in the past, she had in the fall of 1842 suffered the first of a series of debilitating attacks. Her "nerves are much shattered, with tendencies to vertigo," Thomas wrote Elizabeth's brother James — "I endeavor to make it her only care to take [care] of her health."

Meanwhile, Jessie Benton Frémont had given birth to her first child, the Bentons' first grandchild, who was named Elizabeth after her grandmother. As soon as she was able after this event, Jessie showed that she was her father's daughter by setting to work, sometimes with her father's help, to add literary finish to the report John Charles Frémont was preparing of his first expedition West. Their aim was not simply to map the area and sketch possible routes to it, but to describe the country. Here Jessie's literary skill helped to produce a readable, useful guidebook. Throughout the fall and winter of 1842-1843, the C Street home served as a nursery not only for the Frémont baby, but for the Frémont report.

During this same period, Thomas was having difficulties meeting the payments on the new house. Unable to squeeze more than $1000 out of his own means, he had to borrow the balance of $2000 — first a thousand from his friend and Congressional colleague John Miller, and then, in desperation, another thousand from the fur magnate Pierre Chouteau, Jr. in St. Louis. Chouteau readily offered to lend Benton what he needed, and later agreed to extend the note at a reduced interest of 7 per cent. In addition, Thomas worked to realize something from the Woodford County, Kentucky, property, by investing another thousand in a newfangled circular-saw mill to cut lumber on the place. In December, 1842, he went to Baltimore to examine every aspect of the horse-driven contraption. In April, 1843, when Thomas had a chance to watch his wonderful new sawmill in operation on the Kentucky lands, he was so pleased he wrote a testimonial. The machine cut smooth and straight, turning out six hundred feet of lumber in four hours with six horses.[18] Despite these resources, Thomas still had to renew his notes to Pierre Chouteau, Jr., from time to time for years to come.

There was good family-political news from Virginia. Elizabeth's brother James McDowell was elected governor — and McDowell's election was a good omen for Benton's friend and presidential candidate, Van Buren. Weighing his brother-in-law's triumph, and Congressional victories throughout the nation that gave the Democrats a strong majority in the coming House and reduced the Whig majority in the Senate, Benton was sanguine. He predicted flatly that "two years will bring the democracy into power," with Van Buren at their head.[19]

Soon after the beginning of the new year, 1843, a major debate developed in the Senate. The issue, which provoked a violent opposition, was a bill introduced by Lewis Linn to effect American occupation of the huge, disputed Oregon or Northwest area on the Pacific. The measure provided for erecting stockades and blockhouses along the "best" road to Oregon; for a grant of 640 acres to every white, male settler over eighteen who would cultivate the land for five years; and for extending American territorial government over the area north to the forty-ninth parallel. Promptly, Calhoun rose to attack the bill's land-grant provision, which, he declared, would conflict with the joint-occupation agreements with Britain of 1818 and 1827. This complaint was echoed by the scholarly Rufus Choate, who had taken Webster's Senate seat. In reply, Benton argued that the area was *legally* the possession of the United States, and ridiculed "the British pretensions" to ownership — while Lewis Linn quietly corrected, elaborated, and explained. Then, suddenly, *pianissimo* gave way to *fortissimo*. The spare, big-boned Hotspur who was now Calhoun's fellow Senator from South Carolina, George McDuffie, rose to thunder at the whole Oregon idea. Could anyone believe that such a far-distant land would ever form a state in the American Union? "I would not . . . give a pinch of snuff for the whole territory. I wish to God we did not own it." Could anyone believe that farmers from Pennsylvania and New York, or even Ohio and Missouri, would go to settle such a place? "God forbid!" And so on . . . in a roaring speech filled with expostulations and exclamation points. Early in February, nonetheless, the bill passed the Senate, 24 to 22. The New England mercantile-manufacturing and the South Atlantic plantation representatives lined up in opposition, the Middle Atlantic votes were divided, and Yeas came overwhelmingly from agrarian spokesmen of the Northwest and Southwest. The vision of a yeoman-founded Far West Benton had projected twenty-five years before seemed a step nearer realization. But the bill died in the House, and the Oregon question remained unsettled.[20]

Another question involving westward extension also agitated official Washington. Early in his administration Tyler had suggested to Webster that they might win glory for themselves by annexing Texas to the United States. The President had noted: *"Slavery,* I know that is the objection" — but had insisted that annexation of the sprawling Texas republic would benefit North as well as South. In January, 1843, a letter urging immediate annexation appeared in the Administration organ, the *Madisonian,* signed by Thomas W. Gilmer, former Governor of Virginia and now a pro-Tyler Congressman from that state. A copy was sent by Aaron V. Brown, a Democratic Representative from Tennessee, to Andrew Jackson, who replied that he had always favored and still favored the attachment of Texas to the United States, as a matter of *safety* for New Orleans and the West. Jackson's letter was shown about in Washington, though it was not published for thirteen months. Coming as it did during a political stalemate with few great issues to mark off parties, the "Gilmer letter" seemed to Benton like "a clap of thunder in a clear sky." The agitation of the subject was portentous, but nothing was done about it in the short, lame-duck session.[21]

Soon after the adjournment of Congress in March, the Benton family set out for Missouri — Elizabeth stopping off with the children to visit her brother at the Governor's Mansion in Richmond, while Thomas went alone by way of Cherry Grove and Kentucky.

The Bentons' son-in-law, John Charles Frémont, now just thirty, also went his separate way, at the head of his second, enlarged exploring expedition. For guides, the young lieutenant had the hardy, resourceful "mountain men," Thomas ("Broken Hand") Fitzpatrick and Christopher ("Kit") Carson. As part of its equipment, the group took a howitzer firing a twelve-pound ball, acquired from the Army commander at St. Louis, Stephen Watts Kearny. While the expedition was making final preparations at Kaw Landing on the Missouri frontier, a letter came to St. Louis from the Topographical Corps. Opening it, in accord with her husband's instructions, Jessie found that it was an order to Frémont to return to Washington and "explain" his purpose in taking a cannon on an exploring journey. With an imperiousness of decision that would have done credit to her father, the eighteen-year-old Jessie Ann withheld the order, and sent a special messenger with a letter to her husband urging him (without elaboration or explanation) to leave immediately. "Good-bye," Frémont wrote back; "I trust, and *go.*" The expedition was to carry him into the Oregon country, and finally down into the Mexican province of California. It was August, 1844, before he saw his family and civilization again. As Thomas watched his son-in-law's efforts to explore, map, and describe the Far West, he could at last feel that his ideas of Western development "moved."

In mid-June, Benton arrived at St. Louis on the steamboat *Valley Forge,* and joined his family again at Colonel Brant's house. Told of Jessie's hurried letter to her husband, he approved entirely, and wrote the War Department taking responsibility on himself and condemning the recall.[22] There the matter rested.

[5]

THROUGHOUT THE SUMMER AND FALL OF 1843, Benton was immersed in the factional infighting of Missouri politics which his insistent crusade for hard money had precipitated.

During his absence, the heretics under Shadrach Penn had organized a full-blown intra-party opposition. In his *Reporter,* Penn attacked the hard-money Democrats, and fulminated against "the malign influence of the Central Clique" at Fayette. He announced formally for Van Buren, but filled columns with praise of Richard M. Johnson as a Western candidate. In dealing with Benton, however, he limited himself to innuendo. He decried (but published) Whig charges that Benton was a party dictator, and hinted — "nothing would so effectually destroy the popularity of the distinguished Senator, as the belief that he was really attempting to dictate." He suggested blandly that "the elevated position of Col. Benton requires that he should devote his thoughts almost exclusively to national affairs," leaving alone state issues and local party organization. He lamented (but published) rumors of a Benton-Van Buren "bargain and intrigue" for succession to the presidency. And so on, through column after column of carefully contrived intellectual sleight of hand.[23]

The disciples and allies of Old Bullion fought back. The *Inquirer* at Jefferson City cried that "war has been declared." It was a war "in favor of shin-plasters and swindling shops, against half-eagles and Benton mint drops . . . every man to his post!" Throughout the state, Democratic papers took their posts as pro-Benton or anti-Benton (overtly or covertly), with new presses founded at strategic places to further the factional causes. (The press enlistments on each side were about equal.) The Whigs were delighted. In particular, the *Republican* praised Shadrach Penn's "liberal" financial views, and condemned "the doctrine of Benton: to withdraw from the commercial community as much as possible the means whereby it is sustained [paper money credit] in order to prevent commerce from gaining power." More broadly, Editor Chambers's attitude was that of the disgruntled pioneer wife who watched a fight between her husband and a bear — "she did not care one farthing who whipped." [24]

A re-alignment of groups accompanied the dramatic appeals to public opinion. The developments in formal party organization that had been going on for years accelerated in the 1840's, with committees and conventions becoming more regular, candidates adhering more consistently to party designations, and party "tickets" being supplied to voters. Now the intra-party warfare brought with it a proliferation of informally organized but relatively cohesive factional groups. Hards and Softs held rallies and counterrallies, sponsored speeches and counterspeeches, and called caucuses — with leadership in St. Louis taken particularly by Montgomery Blair and his younger, Princeton-educated brother Francis, Jr., or "Frank." Disciplined battles at local conventions and in local party association meetings became the order of the day.

Until mid-July, Benton remained in St. Louis. There a fellow townsman recalled that it was beautiful to see him enter Dr. Potts's Presbyterian Church at Fifth and Walnut, Elizabeth Benton on his arm. The tempestuous politico was always charmingly chivalrous to his wife, and apparently "all the tumult in his stormy soul grew quiet in her presence." But he could be "stormy" in casual as well as political relationships. Once he took a hack from the courthouse in a rain, and was asked to pay a dollar for the six-block ride. Enraged, he protested vociferously and found out the legal fare: twenty-five cents. Paying that and no more, he grandly tossed a half dollar each to two boys standing nearby — "I don't care for the money, but I won't be imposed on." In his dealings with his fellow citizens, Benton eschewed the usual election-

eering arts. Greeting constituents on Fourth Street, he would shake
hands with stately courtesy, but he plainly did not like this part of
politics. He considered his service, not the occupational affability of
the politician, his recommendation to the people.

Visiting one day at a tobacco warehouse, Benton was introduced to
a planter from (Whig) Callaway County. This gentleman failed to hear
the Senator's name, and began descanting on the dishonesty of politicians, including "Tom Benton, the high priest of Locofocoism in Missouri." Was Benton really dishonest? the Senator asked, realizing that
the planter did not know who he was.

"Why," the answer came, everyone knew that he had "exhibited early
at college a strong disposition to *take things* not exactly his own property." This, the *Republican* asserted gleefully in recounting the incident,
was "a stumper," and Benton turned away, "cut to the quick." 25

In mid-July, Benton set out on a two-months tour of the Missouri
interior. Following the practice he had adopted in his tour of 1839, he
avoided formal meetings, talked informally with local party lieutenants
and privates, and outlined his views again and again in long manifestoes. His itinerary included Jefferson City, Boonville on the Missouri
north of the capital, Warsaw in Benton county to the South, Glasgow, a
thriving hemp, tobacco, and apple port on the Missouri upriver from
Boonville, and of course Fayette. While Thomas traveled, an epidemic
threatened his family's health. But Elizabeth took Eliza, Jessie Ann, and
her infant to the country. Ran was staying twelve miles out of St. Louis
on Gravois Creek with a German family to learn the German language,
and Sarah and Susan remained safely at their French boarding school.
In mid-September, Benton returned from Fayette to St. Louis by Missouri River steamboat, an overnight trip. A fellow-passenger remembered him as he sat in the barber's chair in the morning to be shaved
— "a large, robust man of florid complexion." He breakfasted with his
traveling companion, Dr. John J. Lowry, and then walked to the bow,
where he politely acknowledged introductions to bystanders. There he
stood awhile asking about the varieties of timber on the banks, and then
returned to his stateroom. His manner was "dignified, reserved, and by no
means familiar or communicative." This increasing reserve, even on a
political tour, led foes to criticize "the immaculate Benton," as the
Republican called him, as too unbending for a political leader.

Back in St. Louis, Benton played midwife again for a new paper.
Called the *Missourian,* it was to be edited by V. P. Van Antwerp, once

intended as Penn's partner in the *Reporter*. Van Antwerp promised "to keep prominently before his readers the principles of the great party with which he acts, as promulgated by their distinguished supporters." His prospectus, with subscription blanks, went out with a letter signed by Benton, in which he urged systematic, businesslike efforts to get the *Missourian* on a sound basis. By mid-October, Benton could assure Governor Reynolds that the *Missourian* would have "the largest and most general circulation" that any Missouri paper had ever received. But many subscriptions came without money, and Benton asked Reynolds if he could make a loan "as a business transaction" to help tide Van Antwerp over. In passing, Benton noted reports that the Whigs would run no candidates of their own in the 1844 elections, but would support "the *Shad democrats,* which of course will be *fishy.*" He had managed to get a house "fitted up" for Elizabeth and the children during his absence at Congress, and he invited the Governor and his friends to call "whether I am at home or not."

In the pleasant, late-October Indian summer, Benton set out for a short visit at Hannibal and Palmyra to the north in Marion County. There he followed his practice of talking with friends and supporters, while the Whig press railed that he had lined up the party in the region for the Hards and the *Missourian,* and lamented — "Poor Shad! he is already gutted and pickled!! — he no longer swims in Democratic water." [26]

In St. Louis, however, "poor Shad" was fighting back, in the open this time. He ran a series of letters addressed to Benton (ten in all, from October 24 through November 11), in which he fired every round in his arsenal. He plugged the "dictator" theme — you are "a man who has wielded power until he fancies his will is law . . . becoming more unsocial and dictatorial the longer you continue in office." He arraigned Benton for saying that he would not support Calhoun if Calhoun was the Democratic nominee. He condemned Benton for not supporting the establishment of separate Congressional districts in Missouri. And so on . . . fixing all the blame for division in the Missouri Democracy on Benton. [27]

In the midst of this fantasia of factionalism, an event occurred which was to have important consequences for national affairs, as well as for Benton and Missouri affairs. One night at the end of April, 1843, Senator Linn had awakened his wife from her sleep. He had distinctly heard a voice saying — "Prepare, Lewis F. Linn, for this year thy soul shall be required of thee." He refused to accept Mrs. Linn's insistence that he had been dreaming, and asked her to note the incident in her daybook. A little more than five months later, at the beginning of October, he died of a heart ailment at his home in Ste. Genevieve. A week later, a memorial meeting was held in the courthouse in St. Louis, at which Benton spoke briefly in eulogy of his old colleague. He had lost a friend, but Missouri and the West had lost a great spokesman. It was Lewis Linn's tact and wisdom that had secured the Platte area for the state in 1836, despite the fact that it would open previously free territory to slaves. It was Lewis Linn who had been carrying the battle to settle the Oregon country. Now, like Mirabeau of France, he was cut down in the midst of his great project, and his "political legatees" must "take his great measure and carry it through." In Jefferson City, Governor Reynolds appointed David R. Atchison, of Platte County on Missouri's northwestern frontier, to the vacant Senate seat. To Governor Reynolds Benton wrote: "I believe there is general satisfaction with the new Senatorial appointment, and I for one am much pleased with it." [28] Over the years, however, he was to find that he had been much too optimistic.

Shortly before Linn's death, Thomas's brother Jesse Benton had also died. Willing the bulk of his estate to his wife Mary and a share to brother Thomas after his wife's death, Jesse also provided that his personal servants (slaves) should "be free and forever emancipated on the death of my wife & I request all proper measures to be taken to have them sent to the care of Thomas H. Benton or to the children of Thomas H. Benton in Missouri, or to some state where slavery is not tolerated." [29] This was an interesting testament for a man who had lived his life in the South.

Meanwhile, in mid-November, Benton left St. Louis and his family for Washington and new battles in the national political arena.

CHAPTER 13

Thwarted Peacemaker

1843 - 1847

.

O N THE AFTERNOON of December 4, 1843, as Benton and several other Senators were descending the steps of the national Capitol, he was picked out of the group by Congressman Brown of Tennessee — the man who had sent a copy of the "Gilmer letter" to Andrew Jackson to elicit his views on Texas annexation. Now Brown asked Benton to put himself on record. Surely Benton, an early opponent of relinquishing Texas, would take a prominent part now in getting it back . . . ? The reply was warm, abrupt, and perhaps somewhat disconcerting.

"Sir," Benton rumbled, "that movement is, on the part of some, an intrigue for the Presidency and a plot to dissolve the Union — on the part of others, a Texas scrip and land speculation; and I am against it!"

An "intrigue" to control the presidential election, a "plot" to effect disunion . . . this colloquy at the beginning of the new session of Congress was prologue to a new, unfolding drama. For years, by several overland routes and by a Gulf route, "goers" from the United States and immigrants from England, France, and Germany too had been streaming in to the vast plains of the Texas area. During the summer and fall of 1844, some five thousand settlers were to pass through the Texas gateway at Van Buren, Arkansas, alone. Most of the Anglo-American settlers came from the Southern, slaveholding states, many of them from Tennessee (including Benton's old friend Sam Houston) and from Missouri (including two of Benton's nephews). These Southern settlers brought a cotton, slaveholding economy to Texas — though there were Northern and nonslaveholding immigrants also. As the broad lands filled, more and more settlers looked to incorporation of Texas into the United States. Thus filial annexation sentiment in Texas buttressed the annexation campaign in the United States, which was particularly strong in the South and Southwest. Now, in December, 1843, Benton was sure that his encounter with Aaron V. Brown was not a matter of chance. Rather as a busy worker in the movement for immediate annexation, the Tennessee Congressman had begun the conversation as "a thing of premeditation" — and he had indeed gotten Benton on the record.[1]

Nearly three months later, chance did take a hand in the Texas drama. On February 28, 1844, a party of some hundred guests went aboard the new man-of-war *Princeton* for a cruise down the Potomac. Among them were Tyler, Abel P. Upshur of Virginia, who had in 1843 replaced Webster as Secretary of State, Thomas Gilmer of the Texas annexation letter, recently named Secretary of the Navy, and Benton. About four o'clock, on the return trip, most of the guests went forward to watch the fire of a wonderful new big gun called the "Peacemaker." At the last minute, Tyler went back to the cabin. A Lieutenant Hunt whispered to Benton that he could follow the flight of the ball better if he would take a position about six feet back of the breech. The order to fire was given. Then, as Benton described it later, "I saw the hammer pulled back — heard a tap — saw a flash — felt a blast in the face, and knew that my hat was gone; and that was the last I knew of the world, or of myself, for a time of which I can give no account." Regaining consciousness, he saw "the gun itself split open — two seamen, the blood oozing from their ears and nostrils, rising and reeling near me . . . the gun had burst." Thousands of fragments had flown past Benton. Friends lifted him up and led him to the bow, observing "a supernatural whiteness" in his face and hands.* The President had been saved by going to the cabin, and Benton by taking a place behind the gun, though his left eardrum was burst by the concussion. A number of others were killed instantly, among them Upshur and Gilmer. For several days Benton was confined to his room, suffering from the daily recurrence of a slight fever. During this time, as one observer put it, Benton's house was "literally besieged to know the extent of his danger." He was not able to return to the Senate until mid-March. Then, his friend John Fairfield (newly elected to the Senate from Maine) observed, he could by stopping his nostrils "force the air through his ear, making a noise equal to the wind coming from bellows." [2]

* One newspaper report that went the rounds has Benton falling on the deck, supposing himself severely wounded, and then declares that "at this critical moment, while gasping for returning breath, he exclaimed, in a broken voice, to those around him, 'Say to Captain Stockton that this accident has not impaired my confidence in the glorious experiment of the *Princeton,* or lessened my regard for her brave and gallant commander'" (Qu. in *Missourian,* May 21, 1844). The Colonel was an inveterate rhetorician, but this undoubtedly belongs in the Exclamations We Doubt Ever Got Exclaimed Department (Broken Voice Division) — particularly since the exclaimer was unconscious for some time after the explosion.

Despite such pranks, Benton was profoundly impressed by his escape. Friends recalled him referring to it as a sort of providential intervention — with Lieutenant Hunt presumably acting as the agent of Providence.

[2]

THROUGH 1843 AND 1844 the Texas "movement," as Benton called it, had barely moved. After Upshur's death in the *Princeton* disaster, however, Tyler appointed Calhoun Secretary of State. Thereupon the Texas cause and politics in general began to undergo a transformation. By April, 1844, Calhoun had pushed through a treaty providing for immediate annexation, signed by Tyler in Washington and President Sam Houston in Texas. The annexation issue was ready to go to the Senate.

Meanwhile, Calhoun projected some other issues into the controversy. Among the papers Upshur had left, he found a statement by Lord Aberdeen, the British foreign minister. It expressed a general desire to see slavery ended through the world, though it denied charges that Britain was plotting for abolition in Texas. Immediately, Calhoun wrote a long reply which made *slavery* and its *protection* by the Federal government a central concern in the Texas business. This letter "leaked" into the public press. Both Benton and Francis Blair thought that Calhoun had thus shown a determination to make Texas annexation a special, plantation-interest, sectional concern. Both also thought Calhoun's letter a maneuver to weaken Van Buren in the presidential race, because he could never accept annexation on such grounds. Meantime, extremists of the South began to agitate a new slogan — "Texas or Disunion." [3]

These developments were signs of the growth of a plantation economy, society, and politics. As the world's textile industry demanded more and more cotton, the slave labor system spread increasingly into the Southwest. The yeoman or small-producer class Benton championed was increasingly pressed between the expanding plantation-owning class of the rich lowlands and the impoverished-white class of the hill country. There were few well-to-do planters; from their power base of property and position, however, they steadily enlarged their influence and control as an effective interest group. Pulled by the lure of profit, pushed by exhaustion of the soil in old areas, and worried that the growth of population in the North would make them a minority in the nation and in Congress, many planter leaders looked to new lands in the West to make new slave states — though others eschewed expansionist ideas. Over the years, such developments were to bring a sharpening conflict of interests between planter-slaveholding groups on the one side, and free-holding-agrarian groups on the other. As the Bank and currency conflicts had dominated politics in the 1830's, so slavery and slavery-related sectional issues were to dominate the 1840's. In 1844, several state legislatures in the South passed resolutions favoring Texas annexation. In the North, several went on record opposing it.

During the second half of April, 1844, a parade of public letters on the Texas question appeared. Clay opposed annexation "at this time" as likely to lead to war with Mexico. Van Buren questioned "immediate annexation," echoed the fear of war with Mexico, and declared that he would not trim his opinions "for the unworthy purpose of increasing my chances for political promotion." But James K. Polk of Tennessee, who was generally viewed as the "logical" Democratic choice for the Vice-Presidency, declared flatly for *"immediate re-annexation."* At the end of the month, Benton joined the parade in a long public answer to a communication from forty-nine members of the Texas Congress. They were right, he declared, to address their plea for annexation to *him,* "being, as I am, the first opponent of the treaty which dismembered your territory from our Union." He looked in the long run "to the recovery of Texas" as "inevitable." But immediate annexation would revive the (legal) state of war between Texas and Mexico, which was for the moment quiescent. Also, there was the question of the extent of the Texas territory — "I, who consider what I am about, always speak of Texas as constituted at the time of the treaty of 1819, and not as constituted by the Republic of Texas," which claimed an imperial domain including vast reaches of the old Mexican provinces of Chihuahua, Nuevo Mexico, and Tamaulipas. Let us "not repeat the blunder [of 1819], and double the calamity, by the *manner* of recovering [Texas] in 1844." * This blunt and somewhat egotistical manifesto, first published in the *Globe,* was picked up in the national newsmagazine, *Niles Register,* and finally printed in pamphlet form. In May, after others had committed themselves, careful Lewis Cass, advised to seize

---

* In an aside, Benton noted that John Quincy Adams had recently made a declaration on the floor of the House concerning Texas, and proclaimed that this statement absolved Adams "from all censure" for the Adams-Onis treaty by which American claims to Texas had been yielded in 1819, "and places the blame on the majority of Mr. Monroe's cabinet" — including, especially, John Calhoun. Scarcely two weeks later, Benton repeated this absolution on the floor of the Senate.

the chance "to take the wind all out of the sails of Van Buren and
Benton and leave them hard aground," endorsed immediate annexation.

At the Hermitage, Jackson read the Van Buren and Benton letters,
and wrote Blair that he had "shed tears of regret." He was sure Van
Buren's letter would "lose him many western and southern votes at the
Baltimore convention," and he feared Benton's declaration would "enable Penn jnr. to put Col. Benton politically down in Missouri" — in the
forthcoming senatorial election, presumably. Before long Jackson was
convinced that Benton had "led Van Buren into his unfortunate Texas
position." [4] For the first time in twenty years, Benton was in sharp disagreement with "the old chief."

With the stage thus set, the first act of the Texas drama opened in
the Senate. Benton led off in a pyrotechnic attack on the Tyler-Calhoun
treaty, which consumed the better part of three legislative days in the
middle of May. He began with a long (if sometimes misapplied) historical development, quoting showily from such authorities as Humboldt's
La Nouvelle Espagne (in French). He noted that the Administration was
"explicit in presenting the Rio Grande del Norte, in its whole extent,"
as the southern and western boundary of the area to be annexed. But
to call this "Texas" would be to attempt "the seizure of two thousand
miles of a neighbor's dominion," including such purely Mexican towns
as Santa Fe and Albuquerque. More broadly, Benton thundered on,
there was the question of *war*. The "ratification of the treaty would be,
of itself, war between the United States and Mexico." And what a war
it would be! — "unjust in itself — upon a peaceable neighbor — in
violation of treaties and of pledged neutrality — unconstitutionally
made." Turning to domestic political consequences, Benton decried the
timing of the treaty — "its sudden explosion upon us, like a ripened
plot and a charged bomb," just before the Baltimore convention of the
Democratic party. And why? — precisely to give the "bomb" time "to
burst . . . blowing up candidates for the Presidency . . . and furnish-
ing a new Texas candidate, anointed with gunpowder." Apparently,
Tyler wanted "to play Jackson" — but he must take care, for "from
the sublime to the ridiculous there is but a step . . . the hero missed,
and harlequin appears." Finally, Benton spoke of the slavery issue. He
thought about half of the territory *claimed* by annexationists was
unsuited to slavery, argued that the slave-free question was thus in fact
"neutralized," and regretted that "a different aspect has been given to

it." He then outlined his views on slavery in general. *First* — "I am Southern by my birth; Southern in my affections, interest, and connections . . . I am a slaveholder, and shall take the fate of other slaveholders in every aggression upon that species of property." *But* — "I must see a real cause of danger before I take alarm. I am against the cry of wolf, when there is no wolf." *Finally* — "I will not engage in schemes for [slavery] *extension* into regions where it was never known . . . where a slave's face was never seen." This position was far from the all-out, proslavery policy Benton had espoused in his "La Salle" articles of 1829, and in the Benton-Webster-Hayne debate of 1830. In conclusion, Benton noted that for twenty-four years he had found that when he "voted on my own convictions," his action has given "satisfaction to my constituents." He would again vote his convictions. If that brought "the extinction of my political life," as he had been warned it might, "I should have to embrace it." [5]

It was an effective, comprehensive, courageous effort, and it was widely published, widely praised, and widely damned. While nascent free-soilers hailed Benton's words, proslavery leaders thought of him henceforth as a deserter. Calhoun condemned the speech as "a mass of contradictions, resting on baseless assumptions." Warily, seeking middle ground, Buchanan regretted that he had to differ with his old friend's views, and *hoped* that the oration would not injure Benton "in the estimation of his party." The Massachusetts historian and radical-Democrat George Bancroft observed that "the *Whigs* are for once delighted with Benton," who "rule[d] the Senate on the Texas debate." Years later, a Democratic journalist commented more drastically — "the annexation of Texas was the rock upon which Benton split." [6]

The treaty was debated intermittently through the first week of June. During the debate, Benton recalled later, speculators in Texas land and scrip crowded the lobbies ("lobby-ists" again) and operated on the Administration and in the newspapers. Finally, on June 8, the Senate met and argued until nine at night, and then voted. Instead of the two-thirds majority needed for ratification, the treaty got only 16 Yeas to 35 Nays. All the twenty-nine Whig members but one from Mississippi voted Nay, while the twenty-two Democrats split fifteen Yeas and seven Nays, with Benton and Atchison cancelling each other's votes. Though the members from the New England states voted overwhelmingly Nay, party and factional considerations, more than sectional interest group alignments, produced the result. The Democrats who voted against the treaty were all old-school agrarian radicals — Benton, Wright, Niles of Connecticut, John Fairfield, Allen and Tappan of Ohio, and Atherton of New Hampshire. They were promptly and widely vilified as traitors and worse by the Tyler, Calhoun, and pro-annexation Democratic press, including the self-important *Madisonian* in Washington and Penn's noisy *Reporter* in St. Louis.

Two days later, Benton precipitated the second act of the Texas drama with an annexation bill of his own. By this bill, the President would have been authorized to *negotiate* with both Texas *and* Mexico, under *seven* complex qualifications aimed at eliminating potential conflict with Mexico and over slavery. When he saw Benton's bill, Tyler cried out "Alas for annexation!" and Thomas Ritchie in his *Enquirer* at Richmond damned Benton's plan as a "disgraceful trick and humbug." Obviously, the bill could never satisfy the avid partisans of immediate annexation.

In the Senate, the argument grew bitter and personal. Two days after he had offered it, Benton defended his proposal in a long, polemical address, in which he took Tyler and Calhoun as his particular targets. Stressing the importance of friendship and commerce with Mexico, particularly as a source of hard money for the West, Benton insisted that under his bill "offense to Mexico" was "provided against." Furthermore, under a half-and-half division of Texas between slave and free soil, "the danger of future Missouri [slavery] controversies" was also avoided. An answer came, three days later, from the headstrong, heavy-handed South Carolina spokesman, McDuffie — he who had "wish[ed] to God" the United States did not own Oregon, but had emerged as a leading Texas annexationist. He began with personalities, particularly scouting Benton's growing tendency to play schoolmaster to the Senate, "to stand up and say, 'I am Sir Oracle, when I open my mouth let no dog bark' " — "really, this thing of putting senators to school to learn grave questions of statesmanship, after they have reached the age of forty-five or fifty, is rather an awkward business." More seriously McDuffie practically excommunicated Benton from the Democratic party — "in the great division of parties . . .   under what flag shall we find him? . . . the honorable Senator will be thrown out of the Democratic position he has so ably occupied." Finally, McDuffie gave some attention to the Texas bill itself.

As McDuffie sat down, Benton rose. (A large crowd had gathered, including John Quincy Adams, who sat just behind Benton, and remarked that McDuffie's speech was extremely "violent and rancorous." The crowd stayed to hear Benton's reply — spoken, another witness remarked, in a low tone, except for characteristic "occasional and emphatic bursts.") Noting that McDuffie had complained at being called a "neophyte" on the Texas question, Benton defined the term for him, rendered it in six different languages, and asked a page to bring in a dictionary to drive home the lesson. "Neophyte" meant "new plant" — "there [leveling a finger at McDuffie] stands a neophyte! certainly the Senator is a new plant in the Texian garden, his sprouting or taking root there being of quite modern date." Neophytes also were Tyler and Calhoun, who until recently had "never cared a straw" about Texas. He was, Benton admitted, schoolmasterish, "a faint imitation of the older Cato" — but, "here ends the first lesson: I never overtax my neophytes." Still quietly, but with mounting dramatic intensity, Benton turned to a new question, suggesting that for some people, "dissolution of the Union" was "at the bottom" of the Texas agitation — "under the pretext of getting Texas into the Union, the scheme is to get the South out of it," to form a separate, slaveholding "confederacy." (Watching closely, one journalist thought he saw McDuffie "writhe in seeming agony of spirit and body under the charges of disunion.") In a self-consciously self-dramatizing peroration, Benton cried that he would "not fall upon my sword, as Brutus did," if he were defeated on the Texas issue. Instead, "I shall save it, and save myself for another day, and for another use — for the day when the battle of the disunion of these states is to be fought — not with words, but with iron — and for the hearts of the traitors who appear in arms against their country."

The impromptu speech was excited, but overwhelming. Watching Benton "charging home on McDuffie," as he put it, Blair thought the attack "more vehement in manner and unsparing in expression than any I ever heard from Benton." In general, "the effect was electric," particularly when Benton stalked heavily toward McDuffie and gave emphasis to his peroration "by striking a heavy blow on his desk." Attending throughout, Adams thought the onslaught "so merciless and personal that nothing but bodily fear could have withheld the hand of McDuffie from a challenge; but he put up with it, quiet as a lamb." When it was over, Benton and Adams were seen shaking hands with one another, and observers heard Benton say —

"Mr. Adams, you are passing off the stage, and I am passing away also, but while we live, we will stand by THE UNION." *

When news of this incident reached Jackson, "the old chief" could not believe it. He took it as a sign of "derangement" in Benton as a result of the "Peacemaker" explosion.[7] Meanwhile, on June 17, Congress adjourned without acting on Benton's Texas bill.

The emergence of the Texas conflict had brought Benton and Calhoun forward as leading, bitter antagonists in the political arena. The freshman Congressman from Chicago, "Long John" Wentworth, met Benton on the street one evening and told him that he had just come from a visit with Calhoun. At this, Wentworth recalled, Benton became "extremely violent," and declared that it was Calhoun's practice to arrange meetings with young men to infect them with his ideas. Wentworth, however, was not infected. He developed a high opinion of Benton as a man of "indomitable industry, and an iron constitution, and an undying memory," and admired him as a man whose "historical research knew no bounds . . . 'What are the facts?' 'Give us the facts,' were favorite expressions of his." On the other hand, Benjamin F. Perry, a friend of Calhoun's, recalled Calhoun saying of Benton that he ought "to have gone about all his life with quack doctors, and written puffs for their medicines." Indeed, Benton was "the greatest of humbugs, and could make more out of nothing than any other man in the world." [8]

[3]

FOR A FEW, FATEFUL DAYS meanwhile, the conflict had shifted to a new arena — the Democratic convention at Baltimore, May 27 through May 30. Into the first quarter of 1844, the assumption that the nomination would go to Van Buren had persisted. It was shared by men like Polk, who still sought the Vice-Presidency as Van Buren's running mate, and received with pleasure reports "that Benton and the Ohio-men" favored him; and by men like Calhoun, who quietly removed himself from the race. But with the emergence of the Texas issue, the political weather began to change.

* Recalling this incident in a letter to Jackson on July 7, Blair reported it a little differently. He thought Adams had "accosted" Benton to congratulate him, and heard Benton say: "We are too old [for] revolutionary schemes — we must stand by the Constitution and the Union."

The storm center, of course, was Van Buren's anti-annexation letter. In Virginia, Ritchie began blowing up a breeze for Cass as a Texas candidate, a "defection" which evoked "indignation & contempt" in Benton's breast. In Tennessee, testing the wind after a visit to Jackson, Polk began to think of himself as "the most available man" for the Presidency — *if* "my friends in the South and Southwest would propose it as a *compromise,*" in "the state of confusion which exists in the party." In Washington, Polk's agent Gideon Pillow observed that the "foundations" of party were indeed "all broken up here," especially by "the Ultra-discontents, who care but little about Texas and only use the power of the measure as a lever to turn out Van and to kill off Benton as his successor." In this situation, Pillow began actively to stir the breeze for Polk "for the *first place.*" In Washington also, the astute Robert J. Walker of Mississippi was laboring to build a South-Southwest alliance to nominate a Texas candidate.[9] In short, on the eve of the Baltimore convention no man could be sure how the political winds would blow.

The convention opened in a buzz of talk about *Texas, Texas, Texas.* A majority of the delegates were under instructions or bound by pledges to vote for Van Buren. But, promptly after the selection of convention officers, a Southern delegate moved the adoption of the rules of 1832, including the rule requiring a vote of *two thirds* of the delegates present to make a nomination. (This rule had been used before to strengthen the show of support for shoo-in candidates, but now, Benton complained, it was offered to block the selection of the majority choice, to open the door "for the minority to rule.") Debate raged through the afternoon and evening, with the bland, poker-faced, wheezy-voiced, but effective Walker of Mississippi taking the lead for the two-thirds rule. In rebuttal the next morning, Benjamin F. Butler of New York, handsome, intellectual, and oratorical, condemned the "caucusing and contriving by which it was hoped to avert the well-ascertained disposition of the majority of the Democracy." More debate, including an attack on the two-thirds rule by Benton's lieutenant Alexander Kayser of Missouri. All speeches greeted by loud cheers and loud hisses from opposing factions. Passed, 148 to 118 — in a vote which revealed an ominous North-South cleavage, with a number of expansionist votes from the Northwest also being cast for the rule. By this action, Van Buren's prospects were finally doomed. The convention ground its way through seven indecisive ballots — with Van Buren's vote dropping from a clear majority to less than one hundred, and Cass's tally steadily rising, but with stalemate and adjournment overnight the end result.

Behind the scenes, the political managers labored to resolve the deadlock. When some leading delegates from Pennsylvania and Massachusetts offered a "proposition" to Pillow to bring Polk forward for President, the astute Pillow replied that his mentor was available. But he insisted that the suggestion should come from the North "as a *compromise* of all interests." The Massachusetts leader who approached Pillow was George Bancroft, erstwhile partisan of Van Buren, who now feared the triumph of Cass. He also labored until midnight to influence delegates from Ohio, New York, and Maryland. After some hesitation, Walker aligned his forces behind Polk, as a compromise candidate. The next day, May 29, an eighth ballot showed Van Buren 101, Cass 114, and a surprise — Polk 44. Pandemonium, hurried conferences on the floor, followed by the withdrawal of the names of Van Buren and Cass, and the unanimous nomination of Polk. That afternoon, in a "unity" move, Walker proposed that the vice-presidential nomination go to Silas Wright — who was notified through Professor Morse's newfangled telegraph line, recently strung between Baltimore and Washington. But Wright declined, and the honor went to the colorless George M. Dallas of Pennsylvania.

With these developments, American party history was made. The convention system had largely achieved the character that was to mark it for generations to come, particularly in the strategic role played by political managers as political brokers, at the expense of principled leaders or advocates like Benton, and in the increased role of out-of-doors maneuvering. In addition, the first "deadlock" had been resolved, in the first "stampede," which brought nomination to the first "dark horse."

The nominations settled, the convention built its platform, with the convention leaders seeking compromise on this question as they had in the candidate. An old and a new issue, "re-occupation of *Oregon* and the reannexation of *Texas* at the earliest practicable period," were skillfully blended in the same plank — *Texas* to appeal to the South and Southwest, *Oregon* to appeal to the Northwest.

As the convention adjourned, a delegate from Missouri rushed forward and took the rostrum just vacated by the chairman. The delegate was Arthur Magenis, Benton's long-time personal friend and agent, who cried out, to those who would listen: "I bear no part in the responsibility of what [this convention] has done. It has committed a gross

fraud . . . upon the democratic party . . . I go against it — Missouri
will go against it — I denounce it." In fact, Missouri did not "go against
it." Democratic rallies in the state ratified the nominations, and the
pro-Benton *Missourian* placed the names of Polk and Dallas at its masthead, calling Polk a "Young Hickory."

Still, Magenis had probably expressed publicly some of Benton's private sentiments. Benton was not a delegate (he had announced that he
would not serve), but he had followed the proceedings closely. Years
later, he described the convention as the consummation of a "BOLD
INTRIGUE FOR THE PRESIDENCY," planned and "worked to a pattern"
to *"blow Van Buren sky high."* The result had marked "the starting
point in a course of usurpation which has taken the choice of President
out of the hands of the people, and vested it in the hands of a self-
constituted and irresponsible assemblage." Thus, "the elective principle
of our government [was] suppressed, and the people [lost] control
over the selection of the man who was to be their President." [10] Actually,
the chain of events was not so deliberately "worked to a pattern" as the
suspicious Benton alleged. An involved conflict of interest groups and
factions, an intricate concatenation of circumstances, and a final compromise, combined to produce the result. Nonetheless, the plantation-
slaveholding leaders had played a major part in the beginnings of a great
transformation. This transformation was to change the Democracy from
the agrarian-based party it had been under Jackson, to a party led increasingly by an emerging faction of political brokers, who moved
toward positions of party power at the expense of the Van Buren-
Benton radicals *and* the Calhoun extremists. These leaders, however,
proved increasingly sensitive to the demands of the plantation-slave-
holding group, and the infusion of former Whig planters into the
Democratic party increased as the years passed. Thus, with the Texas
issue and its consequences, the political center of gravity of the party
shifted.

Publicly, Benton's reaction to the nomination was that of a regular
party man. He dispatched a manifesto to the *Missourian,* declaring that
"neither Mr. Polk nor Mr. Dallas had anything to do with the intrigue," and urging that "all hands attend to the election, and give us
our full majority." For the rest, "the time will come" — the *people*
would "teach the Congress intriguers to attend to law-making, and let
president making, and unmaking, alone in the future." Hoping to speed
the process, Benton did offer in the Senate (in vain) a new version of his

twenty-year-old Constitutional amendment to place the *selection* of presidential candidates and the *election* of presidents in the hands of the mass of the people — to "do away with the machinery of all intermediate bodies to guide, control, or defeat the popular choice," whether "a national convention," or electors. In July, Van Buren urged support for Polk and Dallas, and Calhoun fell in line. He was relieved that the party was, at long last, freed of "the dangerous control" of the Van Buren-Benton "dynasty."

In fact, Polk had fair claim to party support. For years a party leader in Tennessee, where he had served as governor, he had made his mark as an all-out pro-Jackson Congressman and Speaker of the House in the 1830's. Of middling height, broad countenance, deep-set eyes, serious mien, but graced by a winning smile, he was also of middling ability and intellect, no creator of great ideas and sometimes slow to seize them when put before him, but practical and factual, conscientious, and a hard worker. Contrary to Whig canards that he was a nobody — "Who is James K. Polk?" — he was well known, with reasonable prospects of presidential stature.

The Whigs, meanwhile, had nominated the anti-annexationist Clay. A contemporaneous cartoon pictured the contest as a FIGHT BETWEEN THE KENTUCKY COON & THE TENNESSEE ALLIGATOR — with a caricatured Benton, carrying a bag of MINT DROPS, noting that the coon (Clay) was indeed "a ROARER." The electoral battle lines were drawn.

In mid-July, Benton arrived in St. Louis. In the spring, after Thomas had been injured in the *Princeton* disaster, Elizabeth had returned to Washington. Now, fearing a recall to a special session in September, Elizabeth was reluctant to go West again, particularly because her health had been improved at the C Street home, and also because she wanted to see the play, *The Western Division,* when it came to Washington.[11] But Thomas had to go, to canvass for the national ticket — and to face an election of his own, in which the "extinction" of his political life he had referred to was a clear possibility.

[4]

IN MISSOURI, the party lesions that had broken out on the hard-money question were inflamed by the new Texas issue. The press war continued, with the anti-Benton *Reporter* under Penn now effectively balanced by the pro-Benton *Missourian* under Van Antwerp in St. Louis.

Depression had given way to prosperity in the state, and conflict over economic policy was somewhat muted. The *Inquirer* at Jefferson City quoted an enthusiastic traveler — "labor and enterprise are well rewarded; the necessaries of life are abundant and cheap . . . If there is a place on earth which deserves to be called the poor man's heaven, it is the democratic state of Missouri." In this situation, a new conflict of interests relating to slavery and slavery extension was to come increasingly to the center of the political arena in the state. In 1844, the attack on Benton thus began to center on the Texas issue. Undoubtedly, public opinion in the state favored annexation in some form, and Benton's enemies now accused him of being "merely actuated by contemptible jealousy of Calhoun" in his Texas course, or (by innuendo) of taking Mexican, English, or French gold! Counterattacking, the *Missourian* published Benton's *Enquirer* articles of 1819 on Oregon and Texas in a long pamphlet, and offered a blunt slogan — *"Benton or no Benton:* MAKING UP THE ISSUE, AND THROWING OFF THE MASK." The pro-Benton forces dominated the state convention in April, thus retaining the increasingly potent symbol of party regularity. The convention urged all good Democrats to vote for no Assembly candidate "who will not *pledge himself"* to support both Benton and Atchison for the Senate.

Soon after his arrival in July, Benton began his canvass of the state, traveling up the Missouri to Boonville. There, in a three-hour address, he declared that he was passive concerning re-election for himself. He then spoke out for Polk, especially lauding "Young Hickory's" announced intention to serve only a single term. Hoping to minimize sectional conflict, he, Benton, *"was in favor of seeing the democratic candidate for 1848 taken from the North."* He broadly suggested that that candidate might be the old faithful radical Silas Wright. Yielding nothing to local opinion, Benton went on to damn "Mr. Tyler's Texas Treaty," as designed to present the acquisition of Texas as "wholly directed to the extension, perpetuation, and predominance of slavery." From Boonville, Benton went on up the Missouri to the Platte country on the northwest frontier — busy "putting an end to the Texas fever" in Atchison's bailiwick, the *Republican* suspected. Not until the evening of August 9 did he return to St. Louis.

The state election campaign, meanwhile, ran its course. The Whigs, "Bent-on beating Benton," as one of their campaign transparencies put it, had concentrated on the Assembly races, leaving the gubernatorial and Congressional contests to the Softs. In pre-election torchlight parades, Benton was lampooned in verse, to the tune of "Remember Sinful Youth" —

> *Tom Benton take the track,*
> *You must go, you must go,*
> *Take your gold in your cravat,*
> *We have had enough of that. . . .*

In the August voting, the Whigs did increase their Assembly representation sharply. The possibility emerged that a Whig-Soft combination might force Benton to "take the track."

From mid-August to mid-September, Benton traveled to his Woodford County, Kentucky, farm. In his absence, there was intense maneuvering looking toward the Senatorial election, during which the Softs brought the squat, stump-legged, forceful freshman Congressman from Illinois, Stephen A. Douglas, to St. Louis to address an anti-Benton rally. At the Hermitage, Jackson watched such developments with regret. His affection for Benton was "not abated," he wrote Blair, and he hoped their mutual friend would triumph — though he regretted that, with *Texas* the great issue in the national election, "Col. Benton's speeches has injured the Democratic cause more than all the whiggs." Indeed, as Jackson noted, thousands of copies of Benton's Texas orations had been distributed by the opposition, "all over the Union."

Back in St. Louis, Benton remained passive in the face of attack. At the beginning of October, he attended another statewide Democratic meeting, going with other partisans up the Mississippi by chartered steamer to Hannibal. The next day, at a spot on the river's bank about a mile north of town, the crowd gathered. It was a festive scene, marked, the *Missourian* reported, by "powerful and eloquent speeches, spirit-stirring music, and the occasional report of a 'big gun.'" The chief speech was, of course, given by Benton, who called for a majority of ten thousand for Polk and Dallas in Missouri, and reviewed again the Texas question. When he had finished, he was asked if he knew Polk personally. He responded that he had known Polk from his Tennessee days thirty years ago, and also his grandfather and father, for whom he had pleaded a land case. During the pleading, the teen-aged James K. Polk had sat in the room listening.

Through the rest of October and into early November, Benton divided his time between St. Louis and trips outstate, politicking always. He was sure that on Texas "the people of the State — both parties exclusive of the *Softs,* who are *Calhoun men* — are with me." While intriguing was going on "to operate on individual members" of the Assembly, he knew of only four Democrats who would certainly oppose him, though Claiborne Fox Jackson (of the Fayette group) was "fished for." He summed up in mid-October, in a speech to a Democratic rally at Colonel Brant's tobacco warehouse in St. Louis. It was a sarcastic oration, full of hammer blows and spreading Bentonian rhetoric. He would, Benton protested, avoid all reference to himself, if possible — but "in my long Senatorial service I have acted a part on every public measure which can now claim public attention." The Democratic platform planks on Oregon and Texas, for example — "alas! these are my own measures! children of twenty-five years ago! and then treated as humbugs! and their author ridiculed as a visionary projector! . . . Five and twenty years ago, I put these two balls in motion! Solitary and alone I did it! Millions now roll them forward!" This settled, he lashed out at the whole Tyler-Calhoun-Texas "intrigue," reiterating, elaborating, and reinforcing his established position. Once again, he had made it clear that he was not yielding on the Texas issue. But once again also, he had exhibited the flowering egotism that increasingly characterized his public behavior, a trait which over the years was bound to lose him friends and make enemies. Privately, Benton exulted that he had made his position clear, and revealed that "I was ready to die politically upon it." As for *"the Calhoun crew,"* or new Softs, "I place them at defiance." [12]

On Monday, November 4, the citizens of Missouri went to the polls again. When Benton presented himself at the Fourth Ward election station, his vote was challenged by a Whig on the ground that he was not a bona-fide Missourian. Benton had to swear that he considered himself a resident of the state — what "malignity," the *Missourian* cried. Despite Whig "malignity," Missouri gave Polk and Dallas the ten thousand majority Benton had urged. Nationally, the Democrats also triumphed, in a close vote which provided no clear mandate for Texas or Oregon. In the critical state of New York, the Democratic plurality was only 5000 out of 486,000. Benton was convinced that Polk won there only through the influence of Wright, who in the interest of his party had agreed to leave the Senate, "which he liked," and run for governor, "a place to which he was absolutely averse." Had the vote of New York gone to Clay, he would have won. Nonetheless, in a sober

election, the Democrats had avenged the ballyhoo and buncombe defeat
of 1840. But during the election canvass the old Benton-Van Buren-
Blair radical leadership had been largely displaced, and before the year
was out, Van Buren noted "the rush of unsound men for the loaves and
fishes" of victory. Factional sour grapes, perhaps. But in New York,
1844 also marked the decline of the agrarian, popular democracy, and
the ascendancy of William L. Marcy, political broker who followed
the star of the rising middle classes.

On November 8, Benton left for Washington. The Senatorial election contest moved to its conclusion in his absence. Frantic anti-Benton stratagems were tried, with "Fox" Jackson and "Davey" Atchison,
both of whom had publicly opposed Benton on Texas, both "fished
for." The "Fox" resisted and got the Speakership of the House in
recompense, while Atchison carefully maintained an attitude of high
"disinterest." In the assembly balloting in late November, Atchison was
easily elected to fill the remainder of Lewis Linn's unexpired term. Benton also won, with 74 votes to 57 for a motley Soft, Whig, and individual opposition. It was a close thing, but a victory; and victory
promptly enhanced the prestige of "Glorious Old Tom Benton," as the
Inquirer at Jefferson City proclaimed him. Papers and public meetings
in Missouri, and finally presses as far apart as Massachusetts, Maine,
and Maryland, boomed Benton for the Presidency again. "Of all men,"
a Boston paper summed up in a happy account of the Missouri election, "we should prefer to see Thomas H. Benton in the Presidential
chair." [13]

[5]

BACK IN WASHINGTON Benton found his family all well, and Elizabeth "far better than she has been in many years — I am now relieved
of great anxieties about her."

Before the Texas drama and politics claimed him, Benton gave some
time to the holiday social life. At the end of December, he attended a
gala all-male dinner party given by Richard Pakenham, the British minister, along with Senators Fairfield, Woodbury, Allen, and Haywood; the
painter-inventor Samuel F. B. Morse; Lieutenant Frémont (back from
his glorious expedition); and others. The guests sat at table two hours,
enjoying nine courses, all carefully listed by Fairfield in an awed letter
to Mrs. Fairfield — soup, fish, sweetbread with tomato sauce, "chicken

curiously cooked," *"je ne sais quoi,"* ducks, boiled ham, lobster pie, and saddle of mutton, followed by ice cream, cakes, grapes, and so on. The conversation was pleasant, lively — and light. On New Year's Day, 1845, Benton paid a call on ex-President Adams, "the first in a period of twenty-five years," the New Englander noted (not quite accurately) in his diary. Two days later, Adams returned the call, finding Benton at his C Street home with Elizabeth, three of his daughters, and Lieutenant Frémont.[14]

Meanwhile, the third act of the Texas drama was at hand. Arguing that the elections *were* a mandate for immediate annexation, Tyler asked Congress for a joint resolution to put into effect the rejected Texas treaty. McDuffie in the Senate and Douglas in the House offered bills for this purpose. Persistently, Benton re-introduced the gradualist bill he had offered the previous June. Rallying his forces, Calhoun cried that if annexation failed, "Benton will be responsible" — "he seems bent on doing all the mischief he can." Papers like the *Madisonian* and the *Enquirer* at Richmond were "coaxing, wheedling, and imploring Col. BENTON to come out flat-footed like POLK," the *Republican* noted. In January, 1845, Benton commented in a private letter on the state of public affairs:

> *Item* — "The real friends to the acquisition of Texas have a hard time of it between two parties one of whom is utterly hostile to the whole measure, and the other fatally bent upon using it for selfish and sinister purposes."
>
> *Item* — "Mr. Polk's administration is not to be, 'sleep on a bed of roses.' Do not be surprised if you see two conventions in session for the dissolution of the Union before his four years are out. Massachusetts and South Carolina are each in a bad state, and each creating a bad feeling around them . . ."[15]

Concerned for "peace and harmony," and perhaps also about opinion in Missouri and his place in the party, Benton decided to offer a Texas compromise. Early in February, he proposed a new bill. A state, "formed out of the present republic of Texas," was to be admitted as soon as the terms could be agreed on by the United States and Texas, and the terms of "said admission and cession" were to be arranged by negotiation. This new measure listed no "conditions," such as those he had proposed in June, Benton pointed out — first, because of the difficulty of getting agreement on them, and second, because any action "must devolve upon the new President," Polk, in whom the Senator had full confidence. But in omitting the conditions from the bill, "I do not withdraw them from the consideration of those who may direct the negotiation." The assent of Mexico to annexation as such might be unnecessary, he admitted, but no one should assume "her assent to a new boundary line to be unnecessary." The radicals were enthusiastic — Blair, Fairfield, Niles; John Dix, who had replaced Silas Wright in the Senate, and who thought Benton had "conceded much in the most manly and conciliatory manner"; Gideon Welles of Connecticut; and others. Plantation politicos, however, were adamant, and Calhoun labored to block "Benton's humbug," despite the fact that he was confined to his lodgings with an emaciating fever and pneumonia. The *Madisonian* ridiculed the plan as the same old mouse, minus its tail. It was an "amputated vermin," offered as a ruse to thwart immediate annexation.

In late February, the House sent up a measure for annexation without the complications of negotiation. With the session's end only a week away, the choice before the Senate was — Benton's plan, the new House measure, or stalemate. This situation gave rise to talk of still another compromise. The New York antislavery editor Horace Greeley wrote that Benton's bill and the House bill were to be combined, and commented caustically if not quite fairly that the purpose was to give Benton "an excuse for a retreat," a chance to make a "juggle" with his New York allies. In fact, under the adroit direction of Walker of Mississippi, a compromise was arranged. At the moment of crisis, the political brokers took over, outmaneuvering Benton radicals and Calhoun extremists to mark a prudent path between party antipodes. A proposal for a joint resolution was accepted by Benton and his friends, giving the President his choice between the House's cut-and-dried annexation offer and Benton's negotiation scheme. In a tense evening session on February 27, 1845, the Senate considered Walker's amendment to add Benton's bill, word for word, to the House measure. It was a dramatic moment — all the lamps lit; the lobbies filled with members of the House and spectators; and a rustle of talk to add excitement. Looking on, Aaron V. Brown, of the portentous Capitol-steps conversation with Benton, thought the spectacle sublime. The debate lasted for about two hours, with Benton breaking the tension with a touch of humor toward the end. At the last minute, Miller of New Jersey offered as a substitute the bill, word for word, which Benton had proposed in June, 1844.

MR. BENTON (*from his seat*): The Senator from Missouri will vote against it. (*Laughter*) . . .

MR. MILLER said that the speech delivered by the honorable Senator had made a strong impression upon him, and he hoped the Senator would not destroy his own child.

MR. BENTON (*from his seat*): I'll kill it stone dead.

(*General laughter, with an attempt at cheering, suppressed by the President.*)

The Senate approved the compromise by a hairline, 27 to 25 votes, and the next day the House concurred. In each case the deed was done by Democratic votes, plus a handful of Southern Whig recruits.[16]

Four days later, Congress was due to adjourn, and Tyler was due to relinquish his office. His successor was in Washington, Polk and Mrs. Polk having arrived in mid-February and settled at Coleman's Hotel. There Benton, Elizabeth, and their daughters had called on the President-elect and his lady. The Reverend Mr. Sproule, pastor of the Presbyterian church which Jackson had attended, had spoken to Thomas and Elizabeth Benton "to know *before hand*" whether the Polks would attend his church, so that "a suitable pew, &c may be in readiness," and Benton wrote Sarah Childress Polk to ask her answer. Clearly, Benton wanted to establish friendly relations with Polk. But there was, of course, more to Polk's appearance in Washington than the problem of church pews. He was anxious for Congress to move toward annexation in the current session, and he used his influence to this end while he waited for his inauguration. Enemies charged that he reinforced this influence by promises and threats in relation to appointments, cabinet personnel, and other favors.

In the four days that remained in his term, meanwhile, Tyler acted. Seeing the Texas issue as an urgent one, pressed by the persistent Calhoun, and concerned for a place of honor in the pages of history, he decided *not* to leave the matter to Polk — and he chose the House plan over Benton's scheme. On the evening of March 3, in the last hours of his term, he sent a message to the American Chargé d'Affaires in Texas, ordering him to proceed under the House plan. Formal admission of Texas as a state remained to be accomplished, but the basic decision had been made.[17]

The radical Democrats were outraged. Some, like Blair and Senator Tappan, claimed that the compromise Texas bill had been passed by fraud, and Benton later echoed the charge. The votes of Senators Dix, Tappan, Allen, Haywood, and Bagby were given, according to this charge, only on the basis of two assurances — first, McDuffie's declaration that his friends Tyler and Calhoun would not have the "audacity" to act on the matter, and second, alleged commitments by Polk to Blair and Haywood that he would proceed under Benton's negotiation plan. Without the votes of Benton and his followers, no Texas bill could have been passed. Probably, however, no such guarantees were given. Certainly McDuffie was on his own when he underrated the "audacity" of Tyler and Calhoun, and Polk and his political associates stoutly and convincingly denied that he had made any commitments. Still, the radical Democrats felt bilked, baffled, and bitter.[18]

On March 4, 1845, Polk took the oath of office. The day was marred by a driving rain, and he had to deliver his inaugural address to "a large assemblage of umbrellas," as John Quincy Adams put it. Faced with accepting or reversing Tyler's Texas decision, Polk let that decision stand. Four days after the inauguration, the *Republican* in St. Louis noted that the fateful message to Texas had passed down the Ohio some time before, "as fast as steam and special appliances would enable it."

In the aftermath of the Texas drama, Polk undertook the chores of cabinet making and patronage distribution. As Benton had predicted, he enjoyed no "sleep on a bed of roses." Instead, his political bed was a party divided into three factional groups — a "Left" of agrarians and radicals like Benton, increasingly concerned over slavery and wary on Texas annexation; a "Right" of plantation partisans dominated by Calhoun, passionately determined to protect slavery and to effect immediate annexation of Texas; and a "Center" of the Walker-Buchanan-Marcy stripe, basically political brokers, but ready to concede much to plantation demands, and pro-Texas. At first, Polk made offers or pseudo-offers to all factions. In December, he had tendered the Treasury post to Wright, though there was some question of his sincerity in this, since he knew that Wright was determined to serve his term as Governor. The offer was ejected, and Polk in turn rejected the names of two other New York hard-money radicals suggested by Van Buren and Wright. Meanwhile, Polk on two occasions offered the post of Minister to England to Calhoun — who, if he had not declined, would have thus been removed from the domestic political arena. After these preliminary tacks, Polk listed the self-important, old-maidish Buchanan for State, rewarded the indefatigable Walker with the Treasury, flabbergasted the radical New Yorkers by naming Marcy to the War Department, and sought balance again by naming the lesser radical Bancroft to the Navy post. The Attorney Generalship was given to John Y. Mason, a member of the Tyler cabinet and a friend of Calhoun. As Postmaster General, Polk chose Cave Johnson of Tennessee, his close friend and political agent. At its launching, the new ship of state was designed as a vessel which would pursue a middle course, though ready to veer to the winds of plantation group demands.

The radicals accepted the results publicly, but stormed privately. In New York, Van Buren cried out at the "injury done to Mr. Wright, and the Democracy of the State"; the appointment of Marcy would "infuse new life into a faction bent on [Wright's] overthrow, which was fast dwindling away." In Tennessee, Old Hickory regretted that the New York radical Azariah C. Flagg had been rejected for the Treasury, and warned Young Hickory against Walker as a speculator, "surrounded by so many speculators." [19]

In dispensing patronage, Polk again sought the "Center," and again failed to please either "Right" or "Left" factions. In Missouri, however, Benton fared well. His friend, the *Missourian* editor V. P. Antwerp, was made Receiver of Public Monies in Iowa, and his former "right and left bowers" on the paper, John M. Wimer and Thomas T. Gantt, were made Postmaster and United States Attorney, respectively, in St. Louis. Reporting these events, the *Republican* deduced "that *Softism* and *Calhounism* are both in exceedingly bad standing at Washington." An enraged Shad Penn, now openly pro-Calhoun, protested to Calhoun that he had gone to Washington and "received assurances from the President that he would pause in the appointment of Bentonians to office," but these assurances had been violated.[20] Apparently, Polk was willing to use patronage in an attempt to placate Benton personally in Missouri.

On the national scene, however, Benton had reason for complaint. For some time an antagonism had been developing toward Blair's Washington *Globe*. Calhoun's confidant Duff Green warned that "if you give Blair, Benton, and Wright three years to organize and pack another convention, [then] whoever the *Globe* nominates will be the Democratic candidate . . . This is the crisis of the slave holding interest." Polk complained to Jackson: "the truth is, Blair is more devoted to *Col. Benton* than to the success of my administration." Despite "solicitude" from Benton, from Van Buren, from Silas Wright, and from a vehemently protesting Jackson in Tennessee, the old-Jacksonian organ was marked for extinction. After some complex maneuvering and financing, the deed was accomplished. In May, the *Globe* surrendered to a new sheet called the *Union,* edited by the experienced, wily, but aging (sixty-six), often idiosyncratic *Enquirer* man from Virginia, Thomas Ritchie. In what Benton later called a piece of "hugger-mugger work," Polk had replaced the old radical dreadnought with a new vessel he thought would follow his own cautious course.

This sideshow to the Texas drama gratified Calhoun, and was hailed joyfully by Penn in Missouri. At last, Shad cried, Benton's "influence and control" through the columns of the *Globe* were over; henceforth, he would occupy a "secondary station." At the *Republican,* A. B. Chambers admitted that "the undried copy may not go directly [from Benton] into the hands of the compositor," as it had in the heyday of the *Globe,* but the ghost-editor Senator was still "one of the leaders and master spirits" of his party. He had the "obedience, subserviency and blind adhesion of the Locofoco [radical] party in Missouri such as no man in the Union can boast of," and he was also "in fact head of the northern branch of the Locofoco party, or at least of a large, energetic, and influential portion of it." In short, his strong power base in Missouri and his long-standing influence nationally would preserve him. He could not be "killed off by the loss of a single paper," and Polk knew this too well to risk "any act or measure which will drive him into opposition." [21]

His effort to save the *Globe* was Jackson's last attempt to mix in national politics. Old age and illness were overtaking him, and on the morning of June 8 he lay in his high-posted bed at the Hermitage, exhausted, dropping into unconsciousness. Friends, relatives, and slaves gathered. In the late summer afternoon, the old man suffered a slight convulsion; his breathing grew faint, and he died.

A few days before his death, he had sent a last message to Benton. Committed to William B. Lewis, the message was written out nine months later by that gentleman, who tried to remember the precise words.

"I thank the Colonel for his kind recollection of me in my old age and sore afflictions; it would give me great pleasure to see him once more, but that, I fear, is impossible, as my life is rapidly drawing to a close," Andrew Jackson had said in a deep, solemn voice, and paused. "The Colonel is not only an able and distinguished statesman, but a warm and sincere patriot, and his country is under great obligation to him. I feel grateful for the able and efficient support he gave me during the whole of my Administration, and I beg you, when next you see him, to remember me to him." [22]

The "old chief's" death marked the end of an era. The political movement he had led had split on the rock of Texas annexation, and the related, newly emergent conflict of interests over slavery extension. In that division, the agrarian radical disciples of Jackson were losing the leadership of their party.

[6]

WITH THE TEXAS QUESTION SETTLED, another issue of Westward expansion appeared at the center of the political arena. This was the question of American claims to the vast Northwest or Oregon area — claims Benton, Linn, and other enthusiasts had advocated again and again, unsuccessfully. Throughout the rest of 1845 and the first half of 1846, Benton was engrossed in the Oregon issue. As it developed, he cast and recast his attitude toward the new Administration.

The stream of men, women, and families going to Oregon, like the stream of immigration to Texas, had greatly increased in the 1840's. The flow had begun many years before with a few fur traders and a few hardy missions. It had gone forward under the aegis of businessmen like Astor and William H. Ashley and other fur magnates with whom Benton had been associated, and religious leaders like the hardy missionary-physician Marcus Whitman. Stimulated by the constant pressure of the population to the West, and by reports and route-maps that followed expeditions like that carried through by Frémont in 1842, the flow by the mid-1840's had become a flood. On foot, on horseback, and in great white-covered wagons, despite sun and thirst and snow and cold and Indians and mountains, thousands of "goers" had followed the long, rugged Oregon trails through the South Pass, and pushed on to the Northwest and the Pacific slope — "Oregon or Bust." Unlike the Texas settlers, nearly all of the Oregon immigrants came from the free-state North — though many were from Missouri, including friends and acquaintances of Benton's there. The flood of immigration, and the explosive possibilities of continued American-British joint occupation, made some settlement of the Oregon problem imperative.

At the beginning, Benton and Polk appeared to stand as antagonists on an important aspect of Oregon policy. In his inaugural address, the new President took a position that was interpreted as an endorsement of the most extreme claim to the area, up to the border of Russian territory at 54° 40′ latitude. Any attempt to enforce such a demand would have provoked violent British opposition and the threat of possible war abroad, and in addition a factional crisis at home. As the controversy developed, the Washington letter writers reported that the more modest *"line proposed by . . . Col. Benton"* was 49° latitude — an extension of the established border between the Louisiana Purchase area and Canada. In St. Louis, the *Republican* opined that "if the wishes of the southern and most potent part of the [Democratic] party be consulted," there would be a settlement in the neighborhood of 49°: the Southerners had Texas and wanted no war over Oregon. In fact, behind the scenes, Polk and his cautious Secretary of State, Buchanan, were feeling their way, asking advice as they went. One of the men Buchanan consulted was Benton, who argued firmly for 49°. An exploratory offer on this line was made to the British minister, Richard Pakenham, but he rejected it. Meanwhile, the "Fifty-four Forties," led by Lewis Cass and echoed in scores of Democratic presses, set up a clamor, and the Oregon cry swept the Northwest as the Texas cry had swept the South and Southwest. Before this "storm" (as Benton put it) the Administration "recoiled." [23]

With the Oregon question thus in balance, Benton concerned himself with other matters. He saw his son-in-law John Charles Frémont depart for his third expedition, directed to explore certain river sources and other areas in the Far West. In May Frémont left Washington, in June he collected a company of *voyageurs* at St. Louis, and summer saw him well on his way. He was to be gone more than two years. His explorations were to take him into Oregon, deep into the north-Mexican province of California, and deep into a fantastic set of politico-military adventures. Once again, Benton could feel that his grandiose ideas of Western "destiny" were being given practical effect. He himself, however, went prosaically to his Kentucky farm, where he stayed until late August.[24]

After his return to Washington, Buchanan consulted him again on the Oregon issue, and asked him to talk the matter over with Polk. Remarking that he had "nothing to do," Benton said he would call whenever the President invited him. Some weeks later, at the end of October, a meeting finally took place. Benton's "manner and conversation were altogether pleasant and friendly," Polk noted happily in his diary. Polk declared that he was *now* "disposed to assert our *extreme* right to the *whole* country." But, Benton argued, the British had the same claim to the Fraser River (north of 49°) by discovery, exploration, and settlement that the Americans had to the Columbia River (south of 49°). The two men agreed, however, that a year's notice of termination of the British-American joint occupation Convention of 1827 should be given. The discussion then turned to California, and Frémont's expedition, Benton declaring that Americans "would settle on the Sacrimento River and ultimately hold the country." On this note of manifest destiny, the conversation ended — "very pleasantly," the President noted, with satisfaction and perhaps relief. A beginning had been made toward bridging the political estrangement.

Still, on the Oregon boundary, as on Texas annexation, Benton found himself increasingly aligned with Whig opinion, and reports persisted that he stood in general opposition to Polk. In Faneuil Hall in Boston, Webster came out for 49° and against war, while in Washington, the Whig *National Intelligencer* favored 49°, and cited "the present leading and most intelligent member of the democratic party in the senate," Benton, as authority. In St. Louis, the *Missourian* cracked that "official crumbs" of patronage would not buy Benton's support. Calhoun's friend Duff Green thought that Benton was planning to bring his brother-in-law James McDowell into the Senate from Virginia, when with the aid of other friends like Allen, Bagby, Fairfield, and Dix, he would try "to set up for himself, and by throwing himself between you [Calhoun] and the administration assume the control of the government." Despite their "very pleasant" conversation, Polk still fretted at reports that "Col. B. would oppose my administration, whenever a fair pretext to do so occurred." [25]

Though Benton had hoped that McDowell would be elected to the Senate, he was disappointed. Early in 1846, however, Representative William Taylor died, and McDowell was chosen to fill the vacant House seat, which he occupied until 1851.

When the Congress elected in 1844 met, the Oregon issue promptly came to the fore again. It was a long session, which ran from December, 1845, into August, 1846. There were strong Democratic majorities in both houses, with Democrats particularly outnumbering Whigs in delegations from the South. In the Senate, Webster and Calhoun were back. Graying, growing gaunter with the years, but still an immensely effective leader, Calhoun had been brought forward by his friends in the apprehensive South particularly to counter the threat

that Benton would emerge as the "prominent and pernicious" spokesman of the Democracy. Once again, Benton was made chairman of
the Committee on Military Affairs, and once again he was placed on
Finance, under Calhoun.

In Congress, and in the nation as a whole, the Oregon conflict raged
anew. In his message, Polk urged an end to the British-American joint
occupation agreement, and asserted claims to the "whole" area — up to
54° 40′, presumably. In echo fortissimo, renewed demands for the
"whole" of Oregon were voiced by the Congressional "Ultras," led
by the imposing Lewis Cass, in the Senate now from Michigan, and such
rising political brokers as pugnacious Edward Hannegan of Indiana in
the Senate and stumpy Stephen Douglas in the House. New talk of *war*
rumbled like ominous thunder, and Polk worried over reports that Britain was already engaged in "warlike preparations." In this tense atmos-
phere, a dramatic slogan swept the land — "Fifty-four Forty or Fight!"
Unmoved, Benton stood by 49°. He remarked to Van Buren that "things
are getting a little serious with G. B." — but he believed that a peaceful
and honorable settlement could be achieved "by a union of calmness,
firmness and moderation." Throughout, Benton clung to this expectation of peaceful settlement. Thus, he opposed a bill for a sharp increase
in the Navy — he had "not made any war speeches," he declared, and
he did not want any "war measures." He took this position despite the
fact that he knew the "Fifty-four Forty or Fight" cry was immensely
popular in his own Missouri, which had sent so many immigrants to
Oregon. Meanwhile, Calhoun was also plumping for peace. He who
had been so avid for Texas was by no means so hot for Oregon, and he
too labored to counter the activities of the "Fifty-four Forties." [26]

Thus the stage was set when, in February, 1846, the Senate took up
the Oregon problem. The issue on the floor was a resolution calling on
the President to terminate the British-American joint occupation agreement. The House had already passed a resolution to this effect. Speaking
briefly and to the point in an otherwise long-winded debate, Benton
noted that in 1827 *he* had voted against renewal of the joint occupation agreement, "not altogether, but almost solitary and alone." Now,
he urged that notice be given as a "first step" toward the settlement of
the Oregon problem; it would be "a peace measure" which would
make the British "treat, not fight." The "Fifty-four Forties" showed no
such restraint. When a Senator suggested that the President might settle
for 49°, if the British made such an offer, "that gallant little hotspur

Hannegan" (as one observer described him) pounced on the idea in full cry. If the remarks of the Senator "speak the language of James K. Polk," Hannegan trumpeted, "James K. Polk has spoken words of falsehood, and with the tongue of a serpent."

In the clash of groups and factions and the hurly-burly of debate, the President was again in a difficult situation. Privately, the harassed executive was veering toward the idea of settling on the 49° line. In mid-March Benton had called on Polk again and declared that he would support a treaty on that line. The President had responded that he would not take the initiative for 49°, but "would say to him confidentially that if the parallel of 49° was offered," he would submit such an offer to the Senate for "previous advice" before he acted. In early April, at another meeting, Benton suggested that Polk should take the lead for 49°, and this time the President agreed. His *public* position, however, remained as he had given it originally in his message — for the "whole" of Oregon.

The debate continued in the Senate. On March 31, Cass launched his major oration, in which he broadly condemned the partisans of 49° as pusillanimous, if not unpatriotic, and insisted that American claims be enforced "from California to the Russian boundary." The next day Benton replied in a slashing attack on the "Fifty-four Forties." Perhaps he was being schoolmasterish again, he admonished Cass and his allies, but as an old Oregon partisan, he knew that the history of the region would support no American claim to 54° 40'. He affirmed that *he* was the true friend of the Administration on the Oregon issue. Later, he exulted that in the Oregon debate he had "cut Cass for the simples, sir, and cured him." He explained that "simples" were a physical and mental blindness that afflicted horses in Missouri, curable when a veterinary cut a certain nerve. Finally, near the end of April, after amendments and House-Senate conferences, a resolution was adopted authorizing the President to give notice at his discretion.[27] On May 21, Polk sent the notice. The joint occupation policy Benton had so long opposed was at an end.

The next item of Oregon business was to extend American protection over settlers in the area. A bill similar to Lewis Linn's abortive proposal of 1843 had been pushed through the House by Douglas. Polk told Benton that he "would be grateful if he would take charge of the Bill" in the Senate. Instead, Benton chose the occasion to deliver a final summary of his view of the Oregon issue as a whole, in a massive oration that consumed parts of three days near the end of May. He ranged from history, geography, topography, and the strength and extent of British and American claims, to settlement, Oregon as the route to India, and commerce. As to the boundary crisis, he insisted that the United States should act on a maxim attributed to Jackson: "Ask nothing but what is right — submit to nothing that is wrong." He declared that "we must now introduce the gentlemen of 54-40" to the facts of the boundary issue, to show them that to demand any territory north of 49° would be to demand something not "right." (Perhaps some gentlemen had been taken in by the "superficial glosses" of "books compiled in closets," which were "generally shallow, of no use to the informed, and dangerous to the uninformed, whom they led astray.") As to northern Oregon, he would not even ask the British for it, "much less fight for it." And so on . . . nothing new, but information in crushing weight (although not always totally accurate), and a spicing of invective. Once again, Benton was acting as an advocate, responsible statesman, and one-man propaganda engine. Powerfully, ponderously, polemically, laboring to get "public opinion to come up with him," he was hammering away at the "rightness" of 49°. His speech was widely reprinted, and distributed as a pamphlet.

Before the protection bill was acted on, the Oregon conflict entered its third phase. At the beginning of June, the British government proposed an agreement on the 49° line, with a dip south at the Strait of Juan de Fuca to give the British Vancouver Island, while the United States got Puget Sound. Here was an opportunity to settle the matter, but an opportunity hard to seize for an Administration still publicly committed to the "whole" of Oregon and subject to the influence of the "Fifty-four Forty" group in its own party. As Benton later recalled, "a device was necessary" as a way out. The device was the one Polk and Benton had discussed earlier — to ask the Senate for *advice,* before any treaty was concluded. This threw the responsibility for the treaty, and the responsibility for peace or war with Britain, on the Senate. There, fortunately, the ground for accepting 49° had been well plowed, seeded, and watered by Benton and others. At the critical moment, Benton's efforts were to bear fruit. The terms and relevant documents were submitted, advice to accept was given by a 38-to-12 vote, and the treaty was submitted and formally ratified by a 41-to-14 vote — all in a few days in mid-June. In both votes, Yeas came from peace-minded Democrats like Benton, and from Whigs, while angry Nays were spoken by

"Fifty-four Forties" from the Northwest like Cass and Hannegan, and by Atchison of Missouri. The Oregon question was settled, and substantially on the terms Benton had urged again and again in the long months of doubt.*

Within his own party, Benton was subject to fierce attack for his course on Oregon. Not only did old allies like Allen of Ohio and Fairfield of Maine disagree with him on the boundary, but he and other friends of 49° were also castigated by "the official organ at Washington City," the *Union,* as he put it later, "and the five hundred democratic papers" which followed its lead. One such paper was the *Pennsylvanian,* the special organ of James Buchanan, who toward the end of the controversy had trimmed toward the popular 54° 40′ position.[28]

During the long session, meanwhile, the restored Democracy turned to the restoration of some Democratic policies. With Polk's support, measures were introduced to lower the tariff, to re-establish the Independent Treasury system, and to graduate the prices of the public lands. The greater leader on the tariff was Secretary of the Treasury Walker, who shared generally the free trade view of Calhoun. A bill was finally passed in July, 1846, by predominantly party votes, which reduced the duties of 1842 sharply and made the act in effect a tariff-for-revenue measure. Despite strong objections to its free-trade tendencies Benton supported the bill out of party loyalty — as the Administration proposes it, he remarked to Gideon Welles, "let them have it." The bill to re-establish the Independent Treasury followed a smooth course, and was carried by party majorities in August, 1846. It was carried in

* Recalling these events years later, Benton declared that he had "proposed" to Polk the "device" of submitting the terms of the treaty in advance. He also reported that he undertook to help carry the matter through, particularly by talking with "all" the Whig senators to make sure that they would support the Democratic President as a counterweight against the Democratic "Fifty-four Forties." Finally, he says, he and the President "had many conferences" about this strategy, particularly on the night before the submission, in which the President sought "to get himself re-assured" as to Whig support (Benton, *View,* II, 674-675). All this seems to exaggerate the case considerably. Long before the British offer was made, Polk had determined to submit any such offer to the Senate for advice, and this scheme was apparently his own idea; when the time came, he did speak with Benton as well as with other Senators, but he records only one interview after the British offer, and that on the morning of submission to inform Benton what was planned (Quaife, *Diary,* I, 287, 463). As to Benton talking to the Whig Senators, he may well have done so, though the evidence I have seen does not clearly confirm or disconfirm his statement. In any case, Benton's repeated defenses of 49° must have helped prepare the foundation for the success of the "device" when it was sprung.

emasculated form, however, for it omitted the specie payment or hard-money features for which Old Bullion had fought in the original act of 1840. The Walker tariff remained in effect until 1857, and the Independent Treasury system, supplemented by a new banking structure in the 1860's, remained as the heart of the national fiscal system for nearly seventy years. Land bills were passed in both houses, but differences between them produced a deadlock and failure.

Despite legislative successes, Polk still worried about factionalism in his party. Repeatedly he fretted in his diary that Benton, or the increasingly "irritable" Calhoun, or some other powerful party leader, would soon come out in opposition. On March 4, 1846, the first anniversary of his Administration — "Col. Benton feels that he lost cast[e] with the Democracy on the Texas question, and feels sore and dissatisfied with his position. . . . I am left without any certain or reliable support in Congress." Again in March — "My fear is that these factions [for Cass, for Silas Wright, for Calhoun] looking to the election of my successor in 1848, will so divide and weaken the Democratic party by their feuds as to defeat my measures." [29] The factional clouds were probably not so dark as the fretful Polk painted them, but he certainly had no one whom he could depend on as Jackson had depended on Benton from 1829 to 1837.

[7]

WHILE THE OREGON CONTROVERSY RAGED, Benton had been deeply disturbed over family affairs.

The first difficulty was a crisis in the marriage of his niece Sally and Francis Thomas. Soon after the wedding of young Sally and the middle-aged Francis, signs of strain appeared, and Thomas began to complain that Sally had conducted herself "improperly" with Lewis Linn before her marriage. In May, 1844, Thomas had written a bitter letter to Benton, damning Benton as an "unscrupulous demon" who had connived at the "seduction" of his niece, and then "basely united with his wife, to persuade and prevail upon an unsuspecting and confiding man [Francis Thomas] to take her in marriage." In March, 1845, Francis Thomas went so far as to publish a fifty-two page pamphlet airing the whole matter as he saw it. This pamphlet reproduced intimate letters and reported (alleged) intimate interviews. Its burden was that Sally, while she was living with her Aunt and Uncle Benton, had been "seduced" by Lewis Linn, that she had then "set her cap" for Francis Thomas, and that Benton and Elizabeth had labored "to encourage and promote the connexion." After the Thomas-McDowell marriage, and while he was campaigning (successfully) for the governorship of Maryland, the aggrieved husband continued, Sally had had "improper interviews" and "unlawful intercourse" with three or four different young men. As a result, Thomas went on, Sally had become pregnant and had on the night of September 21, 1841, induced an abortion; the next morning, the embryo was found "under the head of the bed, wrapped in her underclothing." All these charges were vigorously denied by Sally, who admitted a pregnancy and miscarriage in 1841 but insisted that the child was her husband's. Though Sally may have been innocently flirtatious with Linn, there was no truth in the charges of "seduction" or other wrongdoing.

The publication of this "mélange of morbid feeling and scandal" touched off a series of events. First, in Washington, a libel suit, *U.S.* vs. *Thomas;* next, a public meeting in Lexington, Virginia, testifying to the "exalted character" and the "purity and virtue of Mrs. THOMAS"; third, a divorce suit by Francis against Sally in Maryland; fourth, a countersuit by Sally in Richmond, where she was staying with her father James McDowell (then still Governor of Virginia) and her mother; finally, a politically consequential rift between Benton and Mrs. Linn's brother, Congressman James Relfe. The divorce was accomplished by the beginning of 1846. Later, Sally married a Presbyterian minister, John Miller of Princeton, and lived a long and happy life with him.

Throughout the libel suit, Benton acted as the family's manager. He arranged for counsel to assist the public prosecutor, and consulted at least five attorneys for this purpose. At the beginning of October, when Francis Thomas called on the President of the United States to ask him "to order a *nolle prosequi*" in the case, he claimed that Benton was the real "prosecutor" in the matter. Polk refused, the suit went on, and Benton kept busy with its "prosecution." Reporting to James McDowell that Thomas was behaving like "a fool," Benton looked forward to the trial "as the happy time which is to crush *in toto* this blasted wretch, and to annihilate him, and immolate him, here upon the selected theatre for spreading his defamation." The "immolation," however, was postponed from session to session of the Court, in the law's typical delay. Finally, in March, 1847, in the District of Columbia Circuit Court, Thomas's attorney publicly abandoned all attempt to substantiate Thomas's charges, and with this vindication the prosecution entered a motion for *nolle prosequi*.[30] The kindest interpretation of Thomas's part in the scandal was that the Governor of Maryland was "deranged." *

In a second visitation of distress, both Benton and his wife were afflicted with poor health. He had had sciatica; through October, the "agony" began to "abate," though for some time he felt "a dull pain, with stiffness and weakness," a pain which extended "from the hips to the foot, and makes walking tedious and tiresome." At sixty-three, he was beginning to experience the ills of age. He was, however, less concerned for himself than for Elizabeth. Throughout the fall and winter of 1845-1846, he watched and worried over her failing health, reporting her condition regularly to her brother in Virginia. She was affected with slowness of speech, and "the whole machine, mind and body, works slowly and feebly, and seems like it might stop." She grew "more cheerful" after her husband's return from Kentucky, ceasing "to see the gloomy image of death before her"; but still the whole household had to be run to give her "quietude and composure." By late October "our dear Betsy" was "strengthening and improving." Toward the end of December she suffered another "attack." Though she was soon again in the parlor, seeing friends, and was able to ride out in the carriage and even walk a few blocks in good weather, she was still the victim of "languor, weakness, and some depression of spirits." In Janu-

---

* In 1844, James McDowell had been given a letter Thomas had written a Dr. William Tyler in 1843, accusing the physician of administering "poisonous drugs . . . to debilitate, disable, and derange me," and warning Dr. Tyler to leave Frederick, Maryland — "Remain! and may the bitter scorn of man be my portion if I do not send you to your God" (Note by James McDowell, and Enclosure, [Francis Thomas] to Dr. William Tyler, Frederick, November 31 [sic] 1843, Benton Papers, MoHS). Later, a story was told (probably apocryphal) of a session of the Maryland legislature, addressed by Governor Thomas, with Senator Benton and Governor McDowell present. Diverging from state business, Thomas began to discuss his marital troubles, absolved Sally "as pure as an icicle from the frozen north" [!], but declaimed that the McDowell men were out to torture him, and cried — "Let them come! Let them come, I fear them not — from Bully Benton to the blackguard McDowell!" Sensation, according to the story, with Benton starting from his seat in a fury, demanding "protection from the Legislature, or I will protect myself!" — whereupon the Speaker called the Governor to order, and the uproar subsided (Thomas and Williams, "Francis Thomas," 283). Wonderful, and perhaps even true — but certainly it was true that Thomas suffered in the 1840's from paranoia, though he later rehabilitated himself and played a distinguished role in his State.

ary her physicians diagnosed her illness anew as epilepsy — and the
family felt relieved "that all danger of anything sudden is now removed."

For eight more years, Elizabeth Benton lived on — a semi-invalid. All
this time Thomas gave her tender care. One family friend remembered
him carrying Elizabeth into the parlor to see callers when she was
unable to walk, and a South Carolina relative thought it "touching" to
see her sitting at the head of her table at a dinner party, "and he, with
the most delicate tact, dispensing those courtesies which, under other
circumstances, were her duty." Never was Elizabeth to regain the
bright, youthful charm that had won the admiration of all who knew
her.*

In the midst of these trials, Benton continued to face financial
stringencies. Through 1845, he had to renew and renew again his notes
to Pierre Chouteau, Jr., in three items of $1666.66 for periods of nine,
twelve, and fifteen months, and he was distressed when the manager of
his Woodford County farm failed to make expected payments. Finally,
in 1846, he sold a plot of land in St. Louis to Joshua Brant for the
handsome price of twenty-four hundred dollars —and at last saw his
way out of the burden of debt the purchase of his Washington house
had imposed.[31]

During the long Congressional session, meanwhile, Benton was marked
again by a number of observers. The Whig leader from New York,
William H. Seward, met him at the British embassy in January, where
Seward had gone to call with the English traveler Sarah Mytton Maury.
Seward introduced the Englishwoman and Benton, who "pleasantly
summoned his wife, a modest, venerable lady," as Seward put it. Reporting her travels, Sarah Mytton Maury offered a more extended account of Benton. In general and especially when speaking, she noted, he
had "much senatorial dignity — is rarely excited; his action and ges-
tures are expressive; his speech slow." In appearance, he was "of
robust and muscular frame, somewhat inclined to corpulency"; his
features were striking, and his forehead "very massive." In manner, he
had "that gentle self possession . . . which is so usual in those who are
conscious of superior strength." In conversation he spoke "on all topics

---

* In his account of his career written on his own deathbed, Thomas declared
that Elizabeth was "struck with paralysis in 1844, and from the time of that
calamity her husband was never known to go to any place of festivity or amusement" (Benton, "Auto-Biographical Sketch," vi.). This, of course, both over-
simplified Elizabeth's case and overstated its effect on Thomas.

openly and fully, and invariably listens with attention to the remarks of others."

Another estimate was offered by Benjamin F. Perry, who saw service as Governor of South Carolina. He too was "very much struck" with Benton's "imperial air and noble person," and thought him "the most remarkable looking man in the Senate." He found Benton in a personal meeting very "cordial." His "kindness and devotion to his wife and children were touching and beautiful." It was hard to believe that he was "the bad hearted man" some painted him as a result of a "disparaging report" of his career at the University of North Carolina — "it is very rare that domestic virtues are linked with crime." Still, he was certainly "excessively impressed with his own greatness, and intellectual powers," as shown by some remarks that Perry recalled (surely with some exaggeration) Benton making:

"Yes, sir, I never write or speak on any subject till I have thoroughly mastered it."

"Yes, sir, [my daughters] are accomplished girls: I educated them myself, and they are capable of conversing with any of the crowned heads of Europe, and in their own language, sir."

"[The President] knows very well that he did not understand the Oregon question till I explained the matter in my speech."

The Massachusetts gentleman-scholar and Senator-to-be Charles Sumner also observed Benton in April, 1846. Originally biased by Whig legend, he "was not prepared to find [Benton] as much of a courtier in his manners, and as full of the stores of various learning," [32] as he was in fact.

[8]

THE EPILOGUE OF TEXAS ANNEXATION was a crisis between the United States and Mexico. In March, 1845, Mexico broke off diplomatic relations. Long-standing, unsettled damage claims by American citizens further complicated the matter. In addition, the Administration argued that Texas ranged south and west to the Rio Grande River, while Mexico insisted that the proper border of Texas lay north and east of this, along the Nueces River and a line approximating 100° longitude. The war Benton had predicted did not immediately flare, but the situation was ominous.

Despite the "new difficulties in Mexico," Benton was optimistic. He thought the United States and Mexico "must settle," sooner or later. In February, 1846, he reported in a private letter to Pierre Chouteau, Jr., that he was pushing the idea that the private American claims against Mexico should be paid from the United States Treasury, as "an equivalent" to Mexico to serve as groundwork for negotiations "for a new boundary & for terminating all differences between us." Something like this must "eventually be done," and Chouteau could expect "the settlement of the claims" of Auguste Chouteau and Jules DeMun in which he was interested. The only questions were, *When?* and *How?* [33]

The Administration also hoped to ease the tension — *and,* perhaps, to accomplish something more. The President thought the vast Mexican areas of *Alta California* (including the valuable San Francisco Bay) and *Nuevo Mexico* might be purchased and added to the United States, for some twenty or twenty-five million. These expansionist notions, reminiscent of Jefferson's purchase of Louisiana in 1803, were as pacific as they were grand. In October, 1845, and again in March, 1846, Polk and Benton discussed them in the White House study, and the President noted happily that "Col. B. entered very fully into all my views." One John Slidell was sent to Mexico to negotiate on these "views," but Polk informed Benton that the Mexican government refused to receive Slidell.

At the beginning of May, Polk and Benton again discussed Mexico, and Polk noted Benton's "decided aversion to a war with Mexico if it could be avoided consistently with the honor of the country." As in the Oregon controversy, Benton stood for peace.

Meanwhile, a fateful series of events occurred. In August, 1845, American troops under Zachary Taylor had been sent to Corpus Christi, on the south bank of the Nueces near its mouth. In March, 1846, these troops were ordered to move on to the Rio Grande, near which they remained despite a warning from the Mexican commander at Matamoros. In April, a scouting party was ambushed just north of the Rio Grande by Mexican troops, with many American casualties. When news of the encounter reached Washington in early May, Polk acted. He had already decided to ask Congress for a declaration of war, and he used the incident on the Rio Grande to strengthen his plea. Before he sent the message, he consulted Benton and other Congressmen —and heard Benton declare flatly that he would "vote men and money for defence of our territory," but was "not prepared to make aggressive war on Mexico"; that he "disapproved the marching of the army from Corpus

Christi to the left bank of the [Rio Grande] Del Norte"; and that he "did not think the territory of the U.S. extended" beyond the Nueces. In short, Benton rejected Polk's later-to-be-notorious contention that Mexico had "invaded our territory and shed American blood on American soil," that war "exists by the act of Mexico."

This interview was on the morning of Monday, May 11, 1846, and the message was sent at noon. Within a few hours, the House had fulsomely responded with a bill that echoed Polk's declaration of the pre-existence of war and its origin, and provided for troops and money. In the Senate, the message was debated . . . and debated. Calhoun urged deliberation, while Lewis Cass hailed Polk's "manifesto" as one in which he "cheerfully" concurred. Benton argued that the message really dealt with "two distinct subjects," the defense of the nation, which was military, and a matter of the relations between the United States and Mexico, or war. He suggested that the *first* matter be referred to the Military Affairs committee, and the *second* to the Foreign Affairs committee. And so on, through the afternoon, without result.

That evening, Benton was again invited to the White House. There he saw not only Polk, but also Secretary of State Buchanan and Secretary of War Marcy. Despite an hour's argument, Benton refused to change his stand, and insisted that "in the 19th Century war should not be declared without full discussion and much more consideration than had been given to it in the Ho. Repts." On the eve of a major war, Polk found himself without the full support of the veteran, influential chairman of the Senate Military Affairs committee.*

* Years later, the chief historian of the war summed up the leadership situation in the President's party during the critical war period as "a triangular fight — Benton, Cass, and Calhoun. Benton had remarkable powers and seldom failed to be a Democrat, a Senator, and a patriot, but he was egotistical, moody, overbearing, passionate; he despised Cass, he more than hated Calhoun, and he treated his fellow Democrats in general as minions. Cass, a courtier and somewhat a scholar, lacked parliamentary experience, drew more timidity than courage from his Presidential hopes, and possessed no political convictions to reinforce his talents. Calhoun's high character, rare intellectual strength, and frank, affable manners made him personally the most influential man at the capital; but his judgments were erratic, and he aimed to stand aloof, with a following of about four Senators, as a balance of power faction . . . for him there seemed to be only one region in the world, one state in the south, and only one public man there. Cass was loyal to the Administration, Benton helpful but domineering, and Calhoun unfriendly. Not a very firm tripod, this, to support a government engaged in war" (Smith, *War with Mexico*, II, 282-283). This account exaggerates somewhat — and it must be added that Polk became President in the first place only as a result of the disorganization and "triangular fight" in his party.

The next day, in a floor debate that lasted until 6:30, Benton pleaded that peace was still possible, that "the door was open for an adjustment of our difficulties." When the vote came, however, he answered Yea, and the bill was passed, with only two Whigs voting Nay, while Calhoun abstained. Afterwards Benton remarked that many affirmative votes were given by members "extremely averse to this war," who acted out of a feeling of "duresse in the necessity of aiding our own troops."

Years later, Benton placed the Presidential explanation of the war in perspective. Its actual origins, he maintained, lay in three preceding factors — *first,* "the incorporation of Texas, with which Mexico was at war"; *second,* "the immediate advance of the army to the frontier of Texas"; *third,* "the further advance of the American troops," across the Nueces, and on "to the left bank of the Lower Rio Grande, then and always in the possession of Mexico." It was only "under these circumstances that the Mexican troops crossed the river, and commenced the attack." [34]

While Benton co-operated with Polk in prosecuting the war, he also constantly sought ways toward peaceful settlement. Again and again, serving as a sort of informal, personal chief of staff, he visited Polk and gave advice on problems ranging from the revision of militia legislation to make it workable, to war-and-peace strategy in general. Once more, in the fall of 1846, he failed to go to Missouri — though he did visit briefly in Philadelphia, and spent some time in September and October with business at his Kentucky farm.

In November, Benton was occupied with several long conferences with the President. In a frank though cutting manner he passed judgment on the formal military commander in Washington, the aging Winfield Scott ("no confidence in him"), and on the chief commander in the field in northern Mexico, Zachary Taylor ("unfit for command"). Both these major generals happened to be Whigs. More significantly, Benton proposed a grand war-and-peace plan of his own. So far a limited strategy had been followed, aimed at seizing the loosely held north-Mexican provinces of California, Nuevo Mexico, and Chihuahua, and then outwaiting the Mexicans. Benton denounced this policy as unsuited to "a go-ahead people," and proposed that "a bold blow be struck," through the seizure of the Gulf Coast city of Vera Cruz far to the South, followed by "a rapid crushing movement" on Mexico City itself. First offered on November 7, this suggestion was discussed, elaborated, and reiterated in successive White House interviews. In these interviews, Benton suggested that a high-level, bipartisan commission, authorized to make peace, should be sent with the military headquarters. He also proposed that "there ought to be a Lieutenant General of the army who should be General in chief," and who would be "a man of talents and resources [political and diplomatic, presumably] as well as a military man." He declared himself ready to serve on the commission, and to act as Lieutenant General, if such an office were created by Congress, and the President declared *himself* ready to make the appointments. Meantime, Polk discussed the matter with his cabinet. Doubts were raised concerning the proposed march on Mexico City (the special feature of Benton's plan), though an expedition to Vera Cruz was agreed to.

Earlier, Benton had developed more fully the political aspects of his plan. He prepared an eleven-page document, written as though it were a letter to a Commander in Chief in Mexico. The "inhabitants" there should be treated with studied *kindness*. To the people, and to captured Mexican officers, assurances should repeatedly be given that "the war itself is only carried on to obtain justice, and that we had much rather procure that by negotiation than by fighting." Certainly, it should be easy to play on divisions "in a country so divided into races, classes, and parties as Mexico," the Missouri Machiavelli went on. "Between the Spanish who monopolize the wealth and power of the country," he declared, "and the mixed Indian race who bear its burthens, there must be jealously and animosity," and there must be some parties more "liberal" than others. All rifts in the community should be utilized "in bringing about an honorable and a speedy peace." It should be made clear to "the Mexican nation" that it was the President's wish to establish "the future friendship and commerce of the two countries."

Events proved Benton right in his opinion that, though procrastination suited the Mexican temperament, it was "utterly unsuited to the temper of our people." But he exaggerated in later giving himself nearly full credit for the development of any more active strategy — and nothing came of the peace commission idea as he had originally planned it.

During one of their talks, Polk asked Benton to accept an appointment as Minister to France, but Benton promptly declined. He had never wanted "to engage in the Foreign service," and had therefore refused other missions abroad that Jackson and Van Buren had tendered him in previous years.[35]

Meanwhile, events elsewhere were occurring which were to have an important effect, directly or indirectly, on Benton.

While he was busy in Washington as a would-be peacemaker, his son-in-law in the Far West was active as a stormy warrior. Arriving in California in January, 1846, Frémont had been greeted by the Mexican *"prefecto"* with a sputter of hostile letters and a show of force. Discreetly, Frémont had retired to the wild Tla-math or Klamath Lake region in the Oregon country. Early in May, a messenger managed to find him in the wilderness. The messenger brought letters from Benton and others, dispatches, and oral communications from Administration officials concerning the rising tension between the United States and Mexico, and fears of British or French aggression on California. All this Frémont took as warrant for returning to the Sacramento Valley, and standing there as a potential "protector" of American interests as he saw them. In California, an intricate series of revolts, near-revolts, and military skirmishes was developing. In June, a group of Anglo-American settlers proclaimed an independent "Republic of California" under a hastily designed "Bear Flag," and Frémont's explorer company happily granted them "protection." Before long, the "Bear Flag" was hauled down and the United States flag boldly hoisted in its place. This, and some more fighting which now appeared as a part of the general war with Mexico, resulted in the destruction of the (effective) power of Mexico and in California's (effective) "incorporation with the American republic," as Benton put it later. Thus, with the thirty-three year old Frémont playing a leading role, California was to fulfill what Benton thought its "destiny."

In Washington, Thomas and Jessie received private letters from John Charles detailing these adventures. Promptly, Benton decided to chronicle and "justify" the "operations" of his son-in-law in a letter to Polk which was made public to the nation in *Niles Register*. In addition, Benton in another public letter urged wounded survivors of the expedition or the widows of nonsurvivors to "send petitions to me," or other Congressmen, "and have nothing to do with agents," or lobby operators in Washington who would take claims for a fee. Even the *Republican* in St. Louis had to praise this action. Meanwhile, Jessie Benton Frémont wrote her "dearest husband" an ecstatic private letter. She informed him of his promotion to the rank of Lieutenant Colonel, girlishly awed and happy (she was barely twenty-two) at the right "to call you Colonel." There was, she reported, no envy over his lightning advance "in eight years from an unknown second lieutenant," except "from some of the lower order of Whig papers who only see you as Colonel Benton's son-in-law." She noted that "father absolutely idolizes Lilly [little Elizabeth Benton Frémont, aged three-and-a-half] . . . and then you should see his pride in you!" Although "mother's health" was "worse than ever during the winter," even she seemed "well again" by summer.[36] While the whole family waited expectantly for their explorer's triumphant return, there was glory for everybody.

Politically, Benton could remark a shift in the Administration which was an index of the times. In September, Louis McLane had resigned as Minister to England, and was replaced by George Bancroft, who resigned as Secretary of the Navy, and was in turn replaced by the ex-Tylerite John Y. Mason. Thus, the only old-radical member of the Cabinet was removed from that body and its counsel.

When the Congress of 1846-1847 convened, Polk decided to try Benton's Lieutenant General idea. A Senate bill to create the office was introduced in mid-January, 1847, by John Dix of New York, who was now Benton's C Street neighbor and friend. The bill was promptly attacked on two grounds. The opposition cried, first, that no mere contemporary should have a rank previously held only by George Washington, and charged, second, that the bill was part of a maneuver by Polk to arrange his successor (Benton, presumably). Ten days later, Benton scouted this charge. All he and Polk had in mind, he insisted, was a mission to "show the deceived people of Mexico that just and honorable peace is all we want." There was no "ulterior and covert design" to boost any man for the Presidency. Meanwhile, the plan to bring Benton into command as joint military-diplomatic leader was tabled, 28 to 21. The opposition consisted chiefly of the Whigs and of Calhoun's personal Democratic faction.

This miscarriage was followed by lengthy recriminations. While Calhoun exulted in the failure of the effort "to build up, through Benton, the old Van Buren party," Polk blamed Calhoun for strangling the bill; and before long Buchanan was noting "the open defection of Calhoun from the Administration." But Benton thought that Buchanan himself, and Secretaries Marcy and Walker too, had labored "covertly" to defeat his war-and-peace plan and appointment (lobbying, presumably); and he spoke with "some excitement" about the matter to Polk, who pooh-poohed the whole idea. Buchanan admitted that he had "opposed placing any civilian at the head of the Army," but denied any

attempt to influence Congress. The Whigs feared that Benton as commander in Mexico would necessarily win glory that might otherwise go
to their major generals, Taylor and Scott — who was even then preparing to lead the long-delayed expedition to Vera Cruz. Thus, considerations of factional, personal, presidential and party advantage, quite as
much as concern for the wisdom of the proposal, had deprived Benton
of his chance to undertake his military-diplomatic mission.

Despite its failure, the Lieutenant General bill seemed to mark better
relations between Polk and the radical Democrats. To Van Buren,
Benton wrote that it was "strange that Mr. Polk finds his reliable and
disinterested support from your friends." But the President had begun
"to see it," and wished "to give public evidence of it — hence certain
embassies offered, and the lieutenant general." [37]   The first week in
March saw a sequel to the Lieutenant General story, when Benton was
appointed and confirmed as a *Major* General. He agreed to take the
commission only under certain conditions. He had "no desire to go to
Mexico simply to have a plume & a bunch of feathers in his hat," he
told Polk, and wrote him more formally that he would accept only if
he were given "the powers which I deem necessary to success" — "the
command of the army, *and* authority to sign preliminaries of peace."
The President and cabinet considered these "stipulations," and finally
(with Buchanan playing the leading role) pieced together a letter declaring that it was impossible to name "you — a junior Major General
— to the chief command of an Army in the field." Thereupon, Benton
declined the appointment. The next day, he saw Polk, and refused to
reconsider. Still, the President noted, "he was in a pleasant humor and
his conversation was in a friendly tone." [38]

In January, meanwhile, Benton was involved in another abortive
effort for peace. A free-lance adventurer in diplomacy named Alexander Atocha brought him letters from Mexican leaders which seemed
to suggest that peace might be arranged. In a pair of stiff, formal notes,
Benton brought the Atocha letters to Buchanan's attention, and read
them personally to Polk, translating from the Spanish as he went
along. After lengthy deliberations, Polk dispatched Atocha to Mexico
to propose a peace meeting, but in Mexico Atocha was met coldly by
both people and regime.[39]

All efforts at peace had failed, and the war went on.

CHAPTER 14

Days of Wrath

1847 - 1849

THE BACKWASH OF WAR brought an angry revival of the slavery controversy in a new form. This conflict was to dominate politics for years to come, and to pit Benton and Calhoun against one another again as leading antagonists in the legislative struggle.

In 1846, and in 1847, Polk asked Congress to authorize a special loan, first of two million and then of three million dollars. With these funds, he hoped to induce Mexico to end the war, *and* to cede to the United States the vast, Mexican-held or Mexican-claimed domains from Texas through Nuevo Mexico to California. In the House, a *"proviso"* was attached to the loan bills — *that any territory that might be acquired should be forever closed to slavery.* This stipulation was called the "Wilmot Proviso," after its author David Wilmot, an antislavery Pennsylvania Democrat. Thus a conflict was precipitated far more portentious than the Mexican War itself. This was the divisive issue of slavery, slavery extension, and slavery restriction.

When the question came before the Senate in February, 1847, an all-out attack on the Wilmot Proviso doctrine was launched by the indefatigable Calhoun. He condemned slavery restriction as hostile to the interests of "the slaveholding States," as "a question of safety, of self-preservation," of the structure of the Southern society, economy, and culture. He proposed a set of formal resolutions declaring that Congress "has no right to make any law, or do any act," which would "deprive the citizens of any of the States of this Union from emigrating with their property [slaves], into any of the territories"; and that any such act "would tend directly to subvert the union itself." The "slaveholding States" were "already a minority" in every part of the political system except for their still-equal representation in the Senate, he cried, and destruction of this balance by the addition of new nonslaveholding States would bring "a day that will not be far removed from political revolution, anarchy, civil war, and widespread disaster." The "Wilmot

Proviso" was now matched with the "Calhoun Resolutions." Immediately, Benton rose to his feet in protest. "We have some business to transact," he pointed out in his pragmatic way — "if anybody thinks that I am going to lay aside the necessary business of the session to vote on such a string of abstractions, he is greatly mistaken." There followed a bitter exchange between the slender, cadaverous, reserved Calhoun and the bulky, florid, impetuous Benton, who denounced Calhoun's "firebrands" with all his accustomed vigor. When Calhoun remarked, sarcastically, that he had thought his colleague, as "the representative of a slaveholding State," would have been found in support of the Resolutions, Benton boomed a rejoinder.

MR. BENTON: I shall be found in the right place. I am on the side of my country and the Union.

Thus the angry colloquy ended. No action was taken on the "abstractions," which remained a political storm center for some time to come.

Finally, the Wilmot Proviso issue came to a vote in the Senate. The session of 1846-1847 was nearing its end, and in an effort to finish its business the Senate sat late into the night of March 1-2. About one in the morning of March 2, the weary members rejected the antislavery Proviso to the loan bill, 31 to 21, with Benton voting with the Nays.[1]

In voting against the Wilmot Proviso, Benton put himself in an anomalous position. He was in step with Polk, who thought the Proviso "mischievous & wicked agitation," and with the political brokers like Cass, Hannegan, and others. He was at least on the same road with his arch-enemy John Calhoun, and other champions of slavery. But he was out of step with radical Democrats like Dix, Fairfield, Niles, and others, who voted Yea, and with his old friend and presumed candidate for the Presidency, Silas Wright, who thought the slavery restriction principle "clearly right . . . expedient . . . necessary." He was also in disagreement with his friend Blair — who in his retirement was taking busmen's holidays by visiting the Congress he had once reported, sitting behind Benton in the Senate chamber. More significantly, he was out of step also with rising antislavery public opinion in the North, the section with which he was becoming increasingly identified. The Wilmot Proviso had sparked a popular movement, and in free state after state it was endorsed in public meetings and in legislative resolutions. Practically, of course, it would have been tantamount to political suicide for a slave state Senator to support the Wilmot Proviso. But Benton had larger reasons for his position. In terms of national policy, he saw the Proviso *and* the Calhoun Resolutions as twin evils. As he put it in perspective later, they were "two halves of a pair of shears, neither of which could cut until joined together"; but thus joined, "the map of the Union was in danger." In addition, he believed, the slavery-restriction Proviso was "nugatory, and could answer no purpose," because the territory it was meant to cover was *already* free under *Mexican law,* and free in fact. The whole "slavery agitation," Benton thought, portended a violent new "sectional struggle." He wanted no part in such doings.[2]

At the end of March, after adjournment, Benton concerned himself with another slavery-infected issue. A bill for an Oregon territorial government had failed, because it contained a provision prohibiting slavery in the area. Now Benton wrote a public letter to the settlers in Oregon, explaining why they had been left without a government. He showed a draft of the letter to Polk, who was fearful that it might "incline" the people of Oregon to set up a government of their own. But Benton persisted, and Polk lamented that, knowing Benton's "utter impatience of contradiction," he could not hold him back. Though "General Benton," as Polk now called him, agreed to think the matter over, he finally decided to go ahead, sending the document by John Shively, whose appointment to carry mail to Oregon he had proposed. The letter's salutation was "MY FRIENDS — for such I may call many of you from personal acquaintance, and all of you from my thirty years devotion to the interests of your country." It declared that the efforts to set up a government had failed on the violence of Southern objections to the slavery-exclusion clause, "copied from the [Northwest] ordinance of 1787 — the work of the great men of the South, in the great day of the South, prohibiting slavery in a territory far less northern than yours." It then condemned the "author" of the new slavery controversy (Calhoun), and promised action in the next session for a territoral government.[3]

Launching again the attack on the arch-enemy Calhoun, this manifesto was apparently aimed in part at driving him further from the Administration and party standard. But it also showed Benton's persistent, practical interest in Westward advance and settlement. When the Oregonians organized a provisional government, they honored Benton by naming one of their first counties (in the rich Willamette Valley) after him.

In the capital, political speculation ran wild. Polk, feeling insecure and persecuted, agreed with Benton that "the Democratic party in Congress were in a most distracted and feeble condition" — with Calhoun, "perfectly desperate in his aspirations for the Presidency," seizing upon the slavery issue "as the only means of sustaining himself." Furthermore, Polk added, the radical and New York Democrats, pushing Silas Wright, "would be rejoiced at the opportunity to take issue with Mr. Calhoun on such a question." There was, Polk cried, "no patriotism on either side." Contrariwise, many Calhoun partisans were torturing themselves with nightmares of Benton's ascendancy. Hearing rumors that Walker was "getting very sick" and might have to resign as Secretary of the Treasury, one Calhounite wailed that "in that event Benton might become Dictator of the Administration." Another thought "something must be done to head Mr. Benton" in his effort to develop an "alliance with the North." [4]

On March 18, Benton gave his oldest daughter Eliza in marriage to William Carey Jones of New Orleans. The wedding was held at the family's C Street home, and attended by many prominent guests, including President Polk and his lady. The President escorted the bride to the supper table after the ceremony. Ten days later "General Benton" called at the White House to suggest that his new son-in-law be named a Chargé d'Affaires abroad,* but Polk offered no encouragement.[5] Now, Thomas and Elizabeth had with them regularly only their youngest daughters Sarah and Susan, and their son Randolph — and he was often away at school.

[2]

THE SUMMER OF 1847 Benton spent in Missouri, politicking mostly, and in Kentucky at his farm. In the fall, he returned to Washington — where he faced a new crisis in his personal affairs.

When Benton had reached St. Louis early in May, 1847, he found his party, locally, jubilant. The previous year, the bitter-end anti-Benton leader, Shadrach Penn, had died,† and this plus the settlement of the Texas and Oregon issues had made a new accommodation between old factional enemies seem possible. The *Reporter* and its erstwhile rival

---

* This was, on the evidence I have seen, the only instance in Benton's long career in which he sought office for a family connection (cf. Meigs, *Benton,* 381) — and he does not seem to have pushed this matter.

† The year 1846 had also brought the death in St. Louis of Benton's old friend, dueling second, and staunch political ally, Luke E. Lawless.

the *Missourian* were combined to form a new paper, called (like the new national organ) the *Union*. At first the *Union's* editor was Benton's friend John H. Tice of the old *Missourian,* but later Tice gave way to Samuel Treat, Penn's former understudy on the *Reporter.* Still, unity persisted, and in April, 1847, the Democrats had swept the St. Louis city election. The victory was won over the old Whig party, and over a new "Nativist" faction which labored to stir sentiment against the German immigrants who were filling the city. The Democrats, particularly utilizing a new pro-Benton German-language paper *Anzeiger des Westens,* made a special appeal to the German-Americans. Increasingly, these immigrants were to become an important element in Benton's power base in St. Louis.

Two days after his arrival in St. Louis, Benton spoke at a dinner of the local chapter of the Sons of Temperance. It was "a chaste, appropriate, and eloquent speech, which elicited the most rapturous applause," the *Union* reported, adding that it was happy to see men of such "widespread influence" aiding the cause of sobriety. Willing to eat and speak for reform, Benton declined an invitation to a public dinner in his honor — he had "not yet given up" his rule against such affairs.

From such pleasantries, Benton turned to the thorny issues of politics. A meeting of Democrats in Howard County in the heart of the state had nominated him for the Presidency. Replying that he was "pained" at the proposal, Benton reminded his followers that he had in 1844 called for a Democratic candidate from the North. More than ever, these "sentiments" were appropriate, now that Calhoun's "firebrand resolutions" showed that men from the South wanted to make "a new political test" on slavery. The "election of 1848 is the crisis"; for "the good of the Union and of the party," the candidate must be from the North. Thus bluntly did Benton, again, count himself out.

In mid-May he elaborated his views at a meeting in the Rotunda of the courthouse, before an overflow crowd of thousands. It was a slashing, hour-long address, warmly applauded during and after its delivery. Apparently, Benton offered it as a keynote exposition of his position for the 1840's, as his "MEN" or "MONEY" speech of 1835 had stood as a keynote for the program he advocated in the 1830's. After reviewing in detail his bold course on Texas and Oregon, he blasted "the slavery propagandist resolutions" of Calhoun. They contemplated, he thundered, "a subversion of the Union," and proposed in effect "the abolition of all compromises, past and future, on the slavery question." Indeed, "they go the precise length of the northern abolitionists, and with the same practical consequences, only in a reversed form." He had already "sounded the alarm." It was now up to "the people of the United States — all the friends of the Union — to do the rest," for there was now no Jackson to preserve the Union "by a voice, like the command of destiny." Thus bluntly did Benton join the new slavery issue in slaveholding Missouri. Thus boldly did he stand forth as the advocate of the cause of freedom, the Union, and harmony.

In mid-May also, Benton had word of his son-in-law Frémont in far-off California. The news was brought by Kit Carson, who had been on his way from California since February, carrying dispatches to Washington. The cool, observant, barrel-chested, sharp-eyed mountain man, lacking in "book learning" but filled with practical lore of the great West, had never met Benton. Now he "had the honor of an introduction," as he put it later, and was pleased when the august and polished Senator invited him to stay at the family's C Street home when he reached Washington. The news Carson brought was good. It included letters describing the loyalty Mexican-Californians were developing toward the United States, and Frémont as its symbol. Indeed, verses were being sung in the streets to guitar accompaniments:

> *Vivan los Estados Unidos,*
> *Y viva el Coronel Fremont.*

The mountain man stayed in St. Louis for about a week. For decades Benton had been in the habit of entertaining trappers, traders, adventurers, Indian chiefs, and explorers at his St. Louis home, to get their impressions of the Far West. Now a friend who called on Benton at Joshua Brant's found him deep in conversation with Carson, the two surrounded by maps and charts, discussing routes to the Pacific. One tale the dispatch-bearer might have told in the conversation concerned an Indian attack on the party's camp one night on the Gila River. When the Indians surrounded the little group, firing arrows at them, Kit Carson directed his men to hold their pack saddles in front of them, neither speak nor return fire, wait until the Indians approached, and then use their rifles as clubs. The Indians came no closer, and left before morning; no one in the party was hurt. No wonder Benton gave "Mr. Christopher Carson" a note of introduction praising his "skill and courage," as well as his "fidelity, generosity, and truth."

On the strength of the letters Kit Carson brought, Benton undertook to deny Washington rumors that dissension had developed between Lieutenant-Colonel Frémont and Brigadier-General Stephen Watts Kearny, who had reached California with a detachment of American troops after Frémont had established himself there. Now Carson's letters, Benton declared, showed that these reports were false — harmony reigned. Unfortunately for Benton and his son-in-law, events were to contradict him.

At the end of May, Benton traveled to Jefferson City to address the Cole County Democracy, and through "the art of printing" the people of Missouri. He reviewed his long record in the Senate, taking particular pride in declaring that the financial system he had advocated was proving itself under the stress of war — "banks paying specie; shin plasters gone; gold aplenty! and all without a regulator! without a King Bank!" Reviewing the "new slavery question," he warned again that it would produce a division like the North-South split that had just riven the Methodist Episcopal church. It would break parties on sectional lines, and bring finally "the destruction of the Union." He thought that Missouri, "for one slaveholding State, will not follow the lead of the slavery propagandist resolutions." As lagniappe, he offered a story to symbolize the pride he and his family felt in his Missouri. Important triumphs were at last being reported in the war. At Buena Vista in the north Taylor's troops had scored a smashing victory, and Scott's forces had landed at Vera Cruz and begun a long march to Mexico City, routing a determined Mexican stand at Cerro Gordo. The "crushing movement" on the capital Benton had proposed was at last in progress. All these triumphs had been greeted in Washington by a grand "illumination" of streets and buildings, Benton noted. His own home had been decorated and lit up, with legends *Cerro Gordo* and *Buena Vista* to the left and right, and in the center a flag that had been carried by Colonel Frémont and his Missouri men to the lofty peaks of the Rockies. His daughters had done this display, Elizabeth being confined to her bed, and Randolph having come West with his father. All, of course, "had heard that he was a teacher to his children; this illustration would prove that he had taught them to honor the State which had honored their father." With this little masterpiece in the conjunction of propaganda symbols, Benton concluded his address.

Back in St. Louis, he declined an invitation to serve as a delegate to a "Rivers and Harbors Convention" called to meet in Chicago. The approach of summer heat in Washington made it "imperative" that he make some arrangements for Elizabeth Benton's health. By failing to go to the Chicago convention, Benton missed hearing a felicitous address of welcome by a man the press listed simply as "Mr. Lincoln" — recently elected from the Springfield district as the only Whig in the Illinois Congressional delegation.

Through the first third of July, Benton stayed on in St. Louis. Early that month, the New York merchant and bitter-end Whig Philip Hone, with his daughter Margaret, visited St. Louis. He was surprised when "the great gun of the West" (Benton, whom Hone had scourged verbally often and bitterly in previous years), made himself agreeable, calling for the Hones in a carriage and showing them about the growing city.

The residents of the town were meanwhile busy preparing a grand reception for a group of returning Missouri volunteers. These troops, under Colonel Alexander W. Doniphan, had fought brilliantly in a long march through the northern Mexican provinces. The ceremony took place in front of the magnificent Planters House Hotel, on July 2. Despite the advancing heat and the press of the huge crowd, it was a happy occasion. Giving the chief address of welcome, Benton offered a glowing tribute to "your march and exploits," through rough, little-known terrain, and he particularly praised the regiment's part in the bloodless conquest of New Mexico under General Kearny. To this address, Colonel Doniphan himself responded warmly — "if the honorable senator's [*turning to Mr. Benton*] plans had been adopted, the war would have terminated long ago."

Ten days later, Benton and his son Randolph left for Washington, by way of Kentucky. As they traveled, the University of Missouri held its commencement exercises in its stately-columned chapel, and awarded Benton *in absentia* a Doctor of Laws degree. The man who had failed to graduate at the University of North Carolina now had an honorary doctorate. All told, Benton's Western trip had been a pleasant, triumphal one, a happy sojourn of political harmony and personal deference.[6]

In the fall, however, Dr. Benton became again the subject of bitter, national political speculation. On August 26, Silas Wright died suddenly at his New York farm, at the early age of fifty-two. Thus the Benton-Van Buren-Blair group lost their "democratic candidate for 1848 taken from the north." It was a staggering setback, "a severe blow," Calhoun noted gleefully. One of the New York radicals, seeking

a way out, insisted that the party could stand no more second-raters
like Cass, Buchanan, or Levi Woodbury, and wrote Van Buren that
"the democracy must fall back on you or on 'Old Bullion.' " For some
time, Van Buren and Blair hoped Benton would now permit himself to
be drafted, but he would not run. Meanwhile, a paper in Louisville reported that in an informal conversation in Kentucky Benton had spoken
of the war, "and became immensely excited — perfectly infuriated" at
the Administration's failure to take the opportunity "of making an
advantageous and honorable peace." Thus, it was clear "that Mr. Benton is preparing himself for a terrific attack upon the administration" in
the Senate, on the "peace" issue. This article evoked a curt note from
Benton — "Gentlemen . . . I have to request that [your] paper be no
longer left at my house." But Calhoun, at his Fort Hill plantation in
South Carolina, noted that "Benton is denouncing the administration,
whether to break with them, or control them is uncertain; probably the
latter." [7]

In mid-August, Thomas brought Elizabeth from Washington to Kentucky. While he was in the capital, he called twice on Polk, who found
him "pleasant and agreeable," despite the rumors of dissension.
Through the last hot days of August, all of September, and the first half
of October, Thomas and Elizabeth stayed on at their Kentucky farm,
with Elizabeth's health remaining precarious but not critical. Thomas
sold 300 acres of land adjoining his sawmill tract, and wished he had
sold the main tract too, "as we wish to transfer all to Missouri." In mid-
October, he and Elizabeth returned to Washington — "Mrs. Benton
standing the journey quite well," Thomas wrote a friend, "which has
been of advantage to her spirits, & in some respects her health is improved, tho the attacks still continue, tho greatly mitigated from their
first violence." [8] In keeping with the happy spirit of the season, even
Elizabeth seemed better.

Far away in California, however, fortune's wheel had turned against
Frémont — and the turn was ominous for Benton. Authority in California had been vested by the *Navy* in Commodore R. F. Stockton,
who had sworn Frémont and his men into the Navy, and appointed Frémont civilian governor. This odd arrangement was later complicated by
the arrival of Brigadier General Kearny, who also claimed supreme
authority over California from the *Army,* and sought to bring the impetuous Frémont under his control. Stockton and Frémont had worked
well together. Kearny was a martinet, a West Point routineer, though

capable, and he and Frémont could not get along; in addition, Frémont felt that Kearny's West Point officers, whose advancement had been slower than his, were jealous and hostile. A tangled situation thus developed, out of bureaucratic bungling over lines of authority, Frémont's own impetuosity, vainglory, and often ill-advised judgment, and West Point inflexibility and pride. In this conflict of legitimacies, Frémont cast his lot with Stockton. Thereupon Kearny accused Frémont of insubordination and finally of mutiny, and brought him back to civilization in August, 1847, to face a court-martial.

All his intense family loyalties stirred, Benton rushed to the rescue, as he had done for Sally McDowell. Acquittal would be easy, in his opinion, "but you are entitled to credit for your conduct," he told his son-in-law. Counsel would have to be employed, but it would "be more nominal than otherwise, as I shall do the work. . . . I will be with you to the end, if it takes up the whole session of Congress." The result would be a triumph, and Frémont would "realize what Lord Palmerston said to Mr. Van Buren when he was rejected by the Senate, 'that it was an advantage to a public man to be, in the course of his life, the subject of an outrage.' " Indeed, "the enemy is now in our hands, and may the Lord have mercy upon them; for I feel as if I could not." In his headlong, egotistical, driving way, Benton had no doubt about the "right" of the situation.

The "outrage" stirred up a furor. In Mexico, Zachary Taylor expected "a great blow-out," thought it might be settled "by mutual explanations & concessions as they are all politicians," but opined that "Benton will be most difficult to satisfy." In Washington, a worried, valiant Jessie Benton Frémont visited Polk and pressed him on the matter; Kit Carson discussed it with him; and in August and again in October the question was canvassed at length by "General Benton" and Polk. The President — quite properly, Benton thought — refused to commit himself on the court-martial, while Benton confined himself to insisting that all charges made at any time be specifically listed for trial. His "deepest concern in this life was to see justice done to Col. Fremont."

Late October brought another complication, when Randolph Benton, not quite eighteen, called on the President to ask for an appointment as a lieutenant. The President demurred, whereupon Randolph rose to his feet, became "impertinent" and "excited," and insisted on a yes-or-no answer — which Polk refused. Then, Polk noted in his diary, Randolph banged out, "swearing profanely . . . 'By God' he would do something." The harassed Polk thought he had been drinking, and was sure he was "in all respects worthless." Meanwhile, Benton's son-in-law William Carey Jones, who still stood in the President's eyes as "an applicant to me for office," became assistant counsel in Frémont's case. Despairing at so much difficulty with so many members of Benton's apparently ubiquitous family, Polk predicted morosely that Benton would "become my enemy because all his wishes in reference to his family and their appointments" were not gratified.

The great court-martial began on November 2, 1847, in the glow of a late Washington Indian summer. At the capital Armory, it wound its involved, tedious, explosive way through November and December, into the wintery month of January, 1848. Conflicting and hostile witnesses gave hundreds of thousands of words of conflicting and hostile testimony before the thirteen officers of the court. The principals, Kearny and Frémont, sat calmly, while Benton maintained a vigil-like scrutiny of the proceedings. In the testimony, he revealed General Kearny as an unreliable witness with a spotty memory, and took the offensive against the accuser. Toward the end, he charged Kearny with looking "insultingly and fiendishly" at Frémont. The result was an angry clash between the General and Benton, who boasted that he had stared back at Kearny "till his eyes fell — till they fell upon the floor!" For this bit of bluster, Benton was rebuked by the presiding officer. Finally, on the last day of January, 1848, the last scene in the somber, gold-braided drama was played. The court-martial found Frémont *guilty* on all charges, and sentenced him to dismissal from the service. Noting the unusual circumstances, six of the thirteen officers recommended executive clemency. The President and his cabinet worried the matter into mid-February, and then Polk announced that he found Frémont guilty of insubordination though not of mutiny. But he was canceling the punishment — Lieutenant Colonel Frémont "will resume his sword, and will report for duty." While these decisions did not hurt Frémont's reputation nationally, and even enhanced it, they were too much for the high-spirited young officer. He, like Benton, could not brook the challenge to his honor in the implication of guilt. He resigned from the Army in disgust.

Fiercely loyal to his son-in-law, Benton thought the decisions of court and President another outrage. His pleasant relations with Polk, repeatedly strained by politics before, were now broken off altogether. There were no more intimate talks at the White House; the President in his diary referred now to "Mr. Benton" or "Col. Benton" instead of "General Benton"; the two men saw each other almost every Sunday at church, but Polk complained that Benton "never speaks to me as he was in the habit of doing." From the day he had approved the sentence of the court-martial, Polk lamented in summary, "Col. Benton . . . has been exceedingly hostile to me." [9]

In mid-January, meantime, Thomas's third daughter had been married. With Frémont in California there had been a twenty-one-year-old Kentuckian named Richard Taylor Jacob. He had come to Washington for the court-martial, and had met Sarah Benton. On January 17, 1847, at the Bentons' home, Richard and Sarah were married, and the young man soon took his bride to Missouri, where he set up as a gentleman farmer. This time, though the court-martial was as yet still in progress, there was no President Polk at the wedding to take the bride in to supper.

It was a dark season. Even Thomas's old friend Francis Blair thought him "absolutely possessed with the Kearny conspiracy against Frémont." [10]

[3]

THUS ABSORBED, Benton had given little attention to politics and legislation. Before Congress convened in December, 1847, he had written Polk that he would not again take the chairmanship of the Military Affairs committee, because he thought Secretary of War Marcy had behaved unfairly in the Frémont case, adding new and improper charges to Kearny's list. When in January, 1848, argument raged in the Senate over war and sectional issues, men like Dix and Niles who looked to Benton's leadership regretted sorely that he was "not at his post . . . to save what remains of the principles of the Democratic party." [11]

The new Congress contained some striking figures. The squat but politically agile Douglas of Illinois had been advanced to the Senate. There he was ideologically flanked by the cool, polished plantation leader and ultraslavery-extensionist Jefferson Davis of Mississippi — fresh from a dashing career in the war with Mexico — and by the antislavery leaders Hale of New Hampshire and Hamlin of Maine. The latter replaced Benton's old friend John Fairfield, who had died. In the House, the freshman Whig from Illinois, Lincoln, was to gain a flicker-

ing fame in his single Congressional term by offering a resolution demanding that Polk indicate the "spot" on which the war's first blood
had been shed, and say whether it was traditionally Mexican or American. In the mid-term elections the Whigs had won a majority in the
House, with their greatest gains in the free-state North, while the Democrats had strengthened their majority in the Senate by slight gains in
the slave-state South. The elections had apparently reflected some un-
popularity for "Mr. Polk's war," particularly in the North.

Although Davis and Benton were at political antipodes, Jefferson
Davis's wife Varina admired Benton as a senatorial performer. He was
"courtly," even to enemies, she recalled, and possessed "rare personal
dignity," despite the fact that as he grew older he grew "so stout," and
despite his "swelling" oratorical manner. He went after an opponent,
Clay, for example, when he was in the Senate, or Calhoun, "as one would
hunt a hare," and the opponent was "doomed." Clay, whom Varina
Davis thought "impressive" but lacking in Benton's "leonine character,"
would fight back, while the "prophetic" Calhoun, at whose feet Jefferson Davis sat, "never willingly engaged in these tilts." But Benton had
more than "burning eloquence, keen satire, and exalted romanesque
declamation." He was steeped in "statesmen's lore," he "had reasoned
out his policy," and he "was entirely sincere in his opinions," Varina
Davis recalled. She went to hear him speak not only for the pleasure of
it, but because his discourse made her "feel profound," and gave her
and other women "a cheap and charming education" in American politics.[12]

By February, 1848, Benton had begun to play something like his old
part in the legislative proceedings. Toward the end of the month, he
broke in to the Senate debates to make what he called "a painful announcement." In the House, John Quincy Adams had "just sunk down
in his chair," and had been taken into an adjoining room, "and may at
this moment be passing from the earth." Benton moved that the Senate
immediately adjourn. Two days later, Adams died in the anteroom at
the Capitol. The chief eulogies in the Senate were given by John
Davis of Adams's Massachusetts, and by Benton. With more than a
quarter of a century of service, Benton was now the senior Senator, "the member of this body longest here," as he described himself.
As such, he had been asked by the Massachusetts delegation to speak the
Senate's final tribute to Adams. On February 26, a funeral ceremony
was held in the House chamber. The coffin, covered with black velvet

and ornamented with silver lace, was carried by twelve pallbearers, with Benton third in line on the right, opposite Calhoun, who was followed by Chief Justice Taney of the Supreme Court.[13] Again, politics and death had produced strange associations and relationships.

February also brought the end of the War with Mexico. A curious set of negotiations conducted by an American agent whose authority had been withdrawn produced a treaty signed at Guadalupe Hidalgo on February 2, 1848. After some hesitation, Polk sent this document to the Senate on February 22, where it faced powerful critics. A majority of the Senate committee on Foreign Affairs, led by Benton and Webster, objected that the treaty had been negotiated without authority, and proposed a fresh commission to settle the matter in form. In addition, Polk thought Benton objected on the ground that "the true boundary of Texas was the Nueces instead of the Rio Grande," as provided in the treaty, and was apt in any case "to think that nothing is done properly that he is not previously consulted about." [14] But ratification finally came on March 10. The treaty added hugely to the American domain. Settling the Texas dispute, it also brought in to the United States the immense former Mexican areas of Alta California and Nuevo Mexico.* Thus, the Oregon agreement and the Mexican cession together made the Pacific from Puget Sound to San Diego an American ocean. In return, the United States was to pay all claims by its citizens against Mexico, and pay fifteen million dollars to Mexico.

This territorial settlement was a prelude to renewed political unsettlements. What sort of government was to be provided for the new domains? Were they to be open to slavery, closed to slavery, or left to decide for themselves? Were the laws of Mexico forbidding slavery in California and Nuevo Mexico to stand?

The need for government in the new Territories had been impressed personally on Benton. During the winter Joseph Watt, a former Missourian who was an early Oregon immigrant, had come to Washington. Denied interviews by Polk and Marcy, he had come to the man he recalled as "Burly" Benton, and had been admitted to the "little brick house" on C Street by a Negro servant. Conversing with Benton in his study, Watt remembered his exclaiming:

---

* The "Alta California" of 1848 was all of the present state of California, and the "Nuevo Mexico" of 1848 was all of the Mexican territory ceded from the (disputed) western boundary of Texas to the eastern boundary of California, north to 42° latitude, including substantially the present states of New Mexico, Arizona, Nevada, Utah, and part of Colorado.

"Ah, yes; we know all about Oregon. My son-in-law, Colonel Frémont, has traveled all over that country. The country is, or ought to be, under everlasting obligation to him for the information he has given."

When Watt ventured that Frémont had not done quite so much for Oregon, Benton stormed across the floor, rubbing his hands — "Perhaps I don't know the movements of my own son-in-law!" Hastily reassured that Frémont had rendered important services, Benton became calm again. The two men discussed the problems of the far-off area, with Watt stressing the imperative need for regular territorial government. The Senator agreed, but warned: "There are a great many things to contend with, I am afraid."

More prosaically, in May, Benton received two letters from Oregon in a packet sent the President. These, he remarked to Polk in a stiffly formal acknowledgment of their delivery, showed "the unhappy condition of Oregon," suffering devastating Indian wars, and "the necessity for law and government." [15]

But for all its impressive roster of members, Congress found no solution, although several attempts at finding one were made.

First attempt: A Senate bill to provide territorial government for Oregon. To this bill, on May 31, Hale of New Hampshire offered a "Wilmot Proviso" slavery-prohibition amendment, which drew a sharp protest from Benton. He recalled the "plague of frogs" described in the Bible — "You could not look upon the table but there were frogs, you could not sit down at the banquet but there were frogs, you could not go to the bridal couch and lift the sheets but there were frogs!" So it was with "this black question, forever on the table, on the nuptial couch, everywhere!" He wanted to get on with the *practical* problem — *territorial organization*. Long, angry, involved, inconclusive debate, with Jefferson Davis of Mississippi and John Dix emerging as particular antagonists.* Long, juridical-metaphysical speech by Calhoun, which made doctrine for future crises. The extension of American authority over *all* the new lands, "carrying with it the Constitution, with its overriding control over all . . . laws and institutions," guaranteed protection for slave property and precluded slavery restriction measures, whether by pre-existing Mexican law, or Congressional enactment, or territorial legislation. Confusion, and stalemate — with Benton wait-

---

* Thirteen years later, in the clash of civil war, Jefferson Davis was to serve as President of the Confederate States of America, and John A. Dix as a major general in the Union Army.

ing "patiently," as he put it later, for some "conciliation" that would get Oregon a government.

Second attempt: An embracing compromise, fathered by the Whig leader John Clayton of Delaware and midwifed by a special committee of eight, with its membership carefully balanced between North and South, Democrat and Whig. After prolonged debate, ending with a twenty-one-hour session on July 26 and 27, a bill for territorial governments, which in effect left the slavery issue to the courts, was finally shaped and adopted. But it was tabled in the House.

Third attempt: On July 31, a modest proposal by Benton, to provide governments for Oregon, California, and New Mexico, "copied from the act of 1804, relating to Louisiana, in effect that the people should be governed according to the existing law" — which, as Benton understood provisional law in Oregon and Mexican law in California and New Mexico, prohibited slavery. Result — nothing.

Fourth attempt: A house bill to organize Oregon alone, *with* the Wilmot Proviso. A spirited debate in the Senate, crackling on through a night session until ten o'clock —with Benton again refraining from combat. Motion by Douglas to graft on to the slavery section a provision extending the Missouri Compromise line to the Pacific; adopted 33-21. Back to the House; rejection of the Missouri Compromise proviso; insistence on the Wilmot Proviso. In the Senate again on August 12; with a weary Congress, further wearied by the hot days and nights of a Washington August, driving toward adjournment. Talk, motion and countermotion, procedural snarls — until a disgusted Benton cut boldly into the struggle with a simple motion — that the Senate recede from its Missouri Compromise amendment, thereby clearing the way for the original Oregon bill, including the Wilmot Proviso. Passed, 29 to 25, with the Yeas including Benton, the slavery restrictionists like Dix, the political brokers led by Douglas, and a number of Whigs led by Webster, while Calhoun, plantation-partisans of the South, and Atchison of Missouri voted Nay. At last, Congress had managed to provide a government for Oregon.

During the debate on the Oregon bill, Benton summed up his course in the session, and engaged again in combat with Calhoun. He had "patiently waited with an anxious desire to adopt some measure of conciliation," and he had reluctantly voted for proposals he did not approve, such as those of Clayton and Douglas, "in order to put an end to the question." Convinced that he had "now done enough to secure conciliation and compromise," he insisted that the House bill be accepted *proviso and all,* as the only way to get a government. In reply, Calhoun decried what he called "a fixed majority" in Senate and House opposed to further "conciliation" of the slave-state minority; damned "any southern man" (including, presumably, Benton) who would not take an all-out proslavery course; and called on the South "to show that, dearly as she prizes the Union, there are questions which she regards as of greater importance." But this time Benton refused to be drawn. All "this talk of disunion was idle," he declared —

> . . . *a tale*
> *Told by an idiot, full of sound and fury*
> *Signifying nothing.*[16]

Back in South Carolina after the adjournment, Calhoun resentfully blamed the "defeat" of the plantation-minority on two "traitors to the South." These were Benton of Missouri, and that gentleman's old Tennessee crony, Sam Houston,[17] who had entered the Senate from Texas.

Meanwhile, Benton was involved in another senatorial fracas. The President had nominated Brigadier General Kearny to be Brevet Major General. At the end of July and the beginning of August Benton made this nomination the occasion for a speech which ran through parts of *thirteen* days. He reviewed again, and bitterly, all the issues of the famous court-martial, mixing a showy array of documents, documents, documents, with a stinging and often malignant polemic against Kearny — "human crime can rise no higher." It was an effective, if headlong, harangue, in which Benton manifested all the wrath he felt at his son-in-law's "persecution." In the end, however, the nomination was confirmed.

This debate brought Benton into another verbal clash, with Calhoun and with his Carolina colleague Andrew Butler. In the wake of the harsh words, the fiery Senator Butler sent a challenge to a duel. Imperiously, Benton refused to accept it, because it had been brought by the Mississippi Senator Henry S. Foote, a popinjay with whom Benton had not been on speaking terms "until quite recently," and because Foote had brought it "on a Sunday night, and delivered it under circumstances to alarm the whole family." [18] Thus animosities based on family loyalty, and animosities founded in political and sectional conflicts, had merged.

On August 14, the acrimonious session finally adjourned. "The members," the Washington *Union* declared, "have gone to their constituents to give an account of their stewardship." Well they might, for the session had marked a nadir in the history of Congressional accomplishment. On the eve of adjournment, Benton had made a facetious but evocative objection to giving time to a bill to provide more ventilation for the Senate chamber. "No, sir," he had cried, "no more ventilation! We have quite wind enough, sir! Yes, sir; quite wind enough!"

After the adjournment, Benton was involved again in the interminable affairs of John Charles Frémont. He was planning a fourth, privately promoted expedition to the Pacific. He wanted to finish the surveys that had been interrupted on his earlier expedition, and to investigate the possibility of a central road or railroad route to the new lands. Taking Jessie with him, Frémont quit Washington for St. Louis in late August. While Jessie stayed at St. Louis, he then went on with his party into the mountains at the headwaters of the Rio Grande River in the New Mexico country. There, under the lash of raging snowstorms and hostile Indians, in the dead of winter, the expedition came to disaster. A third of the men died, and all of the equipment and animals were lost. After a stopover with Kit Carson, who had settled at Taos, in New Mexico, Frémont managed to push on in the early months of 1849 to California.

With Frémont, Benton sent a long proclamation-letter to "the People of California." Congress had failed to give the settlers a government and, Benton declared, with the end of war, there was no proper authority behind "the edicts promulgated by your temporary Governors (Kearny and Mason, each an ignoramus) . . . the laws of a conquered territory remain in force, until altered by the proper legislative authority." The only "sanction" on which law in California could rest was "the will of the majority" of the people there — "I recommend you to meet in convention — provide for a cheap and simple government — and take care of yourselves, until Congress can provide for you." He knew that "the emigrants want land," and eventually grants would be made, "probably according to the Oregon bill that passed the Senate some years ago — 640 acres to each head of a family (widows and young men over 18 being included) — 160 acres to the father for each child under 18, and the same to the wife." Meanwhile, a local government could establish such a land program for itself. The settlers should know, Benton continued, that the question of carrying slavery to California was currently agitating Congress. When "you become a State, the entire and absolute decision will be in your own hands"; meanwhile, "in your present condition, and with your paucity of numbers, I would recommend total abstinence from the agitation of the question." In September, the text of this imperious letter was published in several newspapers. The punctilious Polk gasped at such an "extraordinary" attempt "to speak as from one in authority." But the St. Louis *Union* reported that Benton's letter won "general approbation" from the Californians, who in effect adopted the plan Benton had proposed. They called a convention in September, 1849, wrote a constitution prohibiting slavery, and established a *de facto* government.

Back in St. Louis meanwhile, a final touch of bitterness completed the saga of Kearny and Frémont. Ill, Kearny had returned to the city, and on his deathbed sent a message to Jessie Benton Frémont saying that he would be grateful for a visit. But the high-spirited Jessie sternly refused. Her second child and first son, Benton Frémont, had died from a heart ailment she thought had been caused by the anxieties of the court-martial during her pregnancy. Between her and Kearny, Jessie declared, there would always be a little grave she could never forget.[19]

[4]

WITH THE PRESIDENTIAL ELECTION in the offing, the usual maneuvering had filled the political arena. To Polk's disgust, Buchanan had played the game from his cabinet post, turning, trimming, striving to catch the sentiment of the crowd. The radicals had staked all on Silas Wright, and even opponents had conceded that he was an almost sure winner; but his sudden death had left the Benton-Blair-Van Buren group without a champion. There was support for Levi Woodbury, whose position on the Supreme Court gave him a convenient availability. But the outstanding entry appeared more and more to be Lewis Cass of Michigan, slow, lethargic, but steady. In December, 1847, he had gained a lap on other contenders by an adroit handling of the slavery-versus-Wilmot Proviso issue. He declared in a public letter that the question of slavery in the Territories was not for Congress to decide with "despotic power" — instead, the matter should be left *to the inhabitants of the Territories themselves,* and the inhabitants could decide even *before* they had statehood. This doctrine, or "dogma of squatter sovereignty" as Benton called it, was not new, and Douglas was to emerge later as its great exponent. Cass, however, gave it its first full exposition. It fitted well the ways, needs, and hopes of the political brokers in his party.

Still, there was no assurance of Democratic victory with any candidate. Within the party, the old factional divisions remained, and the Whigs had two leaders who had caught the public imagination on the battlefront, Zachary Taylor and Winfield Scott. The Whig managers passed over Clay again and entered the race with another military hero, run again with platitudes as a program — "Old Rough and Ready" Taylor.[20]

The Democrats of St. Louis adopted a resolution regretting that they could not urge for the Presidency "one who has now, for a quarter of a century, filled a space in the affairs of his country which can be claimed for no other man . . . THOMAS H. BENTON." But "we have been taught, by his precept, to do 'everything for the cause — nothing for men,' " and Benton was still not available.[21]

The great question was what the New York disciples of Van Buren would do. Disgusted with Polk for allegedly reviving the conservative, Marcy, "Hunker" faction with patronage, and on the outs with the President on the Wilmot Proviso issue, the radical, "Barnburner" faction was in no conciliatory mood.* Both New York groups chose delegates to the National convention. The Barnburners boasted brilliant leadership — Senator Dix; John Van Buren, distinguished in his own right as well as by parentage; the portly, laborious former Congressman C. C. Cambreleng; Preston King, "cool, calm, and resolved," as the editor of the *Pennsylvanian* remembered him; and a quick, charming young lawyer, Samuel J. Tilden. But, as young Frank Blair warned in St. Louis, it was not just a matter of New York. The slavery-restriction men included "a large portion of the Democrats of every free State." It was the old tripartite factionalism of the party again, exacerbated — slavery *extensionists,* slavery *restrictionists,* and the political brokers. The issue, as the radical Democrats saw it, was not *abolition,* in the interest of the Negro, or simply a *territorial* question and the national balance of power. The question was rooted in the value of *free labor* as a way of life — the rights, chances, and hopes of yeomen farmers and urban workingmen. Opposition to the spread of the slavery system was, in their perspective, keeping faith with the popular, libertarian, and agrarian interests and doctrines of the old, democratic, or Jacksonian

---

* "Hunkers," because they were alleged to lack principle and "hanker" or "hunker" after office at any cost; "Barnburners," because they were said to be so radical they would, like the Dutch farmer, burn down the barn to get rid of the rats.

radicalism — and Benton largely shared these perspectives. Expansively, as if in echo of Benton's keynote of the 1830's, "whether PEOPLE, or PROPERTY, shall govern," the Brooklyn radical Democratic editor Walt Whitman posed a fundamental issue "between *the grand body of white workingmen, and the millions of mechanics, farmers, and operatives*" on the one side, and a "few thousand rich, 'polished,' and aristocratic owners of slaves," on the other side. Who was to have the new lands and their new opportunities — freeholding farmers, and free workingmen in the towns, or great plantation owners, with slave labor as their property? Here was the basic conflict of interests. Here, headed not by Abolitionists but by the practical New York and other political leaders, was a new antislavery crusade.*

Tied thus to the free labor system, the slavery issue took on meaning for free laborers. For years, urban workingmen had been indifferent to the Negro and his lot, but now many workingmen, unions, and labor papers gave active aid to the free-soil movement, though they were by no means unanimous or all-out crusaders.[22]

In this complex clash of interests and leaders, as it was reflected in the election maneuvering, Benton's own position remained anomalous. The St. Louis *Union's* correspondent in the capital noted Benton "stood aloof, and with becoming delicacy declined to express any preference." [23] He was pulled one way by opposition to slavery extension, ties of political association, and personal friendship. But he was pulled another way by fear of "agitation," a deep concern for the Union, and a necessary consideration of Missouri public opinion.

The Democratic convention met at Baltimore near the end of May. A sharp debate at the beginning of the sessions over whether to seat Barnburners or Hunkers from New York ended in a deadlock, with neither delegation getting places, and South Carolina had sent no representatives. Thus, with the leading spokesmen of the great polar opposites out of the arena, the basic controversy and the basic power-struggle was muted. The convention was able to nominate a broker-candidate without difficulty, Lewis Cass; and to adopt a broker-devised, platitudinous platform, which carefully evaded commitment on the slavery conflict. The convention also established a new device of

* Some years later, these doctrines were to be advocated by Abraham Lincoln. But in 1848, Representative Lincoln was ridiculing "free-soil" protagonists, and playing Whig party wheel-horse, stumping Massachusetts on behalf of the then meaningless candidacy of Zachary Taylor. It took another great slavery-issue debate, six years later, to rouse the Illinois Whig to free-soil activity.

American party organization, which gave added influence and power
to the party's new broker-leaders — a permanent National Committee,
set up to supervise the campaign and carry on party business between
elections. A sop was thrown to the radicals in the vice-presidential nomination, which was given to Francis Blair's special protégé, the Mexican
war hero, General William O. Butler of Kentucky. The proceedings
could hardly have been pleasing to Benton. In retrospect, he called the
convention another show staged by "the trained intriguers," who were
consolidating their "virtually supreme power over the *selection*" of the
President, however he might be *"elected."* Immediately after the nomination, however, Benton went with Sam Houston to Baltimore. Escorted
from the depot to Cass's hotel suite by the convention arrangements
committee, he offered Cass his congratulations. Back in Washington, a
ratification meeting marched in procession, with a band, to Benton's
house, where he pledged Missouri's support to the convention nominees.[24]

Early in June, Cass resigned his Senate seat and began a long
hegira from Washington to his Michigan home. He invited a number
of politicos to go with him, including the chairman of the new National
Committee (the broker-minded Ben Hallett of Massachusetts), Senators
Allen and Houston, and Benton — who joined the travelers at Philadelphia on the evening of June 7. At Philadelphia, the candidate made a
brief address from the steps of his hotel. Responding to calls from the
crowd, Benton also spoke briefly, expressing "his intense gratification at
standing by the side of Lewis CASS, as the bearer of the Democratic
banner" — so the *Union* in St. Louis reported it. On June 9, the group
arrived in New York. There the Mayor and City Council welcomed
them, and a vast crowd greeted them with cheering, gunfire, and flags.
The routine again, with Cass speaking, and "Mr. Benton, being loudly
and repeatedly called on," adding his "few remarks" for the nominee.
Later, after the party had settled at the Astor House, another crowd set
up a call for the candidate, and for Benton, who finally appeared to
express his thanks for this spirited welcome on what was his first visit
to New York. The triumph was capped by a grand open-air rally, where
Cass, Benton, and others spoke to a crowd estimated at twenty thousand.
From New York the candidate went on through Buffalo to the West —
while the Colonel returned to Washington.[25]

This orgy of ostentatious party unity made good propaganda for the
regular-party press — but it failed to persuade the New Yorkers.

Though he was in New York City while Cass's suite was there, the stalwart radical Azariah C. Flagg refrained from calling on Benton, "or any of the Court of Louis Philippe," as he put it to Van Buren. He thought Benton's support of Cass "unworthy of his public career." The New York *Post* of William Cullen Bryant asked if Benton had come to the metropolis "to propose over the grave of Silas Wright a disgraceful co-operation with his assassins" — the Hunkers, blamed by the Barnburners for Wright's tribulations during his service as governor. Across the state, a prairie-fire movement developed for a separate radical nominee, and a Barnburner state convention was called for late June in Utica. In frequent consultation with the older radical leaders, Benton spoke against separate organization. But the younger men, like Preston King, John Van Buren, Wilmot of Pennsylvania, and Welles of Connecticut, pressed for action. Finally Martin Van Buren gave in to the desire of "the Radical Democracy of the State" to nominate him at Utica. A third candidate was in the field on a free-soil program.

Once again, Benton was put in a strange position. He agreed "in principle with the Utica convention, and was for keeping free territory clear of negroes." But he had to look to his power base in slaveholding Missouri, and he reminded Blair "his was a location which required that he should have the advantage of favorable circumstances to act successfully in support of what he wished." In July, he wrote a "Private" letter to Cass, suggesting that the Utica nomination "may do us no harm — that it may cut as much one way as the other," adding that he would go out to Missouri "soon after the rise of Congress." In St. Louis, meanwhile, the *Republican* declared darkly that now Benton would withdraw his support of the ticket. Publicly, editor Samuel Treat of the *Union* scouted such reports — "strong as has been his attachment to Mr. VAN BUREN, Col. BENTON will take bold ground against the New York defection." Privately Treat, who had been named to the Democratic National Committee, expressed angry suspicions. He "insisted" that Benton could have prevented the "defection" by visiting Van Buren at Kinderhook, which he had refused to do when he was in New York. Before long he was convinced that Benton's participation in the canvass had been "half-hearted." [26]

Through the summer, the free-soil movement gathered support. Many former Whigs, like the brilliant, fortyish Salmon P. Chase of Ohio, had long feared Zachary Taylor as "a large slaveholder," leaning toward "the Calhoun opinion of slavery." Others — Democrats, old Liberty

Party advocates, and "conscience" Whigs, men like the imposing, sonorous Charles Sumner of Massachusetts, the craggy, Biblical Joshua Giddings of Ohio, Owen Lovejoy of Illinois, and lesser figures — were ready to join the Barnburners in a new slavery-restriction party. On August 9, a convention of some 465 "delegates" met within a mass meeting of ten thousand at Buffalo, formed a Free-Soil party, and nominated Martin Van Buren for President and the polished, capable Charles Francis Adams (son and grandson of former chief executives) for Vice-President. Some of the enthusiasm and dedication of this gathering was promptly conveyed to the public in a *Phonographic Report* (shorthand) of the proceedings, prepared by one Oliver Dyer. Again, new issues had brought old party enemies under the same banner. In New York, Dix reluctantly accepted a "Free-Soil Democratic" nomination for governor, while Francis Blair bolted and lent his pen to the Free-Soil cause. (He remarked, meanwhile, on the "apathy of the voters" toward the old major parties and their candidates, both cautiously playing political broker and avoiding any commitment on the critical new issue.) In Missouri, young Frank Blair established a campaign paper boldly called the *Barnburner,* and Frank, Montgomery Blair, and others did all they could toward an (abortive) Free-Soil ticket. The incipient Free-soilers in Missouri invoked the name of Thomas Benton, as well as those of George Washington and Thomas Jefferson. But Benton lent no aid to the movement, and the great question remained: Where did the Missouri oracle really stand? [27]

Through August, September, and October, rumors flew. "It is said," a St. Louis Whig remarked at the beginning of September, "that Col. Benton will be here in a few days and will 'define his position' so then the faithful will know what to do." The *Union* ran reassuring little articles, and denied inferences from Benton's vote on the Oregon bill that he was a "Wilmot Provisoist" who "sympathizes with the VAN BUREN defection." But from July through October Samuel Treat was unable to produce any direct statement from Benton. Toward the end of October, the *Republican* noted that the silent Senator had finally left Washington, but opined that he would "make his way West, if he comes at all, in no great haste" — the man who had "once said of General CASS that he had 'cut him for the simples,' " now showed no "disposition" to help Cass to the Presidency. In fact, Benton was taking a very long and leisurely political "walk." From Washington he went with Elizabeth to Lexington, Virginia, where they arranged for the sale of the last of their family property — "of course, low price & slow payment, except a trifle of $500 in hand." They planned to go on to Woodford County, Kentucky, to sell "our remaining tract" there. But they were in no hurry, and Benton advertised the auction at Versailles for November 6, after the election. In St. Louis, Samuel Treat had to announce in the *Union* that "business" would "detain" Benton "for a few weeks, so that he will be unable to come here this fall." [28]

The voting in November made "Old Rough and Ready" the President-elect, in a close contest. Thirty states participated, with Texas, Florida, Iowa, and Wisconsin being added to the roster since 1844; but the total popular vote showed only a slight increase over 1844. There was no clear sectional alignment, each candidate winning a nearly equal number of free and slave states. The Barnburner-Hunker split gave New York to Taylor, though the combined Democratic and Free-Soil vote was well above the Whig vote. If the Empire State had gone Democratic again, Cass would have been President.

The Whigs were jubilant, the regular Democrats discouraged, and Van Buren at least well satisfied. The Free-soilers had elected thirteen Representatives, and a Free-Soil–Democratic alliance in Ohio later sent Chase to the Senate to replace Allen. Generally, Van Buren thought the movement had achieved "much more than there was good reason to expect." He looked forward to victory for a Northern-oriented, free-soil, radical Democracy in 1852 — *with Benton as rallying point and candidate.*[29]

In fact, however, Benton's developing antislavery convictions and refusal to follow a proslavery course in the Senate, and his break with Polk and long walk away from Cass in the presidential canvass, alienated him further from the new men of power in a Democratic party that was to become more and not less proslavery in the future. Henceforth, Benton found himself increasingly linked with a few New York and Northern allies. The great party stalwart and advocate of the 1830's was increasingly isolated from the main stream of national Democratic politics.

[5]

ALTHOUGH CONGRESS went through the legislative formalities in the short session of 1848-1849 — with Benton and Dix occupying seats side

by side, as though in token of their growing intimacy — the important
events of the season took place outside the Congressional halls.

In December, while Congress marked time, Blair paid a call on his
"old friend, the father of the Senate." It made Blair "melancholy to
perceive how thin and white his temples are growing" — Benton was
sixty-six. He was, however, "strong and vigorous with all the look of
resolution in his face that ever characterized it." During the visit,
Elizabeth Benton "tottered in," Blair remarked sadly, "the very ghost of
her former self."

The reporter of the Free-Soil convention, Oliver Dyer, also admired
Benton's vigor as he watched him in the Senate. He particularly noted
Benton's "romanesque" countenance, "with the blended expression of
the eagle and the lion" — "in mind, dignity, and patriotism he was a
Roman Senator of the highest type; and in physique, temper, and
ferocity he was a Roman gladiator." When thoroughly angry he was
most dangerous, for he "used his anger as a wrath-power wherewith to
propel his mental machinery." His famous egotism was also "vigorous"
— "so vast, so towering, so part and parcel of the man, that it
was," Oliver Dyer thought, not really "offensive" at all, but "a sort of
national institution in which every patriotic American could take a
just pride."

Two tales of Benton's institutionalized egotism became part of Missouri folklore. One tells of a party in Washington, where drinks were
served. After a few rounds, the guests sought to top one another in
speaking Benton's praises — "the greatest Senator in the United States"
. . . "not only the greatest Senator in the United States; he is the
greatest man in the United States" . . . "the greatest man not only in
the United States, but in the world" . . . "not only the greatest man
in the world, but he is the greatest man who ever lived" . . . "not only
the greatest man who ever lived, but he is the greatest man who ever
will live." At this point, the story concludes, Benton rose, bowed, and
intoned: "My friends, you do me but simple justice." The other story
recounts a conversation after Benton had made a speech in St. Louis.
"Senator," said a man who brought a young boy with him to the
platform, "this boy walked 200 miles to hear you." "Young man,"
Benton is supposed to have replied, "you did right." [30]

These tales are probably not literally true, though they indicate the
extent to which Benton's self-esteem had become a legend, and catch
some of the robust sense of humor that characterized the man.

Neither the "vigorous" Benton, nor any other leader, could get any constructive action out of Congress. In his last annual message, Polk invoked "the great republican maxim" of Jefferson and Jackson, "that the will of the majority, constitutionally expressed, shall prevail [as] our safeguard against force and violence." He then pleaded for action to establish territorial governments for California and New Mexico, avoiding "geographical divisions, and heated contests for political power." Exhortation, however, was in vain. Given the economic, social, doctrinal, and political conflicts raging in the nation — given the party, factional, and personal alignments and animosities in Congress — given the breakdown of party action and program — given Polk's indecision, and the weakness of presidential leadership without party support — there was in fact no "will of the majority" to "prevail." Both majority rule and broker rule had broken down. Abortive proposals were to be the extent of Congressional efforts.

Early in the session, Benton and Clayton joined to press the cause of territorial organization. The Democrat and the Whig had each received petitions from a convention "of the people of New Mexico" at Santa Fe, praying for a government. Now Benton asked that the petitions be referred to Douglas's Committee on Territories, and Clayton seconded the motion. But Calhoun was promptly on his feet to express his slavery monomania again, charging that the petition showed "disrespect to one-half of the people of this Union" — the New Mexicans had resolved that "we do not desire to have domestic slavery within our borders." After another bootless debate, in which Benton was unusually calm and conciliatory, the petition was referred. But no action resulted.[31]

Recent events in California underscored the need for government there. In January, 1848, gold had been discovered by workmen who were building a sawmill for a Captain Sutter in the Sacramento valley. Before the year was out, other strikes had been made, and the exhilarating news had spread throughout the nation. In his message to Congress, Polk had confirmed the "extraordinary" accounts of "extensive and valuable" gold deposits, adding that "nearly the whole of the male population of [California] have gone to the gold districts." By the turn of the year, a "rush" to California had begun that was to fill the province with eager prospectors. Still, Congress found it impossible to give California a government.

In February, 1849, Benton presented the Senate with a bill on another, though related, subject. His friend Blair had noted at the end of January that Benton had been absent from the Senate the last two or three times he had visited there — "hence I surmise that he is busy rummaging and writing," for absence from the debates was "a sign always of gestation with him." The product of the gestation was a grand scheme for a "central national road" to run from the Mississippi River to San Francisco Bay, with a branch to the lower Columbia River in Oregon. The route was to consist of "iron railways, where practicable and advantageous," and of common roads "macadamized, or otherwise constructed," where railroads were not practical. An "inland communication between the two sides of the continent," Benton argued, was now a national necessity. He had advocated such communications thirty years ago, before the age of railroads, and recently Frémont had shown the practicality of such routes. The work must be a national effort by the national government. Benton was against any proposal to "make a great national work of this kind a matter of stockjobbing," to the profit of "individuals or of companies," at the expense of "the American people." There was, of course, no action on this new proposal, either, at the moment. But the idea of a road or railroad to the Pacific was gaining currency at the time. As early as 1844 the New England capitalist Asa Whitney had proposed a privately built railway west from Lake Michigan, and other suggestions flowered through the 'forties and 'fifties. In 1849, a Missouri Pacific Railroad was chartered in Missouri; but its construction lagged, and never quite caught up with its title. Thus, Benton's plan for a government road appeared as one scheme among many. It like the others was soon involved in controversy over what route any railroad should take — northern, southern, or central.[32]

Meanwhile, other events were in progress. Under Calhoun's leadership, spurred by proposals in Congress to abolish the slave trade in the District of Columbia, a number of Southern Congressmen met in caucus in December, 1848, and January, 1849. There they discussed what they called the "aggression and encroachment" of the "North against the South on this most vital subject," slavery. There they prepared a document later known as the "Southern Address." It announced that "the Federal Government has no right to extend or restrict slavery, no more than to establish or abolish it," and demanded that men of the South "shall not be prohibited from migrating with our property into the Territories of the United States, because we are slaveholders." Despite

its show of nicely balanced tone, the "Southern Address" was viewed by
Benton as part of an "ominous movement," a new threat to the Union.
He had refused to attend the Southern caucuses, although he was from
Southern, slaveholding Missouri. He refused to sign the "Southern Address" — as did his friend Sam Houston, although *he* was from Southern, slaveholding Texas. The movement, designed to strengthen the
solidarity of the proslavery interest group, was also "ominous" to Benton's personal political future. One of the caucusers, one of Calhoun's
avid aids, was Benton's colleague David Atchison. The running antagonism between Calhoun and Benton in Congress was now to be dupli-
cated by running antagonism between Atchison and Benton in Missouri
politics. Before long, the "Southern Address" planter-partisans came to
regard Benton as the great obstacle in their path, and determined on his
political extinction.[33]

In Missouri, concurrently, a revived, concerted, and determined opposition to Benton was organizing. Its leaders included not only Atchison, but proslavery members of the old Fayette group, including many
of Benton's erstwhile allies, and the ubiquitous *Union* editor and party
national committeeman Samuel Treat himself — who worked covertly,
although he was in regular correspondence with Calhoun and the Mississippi Senator who was emerging as Calhoun's chief axe-man, Henry
S. Foote. The new factionalism was fairly launched with the adoption
by the Missouri State Assembly in early March, 1849, of a set of
resolutions known as the "Jackson Resolutions," after Claiborne Fox
Jackson. These resolutions, from first to fifth, proclaimed the extreme
Southern, proslavery position and *instructed* the Senators from Missouri
to "act in conformity" with them.* The Jackson Resolutions spoke the
interests of slaveholding planters, and echoed the doctrines of Calhoun,
from the "firebrand" resolutions of February, 1847, to the "Southern

---

* The Jackson Resolutions declared, subtly, legalistically, but plausibly, many
of the key points in the proslavery doctrine. They denied that Congress had
authority to legislate on slavery in the states or in the Territories; proclaimed that
citizens of any state had the right to emigrate to the Territories "with their property" (including slaves), and that denial of this right would "alienate" the various
portions of the Union and "tend . . . ultimately to disunion"; argued that "ag-
gressions" motivated by "anti-slavery fanaticism" in the North released the South
from any moral obligations under the Missouri Compromise of 1820; maintained
that prohibition of slavery in any area was solely for "the people thereof," in making a state constitution or through state legislation; and pledged Missouri to
"hearty cooperation with the slave-holding states" against "encroachments" by the
North.

Address" of January, 1849. Certainly Benton, still loyal to the interests of freeholding farmers and increasingly opposed to slavery and slavery extension, could never "act in conformity" with them. Later, he charged flatly that the Jackson Resolutions were a Calhoun-inspired conspiracy to "instruct" him out of his Senate seat, or defeat him for re-election in 1850-1851. Of course, Benton and his friends were aware of the Missouri "ominous movement." As early as January, Montgomery Blair had scouted a "plot" by which "Fox" Jackson had agreed to drop a plan to run against "Davey" Atchison for the latter's Senate seat, in return for an agreement from Atchison to help the "Fox" in an attempt to put down Benton when *he* came up for re-election. In Washington, Francis Blair noted that Benton was "aware of these origins and will go through the State on horseback next summer to visit the Sachems." [34] In fact, he was to appeal against the "Jackson Resolutions" not only to party "Sachems" but to the mass of the electorate. His "wrath-power," recently dissipated in Frémont's cause, was now aimed squarely at the slavery-extensionist group in his party, at Calhoun, his disciples, and his purposes.

Meanwhile, the troubled Administration of James K. Polk was drawing to its close. It had begun with Benton suspicious of Polk, though ready to make friends; it ended with both the Senator and the President suspicious of each other, and not disposed to make friends. In the interim, there had been a long period of confidence, during which the industrious, conscientious, but narrow and sometimes petty Polk had gained much from the advice of the bold, broad-thinking, if often self-willed and vainglorious Benton. In particular, Young Hickory owed Old Bullion a debt for his far-sighted counsel and practical aid in the Oregon settlement and the conduct of the War with Mexico. It had been a curious but productive conjunction of talents and personalities in leadership. From the time of the court-martial, however, such communion had ceased. Bitterly, Polk recorded in his diary that Benton "would never have quarrelled with me," except for the anger that had grown out of Frémont's case. Years later, Benton managed a kinder and more penetrating summary. It was Polk's *"misfortune,"* he recalled, "to have been brought into the presidency by an intrigue, not of his own, but of others." Thus he had been surrounded by a cabinet and advisers who were "intriguers"; because "his own will was not strong enough for his position," he often vacillated, although "he became firm and absolute where his judgment was convinced and patriotism required decision."

The acquisition of California and New Mexico "were the distinguishing events of his administration." But the War with Mexico was "the great blot," for it could have been avoided, and its territorial "fruits" achieved by peaceful means.[35]

Three months and eleven days after he had surrendered the Presidency to the Whigs' second military hero, Zachary Taylor, Polk died at his Tennessee home — careworn, exhausted, denied the repose of private life he had so long hoped for.

In mid-March, 1849, Benton had gone to New York for the second time. This time it was to bid *bon voyage* to his daughter Jessie, who was on her way to California to join her husband. She would go by ship to Panama, then up the tropical, fever-infested, tortuous Chagres River, then overland by mule train to the Pacific, and finally by ship again to the New Eldorado. Returning to Washington and his family, Benton watched the quadrennial overturn of the government service. Out went Democrats, in came Whigs. Though he was formally in opposition, he made bold to suggest to the new Administration a Missouri acquaintance as a possible purveyor of American hemp for naval ropes. More significantly, Benton's second son-in-law, William Carey Jones, was named secretary to a commission to consider the American-Mexican claims.[36]

Toward the end of April, Thomas and Elizabeth left for St. Louis. Elizabeth soon returned to the East, but Benton stayed in Missouri, launched on a political voyage that was quite as uncertain and dangerous politically as Jessie's trip to California was physically.

CHAPTER 15

High Wall

1849 - 1851

IN MISSOURI, Benton labored to counter the proslavery "ominous movement." From the beginning of May through early November, 1849, he traveled from county to county, prosecuting a grand, formal "appeal" to *the People of Missouri* against the Jackson Resolutions. He began with a blunt manifesto in the press on May 9,[1] and went on to advocate boldly the policies he believed right.

The issue he made was to stir the state for years to come. The power of legislatures to instruct Senators was an established part of Democratic dogma, and Benton himself had supported the right. But now he insisted that an appeal from the Assembly to the public for a final decision was also good democratic doctrine. He had not been in Missouri for two years, and Montgomery Blair feared that Benton would find it "uphill work to maintain his principles and his position in such circumstances." But, Montgomery wrote Van Buren, he counted on "an old-fashioned Benton fight," and the opening shot in the war had been "more decisive than I had expected . . . this will, I hope, make him President if he fails of being Senator again." [2] The climactic events of the conflict came in two tremendous speeches, both published in the press and as meaty pamphlets. The first was at the governmental capital of the state, Jefferson City, where on May 26 Benton spoke from a flower-decorated speaker's stand in the House of Representatives hall. The second came at what was now the political capital of the anti-Benton group in the state, Fayette, on September 1. Both addresses were long, forceful, heavy with documentation, polemical — all Benton and no compromise.

At Jefferson City, Benton began with an all-out blast at Calhoun and at the Jackson Resolutions. He damned Calhoun as the "prime mover and head contriver" of the new slavery controversy, and the Missouri Resolutions as "copied from those of Mr. Calhoun." To "understand *their* design, you must understand *his* design," which was co-operation of all the slave states on the slavery question, looking finally to "the subversion of the Union." Rejecting the Calhoun-Jackson Resolution contention that Congress had no authority over slavery in the Territories. Benton asserted that "Congress *has* the power to prohibit, or admit slavery." He thought the Wilmot Proviso unnecessary, and likely to cause tension between South and North. But, he insisted, it was only a reformulation of the antislavery clause Thomas Jefferson had drawn for the historic Northwest Ordinance of 1787 — "I think Mr. Jefferson, and not Davy Wilmot, was the author of that proviso, and that it should bear his name, and not Davy's." He went on to a legalistic examination of "the political metaphysics of Mr. Calhoun," insisting that legislation up to and including "the Benton proviso, if you please" (for Oregon), plus Mexican law, *left no territory in which the slavery question was actually open.* This was the "practical point." All the rest was "abstraction! and no reality, substance, or practice in it!" As to slavery itself, Benton now declared flatly that he was "against the institution" — "if there was no slavery in Missouri today, I should oppose its coming in; if there was none in the United States, I should oppose its coming into the United States; as there is none in New Mexico or California, I am against sending it to those territories." This stand, so far from Benton's position in the Missouri controversy of 1820, was strong doctrine for Missouri in 1849 — but "these are my principles."

Rhetorically, Benton reached a peak in a phrase which he repeated in future speeches, a phrase which was soon widely quoted. "Now I have them," he cried after his final attack on Calhoun and his Missouri minions — "and between them and me, henceforth and forever, *a high wall and a deep ditch!* and no communication, no compromise, no caucus with them." Thus, he ruled out any new accommodation between the newly developed party factions.[3]

The manifesto, warmly applauded in the hall, brought a warm response from partisans in Missouri and nationally. In the press, in several pamphlet reprints including one in German published by the *Anzeiger des Westens* in St. Louis, "Col. Benton's Great Speech" was widely read. In county after county meetings passed resolutions supporting Benton's position. The address was also praised in papers from New York to Pittsburgh, from Albany to Chicago. From Lindenwald, Van Buren wrote Francis Blair that "the Col.'s speech could not have been better." But planter partisans were apprehensive and angry, and from Mississippi, Foote warned Calhoun that the speech would "do us much harm, if it is not seasonably countered." At Fort Hill Calhoun complained "that Benton has openly deserted [the slavery cause] and that he pours out his venom against me . . . he strikes at the South and its cause through me." [4]

From Jefferson City, Benton traveled north and west through the heat of June, July, and a blazing August. He spoke first in the central Missouri River counties with a heavy slave population — Boone, Cooper, and Howard. He went on finally to the frontier counties to the northwest, David Atchison's home ground: Jackson, Clay and Buchanan. At courthouses, in church buildings, in the open air, he advocated his views and blasted his enemies. He declined invitations from a dozen or more counties, where there were few slaves, to concentrate his effort in slaveholding territory. At Columbia, Governor Austin A. King also spoke; he had favored the Jackson Resolutions, but he now committed himself fully for Benton. At New Franklin, members of the Fayette group of politicians, including Claiborne Fox Jackson himself, appeared; some feared violence, but the opposition made no disturbance during Benton's two-and-a-quarter-hour oration. At Glasgow, a journalist noted, Benton "made 'killing work' of the Fayette Clique, who were out in full force." It was also demanding work for a man of sixty-seven, traveling mostly by horseback over difficult trails or dusty roads.[5]

The greatest excitement occurred at Liberty, in Clay County near the big bend of the Missouri River. There Benton came up against the active, bitter opposition of James H. Birch, one of the inner group responsible for the anti-Benton campaign, and a recent appointee to the Supreme Court of Missouri — as a reward, Benton charged, for his part in the anti-Benton "conspiracy." A rough-and-tumble antagonist, Birch was a ready (if not exact) man in vulgar polemic. The Senator's appearance at Liberty was by invitation, and the courthouse had been reserved for the occasion at two in the afternoon, Monday, July 16. But at ten that morning, Birch and a group of followers began a "meeting" of their own at the courthouse, which dragged on through a long, vituperative, wandering speech by the Judge, soon reprinted in pamphlet form as a *"Reply"* to Benton's appeal. It was an odd answer that ignored the Jackson Resolutions entirely to trumpet the "RIGHT OF INSTRUCTION," raise the diversionary cry which became the keynote of the anti-Benton propaganda, "OBEY OR RESIGN," attack Benton's personal honesty, and link "Benton and the *Abolitionists*." The pro-Benton leaders thought the ten o'clock meeting and its interminable oratory a "stratagem" — to prevent the meeting scheduled for Benton, or precipitate a fight. Refusing to be drawn, they shifted their meeting to a grove near the town. After the gathering at the courthouse had thinned out to a reliable anti-Benton group, resolutions condemning Benton's appeal were rushed through. Immediately, pre-printed handbills were circulated, declaring that Benton and Birch had *met* at Liberty, and that the meeting had then rejected the appeal! The "stratagem" enraged Benton's partisans; and it apparently angered Benton too, for a bitter sequel followed.

This was a libel suit brought by Birch against Benton. The plaintiff alleged: *First,* that on July 16, in front of Green's tavern at Liberty, Benton had said of Birch: "I wonder when the damned scoundrel whipped his wife last?" *Second,* that on August 4, on the porch of Gaines Hotel at Platte City, Benton had elaborated the wife-beating charge: "he knocked out three of her teeth . . . he whipped his wife until the blood ran down to her heels"; *Third,* that Benton had called Birch a "cur dog . . . yes, a damned sheep-killing dog," brought out to speak against him, and had suggested broadly that the quarrels with Mrs. Birch were due to the Judge's "keeping his own negro wench." Such remarks, Birch charged, were false, slanderous, and damaging. Benton admitted that he had made the wife-beating accusations, while denying the bloody elaborations of the theme, but maintained that it was true, and generally known, that Birch beat his wife frequently, and therefore that another assertion of the fact could not damage him; he admitted to the "cur dog" epithet; and he admitted that he had said the difficulty between Judge and Mrs. Birch concerned a Negro girl, but denied that he had implied adultery between the Judge and his slave, as charged. The case of *Birch* vs. *Benton* became celebrated — or notorious. It was not finally brought to trial until May, 1855, when a jury in Benton's absence awarded $5000 damages to Birch. But in January, 1858, the Supreme Court of Missouri found error. Special damages had not been proved as a result of the wife-beating charges, and other charges had not been proved at all. The case was remanded, but before it could be heard again, the defendant had died.[6]

From the frontier counties Benton returned to Boonville, in the center of the state. There, at the end of August, he paused briefly in his journey, and wrote out two long manifestoes to those of "The People of Missouri" he could not reach personally.

His war on the Jackson Resolutions was creating an immense stir. In St. Louis Samuel Treat had retired from the *Union* and resumed his law practice (for reasons of personal health, he said), though he did not retire entirely from politics. The new editor, Richard Phillips, supported Benton in the "contest between THOS. H. BENTON and JOHN C. CALHOUN, on a great national question." He maintained that "Col. Benton cannot be put down," because "his opinions" were those of "a majority of the people." But Benton's enemies called him "renegade, traitor, abolitionist, apostate, liar." Someone at Platte City called him a *"God dam'd liar."* The *Metropolitan* in St. Louis approved this epithet even though it was edited by "a *minister,"* the *Union* commented dourly — "who will not be *charmed* with this mode of conducting a controversy?" On the other hand, private letters, reports of mass meetings and rallies, resolutions, and other signs of "public opinion" convinced not only Richard Phillips at the *Union* but many Whig observers, too, that "old Tom holds the majority by large odds," as a frontier county correspondent put it. This, despite the fact that most of the Democratic presses in the state had lined up for the instructions, and against Benton's appeal.[7]

Beyond Missouri's borders, Foote and Calhoun joined the fray. In a pamphlet-letter Foote plugged the old charge of "treachery to the South," and particularly damned Benton for attacking the purest statesman of the day, Calhoun. The "traitor" was talked of again for the Presidency, Foote noted, but insisted that because Benton was for the Wilmot Proviso and a Free-Soiler (!), the Democratic party "will never take up Mr. Benton for the presidency! *Never! Never!! Never!!!"* He would not even be returned to the Senate from Missouri. In frequent correspondence with Atchison, Congressman James S. Green, Treat, and others in Missouri, Calhoun had decided to "repel" Benton's attack on him. There was "no hope of bringing the North to a sense of justice, but by our united action," he noted privately — within the Union, if possible, but the slave states must be ready "to resist rather than submit." In an elaborate "Address" to the people of the South, published in the press and in pamphlet editions, he labored further to unify the plantation interest group around hostility to Benton. Urging Treat to get the "Address" distributed in Missouri, he added a final word on Benton. He had been "false to the South for ten years," Calhoun declared, "and can do us much less injury in the camp of the abolitionists than he could in our own camp." [8]

At last Benton took his appeal to Fayette, the anti-Benton political capital, in one of Missouri's chief slaveholding counties. News that he intended to speak there brought threats against his life. But Benton had never been wanting in physical courage, and he was determined to say his piece. The "speaking" took place in the chapel on the Central College grounds, on September 1. An admirer later recalled the scene when Benton arrived — "he entered, walked majestically to the stand, and as he did so a tumult of discordant sounds from his opponents broke forth — braying, whistling, yelling, and groaning, which lasted for several moments." Impassively, Benton "removed deliberately first, his broad-brimmed white beaver hat, and next his black silk gloves, and . . . facing the crowd looked round upon it with unblanched face and haughty defiance." His address lasted more than three hours, and within fifteen minutes "the insulters were cowed," and "all outrage ceased." He began imperiously. "My friends," he intoned, "and in that term I comprehend those who come here to hear the truth, and to believe it, and none others . . ." The rest was a total review of the issues as Benton saw them, and a total polemic.

At the beginning, Benton scouted a "fundamental falsehood." This was the charge, launched by Calhoun and his followers, that the North sought the abolition of slavery in the states. In fact, Benton trumpeted, the abolition falsehood was agitation again, a "barefaced attempt to pick a quarrel, for a wicked purpose" — to unite the South against the North, and eventually to disunite the nation. The *North* was now the friend of Missouri and the *West,* because "the men of the North are workingmen, and they feel for workingmen in other places," including "the man who waters the soil with his sweat, and makes an improvement in the wilderness." Here Benton echoed old Jacksonian class appeals, and heralded political alignments to come. Reviewing the history of the Southern caucuses during the last session of Congress, and their Missouri parallels in the Jackson Resolutions, Benton stigmatized their progeny as a new *"nullification."* That was an "odious, and treasonable doctrine" — "the assertion of the right of the minority to govern the majority — to do so by military violence — to resist acts of Congress by force." A toast befitting such doctrines had recently been proposed in South Carolina: "THOS. H. BENTON: *Caesar had his Brutus, Charles I his Cromwell, we have a Benton:* let *us* profit by their example." Such "killing" sentiments coincided, Benton trumpeted, "with what is going on here" — "knives are carried for my benefit, and revolvers prepared to give me six, out of the half dozen bullets they contain." In short, "my life is wanted!" because "I am an obstacle to nullification." These "killing" observations contained a good portion of melodramatic exaggeration, but certainly Benton's *political* life was "wanted."

Plunging on, Benton offered an extended, detailed, devastating review of the Jackson Resolutions, clause by clause, in context. In peroration, he declared that the resolutions and their accompanying instructions to him had been passed — "For alarm and agitation at home. To fire the people. To stir them up. To hold them to the attack upon Benton and the North." The author's real purpose must be clear — "knowing that I would not obey them, they provided in advance" the foundation for the new anti-Benton campaign, with stump speakers, newspaper writers, pamphleteers, letter writers "all repeating the fundamental falsehood of 'abolition of slavery in the states,' and all shouting the wolf howl, 'obey or resign.' " Against this "conspiracy . . . fraud . . . corruption," he had launched his "appeal." Now, he cried, taking the offensive, "the resolutions should be repudiated as a disgrace to the state."

The Fayette speech, with all its attendant circumstances, marked the apogee of the appeal. It was Benton at his best — courageous, self-possessed, effective; despite its repetitions, filled with close, reasoned, specific analysis of issues and the Calhoun-Jackson Resolution doctrines; little given to the domineering and dealing in extraneous personalities that had begun to characterize Benton; bold and forthright, and yet linked to the predispositions of his larger public; exhaustive, historical, and factual, and yet simple and dramatic. In short, it was one of the major propaganda efforts of his life. The text filled columns in the newspapers, and thirty-two pages of small, double-column type in one of its pamphlet editions, which were distributed by the tens of thousands. The *Union* called it "by far the most important document of the contest." [9]

For six weeks more, Benton traveled the state. In county after county, through Pettis, Benton, Polk, St. Clair, Morgan, and Franklin, to his farthest south and west on the frontier at Springfield in Greene, he elaborated his Fayette themes. Then, after a long visit at Jefferson City, he returned to St. Louis in mid-October.

After nearly five months, some of the effects of the "appeal" were beginning to come clear. The *Union* was sure that Benton was "sustained by a large majority of the Democratic party." He had indeed drawn large crowds and enthusiastic welcomes, while meetings in every part of the state had adopted resolutions in his support. The apparent effect of his advocacy on public opinion seemed to produce results among political leaders. Before the year was out six state Senators who had voted for the Jackson Resolutions repudiated them and endorsed Benton's appeal, while three of the state's five Congressmen supported him or remained "mum." The influential *Inquirer* at Jefferson City was all out for him, and many other Democratic papers now followed its steady lead. (Toward the end of the appeal campaign, the *Union* began to vacillate, and announced that "personally, BENTON and ATCHISON are alike to us," but by mid-1850 it had returned to the Benton standard.) Throughout his canvass, meanwhile, Benton had been stalked or attacked from afar by such able or persistent enemies as Atchison himself, "Fox" Jackson, Birch, and Congressmen Green and Hall. Their counterappeal, to proslavery interest groups in Missouri, was effective. In addition, the *Republican* thought that most of the township *"strikers* — the active men at the polls, and in meetings," seemed determined to put Benton "down" and elect "one of their number" in his place. This growing group of professional political brokers, ambitious, not deeply concerned for matters of program or policy, was certainly affronted by Benton's increasingly imperious and overbearing manner, and disturbed by his potentially disruptive proclamation that between him and his party opponents there must be "a high wall and a deep ditch." Many younger, lesser, party leaders who had "chafed under his treatment" for years sought revenge. Also, the political organization that had grown up about the state bank and its branches fought him.[10]

A remarkably probing and apparently balanced estimate of the conflict was offered by a Platte country free-soiler. In a letter to Salmon P. Chase of Ohio, this observer spoke of "extraordinary exertions now going on to defeat Col. Benton" — "excitement and agitation" was "fully equal to a presidential campaign." While Benton's enemies damned him as a "scoundrel," "Barnburner," "abolitionist," "Free Soiler," he counterattacked "in no unqualified terms." It was unfortunate that he indulged "so much in profanity: it looks certainly very bad, especially so in a statesman." Still, "the *people*" would surely "sustain" him. There was, however, grave danger that the *Assembly* would "drop" him and "send in his place another such dough-head and Slavery Propagandist as General Atchison." If Benton was re-elected in 1850, "you can be assured that the anti-slavery influence is gaining ground in Missouri." [11]

[2]

FOR A BRIEF INTERLUDE, Benton now turned from slavery politics to railroad politics. A grand convention had been called at St. Louis to give Western men a chance to discuss the railroad problem, and if possible agree on a program; and Benton attended to advocate the railroad plan he had submitted in Congress.

The meeting took place against a background of immense development. In the 1840's, the nation's population jumped from about 17,000,000 to about 23,000,000. Though the thirty states were still half free and half slave, the *population* of the free states greatly outnumbered that of the slave states, and was steadily gaining. In the North, at an ever-accelerating pace, new technologies and new enterprises were transforming an agrarian, rural, simple commonwealth into an industrial, urbanizing, complex society. The old Arcadia was doomed; a new society of Enterprise was taking its place. In Missouri, new commerce and industry, a huge immigration, and a rising birth rate produced a population increase from about 383,000 in 1840 to about 682,000 in 1850, while the population of St. Louis increased fivefold to 77,860. The village Benton had entered in 1815 was becoming a metropolis. In this onrushing development, more and more schemes for a Pacific railroad were offered. These included the proposed northern line from Lake Michigan, Benton's central route, and now a suggested southern road from Memphis. These alternative proposals stirred intense conflicts among sectional interest groups, and were seized upon and cried up by rival political spokesmen. Emerging as a leading statesman in the West and a presidential aspirant, Douglas of Illinois sought a grand compromise. He suggested a northern trunk road with privately-built branches to Chicago *and* St. Louis *and* Memphis.

The sponsors of the convention were eager to have Benton there. The invitation was taken to him at Joshua Brant's house by John Darby, a Whig leader, who knew that Benton had once opposed railroads in

favor of waterways, but also knew that the Missourian now opposed
Stephen Douglas's budding ambitions. The reply Darby recalls Benton
giving was warm — "I shall be there, sir; I shall attend the convention.
. . . Douglas never can be president, sir. No, sir; Douglas never can
be president, sir. His legs are too short, sir. His coat, like a cow's tail,
hangs too near the ground, sir."

More than eight hundred delegates convened in the Rotunda of the
courthouse in mid-October. They were mostly from Missouri and Illinois, with twelve other states represented to various degrees. On the
second day, Benton was "called for loudly and repeatedly from all parts
of the house," and "took the stand amidst most rapturous applause."
He gave a long, resounding, rolling speech, arguing with documentation
and passion for his proposed central route between latitudes 38° and
39°. He wanted a national road in fact as well as name — "national in
its location, by being central — national in its construction, being made
by the nation — national in its title, by belonging to the nation." In
peroration, he proposed a huge statue of Columbus on a Rocky Mountain peak overlooking the road, "pointing with outstretched arm to
the western horizon, and saying to the flying passenger, there is the
East! there is India!" The speech was enthusiastically received, interrupted with bursts of cheering, and its grand peroration brought a
thunder of applause.*

In the end, however, dramatic advocacy was vanquished by adept
political footwork. Douglas had been busy circulating and politicking
among the delegates, and in its final resolutions the convention endorsed his catch-all proposal.[12]

Through the rest of October and into November, Benton prosecuted
his Missouri appeal. The day after the railroad convention adjourned,
he spoke to what the *Union* called "a vast concourse of citizens" in
front of the courthouse. That night, in the Rotunda, Judge Birch and
Congressman Green excoriated the Senator at an anti-Benton meeting,
calling upon the *"servant* of the people" to abide by the "instructions"
— of the legislature. After the courthouse steps meeting, a bitter letter
appeared in the press. One Ferdinand Kennett, steamboat operator,

---

* Years later, romancing again, Jessie Benton Frémont recalled that this peroration caused men to smile significantly at each other, suggesting that too much
thinking on the subject had warped Thomas Benton's mind (Frémont, "Biographical Sketch," in Frémont, *Memoirs,* I, 2). In 1868, a statue of Thomas Benton
was erected in Lafayette Park, in St. Louis, with the closing words of the peroration inscribed on its base (*Missouri Republican,* May 26, 1868).

and a leading Soft in the old financial-policy fights, wrote that before the meeting he had requested the pro-Benton Congressman Bowlin to give Benton a paper asking whether he would vote to admit a state *south* of latitude 36° 30′ if the state recognized slavery. On receiving the paper, Benton "threw it from him with apparent scorn," Ferdinand Kennett complained, and he condemned this action as a "personal insult" from a man who clothed himself with the "mantle of age and Senatorial dignity." [13] Perhaps Benton sought only to dramatize the "high wall" between him and his opponents. But certainly he offended people of all sorts with his bursts of imperious behavior.

From St. Louis Benton traveled by carriage, with a driver, through the counties along the Mississippi to the Iowa line, repeating in two- and three-hour speeches the points he had made in his Western swing. Passing through St. Louis again at the beginning of November, he swung south, speaking to huge crowds at Ste. Genevieve and Jackson. There he was answered by a local leader named Lewis V. Bogy, who declared flatly that Benton was simply "cracked, or crazed," the victim of "an entire conviction of his own greatness." [14] Through the whole campaign up and down the Mississippi, Benton carried the contest into enemy country again. All but one of the nine counties he visited had heavy slave populations.*

Finally, in early November, Benton left by steamboat from Cape Girardeau for Washington, the coming Congress, and his family. The great "appeal" to "the People of Missouri" was over.

---

* Years later, John Darby attributed a high-flying, often-quoted summary of his campaign in the Southern counties to Benton. To an auditor who congratulated him on the response to his speech, Thomas Benton is supposed to have replied: "Always the case, sir. Nobody opposes Benton but a few black-jack prairie lawyers; fellows who aspire to the ambition of cheating some honest farmer out of a heifer in a suit before a justice of the peace, sir — these are the only opponents of Benton. Benton and the people, Benton and [the] Democracy, are one and the same, sir; synonymous terms, sir; synonymous terms, sir." These words catch some of Benton's expansive, rhetorical spirit, and his increasing tendency to identify himself with "the people"; but the famous account is certainly not accurate. It greatly underestimates the anti-Benton campaign, which Benton understood quite realistically, and Darby's memoir here also diverges from the evidence in other, incidental aspects. A Whig, long anti-Benton, Darby was writing years after the fact, and was probably eager to make a good story, and to exaggerate Benton's flamboyance and egotism.

[3]

AT LAST, in an angry, momentous, intricate legislative struggle, which
was to run into the late fall of 1850, some settlement of the slavery-
territorial issue was to be accomplished.

The capital in which the first Congress under Taylor met was still a
city of "Magnificent Distances," and little else magnificent. So, at least,
the new Whig Senator from New York, William H. Seward, saw it —
and added that the town's 40,000 inhabitants still had to travel by
unpaved streets, dusty in summer, muddy in winter. But Seward was
impressed by his colleagues, as he looked them over in the little semicircular Senate chamber. On the left of the main aisle, he saw "the
portly form of General Cass . . . the towering bulk of General Houston . . . the classic head and genial face of Colonel Benton; the long,
gray locks and sharp, attenuated face of Calhoun; the erect, slender
figure of Jefferson Davis . . . the energetic, black-clothed 'Little
Giant,' Douglas." On the right, there were "the massive head and great
deep-set eyes of Webster," and "the tall and courtly figure of Clay"
— back in action after his long retirement. Mrs. Seward particularly
noticed Benton, "one of the finest looking men in the Senate." [15]

The new Congress was slow in getting to work. Both Democrats and
Whigs were divided on the slavery issue, and interest group and factional maneuvering were to dominate the session — "for all practical
purposes of legislation, we are already nearly in a state of disunion,"
Benton remarked. In the House, where thirteen Free-soilers held a
balance of power, it took sixty-three ballots to elect a Speaker, with the
place finally going by plurality vote to a Democrat. As a result of this
strife, it was the day before Christmas before Congress could receive
Taylor's first message.[16]

The message surprisingly showed the beginning of a strong, nationalist presidential policy. Averring that California would soon seek admission as a state, Zachary Taylor urged that it be accepted — with its
free-soil Monterey constitution, presumably. He suggested that New
Mexico, which would soon be ready for admission as a state also, be
admitted when the time came — again, presumably, as a *free* state.
While each issue was thus considered in order, on its merits, "we should
abstain from the introduction of those exciting topics of a sectional
character," such as the Wilmot Proviso pro and con, disunion cries, and

other wars of words and sectional posturings. An aside on the veto power was taken as an indication that Taylor would *not* veto a Wilmot Proviso measure, *if* it were passed. In peroration Taylor proclaimed himself a firm Unionist, ready to protect national power and integrity against any threat. For a Southerner, a slaveholder, and a man who had committed himself to little during the campaign, this was strong doctrine. Its practical core was its recommendation that California be promptly admitted as a (free) state. This was anathema to plantation extremists, who also recoiled from the nationalist tone of Taylor's pronouncement and from other free-soil portents they found in it. But Benton thought the new Whig President "comprehended the difficulties of his position, and was determined to grapple with them," through "frankly and firmly presented" remedies.[17] Benton's friend John Clayton, formerly Senator from Delaware, and now Secretary of State, had had a hand in drafting the message.

Still, New Year's Day, 1850, passed with Congress given over to little but sectional bickering and angry harangues. On New Year's Day, Thomas and Elizabeth Benton received callers at their C Street home, among them Senator and Mrs. Seward of New York. Seward found Benton "very agreeable," and Mrs. Seward enjoyed "a cup of chocolate" with Mrs. Benton.

Soon after this, Benton was involved in a pair of angry, portentous Senatorial side-skirmishes. The first came when Atchison presented the Jackson Resolutions and asked that they be printed. Immediately, Benton was on his feet to cry that "these resolutions do not represent the sentiments of the people of Missouri," and to denounce their assumption that the present Union was "a league," like "the old Confederation." In reply, Atchison proclaimed ominously that "when the time arrives," the people of Missouri would sustain "every sentiment" the Assembly had enunciated. Without objection, the controversial Resolutions were then ordered to be printed. The second skirmish concerned a dispute over the extent of the state of Texas. Benton proposed that the Texas-New Mexico boundary be drawn "four degrees east of Santa Fe." Thus, Texas would cede to New Mexico 200,000 acres of disputed, unsettled land, which might through "donations and pre-emptions" give New Mexico more "settlers — a home population." Finally, Texas would be compensated with $15,000,000 of Federal "stock." These suggestions drew a violent response from Henry S. Foote. He passionately condemned transferring territory from slaveholding Texas to the Federal domain, where it might end up free soil. Veering from issues to personalities, as was his wont, Foote added a bitter personal attack on Benton — who rose majestically from his seat and left the chamber. "See," the Mississippian cried, "he flies," just as Foote was about to compare him to "that degenerate Roman senator," *Catiline!* [18] In the weeks to come, Foote was to return again and again to passionate personal attacks on Benton, topping his vilifications with allusions to Benton's early disgrace at the University of North Carolina, fifty years before.

At the end of January, 1850, a new direction was given to the debates — by Henry Clay. Aging, his face deeply lined, stooped, Clay was still appealing, still a master of parliamentary footwork. The veteran Whig Senator, in effect rejecting the Whig President's proposals, and moved perhaps by a desire for a glorious personal triumph to finish his career as well as by his own conception of how to save the Union, essayed again the role of "Great Compromiser," and offered a plan of his own. Summing up later, Benton thought Clay's compromise an appeasement of the plantation South, "a *capitulation* to those who threatened secession." The compromise entailed eight connected resolutions, which provided, *first,* that California should be admitted as a *state,* without Congressional "restriction" on the "exclusion or introduction of slavery"; *second,* that two *territorial* governments for the rest of the Mexican-ceded areas should be established, without Congressional action concerning slavery; *third* and *fourth,* for a settlement of the Texas-New Mexico boundary; *fifth,* that it was "inexpedient to abolish slavery in the District of Columbia," but that it was, *sixth,* "expedient" to prohibit the "slave trade" there; *seventh,* that a " more effectual" law should be passed for the return of fugitive slaves to their masters; and, *eighth,* that Congress had "no power" to restrict "trade in slaves between the slaveholding states." The "compromise" lay in the notion that all these provisions be accepted *together,* with the various proposals representing a *quid pro quo* between free North and slave South. Eloquently, Clay argued for his new compromise, calling for "forbearance," "magnanimity" by the Northern majority toward the Southern minority, and "concession."

These resolutions and related matters were debated vigorously through February, March, and April.* Support came from Cass, Douglas, Hous-

* A copious, detailed, lucid, probing analysis of the Congressional debates through 1849-1850 and their context is offered in Hamilton, *Zachary Taylor:*

ton and Foote, all Democrats, and from the veteran Whig, Webster. But sharp opposition was expressed by many Whigs, including Seward, who dramatically called on a "higher law" as sanction for antislavery policies; by the Free-Soilers Chase and Hale; and by the die-hard planter partisans Davis and Calhoun. On March 4, too ill to speak, Calhoun sat grimly as his address, demanding elaborate new Constitutional protections to the South as the price of Union, was read for him. In endorsing the compromise, Houston knew he was parting company with his old friend Benton. He did so reluctantly, offering a sentimental tribute to the man who, thirty-six years before in the War of 1812, had been "the first field officer I ever had," and over the years had always "treated me with frankness, with kindness, and with justice . . . and friendly esteem." [19] The "Great Debate," one of the greatest in Congressional history, was making new political alignments — though the personal friendship between Benton and Houston continued.

While the controversy raged, Calhoun's illness deepened, and on March 31 he died. Though as senior Senator he arranged for the Congressional obsequies, Benton refused to join Clay, and his and Calhoun's exact contemporaries and long-time antagonists Webster and Cass, in the customary eulogies to the deceased. He maintained, or so John Wentworth of Chicago recalled it, that Calhoun had "died with treason in his heart and on his lips." [20] Toward no other man did Benton set his heart so bitterly, in life or in death.

Through February and March, Benton had refrained from major participation in the debates. When Seward made his "higher law" speech, Benton shut a book he had been perusing to wonder at this "new novelty." But at the beginning of April he concluded that "the progress of the question" had reached "the point when I must enter the discussion." He addressed himself to a single object — the admission of California as a (free) state, on the basis of "a separate consideration, and an independent decision, upon its own merits." He did not want to "mix up" this issue "with all the questions which the slavery agitation has produced," making "one general settlement of the whole," which was, of course, Clay's plan. He objected because the proposed "lump" was a piece of *"log-rolling* — a term which needs no definition in this assembly."
He was ready to act on the particular matters at issue, which he

---

Soldier in the White House, 270 ff.; and I have made full use of this account. The evidence, I think, supports Hamilton's interpretation of the momentous events of 1850.

listed, including territorial governments "in New Mexico, and the Great Basin," or Utah; and since slavery was "extinct" there and could not be "revived," he would "vote them governments without any provision on the subject of slavery." But he did not want admission of California made "dependent" upon the "precedent settlement" of such matters, with the chance that admission might thus be delayed or lost. He knew that "the spirit of compromise is good"; but he objected to Clay's "concoction . . . called a compromise," and denounced any "surrender" to a "threat" by which a "minority in Congress [might] control or awe the majority." He was "for open and independent voting upon every point," beginning with California. This contribution was relatively short, carefully circumscribed in its range, and moderate. But it aligned Benton against Clay, and for the piecemeal process of settlement Taylor had proposed. This, plus the free-soil overtones of the speech, further enraged the planter-Democrats against him.

In a calm, friendly answer to Benton, Clay agreed that admission of California could pass Congress on its own, but insisted in effect that for that very reason it should be linked with "other subjects equally important" to "the great object of quiet." The debate continued for another ten days, with Benton playing a full, persistent part — though he revealed throughout what he called "the extreme disposition I have to get on harmoniously," particularly with Clay and Webster, who treated him in kind.[21]

A curious alignment was developing in the Senate, in which Benton appeared in an odd role. The debates were revealing that, in the breakdown of parties, Clay had the support only of Webster and one other Senator among the Northern Whigs, and of a scattering of Southern fellow-partisans. He could, however, count on most of the Democrats, led to his standard by the political brokers Cass and Douglas, with the latter working particularly effectively in the lobbies and behind the scene, and by Southerners like Foote, who was now impelled to abandon Calhoun's doctrines to defend slavery *and* the Union through the compromise. On the other hand, Taylor's plan for a piecemeal settlement won the overwhelming allegiance of northern Whigs, including the antislavery leader Seward, and of radical Democrats like Benton and Hannibal Hamlin of Maine. At first, the differences between the two approaches had been slurred over. But when the distinction finally became clear, the battle lines drew tighter. More and more, Benton, the Democratic Senator from slaveholding Missouri, emerged as the apparent floor leader for the procedure advocated by Taylor, the Whig President; while Douglas, the Democratic Senator from free-soil Illinois, emerged as the effective political manager supporting the proposals of Clay, the Whig veteran. A Democratic observer from New Jersey recalled that he was "amazed" that most of the Whigs were "following the lead of Mr. Benton." When he congratulated the Whig senator from New Jersey on his "very remarkable choice of a leader," that gentleman agreed "that it certainly was an unlooked for change, but circumstances had rendered it necessary." An old colleague and friend of Benton's, former Senator Haywood of North Carolina, wrote Van Buren: "Who believed a short while ago that Gen'l Taylor would find himself thrown upon Benton to support his Adm'n? against Whig-Chiefs like Clay & Webster?" A paper in Clay's Kentucky commented on "the singular spectacle . . . of *Thomas H. Benton* leading the forces of a Whig Administration upon a particular subject," while Clay stood "in an attitude of hostility to that Administration." [22]

On April 17, the proceedings were interrupted briefly by a melodramatic scene. The Senate was considering a motion by Foote to refer Clay's *"hotch-potch,"* as Benton called it, to a select committee of thirteen. Benton, fearing "hugger-mugger work" in the committee, was doggedly proposing amendment after amendment to restrict the scope of any such committee. When Benton referred briefly to the Southern Address of 1849 as "agitation," Foote bounced up to defend the Address against Benton's "extraordinary denunciation," as he called it. Ever voluble, niggling, and sarcastic, Foote was "a little man of nervous excitability," as one observer noted, and capable of being "intolerably wearisome and offensive," as another recalled. Of a stamp calculated to irritate the massive, grandiose Benton in any case, he had capped his long course of harrying Benton with an attempt to have him removed from his place on the Foreign Affairs and other committees.* Now he worked up to another peroration in personalities. Who was it, he asked, who attacked the Southern Address and its subscribers? Who was this "calumniator"?

---

* The persistence with which Foote had indulged himself in extreme personalities at Benton's expense, in the debates, led some observers to conclude that he had been "appointed" by a clique or council of planter partisans to goad the Missouri "obstacle" to planter policies (Cf. Meigs, *Benton*, 392-401). There is no direct evidence for this, and it is hard to know who would have made such a designation. Also, by the time of his great assault on Benton, Foote had broken with the position espoused by Calhoun, Andrew Pickens Butler, Jefferson Davis, and other plantation fire-eaters. Finally, it seems likely that he was capable of taking the task on himself at his own initiative, and that he had in fact done so.

It was "a gentleman long denominated the oldest member of the Senate — the father of the Senate . . . a gentleman who, on a late occasion —"

Here, Senator Foote suddenly broke off. Benton had stood up at his desk, pushed his chair violently from him, and started walking down the passage behind the bar toward Foote's seat. Now Foote backed down the aisle toward the Vice-President's dais, drawing and cocking as he did so a five-chambered loaded revolver. At first Benton, checked by his old friend Senator Dodge of Wisconsin, had started back toward his seat, but when he saw the pistol he turned and followed the retreating pistol-wielder down the aisle. Pandemonium . . . Senators leaping from their seats . . . calls for the Sergeant-at-Arms . . . cries for order . . . while Dodge tried forcibly to detain Benton, and a number of other Senators surrounded Foote. But Benton would not be restrained and continued his advance toward Foote, who crouched by the Vice-President's desk, pistol still pointed at Benton. As he strode forward, Benton called out in what one observer remembered as a "loud and defiant" voice:

"Let him fire! Stand out of the way! I have no pistols! I disdain to carry arms! Stand out of the way, and let the assassin fire!" But while Foote still held his gun, he was nearer fleeing than firing.

Finally, Senator Dickinson of New York confiscated the revolver and locked it in his desk, and both Benton and Foote were persuaded to return to their seats. Blandly, Clay intoned, "I hope that order will be preserved." Immediately, Benton rose in his place:

> MR. BENTON. We are not going to get off in this way. A pistol has been brought here to assassinate me . . .
> MR. FOOTE. I brought it here to defend myself.
> MR. BENTON. Nothing of the kind, sir. It is a false imputation. I carry [no pistol], and no assassin has a right to draw a pistol on me.
> SEVERAL SENATORS. "Order," "order."
> MR. BENTON. It is a mere pretext of the assassin. Will the Senate take notice of it, or shall I be forced to take notice of it by going and getting a weapon myself?

The Senate established a committee of seven to investigate the affair. Benton peppered its chairman (the Whig Senator from Maryland, James A. Pearce), with letters, expressing his willingness to testify; insisting that Senators Dodge, Jones, Bright, Bradbury, and Hamlin, all Democrats, be called as witnesses; complaining that the committee was putting himself and his antagonist "very much on a footing"; and insisting that the committee consider his charge of premeditated malice on Foote's part. He urged District Attorney Tindall of Washington to bring the matter before a grand jury for criminal action. At the end of July, Pearce's committee reported. It condemned Foote for precipitating the threat of violence by introducing "offensive and insulting" personalities without "any sufficient provocation," noted that Benton had conducted himself "for a long time with great forbearance," but rapped him for finally responding in kind. It absolved Foote of "any design or desire to assassinate Mr. BENTON," but condemned him for "wearing arms" in the Senate, while it held him justified in the belief that Benton intended to "assault" or "intimidate" him. As to action, the committee forebore recommending any — and there the matter dropped.

Public reactions to the fracas divided along lines of pre-established bias. A contemporaneous cartoon of the SCENE IN UNCLE SAM'S SENATE showed a rotund Benton baring his expansive chest to a diminutive, crouching Foote, and a lady in the gallery crying, "Oh, I shall faint!" as a gentleman there rushed for the door exclaiming *"Sauve qui peut!"* while a suave, unmoved Clay punned, "It's a ridiculous matter, I apprehend there is no danger on foot!" Northern and antislavery partisans condemned Foote from press, platform, and pulpit, and demanded his expulsion. Southerners argued that their champion was only defending himself. Compromise men like Cass, Douglas and Webster clucked but carefully refrained from criticizing him.[23]

The day after the encounter, a calmer Senate returned to business. Immediately, Benton moved that "all the previous orders be postponed," and that the Senate take up instead a separate bill to admit California as a state. This would have given the California question as such precedence over Clay's resolutions, and over Foote's motion to refer these and related matters to a committee. Following some involved parliamentary maneuvering and confusion, Benton's motion was tabled, by the close vote of 27 to 24. After this critical decision, and after all restrictive amendments, including Benton's, had been rejected, the Senate finally referred the entire conflict to a "Committee of Thirteen," with Clay as Chairman. Three weeks later, the committee reported an all-or-nothing "Omnibus Bill." It proposed to admit California as a *state,* provide *territorial* governments in New Mexico and Utah without action on slavery, and adjust the Texas-New Mexico border. As part of the package, it also included a more stringent plan for the return of fugitive slaves, and a provision to abolish the slave trade in the national capital.[24]

The first round had gone to Clay and his Democratic Southern allies. But through June and July the balance seemed to shift toward Taylor, Benton, and the anti-compromise forces. In the debates, and in the nation's press, the issues were gradually clarified — while the crisis sharpened. In the Washington *Republic,* the Administration paper, a new editor drew the line clearly between Clay's Omnibus, and Taylor's plan to admit California first and then settle the other issues on their merits. No *territorial* proposal could pass, the *Republic* argued, "without bringing up the . . . proviso," and in the "agitation" that would follow, stalemate might again ensue. In addition, controversy over various aspects of the "Compromise" portended charges of "bad faith." Already, the Washington *Union* was proclaiming that Clay's Omnibus Bill would open New Mexico and Utah to slavery, while Northern papers predicted a gain in free soil. If New Mexico were admitted as a *state,* the *Republic* declared, then the Supreme Court could settle the Texas-New Mexico boundary dispute — which was flaring dangerously, with militia and troops lined up on opposite sides. Through it all, Taylor held firm to his position, with his veto power in reserve as a final weapon.

Meanwhile, Benton planned a new review of the issues. Ever more Whigs were recognizing his role as a leader seeking to marshal Congressional support for Taylor's position. When Seward had Benton and two other guests to dinner on June 8, Seward was happy to hear that Benton planned on June 10 to "give us his fire." [25]

The "fire" came in a short motion and a long speech. The motion was to postpone consideration of the California-Texas-New Mexico-Utah legislation until March 5, 1851 — that is, until the life of the sitting Congress had expired. The speech ranged over the whole field, with its focus a probing analysis and sharp polemic against Clay's proposal. Counting on his fingers, Clay had listed "five gaping wounds" in the nation which he wanted to heal. Benton suggested that if Clay had had more than five fingers to a hand he might, for propaganda purposes, have listed more than five "wounds." Such propaganda was designed to carry "five bills taken from our files, altered just enough to spoil each, then tacked together, and christened a compromise," which was "to be swallowed, and swallowed whole." Thus, the Committee of Thirteen would govern the Senate, and the Senate would govern the nation! But, Benton trumpeted, the Omnibus was a "monster," in which the long-overdue admission of California as a state was made "the scapegoat of all the sins of slavery," from the ever controversial territorial question to the thorny Texas-New Mexico boundary issue. With all this "packed upon her back," innocent California and her plea for admission was likely to be "sacrificed under the heavy load." Offering next a learned geographical-historical argument for his own Texas-New Mexico border bill, Benton then turned to the slavery issue as such again. He declared himself flatly opposed "to the extension of slavery," which, he maintained, the Omnibus Bill would effect, by transferring seventy thousand square miles of territory from New Mexico to slaveholding Texas. He was a small slaveholder still, and would pick no quarrels with those who supposed slavery "a blessing"; but "I deem it an evil, and would neither adopt it nor impose it on others." He believed that emancipation was impractical, but the very "incurability of the evil" of slavery was the greatest objection to its "extension." In conclusion, Benton argued with some levity that Clay's attempted "anodyne" had only produced a "fierce contention" in the Senate, in which even "the great peacemaker himself [Clay] fares badly — stuck all over with arrows." It was time to end "this comedy of errors," and get on with the "public business," taking up the issues "one by one," and deciding them accordingly.

Pointed and insistent, the speech was one of the strongest critiques of the session of Clay's plan. In the national political forum, Benton had boldly reiterated his opposition to slavery as an institution, and to slavery extension by any means — the only Senator from a slave state to do so.* The speech was printed in a fifteen-page pamphlet to stir public opinion, as it had stirred comment during its delivery. It was a "powerful onslaught," Seward thought as he listened to it, particularly in the "satire and ridicule" directed at Clay and the committee, "which I think will do more execution than heavier metal." Though "prejudices strong and hateful resisted the speaker" at the beginning, Benton had "brought laughter and almost cheers from his hearers continually." Nine days later, Seward remarked that Benton was "enjoying the fame of his speech with the gratification of a schoolboy." [26] Having delivered his "fire," Benton did not insist on his motion to postpone, and on June 12 he withdrew it, to make way for a strategy of attack-by-amendment.

---

* While the views of Benton and those of his friend from Texas, Sam Houston, were close, Houston still supported the Omnibus Bill, including those portions which Benton construed as effecting slavery extension.

The next day, the Senate saw a brief, personal, angry altercation between Benton and Clay, in which each charged the other with delaying the business of the session and with various kinds of irresponsibility.

The combat in Congress ran its course — until suddenly, on July 9, Zachary Taylor died. Nearing sixty-seven, worn by his effort to maintain a firm policy in office, Taylor fell victim to an intestinal ailment (acute gastroenteritis) which was probably traceable to the capital's water or milk supply. At an elaborate funeral on July 13, Benton acted as one of the pallbearers. Meanwhile, on July 10, Millard Fillmore took office as President of the United States. The death of Taylor, Benton declared later was "a public calamity" — "no man could have been more devoted to the Union, or more opposed to the slavery agitation," and "his election by a majority of the people" gave him great potential "power" in the settlement of the issues. The accession of the colorless Fillmore brought not only a new Cabinet, headed by Webster as Secretary of State, but a new policy tack — support for Henry Clay's plan. No longer was the White House to stand as a center of independent leadership, a center of opposition to concession or appeasement of the demands of the plantation-slavery group. The power of party leadership and patronage was now with Clay, and the threat of the veto power no longer menaced his proposals.[27] In this situation, Benton found himself further isolated politically. Alienated from the bulk of his party, playing a largely independent role, he no longer had an ally in the White House.*

The third round of the debates, through the hot and humid summer and into the fall, found Benton nonetheless a persistent participant. Thus, in mid-July, he mounted another long attack on Clay's Texas-New Mexico boundary bill, mixing a display of historical and geographical knowledge with polemical and dramatic forensics.

This new encounter with Clay was watched with interest by the spinsterish, middle-aged Swedish traveler, Frederika Bremer. She had

---

* One biographer of Benton, depending on a letter from the Colonel's son-in-law, Richard T. Jacob, written in his old age, has Taylor conferring with Benton on a special message to Congress he was preparing, to reiterate his views and make clear his opposition to the Omnibus Bill, and further has it understood between the two men that Benton would defend the message in the Senate (Meigs, *Benton,* 390). The President was apparently planning such a message, but he did not consult with Benton, who at the end of 1850 had to write Taylor's Secretary of State, John M. Clayton — "Can you, in any way, let me know the purport of that message which you were to draw the Sunday before Genl. Taylor's death?" (Benton to Clayton, December 8, 1850, Clayton Papers, L. of C.). Once again, the memoir fails to correspond with the evidence.

heard that the Missourian was "highly esteemed for his learning, his firmness, and his courage." But she had been chilled by stories of the duel of 1817 in which he had "in cold blood shot his man," Charles Lucas. She placed him (quite erroneously) in "the population of 'the Borderers,' " as one who had "accustomed himself to go with pistol and bowie-knife." Now, more realistically, she saw the actual Senator as "a strong-built, powerful, broad-shouldered, broad-chested man," with a "lofty" forehead, "lively, but cold, gray eyes," between which "shoots forth an aquiline nose." In society, she had found him "candid, extremely polite, and kind," but still she could not get over "a repulsion to that cool, blood-stained hand" — "if it were not for this, I should like to see more of the man." She thus interpreted Benton's new attack on Clay's proposals as "a single combat between the lion of Kentucky and the hawk of Missouri," during which the hawk labored "with a real lust of murder" — "I saw before me [again!] the cold-blooded duellist." When Benton declared that he would "dissect" the committee's bill, as Frederika Bremer recorded it, she thought "he turned up his coat sleeves, perhaps unconsciously, as if preparing himself for an operation which he should perform with gusto." That "the lion of Kentucky felt the claws and the beak of the hawk, I could see." In the evening, she was astonished to find that many persons had taken the attack as a "regular treat" — "what taste!" [28]

Despite the Clay-Fillmore alliance, it still proved impossible to drive the Omnibus Bill through as an omnibus. Finally, disgusted and exhausted, Clay left in August for two weeks of rest and sea-bathing at Newport. Thereupon Stephen Douglas emerged as full floor-and-lobby leader for the disassembled parts of the old vehicle. [29]

The dismantling had begun when amendments stripped from the Omnibus Bill everything but the Utah provision. In a little speech that provoked laughter, the Colonel chided the compromise leaders. "Their vehicle is gone," he cried, and, changing the metaphor, "the omnibus is overturned, and all the passengers spilled out but . . . Utah!" As July gave way to August, the Utah territorial measure was readily passed without explicit provisions concerning slavery, with Benton voting Yea, and thus breaking company with the free soil doctrinaires of whatever party, like Chase, Hamlin, and Seward, who led the Nays. Through August, other decisions followed in order. The Texas-New Mexico boundary bill was carried, 30 to 20, with Benton joining a motley list of Nays that included Chase, Seward, Atchison, and

Davis. The admission of California was accomplished, and this time Benton joined free-soilers and political-brokers to vote Yea, while slavery partisans from Atchison to Davis and Foote cried anguished Nays. Identical with the Utah bill, the New Mexico territorial bill also passed — Benton Yea, free-soilers and a scattering of Whigs making the Nays. The new, stronger bill for the return of fugitive slaves was passed by the low vote of 27 to 12, and Benton was among the many not listed in the final roll call. Finally, in mid-September, the bill to end the slave trade in the District of Columbia was adopted, 33 to 19, the Yeas including Benton, the Nays consisting of planter-partisans both Democrat and Whig. Passed by the House and signed by the President, the bills were all law by September's end.

Later, Benton (who seldom dodged an issue) explained his refusal to vote on final passage of the fugitive slave bill. He was ready, he declared, to support some necessary revisions to the old act of 1793. But he thought the final measure freighted "with such multiplied and complex provisions" as to make it "inexecutable," except at nearly prohibitive "cost and trouble"; and he also thought the act was "attended with an array and machinery which would excite disturbance, and scenes of force and violence, and render the law odious." Experience under the act, Benton claimed later, "verified all the objections taken to it."

As the great events in the Senate drew to a close, Benton indulged himself in a mordant comment. The voting, he argued, had proved him right in his complaints against the Omnibus approach. An analysis of the roll calls on the California, New Mexico, Utah, and boundary questions, he claimed, showed that those "who voted for all the four measures amount to just seventeen!" Thus he vindicated the right to take measures separately, the "right to resist a measure, come from whom it may," even "the Senator from Kentucky." Four months had been wasted and California admission endangered while legislative "cats and dogs had been tied together, scratching and biting." But when they were loosed again, "every one of them ran off to his own hole and was quiet." This speech drew pleasant "Laughter" from many members, a mild remonstrance from Clay, and a violent tirade from the Mississippi Hotspur, Foote. This polemic Benton answered with neither word nor deed.[30]

Congress finally adjourned on September 30, 1850. Just twenty days before it did so, it received as one of the first Senators from newly admitted California Benton's son-in-law John Charles Frémont. Thus

Jessie Benton held a rare, perhaps unique privilege, being at once a Senator's daughter and a Senator's wife. For his part, Benton could think back thirty years to another fight for the admission of another frontier state, Missouri, which had made *him* one of its first Senators. But in that battle, he had taken the opposite side on the slavery-restriction issue from the one he and his son-in-law now held.

The great debate and the protracted voting revealed again the peculiar political isolation Benton had come to. Once a great party leader and stanch party man, he had, since he had struck the Texas "rock," found himself increasingly unable to sail with the main currents in his party. Utterly estranged from planter-Democrats but willing to enforce Constitutional protections on slaves as property, unable to go along with the South-inclining political brokers but led sometimes to vote with them by his own aversion to agitation of the slavery issue, he was closest to the antislavery radical Democrats, but unable to go all the way with them. Outside the party main streams, he was not planter-Democrat, broker-Democrat, or quite a Free-Soil Democrat either. His peculiar place reflected, of course, the conflict between slavery and nonslavery interest groupings within his power base in Missouri, and the conflicting elements in Benton's own backgrounds and convictions.

Before long Clay was credited, despite the failure of his Omnibus Bill approach, with a Union-saving compromise. Time, however, was to prove this a superficial interpretation. Immediately after the fact, Benton dissented. Writing to Taylor's old political mentor and Secretary of State, John Clayton, he reiterated his conviction that "Taylor's policy was right," and expressed fears that Clay was "destroying the Union with his humbug compromises." [31]

[4]

IN MISSOURI, the political storm had continued to rage. The battle of conflicting groups, feuding factions, striving leaders, and diverse doctrines had persisted through the winter, spring and summer — with Benton's antislavery, pro-Union convictions, and his political life, the great questions at issue.

Both Benton and anti-Benton factions were busy. "We must keep up the fight without ceasing, every man that can speak must take the stump, every man who can talk do so, every man who can plan must do it," Atchison wrote to Birch — "we must have men in every meeting, in every grogshop and upon every cellar door, we must fight upon every spot." He intended to devote himself "to this cause soul and body, with an eye single to the overthrow of the old apostate and Traitor." In St. Louis, Montgomery Blair and other pro-Benton leaders sought to make support of Benton a "test" in the nominations for the city elections of April, 1850. The influx of German and Irish immigrants and work-ingmen, and the rise of the new slavery issue, had changed St. Louis from a Soft center to a pro-Benton factional stronghold — though the Whigs still won the April election. At the *Union,* Richard Phillips swung back to Benton and posed the issue as "BENTON AND THE UNION, OR DISUN-ION." At Jefferson City, James Lusk and his *Inquirer* remained steadfast, and also proclaimed a Union-disunion issue.

Still, there was talk of accommodation between Benton and anti-Benton groups. Receiving such proposals himself in Washington in March, 1850, Benton penned a stinging rebuke — "I would sooner sit in council with the six thousand dead who died of cholera in St. Louis, than go into convention with such a gang of *scamps.*" He insisted on "a clean Democratic ticket — no taint of Calhounism"; he thought such a ticket could win, but he wanted "no timid or selfish calculations about losing elections"; with a "clean" ticket some might be lost, "but still the great point would be gained." Determined, demanding, and imperious, Benton's "Scamp Letter," as it was soon widely known, showed that he would not retreat from his "high wall and deep ditch" stand. On the other hand, some pro-Benton leaders, particularly Frank Blair in St. Louis, thought the Whigs would support the veteran Senator. But Benton had made no politic overtures in this direction, and had instead main-tained an unyielding attack on the still-reigning hero of the Whigs, Clay. Whig spokesmen generally urged a hands-off policy, in the hope of eventual Whig triumph.[32]

The election in which Assemblymen would be chosen was set for August 5. As the weather grew warmer through the spring and fall, so did the political contest, with Benton's allies launching a renewed "ap-peal" to the mass of the people — through a special campaign paper called the *Old Bullion,* as well as through the *Union,* the *Anzeiger des Westens,* the *Inquirer,* and other established sheets. The press campaign was supplemented by organization, by public meetings, and by a flurry of pre-election rallies aimed at getting out the vote. It was three weeks before any adequate analysis of the returns could be made. In Washing-ton, Benton scanned private dispatches from friends, including Lieutenant Governor Thomas L. Price. Finally, at the end of August, the *Metropolitan* in St. Louis offered a summary which proved substantially accurate, though it overestimated the anti-Benton strength slightly. Counting both Representatives and Senators (including seven holdovers), the Assembly line-up would be: "Whigs 65; Benton Free-soilers 54; Anti-Benton Democrats 42." No party or faction had the majority of eighty necessary to elect a Senator, and the grand outcome was still in doubt.[33]

The voting followed old divisions between Enterprise and Arcadia, now qualified by newer divisions between slave soil and free soil. The Whigs won substantially all of the long-settled, mercantile, prosperous-farming, mining, and (now) manufacturing counties. They also carried eleven and split in four of the twenty-one heaviest slaveholding counties, many of which were also important commercial centers. The anti-Benton Democrats split in five and carried four of the heaviest slaveholding counties, and also won in some areas where attachments to local leaders probably determined the outcome. The pro-Benton Democrats, as they had done ever since the 1830's, swept county after county where freeholding, small-farming, free soil agriculture predominated; and also, as a result of local deals, registered partial victories in two heavy slaveholding counties. There were many local and complicating factors operating, but Benton's old-Jacksonian appeal on the new slavery-extension issue had apparently won him nearly cohesive agrarian support.*

* Some more detailed consideration of the whole election picture may be useful. The chief mercantile counties included St. Louis, of course, Jackson and Clay in the far west, Marion (including the town of Hannibal) to the north, Boone, Cooper, and others in the center of the state, and Ste. Genevieve and others in the southeast. Mining was still concentrated in the St. Francis-Washington County area, with lead now supplemented by iron. The slavery concentration ran west along the Missouri from Callaway, Boone, Howard, Cooper, Chariton, and Saline to Lafayette, Jackson, Clay, Platte, and up the Mississippi from St. Charles through Lincoln, Pike, and Ralls to Marion and Lewis, with the two belts joined by the nonriver counties Randolph and Monroe; and slavery was also important in Cape Girardeau, Mississippi, and New Madrid on the Mississippi River to the south. As the heaviest-slaveholding counties, twenty-one out of one hundred, I have taken (generally) those that showed in the 1850 census fifteen hundred or more slaves and/or slave population, of 20 per cent or more of the whole. The small-farming counties, where merchandising and slavery played little part, made up the mass of the state's area; they lay mostly away from the great river lines, though they included such important river-bordered but hilly counties as Jefferson, Franklin, Gasconade, Osage, Cole, and others. The summary offered here is the product of my own calculations and analysis, based primarily on the (state) House of Representative election results, as revealed in the party-factional alignment in the session; but I have also tested the pattern found there against a county-by-county check of the Congressional election returns, and against the alignment in the

The Benton, anti-Benton and Whig stand-off prompted rumors of a deal in the Assembly. One report, dispatched privately, said that leaders of a Whig group centering around Henry S. Geyer of St. Louis were consulting busily with top Antis about a "bargain," the heart of which was that if the Antis could not elect one of their own as Senator they would "support Mr. Geyer," a Whig who was "a supporter of the Jackson resolutions!" After the popular voting, the proslavery, anti-Benton, violent *Metropolitan* in St. Louis suggested publicly that the Antis might "support Mr. Geyer," as a man who was sound on slavery.[34]

In mid-October, both Benton and Atchison arrived in St. Louis — on separate boats. Benton went promptly to Boonville to join his family, who had been staying for some time at the home of Joshua Brant's son Henry. After a ten-day rest, Thomas and Elizabeth went to Jefferson City for a week, and thence returned to St. Louis by steamboat at the beginning of November. In St. Louis, Benton planned to make one major political speech, before he left again for Washington and the short session. He spoke in the Rotunda of the courthouse, Saturday evening, November 9. The hall was filled "to suffocation" by a "living mass of anxious listeners," the reporters noted, while thousands stood outside clamoring for admission. At about seven o'clock, accompanied by Montgomery Blair who was the chairman for the evening, Benton forced his way through the dense throng to the speaker's stand. Cheers, shouts, and mounting waves of applause echoed through the hall. In a typical Benton grass-roots oration, factual and exhaustive but electric and polemical, Benton began with a summary of the recent Congressional session, spiced with an attack on Clay for delaying the proceedings by his Omnibus scheme. He then went on to the Missouri situation, declaring that his "Appeal" on the slavery agitation issue had first "waked up" the people and then been "sustained." At Jefferson City he had analyzed the election returns in detail, and he insisted that public opinion was strongly against the Jackson Resolutions, and that the Antis were a "miserable minority" among the people themselves. *Every* anti-Benton victor had "got his election by a combination with the Whigs, or by votes from Benton men under pledge to go with a majority of the democracy [in a district]." As to the coalition of Antis and Whigs, "we will make the

state Senate. The evidence available seems to preclude anything more than the approximation presented here, but not even this has been attempted previously.

Whigs a *bill of sale* of all the Nullification and old Soft Democrats
. . . but without recourse." Thus to his "high wall and deep ditch"
speech, and to his "Scamp Letter," the unyielding, ever-courageous
Benton added the polemic that was to become famous as his "Bill
of Sale" proposal. As to his personal prospects, he was less certain. He
spoke of his thirty-year Senate career in the past tense. He valued
"solid popularity, the esteem of good men, for good actions," but he
added defiantly: "I despise the bubble popularity that is won without
merit and lost without crime." He would advocate measures, but he
would not solicit office. Issues, policies, were the important matters, and
here Benton could report a triumph. Personally, "I claim nothing." [35]

The speech caused a tremendous stir. At the *Republican,* A. B. Chambers damned it as final evidence that Benton had "thrown himself into
the hands of Northern men and espoused Northern principles." He
condemned Benton's explanation of his refusal to vote for the Fugitive
Slave Bill as unlikely to satisfy "any slaveholder in Missouri" — especially in view of the fact that Benton's great rival, Douglas, was stumping neighboring Illinois for the law. In Illinois, Douglas's organ at
Springfield also attacked the address and predicted Benton's "political
overthrow." In a speech at Platte City, Atchison declared a renewed
"war to the knife." The Rotunda meeting had stirred the opposition to
new heights of anger, with the Antis "making very ugly epithets upon
the old gentleman," as one observer in St. Louis put it quaintly. The
Swedish traveler Frederika Bremer, making a swing through the great
West, thought Benton's stand incredibly "bold" for slaveholding Missouri, and admired him for his magnificent candor. Everywhere Miss
Bremer went in St. Louis, she heard a buzz of talk about the "great
speech." [36]

Five days after the Rotunda meeting, Benton made a different kind of
address to a different audience. To compensate for the "dearth of intellectual entertainment" in St. Louis, the directors of the Mercantile Library had planned a course of lectures. Anxious to start with a good
crowd, they had asked Benton to open the series. Speaking to an overflow audience of men and women at Wyman's Hall, he talked for more
than an hour on "The Progress of the Age." He began with social and
political progress — "man . . . never before was so fully valued for
his own worth," he declared. In the American democracy, "the labouring man, the farmer, the merchant, the manufacturer" conversed on
national and international issues and decided them. Thus democracy had

brought a *"New Power"* — "public opinion . . . offspring of knowledge and freedom, more powerful than fleets and armies, more effective
than laws and scaffolds, that power above which no man can place himself." From such panegyrics, the orator turned to technological progress,
particularly "the Steam Engine." Railroads would eventually extend
from the Atlantic to the Pacific, and from Hudson's Bay to the Gulf of
Mexico, meeting incidentally at St. Louis. Such transportation facilities
would promote immense developments in agriculture, manufactures,
commerce, inventions, and "machine power." In fifty years the city's
population would approach a million, and the nation's would reach
ninety million, with "every operative, from further perfection of machinery, standing for fifty men." In this picture Benton saw St. Louis as
"the absorbing center of the American continent," on "the continental
crossroads." This expansive encomium to Jacksonian democracy and
modern technology, representing two sometimes conflicting themes in
Benton's thought, was well received by his "intellectual" audience. The
whole occasion was a brilliant success.[37]

The next day Benton left for Washington. As he traveled, the
Union predicted that the Assembly in January would give him another
term in the Senate. His visit, and "his frequent interchanges of opinion
with his fellow citzens," had aroused the people again. The legislators
would feel bound to "obey" their wishes in the Senatorial voting.

[5]

WHATEVER BENTON THOUGHT of his prospects in Missouri, he was
promptly and fully active in the short session of Congress. On the second
day of the session, he announced his intention to introduce *eight* bills.
These included a revival and revision of his graduation-donation plan,
and a bill "for the location and construction of a national highway,
consisting of a railroad and a common road, from St. Louis to San
Francisco." Neither measure came to a vote, but Benton made long,
strong speeches for them, once again utilizing the Senate floor to advocate and popularize great projects. His railroad and "Grand National
Central Highway" speech was printed in a pamphlet, with appendices.[38]

The future was to see action on both the land and railroad ideas
Benton had advocated so vigorously. In a Pacific Railroad Act of 1862
and other developments, much of his project was to be realized —
though not his agrarian plea for a common road for poor immigrant-

settlers as well as a railroad, or his democratic plea to avoid "monopoly and private interest" jobbing by making the whole a government work, or the particular route he proposed. In a Graduation Act in 1854, and a Homestead Act in 1862, much of his land vision was to be realized, though again not in exactly the form he proposed.

On February 6 and 14, Benton engaged in a spirited debate on a Missouri subject. He sought leave to introduce a measure to grant 2 per cent of Federal land revenues in Missouri to the state for building railroads within the state. The discussion involved him again in long altercations with Clay, and with Foote and Jefferson Davis. When he called for the Yeas and Nays on request for leave to introduce his bill, leave was denied. This was his final individual act in the session. He answered roll calls through February 20, but a series of Yeas and Nays thereafter to the end of the session on March 3 found him absent. He was ill, confined to his C Street house with a "fever which locates itself in his head," Francis Blair noted when he called on February 25. Blair did not see his old friend because of physician's orders that the patient must be "kept quiet," but when he called once more late in the evening he learned from Elizabeth that Thomas was no better. He would not be able to return to the Senate. Blair thought this would cost the government "a million," because there were all sorts of plundering schemes on foot.

An unkinder evaluation had been offered earlier, during the Senate debates. Perhaps anticipating or hoping for a defeat for Benton in the Missouri Assembly, Downs of Louisiana in a floor exchange with Benton had started to quote something "once said of another great man, 'but yesterday he might have stood against the world'" — and had broken off. Quite amiably, Benton had called for the rest of the passage, which he said he had by heart, and Downs had at last responded with Shakespeare's lines:

> *But yesterday the word of Caesar might*
> *Have stood against the world; now lies he there,*
> *And none so poor to do him reverence.*[39]

In Missouri, meanwhile, the Senatorial election battle reached its climax. The Assembly met in Jefferson City, and got down to business in January, 1851. "The hotels are filled with visitors," a Whig member noted, "and the outsiders are as much engrossed in the election as members." A three-day struggle to elect a Speaker in the House ended ominously for Benton — enough anti-Benton Democrats joined the Whigs to make a majority for the Whig candidate. On January 9, the candidates for the Senate were officially offered in the Assembly. The night before a Democratic caucus, nominating Benton, had resolved in high Bentonian style to "support him for that office until he is elected, defeated, or until the present Legislature ceases to exist." The anti-Benton Democrats named lame-duck Congressman James S. Green as their champion. The Whig choice was Henry S. Geyer.[40]

The next thirteen fateful days were a fantasia of balloting in joint session by day, and caucusing by night. The first ballot on Friday, January 10, showed Geyer 64, Benton 55, Green 37. Fifteen ballots on Saturday into a night session, and another six on Monday into another evening session, showed no substantial change. Meanwhile, joint meetings of the Democratic factions were held, but the *Republican* reported that the Antis remained "fierce" against Benton, while the "Bentonites" insisted on "Benton or Nobody." Thus, the joint caucuses only "built the high wall higher, and dug the deep ditch deeper." Indeed, A. B. Chambers charged, the pro-Benton men hoped to see the session end *without an election,* because they believed that two years more "of *agitating"* might "restore Col. BENTON to a majority." On the other side, the *Union* predicted that the Antis would finally be found "knocking under to the Whigs." Further ballotings on January 14 and 16 failed to change the situation.

On January 17, on the twenty-sixth ballot, a break came. Six Antis voted for Geyer, and his total rose to 70. On January 20 and 21, the anti-Benton Democrats tried a final maneuver, dropping Green and scrambling first to one and then to another alternate candidate. But this maneuver failed. On January 21, a night-session thirty-ninth ballot showed Geyer 77 — three short of a majority. Meanwhile, the ambitious Geyer had written a public letter denying the power of Congress to legislate on slavery in the territories — an utter "abandonment," the *Union* charged, of Whig principles as expressed by leaders like Clay, Webster . . . and Fillmore. The tension rose. Finally, on a fortieth ballot on January 22, enough Antis swung over to make the total read Geyer 80, Benton 55, Stringfellow 18. The proslavery Whig was declared elected. To the end, Benton's forces remained firm, and his vote on the last ballot was the same as it had been on the first.[41]

By telegraph, the news was carried throughout the state and the nation. *Benton is Beaten!* the *Republican* cried in ecstasy; and Editor
Chambers added a line Editor Benton had used in the *Enquirer* thirty
years before to hail Missouri's admission as a state: "The 'long agony is
over.' " The "Bill of Sale" of the "Nullifiers" to the Whigs "has been
signed and delivered," the *Union* railed — " 'SCAMP' DEMOCRACY AND
HYPOCRACY [sic] — BARGAIN, SALE, AND CORRUPTION!" It only remained to be seen what was *"the price of their treason."* * A proslavery
enthusiast in Jackson County exulted: "This result forever seals the
fate of Benton, the charm of the old tyrant is now broken, by his own
acts he has blighted his own prospects." After thirty long years (no
man, to that time, had served continuously in Congress for so long), it
was a great day for Antis, Whigs, and Benton's enemies in general.
There was a final irony in the selection of Geyer as Benton's successor.
On the same day some thirty-five years before — October 2, 1815 —
the two new arrivals had signed the Roll of Attorneys in St. Louis.
Since then, Geyer had emerged as a political and personal "bitter
enemy of the Old Senator," as one contemporary put it.[42]

In Washington, portents of the result had preceded reports of its
accomplishment. Much interested in the question of "Col. Benton's election," Salmon P. Chase had overheard in the Capitol corridor "one slaveholding democrat expressing to another . . . a strong wish that [the
Missouri Anti-Benton men] would vote for the Whig candidate, if sound
on the slavery question." In spite of himself, Francis Blair "got the
blue Devils," as he put it to Van Buren, when he heard the news of
Benton's defeat. He "tried to argue myself into the belief that it was
all for the best — but when I came to look the Senate through and
see how entirely our strength had vanished there — how it had disappeared from the House — how extinct at the other end of the Avenue
[the White House] — my philosophy could hardly hold me up." Despite

---

* Whether there was in fact a direct Whig–Anti-Benton "BARGAIN," with a
"price" paid the Antis, cannot be definitely determined on the evidence I have
been able to find. The *Republican* denied (of course) any such "combination,"
though later the Whigs did assist the Antis in frustrating a Benton Democratic
move to get the Assembly clearly to repudiate the Jackson Resolutions. If there
was a deal, it could have been worked out orally before the Assembly met, or at
the Assembly, without any incriminating documents being written to provide evidence for later research. Certainly, the vote for Geyer was itself at least a cynical
alliance of some Antis with the Whigs.

his "blue Devils," Blair thought the next step was to propose Benton for the Presidency.

In the Washington *Union,* Benton himself could read an ostensible epitaph to his career. "He had made an issue with the Democratic party," and "an issue with the people of his own State," the *Union* declared, and the verdict had been "rendered." [43]

PART V

Long and Bitter War

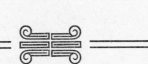

Sail, sail thy best, ship of Democracy.
Of value is thy freight, 'tis not the Present only,
The Past is also stored in thee.

— WALT WHITMAN

CHAPTER 16

Freedom . . .

1851 - 1855

ILL, DEFEATED for re-election, politically isolated, Benton might well have retired. He was sixty-nine, his enemies proclaimed that his "political existence" was finished, he had served industriously and well for thirty years in the Senate, and he deserved respite and rest. But, by temperament and by conviction, he was not one to let go so easily. He determined again to carry his views to the people, and for the rest of his life he pursued a final, dramatic advocacy on three broad fronts.

He directed his first efforts to Missouri. In March, 1851, as soon as his fever had abated, he left his family and his comfortable Washington home for St. Louis, to prosecute what he called "a long and bitter war" against the Whigs "in front," and their formerly "Soft," now "Rotten" Democratic allies on the "rear." Determined to represent Missouri in Congress again, he declared that he would not sell his house in Washington, *as I mean to reoccupy it.*" As he traveled down the Ohio River by steamboat, a fellow Missourian saw and remembered him — "a white-haired man of grave demeanor and distinguished presence," who offered "some pleasant remarks" about the landing the boat was making. The names of Clay, Webster, Calhoun, and Benton were familiar "as the greatest men of the day"; and Benton's fellow passenger was pleased to see the ex-Senator "dressed as a recognized statesman of the day should have been, in black, swallowtail broadcloth coat, cloth pantaloons, satin vest, stiff silk hat, and low shoes with white stockings." Benton's face was still spotted with marks of his recent illness, which his fellow passenger recalled as varioloid, or mild smallpox.

In the first battle of his war, Benton labored to strengthen his power base in St. Louis by projecting himself into the municipal elections. Whig, anti-Benton or "National" Democratic, and pro-Benton slates were all in the field. Through the first week of April, 1851, Benton spoke at the courthouse and in ward meetings, and electioneered at the polls for the pro-Benton candidates. The *Republican* damned him for descending into municipal politics, and shrilled that his support among Irish and German immigrants linked him with "Socialism, Red Republicanism, Infidelity, Communism, Free Soilism, Anti-Catholicism, and every other ism!" Guessing that 40,000 out of the 80,000 inhabitants of St. Louis were Irish or German born, Representative Bowlin (who had turned anti-Benton) huffed that Benton had come all the way from Washington to appeal "for the Free Soil candidate," by "pandering to the foreign prejudice against slavery." Clearly, the conflict stirred by the Jackson Resolutions had not abated in Missouri. The Whigs, led by the able incumbent mayor Luther Kennett, won the city elections — but the pro-Benton Democrats utterly overwhelmed the Antis. At the outset of his war, by coming "down to mingle" at the local roots of politics, Benton had helped lay a foundation on which he was to build later.[1]

In Washington again through the spring and summer, Benton turned to a second phase of his new appeal — national politics. With a presidential election due in 1852, men like Blair, Van Buren, Preston King of New York, Wilmot, Chase, Hamlin of Maine, and Welles of Connecticut — all now identifying themselves as antislavery Democrats — looked to Benton as the potential "torchbearer" of the "true Jackson democracy." Once again, however, Benton refused flatly to enter the contest. Nonetheless, he feared a "double Hunkerdom" headed by Cass and Clay, hoped to influence the outcome, and suggested that with a little "warping" Levi Woodbury of New Hampshire (whose daughter "Minna" had married Montgomery Blair a few years before) could be made a candidate in the Jackson-Van Buren tradition.* But in September, 1851, Mr. Justice Woodbury most inconsiderately died. After some groping, a possible substitute was found in William O. Butler of Kentucky, a slaveholder who opposed slavery extension, the Democratic vice-presidential candidate in 1848. Though Benton thought Butler highly available as "a *new man*" who had not been "mixed up with late events," the Kentucky dark horse ran poorly in critical trial heats and had to be scratched. In the long run, Benton and his allies found themselves without a candidate.[2]

When the Democratic convention met in 1852, a long deadlock developed, with the "logical" candidate Cass and the "most available

---

* Ten years later, Hamlin, Chase, Montgomery Blair and Welles were to sit in Lincoln's cabinet, as Vice-President, Secretary of the Treasury, Postmaster General, and Secretary of the Navy, respectively.

candidate" Douglas, as the *Republican* correspondent put it, standing each other off; until finally, on the forty-ninth ballot, the delegates settled for another dark horse, Franklin Pierce of New Hampshire. The Whigs contented themselves with another general — "Old Fuss and Feathers," Winfield Scott.

Through the rest of 1851 and most of 1852, meanwhile, Benton pressed his political war in Missouri. Taking a house for himself and his family at the corner of Sixth and Walnut Streets in St. Louis, he stayed in Missouri from November, 1851, to August, 1852, except for one brief visit in the East. "In no very amiable mood," the *Republican* noted, "at the beginning of his seventy-first year," he launched "a contest as fierce, vindictive, and implacable as was ever waged," for "the mastery of the party in Missouri." More succinctly, David Atchison commented — "the d——d old Rip! He's got enough in him to make five Roman tyrants!" In rallies and private conversations, and through the press, Benton carried the war to his enemies. Noting talk of a new reunion in the Democratic party, he made his terms clear in a public letter he dispatched in mid-December. Any union must rest on "principle" — *first,* complete repudiation of the Jackson Resolutions; *second,* repudiation of the votes some "recreant, self-called Democrats" had given for Geyer in the last Assembly; *third,* acceptance of "the right of instruction," but only "according to the will of the people," not according to legislative "sovereignty"; and *fourth,* repudiation of the "new dogma . . . that Congress has no right to legislate upon slavery in the Territories." Clearly, as the *Republican* remarked, Benton's terms to the Antis were "unconditional surrender."

In another keynote address in March, 1852, Benton elaborated. He spoke at the Rotunda of the St. Louis courthouse, ostensibly to aid the pro-Benton campaign in the new municipal elections. Actually, he used the occasion for a speech which was a far-flung mixture of philosophy, broad wit, and dramatic appeal. He began with a weighty discussion of political parties. "Inherent in all free states," parties were rooted "in the different natures of different men, one part of whom fear tyranny in the government, and another part fear licentiousness in the people." This had been the "dividing line" between Federalists and anti-Federalists when the Constitution of 1787 was debated, and again between broad constructionists and strict constructionists in the Bank war. The second party (of course) was designated "Democratic," "derived from the

Greek, and almost the pure Greek itself, *'Demos-Krateo'* 'the people —
to possess, to govern.' " * Next, Benton turned to a facetious account of
the union of certain "trading Whigs" with certain "renegade Democrats." In some cases this had been a public "wedding," in others not.
But "the intercourse ha[d] been clandestine and incessant [Laughter].
They met together in dark places, and they act together as man and
wife, whether lawfully married or not [Laughter]." This combination
had given Democratic Missouri a representation of "one Nullifier [At-
chison] and one Nullity [Geyer] in the Senate, and one Democrat and
four Whigs in the House." But the beginning of "redemption" was at
hand, in the city election contest — "begin tonight . . . Repair to your
wards this evening. Let every man do his duty . . . 'To your tents, oh,
Israel!' " Though he gave little attention to city affairs, Benton did
essay an old-Jacksonian class appeal in a reference to the condition of
certain streets under the Whig incumbent and candidate, Luther M.
Kennett — "I leave out the principal streets, where merchants and
bankers congregate, and speak of those which the working population
have to traverse early in the morning and late at night . . . something
that looks like a mud canal, with a little tow path on the one side
. . . and there your working population tread their way, one by one,
in Indian file, the head man looking out for breakers." Clearly, Benton
had lost none of his orotund oratorical flair. Nonetheless, another
three-way contest brought another Kennett-Whig victory.

A new point, meanwhile, was given to Benton's war. A rally in St.
Louis proposed him as a candidate for the national House of Representatives from a district that extended across twenty counties in the
southeast portion of the state, from St. Louis to the Arkansas border.
He agreed to run; and through the spring and summer he was busy
speaking at county seats and other towns, in a campaign which was a
small replica of his "appeal" of 1849. As he pressed it through the intense heat of June and July, traveling sometimes on horseback, sometimes by Mississippi River steamboat, he showed that despite his seventy
years he still possessed all the drive that had always characterized him.
Throughout he was harried by his anti-Benton Democratic opponent, the
bitter, vindictive Lewis V. Bogy, who had ridiculed Benton as "cracked"

---

* It is interesting to compare this Macaulay-like, psychological analysis with the
Madison-like, socio-economic account of parties Benton had offered in his St.
Louis speech of July 18, 1835, when he proclaimed that the foundation of parties
was "in the radical question, whether PEOPLE or PROPERTY shall govern;" it was "a
question between MEN on the one side and MONEY on the other!"

in the 1849 campaign. He now charged that Benton was determined to "rule in his own way," or "ruin in his own way." He also denied that he, Bogy, was a "Nullifier," as the Benton men had alleged.*

In the canvass, Benton underscored the policies he advocated. At the center was the repeal or "expunging" of the Jackson Resolutions, and the defeat of local "demagogues" like Atchison, Green, "Fox" Jackson, and Birch, who strove "to hitch Missouri to the car of nullification." (Surely, Benton commented, he could handle these "little Anties of Missouri," for "Benton had fought with *men* . . . with Clay, and Webster, and Calhoun," and with the *national* "demagogues" like Cass, Buchanan, Marcy, "old Father Ritchie" and Douglas). He pledged continued efforts for legislation to guarantee every family a "homestead," and urged again his project for a road-and-railroad system on "a direct line from St. Louis to San Francisco." He was happy to be a candidate for that branch of Congress directly elected by "my real friends — the people." It gave him a chance to join battle against the current trend which was "slipping away the power from the immediate and responsible representatives of the people to those whom they neither elect nor control — from the many to the few — converting the government into an oligarchy instead of a democracy." But enough — "my Senatorial life of six Roman lustrums, seven and a half Greek olympiads, has shown what my principles and conduct are." The people must judge Benton accordingly, and then decide.†

All Benton and no compromise again, he scouted renewed attempts at factional accommodation. Insisting that when factions like the Softs had broken with the Democratic party in the past, the party had grown stronger with the people, he bluntly invited the Antis to "form their separate organization." Let them "run their separate candidates for everything; it will form the grand sewer, the *cloaca maxima,* to carry off all the filth from the democratic camp!" Once cleansed of the "lep-

* Like many other anti-Benton Democrats in Missouri in the 1840's and 1850's, Bogy was to espouse the Confederate, slavery cause in the Civil War — though he kept rather quiet about it. He was elected Senator from Missouri in 1872, and served without distinction.

† In his later campaigns, Benton referred to himself occasionally in the third person. This led one memoirist to record that he always did so, "and by the formal and courtly title of Ben-ton," with "the second syllable being pronounced as distinctly as the first, without Mr., or Colonel, or any other prefix" (Grissom, "Personal Recollections," 131). Other memoirists have the Colonel giving his name a sort of country pronunciation — *Bane*-ton. Once again, the contemporaneous record is not quite so colorful as the reminiscences.

rosy" of "nullification treason," the true, people's Democracy would triumph again.

In one instance issues of policy were mixed with personal encounter. At an open meeting at Bremen, in north St. Louis, where Benton spoke briefly, a Whig candidate for Assembly named E. C. Blackburn undertook to answer him. In the midst of his remarks, the young man was interrupted by Benton, who rose majestically but angrily to accuse Blackburn of having misrepresented what Benton had just said. A bitter exchange ensued.

> BLACKBURN: I did not come upon this stand to be insulted. You, Colonel, are an old, gray-headed man, and you cannot, and shall not, urge me to forget myself, or what is due to your years . . .
> BENTON: I further understand that you have, during this canvass, charged me behind my back with being an Abolitionist and a Free Soiler. Did you do it, Sir?
> BLACKBURN: I did not call you an Abolitionist, Sir.

With this, Blackburn was allowed to finish his remarks. When he did so an unrelenting Benton took the stand, glared at his hapless adversary, and resumed the inquisition.

> BENTON: Did you call me a F-r-e-e S-o-i-l-e-r?
> BLACKBURN: I might have done so, and I believe I did.
> BENTON: Then, at last . . . after much hard work, I have got him to admit so much. Now, I say again, the charge is false, from beginning to end — from the mind that conceived it to the tongue that uttered it — and unless the author is like the man who had no soul, and was refused admission into h-ll because they admitted no one without souls, he will retract it.

But Blackburn would not retract, and declared bravely that he would not "pander to the prejudices or passions of . . . the honorable ex-Senator."

Certainly, Benton had struck hard, even for him — at the time of the Bremen meeting, he was still suffering from the effects of a family tragedy. But other leaders without his personal reasons for sensitivity behaved with similar rancor though less bravado. In the contest, the issues were fundamental, intensely felt, and highly personalized.

The rancor was reflected in the press, and in the speeches of other campaigners. The *Republican* raked Benton as "an old Fogy," whose "influence" was gone — "his hand was uplifted against every prominent man in public life." The anti-Benton *Times* and the pro-Benton

Anzeiger des Westens were equally vehement, as were speakers like Frank Blair and Alexander Kayser, who often campaigned in his native German for his German-American audiences. When the *Union* failed to keep pace, a lively sheet called the *Missouri Democrat* was established to press the campaign. Its chief editor was a twenty-six-year-old Kentuckian named B. Gratz Brown, a cousin of Frank Blair's; Brown held degrees from Transylvania University and Yale, and proved himself a brilliant, slashing politico-publicist. The *Democrat* held on after the campaign, and soon absorbed the declining *Union.**

The people voted on August 2, 1852. Even A. B. Chambers at the *Republican* had to admit that Benton had "made a Duke of Wellington affair of it — a perfect Waterloo defeat to us — and that too, we believe, solely by the aid of Blucher and the Prussian forces." Indeed, what Bowlin had called "the foreign prejudice against slavery," and the forces of "white labor" or other workingmen who had been drawn into the city's new industries, were apparently decisive in giving Benton a new power base in St. Louis. But the "Duke of Wellington" marched victoriously through most of the other counties too. Though he lost such slaveholding, mercantile, or mining centers as St. Francis, Ste. Genevieve, Mississippi, and New Madrid, Benton carried the rest of the counties outside of St. Louis over his combined Whig and Anti opposition. He would return to Congress as a Representative from Missouri — though he would not actually have his seat until December, 1853.

At a grand victory celebration at the courthouse, Benton hailed this vindication of the "appeal direct." It was a triumph for the "no caucus, no convention" principle which eliminated the opportunity for "juggling," of the sort that went on at conventions and elections by legislatures. Such "direct voting" must be established universally, "if our elections are not to degenerate into empty form and criminal substance." Although Benton had earlier, albeit parenthetically, declared that he preferred Franklin Pierce to "any who were thrown away" at the Democratic presidential convention, A. B. Chambers in the *Republican* noted that his victory address made no reference to Pierce's candidacy. More significantly, the speech raised a problem and then passed it by. This was

* This *Democrat*, after endorsing Buchanan for President in 1856, turned gradually Republican, and was to offer stalwart support to Lincoln in the difficult days (particularly difficult in Missouri) of civil war. In 1875, the *Democrat* merged with a rival paper called the *Globe*, as the *Globe-Democrat*. In 1919, the *Globe-Democrat* bought the *Republican's* successor, the *Republic*, thereby becoming the only morning newspaper in St. Louis.

the question of *how,* under a "no caucus, no convention" procedure, the Democrats were "to take effective measures . . . to concentrate the vote of the party," as Benton himself had put it during the factional confusions of the 1830's. For the moment, however, "the crowning ornament of victory" was perhaps enough.

In the East, Van Buren declared that the triumph had "refreshed me very much," and Blair rejoiced that Benton "was restored to his power in his state again." In Washington, "Father Ritchie" had retired at the *Union,* and a new editor seeking new harmony hailed Benton's victory along with other Congressional successes as a good omen for Pierce. In the absence of the disruptive issues and party splits that had brought defeat in 1848, dark horse Pierce did run well ahead of war horse Scott in the November balloting.[3]

[2]

IN THE MIDST of his political engagements, Benton had found himself again and again face to face with illness and death — in his own family, and among his old Congressional colleagues.

His great concern was always for Elizabeth, whose health steadily declined. She was free from suffering, and in Washington tried to walk two blocks every evening after sunset, to vary the monotony of household life and to refresh herself with a glass of soda water. But she was increasingly feeble, and shattered by terrible paralytic shocks. She moved about little, found it impossible to write letters, and was scarcely able to speak intelligibly. When an old friend asked after her, she was gratified. But, Benton had to tell Van Buren, it was "a mournful gratification, almost always reducing her to tears — making her remember what she was & feel what she is." [4]

Near the beginning of the 1852 Congressional campaign in St. Louis, Randolph Benton was taken ill. "His disease," Thomas wrote Jessie Benton Frémont, who was in London with her husband, "had all the violence of cholera, though bilious, and quickly set his bowels on fire with inflammation." The next day, March 13, Randolph was delirious. He was visited at the Walnut Street house by his friend Father Pierre Jan de Smet, and on the night of March 16, he declared his desire to be taken into the Catholic Church. Going to Randolph's room after Father de Smet had left, Thomas talked with his son, who was worried about his Presbyterian father's reaction to the decision — "I intended to do it long ago, but did not know whether you would like it." The father replied that what made his son happy, made him happy, and Randolph cried: "Thank God I am happy!" Indeed, Benton wrote Father de Smet later that night, "it is the first feeling of relief I have had in these five terrible days and nights." At sunrise the next morning, March 17, 1852, John Randolph Benton died, aged twenty-two years and four months. The sudden death of his only remaining son was a deep affliction to Thomas Benton. His friends noted that he was "dreadfully oppressed," and Minna Woodbury Blair observed that "his firm nerves shook, till he could hardly stand."

Nor was the death of Randolph the only burden he carried. He was, in addition, arranging for the re-interment of members of his family in the new Bellefontaine Cemetery north of St. Louis. The undertaker asked his occupation, but he knew "what occupies my thoughts and cares — gathering the bones of the dead — a mother — a sister [Polly] — two sons [McDowell and Randolph] — a grandchild [Benton Frémont] — planting the cypress over assembled graves."

All this left Benton little spirit for political rough-and-tumble. Never an adept in the politician's cajolery, he found it more than usually impossible to spend his time conciliating individuals by walking the streets, visiting at public places, standing at corners. Yet he knew he must go on, and he did. But his work, as he himself put it, was "that of the sick lion, sick at the heart, reposing in his lair, only leaving it when the hunters and their pack bayed too closely." Moved by the goad of his afflictions and depressions, he knew he sometimes struck excessively hard at his "assailants," as he did in his exchange with E. C. Blackburn. Ignoring his personal distress, his enemies arraigned him for an "overbearing, brow beating" style. But it was the "style" of a harassed, doubly driven, aging man.[5]

In 1852 also, Henry Clay and Daniel Webster died, leaving Benton the only survivor of the great Senatorial quadrumvirate, Clay, Webster, Calhoun and Benton. Benton had fought bitterly with all of these colleagues, but he had respected them as adversaries; and the falling-away of so many men of his generation left him in an ever more isolated and melancholy situation.

After the August election, Benton returned to Washington, leaving Elizabeth and their daughter Susan in St. Louis. In the capital, his friends found him improved in appearance. He had "lost the heavy encumbered look of age" for an "alacrity of look and carriage," and "his flesh was reddened and hardened & his spirits buoyant & he was altogether a new man," Francis Blair noted. Benton talked "of playing the part of Dandolo, 'the octogenerian chief' celebrated by Byron," and Blair thought he had a good chance of doing it.

Still, as he labored in his third-floor study, Benton lamented the absence of his family and grew somber again. Letters assured him that Elizabeth was much as she had been, feeble, but still able to amuse herself at the Christmas season by planning holiday events for the grandchildren of the household. But the family was too much scattered — Elizabeth in St. Louis with Susan, still unmarried "but not unsought"; Jessie in Paris; Eliza with William Carey Jones in far-off California, where that young lawyer had done well in land cases; and Sarah with Richard Taylor Jacob, now a prosperous farmer, in Missouri. With so much of his family so far away through the winter of 1853, Thomas admitted to "spells of depression which instead of being removed by time only seem to fall more heavily upon me." The death of the wife of an old friend reminded him that "few of our comrades of fifty years ago still survive."

It was a dark season. He found consolation only in "feeling that we are soon to follow," and he thought again of how he had been busy in St. Louis, "preparing the narrow bed which is to be our long home." [6]

[3]

NOT CONTENT with immediate political action, Benton had turned to a third front to advocate his views. Looking to national public opinion and the long future, he had in May, 1851, started a book. Thereafter he kept at it steadily, growing increasingly absorbed in the job and his enlarging conception of the work.

At the beginning, he envisaged only publication of portions of his speeches, "with historical notes." Thus, he told his friends, he hoped to give "an inside view" of politics during the thirty years he had served in the Senate — a view "no outsider, nor anyone *post hunc diem,* can ever give." In addition, he would use the papers of Andrew Jackson that had been entrusted to his friend Blair, and he hoped thus to fulfill a promise to Jackson "to take care that his presidency should go down *right* to posterity." Month after month he labored. As he worked he enlisted the aid of other public men, pleading, demanding, cajoling, calling for documents, for recollections of events and personalities, for criticisms. The list of quasi-collaborators was long — old friends like Blair, Van Buren, Taney, Benjamin F. Butler of New York and Woodbury before his death; and new friends and lesser acquaintances like Chase, Hamlin, Bedford Brown of North Carolina and others. In August, 1851, writing Montgomery Blair, Benton referred to the book as "my 'Thirty Years View.' " By October, he had learned to read the miserable meanders in which Van Buren penned his dozen-page critiques, and urged him to "scrawl away without restraint." He carried "a winter's work" with him to St. Louis at the end of 1851, and resumed the task in Washington after his return. Though he complained in 1852 that "I have rather too much writing to do," he persisted in his search for more materials.

Looking to the problem of publication, he asked John Dix to call on the "principal publishers" in New York. He wanted "a work for the people, for the masses," and therefore, "one volume and a moderate price." He hoped for "the sale of millions of copies." * By July, 1851, a contract was signed with D. Appleton and Company, one of the outstanding houses in the nation. It prescribed a single octavo volume — though the work was actually to appear in two large volumes.

As he wrote, Benton's conception of the book developed and took its place in a larger context. He envisioned "an object from beginning to ending, to establish and maintain the democratic party upon the basis of principle." Lamartine had done "justice to the Girondists," Carlyle to "Cromwell and his puritans," and Benton hoped to do the same for Jackson and the radical Democratic tradition. He saw his book as one of three jobs he had on his hands at once. The others were "the redemption of Mri. from whigs, rottens, and nullifiers," and "some hand" in national political developments.

Special problems arose as Benton wrote, and he met them zestfully. When he came to "the combination of Clay, Webster & Calhoun" against the nomination of Van Buren as Minister to England, he asked the New Yorker for permission to print the letter he, Benton, had written on that occasion, because it showed that though "close friends, we were independent and acted like men to each other." † Planning

---

* A doubtless apocryphal story on this matter (Dyer, *Great Senators,* 209) says that Benton answered his publishers' question as to how many copies they should print thus: "Sir, they can ascertain from the last census how many persons there are in the United States who can read."

† This was the letter in which Benton had told Van Buren bluntly that if he would oppose the "dynasty of '98 (federalists)" on basic issues, he would be

character-sketch chapters of "the friends who have departed," he had written one about Nathaniel Macon and sent it to North Carolina friends "for the verification of some details," and he wanted help from Van Buren and Blair in drawing up something similar for Silas Wright. In the course of composition Benton read Alexis de Tocqueville's magistral *Democracy in America,* considered his influence, and was appalled. He was "authority on American democracy in Europe, and with the federalists here, and will be with our posterity if they know nothing but what the federalists wrote." During his visit, Tocqueville had followed the anti-Jackson papers, and listened to anti-Jackson talk, "and framed his book upon it, and evidently in good faith." Certainly, Tocqueville was the best of the European commentators, and his book "pass[ed] for candid & intelligent." But, Benton cried, "what a figure we are to make if we do not write for ourselves!" *

Concerned to avoid "errors" of partisanship himself, Benton sought aid from former opponents. He corresponded with the veteran Whig Senator from Delaware, John M. Clayton, for example, and made arrangements to meet him. Given the immediate political situation, however, he declined an invitation to visit Clayton at his home, and suggested that they meet "accidentally" at Barnum's in Baltimore, "my usual stopping place there"; and he named a day and time. During Henry Clay's last illness, Blair visited him in Washington, and found him apprehensive about the treatment he would receive in Benton's book. When Blair assured Clay that Benton would refute the "corrupt bargain" charge concerning the election of Adams in 1825, "a beam of sunshine went over [Clay's] face." Surely, Benton declared, "there is a time when political animosities are to be obliterated under the great duties of historical truth."

"worth contending for" for the Vice-Presidency; if he would not, there would be "nothing between them and you worth contending for" — "as for myself, when I find myself on the bridge of Lodi, I neither stop to parley, nor turn back . . . Forward, is the word."

* In the first volume of his work, Benton was to devote all or parts of four chapters, more than a dozen closely written pages, to various "errors" he thought Tocqueville had committed — in relation to the groups and classes supporting Andrew Jackson; removals from office and patronage in the Jackson Administration; the character and place of the House of Representatives as an agent of direct democracy in the United States; and the Bank of the United States (Benton, *View,* I, 112-114, 159-163, 205-208, 226-229). The Missourian quoted the Frenchman copiously, and then scored his "errors" with a typically Bentonian array of "facts," interpretations, and impassioned rhetoric.

By the summer of 1853, the public had a foretaste of the great work. In the *Post* in New York on July 7, and in the *Union* in Washington on July 12, a chapter appeared. It was Benton's colorful account of the duel between Clay and Randolph in 1826, "the last high-toned duel that I have witnessed." The friendly, anti-slavery Democrat who edited the *Post,* William Cullen Bryant, promised regular publication, and even the unfriendly A. O. P. Nicholson of Tennessee, who had become the *Union's* third editor, suggested that "the anxiety of the public" to see the book would be "greatly increased by a perusal of the extract." The *Post* ran chapters through April, 1854, almost thirty in all. It paid Benton ten dollars a column for his contributions, which generally ran a column or two a week.

Throughout the fall, Benton stayed at it. To Alexander Kayser in Missouri, he commented that "Thucydides says his work was not written to be recited and applauded in the theatres, but for a 'perpetual possession,' " and added modestly, "mine is written with the same view, but without any expectation that it will last so long." He lamented that while Thucydides had had "thirty years of uninterrupted leisure," and still did not finish his thirty years of history, he, Benton, had only "a couple of years with continued interruptions." In November, 1853, Blair stopped off at the C Street house, where he found Benton "labouring most strenuously . . . from dawn to dusk again he is at work." He observed that Elizabeth sat at Thomas's side while he wrote, and that she was scarcely able to rise from her chair without falling unless Thomas assisted her. Touched by such "conjugal tenderness," Blair wondered that Benton exerted himself so well "under his depressed feelings," and drove on with his writing.[7]

Finally, in the spring of 1854, the first volume of the *Thirty Years' View* was published. It began with a preface in which the author disavowed "animosities" against "those with whom I have differed." It carried on, for 739 pages, the story of the "Working of the American Government" (as Benton saw it) from the "agitating question" of Missouri admission in 1820 to the end of Andrew Jackson's administration. The pages were large, and the type was set in double columns; all told the work ran about 665,000 words. It was offered in several bindings ranging from cloth to an elegant half-calf, tooled, gold-stamped, with blue-and-brown-marbled end papers. The price was popular, considering the size of the book — $2.50 for the cloth edition. No "sale of millions of copies" occurred, of course; but the *Democrat* in St. Louis

reported that the pre-publication *"subscription"* was "the largest that
was ever known to any work in Europe or America." Later reports put
the original sale at 50,000 to 65,000 copies — an immense number for
the time.*

The reaction of readers was various. In Congress, the *Thirty Years'
View* was fulsomely quoted — often against its author-legislator. The
Virginia zealot for scientific agriculture and extreme proslavery politics,
Edmund Ruffin, thought the volume "a huge monument of self-eulogy"
— no surprise from an author who had never been anything but an able
"scoundrel" — "the certain fact of his having stolen money, & by
means of a false key, when 19 years old, & a student at the University
of N.Cᵃ though perhaps his only felonious act (in law), was by no
means his most dishonest or immoral act." The New York poet and antislavery editor William Cullen Bryant, on the other hand, declared that
"the literary execution of this work, the simplicity of its style, and the
unexceptionable taste which tempers all its author's allusions to his
contemporaries, have been the subject of universal admiration." He also
praised the work as a practical "handbook" of "the great principles of
public policy" the radical Democrats had represented in the days of Jackson — it was "convenient to turn to these pages to see how the party
professing to be Democratic has departed from these great principles."
Through the summer paper after paper, North and South, political, nonpolitical, and religious, ran reviews praising the work. A balanced account was offered in the new monthly, *Harper's Magazine*. The book
was sure to be regarded "by men of all parties as a valuable commen-
tary" on an era during which "a direction was given to the measures
of Government [popular democracy, presumably] the influence of
which will be felt in remote ages," the anonymous reviewer wrote. As a
"prominent actor" in the events, Benton had been "gifted with . . .
sufficient personal ambition to give intensity to his powers, but not so
overwrought as to dim the clearness of his perceptions." He aimed at
"fairness and accuracy" and achieved "the baldest honesty," but he was
too involved "to affect the dignity of the philosophic historian"; thus the
book was "warm with party heats," and gave the author's views with
"frankness and ardor." Over all, it was a "rough, commanding, im-

* Inquiry to the successors of D. Appleton and Company as to the sales of the
Thirty Years' View, and other works Benton published subsequently with the firm,
failed to elicit any information: "it is presumed that [the records] were destroyed
by fire in the offices of D. Appleton and Company at the turn of the century"
(Letter from C. E. Nelson, New York, May 5, 1948).

pressive outline — often dashing in an excess of coloring — never attempting the minute and delicate finish of the literary artist."

At best, the book showed insight, intensity, and eloquence — at worst, distortion, dullness, and pomposity. In its 165 chapters, crammed with information and rhetoric, there was substantially more best than worst. The work offered an "inside view," but it was always Benton's "inside view," often revealing but sometimes slanted or inaccurate — no surprise, since the "scientific revolution" in historiography was yet to come. There was some autobiography, more than usual in a "history" but less than in most "memoirs" of the period. As a testament of faith in the spirit of popular democracy, economic, social, and political, the volume clearly "voted" for Jackson (and Benton), yet it was not on the whole narrowly partisan. The reports of speeches inserted into the text, as in the work of the author's admired Thucydides, gave the whole a contemporaneous flavor. The prose leaned to long, involuted, marching sentences, which probably reflected Benton's reading of Gibbon and Macaulay; but generally the sentences *did* march. The total effect was vigorous, muscular, and supple, like the style of the author's speeches, but more economical, less argumentative, and moderated. Finally, the sprawling volume was somehow unified by Benton's feeling for the sweep of his era, and by the drive of his personality.

He hoped that his book would have a timely impact for "direct" democracy. He announced that "this work [is] intended to show the capacity of the people for self-government, and the advantage of extending — instead of restricting — the privilege of the direct vote." Away with canards like Tocqueville's "fanciful theory" that the United States risked "perishing miserably among the shoals of democracy." In another contentious chapter Benton summed up his persistent attack on "irresponsible" conventions, "conducted by a few adroit managers, who baffle the [presidential] nomination until they are able to govern it, and to substitute their own will for that of the people." Believers in democracy "should press the constitutional amendment" he had so often urged. Over-all, the book was a ringing re-statement of the anti-Bank, hard-money, agrarian doctrines Benton had advocated in the 1830's. In the long course of history, Arcadia was bound to fall before developing Enterprise, before the onrush of commercial, manufacturing, and business expansion. But in their battles over economic policy, Benton and other radical Jacksonians had furthered the growth of popular, effective, political democracy; and had also planted deep the roots of re-

sistance to the Hamiltonian system Clay and Webster had espoused, of
hothouse, government-sponsored, monopoly capitalism. In so doing, Benton had helped to carry forward the Jeffersonian ideals of equal rights
and equal opportunity, had helped to shape and strengthen the American democratic, libertarian tradition. Again and again, this tradition
spoke through the pages of his book.

Whatever its critical reception or political effect, Benton was elated
that his *Thirty Years' View* had "an immense sale." The publishers
gave him "the largest share of the profits by 3 1/3 percent that was
ever allowed to an American author." [8]

[4]

IN BOTH STATE AND NATIONAL political arenas, meanwhile, Benton
was busy. With the inauguration of Pierce in March, 1853, the political conflict entered a new phase nationally and in Missouri; and a
momentous session of Congress in 1853-1854 was to give it still another
direction.

At the beginning, rumor had it that Pierce would name Benton to a
diplomatic post, or support him for Speaker when the new House met.
At a reception Pierce gave at the White House, journalists noted that
Benton was most agreeable, "and apparently on the best possible terms
with the master of the house." The cabinet Pierce named soon made it
clear, however, that his Administration would not go Benton's way. The
antislavery Democrat John Dix was considered briefly for state and
then dropped — "if Dix is in," one of Douglas's lieutenants had groaned,
"then Blair, Benton, and Van Buren are in." The chief figures in the
cabinet were the aging, ponderous, epicurean Hunker, Marcy, at State;
the thin, precise, stiff slavery extremist, Jefferson Davis, at War; and
the wily ex-Tylerite Caleb Cushing as Attorney General. In the patronage distribution, jobs were found for one Anti after another in Missouri,
despite Benton's protests — "the scoundrel" Birch, ex-Congressman
Green, and particularly anti-Benton editors like the vituperative John
Loughborough in St. Louis and the persistent Joseph Ament in Hannibal.* In Washington Pierce parleyed with Atchison, the tight-lipped,

---

* A few years before, Ament had employed an apprentice in his early teens,
named Sam Clemens, who in 1856 left Hannibal for St. Louis, became a steamboat pilot, and finally won a reputation which bracketed him with (and above)
Benton as one of the two most famous Missourians of their century.

capable Congressman John S. Phelps (who had represented himself as
pro-Benton, only to emerge as what the *Democrat* called Douglas's "fu-
gleman" in Missouri), and a new Congressman elected as pro-Benton but
now following Phelps, James Lamb. Bilked again, Benton and his allies
cried out against the latest "canine insurrection (Phelps & Co.)," and
lamented that *"innocent* Lamb" had been devoured by the "cunning old
wolves."

In Missouri, the situation grew more difficult. Angrily, Gratz Brown
at the *Democrat* damned the defection of John "S(ly)" Phelps and
others, and complained that "no man, since old King Lear, has had so
much cause to rail against treachery" as Benton had. In Jefferson City
the governor, Sterling Price, took the state printing from James Lusk
at the pro-Benton *Inquirer* and gave it to the anti-Benton *Examiner.**
Thus, Whig observers chortled, Price and Benton were "now fairly pitted
against each other." In April, 1853, Benton returned personally to prosecute his war again on the Missouri battlefield.[9]

Launching his third battle, Benton mixed railroad politics and slavery
politics. He had already had printed at the *Democrat* a long pamphlet
summarizing again his plan for a railroad and "a plain old English road"
for farmers to the Pacific. Having failed to persuade Jefferson Davis in
Washington to dispatch an army expedition to explore the central
route, he arranged in Missouri "a little pioneer party" of his own.
(Later, Davis did send out explorers, and brought the Administration
to sponsor an extreme southern route). At the end of April, Benton
went to the Missouri frontier with his friend Edward F. Beale, who
had been named Superintendent of Indian Affairs for California. On
the frontier he saw Lieutenant Beale strike west, with a few companions,
on muleback. On his way to his California post, he would traverse
the open country due west of Missouri and go on through Utah Territory
along the route suggested by Frémont, to estimate its feasibility for a
railroad. Meanwhile, Benton stayed several days at the frontier to speak
at Kansas and Westport (the two towns that later merged into Kansas
City), and at Independence, about "that *'American road to India'* . . .
a cherished vision of mine for thirty-eight years." Everywhere he was
well received, with city councils passing resolutions of welcome and

---

* Perhaps Price was partly moved by an *Inquirer* article praising a new novel,
Uncle Tom's Cabin, for giving a "wonderful" insight into some aspects of Southern
society. A decade later in Missouri, General Sterling Price, CSA, commanded southern troops which faced Union troops commanded for a time by General John
Charles Frémont, USA.

greeting committees meeting him at the steamboat landings. By fall, he could claim that Beale had found "the Central Route" to be "good for roads and settlements, and inviting the hand of the farmer to improve it."

In mid-May, Benton returned to St. Louis, where he made arrangements to take his family back to Washington. Replying to proposals that he stand for the Senate again, in opposition to Atchison, whose term would soon expire, he announced that he was at the people's "service" for the seat. However, he would not "canvass" because he did not feel the "personal interest" which the word implied. He was interested rather in issues. He reminded the people of the northwest counties that the spirit of Nullification had opposed the organization and settlement of the area to the west of Missouri, which ran to the Continental Divide and north to Canada and was known as "Nebraska," "because it was free soil." Now, this same spirit of Nullification also clandestinely supported "a southern sectional [railroad] route because it would be on slave soil and accommodate the Southern States."

The reaction to Benton's railroad and Nebraska campaigns reflected the party confusions of the day. Privately, Atchison had written of Nebraska — "I had rather see the whole territory sunk into hell, than to see it organized as free territory." (Before long, conditions in Nebraska were to approximate those of hell, with Atchison playing Mephistopheles). Now he cried out to Samuel Treat — "of all the humbugs the old sinner [Benton] has ever mounted, of all the lame, blind, wind-broken and spavined hobbies the old villain ever bestrode, he has now mounted the most shabby, his 'sitting astraddle of the big gun when it bursted' was nothing to it." More literately, in a campaign pamphlet, Atchison charged Benton with advocating the Pacific railroad and organization of the Nebraska area only to win Free-Soil votes, and make himself "the recognized champion of that very free soil faction." On the other hand, one Whig Assemblyman thought the railroad issue so important that he declared that Benton's return to the Senate had "now become a State necessity." But the *Republican* cracked that Benton never *did* anything for any railroad, and only *talked* about it.[10]

In May, Benton left with his family for Washington. There he labored through the second half of 1853 with his book, and watched developments in the national political arena. At the end of 1853, he entered that arena again, taking his place in the House of Representatives. The drawing of lots gave him a seat in the front row, immediately to the left of the center aisle.

He stood out as an unusual figure in the House. The Chicago member Long John Wentworth recalled that ex-Senator Benton commanded from many members the same veneration that had been accorded to ex-President Adams when he had entered the House years before. A journalist who made "Off-Hand Takings" of members remarked on Benton's "iron will" that had enabled him to defeat the "army of demagogues" in Missouri, and on his "magnificent head" and "face beaming with intellect." At home, Benton was the center of an admiring circle. On New Year's Day, 1854, the New York Whig Senator, Seward, stopped off to see Representative Benton, and found him with two of his daughters, "all surrounded by Democrats fierce for his return to the Senate" — "I joined heartily, to their surprise." Three days later Seward walked home from the Capitol with Benton, and went with him two doors up C Street to the house then occupied by Jessie Benton Frémont, whose husband was on a winter exploration of the central railroad route to California — his fifth and last expedition. Like her famous father, Jessie was "noble spirited," Seward noted, with "much character," and "very outspoken." [11]

In the House, Benton gave detailed attention to concerns of local, special interest to his St. Louis-centered constituency. *Item:* The arsenal in St. Louis should be moved to Jefferson Barracks south of town, and the thirty-seven acres of ground sold to the City for a park; for St. Louis lacked "a place for recreation," where the people could "go for health and amusement." *Item:* An appropriation of one hundred thousand dollars to complete the custom house at St. Louis; what had been "a little French village when I went to the place," had become "a great city, of one hundred thousand souls," and a key river port. *Item:* A bill from the Military Affairs committee, to grant a right of way through the arsenal and Jefferson Barracks tracts for a proposed St. Louis and Iron Mountain Railway. . . . And so on, through issue after issue.[12] Such solicitude for the St. Louis mercantile community was in marked contrast to Benton's old agrarian perspective, and in the past he had shown minimal interest in legislative pork. But slavery and the Union were now the great issues. Benton was laboring to build a new power base from which he could carry on the fight, and he adapted himself to the interests of new pro-Union, antislavery groups, like much of the St. Louis business community. In this adaption, he undertook the increasingly typical Congressman's role as errand-boy for local interest groups.*

Meanwhile, a new proposal cut into the special interest, small change politics that had been the business of the House. Soon known as the "Kansas-Nebraska Bill," it provided for *two* new Territories in the area then known as "Nebraska." By the Missouri Compromise legislation of 1820, all of the area north of latitude 36° 30′ (the line of Missouri's southern boundary) was closed to slavery. In January, 1854, Douglas reported to the Senate a bill which, after a series of politics-inspired metamorphoses, provided for the effective repeal of the Missouri Compromise restrictions in Kansas and Nebraska, and for the acceptance or rejection of slavery "by the people" of the Territories "in their own way." An amalgam of many ideas, the bill had many political facets. It built on the interest of the plantation class in opening new lands for slavery extension. It marked the hopes of the adroit, ambitious Douglas as a perennial presidential candidate to curry favor with this important group, as well (perhaps) as his desire to satisfy the interests of settlers, land speculators, and magnates by clearing the way for a railroad from Chicago to the Pacific. It accorded with the concern of Douglas's particular friend, the persistent and truculent David Atchison, to get the restrictions of the Missouri Compromise repealed and open the area immediately west of his Missouri bailiwick to slavery. On the other hand, the measure enraged old-Jacksonian champions of the freeholding class, like Benton, Van Buren and the Blairs, and, of course, free-soilers like Wilmot, Chase, Charles Sumner and Welles. In the North generally, the proposal was greeted with mass protests. The apparent peace that had followed the Clay-Douglas "compromise" of 1850 was shattered. Under the proddings of Davis and Douglas, Pierce made the bill an Administration measure, while the *Union* proclaimed it "a test of Democratic orthodoxy." Thus began a course of yielding

---

* These aspects of Benton's activity were practically ignored by earlier biographers, who apparently saw no need for inquiry into the details of his House career as a means of characterizing his work during this period. One notes his "indomitable energy" in minor matters as well as major, but offers no summary analysis (Roosevelt, *Benton*, 306-313), while another focuses almost entirely on his "elaborate arguments on two matters of the greatest moment" (Meigs, *Benton*, 425-433). Both Roosevelt and Meigs seem so anxious to place Benton on a pedestal as a *statesman* in this period, that they lose sight of him as a working *politician*, who knew that success as a politician was a prerequisite for success as a statesman.

that was to establish the Chief Executive as the pliable President Pierce
— weak, South-dominated, and indecisive.

For his part, Benton reacted vigorously. In a long conversation with
Seward, he urged all antislavery men to "save ourselves from Douglas'
bill" by remonstrations throughout the North "in public meetings and
in legislative resolutions." [13] On April 25, before the bill was formally
taken up by the House, Benton attacked it in a long, passionate, historical, polemical speech, which was soon distributed as a pamphlet to stir
public opinion to remonstrations.

At the beginning, Benton reiterated his loyalty to the Missouri Compromise itself. He "had stood upon it above thirty years, and intended
to stand upon it to the end — solitary and alone, if need be; but prefer-
ring company." Parenthetically, he condemned the efforts of "public
printers" as "intermeddlers" in legislation (the *Union,* presumably) to
require Democratic members, "under the instant penalty of political
damnation," to support "every bill which they call administration." He
recounted the fable of *L'âne et son maître,* with its moral — " 'A caution
to all asses to take care how they undertake to scare their masters' (Great
applause)." The Missouri Compromise was to be "abrogated" in the
name of the new-found doctrine of "squatter sovereignty," or determination of the slavery issue by the people in the Territories. But in better days, Congress had repeatedly refused "to 'impair' " the old slavery
compromises, Benton trumpeted — "Oh, squatter sovereignty! Where
were you then? . . . The mare's nest had not then been found in
which has been laid the marvelous egg out of which has been hatched
the nondescript fowl, yclept 'squatter sovereignty.' " Yet now this idea,
mixed with others in "a farrago of nullities, incongruities and inconsist-
encies," was "injected into the belly of the bill," a "little stump speech,"
to become the heart of "a bulging attempt to smuggle slavery into the
Territory." But, Benton objected, "the Territories are the children of the
States . . . minors under twenty-one years of age." It was the business
of Congress "to take care of these minors until they are of age." He
was opposed to trying to palm the decision off on the children
Territories, opposed to "this shilly-shally, willy-won'ty, don'ty-can'ty style
of legislation." Indeed, he declared in crescendo, he objected to the
whole measure as "an amphibological bill," and "amphibology" . . .

Here the gavel fell, signifying that Benton had used the hour allowed him under the rules. Immediately Long John Wentworth was on

his feet, declaring that he would yield as much of an hour *he* had as Benton needed. *Objection!* from a member from Georgia, and others. Angry debate over the rules and precedents, until finally —

> MR. WENTWORTH: I wish, at the outset of my remarks, to know if at any time during this Congress or any other, when any member of this House has obtained the floor, and another gentleman has requested a short portion of his time to finish his speech, that request has ever been denied by the House?
> MANY MEMBERS: Never, never.
> MR. WENTWORTH: . . . I want the whole country to understand that the oldest man living in Congress, the man who was here when the Missouri Compromise was adopted, and the only man in the whole Congress, is now refused a courtesy which has been refused to no other living man.

More wrangling, with "cries of 'Order!' 'Order!' " appeals from the decisions of the chair, wrathful expostulations, all taking up more time than Benton would have consumed in delivering the rest of his speech — Benton meantime standing impassive in all his bulk, saying nothing. Finally, a *pro forma* amendment by Wentworth as a device within the rules to allow Benton to proceed.

> MR. BENTON: "Amphibology," sir, "amphibology"; that was the point where I left off . . .

Shouts, and more disorder . . . until finally Benton was able to go on. Yes, "amphibology" was "a cause for the rejection of bills," and "we should reject this bill for [that] cause, if for nothing more." He knew that, by the bill, "the slave States expect . . . the extension of slave power, and slave population." But, the Cassandra-Congressman warned, slaveholding settlers were likely to be outnumbered by non-slaveholding settlers. In any case, placing the slavery decision in the Territories was likely to produce contention and violence there, "and the destruction of the peace of the country."

This dramatic speech evoked an excited response. Antislavery members rushed to Benton to shake his hand in congratulation. In the Senate, Seward noted reports that Benton was "making a great anti-Nebraska speech in the House — I would rather be there than here." But the *Union,* attacked, fired column-long broadsides at the "former idol of his party," for now "aiding the abolitionists in their war upon a bill intrusting the domestic affairs of the people to their own care and oversight!" Nationally, the speech was widely discussed. The *Democrat* in St. Louis declared that Benton had stripped "the Douglas fraud . . . naked in its many deformities," and hailed Benton as the only Congressman from slaveholding Missouri to oppose the measure. In New York, the *Times* pictured Benton as a "lion" whose roar could scatter herds of politicians. An anonymous author in Boston published a long poem called "Nebraska," which devoted forty-four lines to Benton, including —

> *Behold that tall and Senatorial form,*
> *A noble soldier harnessed for the war! . . .*
> *No northern doughface with a cotton heart,*
> *He is the southern Nestor of the race;*
> *The king of statesmen since the* TRIO *died. . . .*

The debate crackled on through the rest of April and into May, with Benton subjected to regular attacks from Southern members. He was apparently stimulated by the fight. He declared that a brief absence during a two-day continuous sitting on May 11-12 "was neither on account of age or infirmities" — "for I never felt better!"

Toward the end of the debate, on May 19, Benton delivered another major speech. He noted that a Georgia member had alluded to possible *future* applications of the "principle" of the bill, which led him to vote for it "as a southern man." What were these "ulterior operations" of the bill, Benton asked, "containing a principle to be asserted in future?" He found the answer in two diplomatic endeavors of the Administration. *First,* there was the mission to Mexico of James Gadsden (expansionist from South Carolina, protégé of Jefferson Davis) seeking to buy Mexican territory which would "make five or six States of the first class." True, James Gadsden had come back with "a small slice only of the desired territory," but he might have "better luck on a second trial" to acquire new territory and convert it from "free soil" to "slave soil." *Second,* there was the "grand movement" led by Pierre Soulé (reckless Louisiana fire-eater, the ambassador in Madrid) to buy Cuba from Spain, "and a rumpus kicked up if the island is not got" — for further slavery expansion. These, Benton proclaimed, were "indexes" to what the Georgia member may have had in mind, when he spoke of the future. . . . In fact, Benton was substantially right in both his charges of "ulterior operations." Frantic, South-inspired "grand movements" *were* under way to acquire parts of Mexico and all of Cuba as potential future slave areas.

Finally, toward the end of May, 1854, the Kansas-Nebraska Bill passed in the House, as it had already passed the Senate. The Yeas comprised 101 Democrats from both North and South, and twelve Southern Whigs. There were an even 100 Nays, which included 42 Northern Democrats, nearly all the Northern Whigs, and the four Free-Soil Democratic members. On May 30, the bill was signed by President Pierce. The dramatic lack of party cohesion in the vote, and the equally dramatic sectional cohesion, was an omen of the effect the Kansas-Nebraska Act was to have in the nation. In the North, a crescendo of protest from meetings, press, and pulpit arose. "We would belie our convictions of democracy did we not oppose slavery's extension over new lands," a labor paper in Cincinnati proclaimed. In Chicago, Douglas faced hostile crowds; while in Springfield, ex-Congressman Lincoln was stirred from comparative apathy concerning slavery to a firm stand against slavery extension. The wave of protest against the Kansas-Nebraska Act, as a Southern, slave-power aggression, laid foundations for the disorganization of old political relations, and the emergence of new sectional and party alignments.[14]

In the House, Benton addressed himself to one more important question. This was what he called a "demand" from Pierce for ten million dollars to pay for the land purchase James Gadsden had arranged with Mexico, a strip some hundred miles deep along the southern border from El Paso, Texas, to the bottom tip of California. The immediately foreseen use for this sliver of Mexico was to open a better route for an extreme southern railroad to California. The President's "demand," Benton insisted, citing Saxon tradition, Magna Carta, and Montesquieu on the power of "the people's representatives" over the "public purse," was like "the imperious command sometimes heard in the highways: stand, and deliver!" In addition, he attacked the railroad aspects of the Gadsden purchase, and argued again for "the fine national route on the parallels of 38 and 39." The Gadsden route was "too far South," and through country "so utterly desolate, desert, and God-forsaken, that Kit Carson says a wolf could not make his living upon it." And for this, the House was "commanded" to "stand, and deliver" ten million dollars! — which it finally did.[15]

In the House from December, 1853, to August, 1854, Benton had utterly alienated himself from Pierce's regime. Elected as a Democrat, he had violently attacked the great measures which had been made "test[s] of Democratic orthodoxy" by the Administration and its organ. The *Union* announced flatly that "the hostility of Colonel Benton to the administration is no secret to anybody," and damned him as a "Whig adjunct and abolition ally." * But genuine Abolitionists like James Birney and William Goodell, editor of the American Anti-slavery Society's *Emancipator,* would have none of him, and lamented "the mischievous tendency of his being put forward as a candidate for the *Presidency."* Indeed, Birney wrote an article "exposing" Benton and sent it to Horace Greeley for his *Tribune.* But the antislavery Whig editor refused to print an attack on a man who was "now doing good" as "a Samson falling and carrying down the pillars of the [slavery] temple with him." A sub-editor summed up: 1854 was no time "to overhaul the past faults of Col. Benton — he is now acting on the side of freedom, and why repel the aid of such a man?"

Of course, Benton had not become a "Whig adjunct and abolition ally." He still thought of himself as a Democrat, but he worked for sectional peace, the Union, and the restriction of slavery. He was willing within limits to work with other men who sought these ends, regardless of party labels. What he called "the disposition in some to injure me in every way on account of [my] Nebraska speech," brought him into even closer sympathy and communication with Free-Soil Democratic leaders like Chase and Sumner.[16] But though he was ready to "act with" these men and antislavery Whigs like Seward, he did not, as they soon did, drop his Democratic party identity.

In Missouri, meanwhile, with the chief warrior occupied in Congress, the fourth battle in Benton's "long and bitter war" was fought. In May, 1854, he was announced as a candidate for re-election to the House, subject to "a primary election," and as a candidate for the Senate. Throughout his House constituency, which had been cut in a redistricting to St. Louis city and county, and throughout the state, the usual campaign raged, with faithful Assembly candidates hastening to pledge themselves to Benton for Senator. The *Union,* looking on from Washington, pre-

---

* In April, Benton had given vent to his hostility toward the Administration in an amusing way. When an anti-Benton man was named Postmaster in St. Louis, Benton announced that he would receive nothing through that office — "my correspondence will go through the express line of Adams and Co., who generously offer to fetch and carry for me, gratis, and their office will be my Post-Office" (Washington *Union,* April 25, 1854). This was possibly the only time a United States citizen boycotted the United States Post Office — but it was typical of Benton's magisterial ways. Perhaps he feared, with some reason, that his political enemies at the Post Office might tamper with his mail.

dicted that the Missouri contests would "forever settle the destinies" of Benton as an effective political leader.

The "primary election" was offered as a solution to the problem posed by Benton's "direct voting" stand of 1852 — how to concentrate the party's strength on a candidate without caucuses or conventions. Before the local elections of 1853, the *Democrat* had suggested such a direct choice by the people, in an editorial which the *Republican* hinted was written by Benton. In June, 1854, a full scale "Primary Election" plan was announced by the party Executive Committee in St. Louis. Three judges for each polling place in the wards and townships were designated by the committee, and "all legal bona fide Democratic voters" were invited to choose nominees for the various offices from among the candidates who filed. Returns were to be certified by the judges, and the Executive Committee would announce those with the most votes as the "Candidates of the Democratic Party." Careful arrangements were made for the challenge of voters. Here, under the private auspices of the local party committee, was a practical application of the doctrine of the popular *selection* of candidates Benton had so often advocated.

Publicized well in advance, this primary took place on Saturday, June 24. More than 4500 partisans voted.[17] No one filed against Benton for Congress, but there were lively contests for the Assembly posts.*

In Washington, Benton responded to notice of his nomination in a pamphlet-letter to his constituents. He was glad to see both Whig (Luther Kennett, long-time Mayor of St. Louis) and "Nullifier" (Trusten Polk) candidates in the field against him. He damned the anti-Missouri Compromise portions of Douglas's Kansas-Nebraska bill as the spawn of a "night caucus of eight nullifiers" in Congress, designed "to

* This may have been the first instance of a direct primary election in which balloting was done at polling places. Many students have found the origin of the direct primary in Crawford County, Pennsylvania, about 1868. Evidence has been unearthed to show, however, that a primary procedure was developed by the Crawford County Democrats as early as 1842, as a way to "hush . . . the cry of bargain and sale, packed conventions," and so on (Booser, "Origin of the Direct Primary," *National Municipal Review,* XXIV [April, 1935], 222-223). But an examination of the details of this primary reveals that voting was at afternoon *meetings* "in the several districts [?] of the county," while in the St. Louis primary voting was at *polling places* kept open all day in each ward and township — an important difference. On the data, I have been unable to determine to what extent if any Benton was responsible for launching the primary idea in St. Louis, beyond the suggestion that he was responsible for the first editorial. The full direct primary under *state law,* rather than party aegis, made its first appearance in Wisconsin in 1903, whence it was widely copied.

govern the next presidential election, and to 'kill off Benton.' " He had hoped for "an interval of repose before I die," but he could not give way to "Nullifiers" without a fight.[18]

In St. Louis, the campaign for Kennett developed against a background of shifting political alignments. Throughout the nation a new political group had been organizing, appealing to "nativist" sentiments against the growing flood of immigrants, and offering itself as a new rallying point for voters confused by the confusion of parties. Self-called the "American party," it was more generally dubbed "Know Nothing," because members of its many secret lodges were supposed to parry questions by saying, "I know nothing." In St. Louis, where many "natives" were disturbed by the massive Irish and German immigration, the Know Nothings quickly developed a following. In this situation, Benton's friends charged, Kennett played "wiry politician," appealing to Irish and German votes as a *Whig,* and standing as an "ultra nativist" in a bid for "American" votes! Nationally and locally, the old Whig party was being buffeted by what the *Democrat* called "the Nebraska thunderstorm." Proslavery and antislavery groups within the party were pulling apart. Unable to meet the new issue, with its leaders increasingly quick to combine with any likely faction or group, the Whig party was on the eve of disorganization. But the Kansas-Nebraska issue was to bring defections not only from the Whigs but from the Democratic party too, and finally align it as almost wholly proslavery.

All this was a part of a great political sea-change. It was produced by the revived conflict of interests over slavery and slavery extension which followed in the wake of the Kansas-Nebraska bill, and which swept through national politics. In the sea-change, another new party was emerging, which took a firm slavery-restriction stand, adopted the old-Jeffersonian name "Republican," and became major. At the moment, in St. Louis, party confusion enabled Kennett to emerge as the candidate of an ominous Know-Nothing–Whig coalition. The Washington *Union's* correspondent in Missouri predicted (gleefully) that unless Benton made an "appearance in our midst," the Know Nothings would ruin him.

Election Day, Monday, August 7, 1854, was marked by violence and riots. Street fights raged between some Know Nothing followers and Irish-Americans, and the office of the *Anzeiger des Westens* was attacked. The rioters were dispersed by troops, with many wounded and some reported killed.

The election was a defeat for Benton. In a vote of nearly twelve thousand, he ran not quite a thousand behind the ambipartisan Kennett, while Polk collected a miserable 378. In the Assembly contests the pro-Benton Democrats and the Whigs split evenly in the St. Louis area, with Frank Blair and Gratz Brown among the pro-Benton winners. The statewide returns showed pro-Bentons, anti-Bentons, and Whigs nearly evenly matched. In St. Louis, the results were generally attributed to the Know Nothings. By his duplicitous devices, Kennett had won a "strict" Know Nothing vote almost twice as large as his straight Whig vote, and a coalition vote almost as large as his Whig vote. While Benton ran only 53 votes better in St. Louis than he had done in 1852, Kennett topped the 1852 Whig total there by more than 1700.[19]

Three months after the election, Benton paid a brief visit to Missouri. He came by way of the Baltimore and Ohio railroad to Cincinnati, and then on by stage, reaching St. Louis in mid-November. When news of his arrival spread, he was called upon by "hundreds of his fellow citizens," who found him in good health, the *Democrat* reported — "his bearing [was] erect, yet his locks silvered with the frosts of time." He seemed to be pleased with the hero's welcome he received from "the sturdy mechanic, and the hard working laborer, dusty with toil, and the industrious merchant, and the wealthy citizen, politicians and patriots, friends and connections, rich and poor." During his short visit, he offered his definitive comment on the Administration. He did not condemn poor Mr. Pierce, "but the nullifiers who rule him, and who have brought things to their present pass — the harmony of the Union destroyed . . . and his own Administration run into the ground."

In St. Louis, Benton sat for a bust by a local sculptor, James Wilson McDonald. The product was hailed by Gratz Brown as *"Old Bullion! Alive in Marble"* — it expressed fully "that powerful and uncompromising quality which has enabled the old man so often finally to triumph." The artist had indeed presented Benton dramatically and in fine detail. By Christmas twenty plaster casts of the statue had been ordered.[20] It showed Benton with his unusually large head thrown slightly back on his massive shoulders, his high forehead lined, his bushy eyebrows and deep-set eyes setting off his long, slightly aquiline, narrow nose, the whole given warmth by a mouth thin-lipped but suggesting a smile, and seeming small in a heavy chin. The artist even caught the starched, formal, gentlemanly effect of Benton's winged collar and stiff ruffled shirt, set off with a bow tie. The marble original was presented to the St. Louis Mercantile Library, where it was given a place of honor for more than a century to come.

By the end of November, Benton was on his way back East, to tend to Congressional and other business. In his absence again, the fifth battle of the political war he had launched in Missouri was fought out.

This battle was the Senatorial election in the Assembly. With Benton Democrats, anti-Benton Democrats, and Whigs represented in stand-off proportions, various deals were rumored or proposed. A first balloting in January, 1855, showed Benton 41, the Mexican War hero, A. W. Doniphan (Whig) 57, and Atchison 56. Repeated later ballots brought little change, despite suggestions that Doniphan give way to the venerable Columbia leader James S. Rollins as a *"true blue* Whig," or Union man the pro-Benton group could support.*

At the end of January, an exchange occurred which symbolized the whole Benton–anti-Benton contest. The Senator from Pike County, Peter Carr, delivered a long diatribe in which he arraigned Benton as always "defiant and overbearing . . . cold, distant, haughty, and repellent"; since 1844, Democrats "of the slaveholding states . . . [had come to] look upon him as the *leper* of an ancient time was regarded, and cry out, 'unclean! unclean!' " This studied harangue was too much for Representative Frank Blair, who lashed back, impromptu, declaring that contrary to Carr's assertion, Benton was not "politically dead . . . but liveth," advocating right policies and great projects, like the Pacific railroad — in which he would triumph, "in spite of the opposition of . . . traitors in our own State," and of "the miserable puppet we call our President." *Some* rejoiced that Benton might no longer be in the service of Missouri, and so "wicked and foolish men rejoiced when Aristides the Just was banished." † But "when the danger arose, the great Athenian was recalled to save the state." So would the great Missourian be recalled, to face "the dark cloud [which] is looming up in the horizon, threatening destruction to the Union." Each of these

---

* Despite their affiliation with opposing political parties, Benton and the "father" of the University of Missouri were on personally friendly and confidential terms. Near the end of 1851, for example, Benton had written a letter to Rollins which concluded, "your friend and well-wisher in everything" (*Missouri Republican,* December 11, 1851), and he always held the Columbia leader in great respect. By the 1850's, their views on slavery extension and the Union were growing closer and closer together.

† Fifth-century B.C. Athenian leader, banished and then recalled in the war against Persia; one of the commanders at the battle of Marathon, later chief archon in Athens, and the classic example of integrity in public life.

showy, unbending orations was given pamphlet distribution to enspirit the faithful.

In the face of such strongly focused, personalized loves and hates for Benton, no bargain, deal, or compromise was possible. After a forty-first ballot at the beginning of February, 1855, revealed a continued stalemate in which no one could win a majority, the joint session adjourned without electing a Senator and did not reconvene.[21] When Atchison's term expired in March, his seat was left vacant. Though Benton was never to return to the Senate, it was two years before anyone else was elected to the place.

[5]

AS A LAME DUCK MEMBER, Benton took his old front row seat in the House for the short session of 1854-1855. The lottery this time placed next to him a freshman Representative from New York, the later-to-be-notorious William Marcy Tweed.

Though Benton attended to the routine business of Congress, his great energies went to his railroad project. He advocated his central national highway to the Pacific, not only in the House, but in a series of "discourses" at "institutes," library associations, and other forums along the Atlantic seaboard. He began in Baltimore the day after Congress convened, went to New York in mid-December and thence to Boston, Providence, and Hartford, returned to Washington on Christmas Eve, and then left again for a final address at Philadelphia six days later. Ready to speak "everywhere to rouse and unite the people in so great an enterprise," he traveled on two conditions: no public receptions and no pay — and compared himself to Peter the Hermit in his new crusade. He repeated all his old arguments, from geography and topography to pre-emption rights to provide "freeholds" for settlers, and as usual offered a copious and colorful supply of information mixed with grand speculations — including the wild prediction that trains would one day fly along the central route at "a speed of an hundred miles an hour." There was, however, one new text in his Peter the Hermit preaching. Convinced that the clash of "political and sectional interests" in the legislative struggle made hope for a publicly built road vain, he now proposed that the line might be constructed by "enlightened capitalists." He had in mind men like the merchant, manufacturer, and anti-Nebraska Whig Abbott Lawrence, and other "solid names" with whom he had discussed the matter in Boston. Such "enlightened capitalists" should ask, and have, "nothing from Congress but the right of way through the public lands."

The New York and Boston appearances were particularly gala. At the new Academy of Music in New York, a crowd of six thousand filled the hall for the first time. Benton was accompanied to the stage by William Cullen Bryant; the advocate of education for workingmen, Peter Cooper; the historian George Bancroft; and politicos like Mayor Fernando Wood and John Van Buren. He wore what Greeley's *Tribune* described as "a capacious cloak," which gave "dignity to his portly form and good-natured face." At Tremont Temple, in Boston, he remarked that he had found such a warm welcome, such warm hearts and homes, in his first visit to New England, that it made him forget the December cold. The Boston *Courier* praised "the GREAT MISSOURIAN'S" speech as "terse, clear, and engaging," and thought his "dignity of person" like that of Webster. At the end of his Boston address, Benton was given a check for two hundred and fifty dollars, which he promptly endorsed back to the sponsoring society.

In his new advocacy, Benton followed procedures that he had developed and practiced through more than thirty years. Although he generally had a prepared text, he did not read, but spoke. He had developed an immense facility, his friend Gratz Brown recorded, for writing out a speech carefully, "and then deliver[ing] it without reading, and without getting it by heart, always following the written speech, even to its very words, but also throwing in additional illustrations to enliven the subject," and all without looking at the text or a note. Thus an address that might in a printed version seem likely to take no more than an hour to deliver, would actually consume two hours, because of Benton's "deliberation of speaking — proper pauses — sometimes interruptions for applause" — and the added illustrations. Also typically, Benton published his Baltimore, Boston, and Congressional railroad speeches in pamphlet form for general distribution. In his thirty-two year career in Congress, more than seventy-five of his speeches were thus printed. His Congressional railroad speech of January, 1855, was the last of the list.[22]

In the House, Benton gave conscientious attention to a generally dull session. He particularly scrutinized innumerable bills which he considered give-aways of government lands or funds to the "ravenous wolves" of special interests.* He stayed up most of the night studying one such proposal, and in the next day's debate found himself well-informed but quickly becoming "dreadfully hoarse." He had caught cold, and could "do little better than bark! but it is a case to justify barking." Scouting a petition for a land grant to build a "subterranean telegraph" to the Pacific, he argued that the Digger Indians through whose lands the telegraph would pass would dig the wire up to make hooks to spear lizards. Thus the line would be "a God-send to the Indians, but destruction to the lizards (Great Laughter)," and a profligate waste. More seriously, he damned the "dreadful misconduct" of the Administration, the War Department under Jefferson Davis, and the "school-house" (West Point) officers in the field, in the conduct of spreading, "calamitous Indian wars" with the Jicarilla Apache and Sioux, and asked (in vain) for "conciliatory means . . . to restore peace." Throughout he was amiable, though insistent, and many members treated him amiably in return. But the tension over the slavery issue was always latent, and to planter extremists and Administration stalwarts Benton's very presence and what he stood for was a constant goad. Parts of his railroad speech in particular were provocative, for there he touched again the sensitive slavery-sectional conflict, and again attacked the Pierce regime.

On March 3, the session was to end — and that end was bitter for Benton. The House was unable to finish its business, and it worked through Saturday night and Sunday morning, March 3 and 4, with the calendar day still officially March 3. At a roll call on Sunday morning, Benton appeared in the doorway and addressed the chair. He was often inclined to punctilio, and now he was punctilious about the fact that he was no longer legally a member of the House.

> THE SPEAKER *pro tempore:* Was the gentleman within the bar when his name was called?
> MR. BENTON: No, sir. I am here, sir. I appear outside the bar, sir, as an ex-member of Congress, to protest against any man calling my name. If any man calls my name, I will sue him, sir.
> THE SPEAKER *pro tempore:* The gentleman from Missouri is out of order.

* The 1850's marked a high point of petty scheming and activity by "contractors, speculators, stockjobbers, and lobby members," as James Buchanan called them, all anxious "on any and every pretext to get their arms into the public treasury." The 1850's were a decade of crisis for the Union — but they were also a decade of rehearsal for larger give-aways in the "Great Barbecue" plunder politicians were to serve up to more ambitious "jobbers" in the decades immediately following.

MR. BENTON: Yes, sir. And if the Sergeant-at-Arms attempts to arrest me [to compel attendance at the session the Missourian maintained was ended], I will sue him, sir.

THE SPEAKER *pro tempore:* If the gentleman from Missouri is not a member of the House, the Doorkeeper will keep him outside the Hall.

(*Roars of laughter, and cries of "Good!"*)[23]

Thus ended the Congressional career of Thomas Benton — amid the rancor engendered by the revived, fateful slavery controversy.

[6]

STRIPPED AS HE WAS of much of his old power and prestige in public life, Benton also suffered personal tragedies, which overmatched his political reverses and deprived him of many of the remnants of his old, happy life.

Through the winter and spring of 1854, Elizabeth Benton's illness had deepened, and kept her confined to the family's Washington home. She had lost the power of speech, and her only joy seemed to be in her devotion to her husband, to be with him as he worked, and sometimes to place her hand in one of his as he read. While he was busy in his study, she would sit nearby, silent, almost listless, and yet evidently grateful for his company. Except in the line of duty, he seldom went out, and political friend, foe, and neutral alike (for example, a New York *Times* correspondent who visited the family) remarked on the care and affection this street-lion house-lamb showed his wife. In the summer of 1854 (she was sixty on July 8), Elizabeth's health had seemed to revive, and in a hopeful spirit Thomas had left for Missouri in mid-August, his youngest daughter Susan accompanying him. On the way he was called back by news that Elizabeth had suddenly grown worse. Before he could return to her, she died — on Sunday evening, September 10, 1854, quietly, without pain.

Though he had long expected this event, Thomas was deeply distressed that it should have happened while he was away. "That I should have been absent at that moment!" he cried — "I who had always been with her, and striving to keep every sorrow from her heart!" She had accepted her husband's leaving for Missouri. But near the end, she had led Jessie to Thomas's chair in the living room, thus silently saying that she wanted him recalled. In Thomas's absence, the funeral was held at four in the afternoon, September 12, at the family's residence. The ceremonies were conducted by the family's pastor, the Reverend Mr. Ballantyne of the First Presbyterian Church. One of the pallbearers was the old family friend, Francis Blair. The funeral procession was attended by what the *Union* called "a vast concourse" of Elizabeth's admiring and sorrowing friends. A second service and final interment was planned for St. Louis in the spring, with burial in a cemetery plot Thomas and Elizabeth had marked out.[24]

During the short session, in 1855, another tragedy struck. On the morning of February 27, Benton left the C Street house to attend the session. His daughter Eliza, who was visiting with her father, went into his study about noon, and was astonished at how warm the room was, considering that the fire had been put out, and the day was uncommonly cold. But she left and closed the door after her. Later, smoke was seen coming from the crevices of the study door, and from the bedroom adjoining it. Immediately Eliza and a servant opened the study door, and found the contents in flames. They had to retire to save their lives, and some passers-by who came in and tried to save Benton's papers in his study were nearly suffocated. Fire companies were called, but they were unable to save the interior of the house or its contents. The dwelling Jessie Benton Frémont had nearby was saved — as were the other neighboring houses. Called from the Capitol, Benton could only stand in the cold street while the flames consumed most of his personal, business, and public papers, and his cherished books. He was offered hospitality by friends, acquaintances, and even Franklin Pierce himself at the Executive Mansion — but he declined, and settled at the Frémont house. The fire had apparently begun some days before, in a defective chimney. On the Sunday before it was discovered, Susan had told her father that she had noticed smoke in her room, which was above his, but it did not occur to them that some woodwork within the walls might be smoldering. None of the loss was covered by insurance, but Benton did not so much regret this — "I have enough to live on," he told the *Union* in an interview. What he did feel was the loss of irreplaceable things — "the bed on which my wife died, on which I sleep; her clothes, which were in a trunk setting at the head of it; the articles which she prized most, around it — the last things I saw at night, and the first in the morning." Years later, Jessie remembered her father saying — "it makes dying easier, there is so much less to leave."

Through the winter, Benton had been working on the second volume of his *Thirty Years' View*. Among the papers that were burned was his manuscript, and of course all his notes for the book. With characteristic determination, Benton told his publishers that he would "go to work and work incessantly" to rewrite the lost pages.[25]

In the last week of March, 1855, accompanied by his daughter Susan, Benton made the sad journey West to arrange for Elizabeth's final interment. Services were held the day after their arrival, March 26. The second Presbyterian Church at Fifth and Walnut was filled with family friends and prominent citizens, including the judges of the State Supreme Court in a group. When the pallbearers, headed by Montgomery Blair, carried Elizabeth's body into the church and placed the coffin on a table in front of the pulpit, "all eyes were directed to the noble form of the chief mourner," who "was convulsed with emotion." The aging, afflicted Thomas Benton "sat with his head somewhat bowed down," his old political rival Abiel Leonard observed, "holding his hat so as to cover his face. . . . What must have been passing in the mind of a kind husband, sitting by the remains of a deceased wife, with whom he has lived for upwards of thirty years!" While Leonard "restrained" his own feelings "with difficulty," others in the church shed tears of sympathy. A long funeral sermon was preached by the Rev. N. L. Rice. He chose as his text Luke 10:42, "But one thing is needful" — faith, the Reverend Dr. Rice elaborated, in Christ as Prophet, Priest, and King, a faith that had been "strikingly illuminated in the life of the deceased." She had also combined a "cultivated" intellect with "firmness of purpose and great moral courage," and "an amiable and affectionate disposition." The closing hymn was a favorite of Elizabeth's, "Jesus, Lover of My Soul."

From the church, a procession of carriages made its way to Bellefontaine Cemetery. There, on "a beautiful eminence, on the 'sunset side of the Father of rivers,' within the family enclosure," Elizabeth Benton was buried — alongside Thomas's mother Nancy, and his sons McDowell and Randolph. Despite the chill March wind, Thomas and Susan remained until the last spadeful of earth was placed on the grave.

For another week, Thomas and Susan stayed in St. Louis, at Joshua Brant's residence on Washington Avenue. Then at the beginning of April, aboard the *Crystal Palace,* they left for Washington, accompanied by Frank and Montgomery Blair. Montgomery planned to leave St. Louis permanently, to settle with his father at Silver Spring.[26]

Soon after, in Washington, Susan Benton was married, to Gauldrée de Boileau, Secretary of the French Legation. After the wedding on June 2, "a splendid entertainment" was given at the Frémont residence on C Street, with a large circle of friends present.[27] The marriage left Benton with none of his daughters living with him, though they visited him frequently. As old age advanced upon him, Thomas found himself more and more alone.

CHAPTER 17

. . . and Union

1855 - 1858

THE NEXT YEAR OF BENTON'S life, through 1855 and the spring of 1856, was devoted chiefly to writing. Day in and day out, week after week, month after month, he labored, first at the Frémont residence and later at his rebuilt C Street home, rewriting the portions of his *Thirty Years' View* that had been lost in the fire.

He followed the same procedure he had used in preparing the first volume. From his study came a barrage of appeals for documents, for spot-checks on some piece of information, and for recollections. From Van Buren he solicited sharper criticisms as "the effectual way of helping a friend," and added — "it has been the hardest lift of my life to undertake to make up what is lost, but I have a spirit that won't give up, and a body that holds out well thus far." Poring over *Niles National Register,* he condemned its editor for filling his publication "with everything the Whigs said and did to hurt us." Thus, "to an ordinary compiler of history he would do us much hurt." So hurried and engrossed was Benton that he declined all requests for speeches or lectures, and refused invitations to go out — "I rise at daybreak and work till midnight, with an interval of one or two hours recreation on horseback."

At the end of May, 1856, the book was published, 788 pages long. Though Gratz Brown thought it would rise above the petty bickerings of politicians like "the Parthenon of Athens," it was not so successful as its predecessor. It showed signs of Benton's having lost his documents when his house burned, and of his hurried, almost harried rewriting. Its chapters were of uneven merit; the space allotted to various portions of the story was out of proportion to their importance or their time span; and an undue number of words was lavished on matters of secondary importance, or on the Colonel's crotchets. Despite his effort to be "correct and impartial," he offered a highly dubious if brilliantly written recasting of his theory of Texas annexation as a prefabricated plot or "charged bomb," and generally portrayed John Calhoun as a sort of infernal machine of politics. Still, the book contained a mass of information, some of it "inside," and it was shot through with powerful narrative writing and probing insights. As a monument to Benton's continuing faith in popular democracy, it stood forth like the Agora if not the Parthenon. The narrative ended with the "compromise" of 1850, and an account of Southern disunion movements. In a last, brief chapter, Benton tried to focus the whole work on the great issue of the day — "the sentiment of political nationality! and whether it is to remain co-extensive with the Union, leading to harmony and fraternity, or divide into sectionalism, ending in hate, alienation, separation, and civil war?" If his book helped the people "open their eyes to these dangers," and *act,* "then this View will not have been written in vain." [1]

In any case, he had finished. The fire had delayed him, but his will and energy had enabled him to complete the task only six months after the time that he had originally planned.

[2]

THROUGHOUT HIS LABORS on his political testament, Benton watched the currents of contemporaneous politics too, and he was soon to undertake another battle in his "long and bitter war."

The blazing new conflict of the day was an outbreak of violence in Kansas. With the status of slavery to be settled there by "popular sovereignty" or local decision, both proslavery and antislavery immigrants rushed into the Territory. But Benton's old Missouri foes, Davey Atchison and B. F. Stringfellow, did not stop there. Shrieking against Yankee "abolitionists," glorying in the name "Border Ruffians," they lashed their followers to deeds of increasing violence, and led foray after foray of proslavery Missourians into the area. By violence and terror the decision of "squatter sovereignty" was to be made a proslavery decision. The antislavery settlers fought back, emigration from New England was accompanied by shipments of Sharp's rifles, and massacre and pillage swept the plains. The bitter fruits of Douglas's legislative masterpiece, as administered by Pierce, were — "Bleeding Kansas" and (local) civil war.

Reading news of "the operations upon Kansas," Benton was horrified. The "climax of nullification rule," nationally, was "the assumpsit, by the Administration, of all the lawless conduct in, and on Kansas." Noting the new phenomenon of "elections governed by violence and terror," Benton urged Bryant at the *Post* to give the matter space — not only the Kansas elections, but also the Congressional elections in St. Louis in August, 1854, and in Louisville in August, 1855. Such violence raised "a question between the Constitution, the laws, and representative government on one side," and ruffian rule on the other.

The conflagration in Kansas produced dramatic reactions in Congress. In May, 1856, Sumner of Massachusetts delivered a long, bitter speech on the "crime against Kansas," condemning the "slave oligarchy," the Administration, and Douglas and the Northern "doughfaces." After the address, Benton congratulated Sumner warmly — "you had all three of them at once on the point of your spear." Two days after his speech, Sumner was attacked at his Senate desk by Representative Preston Brooks of South Carolina, who beat Sumner again and again with a heavy cane until Sumner collapsed insensible to the floor. Seriously injured, he spent the early part of a three-year convalescence at Francis Blair's house at Silver Spring. Benton's reaction to this assault was all for Sumner. Noting that Brooks had had the approval of other planter Hotspurs who helped him or stood by, Benton cried that the attack was part of "a conspiracy; yes, sir, a conspiracy" — "these men hunt in couples, sir." [2]

Amidst such rehearsals for civil war, the presidential election of 1856 approached. Once again old-Jacksonians talked of Benton as a candidate. In the violent agitations of the day, he was emerging as a "conservative." Friends argued that his "moderation" recommended him, as did his "firm opposition" to the Know Nothings. But the veteran would have none of it, especially now that "all statesmanship [was] reduced to a *hurrah* on one side or the other of slavery." He thought that *"a new man, unconnected with the agitation, is what the country wants."* The Republican party, damned as "Black Republican" by its enemies, nominated a "new man" — Benton's son-in-law, John Charles Frémont. Among the Republican leaders were old friends and allies of Benton, like Blair, Bryant, Hamlin, Chase, Seward, Sumner, Welles, Benjamin F. Butler of New York, John Niles, and Wilmot. Many of Benton's old-Jacksonian friends saw support of the new antislavery Republican party as the only practical way to keep faith with their radical-Democratic convictions. In addition there were ex-Whigs like Lincoln of Illinois and Greeley, and the adroit political managers Weed of New York and Cameron of Pennsylvania. But Benton would not participate in the new movement, which he feared as sectional and a threat to the Union. He counseled Blair sternly against joining the new party. Though Benton and Frémont remained intimates and were in essential agreement on slavery, Benton urged Frémont not to accept the Republican nomination. Putting loyalty to peace and the Union above loyalty to family, Benton refused flatly to support his son-in-law for President. Meanwhile, the Know Nothings named an "old" man, ex-President Fillmore, whose nomination was ratified by a moribund Whig party.

Still hopeful for conservative salvation through the old Democratic party, Benton attended the Democratic national convention in June, 1856, as a visitor. In his parlor in the Broadway Hotel in Cincinnati, he received a steady stream of callers. He was, the *Democrat* reported, quite "the lion of the town." In earnest conversations, he campaigned "hard and hot" for — James Buchanan, as a man unconnected with the recent slavery agitation. (He had been out of the country, serving as Minister to Great Britain.) At the same time, Benton was "death and woe" on the ambitions of Pierce and Douglas —

"This administration is weak and corrupt," he would tell his visitors. "The President don't know his own mind for one hour."

"Mention the name of Douglas," he would continue, "and every bad passion is aroused; he is a political filibuster." * The North was "incensed, very justly, at his conduct [in reviving] slavery agitation."

It was true that Buchanan was "never a leading man in any high sense," Benton would agree — but "the effect of his nomination would be to restore peace."

After seventeen ballots, Buchanan was nominated, with strong Northern support. At Buchanan's victory, the *Democrat's* correspondent reported, Benton was seen "rubbing his hands with gratification." He had done more to secure the outcome "than all the outside influences in the city." It was a curious commitment — Benton and the "old Buchaneer" had been on ill terms politically and personally for a dozen years. But Benton's Missouri followers now hailed BUCHANAN AND BENTON as new twin leaders in the cause of sectional peace.[3]

From Cincinnati, Benton went to Missouri, where a pro-Benton, anti-Benton, Know Nothing battle was in prospect. Encouraged by a smashing victory by John How and others over Know Nothing "intolerance" in the St. Louis elections of April, a revived "Benton Democracy" had nominated Benton for Governor and Frank Blair for Congress from the St. Louis district. Though young Blair had been in "exceedingly off

* In the old sense of freebooter, or military adventurer, acting irregularly and without discipline.

humor" with Benton for keeping him from launching a pro-Frémont, Republican movement in Missouri, Blair, Brown, Thomas L. Price, and others were optimistic for a return to power with Benton. On the other hand, Atchison, Green, Phelps and others were confident of drawing "a majority of heretofore *Bentons*" into their Democratic faction. Both "National Democrats" and Know Nothings slated candidates against Benton for Governor — Trusten Polk and Robert C. Ewing. At first Benton was reluctant to make the race, but the nomination of Buchanan decided him — "I consider him the safest chance for preserving the peace of the country, now gravely endangered." Having decided, he planned a complete canvass of the state. In this canvass, though he was a candidate for state office, he spoke almost entirely of national affairs.[4]

On his arrival at St. Louis by packet, Benton was greeted with a hundred-gun salute. The welcoming committee found him in good health, with "upright port and vigorous bearing" — despite his seventy-four years, he looked "younger than he did ten years ago." He settled at Barnum's Hotel, where he conversed with a steady stream of visitors. Seeing the new battle in his long war as a possible "turning point" for the whole country, he was apparently ready for another old-fashioned Benton fight.

Two days after his arrival, on June 21, Benton addressed a rally of ten thousand that overflowed Washington Square.* It was the largest political crowd that had to that time ever assembled in St. Louis. The whole speech was pitched to a plea for a renewal of "family harmony . . . and fraternal affection" in the Union. That harmony had been sapped by Douglas's evil bill — and though Benton had known that it would lose him "favor" among some groups in Missouri, he had voted against the Kansas-Nebraska bill, and "of that I am proud! and would not revoke it this day for the honors of the earth (Great Applause)." Harmony had been further weakened by the vacillations of Pierce, who had been ruled by Jefferson Davis — "a martinet, puffed up with West Point science, dogmatical . . . an avowed secessionist" — and the devious semi-Democrat Caleb Cushing — "unscrupulous, double sexed, double gendered, and hermaphroditic in politics, with a hinge in his knee, which often crooks, 'that thrift may follow fawning' — he governs by subserviency," expecially to proslavery extremists. Such forces had hoped to control the Democratic convention, which had met appropriately in a

---

* A whole city block along Twelfth Street, the site of the present St. Louis City Hall.

close, windowless, sweaty den like "the 'black-hole' in Calcutta." The "cohort of office holders" had planned to play "the old game" — "the majority baffled, worried, and tired out," by the two-thirds rule, until the "trimmers" produced some "pet" as the *compromise* candidate." But "real delegates, fresh from the people," had finally carried Buchanan's nomination. Still, lacking "parties founded on principle," the national harmony was further imperiled by "fractional parties" — including, Benton proclaimed dramatically, "one with which the name of a member of my family is connected." He knew that there were insinuations that he would finally support that kinsman; he would "not answer such insinuations by words, but by conduct (Great Applause)." And so on . . . through a characteristically numbered bill of particulars against the Administration, and a discussion of the Kansas-Nebraska Act and other issues in detail. In peroration, Benton referred to the "violence and disorder which overspreads the land," and proclaimed: "I represent the principle of peace — of order, law, and justice."

It was one of the finest campaign efforts in the aging advocate's long career — forthright, full of fire, comprehensive, and yet carefully molded and restrained. Throughout the Missouri canvass, Benton elaborated his St. Louis themes again and again.

From St. Louis, he set out on what the *Democrat* called his "Forty Days' Campaign." Through July and into August, sometimes by train, on other occasions on horseback, or by buggy, he traveled some 1200 miles making more than twenty-five speeches — most of them to huge crowds in the open air, and most of them two hours or more long. He covered every part of the state except the southeast, going through the interior, then down through Phelps's district in the southwest and up through Atchison's domain in the northwest, and finally across the northern tier of counties to Hannibal on the Mississippi, and back to St. Louis. At German-settled Hermann, Benton was greeted by an artillery discharge. At Washington the improvised speaker's platform gave way, and Benton quipped that "it was his prerogative to break through platforms." At Jefferson City, a torchlight procession marched to a meeting of fifteen hundred in the railroad station. At Boonville, a band serenaded Benton at the City Hotel. Going south through a driving rain, crossing a deep ford in the Lamine River, "down sunk the carriage (heavy with a load of Bullion)," the *Democrat's* correspondent with the group reported, and everyone was plunged into water up to his neck. At Bolivar near the troubled Kansas border, the meeting was held in the tent of a traveling circus. At Warrensburg in Atchison's home county, Benton and Trusten Polk spoke from the same platform in front of the courthouse. An auditor long remembered Benton as he stood looking calmly over the crowd of friends and foes — "his majestic form was attired in a handsome tailor-made suit of broadcloth . . . His eyes sparkled at every angle and his face was all aglow with dazzling brilliancy. . . . The sun was hot that day, but those Missourians stood with bared heads for two hours, listening and shouting for Benton." At the rising town of St. Joseph, Benton spoke on a grassy slope, from which he could look west across the broad Missouri into Kansas. At Gallatin on the way east, battalions of Bentonites from eight counties swelled the meeting. Finally, at Hannibal on the Mississippi, the *Democrat's* correspondent summed up. Thriving on the campaign, and the "air and exercise," riding "unfatigued for weeks," with "the power and modulation of his voice improving daily," the white-haired "Great Tribune of the People" had proved himself "a man of iron." Everywhere he had drawn huge country crowds, with a peak of three thousand at Springfield in the heart of Phelps's district. Such "multitudes," the *Democrat* maintained, promised victory, though the election would be close.[5]

But Polk and Ewing had been drawing good crowds too, and Benton faced a formidable double opposition. His enemies, Atchison, Green, Phelps, his former *Argus*-ally Abel "Ratsbane" Corbin (as the *Democrat* called him), who was now acting as an anti-Benton correspondent for the Washington *Union,* the anti-Benton Congressional candidate in St. Louis, Thomas C. Reynolds, and others, were busy electioneering, propagandizing, and organizing. They damned Benton as actually "the leader of the Free Soil or Black Republican party in Missouri." They alleged persistently that his ulterior purpose was some devious intrigue to procure the election of his "Black Republican" son-in-law Frémont. They charged that he had cut short his out-of-state campaign to hurry to St. Louis "to save Blair and his Black Republican associates," for young Frank could be elected only by "the influence of Benton." They admitted that Benton was making "a campaign probably never exceeded in this country by a man seventy-[four] years old," but exulted that Polk, "better versed in local politics," was gaining steadily.[6]

Back in St. Louis, proclaiming himself *"seventy-four* upon the calendar, but *only fifty* upon the turf," Benton addressed another mass meeting. Torchlight processions headed by bands converged on Lucas Market place, on Twelfth Street, and the crowd swelled until the *Democrat* thought it was best measured by "acres." The arrival of Benton at the speaker's stand was "the signal for cheers upon cheers . . . the applause for several minutes was perfectly deafening." He spoke for two hours, without text and without notes. An auditor remembered the occasion, particularly the speaker's "tall, robust, and commanding figure towering above all." He moved little, only occasionally taking a step forward or to one side, or leaning forward "slowly and majestically," only occasionally gesturing with his right hand or arm. But when he indulged in invective, he "raised, pointed, and shook his forefinger or his clenched fist and in a climax brought it down with emphasis." In content, the speech was a total review of Benton's convictions and recent campaign. Utilizing the third person again, he emphasized that "Benton in canvassing the state was actuated by no selfish motive." He intended to do more historical writing — the *Thirty Years' View* was proving profitable as public service never had, and he looked upon "office" as "vanity! vanity! vanity!" He had traveled solely as a peacemaker, "laboring to restore the peace and harmony of the country."

The voting came on Monday, August 4 — the "Fortieth Day." Young Frank Blair was elected to Congress over the "American" and anti-Benton candidates. The *Democrat* rejoiced that St. Louis County would once again be represented by a champion "of the rights of the working men . . . who desired to devote the new territories of the United States to the tillage and agriculture of white freemen instead of slaves." In addition, Gratz Brown was returned to the Assembly. In St. Louis County, Benton ran well ahead for Governor, doing even better than Blair — if he had tried for Congress again, he might well have been elected. But outstate, he ran a poor third, getting slightly less than a fourth of the total vote, and the anti-Benton Trusten Polk was victorious. In Washington, the *Union* hailed "a total overthrow and rout of . . . the Bentonians." [7] Indeed, the proslavery faction had secured control of the state Democratic organization, and the "Benton Democracy" was practically finished as a major political force. The way was cleared for the organization of a Republican party in Missouri in the years to come. It was the last battle in Benton's "long and bitter war" in Missouri.

Soon after the voting, in mid-August, Benton left St. Louis for Washington. He set to work immediately to gather materials for a new historical project — an abridgment, in several volumes, of the debates of Congress from 1789 through the latest session. It was typical of his sanguine, resilient spirit that his defeat for the Governorship should leave him undaunted, and that he should immediately undertake another line of work. Through the autumn he kept at it, declining all invitations to speak, though he planned to give several addresses "intended to be national," *after* the partisan heats of the presidential election had cooled. Holding himself to a rigorous schedule, he allowed himself only his usual recreation, horseback riding — with his pretty, teen-aged granddaughter "Lilly" Frémont joining him along Pennsylvania Avenue on pleasant afternoons.[8]

Meanwhile, political currents flowed around him. The historian-politician Bancroft lamented the state of Democratic party leadership, "this bastard race that controls the organization, this unproductive hybrid begot by southern arrogance upon northern subserviency" — "Oh! for a voice of true democracy!" Unlike Benton, he could not believe that Buchanan would be that voice. Before long, Douglas was assuring Treat in Missouri that, in effect, Bancroft was right. There was no need to fear that "Bentonism" would dominate a Buchanan administration, "no reason to believe that Benton is in favor or will be recognized by Mr. Buchanan." [9]

By November, D. Appleton and Company was ready with the first volume of Benton's *Abridgment of the Debates of Congress,* covering the sessions from 1789 through 1796. In the next few years, fifteen more 800-page volumes were to appear, bringing the record through 1850. The compendium was, and is, a useful work, careful and impartial, extracting the kernels of lasting import from the Congressional chaff, arranging them readably in large two-column pages with topic headings at the top. The contents were epitomized in a painstaking index by speaker and subject, with illuminating footnotes based on historical research, and in later volumes on Benton's own experience. After looking at the first volume, Bancroft predicted that the work would be "the monument of the age."

At the beginning of November, Benton returned to St. Louis for a final appearance in the electoral arena. On the evening before the presidential voting, he spoke at the new lecture hall which had been built at Locust and Fifth by the Mercantile Library Association — an association in which Benton had taken an increasing interest, holding an honorary membership and contributing books. He reiterated that, "at his own hearth and talking as a parent to a child," he had urged Frémont against making the presidential race. He, like Frémont, was "opposed to the extension of slavery into free territory." But he was also concerned about the "danger of disunion . . . more imminent than was generally believed," and he insisted that Buchanan's "pledges to restore fraternal feeling by conciliatory means" made him the "Union candidate." It was Benton's last public address in St. Louis.[10]

Nationally and in Missouri, Buchanan won a handsome victory. Still, the startling feature of the contest was the rise of the Republican party, which carried a third of the popular vote despite the fact that it ran no ticket in eleven slave states — Buchanan 1,838,169, Frémont 1,341,264, Fillmore 874,534. Here were the fruits of the Kansas-Nebraska furor. The Whig party was gone, the Know-Nothing party was soon to disintegrate, and the Republican and Democratic parties were to survive as durable adversaries in a renewed two-party system.

Though Benton soon returned to Washington, his name remained a storm center in Missouri. In January, 1857, the Assembly elected two Senators, one to fill the vacancy left by the Benton-Atchison-Doniphan deadlock of 1855, the other for a full term. Benton's name was put up for both seats in three-way contests, but he commanded less than a fourth of the total votes, and his old enemies ex-Representative Green and Governor-elect Polk won easy first-ballot victories. Sadly, Gratz Brown at the *Democrat* wrote *finis* to the conflict that had agitated the Missouri Democracy since 1844, Benton's courageous but losing struggle within the party against "slavery acting on the aggressive in its efforts to become the absolute power in the state." Gleefully, A. B. Chambers at the *Republican* announced that "Benton's epitaph may now be written," and the *Union* in Washington reprinted this comment as its own.

A little later, controversy raged in the Assembly over a new issue — *emancipation* of Missouri's slaves. When proslavery leaders proposed and carried a resolution condemning the as yet small voice of emancipation in Missouri, Gratz Brown took the occasion to deliver a long speech. It was thoroughly Bentonian in its massive, fact-filled, rhetorical style, but not in its content. Cautiously, but portentously, Gratz Brown argued that emancipation must finally come in the interest of white labor — in the end one system must triumph over the other. When Benton's name was evoked in support of this new movement, he cried out in "amazement" and "outrage." From Washington in late February, 1857, he protested to more conservative friends, like Lusk of the *Inquirer* and former Lieutenant-Governor Thomas L. Price, that the St. Louisans "ought to have cut themselves off from me," before they added "a state slavery agitation to the national agitation." With all his old painful honesty and dogged consistency, he reiterated that "the whole policy of my life" had been "to keep the slavery agitation out of the state." To Brown, and the young, increasingly radical, dashing Frank Blair, this conservative manifesto came as a shock. They maintained that the proslavery leaders had begun the new "agitation" and that Brown had spoken only in defense. Still, they gave continued aid to the cause of "white labor" as they saw it. By 1858 Blair was conferring with Abraham Lincoln in Illinois, while Brown brought the *Democrat* out for Lincoln in a senatorial contest with Douglas. Meanwhile, the breach with Benton was patched, and the friendship between the old man and the young men continued.

The emancipation imbroglio foreshadowed conflicts that were to impose severe tests of all Benton's Missouri friends and foes. Political struggle was soon transformed into civil war. In this war, many of Benton's extreme pro-slavery enemies, like Atchison, Trusten Polk, "Fox" Jackson, Thomas C. Reynolds, and Sterling Price, gave active aid including military service to the secessionist cause. Others like Green and Bogy were sympathizers or accorded the Confederacy passive support. Still others, including Phelps, Treat, and even James H. Birch, basically political brokers or moved by special considerations, cast in with the Union Democracy. Substantially all of Benton's chief friends in St. Louis, like Blair, Brown, O. D. Filley, and How, became Republicans, while many outstate leaders like Price, W. V. N. Bay, Lusk, and ex-Governor King remained Union Democrats. Despite abortive attempts at local civil war, led by Jackson and Price, Missouri as a state remained in the Union. For this result, Benton might have claimed some credit. He had given years of his life to preparing Missouri public opinion to resist disunion. He had labored valiantly to maintain a political organization devoted to resisting slavery extension and maintaining the Union. He had sponsored many leaders who were to fight in that cause.

In 1857, Benton's Missouri friends saw one of these leaders in particular as the personal heir to the tradition Benton had established. He was Frank Blair, whom Benton had once called the "Young Hickory" of Missouri. He had, the *Democrat* proclaimed, all Benton's strong integrity, and an insight into the political history of the United States second only to Benton's, and when finally the cause of freedom triumphed in the nation, "Young Hickory" might be President.[11] This hope went unrealized, but decades later statues of Benton and Blair stood side by side as Missouri's representatives in the Hall of Fame in the national Capitol.

[3]

IN THE WINTER AND SPRING OF 1856-1857, Benton undertook a long lecture tour, giving the nonpolitical, "national" addresses he had projected before the presidential election. His purpose throughout, he proclaimed, was to help "pacify the public mind," to help restore "fraternal feeling" in the nation. He began his circuit of literary societies and lyceums at Boston in late November, and repeated his discourse in fifteen more New England towns in the next four weeks. In the larger cities he generally received a fee of two hundred dollars but always he was willing to leave "the terms" to the local forum. On at least one occasion (at a Mechanic's Apprentices Library Association) he spoke without fee. Though he traveled by railroad, and was used to speaking every day, he found it impossible to accept as many invitations as he received.

The meeting at Boston, in the Tremont Temple, was a personal triumph. Before a full house, with many outstanding citizens of "this modern Athens" in the audience or on the platform, Benton lectured for two hours in what one observer described as a "breathless silence" except for applause. He dwelt particularly on the effects of disunion if it should occur. It would produce two confederacies at first, with two rows of border states, "an angry feeling subsisting between them," and all the apparatus of border police, customs houses, and armies. The old "common glory" of the Revolution and its heroes "would no longer animate the common country"; the loss of a national symbolism would open the way to more "internal disorganization"; the final result would be a collection of "insignificant sovereignties, like the states of Holland and of Italy," all "quarreling with each other." It was this prospect that made him speak out for the Union and the Constitution, avoiding topics of the day "below the Constitution." Indeed, "the Constitution was his platform (Cheers) . . . He wished to maintain that Constitution in letter and spirit . . . (Cheers)." To do so, he had condemned nullification and disunion talk from men of the *South*. Now he would also urge men of the *North* to "cease all irritating measures," like further agitation against "the *institution* of slavery." Such activities simply aided extremists who sought to deceive "the people of the South" into the notion that "the policy of the north . . . is aggressive." This was blunt talk for Boston, where some abolitionists were openly denouncing the Constitution and the Union as "an agreement with hell" — slavery as an "institution." But Benton would not trim in Massachusetts, any more than in Missouri.

His mentor in New England, William C. Todd of the Newburyport Lyceum, was much impressed by Benton's personality. He remembered their first meeting, early in the morning at Benton's room in Tremont House in Boston, "where I found him, not yet dressed, in a loose wrapper, with a cap on his head, sitting at a table writing." Traveling with Benton, Todd also remembered his off-hand and often savage comments on public figures. *Of Tyler:* "A trifling man." *Of Cass:* "Very timid* — afraid to take a decided stand." *Of Douglas:* "Driven into the Kansas-Nebraska bill by the Southerners, Atchison, and others, the fire-eaters of the South, [who] threatened to drop him if he would not take hold of it." *Of President-elect Buchanan:* "It is too true, he is not a firm, decided man — he is too apt to be swayed by others." The Colonel's physique also impressed Todd, who noted that he was five-feet-eleven, that he weighed then 210 pounds, and that despite his age he always stood "erect, with his head thrown back."

From Boston, Benton's schedule encompassed a wide circuit through Newburyport, Salem, New Bedford, Haverhill, Lawrence, and Chelsea in Massachusetts; Manchester in New Hampshire; Portland, Auburn, Waterville, Bangor, Augusta, and Bath in Maine; and Middletown and New Haven in Connecticut. He had copyrighted his address, and he repeated it in lyceum after lyceum, with minor variations.[12]

From his New England tour, Benton went immediately to New York City, where he arrived four days before Christmas. There he spoke at a meeting of the New England Society of New York, at the Astor House, to commemorate the landing of the Pilgrims. He began with some autobiography, especially his mother's influences on him — learning, and abstinence from tobacco, gambling, and hard drink. He then got to his great subject again — "I say, in brief and in short, that the two halves of this Union, the North and the South, were made for each other, as much as Adam and Eve were made for each other (Applause); and I say, 'accursed be the serpent and bruised be his head who undertakes mischief or division between them!' (Enthusiastic Applause)." [13]

After a brief respite in Washington over the Christmas and New Year holidays, Benton took to the road again. Arranging a second New England schedule, he accepted an invitation to stay at the home of Professor

Jared Sparks, the erstwhile president of Harvard, with whom Benton had corresponded intermittently for years. He spoke at Harvard on January 13, at Boston again on January 14, and at other towns in the days that followed. After the Harvard meeting, he wrote Professor Sparks to request a copy of the university catalogue, and "also some Cambridge newspapers that may speak of the Lecture, as *people* want to know how they are talked of." The Boston address, in the Tremont Temple again, was a benefit for the New England Female Medical College. Here Benton spoke glowingly of young women as "natural born physicians and nurses," a fact he had seen evidenced many times in Mississippi River steamboat accidents. On the way back from Marblehead to his head-quarters at Tremont House the night of January 18, Benton was caught in a New England snowstorm. He had often praised the warm hospitality he had met in New England, and now he quipped that he liked even the climate, and would lecture in the region for another three months if he could.[14]

In Washington again by mid-February, 1857, Benton returned to his condensation of the Congressional debates, and made plans. He expected to accept some twenty invitations in upstate New York through the rest of February, and into March, and after that he wanted to go through the Midwest. All this was part of a grand, four-year plan, he confided to Martin Van Buren. He knew that "if Mr. Buchanan continues the policy of the present [Pierce] administration the Union will approach its last days." Thus he labored to prepare public opinion for 1860, when to save the Union would "require all its friends." As to Buchanan, a month from office, Benton could only say: "My position is that of friendly independence, wishing for the best, fearing a little." [15]

The New York tour kept Benton busy through February, through his seventy-fifth birthday on March 14, and into the last week of March. But after New England it was anticlimax. In New England he had been among people whose regional character and politics were much in his own mold — a character of moral fervor and striving, firm and determined, full of admiration for intelligence and learning, yet gracious withal; and a politics of opposition to slavery extension and support for the Union. At the end of March, Benton hurried to New York City to bid his daughter Susan farewell. Her diplomat husband Gauldrée de Boileau had been named French Consul General at Calcutta, India, and was leaving with Susan via New York. All the surviving members of Benton's family, his other daughters and their husbands, gathered for the farewells in a house the Frémonts had taken in Manhattan. The aging paterfamilias was never to see his youngest daughter again.

In the oncoming spring in April, Benton left for the West. He stopped first to visit with his third daughter Sarah Benton Jacob and her husband near Louisville, and then went on to St. Louis, where he visited with old friends. But the visit was brief, and he soon set out, early in May, in his role as peacemaker-lecturer again. His first stop was Chicago, where he was shown about town by Long John Wentworth, his former Congressional colleague who had recently been elected Mayor of Chicago on a Republican ticket. At Cleveland, the *Herald* interviewed Benton and reported that "his powerful mental engine is never idle." Even on a lecture tour he had "a trunk of books" with him as a traveling companion. One of his auditors at Cleveland remarked that Benton, using no notes, spoke for an hour and a half without apparent fatigue. Adding to his regular lecture, Benton expressed a growing apprehension that Buchanan was continuing Pierce's policy in Kansas. Thus Benton traveled on from St. Louis to Washington through mid-May, well received everywhere — though some "ultras" sneered at "the Union-saving business."

Toward the end of May, Benton was the victim of a railroad accident. On the train for Pittsburgh, where he was to deliver his lecture, he felt his car "hobble and jump," and then slam against the ground. The forward axle had broken, and the car had fallen on its side. Benton suffered a bleeding cut on his head, and his shirt front was covered with blood; more seriously, the seat on which he had been sitting had fallen on him, and he had suffered a painful bruise four or five inches wide across his back. He went on and made his address, despite a high fever, which required him to hold on to a chair to stay standing. Back in Washington, he was confined to his home for three weeks. Still, he labored at his worktable to meet his publisher's deadlines — "a toil not without suffering," friends noted — "his back is painful under any protracted sitting, and writing requires all the exertion of his strong will." By July, he was out riding again, sitting "gracefully" astride "the prettiest animal, a glossy black." [16] But the ill-fated Pittsburgh journey marked the end of Benton's lecture travels, and he was not to leave Washington again.

[4]

THROUGH THE HOT SUMMER OF 1857, Benton kept at his literary-historical labors. He pressed on with his *Abridgment of the Debates,* trying to supply material for an additional volume every three months. He also planned a third volume to add to his "inside" *View,* which he hoped would carry the story from 1850 to 1860, and his publishers suggested that he might do a "popular life" of Andrew Jackson. But a new explosion in politics turned him to a new project.

In March, 1857, the Supreme Court had decided the case of a slave named Dred Scott. In this action, Scott had claimed his freedom, advancing as one argument that he had been made free when his master took him into the Wisconsin-Minnesota area, where slavery had been forbidden by the Missouri Compromise of 1820. From 1846 through 1852, the issue had been before the Missouri courts. While it was there, the anti-Benton judges Birch and Napton had considered scoring an anti-Benton *coup* from the Missouri supreme bench by delivering a *"politico-legal* opinion" — to the effect that the national government had no power to legislate on slavery in the Territories, and that even the slavery-restriction provisions of the Missouri Compromise were unconstitutional. In the end, however, Scott's contention was rejected on other grounds. A new case was taken to the Federal Supreme Court in 1856, with Benton's old protégé Montgomery Blair acting as one of the attorneys for Scott, and Benton's senatorial successor Geyer serving on the other side. The nominal defendant was John F. A. Sanford, who had been recommended by Benton for the post of Indian Agent at the beginning of Jackson's first term. The case was decided against Scott, with the leading opinion written by Chief Justice Taney, Benton's one-time radical-Democratic friend and ally. Ranging beyond noncontroversial points on which the case might have been decided, Taney in *obiter dicta* offered the *"politico-legal* opinion" Birch and Napton had toyed with. In his argument, Blair had stoutly maintained the Bentonian doctrine of the power or authority of Congress to legislate concerning any matter in the Territories it fathered. On the other side, Geyer and his fellow counsel had insisted on the Calhoun doctrine that the Constitution protected slaveholders absolutely in their slave property, wherever they might go. In effect Taney chose Calhoun's view, pegging it to the property-rights clause of the Fifth Amendment. Thus he declared the Missouri Compromise restriction on slavery contrary to the Constitution, and void.

This judicial opinion immediately stirred a new conflict of interests in politics, a new storm in public opinion. Passionate protest came from opponents of slavery extension — including Lincoln in Illinois and Gratz Brown in Missouri, who fulminated that the "supreme power" (slavery) now had not only the executive and legislative branches, but the judicial branch too, "under its feet." With an advance knowledge of the result, Buchanan in his Inaugural Address had declared that the great slavery issue would be "finally settled" by the Court. Actually the opinion was substantially equal in its effect to the Kansas-Nebraska Act. It drew sectional tensions tighter, pitched political animosities higher, and gave the Republican party a new issue on which to build.[17]

The most extensive immediate attack on Taney's opinion was fired by the indefatigable Benton. Writing furiously, he prepared an exhaustive inquiry that was to extend to 130 pages of general argument plus 60 of appendices. It carried a nineteenth-century title that was an epitome: *Historical and Legal* EXAMINATION *of That Part of the Dred Scott Case Which Declares the Unconstitutionality of the Missouri Compromise Act, and the Self-Extension of the Constitution to Territories, Carrying Slavery Along With It.* Alternately analytic and polemical, sometimes brilliant, often heavy, Benton's argument in turn was an epitome of his long-settled views on the slavery-extension controversy. He limited himself strictly to the two "political subjects," the constitutionality of the Missouri Compromise and the extension of the constitutional protection over slavery to the territories. Arguing that, under the Constitution, Congress did not have "to look to judicial interpretation for its powers," Benton maintained that the Court had no authority to decide such "political subjects." And, he added, see the practical result of the Court's delivering opinions on a case it had effectively dismissed "for want of jurisdiction" — "far from settling the question, the opinion itself has become a new question, more virulent than the former!" It was based on a "great error." This was the "naked assumption, without a reason to support it, or a leg to stand upon," that the Constitution automatically protected the extension of slave property in the territories and invalidated slave-restriction legislation by Congress. The proper interpretation, Benton lectured the Court, was that "Congress exercised, and rightfully, supreme authority over these Territories," and that "it governed them independently of the Constitution," or its restrictions, "as a father does for his children." This had been the maxim of "the uniform action of all the departments of the Federal Government from its foundation," he continued, expressing his new conservatism again. The cataclysmic *obiter dicta* of the Supreme Court could not be accepted "without reversing that action, and admitting the political supremacy of the Court, and accepting an altered Constitution from its hands." Summing up, Benton remarked that he "performed an unpleasant task, but unavoidable," and invoked again the themes of harmony, the Union, and peace. He had been on "the kindest personal terms" with all the judges of the Supreme Court, but he was forced to speak, for the architect of the Missouri Compromise and the great expounder of "liberty and union" under the Constitution, Clay and Webster, were gone. Of those who had stood where they stood, "I am one of the few — no longer in power, but still in armor when the works of our fathers are in danger." [18]

Full as it was, the *Examination* was not so full as Benton had hoped it would be. While he was working on his manuscript, he was prostrated by a wracking illness, which for two weeks kept him "face to face with death." He amazed his physician, Dr. May, by rising from "what he knew I considered the bed of death (and what he feared to be so)," to go to his table and write. But he had to leave two whole topics untouched.

The "appalling attack" came early in September. First reported as "an obstinate constipation," it was later diagnosed as cancer of the bowel, a deep and painful seizure accompanied by severe paroxysms. Fearing that the illness would indeed be fatal, Benton's intimates cried out at the prospective loss of a friend, which would also be "an inexpressible calamity for the country." But by September 10, the patient could write Buchanan a polite but stiffly formal note thanking him for his solicitude, and declaring that he was "somewhat relieved from the pain." By early October, he was listed as "out of danger" and convalescent, though he himself knew that he held on to life only by a slender thread. Later in October he was able to take short walks, and finally brief rides on horseback — *and* to resume a schedule of work. Still, the disease had proved debilitating even to Benton's rugged constitution. He had not regained his flesh, his strength, or his natural buoyancy.

Soon after his first seizure, Benton wrote a last will and testament. The house on C Street and all its contents except his books were left to his eldest daughter Eliza Jones, while he left his library to his son-in-law William Carey Jones. Out of royalties received or expected from D. Appleton and Company, ten thousand dollars was to go to Eliza, five thousand to his youngest daughter Susan Boileau, and any remainder was to be divided equally among Eliza, Jessie Ann, Sarah, and Susan. His executors were to be his sons-in-law Jones, Frémont, and Jacob, aided by his Washington friends Montgomery Blair and Samuel Phillips

Lee. Before they distributed his estate, they were to pay his (unlisted) debts.[19]

It took more than one onset of illness to kill Benton, however, and he was soon doing a full day's work again. In addition, on the eve of the first meeting of Congress under Buchanan, he sought to exert some influence over that body. At the beginning of December, 1857, he asked his old friend Francis Blair to call for a talk, "as I deem it very material that right LEADS should be taken at the beginning of the session." Such "LEADS" apparently included a resolution to be introduced in Congress arraigning the Dred Scott decision as not genuinely judicial but "political," and thus "illegal and void." [20]

Through the fall of 1857, meanwhile, publication of Benton's *Examination* was anxiously awaited. In New York, Greeley's *Tribune* predicted happily that it would be "terribly severe." By November, Benton himself in a public letter announced that the "thin octavo" was in the press. He also made it the occasion of a new political testament: "FOR ONE, I CAN GIVE NO POLITICAL AID OR COMFORT TO ANY MAN OR PARTY, IN ANY FUTURE ELECTION, WHO SHALL UPHOLD THE OPINIONS OF THE SUPREME COURT," in the Dred Scott case. In St. Louis, Gratz Brown took this as an implied condemnation of Buchanan's Administration. He might have added, but did not, that the letter came very near to "voting" Republican.

The *Examination* was ready for distribution by D. Appleton and Company at the beginning of 1858. Through January, Benton wrote friends over the country, asking aid to get the book "into the hands of the masses." He had written for "a practical purpose, that of giving a rallying point to the friends of the Union." All such could find a new "unity" by opposition to the Dred Scott decision — "there is division enough, and distraction enough in the Nullification party which now commands in the Federal government and which is able to proscribe every man who is not their accomplice or instrument." Here, although in a private letter, was the severest stricture Benton had yet expressed on the Buchanan administration. The opinion of the Supreme Court portended the advance of slavery into New Mexico, the newly created Arizona Territory, Utah, "and all the Territory acquired, or to be acquired to the South." Reassertion of "the power of the people" was "only to be accomplished through the elections," for President, for state legislators who would choose Senators, and for Representatives; and Benton wanted his work to become and remain "a household book . . . until after the next [1860] presidential election." The distribution could be aided by articles in the newspapers, which he urged friends to write. But particularly he hoped friends would arrange with "some of the travelling booksellers to take [the *Examination*] with heart and spirit."

Thus, Benton approached the end of his public life as he had begun it in Tennessee and in Missouri — as an advocate and propagandist, seeking to apply a "powerful lever" to public opinion, on behalf of a cause.

By November, 1857, Benton had considered himself "well recovered," and was working as usual. He expected to finish his *Abridgment* by the next summer, and then to go to work immediately on his plan for a third volume of his *View* — "if I live that long."

Through the cold of winter, he labored steadily at his Congressional digest. Remarking that Benton kept at it through January and February and into March, 1858, the *Union* in Washington hailed the publication of the sixth volume, bringing the debates through 1821, and praised Benton for his determination "to divest himself of all previous prejudices and associations." The work was selling well, the *Union* reported, and suggested that it be placed in all the committee rooms of the Capitol as a valuable reference set. For the rest of March and into April, Benton drove himself to his task, asking that a new supply of the original records be brought to his C Street study — "for I cannot stop." [21]

He knew that he could not stop, because the month in which he had passed his seventy-sixth birthday, March, 1858, brought a return of his illness.

[5]

THE NEW ATTACK forced Benton to leave his study table for his bed — "lying down is my only practical, easy posture," he wrote Joshua Brant in St. Louis. But he converted his bedroom into a writing room, and pushed on with his "great work."

The effects of the cancer grew alternately more and less severe. Early in April, Francis Blair thought Benton "in extremis," noted that he showed a "stoicism almost superhuman," and remarked that "his patience and tenderness . . . and love for his friends increases as vitality decreases." Benton himself was pleased at his continued ability to work, and at "a returning inclination for food," although of "the simplest kind, as milk and rice, and it cold with ice." On April 4 and 5, however, he grew worse, and was kept alive and conscious only by "restoratives" administered by his physicians. Knowing that he had not long to live, he sent for a clergyman so that he might "prepare for his departure." Still he persisted with his work, and conversed cheerfully with friends who came to see him.

Plagued by financial stringencies to the end, Benton made hurried arrangements with Joshua Brant for a loan of one thousand dollars, to meet his expenses. He insisted on making this "a business transaction," with repayment forthcoming "as soon as *we,* that is, the publishers & myself can see how the spring & summer trade opens."

With him in his illness, Benton had two of his daughters and two of his sons-in-law. The news of his September attack had brought the Frémonts back from Europe to spend part of the winter in Washington, but in February, 1858, they had left for California to attend to pressing business there. Their Calcutta duty finished, the Boileaus had been recalled to Paris, where the bright Susan played the piano for the composer Rossini at his Sunday musicales. But William and Eliza Benton Jones had returned from a diplomatic appointment tendered by Buchanan, and settled at the C Street house at the end of March; and Richard and Sarah Benton Jacob came from Kentucky early in April. These four, with Jones playing major-domo, watched over Benton, admitting occasional personal and political friends to the second floor to see him.

One friend who was both personal and political was Francis Blair, who came to the sickroom on the morning of April 6. He found Benton barely able to move hands or feet, and incapable of speaking much above a whisper — but deeply concerned as always with public affairs, particularly a new development in Kansas. The proslavery extremists there had succeeded in driving through, with fraud and force and against the wishes of a majority of the settlers, a proslavery state constitution. To the consternation of the North, Buchanan had upheld this "Lecompton constitution," and in February, 1858, urged the admission of Kansas as a slave state. The result was a new disruption of the Democratic party, with the anti-Administration forces led by a chastened Stephen Douglas. Now Benton whispered to Blair that "the same men who had sought to destroy the Republic in 1850 were at the bottom of this accursed Lecompton business." Indeed, "few events in our history had given him so much satisfaction," as the defeat in Congress of the Lecompton constitution by "the intrepid and incorruptible Douglas Democrats who had resisted the power and the wiles of a corrupt and deluded Administration." Here was a culmination of Benton's increasing dissatisfaction with the Administration, a denunciation flat and direct. At least . . . so it was reported through the New York *Tribune* by Francis and Frank Blair.

Two days earlier, on Sunday, April 4, Benton had seen Lewis Cass. The Michigander, Secretary of State in Buchanan's cabinet, found Benton weak and suffering and sure he would "never recover." Alluding at once to public affairs, Benton had reminded Cass that he had supported Buchanan, and added, "he had not been disappointed and had approved the course of the Administration." At least . . . so Cass remembered the interview when he made a private memorandum of it in his almost illegible scrawl five days later.

On the evening of Friday, April 9, Buchanan himself came to the sickroom. While he conversed with the exhausted Benton, Sarah Jacob stood by. She heard her father whisper to Buchanan that they were friends, though they *had* "differed on many points"; Benton had always known "you would honestly endeavor to do right"; and, he added, "I have that faith in you now, but you must look to a Higher Power to support and guide you." At least . . . so Sarah reported the conversation four months afterwards, through her husband, who made it public.*

Throughout the days of these visits, Benton had continued to suffer. The pain from his cancer was intense, and he grew steadily weaker. Though he felt death always at his back, he labored in a last effort of high courage and dogged determination to finish his *Abridgment*. He was assisted by William Carey Jones, who collected and ordered materials and took whispered dictation from the prostrate compiler. Visitors found books and papers spread over the bed and lying on Benton's emaciated body, as well as on the little writing table at the head of the bed. Though his publishers were only up to the eighth

* Some seven years later, Buchanan recalled Benton's "kind & affectionate sentiments" with gratitude — though he could not really quite remember what they had been (Buchanan to Richard Taylor Jacob, October 28, 1845; cf. also Letters of April 21, 1866, and March 23, 1867, in Moore, *Works*, XI, 405-406, 416-417, 439). Buchanan, who was born in 1791, also prided himself on being the last survivor of the age of "Webster and Clay, of Benton and Calhoun." Though Buchanan, who died in 1868, outlived two other oldsters, Van Buren and Cass, by six and two years respectively, Francis Blair, also born in 1791, outlived Buchanan by eight years. None of these last survivors of an age played the active role in their declining years that Benton played in his.

volume, carrying the debates through 1826, Benton himself was far ahead, working on the Great Debate of 1850. Convinced that "knowledge is power! — especially political power!" and didactically determined to make the lessons of the debates "accessible (and I hope attractive) to the whole reading community," he called attention in a last public letter to Webster's and Clay's ringing defenses of the Union in the debates of June 17 and July 22, 1850. He did finish his vast compendium, by laboring through the day before his death. The posthumous publication of eight volumes brought the work to the projected sixteen volumes and through 1850. Friends and foes alike spoke of "the high, resolute Roman spirit" with which Benton labored, the "Roman fortitude" with which he faced his certain end.

On April 8, Benton wrote Sam Houston to ask that no formal notice of his death be taken in Congress, signing himself, "your old Tennessee friend." On the evening of April 9, Friday, he told his children with him that the solicitude of old contemporaries had made him happy — *"I am comfortable and content."* These were his last audible words, for the next morning, Saturday, April 10, at 7:30, he died.

Two days later, little McDowell Jones, a sprightly lad who had been a great favorite of his grandfather, fell suddenly ill and also died at the C Street house.

Funeral services were held at the house on Monday, April 12. The day had begun angry and overcast. By two in the afternoon, driving torrents of rain were falling on Washington. Still, the rites were largely attended by old friends and public figures, including Buchanan, Cass, other members of the Cabinet, foreign ministers resident in Washington, and many members of Congress. The family was represented by Eliza, Sarah, and their husbands. The father's companion of his middle years, Jessie Ann, and the darling of his later years, Susan, were still far away in California and Paris. As the mourners passed the flower-strewn coffin, they saw Thomas Benton's fine, strong expression as they had known it in the vigor of life, despite the emaciation of his illness. Beside the larger casket was a smaller one, which contained the body of McDowell Jones — "the gray-haired and the sunny-haired are sleeping side by side." A eulogy was delivered by Benton's old Presbyterian pastor, the Reverend Byron Sunderland. The measured, moving poetry of the Episcopal burial service was read by the Reverend C. H. Hall — "ashes to ashes, dust to dust . . ."

From the home Thomas, Elizabeth, and the children had loved, the two caskets were carried to the railroad station. In the gray haze of the unremitting rain, most of the mourners followed the slow progress of the dead through the streets — with the figure of Sam Houston towering above all the rest. At the station the black caskets in black shells were placed in a special car of the three o'clock train for Wheeling, the West, and St. Louis.[22]

[6]

EVEN IN DEATH, Benton was a focus of controversy. It turned not only on his general character and the part he had played in his age, but also more particularly on his deathbed evaluation of the Buchanan Administration.

At the *Tribune* in New York, Greeley offered a high estimate of Benton. The veteran Democrat's incorruptible career was the very type of exalted public service, an exemplar to rising leaders, "who, in this budding era of corruption, are likely to be tested by severer temptations than the statesmen of the past."

Others expressed less favorable reactions. Bitter to the end, ex-President Tyler snarled (privately) that no man "who had played a prominent part in the politics of his own time ever had less of the public sympathy in life or was less lamented in death," than Benton. He had "doubtless aspired to the Presidential succession after Mr. Van Buren." But because they had "thrown [themselves] on the drawn sword of the [Tyler] administration on the Texas question," both had "shared the same fate" — exclusion from the White House.

Setting aside factional animosities, the *Union* in Washington mustered praise for Benton. As a man — "of gigantic intellect, strong physical constitution, and imposing presence; of inflexible will, undaunted courage, immense application, vast erudition, capacious memory, direct manner of thought, and nervous, emphatic eloquence." In private life — "none of that sternness of character and angularity of manner that distinguished him in public. As a husband, he was tender, anxious, thoughtful, and gentle to a degree never exceeded . . . He was as devoted, affectionate, and assiduous a father as a husband." As a public figure — "a man whose name and history are as familiar as household words among the American people."

In Missouri, an old-Whig who had been nominated to oppose Benton for the Senate in 1838 offered Benton as an example to his son. Remarking that he had known many men "far superior to Mr. Benton in natural intellectual endowments," Abiel Leonard added that "this man, by the dint of untiring industry, by never-ceasing labor & an indomitable will, has accomplished much to make himself a name." [23]

Through the spring and summer of 1858, that "name" was a storm center again. Reports of Benton's deathbed interviews with rival political leaders produced a long, undignified wrangle which filled columns in the national press. *What,* the great question ran, *was Benton's political legacy — what his ultimate judgment on James Buchanan and his Administration?* On one side, the Republican Francis Blair insisted that Benton had finally become disillusioned at the President's tacks toward the South, and condemned him. On the other side William Carey Jones and Richard Taylor Jacob, still Democrats, insisted that Benton had remained friendly toward Buchanan and his Administration. Each set of protagonists collected lesser allies. Each told his story at length in the public prints, with Blair having recourse to Greeley's *Tribune* while Jones relied on the Washington *Union* and an elaborate pamphlet he issued. Admitting a long-standing hostility to the Blairs, Jones accused them of "libels" concerning Benton's last opinions to aid Frank in his campaign for re-election to Congress. Of course, Francis Blair replied, Benton would not have condemned Buchanan's course to Jones and others who like him had been "beneficiaries" of the Administration and depended upon it for further employment or favors. But he *had* made such remarks to Frank Blair and other Congressmen; he *had* drawn up a strong set of resolutions declaring the *obiter dicta* of the Dred Scott decision void, and asked Frank Blair, Hannibal Hamlin, and others to sponsor them in Congress; and he *had* expressed an ultimate disillusionment with the Administration. Not so, cried Jones — he had been present at the fateful (whispered) interview with the elder Blair, working at the bedside writing table, and had heard no such thing. And so on, with innumerable side issues being paraded to support the opposing cases.

It is possible that Benton's mind was wandering at the end. It seems more probable that he might have spoken critically of the Administration to the Republican Blair, and also have expressed hopes and generalized sentiments of friendship to the Democrats Cass and Buchanan, in deathbed charity, and in a last attempt to influence national policy.* Certainly, with his attachment to both freedom and Union, Benton could no more have supported the Lecompton constitution than he could the Dred Scott decision — and Buchanan's proslavery reactions to these two issues were the chief indices to the first year of his Administration. Indirectly in public, and directly in private but incontrovertible written expressions at the time his Dred Scott *Examination* was issued, and even before the Lecompton debate, Benton had begun to fear that the Administration was being taken over by "the Nullification party," as Pierce's regime had been.[24] Ever sanguine and ever convinced of his own potentiality, he may have hoped that a deathbed testament from him would have an effect toward reversing that trend.

[7]

IN 1815 THOMAS BENTON, thirty-three, had crossed the Mississippi River and entered the little village on its farther bank. There in St. Louis he had determined to lay "some foundation of character and fortune," and in the years that followed he had more than realized his resolution. During his long and stormy political career, the village had grown to a city of more than a hundred thousand. Now in 1858 its inhabitants put aside old animosities to honor in death one who had grown great among them.

On the afternoon of Wednesday, April 14, the caskets containing the bodies of Benton and McDowell Jones reached the railroad terminus on the Mississippi's east bank. They were taken by ferry across the still-unbridged river, and carried on to the levee, where a committee waited and a company of the National Guard stood at attention. Placed in a splendid hearse drawn by two black horses, the black caskets were carried through the streets, followed by William and Eliza Jones, Richard and Sarah Jacob, and twenty-one St. Louis pallbearers, including old friends and old political enemies alike. While crowds of people bowed their heads in sorrow and respect, the little cortege traveled the few blocks to Joshua Brant's house at Washington and Fourth. There the large and small caskets were placed for the night.

At ten the next morning, Thursday, April 15, a larger procession set out. With a military escort of the Washington Guards ahead and the Washington Blues behind, and the coffin wrapped in the red-white-and-

* This assumes, of course, that none of the disputants was guilty of outright falsification, or *total* distortion.

blue American ensign, Benton's body was carried to the spacious Mercantile Library Hall at Locust and Fifth. On a raised platform, under the brilliantly lighted central chandelier of the black-draped library hall, Benton's body lay in state. Through the afternoon and evening, and through the next morning, thousands came to look their last on the features of the honored dead. Standing by the coffin, Gratz Brown saw that these features "retained the lofty, tranquil, and gentle expression which the Hero's communion with death had left them." In his *Democrat,* he added:

> *Greatness is ended,*
> *An unsubstantial pageant all —*
> *Drop o'er the scene the funeral pall.*

Through the city, memorial meetings were held. The Merchant's Exchange announced that no business would be done in its magnificent new building on the funeral day. Homes, shops, and public buildings were draped in black, and flags in the harbor trailed at half mast. "A deep gloom settled over the Great City of the West," one of the mourners remembered — "it was evident that a mighty man had fallen."

On Friday afternoon, April 16, the funeral services and burial rites were held. From the Mercantile Library, surrounded by an immense crowd, Benton's body was carried to the Second Presbyterian Church at Walnut and Fifth, while McDowell Jones's coffin was brought from Joshua Brant's house. The sky, Gratz Brown remarked, was "mildly veiled by clouds almost tearful, as if in sympathy." In the crowded church, where Thomas had sat with bowed head to mourn his wife Elizabeth three years before, the Reverend Messrs. Brooks, Schuyler, and Cowan performed the funeral services. Outside, a silent and ever-augmenting throng crowded windows, balconies, roofs, terraces, steps, and every foot of the sidewalks. At 2:30 the long Presbyterian services were over. Another procession formed for the final journey to Bellefontaine Cemetery on the outskirts of the city. A hearse with McDowell Jones' coffin went first, followed by six black horses decked with sable plumes drawing another hearse which carried Benton's body. After it came the pallbearers, the family, relatives, and close friends, the arrangements committee, the judges of the local courts, members of the bar, the mayor and the city councilors, members of the school board on which Benton had once served, fraternal orders and fire companies, with military groups and bands interspersed at intervals through the whole. In all, the cortege stretched out for two miles. Everywhere along the route there were immense crowds, more than forty thousand people in all. Old friends and old foes of Benton stood side by side, pervaded with feelings of awe and reverence. Men and women wept like children. Hundreds of watchers fell in spontaneously behind the procession, walking in pairs or driving in carriages. Through the streets decked with flags draped in black, to the accompaniment of funereal music, the long line made its way to the burial lot where Thomas's mother Nancy, his wife Elizabeth, and his sons Randolph and McDowell already lay. Meanwhile, trains shuttled back and forth carrying more military companies from the city to the cemetery.

In late afternoon, at the Bellefontaine Cemetery eminence, the final brief services were said. Under the misting, veiled sky, on the sunset side of the broad Mississippi, Thomas Benton at last found repose as his body was lowered into the grave with his gentle grandchild beside him. Thus, together, "the child and the great man were laid to rest." [25]

Long after the hero's funeral, remembering Benton in life, and remembering him in death, one of his personal and political friends lamented:

"Alas! when will Missouri have another Benton?"

Evidence and Authorities

All particular statements, and all general or interpretive hypotheses in this study, have been made with careful reference to available evidence and authorities. Actual reference notes, however, have been kept to a minimum in the published volume.

With the exception of first citations of journal articles, short titles have been used throughout in the reference notes. Full names of authors, full titles, places and dates of publication, and the like, are given in the classified list of Sources. The following abbreviation forms for items frequently cited have been used:

AC, x/y	*Annals of Congress,* Congress/Session.
CG, x/y	*Congressional Globe,* Congress/Session.
Duke	Duke University Library, Durham.
LofC	Library of Congress, Washington.
MoHS	Missouri Historical Society, St. Louis. Not to be confused with Missouri State Historical Society, Columbia.
PHS	Pennsylvania Historical Society, Philadelphia.
RD, x/y	*Register of Debates,* Congress/Session.
UVa	Alderman Library, University of Virginia, Charlottesville.

CHAPTER NOTES

CHAPTER 1

1. Cf. Jesse Benton to Thomas Hart, April 3, 1786, in Thomas J. Clay Papers, LofC.
2. For Samuel Benton: Boyd, "Some North Carolina Tracts of the Eighteenth Century," and Sims, "An Address to the People of Granville County," June 6, 1765, in *North Carolina Historical Review,* III (Jan-

uary, 1926), 54, 62-65; Tilley, "Political Disturbances in Colonial Granville County," in *Ibid.*, XVIII (October,, 1941), 340, 342, 353, 357; Saunders and Clark, *Colonial and State Records of North Carolina*, V, 591; VI, 343, 399, 405, 1157-1158; XXIII, 626, 627; also Will of Samuel Benton, February 18, 1770, in Wills, Granville County 1746-1771, Oxford, North Carolina; Henderson, *North Carolina*, I, 522; II, 40.

3. For Jesse Benton: Thomas H. Benton, "Auto-Biographical Sketch," i; Indenture of the Watauga Purchase, March 19, 1775, Register of Washington County, Jonesboro, Tennessee; Henderson, *North Carolina*, I, 270-272, 382; Letters of Jesse Benton to Thomas Hart, 1780-1790, in Thomas J. Clay Papers, LofC; Inventory of the Estate of Jesse Benton for the Year 1781, in Jesse Benton Papers, North Carolina Department of Archives and History, Raleigh; Clark, *Records*, XVII, 883, 886-887, 947; XIX, 392; Jessie Benton Frémont, "Biographical Sketch of Senator Benton," in John Charles Frémont, *Memoirs of My Life*, I, 2, 3, and "Senator Thomas H. Benton," in *Independent*, LV, (January 29, 1903), 241.

4. Young, *Genealogical Narrative of the Hart Family in the United States*, 4, 5; Nash, *Hillsboro*, 8, 15-16, 38; Letters of Jesse Benton to Thomas Hart, 1780-1790, in Thomas Clay Papers, LofC; Frémont, "Biographical Sketch," 3.

5. For the period 1782-1790: Benton, "Auto-Biographical Sketch," i; Frémont, "Biographical Sketch," 3, 4, and "Senator Thomas H. Benton," 243; Will of Jesse Benton, State Department of Archives and History, Raleigh; Moore, *Some Memories of My Life*, 8; Nash, *Hillsboro*, 5-6, 89; List of Jesse Benton's Taxable Property, 1788, in Orange County Records, State Department of Archives and History, Raleigh; Clark, *Records*, XXVI, 1312; Jesse Benton to Thomas Hart, December 4, 1782, March 22, August 23, 1783; June 20, 1784; April 3, 1786, Undated (1790?); and Nancy Benton to Thomas Hart, September 25, 1792 — in Thomas J. Clay Papers; Benton, *View*, I, 736; James, *Life of Andrew Jackson*, 37; *CG*, 33/2, 998; Memorandum of Jesse Benton, January 8, 1790; and Receipt, Isaac Roberts to Jesse Benton, September 4, 1790 — in Jesse Benton Papers, LofC; also *Fayetteville Gazette*, January 10, 1791.

6. Bond of Nancy Benton to Thomas Hart, October 26, 1791; Nancy Benton to Thomas Hart, April 25, 1792; Bond of Nancy Benton to Thomas Hart, August 12, 1792; and John Umstead to Thomas Hart, October 24, 1791 — all in Thomas J. Clay Papers, LofC. Also Lists of Taxable Property, Orange County, 1752-1798, State Department of Archives and History, Raleigh.

7. For the period 1790-1798: Benton, "Auto-Biographical Sketch," i-ii; Frémont, "Biographical Sketch," 3-4; "Remarks of Thomas H. Benton," in *National Intelligencer*, December 25, 1856; *RD*, 21/1, 113; article signed OLDCASTLE [Benton], in *Impartial Review and Cumberland Repository* (Nashville), July 14, 1808.

8. Battle, *History of the University of North Carolina*, I, 35, 51, 60, 61,

168-169, 194-195; Faculty Records, 1799-1814, manuscript, University of North Carolina.

9. Manuscript Note, n. d., in Miscellaneous Philanthropic Society Papers, University of North Carolina; Battle, *History*, I, 72-74; H——, "About Thomas H. Benton," in *Charlotte Democrat*, October 1, 1880.

10. Statements at an Investigation, 1799, in Faculty Records, University of North Carolina.

11. Statement of Saunders, Baker, and Cherry, March 19, 1799, Faculty Records, and Manuscript Note, n. d., in Miscellaneous Philanthropic Society Papers, University of North Carolina.

12. Ehrhardt, "Expelled from North Carolina University on Theft Charge, Boy Becomes U. S. Senator," in *News and Observer* (Raleigh), February 5, 1928.

13. Statement of Thomas King, September 1, 1799, in Faculty Records, University of North Carolina.

CHAPTER 2

1. John Umstead to Thomas Hart, August 7, 1800, in Thomas J. Clay Papers, LofC; Tax Book, Williamson County, Tennessee, Franklin, I, 31, 75. Cf. Abernethy, *From Frontier to Plantation in Tennessee*, 144-146, 155, 157 ff., 198.

2. Benton, "Auto-Biographical Sketch," ii; Kossuth R. Plummer to Francis Preston Frémont, April 20, 1918, in Frémont Papers, Bancroft Library, Berkeley; Meigs, *Benton*, 46.

3. Cf. Benton, in *RD*, 21/1, 103; Meigs, *Benton*, 48; and Frémont, "Biographical Sketch," 5.

4. Frémont, "Senator Thomas H. Benton," 241; cf. Ramsey, *The Annals of Tennessee*, 501, 503, 507; and Recollections of Dr. George B. Hunter of Leiper's Fork, quoted in Meigs, *Benton*, 47.

5. Minute Book, Superior Court of Law and Equity, District of Mero, Nashville, II, 513-514; Benton, *View*, I, 736.

6. Tax Book, Williamson County, I, 29-49, 73-93, 75, 96, 118 ff.; Benton, "Auto-Biographical Sketch," ii.

7. Benton to Hardemans, Duck River, December 10, 1804 — copy in Benton Papers, MoHS; original in Possession of Mrs. Glen Owen Hardeman, Gray Summit, Missouri.

8. Minute Book, Superior Court, District of Mero, IV, 28, 53, 57, 58.

9. Benton, "Auto-Biographical Sketch," ii; Minute Book, County Court of Williamson County, I, 206, *passim;* Benton, "A Memoir of Edward Hempstead, Written in 1818," in Washburne, *Historical Sketch of Charles S. Hempstead*, 26; Foote, *Bench and Bar of the South and Southwest*, 161; *Impartial Review*, September 24, 1807.

10. Benton, *View*, I, iv, II, 569; Notebook, in Benton Documents, Miscellaneous Manuscript Files, Missouri State Historical Society.

11. *Impartial Review*, December 6, 1806, and January 3 and May 9, 1807;

also articles signed SIR JOHN OLDCASTLE [Benton], April 14 and May 12 ff., 1808.

12. Minute Book, Superior Court of Law and Equity, District of Mero, IV, 340, 410; Foote, *Bench and Bar,* 162-163; Benton, *View,* I, 736.

13. Cf. Susan Benton to Jesse Benton, "Bon Ton [?] Hall," October 22, 1810, in Jesse Benton Papers, LofC; Will of Nancy Benton, January 19, 1807, in Wills and Inventories, Williamson County, I, 28-29; and Frémont, "Biographical Sketch," 5.

14. Minute Book, Superior Court, District of Mero, III, 428, 433; and IV, 203, 399; and of County Court of Williamson County, I, 303; *Impartial Review,* December 3, 1807; Tax Book, Williamson County, I, 96, 118, 221, 222, 262 ff. Cf. Benton to Hart, March 14, 1807, in Benton Papers, MoHS; and fragment of a letter by Benton, in Miscellaneous Papers, New York Public Library.

15. Benton to Clay, June 22, 1813, in Henry Clay Papers; Abernethy, *From Frontier to Plantation in Tennessee,* 134-135, 209, 227-228, 351-352, *passim.*

16. [Benton], "Sir John Oldcastle's Remarks on the Judiciary of the State of Tennessee," in *Impartial Review,* 1808 — February 11, 18, 25; March 3, 10, 17, 31; April 14; May 5, 12.

17. Gresham, "Hugh Lawson White as a Tennessee Politician and Banker," *East Tennessee Historical Society Publications* (1946), 26-29.

18. "Sir John Oldcastle's Remarks," in *Impartial Review,* 1808 — May 12, 26; June 9; July 14.

19. *Impartial Review,* 1808 — May 5; June 23, 30; July 7, 14, 21, 28; August 4, 18.

20. Benton, *View,* I, 104-106; cf. Bogart and Kemmerer, *Economic History of the American People,* 339-346.

21. For Benton in the Tennessee Assembly: *Journal of the Senate of the State of Tennessee,* 8 Assembly, 1 Session, 3, 4, 5, 9, 11, 17, 18, 22, 35, 84, 87, 93, 110, 153, 160-161, 167, 181, 184, 187, 195-196, 199; *Acts Passed at the First Session of the Eighth General Assembly of the State of Tennessee,* 34-35, 42, 63-74, 148, 151-153; cf. also *CG,* 31/2, 360, and Benton to Van Buren, [1828], in Benton Papers, Personal Miscellany, LofC.

22. Minute Book, County Court of Williamson County, I, 468, 496, 539, 545, 572, 510; Minutes of the Circuit Court, Maury County, I, 116-118; Notebook, in Benton Documents, Missouri State Historical Society.

23. *Ibid.,* entry August, 1811, *passim.*

24. *Democratic Clarion* — November 2, 23, and 30, 1810; May 21, 1811; March 2, 1813; also Benton, *View,* I, 736; Parks, *Felix Grundy,* 92-93; Parton, *Life of Andrew Jackson,* I, 344; Buell, *History of Andrew Jackson,* I, 237.

25. Susan Benton to Jesse Benton, "Bon Ton [?] Hall," October 22, 1810, in Jesse Benton Papers, LofC.

26. Tax Book, Williamson County, I, 262, 343, 345, 420.

27. Frémont, "Biographical Sketch," 5, 6, and "Senator Thomas H. Benton,"

241; Plummer to Francis Preston Frémont, April 20, 1918, in Frémont Papers, Bancroft Library, Berkeley.

28. Wills and Inventories, Williamson County, II, 91-93; Benton to Childress, September 11, 1846, in Jesse Benton Papers, LofC.

CHAPTER 3

1. Benton to Jackson, January 30, 1812, in Jackson Papers, LofC.
2. [Benton], *Addresses on the Presentation of the Sword of Gen. Andrew Jackson to the Congress*, 32-33; Grundy to Jackson, February 12, 1812, in Bassett, *Correspondence of Andrew Jackson*, I, 215; Commission Book, 1807-1812, manuscript, Tennessee State Archives, Nashville, 266.
3. *Democratic Clarion*, 1812 — May 19, 23; July 4, 8; also William P. Anderson to John Coffee, May 19, 1812, in Coffee Papers, Dyas Collection, Tennessee Historical Society.
4. Benton to Jackson, July 4, 1812, in Jackson Papers; and to Clay, October 2, 1812, in Henry Clay Papers — both LofC.
5. Benton, "Auto-Biographical Sketch," iii; *Democratic Clarion*, November 23, 1812; General Orders, Hermitage, November 23, 1812, in Bassett, *Correspondence*, I, 242-243; Fagg, "Thomas Hart Benton," in *Missouri Historical Review*, I (October, 1906), 23.
6. *Democratic Clarion*, December 15 and 22, 1812.
7. Benton to Jackson, "Robertson's Landing," January 9, 1813, in *Democratic Clarion*, January 19, 1813.
8. [Benton], "Journal of a Voyage from Nashville, Ten. to New Orleans in the winter of the year 1813," in the *Clarion*, February 9, and 16, also March 9, 1813. (With the February 9 issue, the name of the *Democratic Clarion* was changed to the *Clarion*.)
9. Benton to Jackson, "Some Miles above New Madrid," February 1, 1813, in Jackson Papers, LofC; also Jackson to James Wilkinson, February 16, 1813; John Armstrong to Jackson, Washington, February 5, 1813; and Jackson to Armstrong, March 15, 1813 — all in Basset, *Correspondence*, I, 275, 276, 291; [Benton], *Addresses on the Sword*, 35-36.
10. *Clarion*, March 30, 1813; Frémont, "Biographical Sketch," 1, 2, 6.
11. Statement of William Quarles, Nashville, July 21, 1813, in Jackson Papers, Chicago Historical Society; also *Clarion*, April 27, 1813.
12. *Clarion*, February 23, 1813; Exchange of Letters, Benton and Lewis, April 22, 23, 26, 27, 1813, in *Clarion*, May 5, 1813; Duel Correspondence Circular, April, 1813, copy in Benton Papers, MoHS.
13. Jackson to Armstrong, May 10, 1813, in Bassett, *Correspondence*, I, 307; also [Benton], *Addresses on the Sword*, 37.
14. Benton to Jackson, June 15, 1813, in Jackson Papers, LofC; *Complete Regular Army Register of the United States . . . 1779 to 1879*, 121, 167, 191; Benton to Armstrong, June 20, 1813, National Archives, Washington.
15. Cf. Fuess, *Daniel Webster*, I, 137-138, 141-142, 146, 148-175; Benton, in *RD* 21/1, 109-110, and in *CG*, 25/2, Appendix 216.

16. Benton to Clay, June 22, 1813, in Henry Clay Papers, LofC.
17. William Carroll to Jesse Benton and Jesse Benton to Carroll, June 11 and 12, 1813; Carroll to A. J. Donelson, October 4, 1824 — in Bassett, *Correspondence*, I, 311, 312; also *Clarion*, June 15, 1813.
18. Benton to Jackson, July 25, 1813, in Jackson Papers, LofC; Andrew Hynes to Jackson and Jackson to Benton, July 16, 19, [28], 1813, in Bassett, *Correspondence*, I, 309-310, 314; Statement of Lemuel P. Montgomery, n.p., n. d., in Jackson Papers, Chicago Historical Society.
19. "Account of a Duel with General Jackson," circular by Benton, September 10, 1813, Tennessee Historical Society; Certificate of James W. Sitler, Nashville, September 5, 1813, in Bassett, *Correspondence*, I, 317; Parton, *Jackson*, I, 394-398; James, *Jackson*, 153.
20. Letter From Benton, n.d., quoted in Parton, *Jackson*, I, 395-396; Benton to Carroll and Carroll to Benton, September 16, 1813, in Jackson Papers, Second Series, LofC.
21. Benton to William P. Anderson, November 22, 1813, in Coffee Papers, Dyas Collection, Tennessee Historical Society; General Orders of Andrew Jackson, September 19, 1813, and Jackson to Willie Blount, November 4, 1813, and to John Armstrong, November 21, 1813, in Bassett, *Correspondence*, I, 319-320, 341, 356.
22. *Clarion*, May 10, June 14 and August 23, 1814; Benton to the Adjutant General, National Archives, and to General Flournoy, July 5, 1814, in Jackson Papers, Benton to Governor Holmes, July 8, 1814, in Benton Papers, Personal Miscellany, LofC; George H. Nixon to Jackson, July 19, 1814, in Jackson Papers, Chicago Historical Society.
23. Benton to Jackson, September 2, 11, 1814, in Jackson Papers, LofC; Thomas L. Butler to Benton, September 12, 13, 15, 1814, and Jackson to Robert Butler, September 17, 1814, in Bassett, *Correspondence*, II, 47-50.
24. James, *Jackson*, 180; Proclamation to the People of Louisiana, September 21, 1814, in Bassett, *Correspondence*, II, 57; Benton to Colonel Hayne, October 4, 10, 1814, and to Jackson, September 28, 1814, in Jackson Papers, LofC; Benton to Jackson, September 18, 1814, in Jackson Papers, Chicago Historical Society; Military Order, Benton, September 20, 1814, in Benton Papers, Personal Miscellany, LofC; Military Order, Benton, September 22, 1814, in Benton Letters, PHS.
25. Benton and Others, to the Adjutant General, October 25, 1814, Jackson Papers, LofC; letter to Benton, October [26], 1814, in Bassett, *Correspondence*, II, 65-66.
26. Memorandum to the Adjutant General, by Benton, January 23, 1815, National Archives; Benton, "Auto-Biographical Sketch," iii; *Niles Weekly Register*, VII (February 18, 1815), 385.
27. Benton to Preston, St. Louis, November 14, 1819, in Preston Papers, Virginia Historical Society; Lamb, " 'Smithfield,' Home of the Prestons," *Virginia Magazine of History and Biography*, XLVII (April, 1939), 110, 124; Sally Miller, "James McDowell," *Washington and Lee University Historical Papers*, V, 49; Morton, *A History of Rockbridge County*,

Virginia, 264, 265. Cf. Nathaniel Hart to Francis Preston, May 13, 1802, in Carrington-McDowell Family Papers, LofC.

28. *Death and Obsequies of Mrs. Elizabeth McDowell Benton,* Pamphlet, Missouri State Historical Society, 2, 8; Benton to Nancy Benton, December 13, 1820, Benton Papers, MoHS; Benton, "Auto-Biographical Sketch," vi; Frémont, *Memoirs of My Life,* I, 67.

CHAPTER 4

1. Benton to James P. Preston, November 14, 1819, in Preston Papers, Virginia Historical Society; Flint, *Recollections,* 110; Beck, *A Gazetteer of the States of Illinois and Missouri,* 326.
2. Benton to William C. Preston, April 27, 1817, in Preston Papers; National Park Service, *Map . . . Showing the Location of Various Historic Sites and Buildings,* 8; Missouri Historical Society, "Earliest Picture of St. Louis," in *Glimpses of the Past,* VIII (1941), 7-9; Benton to McDowell, November 5, 1815, McDowell Family Papers, UVa.
3. Benton, "Auto-Biographical Sketch," iii-iv; "Roll of Attorneys Taken from the Records for the Year 1815 to 1849," Bound Manuscript Volume, Circuit Court for the City of St. Louis; Grissom, "Personal Recollections," *Missouri Historical Review,* XVIII (January, 1924), 141; *Charless' Missouri and Illinois Magazine Almanac, for 1818;* Didier, "Thomas H. Benton as a Lawyer," *Green Bag,* XVIII (November, 1906), 585; Shields, "The Old Bar of St. Louis," in Stewart, *The History of the Bench and Bar of Missouri,* 109-110.
4. Flint, *Recollections,* 184.
5. Violette, "Spanish Land Claims in Missouri," *Washington University Studies, Humanistic Series,* VIII, 168, 172, 175, 177, 183-187; cf. *Missouri Gazette,* 1815-1819, esp. August 7, 1818; also Lucas to Robert Moore, January 5, 1820; to John Quincy Adams, January 24, 1823; to Rufus King, November 14, 1823; to Walter Lowrie, n. d. — all in Lucas, *Letters of Hon. John B. C. Lucas,* 39, 74, 153, 213; Darby, *Personal Recollections,* 30-32; *Land Claims in Missouri,* 24 Congress, 1 Session, House Document 270, 132-160. Cf. William Russell to Rufus Easton [Spring or Summer, 1817], Rufus Easton Papers, MoHS.
6. *Missouri Gazette,* January 25, 1817.
7. Minutes of the Circuit Court, St. Louis, I, 14-21; *Missouri Gazette,* November 1, 1817; Statement by Charles Lucas, August 11, 1817; Benton to Lucas, and Lucas to Benton, November 15, 1816 — all in Lucas Papers, MoHS.
8. Flint, *Recollections,* 184.
9. Frémont, "Biographical Sketch," 29; Darby, *Recollections,* 5-6, 10-11; Flint, *Recollections,* 176, 201, 210; *Missouri Gazette,* 1815, June 17; July 1; August 19; Beck, *Gazetteer,* 185-186, 202; Fagg, "Thomas Hart Benton," 24.
10. Cf. Benton to James P. Preston, May 17, 1817, in Preston Papers; Benton to Robert Wash, March 14, 1821, in Benton Papers, MoHS; *Missouri*

Gazette, November 1, 1817; Billon, *Annals,* II, 67, 194-195, 240-242, 254-255; Scharf, *History of St. Louis,* II, 1474-1475; Frémont, "Biographical Sketch," 8.

11. Rules of the Meeting between J. Barton and T. Hempstead, August 10, 1816, and Statement of Meeting between Hempstead and Barton, August 13, 1816 — both in Benton Papers, MoHS.

12. Benton to James P. Preston, May 17, 1817, in Preston Papers; cf. Jessie Benton Frémont, *Souvenirs of My Time,* 148 ff., and "Biographical Sketch," 7; Paxton, *St. Louis Directory and Register* (1821); Billon, *Annals,* II, 195; and *Missouri Gazette,* March 23, 1816.

13. Benton to William C. Preston, April 27, 1817, in Preston Papers, Virginia Historical Society; *Missouri Gazette,* August 16, 1817; Benton, "A Memoir of Edward Hempstead," 22; Burial Records, Bellefontaine Cemetery, St. Louis.

14. Portrait of Thomas Hart Benton, Oil, 1817, MoHS.

15. For the Missouri political situation: *Missouri Gazette,* August 3, 1816, and 1815-1819, *passim;* Scharf, *History of St. Louis,* II, 1408-1410; especially William Russell to Rufus Easton [spring or summer, 1817] in Rufus Easton Papers, MoHS. A careful analysis of this twelve-page, confidential letter throws an immense light on the actual politics of the day.

16. "Adele de P. Gratiot's Narrative," *Collections of the State Historical Society of Wisconsin,* 265; Proceedings of the First Meeting of the Board of Trustees for Schools in St. Louis, April 4, 1817, Schools Collection, MoHS; Billon, *Annals,* II, 104; Bay, *Bench and Bar,* 3. Unfortunately no file of the *Western Emigrant* is available today.

17. For the first duel and its aftermath: Washburne, *Historical Sketch of Charles S. Hempstead,* 6, 8; Statement by Charles Lucas, Lucas Papers; Lucas to Benton, Benton Papers; Benton to Lucas, Duels Envelope, "Articles Regulating the Terms of a Personal Interview between Benton and Lucas," in Benton Papers — all August 11, 1817, MoHS; also *Missouri Gazette,* 1817 — September 18, 20, 23; October 4; November 1; also John B. C. Lucas to William Lucas, August 18, 1817, in Lucas, *Letters,* 6-7; Lawless to Charles Lucas, August 29, 1819, in Lucas Papers — September 26, 1817, Duels Envelope, MoHS; and Soulard, "The Bloody Island Cross Mark," in *St. Louis-Globe Democrat,* June 25, 1899.

18. For the second duel and its aftermath: Charles Lucas to Benton, September 26, 1817, in Lucas Papers, "Terms of a Personal Interview between Benton Demanding and Lucas Answering," n. d., in Benton Papers, Certificate of Conduct of Lucas-Benton Duel, September 27, 1817, in Lucas Papers, and "Address by Thomas T. Gantt, Based on an Account by Luke E. Lawless," March 14, 1882, Newspaper Clipping, MoHS; *Missouri Gazette,* 1817 — September 27; October 4, 1, 8; November 15; December 27; and July 12, 1820; also John B. C. Lucas to Jason Chamberlin, October 17, 1817; to William Carroll, December 13, 1817; and to John Quincy Adams, January 4, 1821 — all in Lucas, *Letters,* 19-20, 25-26, 65; Cf. Benton, "Auto-Biographical Sketch," v.

19. Indenture from Thomas H. Benton to Jesse Benton, May 18, 1818, in

Jesse Benton Papers, LofC; Benton to James P. Preston, May 20, 1818, Benton Papers, Virginia Historical Society; Original and General Records, St. Louis, F, 289, H, 538; *Missouri Gazette,* September 18, 1818; also May 26 and June 2, 1819.

20. *Missouri Gazette,* October 28, 1815, and November 27, 1818; also John B. C. Lucas to William Lucas, October 12, 1817, in Lucas, *Letters,* 18. Cf. Catterall, *Second Bank of the United States,* 18-21; Walters, "Origins of the Second Bank of the United States," *Journal of Political Economy,* LIII (June, 1945), 115-131; Brown, "Stephen Girard, Promoter of the Second Bank of the United States," *Journal of Economic History,* II (November, 1942), 126-132; Bogart and Kemmerer, *Economic History,* 321, 322.

21. For the Bank of St. Louis: *Missouri Gazette,* 1818 — February 20; March 6, 13; April 24; September 4, 11, 18; and July 21, 1819; also Minutes of the Circuit Court, St. Louis, I, 148-149; Cable, *Bank of the State of Missouri,* 47, 52-54.

22. Benton to James P. Preston, November 14, 1819, in Preston Papers, Virginia Historical Society.

CHAPTER 5

1. Benton to James P. Preston, May 20, 1818, in Preston Collection, Virginia Historical Society; Benton to Edwards, October 27, 1818, in Edwards Papers, Chicago Historical Society.

2. *Missouri Gazette,* August 7, 1818, and January 1, 1819; Billon, *Annals,* II, 104; *Map . . . Showing Historic Sites and Buildings; St. Louis Enquirer,* April 21, 28, 1819 (no complete file of the *Enquirer* is known, and the earliest issues appear to be lost). Cf. Alexis de Tocqueville, *Democracy in America,* II, 119 ff.

3. *St. Louis Enquirer,* June 23, 1819; Beck, *Gazetteer,* 325.

4. Benton, *Selections of Editorial Articles from the St. Louis Enquirer, on the Subject of Oregon and Texas,* 4-8, 12-14, 18-23, 26-27 (references to this series are to this pamphlet, because it is apparently complete, and not to the files of the *Enquirer,* which are incomplete). Cf. Bemis, *John Quincy Adams and the Foundations of American Foreign Policy,* 329-340.

5. *Missouri Gazette,* June 23, 1819.

6. *Niles Weekly Register,* XIV (April 25-August 22, 1818), 141, 153, 180, 194, 225, 242, 273, 313, 329, 377, 396, 428; *St. Louis Enquirer,* 1819 — April 21, 28; May 26; June 9, 16; July 14, 21, 28; August 4, 25; September 15; December 15. Cf. Catterall, *Second Bank,* 22-50, 68-92, 501-503.

7. *St. Louis Enquirer,* August 11, 1819, and January 24, and February 16, 1820; Dorsey, "The Panic of 1819 in Missouri," in *Missouri Historical Review,* XXIX (January, 1935), 80-81; *Missouri Gazette,* February 16, 1820.

8. *St. Louis Enquirer,* June 16, 1819. The entire program as summarized in this section appeared in the *Enquirer* for this date.

9. *Enquirer,* October 27, 1819.

10. *Enquirer,* August 11, 1819; Benton to James P. Preston, November 14, 1819, in Preston Papers, Virginia Historical Society; to Mathew Carey and Son, May 2, 1819, in Benton Letters, PHS; to Ninian Edwards, July 26, 1819, in Edwards Papers, Chicago Historical Society; Original and General Records, St. Louis, H, 465; I, 3, 538; K, 106; B2, 170; also Covenant, M. P. Leduc, H. Papin, T. H. Benton, S. Benton, October 18, 1819, in Benton Papers, MoHS.

11. Cable, *Bank of Missouri,* 58, 62-63, 67, 69; *American State Papers:* . . . *on Finance,* III, 720, 747; List of Stockholders, Bank of Missouri, August 4, 1821, unsigned manuscript in Julius S. Walsh Collection, Benton to Clay, August 24, 1821, in Benton Papers, MoHS; Billon, *Annals,* II, 89; Shoemaker, *Missouri and Missourians,* I, 497. Cf. John B. C. Lucas to J. W. Taylor, December 20, 1822, in Lucas, *Letters,* 280.

12. *Missouri Gazette,* July 21, 25, 1819. Because the files of the *Enquirer* are not complete, it is necessary in this instance to reconstruct developments in the *Enquirer* from their reflections in the *Gazette.*

13. Frémont, *Souvenirs,* 142-143; Original and General Records, St. Louis, H, 361; I, 126; *Benton* vs. *O'Fallon,* in *8 Missouri Reports 650.*

14. Cf. Shoemaker, *Missouri's Struggle for Statehood,* 115; *St. Louis En-quirer,* 1819 — April 7, 14, 19, 28; June 9.

15. *Ibid.,* May 19, June 25, July 14, 1819. Cf. McCandless, *Thomas H. Benton, His Source of Political Strength in Missouri from 1815 to 1838,* 21, 25.

16. Cf. Van Ravenswaay, "Tragedy of David Barton," in *Bulletin of the Missouri Historical Society,* VII (October, 1950), 38-39, 42; *Missouri Gazette,* 1819-1820, especially April 12, 1820; and *St. Louis Enquirer,* 1819-1820, especially April 24, 1820.

17. *Enquirer,* 1819 — July 14, 28; December 8; and 1820 — March 29, May 31; also *Missouri Gazette,* 1819 — July 7, 21; August 11, 18, 21, 25.

18. Benton to Scott, January 15, 1820, Miscellaneous Manuscript Files, Missouri State Historical Society.

19. *Missouri Gazette,* 1819 — March 24, 31; April 7, 14, 21, 28; May 5, 12, 19; June 9, 23, 30; August 2; November 3; *St. Louis Enquirer,* July 21, 1819.

20. Cf. Adams, *Memoirs of John Quincy Adams, Comprising Parts of His Diary,* V, 5; *St. Louis Enquirer,* 1820 — March 29; April 26; May 6, 10; and *Missouri Gazette,* April 29, 1820.

21. *St. Louis Enquirer,* June 14, 1820; *Missouri Gazette,* July 12, 1820; Benton, *View,* I, 8-9.

22. *Missouri Gazette,* June 28 and July 12, 1820; *St. Louis Enquirer,* 1820 — July 5, 12, 19, 22, 26; August 5, 9, 26; Benton to Scott, August 30, 1820, photostat in Benton Papers, MoHS.

23. Scott to Cook, September 18, 1820, and to Barton, September 19, 1820,

in *Missouri Republican,* August 21, 1822; William Christy to Thomas A. Smith, September 21, 1820, in Thomas A. Smith Manuscripts, Missouri State Historical Society; Squires, "A New View of the Election of Barton and Benton," in *Missouri Historical Review,* XXVII (October, 1932), 38.

24. Darby, *Recollections,* 32-33; Squires, "A New View of the Election of Barton and Benton," 45; Lucas to Robert Moore, October 27, 1820, in Lucas, *Letters,* 32.

25. *House Journal,* 1 Assembly, 1 Session, 34-38; *St. Louis Enquirer,* November 4, 1820. Cf. McCandless, *Benton, His Source of Political Strength,* 35-36, 40-41.

CHAPTER 6

1. Nathaniel Watkins to Clay, October 6, 1820, in Thomas J. Clay Papers, LofC; *CG,* 26/1, Appendix 118; Benton, *View,* I, 5-6; Reznêck, "Depression of 1819-1822," in *American Historical Review,* XXXIX (October, 1933), 30-33, 47.

2. Benton to Nancy Benton, December 13, 1820, in Benton Papers, MoHS; and to Mrs. Nancy Preston, n. d., in *Death and Obsequies of Mrs. Elizabeth McDowell Benton,* 2.

3. For Washington and Benton's initiation there: Adams, *Memoirs,* V, 128; *Congressional Directory* (1820), 41; Sargent, *Public Men and Events,* I, 52-55; *Missouri Gazette,* December 21, 1820; letter by Margaret Bayard Smith, in Hunt, *First Forty Years of Washington Society,* 145-146; Lucas to Robert Moore, October 27, 1820, and to Adams, January 4, 1821 — both in Lucas, *Letters,* 30-32, 65.

4. Docket, Supreme Court of the United States, C, 1159; Letters in Carter, *Territorial Papers of the United States . . . Louisiana-Missouri 1815-1821,* 683, 687, 689, 706; *United States Magazine and Democratic Review,* I (October-December, 1837), 83; Louis McLane to Mrs. McLane, January 12, 182[1], owned by Mrs. George Batchelder, Beverly, Massachusetts; Williams to Thomas A. Smith, January 7, 1821, Smith Manuscripts, Missouri State Historical Society.

5. *St. Louis Enquirer,* quoted in *Niles Register,* XIX (February 3, 1821), 571-572. Cf. Benton, *Abridgment of the Debates of Congress,* VI, 712, footnote.

6. For the wedding and wedding trip: Benton to Robert Wash, March 14, 1821, MoHS; Miller, "James McDowell," 51-52; Record of Marriages, 1782-1830, Office of the County Court Clerk, Lexington, Virginia; Benton to James P. Preston, March 20, 1821, Preston Papers, Virginia Historical Society; Benton to James McDowell, April 21, 1821, and Sarah McDowell to James McDowell, July 4, 1821, McDowell Family Papers, UVa; Frémont, "Biographical Sketch," 7; Bay, *Bench and Bar,* 13.

7. Dorsey, "Panic of 1819 in Missouri," 81-85, 91; Hamilton, "Relief Movement in Missouri," in *Missouri Historical Review,* XXII (October, 1927), 63, 65-66, 78, 83, 87. Cf. *Missouri Republican,* June 27, 1825,

and McCandless, *Benton, His Source of Political Strength*, 78-81; also Thomas H. Riddick to William H. Crawford, August 24, 1821, in *American State Papers: Finance*, IV, 758, and III, 720. Cf. also Lucas to J. W. Taylor, December 20, 1822, in Lucas, *Letters*, 280; and [Bates], *Edward Bates Against Thomas Benton*, 10.

8. Original and General Records, St. Louis, I, 178; Benton to Clay, August 24, 1821, in Benton Papers, MoHS.

9. Benton to John Preston, November 21, December 1, 1821, in Benton Papers, MoHS.

10. Benton to James P. Preston, December 16, 1821, in Preston Papers, Virginia Historical Society; Burial Records, Bellefontaine Cemetery, St. Louis.

11. Benton, *View*, I, 116-118, 474-476; "Mark Alexander and His Ancestry," in *William and Mary College Quarterly Historical Magazine*, XXV (January, 1917), 207. Cf. Bruce, *John Randolph of Roanoke*, II, 314; and Waddell, "Thomas Hart Benton," in *International Review*, XII (May, 1882), 495.

12. *AC*, 17/1, 179, 183, 298-309, 317-331, 440, 465, 1788; 17/2, 147, 237-242; 18/1, 431-460, 762, 787, 2617; Benton to Pratte, January 23, 1824, in Chouteau-Papin Collection, MoHS; Ramsay Crooks to Benton, April 1, December 31, 1822, in Porter, *John Jacob Astor*, II, 713-714 (and cf. 732); Calhoun to Ninian Edwards, August 20, 1822, in Edwards, *History of Illinois . . . and Life and Times of Ninian Edwards*, 491; Benton, *Abridgment of the Debates*, VII, 201.

13. *AC*, 17/2, 235, 246-251 ff. Cf. *Missouri Republican*, June 4, 1823; Bemis, *Adams*, 484-487; and *RD*, 18/2, 699-744, 712.

14. *AC*, 18/1, 32-33, 417; Benton, *Speech on the Amendment to the Constitution*, 4, 17, 30; Nancy Benton to Samuel Benton, April 17, 1824, copy in Benton Papers, MoHS; Frémont, "Biographical Sketch," 6.

15. *AC*, 18/1, 582-583; Benton, *View*, I, 102-103. Cf. Hibbard, *History of the Public Land Policies*, 219, 293; Goodrich and Davis, "Wage Earner in the Westward Movement," in *Political Science Quarterly*, L (June, 1935), 161-185; LI (March, 1936), 61-116; Riegel, *Young America*, 88, 144.

16. Stanwood, *History of the Presidency*, 126-131; Anderson, "Jackson Men in Missouri," *Missouri Historical Review*, XXXIV (April, 1940), 304-305; Letter to Jonathan Russell, March 29, 1822, in *Proceedings of the Massachusetts Historical Society*, XLVII, 309-310; Lucas to William H. Crawford, January 27, 1825, in Lucas, *Letters*, 110; *Missouri Republican*, September 4, 1822; Letter from William Plumer, Jr., December 10, 1822, in Brown, *Missouri Compromises and Presidential Politics*, 79.

17. Benton to James P. Preston, December 22, 1822, in Preston Papers, Virginia Historical Society.

18. Calhoun to John E. Calhoun, April 14, 1823, in Jameson, *Correspondence of John C. Calhoun*, 206; Webster to Ezekiel Webster, March 14, 1824, in Webster, *Private Correspondence*, I, 347; Benton to Clay, July

23, 1823, in Clay Papers, LofC; Lynch, *An Epoch and a Man: Martin Van Buren,* 253; Ambler, *Thomas Ritchie,* 83, 94, 97.

19. Letter by Benton, n. d., quoted in Parton, *Jackson,* III, 47. Cf. James, *Jackson,* 383.

20. Speeches, June 3, 1816; March 13, 1817; April 26, 1820 — in Mallory, *Life and Speeches of Henry Clay,* I, 71-73, 76-77, 150; II, 83, 87-88. Cf. Macon to Bartlett Yancey, December 12, 1823, in Yancey Papers, Southern Historical Collection; and Turner, *Rise of the New West,* 137-140.

21. *AC,* 18/1, 535, 536-541, 571, 616, 702, 705-708, 711, 712, 743; Benton, *View,* I, 32, 58.

22. Fitzpatrick (Editor), *Autobiography of Martin Van Buren,* 665-666.

23. Benton to William H. Caudell, March 15, 1822, in Benton Letters, Miscellaneous Manuscript File, New York Historical Society; and to Henry R. Schoolcraft, April 29, 1822, in Schoolcraft Papers, LofC.

24. Nancy Benton to Samuel [?] Benton, January 12, December 11, 1823, copies in Benton Papers, MoHS; Memorandum of Agreement, Thomas, Jesse, Samuel, and Nathaniel Benton, June 20, 1823, Jesse Benton Papers, LofC; *5 Yerger's Tennessee Reports 379;* Benton, *Substance . . . in the Suit of John Smith T ads. Nicholas Wilson.* 3-6; *Missouri Advocate,* April 2, 1825; *Missouri Republican,* July 30, 1823; *Vasseur* vs. *Benton,* in *1 Missouri Reports 296.*

25. Cf. Schurz, *Henry Clay,* I, 228; Nancy Benton to Samuel Benton, March 3, June 23, 1824, copy in Benton Papers, MoHS.

26. Scharf, *History of St. Louis,* II, 1459.

27. *Missouri Republican,* June 27, 1825; Benton to Daniel Bissell and Others, October 1, 1824, in *Ibid.,* October 4, 1824. Cf. [Curtius], *Torch Light,* 13.

28. Cf. Wise, *Seven Decades of the Union,* 77-78, 80; Fitzpatrick, *Autobiography of Martin Van Buren,* 449; Hailperin, "Pro-Jackson Sentiment in Pennsylvania," *Pennsylvania Magazine of History and Biography,* L (July, 1926), 198-200 ff.; Turner, *Rise of the New West,* 148.

29. *Missouri Republican,* August 21, 1822, June 27, 1825, and Benton to Scott, August 28, [1822], in *Ibid.,* January 9, 1870; letters from Nancy Benton, August 15, 1823, copy, Benton Papers, MoHS; from John K. Walker, July 27, 1824, UVa; and from John O'Fallon, November 15, 18, 1824, Smith Manuscripts, Missouri State Historical Society; also Magers, "An Early Missouri Political Feud," *Missouri Historical Review,* XXIII (January, 1929), 261, 262; J. F. Perry to Stephen S. Austin, February 14, 1825, in Barker, *Austin Papers,* II, 1043.

30. For the Santa Fe road and Benton's visit to Jefferson: *RD,* 18/2, 6, 7, 109-110, 341-347, 361; Benton, *View,* I, 48; Benton to Jared Sparks, January 16, 1825, Houghton Library, Harvard University.

31. Cf. Benton, *View,* I, 46-50, Parton, *Jackson,* III, 61-63; Saunders to Bartlett Yancey, January 11, 1825, in Newsome, "Letters of Romulus M. Saunders," *North Carolina Historical Review,* VIII (October, 1931),

449; and Barton to Silas Bent, February 2, 1825, in Bay, *Bench and Bar,* 605.

32. Adams, *Memoirs,* VI, 473-474; Benton to Scott, February 8, 1825, in *Niles Weekly Register,* XXVIII (March 26, 1825), 51.

33. Clay to Benton, December 6, 1827, in *Missouri Republican,* May 20, 1852; and letter from Benton, December 7, 1827, in *Niles Weekly Register,* XXXIII (February 2, 1828), 375-376.

34. Adams, *Memoirs,* VI, 522; Benton to James P. Preston, May 6 [1825?], in Preston Papers, Virginia Historical Society; also *Missouri Republican,* June 27, 1825; Benton, *View,* I, 47-48.

CHAPTER 7

1. *Missouri Republican,* 1825 — April 11; July 18; September 12, 19; October 17, 24; also May 10, 1827. *Missouri Advocate,* 1825 — January 8; February 28; May 6, 20; June 10; July 15, 22; August 13; September 17; November 26; December 3, 10, 24. Cf. McCandless, *Benton, His Source of Political Strength,* 100-101.

2. *Benton* vs. *O'Fallon,* in *8 Missouri Reports 650;* Original and General Records, St. Louis, R-3, 91-92; Benton to Randolph, July 7, 1825, in Hart, "An Affair of Honor," 55, 56.

3. *RD,* 19/1, 15, 19, 51, 696. Cf. Benton, *View,* I, 78.

4. For Benton's land proposals: *RD,* 19/1, 720, 749-754; 19/2, 6, 12, 39-40, 347; 20/1, 23-28, 483-678; Benton, *Speech on the Bill to Graduate the Price of the Public Lands* (1826), 2-6, 11, 12, 16; *Mr. Benton's Speeches, on the Public Lands* (1828), 3-5, 7, 9-21, 25-27, 30; *Commercial Advertiser* (New York), quoted in *Missouri Republican,* January 31, 1828; Benton to Ewing, February 14, 1828, in Benton Papers, MoHS; Adams, *Memoirs,* VII, 173, 194.

5. *RD,* 19/1, 306, 671, 2514; Benton, *Speech . . . on the Mission to Panama,* 1-59. Cf. Carroll, "Politics During the Administration of John Quincy Adams," in *South Atlantic Quarterly,* XXIII (April, 1924), 140 ff.; and Sargent, *Public Men and Events,* I, 106.

6. *RD,* 19/1, Appendix 133, 135; 20/1, 379-385, 394; Macon to Bartlett Yancey, March 31, 1836, in Yancey Papers, Southern Historical Collection, University of North Carolina; *Niles Weekly Register,* XXXVI (June 20, 1829), 265.

7. Calhoun to James E. Calhoun, August 26, 1827, in Jameson, *Correspondence,* 250. Cf. Turner, *Rise of the New West,* 314-321; Wiltse, *Calhoun: Nationalist,* 366-372; *RD,* 20/1, 728-730, 732-733, 765-769, 786; and Benton, *View,* I, 95, 101.

8. *Ibid.,* I, 70-77, 73; Benton to Henry St. George Tucker, July 16, 1826, in *Missouri Republican,* January 18, 1827; Extracts from a Private Journal, April 9, 1826, in Clay Papers, LofC.

9. Brown to Clay, May 12, 29, 1826, in Clay Papers, LofC.

10. For the attack on Benton, and Missouri politics in 1826: *Missouri Republican,* 1826 — February 2, 9, 16; March 16; May 4; June 22; July 20;

August 3, 17, 24, 31; September 7, 14, 21; *Missouri Advocate,* 1826 —
May 20; June 10; July 1, 8, 15, 22; August 3, 10, 17; and [CURTIUS],
"Torch Light," 3, 7, 8, 12, 23-24, 33, 47. Cf. Anderson, "Jackson Men,"
309-311; and McCandless, *Benton, His Source of Political Strength,* 103-
106.
11. Lucas to Adams [September?], 1826, in Lucas, *Letters,* 78; also Adams,
Memoirs, VII, 187-188.
12. *Missouri Advocate,* 1826 — September 14; October 2, 12, 26; November
2, 23.
13. Benton to Ewing, September 4, 1826, in Benton Papers, MoHS.
14. *Senate Journal,* 4 Assembly, 1 Session, 59, 81, and *House Journal,* 132;
William Carr Lane to Mrs. Lane, November 22, 28, 1826, in MoHS,
Glimpses of the Past, VII, 91, 94; *Missouri Republican,* December 7,
1826; Petition for Benton, December 11, 1826, in Benton Papers, MoHS.
15. Burial Records, Bellefontaine Cemetery, St. Louis; *RD,* 19/1, 731; Benton to Alfred Balch, April 30, 1828, Jackson Papers, LofC; Benton to
Finis Ewing, October 25, 1828, Benton Papers, MoHS; *American State
Papers: Finance,* V, 624; *Benton* vs. *O'Fallon,* in *8 Missouri Reports
650.*
16. Perley Poore, *Perley's Reminiscences of Sixty Years in the National
Metropolis,* I, 66.
17. Portrait by Matthew Harris Jouett, Oil, Cleveland Museum of Art, Gift
of Mrs. Otto Miller, 1941. It has proved impossible to determine the
exact date of this portrait, though it must have been painted in 1827 or
before, for in that year Jouett died.
18. Miscellaneous Philanthropic Society Papers, University of North Carolina. Cited in Letter from R. D. W. Connor, April 6, 1949.
19. *Missouri Republican,* February 12 and 19, 1828; Statement of William
Eckert, October 4, 1828, in Clay Papers, LofC.
20. *Missouri Republican,* 1828 — July 29; August 12; December 2; also Benton to [Balch?], August 17, 1828, in Jackson Papers, and Bates to Clay,
October 8, 1828, in Clay Papers, LofC.
21. Benton to Kendall, August 24, 1828, in Miscellaneous Manuscripts, Massachusetts Historical Society.
22. *Missouri Republican,* October 14, 1828; [Bates], *Edward Bates Against
Thomas Benton,* 3, 9-12.
23. Cf. Benton, *View,* I, 47, 111; Macon to Bartlett Yancey, October 3,
1827, in Yancey Papers, Southern Historical Collection; Kelsey, "Presidential Campaign of 1828," *East Tennessee Historical Society Publications,* 5 (1933), 70, 72; Hammond, "Jackson, Biddle, and the B. U. S.,"
in *Journal of Economic History,* VII (May, 1947), 6-8; Dorfman, "The
Jackson Wage-Earner Thesis," in *American Historical Review,* LIV
(January, 1949), 296-301; Sullivan, "Did Labor Support Andrew Jackson?" *Political Science Quarterly,* LXII (December, 1947), 577-578,
580; Schlesinger, *Age of Jackson,* 34-36; Turner, *United States: 1830-
1850,* 28-38; Hailperin, "Pro-Jackson Sentiment in Pennsylvania," 224-
226.

24. Benton to [Balch?], February 22, 1828, in Jackson Papers, LofC; and to Messers Green and Jarvis, August 16, 1828, Houghton Library, Harvard University.
25. Tocqueville, *Democracy in America*, I, 299; Benton, *View*, I, 112-113.
26. Adams, *Memoirs*, VIII, 87-88, IX, 247.

CHAPTER 8

1. Note, February, 1829, in Webster, *Correspondence*, I, 467. Cf. Benton, *View*, I, 111, 119, 121; and Bowers, *Party Battles of the Jackson Period*, 5-6, 8-9.
2. Green to Ninian Edwards, December 22, 1828, in Washburne, "The Edwards Papers," *Chicago Historical Society Collections* (1884), 378; Edwards, *Life and Times of Ninian Edwards*, 508; Wiltse, *Calhoun: Nullifier*, 20-23.
3. Letter to Mrs. Kirkpatrick, March 11, 1829, in Hunt, *First Forty Years*, 290-296; Sargent, *Public Men and Events*, I, 163-164. Cf. Mims, *Majority of the People*, 245 ff.; Schlesinger, *Age of Jackson*, 6; and Ostrogorski, *Political Parties*, II, 45 ff.
4. Benton to J. T. Preston, May 25, 1829, in Benton Letters, New York Historical Society.
5. Cf. Eriksson, "Federal Civil Service Under President Jackson," in *Mississippi Valley Historical Review*, XIII (March, 1927), 519; *St. Louis Beacon*, July 4, 1829, and June 17, 1830; Benton to William S. Hamilton, March 21, 1829, Miscellaneous Files, Chicago Historical Society; and to John Eaton, May 24, 1829, in Benton Papers, Personal Miscellany, LofC; also Jackson to Ingham, March 16, 1830, in Bassett, *Correspondence*, IV, 127.
6. Benton, *View*, I, 159-163; Eriksson, "Federal Civil Service Under President Jackson," 519, 528-529, 531 ff.
7. Articles Signed AMERICANUS, *St. Louis Beacon*, August 1, 8, 1829; Benton to Houston, August 15, 1829, copy in Benton Papers, MoHS.
8. Articles Signed LA SALLE, *St. Louis Beacon*, 1829 — October 7, 10, 14, 17, 21, 24, 28; November 4, 11. Also Jackson to Van Buren, August 12, 14, 1829, "Notes on Poinsett's Instructions," in Bassett, *Correspondence*, IV, 57-61; and *CG*, 28/1, Appendix 484.
9. "Beginnings of St. Louis University," *St. Louis Catholic Historical Review*, I (January, 1919), 99; Benton to Thomas Hardeman, November 22, 1829 — copy in Benton Papers, MoHS; original in possession of Mrs. Glen Owen Hardeman, Gray Summit, Missouri; Burial Records, Bellefontaine Cemetery, St. Louis.
10. For the Benton-Webster-Hayne debate: *RD*, 21/1, 4, 22-26, 31-41, 42 ff., 58 ff., 102-119; DeWitt, "Great Webster-Hayne Debate," in *Olde Ulster*, IX (November, 1913), 332-334; Benton, *Speech . . . in Reply to Mr. Webster, passim; St. Louis Beacon*, 1830 — April 22, 29; May 6, 13. Cf. Benton, *View*, I, 130 ff.; Fuess, *Webster*, I, 366; Wiltse, *Calhoun: Nullifier*, 57; and Bruce, *Randolph*, II, 203.

11. *RD*, 21/1, 146-148, 151-152; *St. Louis Beacon*, April 22, 1830.
12. *Niles Weekly Register*, XXXVIII (April 24, 1830), 153-154; XL (May 14, 1831), 192; Benton, *View*, I, 148-149. Cf. Stenberg, "Jefferson Birthday Dinner, 1830," *Journal of Southern History*, IV (August, 1938), 334-355.
13. *RD*, 21/1, 172-176, 244-245, 428-432, 819-820. Cf. Wiltse, *Calhoun: Nullifier*, 74-75.
14. *RD*, 21/1, 405-427. Cf. Wellington, "Tariff and Public Lands from 1828 to 1833," 180, 183; *St. Louis Beacon*, 1830 — May 27; June 3, 10.
15. *RD*, 21/1, 115-116, 820; *Niles Weekly Register*, XXXVIII (May 22, 1830), 240; Veto Message, May 7, 1830, in Richardson, *Messages and Papers*, III, 1050-1052; Benton, *View*, 26, 167.
16. Benton to [Randolph], May 24, 26, 1830, copy in Benton Letters, PHS.
17. Calhoun to Christopher Van Deventer, May 12, 1830, in Jameson, *Correspondence*, 273.
18. Benton to James P. Preston, April 27, 1830, in Preston Papers, Virginia Historical Society.
19. *St. Louis Beacon*, 1830 — May 13; July 8, 20, 29; August 5, 28; September 9, 16, 23; October 7, 21; November 11; also *Missouri Republican*, July 20, 1830; John K. Walker to Thomas H. Walker, August 5, 1830, in Walker Family Papers, UVa; Benton to Finis Ewing, August 22, 1830, and to Lieutenant Governor Dunklin, October 10, 1830, Benton Papers, MoHS.
20. *St. Louis Beacon*, December 9, 1830; *Niles Weekly Register*, XXXIX (December 25, 1830), 302; Recollections of Edward Dobyns, fragmentary manuscript, and Linn to Henry Dodge, February 15, 1833, photostat in Linn Papers — both MoHS; and Bates to Abiel Leonard, April 4, 1831, in Leonard Manuscripts, Missouri State Historical Society.

CHAPTER 9

1. Benton to A. J. Donelson, December 17, 1829, and Enclosure, in Jackson Papers, LofC.
2. The entire speech of February 2, 1831, appears in *RD*, 21/2, 50-75.
3. Cf. Benton, *View*, I, 204; and Lewis, "Benton's Analysis of His Audience," in *Quarterly Journal of Speech*, XXXV (December, 1949), 443, 447.
4. Washington *Globe*, December 7, 18 and 29, 1830, and February 9 and 12, 1831; Smith, *Blair Family in Politics*, I, 60-62.
5. Benton, *View*, I, 158. Cf. Catterall, *Second Bank*, 205; Hammond, "Jackson, Biddle, and the B. U. S.," 4, 6-8; Schlesinger, *Age of Jackson*, 8-11, 57-59, 76-80; and Macon to Benton, March 7, 1831, in Washington *Globe*, June 17, 1831.
6. Van Buren, *Autobiography*, 403; cf. Wiltse, *Calhoun: Nullifier*, 28-38, 76-83, 94-97; Benton, *View*, I, 181, 182; Benton to Cass, August 11, 1831, in Cass Papers, University of Michigan; and *United States Magazine and Democratic Review*, XLII (July, 1858), 62.

7. *RD*, 22/1, 1310; Benton, *View*, I, 214-216, 219.

8. *St. Louis Beacon*, 1831 — January 27; March 3, 10; May 5; June 2; July 21, 28; September 1; also *Missouri Republican*, August 30, 1831; Memoir by Edward Dobyns, Duels Envelope, MoHS; Benton to Cass [August 21, 1831], in Cass Papers, University of Michigan.

9. *St. Louis Beacon*, October 6, 13 and 20, 1831, and January 5, 1832; also Benton to Finis Ewing, November 12, 21, 1831, in Benton Papers, MoHS.

10. *RD*, 22/1, 118-154; Benton, *Speech . . . on the State of the Currency*, 9, 10, 19, 21.

11. Cf. Memorandum by Biddle, October 19, 1831, and letters from Thomas Cadwalader, December, 1831, in McGrane, *Correspondence of Nicholas Biddle*, 131, 146-161; Benton, *View*, I, 227, 235-239; cf. also Washington *Globe*, 1832 — January 23, 26, 28; *RD*, 22/1, 2164, Appendix 33-73; and Catterall, *Second Bank*, 229-230.

12. For the second battle: *RD*, 22/1, 966-968, 971-972, 1001, 1001-1013, 1045-1047, 1068, 1070-1073; *Niles Weekly Register*, XLII (June 23, 1832), 300-301; Taney, "Bank War Manuscript," cited in Schlesinger, *Age of Jackson*, 87; Biddle to Cadwalader, July 3, 1832, in McGrane, *Correspondence*, 192.

13. Van Buren, *Autobiography*, 625; Veto Message, in Richardson, *Messages and Papers*, III, 1142, 1145, 1153.

14. Cf. *RD*, 22/1, 1293-1296; Washington *Globe*, July 18, 1832; Benton, *View*, I, 256-263; Poore, *Reminiscences*, I, 144-145. Accounts of the Benton-Clay interchange differ, with Benton partisans accusing the pro-Clay *Register of Debates* of biased and inaccurate reporting. The version I have given follows the pro-Benton Washington *Globe* and Benton's own account in large part, and is in other aspects reconstructed from the sources indicated.

15. Washington *Globe*, July 18, 21, 1832; Porter, *Life and Times of Anne Royall*, 164, 165.

16. For the Missouri elections: *St. Louis Beacon*, 1832 — January-June; August 2, 30; October 4, 25; November 15; *Missouri Republican*, 1832 — June 26; July 31; August 7, 14; September 4, 25; November 6; Weston F. Birch to Abiel Leonard, December 22, 1831, in Leonard Manuscripts, Missouri State Historical Society; Benton to Daniel Dunklin, August 24 [1832], and to Finis Ewing, September 4, 1832, in Benton Papers, MoHS; Benton in the Senate, December 18, 1834, *CG*, 23/2, 48; *House Journal*, 7 Assembly, 1 Session, 55.

17. *Missouri Republican*, June 5, 1832; Benton to Ewing, September 4, 1832, in Benton Papers, MoHS; *St. Louis Beacon*, September 13, 1832; Shoemaker, *Missouri and Missourians*, I, 412; Stanwood, *Presidency*, 163-164.

18. Cf. Schlesinger, *Age of Jackson*, 143, 180-189; Pessen, "Did Labor Support Andrew Jackson? the Boston Story," Bower, "Note on 'Did Labor Support Jackson? the Boston Story,'" in *Political Science Quarterly*, LXIV (June, 1949), 268, 271-273, and LXV (September, 1950), 442-

444; Dorfman, "The Jackson Wage Earner Thesis," 300-301, 306; and Benton, *View*, I, 282.

19. For the tariff and distribution debates: *RD*, 22/1, 625-638, 786, 907, 931, 1101-1102, 1111, 1145-1146, 1152, 1164, 1219; 22/2, 462-473, 713-715, 308-309; Benton, *Speech . . . on the Reduction of Revenue, passim.* Cf. Wiltse, *Calhoun: Nullifier*, 153, 169, 183-186; Van Deusen, *Henry Clay*, 253-269; and Wellington, "Tariff and Public Lands," 183-185.

20. Benton to Tucker, February 11, 1833, in "Correspondence of Judge Tucker," *William and Mary College Quarterly Historical Magazine*, Series I, XII (October, 1903), 86; and to Van Buren, February 16 [1833], in Van Buren Papers, LofC.

21. *RD*, 22/1, 61, 208-229; Benton, *Speech . . . in the Senate of the United States, January 24th, 1833, passim.*

22. For the "composite portrait": Poore, *Reminiscences*, 141; Bay, *Bench and Bar*, 5; "The Late Thomas H. Benton," *United States Magazine and Democratic Review*, XLII (July, 1858), 68, 69, 70; Portland *Advertiser*, quoted in *Missouri Republican*, June 12, 1832, and Forney, *Anecdotes of Public Men*, 21; Taney, Bank War Manuscript, quoted in Swisher, *Taney*, 205; Rev. N. L. Rice, *A Funeral Discourse of Mrs. Elizabeth Benton;* Waddell, "Thomas Hart Benton," 481; Frémont, "Biographical Sketch," *passim.*

23. James, *Jackson*, 591, and Buell, *History of Andrew Jackson*, II, 268; Frémont, *Souvenirs*, 88.

24. Benton to Mrs. James McDowell, April 21, [1831], and to Sally C. P. McDowell, February 3, 1832, McDowell Family Papers, UVa. Cf. *Missouri Argus*, August 14, 1835.

25. Benton to Finis Ewing, October 7, 1831, and to Dunklin, March 26, 1832, Benton Papers, MoHS.

26. Benton to Julian E. Sawyer, December 18, 1832, Miscellaneous Philanthropic Society Papers, University of North Carolina.

27. Washington *Globe*, May 30, 1833; Bruce, *John Randolph*, II, 51, 57, 356; Benton, *View*, I, 473-475.

28. *Missouri Republican*, June-July, 1833 — especially June 7, 11, 14, 21; July 9, 16; September 6, 17, 20; also Linn to Henry Dodge, February 15, 1833, photostat in Linn Papers, and Benton to Finis Ewing, July 20, 1833, in Benton Papers, MoHS.

29. Cf. Benton, *View*, I, 374, 379.

30. Power, *Impressions of America*, I, 213-283.

31. *Niles Weekly Register*, XLVI (May 24, 1834), 204; Benton, *View*, I, 415-416; Biddle to William Appleton, January 27, 1834, in McGrane, *Correspondence*, 219; Benton, *Abridgment of the Debates*, XII, 308; Schlesinger, *Age of Jackson*, 103-114; Catterall, *Second Bank*, 314, 316, 323, 328-331; Hammond, "Jackson, Biddle, and the B. U. S.," 12; *CG*, 23/1, 54-83, 87, 271, 292-293, 418-420, 426.

32. Benton, *View*, I, 462; *CG*, 23/1, 453-456; Washington *Globe*, July 12, 1834; Broadsides Collections, LofC; Swisher, *Taney*, 284.

33. Cf. Mims, *Majority of the People,* 103-111.
34. *RD,* 23/1, 1073-1105; Washington *Globe,* 1834 — March 22, 24, 25, 26; April 16; May 2; August 8; Jackson to William Findley, August 20, 1834, in Bassett, *Correspondence,* V, 286; Benton, *View,* I, 470.
35. Washington *Globe,* 1934 — July 9, 22, 25, 28, 29; August 1, 9, 14; and January 5, 1835; also Richmond *Enquirer,* quoted in *Niles Weekly Register,* XLVI (June 14, 1834), 259; and Parton, *Jackson,* III, 297.
36. Cf. Cole, *Whig Party in the South,* 5, 6, 17-18, 29-30, 32.
37. Washington *Globe,* August 27, 1834, and Benton to [?], Fairfield, Virginia, September 21 [1834], in Benton Letters, PHS.
38. *CG,* 23/2, 239 ff.; Martineau, *Retrospect of Western Travel,* I, 109-110, 113, 134-135; Nevins, *Diary of Philip Hone,* I, 150.
39. Washington *Globe,* January 14, 1835; Parton, *Jackson,* III, 580-581.

CHAPTER 10

1. Cf. Spencer, "William L. Marcy Goes Conservative," in *Mississippi Valley Historical Review,* XXXI (September, 1944), 209-210; Gresham, "Hugh Lawson White as a Tennessee Politician and Banker," 30, 36; Hammond, "Banking in the Early West: Monopoly, Prohibition, and Laissez-Faire," in *Journal of Economic History,* VIII (May, 1948), 2-4; Dorfman, "The Jackson Wage-Earner Thesis," 300-301; and Schlesinger, *Age of Jackson,* 120, 191 ff.
2. Cf. Clay to White, August 27, 1838, in Scott, *Memoir of Hugh Lawson White,* 367 (in this interesting letter the Kentucky leader gives an *ex post facto* statement of the strategy of 1835-1836, and tells Hugh White just what his place in it was); also Letters from Benton, April-May, 1835, in Washington *Globe,* April 22 and May 18, 1835; and *Missouri Argus,* July 10, 1835.
3. Washington *Globe,* June 30, 1835, and Benton to Van Buren, June 7, 1835, in Van Buren Papers, LofC.
4. *Missouri Argus,* in *Niles Weekly Register,* XLVIII, (August 29, 1835), 462-463. The issue of the *Argus* for July 24, which must have contained the account of Benton's speech, is missing from the files of the Missouri State Historical Society.
5. Benton Interview, Memorandum by Corbin, n. d., in Corbin Papers, Rutgers College Collection, copy, MoHS; Strother — Benton Letters, August 3, 6, 1835, Van Buren Papers, LofC; *Niles Weekly Register,* XLIX (September 5, 1835), 5.
6. *Missouri Argus,* 1835 — August 14; October 30; also Deed Books, Rockbridge County, Virginia, *passim.* These volumes were examined for me by Dr. E. P. Tompkins, of Lexington.
7. Washington *Globe,* November 21, 28; December 1, 11, 15, 1835. Cf. Riegel, *Young America,* 168; and Fairfield to Mrs. Fairfield, December 5, 1835, in Staples, *Letters of John Fairfield,* 24.
8. *CG,* 24/1, 321, 324. Cf. Benton, *View,* I, 678; and Fuess, *Webster,* II, 50.

9. *CG,* 24/1, 426, Appendix, 444-450, and inscription on cover of pamphlet, *Speech of Mr. Benton, of Missouri, Upon the Subject of the District Bank Charters,* in Benton Papers, Personal Miscellany, LofC.
10. Benton, *View,* I, 677-678; *Missouri Argus,* August 26, 1836.
11. *RD,* 24/2, 610-611 ff.; Benton to Messers David Smith and Others, January 3, 1836, in *Missouri Argus,* February 12, 1836; to Dawson, January 9, 1836, in Moses Dawson Collection, Xavier University Library; and to Messers Dawson and Others, February 27, 1836, in Benton Documents, Missouri State Historical Society; Fairfield to Mrs. Fairfield, February 21, 1836, in Staples, *Letters,* 109.
12. *CG,* 24/1, 77, 79-80, 82-83, 150, 221, 229, 301, 430; Benton, *View,* I, 623.
13. Lawrence to Amos Lawrence, January 8, 1836, in "Letters of Amos Adams Lawrence," *Proceedings of the Massachusetts Historical Society,* LIII, 49-50; *Missouri Argus,* January 29, 1836; Webster to Caroline Webster, Senate, April 29, 1836, in McIntyre, *Writings and Speeches of Daniel Webster,* XVI, 275; also Goodrich, *Recollections of a Lifetime,* I, 430. The memoirist gives no date for this story; however, Niles did not enter the Senate until December, 1835, and Hill resigned in May, 1836; it is thus possible to date the event as probably occurring in the early part of 1836.
14. Sally McDowell to Susan S. McDowell, January 21, March 9, April 22, and undated, 1836, and March 7, 1837; to James McDowell, July 7, 1836; and to Francis McDowell, May 6, 1837 — all in McDowell Family Papers, UVa. Also Benton to Sally McDowell [1837], Benton Papers, MoHS. Cf. [Francis Thomas], *Statement of Francis Thomas,* 7-8, 14-15.
15. Scharf, *History of St. Louis,* I, 595.
16. *Missouri Argus,* 1836 — February 15; July 22; August 19; December 9. Cf. Stephens, "Banking and Finance in Missouri in the Thirties," *Proceedings of the Mississippi Valley Historical Association,* X, 130-131.
17. Cf. James Barbour to Clay, August 2, 1835, in Colton, *Correspondence,* 398; Cole, *Whig Party in the South,* 32 ff.; also Biddle to Herman Cope, August 11, 1835, in McGrane, *Correspondence,* 256; Cleaves, *Old Tippecanoe,* 305-308; and Lynch, *An Epoch and a Man,* 395.
18. *RD,* 24/2, 380-391, 499-502, 504-505; Benton, *Speech . . . on the Expunging Resolution,* 2, 7; Benton, *View,* I, 727-731; Washington *Globe,* January 18, 28, 1837; Schurz, *Henry Clay,* II, 106; Broadsides Collection, LofC; Jackson to Benton, January 17, 1837, in Bassett, *Correspondence,* V, 450-451.
19. Benton, *View,* II, 10-11; *CG,* 26/1, Appendix 121.
20. Farewell Address, in Richardson, *Messages and Papers,* IV, 1513-1517, 1520-1525; Benton, *View,* I, 735; and James, *Jackson,* 719.
21. Benton, *View,* II, 701-702. Cf. Garraty, *Silas Wright,* 141-208.
22. *United States Magazine and Democratic Review,* I (October-December, 1837), 84.

Chapter 11

1. *Missouri Argus*, April 21, 1837; *Benton* v. *O'Fallon*, in *8 Missouri Reports 650*.
2. Cf. McGrane, *The Panic of 1837*, 5-96; Rezneck, "The Social History of an American Depression, 1837-1843," *American Historical Review*, XL (July, 1935), *passim*, 666; Bogart and Kemmerer, *Economic History*, 327 ff., 332, 334.
3. Benton, *View*, II, 9-23, 26-28; *Niles Weekly Register*, LII (March 25, 1837), 54; Cartoons Collection, UVa; *Missouri Argus*, 1837 — June 6; July 11; Jackson to Van Buren, May 12, 1837, in Bassett, *Correspondence*, V, 483.
4. *Missouri Argus*, 1837 — June 2, 30; July 11. Cf. Dorsey, "The Panic and Depression of 1837-1843 in Missouri," *Missouri Historical Review*, XXX (January, 1936), 135-140; and Cable, *Bank of the State of Missouri*, 161, 164, 169 ff.
5. Benton to Van Buren, May 31, 1837, Van Buren Papers, LofC.
6. Special Message, in Richardson, *Messages and Papers*, IV, 1548, 1553, 1556. Cf. Schlesinger, *Age of Jackson*, 231-238, 242-249; Spencer, "Marcy Goes Conservative," 22; and Wiltse, *Calhoun: Nullifier*, 341-352.
7. *CG*, 25/1, 27-28, 44, 100, 141, Appendix 49-55; and 25/2, 264, 267, Appendix 217 ff.; Benton, *Speech . . . on the Bill to Separate the Government from the Banks*, 1-17; Blair to Jackson, March 20, 1838, and Benton to Jackson, April 6, 1838, in Jackson Papers, LofC; Washington *Globe*, March-May, 1838; John Letcher and Benjamin Pierce to Van Buren, May 12, 29, 1838, in Van Buren Papers, LofC; George R. Gilmer to Thomas W. Gilmer, January 28, 1839, in Tyler, *Letters and Times of the Tylers*, II, 295.
8. Cf. Blair to Jackson, October 1, 1837, in Bassett, *Correspondence*, V, 514; Benton to Van Buren, March 23, 1839, and n. d. [1840?], "Private," in Van Buren Papers, LofC; and *CG*, 25/1, 38; 25/2, 378, 384 ff., 390, 391.
9. *Missouri Argus*, January 6, 1838; Benton, *Speech . . . on the Bill Providing for the Reduction and Graduation of the Price of the Public Lands*, 3-6; *CG*, 25/2, 130-149, 305, Appendix 129 ff., 143.
10. Benton to [Joel R. Poinsett], and to Van Buren, n. d., and October 28, 1837, in Benton Letters, PHS, and in Van Buren Papers, LofC; *Missouri Argus*, 1837 — September 27; October 25; November 11; also William R. Gentry, Jr., *Full Justice: the Story of Richard Gentry and His Missouri Volunteers*, 5, 9.
11. Cf. Gentry, 20-25, and Hamilton, *Zachary Taylor; Soldier of the Republic*, 143-146, 282; *CG*, 25/2, 182-183; Benton to Richard H. Gentry, March 10, 1838, Benton Documents, Missouri State Historical Society.
12. *Missouri Argus*, July 18 and October 14, 1837, and January 6, 1838; Burial Records, Bellefontaine Cemetery, St. Louis; Benton, "Auto-Biographical Sketch," ii.

13. Benton to Jackson, December 12, 1837, in Jackson Papers, LofC; cf. *Niles Weekly Register,* LII (March 18, 1837), 33; *Missouri Argus,* 1837 — March 24; May 5; February 15; April 26; July 19, 26; also September 2, 1839, and July 25 and September 14, 1840; Sarah Benton Brant to Samuel Benton, May 30, 1838, typed copy, in Benton Papers, MoHS.

14. *United States Magazine and Democratic Review,* I (October-December, 1837), 86-90; Linn to Silas Wright, April 8, 1837, in Van Buren Papers, LofC, and *CG,* 25/1, Appendix 321; Keyes, *Fifty Years of Observation of Men and Events,* 147, 149, and "A Looker on Here in Verona," in *Sketches of United States Senators,* 29-32.

15. *Missouri Argus,* 1837 — September 23; November 18; December 16, 23; and 1838 — January 13; February 16, 23; March 1, 8; April 5; August 2; also *Jeffersonian Republican,* quoted in "To Promise Yet Not Pay," in *Missouri Historical Review,* XXXV (January, 1941), 265; and *Missouri Republican,* 1838 — May 8, 12; July 27, 31.

16. *Missouri Argus,* August 9 and September 5, 1838; *Missouri Republican,* August 18 and September 5 and 14, 1838; James S. Rollins to Abiel Leonard, November 22, 1838, in Leonard Manuscripts, Missouri State Historical Society; *House Journal,* 10 Assembly, 1 Session, 21-22. Cf. McCandless, *Benton, His Source of Political Strength,* 214-222.

17. Cf. *Missouri Argus,* 1838 — October 22, 31; November 22, 24, 27, 28; also *Missouri Republican,* November 29, 1838.

18. Benton to [Joel R. Poinsett?], n. d., in Benton Letters, PHS.

19. Elizabeth Benton to Sally McDowell, January 2, 1839, in McDowell Family Papers, UVa; also Benton to Jackson, April 3, 1839, in Jackson Papers, LofC.

20. For Benton in Missouri in 1839: *Missouri Argus,* 1839 — May 14, 31; June 28; July 12, 15, 19, 26, 30, 31; August 5, 20; also [Benton], *Letters of Senator Benton to His Constituents in 1839,* 35-39.

21. *Missouri Argus,* July 30 and August 2, 1839; August 21, 1840. Cf. Cable, *Bank of the State of Missouri,* 179-187; Dorsey, "The Panic and Depression of 1837-1843," 143-144, 148-152; McClure, *Opposition in Missouri to Thomas Hart Benton,* 14-18; Darby, *Recollections,* 181-182.

22. *Missouri Argus,* September 28, 1839; Benton to Buchanan, August 17, 1839, in Benton Letters, PHS; and to Magenis, October 4, 1839, in Van Buren Papers, LofC.

23. Benton to Jackson, October 14, 1839, in Jackson Papers, LofC.

24. *Congressional Directory* (1839), 39; Frémont, *Souvenirs,* 57-60, and "Senator Thomas H. Benton," 242-243; William Henry Ruffner, in *Washington and Lee University Historical Papers,* IV, 127-218; Poore, *Reminiscences,* I, 305; Elizabeth Benton to Sally McDowell, December 8, 1839, in McDowell Family Papers, UVa.

25. Frémont, "Biographical Sketch," 7, and Adams, *Memoirs,* X, 257.

26. *CG,* 26/1, 1 ff., 51-56; Benton, *View,* II, 159-162; Wiltse, *Calhoun: Nullifier,* 405 ff.

27. *CG,* 26/1, 141, 145, Appendix 117, 118-119, 121, 122, 140, 141. Cf.

Benton to Corbin, September 16, 1839, in Corbin Papers, Rutgers College Collection, copy in MoHS; and Benton, *View*, II, 64.

28. Benton to Jackson, April 24, 1840, in Jackson Papers, LofC; *Missouri Argus*, April 5, 1839.

29. Benton, *View*, II, 204. Cf. Turner, *United States: 1830-1850*, 477-484; Schlesinger, *Age of Jackson*, 289-298; Cleaves, *Old Tippecanoe*, 314-318; Lynch, *An Epoch and a Man*, 445-448; and Mims, *Majority of the People*, 246.

30. *Missouri Argus*, 1840 — May 19; June 2, 5, 9; August 17; also Lucy Kenny, *History of the Present Cabinet*, Title, 4; Frémont, "Senator Thomas H. Benton," 241-242.

31. *Missouri Argus*, July 13 and 14, 1840; [Benton], *The Missouri Delegation to their Constituents*, 5-7, 12, 13, 14; *Democratic Review* — VII (June, 1840), 478, 485-486, 487; VIII (September, 1840), 197.

32. *Missouri Argus*, September 22, 1840; *Missouri Republican*, August 21 and October 21, 1840; Benton to Jackson, September 25, 1840, in Jackson Papers, Second Series, LofC. Cf. Nolan, "The Labor Movement in St. Louis Prior to the Civil War," *Missouri Historical Review*, XXXIV (October, 1939), 18-27.

33. *Missouri Argus*, 1840 — September 25; October 3, 9, 12, 15, 16, 20; November 3; also [Benton], *Letters . . . to His Constituents in 1839*, 5-10; *Missouri Republican*, October 12, 13, and 14, 1840.

34. Brownson, "Popular Government," in *Democratic Review*, XII (May, 1843), 531-535.

35. *Missouri Argus*, 1840 — November 20, 23, 27; John Dougherty to A. B. Chambers, March 17, and to James H. Birch, March 15, 1841, in John Dougherty Collection, Kansas State Historical Society; William M. Campbell to Abiel Leonard, December 20, 1840, in Leonard Manuscripts, Missouri State Historical Society. Cf. McClure, *Opposition in Missouri*, 18-19.

36. Benton to [Dawson], December 6, 1840, in *Niles National Register*, LIX (January 16, 1841), 310; and December 9, 1840 and January 9, 184[1], in Moses Dawson Collection, Xavier University; Benton to [Corbin], December 7, 1840, in Corbin Papers, Rutgers College Collection, copy in MoHS; *Missouri Argus*, December 15, 1840, ff.

37. *CG*, 26/2, 12, 14-15, 19, 54-57, 138, 198.

38. Benton, *View*, II, 208, 210; Cleaves, *Old Tippecanoe*, 333.

CHAPTER 12

1. Frémont, *Memoirs*, I, 62, 64, 67.

2. Cf. Van Deusen, *Henry Clay*, 342 ff.; Poage, *Henry Clay and the Whig Party*, 37; Chitwood, *John Tyler*, 206, 208-216; Benton, *View*, II, 219.

3. *CG*, 27/1, 79-260, 352, 379, 444, 447-449; Washington *Globe*, 1841 — July 6, 8, 14, 24, 26, 27, 28; Benton, *View*, II, 249; Adams, *Memoirs*, X, 533.

4. *CG*, 27/1, 274, 388, 407, 438, Appendix 327, 331; Benton, *View*, II, 245.

5. Cf. Tyler, *Letters and Times*, II, 249-250; *Missouri Argus*, October 11, 1841.

6. Cf. Frémont, *Memoirs*, I, 67, 68; Nevins, *Frémont: Pathmarker of the West*, 56-71.

7. Benton to McDowell, Postscript by Elizabeth Benton, October 16, 1841, in McDowell Papers, Duke; *Missouri Argus*, 1841 — September 28; October 2; November 9.

8. *CG*, 27/2, 848-850, 960, Appendix 659-661; Benton, *View*, II, 417; Benton to Van Buren, June 8, 1842, Van Buren Papers, LofC; cf. Turner, *United States: 1830-1850*, 503-507; and, for the treaty debates, *CG*, 27/3, Appendix 1-27.

9. Benton to Jackson, March 31, 1842, in Jackson Papers, and to Van Buren, April 14, 1842, in Van Buren Papers, LofC. Cf. Benton, *View*, II, 398; and Van Deusen, *Henry Clay*, 355-357.

10. Keyes, *Fifty Years Observation*, 403; Willis, *Hurry-Graphs*, 179-180; Waddell, "Thomas Hart Benton," 482-483; [Preston], "Personal Recollections," 110-120; Frémont, "Senator Thomas H. Benton," 242; Benton, and Silas Wright, to Van Buren, April 2, 14, 1842, in Van Buren Papers, LofC.

11. Benton to Van Buren, April 17, June 3, 1842, and Samuel Hart and Henry Simpson to Van Buren, June 28, July 30, 1842, in Van Buren Papers, LofC; Smith, *Blair Family*, I, 147, 151, 152; Ambler, *Ritchie*, 227; Benton to Jackson, March 10, 1842, in Jackson Papers, LofC; Schlesinger, *Age of Jackson*, 396, 400; *Missouri Republican*, September 19, 1842.

12. Woodford, *Lewis Cass*, 215-221; Duff Green to Calhoun, August 2, 1842, in Jameson, *Correspondence*, 848; John A. Scoville to Hunter, September 11, 1842, in Ambler, *Correspondence of Robert M. T. Hunter*, 42-48. Cf. Fitzsimons, "Calhoun's Bid for the Presidency, 1841-1844," in *Mississippi Valley Historical Review*, XXXVIII (June, 1951), 44-59; and Buchanan to Mr. Leiper, May 22, 1842, in Moore, *Works of James Buchanan*, V, 254.

13. Benton to Van Buren, April 14, and June 3 and 8, 1842, in Van Buren Papers, LofC.

14. *Missouri Republican*, October 11, 12, and 19, 1842; Frémont, *Memoirs*, I, 117; Nevins, *Frémont*, 116, 211.

15. *Missouri Argus*, 1841 — March 24; April 6, 15; October 26; December 15; also Benton to Thomas Reynolds, May 11, 1841, in Reynolds Papers, MoHS; Dorsey, "Panic and Depression of 1837-1843 in Missouri," 151-157; McClure, *Opposition in Missouri*, 39-43; and *Missouri Republican*, November 1, 8, 16, 17, and 18, 1842.

16. *Missouri Reporter*, November 1, 1842, and editorial reprinted in full, March 1, 1843; Benton to Reynolds, November 1, 1842 [November 7 or 8, 1842], in Reynolds Papers, MoHS.

17. Benton to Reynolds, November 10, 1842, Benton Papers, and to William

L. Sublette, January 30, 1843, Sublette Papers, MoHS; *Missouri Republican,* November 28, 1842, and *Missouri Reporter,* 1843 — March 8, 10, 21; April 19.

18. Benton to McDowell, December 12, 1842, and January 6, February 15, 22, and March 4, and 27, 1843 — all in McDowell Papers, Duke; also Nevins, *Frémont,* 116-119, 623; and *Missouri Reporter,* May 3, 1843.

19. Cf. John Letcher to Benton, December 17, 1842, in Van Buren Papers, LofC; Benton to William L. Sublette, January 30, 1843, in Sublette Papers, MoHS.

20. *CG,* 27/3, 133-134, 155 ff., 171, 199-200, 234 ff., 240, Appendix 138-139.

21. Tyler to Webster, October 11, 1841, in Tyler, *Letters and Times,* II, 254; Chitwood, *John Tyler,* 342 ff.; Jackson to Aaron V. Brown, February 9 [12], 1843, in Bassett, *Correspondence,* VI, 201-202; Washington *Globe,* March 20, 1844; Benton, *View,* II, 581 ff.

22. Benton, *View,* II, 579-581; Frémont, *Memoirs,* I, 64-65; Frémont, "Biographical Sketch," 15; Nevins, *Frémont,* 129 ff.; *Missouri Reporter,* June 15, 1843.

23. *Missouri Reporter,* March-June, 1843 — esp. March 1, 4, 6, 8, 9, 10, 21, 24, 25; April 13, 14, 18, 19, 28; May 25; June 17.

24. McClure, *Opposition in Missouri,* 44-45; *Missouri Republican,* June 20 and October 27, 1843.

25. Grissom, "Personal Recollections," 141-144; *Missouri Republican,* November 9, 1843. This story is given here substantially as it appears in the *Republican,* though I have changed indirect to direct discourse in places.

26. *Republican,* 1843 — July 21, 22; August 7, 17, 30; October 23; November 1, 10; also *Missouri Reporter,* 1843 — August 1, 17, 18, 21, 29; September 12, 14, 25; and Benton to McDowell, August 15, 1843, in McDowell Papers, Duke; Collier, "Recollections of Thomas H. Benton," *Missouri Historical Review,* VIII (April, 1914), 137; Benton to Thomas Reynolds, St. Louis, October 19, 1843, in Benton Papers, MoHS.

27. Penn, *Letters to Col. Thomas H. Benton,* 3-5, 7-11, 20 ff. The available file of the *Reporter* breaks off at September 30, 1843, and it is thus necessary to use this pamphlet reprint of Penn's letters.

28. Linn and Sargent, *Life and Public Services of Dr. Lewis F. Linn,* 115, 368-372; *Missouri Republican,* October 6, 1843; Benton to Thomas Reynolds, St. Louis, October 19, 1843, in Benton Papers, MoHS.

29. Will of Jesse Benton, September 23, 1843, in Jesse Benton Papers, LofC.

CHAPTER 13

1. Benton, *View,* II, 582-583; *Niles National Register,* LXVI (June 29, 1844), 280. Cf. Smith, *Annexation of Texas,* 96-97, 363, 434, *passim.*

2. *Niles National Register,* LXVI (March 2, 1844), 1, 61; Benton, *View,* II, 567-569; Buchanan to Edward Y. Buchanan, February 29, 1844, in Moore, *Works,* V, 448; *Missourian,* March 13, 1844; Fairfield to Mrs. Fairfield, March 26, 1844, in Staples, *Letters,* 330.

3. Benton, *View*, II, 589-590; Blair to Jackson, Washington, May 2, 1844, in Bassett, *Correspondence*, 281-282. Cf. Wiltse, *Calhoun: Sectionalist*, 169-171; Smith, *Annexation of Texas*, 199-218.
4. *Niles National Register*, LXVI (May 4, 25, and June 8, 1844), 153-157, 160, 197, 228; *Annexation of Texas, Opinions of Messrs. Clay, Polk, Benton, and Van Buren*, 3, 4, 12-14, 16; MacCormac, *James K. Polk*, 213 ff.; *Letters of Messrs. Clay, Benton, and Barrow*, 6, 8, 10, 11; Woodford, *Lewis Cass*, 222; Jackson to Blair, May 7 and 11, and June 5 and 29, and to Benton, May 14, 1844, in Bassett, *Correspondence*, VI, 284, 286, 298, 299, 292.
5. *CG*, 28/1, Appendix 474-486; Benton, *Three Speeches . . . on the Annexation of Texas*, 3-6, 7, 9-11, 13, 14, 15, 21, 24, 28, 30.
6. Cf. Calhoun to Francis Wharton, May 28, 1844, and to Andrew Pickens Calhoun, June 23, 1849, in Jameson, *Correspondence*, 593, 768; Buchanan in the Senate, June 8, 1844, in *CG*, 28/1, Appendix 723; Bancroft to Van Buren, Washington, May 24, 1844, in "Van Buren-Bancroft Correspondence," *Massachusetts Historical Society Proceedings*, XLII, 430; "The Late Thomas H. Benton," in *United States Magazine and Democratic Review*, XLII (July, 1858), 65.
7. *CG*, 28/1, 652-657, Appendix 568-576, 589-590, 607-610; *Missourian*, June 28, 1844; Washington *Globe*, June 11, 1844; Richmond *Enquirer*, quoted in Smith, *Annexation of Texas*, 285; *Niles National Register*, LXVI (June 22, July 6, 1844), 272, 295; Adams, *Memoirs*, XII, 56; Blair to Jackson, July 7, and Jackson to Blair, June 25, 1844, in Bassett, *Correspondence*, VI, 298, 300-301.
8. Wentworth, *Congressional Reminiscences*, 16, 20, 46-47; Perry, *Reminiscences of Public Men*, 45.
9. Cf. Polk to Donelson, October 19, December 20, 1843, in "Letters of James K. Polk to Andrew J. Donelson" in *Tennessee Historical Magazine*, I (September, 1915), 234; Ambler, *Ritchie*, 237-242; Benton to [McDowell], May 6, 1844, in McDowell Papers, Duke; Polk to Johnson, May 13 and 14, 1844, in "Letters of James K. Polk to Cave Johnson," 240-243; Pillow to Polk, May 22, 24 and 25, 1844, in Reeves, "Letters of Gideon J. Pillow to James K. Polk, 1844," *American Historical Review*, XI (July, 1906), 835-837, 839-840; Jordan, "A Politician of Expansion: Robert J. Walker," *Mississippi Valley Historical Review*, XIX (1932-1933), 370; also Benton, *View*, II, 585, 588.
10. *Niles National Register*, LXVI (June 1, 8, 1844), 211-216, and 218, 227; Forney, *Anecdotes of Public Men*, 117; Pillow to Polk, May 28, 30, 1844, in Reeves, "Letters," 840-841; Bancroft to Polk, July 6, 1844, in Howe, *Life and Letters of George Bancroft*, I, 253-254; Jordan, "A Politician of Expansion," 370; *Missourian*, 1844 — June 6-13, 15, 20; July 11; also Benton, *View*, II, 581-596.
11. *Missourian*, June 15, 1844; Van Buren to Bancroft, July 3, 1844, in "Van Buren-Bancroft Correspondence," 430; Calhoun to Francis Wharton, July 14, 1844, in Jameson, *Correspondence*, 601; Benton to McDowell, June 21, 1844, in McDowell Papers, Duke.

12. *Missourian,* March 16, April 8, October 5, 1844; *Jefferson Inquirer,* quoted in Dorsey, "Panic and Depression of 1837," 161; Ray, "Retirement of Thomas H. Benton from the Senate and Its Significance," in *Missouri Historical Review,* II (October, 1907, January, 1908), 3; McClure, *Opposition in Missouri,* 68-71, 79-85, 88-89; *Missouri Republican,* 1844 — July 19, 22, 23, 27, 30; August 3, 5, 10, 23; September 11, 16, 18; October 1, 5, 19; *Niles National Register,* LXVI (August 24, 1844), 424; Jackson to Blair, August 15, September 19, and October 17, 1844, in Bassett, *Correspondence,* VI, 314, 320, 325; Benton to [A. R. Corbin?], October 5, 28, 1844, in Corbin Papers, Rutgers College Collection, copies in MoHS; Benton, *Substance of . . . Speech delivered at St. Louis, Saturday, October 19, 1844,* 3, 4, 10.

13. *Missourian,* November 6, 8, 9, and 27, 1844, and January 5, 1845; cf. Stanwood, *Presidency,* 223, and Turner, *United States: 1830-1850,* 528-531; also Benton, *View,* II, 626; Van Buren to Bancroft, November 28, 1844, in "Van Buren-Bancroft Correspondence," 432; Spencer, "William L. Marcy Goes Conservative," 224; *Missouri Republican,* November 21, 22, and 25, 1844; *House Journal,* 13 Assembly, 1 Session, 37-40; McClure, *Opposition in Missouri,* 92-96.

14. Benton to McDowell, December 2, 1844, in McDowell Papers, Duke; Staples, *Letters,* 348; Adams, *Memoirs,* XII, 140.

15. Calhoun to William R. King, December 13; to Thomas G. Clemson, December 27; and to R. M. T. Hunter, December 29, 1844 — all in Jameson, *Correspondence,* 633, 635, 636; *Missouri Republican,* January 28, 1845; Benton to Donelson, January 10, 1845, in "Selected Letters from the Donelson Papers," *Tennessee Historical Magazine,* III (June, 1917), 148-149.

16. *CG,* 28/1, 244-245, 359 ff., 372; Benton to McDowell, February 11, 1845, in McDowell Papers, Duke; Letters to Van Buren — from Blair, February 9 and 14; Dix, February 18; Welles, February 20, 1845 — all in Van Buren Papers, LofC; Calhoun to Hunter, February 14, 1845, in Ambler, *Correspondence,* 75; also Wiltse, *Calhoun: Sectionalist,* 211; Smith, *Annexation of Texas,* 337-345; and *Missouri Republican,* March 8 and 14, 1845.

17. Benton to Mrs. James K. Polk, February 14 [1845], in Polk Papers, LofC; Smith, *Annexation of Texas,* 347-353, and MacCormac, *Polk,* 314-315; Tyler, *Letters and Times,* II, 364-365; Chitwood, *John Tyler,* 360-366; Wiltse, *Calhoun: Sectionalist,* 214.

18. Letters from Tappan and Blair, New York *Post,* July 28, 1848, quoted in *Niles National Register,* LXXIV (August 16, 1848), 105-106; Benton, *View,* II, 636-638; Quaife, *Diary,* IV, 38-47, 49, 51-52, 185; Buchanan to Polk, November 9, 1848, in Moore, *Works,* VIII, 241-242; Smith, *Annexation of Texas,* 348-350; MacCormac, *Polk,* 315-317.

19. MacCormac, *Polk,* 291-292, 322-323, 339; Garraty, *Silas Wright,* 340-342, 345-348; Lynch, *An Epoch and a Man,* 496-497; Wiltse, *Calhoun: Sectionalist,* 218-220; Van Buren to Bancroft, March 7, 1845, in Bassett, *Correspondence,* VI, 361, 405.

20. *Missouri Republican*, 1845 — March 7; April 30; May 30; June 16, 24; Penn to Calhoun, June 26, 1845, in Boucher and Brooks, *Correspondence*, 298-299.

21. Green to Calhoun, March 26, 1845, in Boucher and Brooks, *Correspondence*, 288; Polk to Jackson, March 26, 1845, in Bassett, *Correspondence*, VI, 390; Smith, *Blair Family*, II, 162 ff.; Ambler, *Ritchie*, 246-249, 251-259; *Missouri Republican*, April 25, 1845.

22. James, *Jackson*, 784-785; Schlesinger, *Age of Jackson*, 446-448; Lewis to Benton, March 4, 1846, in *CG*, 29/2, 563.

23. Benton, *View*, II, 660-662; MacCormac, *Polk*, 563 ff.; *Missouri Republican*, May 31 and July 31, 1845; Quaife, *Diary*, I, 69.

24. Nevins, *Frémont*, 202 ff.; Benton, *View*, II, 688-693.

25. Quaife, *Diary*, I, 68-72, 140-142; *Niles National Register*, LXIX (November 15, 1845), 165, 167; *Missouri Republican*, August 21, 1845; Green to Calhoun, September 24, 1845, in Jameson, *Correspondence*, 1054.

26. Benton, *View*, II, 662 ff.; Turner, *United States: 1830-1850*, 551; MacCormac, *Polk*, 579-582; Woodford, *Cass*, 234-236; Benton to Van Buren, December 15, 1845, in Van Buren Papers, LofC; *CG*, 29/1, 251-254; Wiltse, *Calhoun: Sectionalist*, 250-262.

27. *CG*, 29/1, 404-405, 456-460, 577-578, 581-583, 683, 716, 721, Appendix 422-430; letter from John Wilson, July 10, 1846, in Harding, *Life of George R. Smith*, 120; Quaife, *Diary*, I, 286-287, 324-325; *Missouri Statesman*, July 21, 1848, quoted in McClure, *Opposition in Missouri*, 113.

28. Quaife, *Diary*, I, 376-377, 451-460; *CG*, 29/1, 851-855, 857-869, 913-919, 1168-1169; *Niles National Register*, LXX (June 6, 13, July 18, 1846), 220, 234, 314; Benton, *Speech on the Oregon Question*, 1-32; Benton, *View*, II, 674-676.

29. *CG*, 29/1, 45, 85, 1044, 1073, 1094, 1112, 1147-1148, 1196; Welles to Van Buren, July 28, 1846, Van Buren Papers, LofC; Quaife, *Diary*, I, 140-141, 265, 280, 441-442.

30. For the Francis Thomas scandal: Benton to James McDowell, August 15, 1843, October 3, 17, 23, and December 26, 1845, and February 1, 1846; and Augustus C. Dodge to Benton, January 19, 1846 — all in McDowell Papers, Duke; also Benton to Joshua Brant, November 13, 1845, Benton Papers, MoHS; Francis Thomas to Benton, May 2, 1844, Van Buren Papers, LofC; and *Statement of Francis Thomas*, 8-10, 18-23, *passim*; *U.S.* v. *Francis Thomas*, in *1 District of Columbia 243-254*; J. W. Thomas and T. J. C. Williams, "Francis Thomas," in *History of Allegany County, Maryland*, 281-284; *Missouri Republican*, 1845 — April 1, 11, 16; July 23; August 30. Also (Sally McDowell) Miller, "James McDowell," 200, *passim*; and Quaife, *Diary*, I, 51-53.

31. Benton to James McDowell, October 3 and 23, December 15, 26 and 30, 1845, and February 1, 1846; also Corcoran and Riggs, Statement to Benton, March 15, 1845 — all in McDowell Papers, Duke. Also Bay,

Bench and Bar, 21; [Preston], "Personal Recollection," 119; Original and General Records, St. Louis, C4, 534.

32. Seward to Mrs. Seward [?], January 9, 16, 1846, in Seward, *Autobiography,* 773, 775; Maury, *Statesmen of America in 1846,* 95-98; Perry, *Reminiscences,* Second Series, 18-21; Sumner to Bancroft, April 22, 1846, quoted in Schlesinger, *Age of Jackson,* 60.

33. Benton to [Pierre Chouteau Jr.], February 11, 1846, Chouteau-Walsh Papers, MoHS.

34. Quaife, *Diary,* I, 71, 305-308, 325-326, 375-376, 390, 391-392; *CG,* 29/1, 783-785, 795-804. Cf. Benton, *View,* II, 693-694.

35. Quaife, *Diary,* II, 102, 219, 221-228, 231-233, 239-243, 258-265, and cf. 268-270; draft of letter in Benton's handwriting [July 14, 1846], in Polk Papers, LofC. Cf. Benton, *View,* II, 693-694.

36. Benton to Polk, November 9, 1846, and "Operations of Captain Frémont in Upper California," *Niles National Register,* LXXI (November 14, 21, 1846), 173-174, 187-191; Benton, *View,* II, 688-693; Nevins, *Frémont,* 217-304; *Missouri Republican,* November 19, 1846.

37. *CG,* 29/2, 175-177, 185-187, 246-247; Calhoun to Thomas G. Clemson, January 30, 1847, in Jameson, *Correspondence,* 717; Quaife, *Diary,* II, 347, 419-420; Buchanan to Bancroft, February 26, 1847; Blair to Buchanan, November 22, 1849; and Buchanan to Blair, November 27, 1849 — all in Moore, *Works,* XI, 474, VIII, 365-366, 368; also, Benton to Van Buren, January 26, 1847, in Van Buren Papers, LofC; and Benton, *View,* II, 678-679.

38. Quaife, *Diary,* II, 406-407, 409, 416, 418; drafts of letters to Benton, March 9, 1847, and Benton to Polk, March 9, 1847, in Polk Papers, LofC; "Circular to Members of the Senate," by Benton, March 10, 1847, in Van Buren Papers, LofC.

39. Quaife, *Diary,* II, 325-327, 331-334; Benton to Buchanan, January 4, 15, 1847, Benton Letters, PHS.

CHAPTER 14

1. *CG,* 29/2, 358, 453-455, 555, 556, Appendix 326.

2. Quaife, *Diary,* II, 334; Garraty, *Silas Wright,* 394-398; Smith, *Blair Family,* I, 205-206, 218; Benton, *View,* II, 694-700.

3. Quaife, *Diary,* II, 444-445, 447-449; *Niles National Register,* LXXII (May 8, 1847), 148.

4. Quaife, *Diary,* II, 334, 346, 458, 459; III, 74; also Elwood Fisher to Calhoun, May 25, 1847, and J. W. A. Pettit to Calhoun, June 18, 1847, in Boucher, *Correspondence,* 378, 384.

5. Quaife, *Diary,* II, 444-445, 447-449.

6. For Missouri politics and Benton's 1847 visit: St. Louis *Union,* May-August 1847 — esp. May 6, 11, 13, 14, 15, 18; June 4, 12; July 5, 8, 12, 15, 17, 19; August 11; also *Missouri Republican,* June 3 and 10, 1847; Quaife, *Kit Carson's Autobiography,* 119-120; Benton to Colonel

Medill, May 21, 1847, in Benton Letters, PHS; and Nevins, *Diary of Philip Hone*, II, 810.

7. Calhoun to Thomas G. Clemson, September 6, 1847, in Jameson, *Correspondence*, 736-737; E. A. Maynard to Van Buren, August 30, 1847, in Van Buren Papers, LofC; Smith, *Blair Family*, I, 221-222; *Niles National Register*, LXXIII (September 11, 1847), 24.

8. Letters from Benton, August 24, October 22, 1847, Houghton Library, Harvard University, and Personal Miscellany, LofC; Quaife, *Diary*, III, 120-123, 129-130.

9. For the Frémont fracas: Nevins, *Frémont*, 305-326, 329-341; Benton to Frémont, October 3, 7, ?, 14, 1847, in Wheat, "Senator Benton Lays His Plans," *California Historical Society Quarterly*, XIII (June, 1934), 151-154; Taylor to R. C. Wood, September 27, 1847, in Sampson, *Letters of Zachary Taylor*, 136; Quaife, *Diary*, III, 52-54, 61-62, 120-123, 129-130, 197-198, 201-206, 324, 336-339, 442; and IV, 227.

10. Washington *Union*, January 18, 1847; Blair to Van Buren, January 23, [1848], in Van Buren Papers, LofC.

11. Benton to Polk, November 21, 1847, and Niles and Dix to Van Buren, January 20, 27, 1848, in Van Buren Papers, LofC.

12. [Davis], *Jefferson Davis . . . A Memoir*, I, 269-276.

13. *CG*, 30/1, 383, 388-389; Benton, *View*, II, 707-709.

14. Cf. Smith, *War with Mexico*, II, 233 ff.; Quaife, *Diary*, III, 363-368, 370 ff.

15. Robertson, "A Pioneer Captain of Industry in Oregon," *Quarterly Journal of the Oregon Historical Society*, IV (June, 1903), 157-158; Memorandum to Polk (unsigned), C Street, May 28, 1848, in Polk Papers, LofC.

16. For Congress in 1848: *CG*, 30/1, 809 ff., 875, 901, 927, 932, 950, 1002-1005, 1016, 1060 ff., Appendix 684, 686, 871, 876; Quaife, *Diary*, III, 501-502. Cf. Benton, *View*, II, 713-715.

17. Charleston *Mercury*, August 21, 1848, quoted in Nevins, *Ordeal of the Union*, I, 25; Benton, *View*, II, 712.

18. *CG*, 30/1, Appendix 977-1040; cf. Nevins, *Frémont*, 342; Quaife, *Diary*, IV, 59-60; Blair to Van Buren, August 13 and 14, 1848, in Van Buren Papers; also Benton to Andrew P. Butler, August 14, 1848, Benton Papers, Personal Miscellany, LofC.

19. Benton, *View*, II, 719-721; Nevins, *Frémont*, 342-372; *Niles National Register*, LXXIV (October 18, 1848), 244-245; Quaife, *Diary*, IV, 136-137; St. Louis *Union*, April 3 and October 17, 1849.

20. *Niles National Register*, LXXIII (January 8, 1848), 293; Schlesinger, *Age of Jackson*, 450 ff., 457-460; Nevins, *Ordeal of the Union*, I, 29-30, 189 ff.; Woodford, *Lewis Cass*, 250-254; Benton, *View*, II, 722-723.

21. Francis Blair, Jr., *Address, Resolutions and Proceedings of the Democracy of St. Louis*, January 8, 1848, 4.

22. *Missouri Republican*, May 1, 4, 22 and 26, 1848; Forney, *Anecdotes of Public Men*, 324; Dix, *Memoirs of John Adams Dix*, I, 231; Schlesinger, *Age of Jackson*, 451-452, 462; Rayback, "The American Workingman

and the Antislavery Crusade," in *Journal of Economic History*, III (November, 1943), 152-163.

23. St. Louis *Union*, June 7, 1848.

24. *Missouri Republican*, May 24, 1848, and Baltimore *Sun*, quoted in *Missouri Republican*, May 30 and June 1-3 and 5, 1848; Benton, *View*, II, 722; Washington *Union*, June 1 and 8, 1848; St. Louis *Union*, June 7 and 30, 1848.

25. Washington *Union*, June 9, 10, 11, 14, 15, and 20, 1848; St. Louis *Union*, June 16, 17, and 19, 1848.

26. Flagg to Van Buren, June 19, 1848; Benton to Van Buren, May 29, 1848; and Blair to Van Buren, June 26, 1848 — all in Van Buren Papers, LofC; Van Buren to Dix, June 20, 1848, in Dix, *Memoirs*, I, 233-234; Benton to Cass, *"Private,"* [June] and July 10, 1848, in Cass Papers, University of Michigan; Washington *Union*, June 14, 1848; *Missouri Republican*, 1848, June 5, 6, 13; St. Louis *Union*, June 30, 1848; notes by Treat, July 3, 1848, and n. d., on letter from Cass, Treat Papers, MoHS.

27. Cf. Chase to Sumner, April 24, 1847; to John Thomas, June 24, 1847; to Preston King, July 15, 1847 — all in Bourne, *Diary and Correspondence*, 116, 118-119, 120-122; Dyer, *Phonographic Report*, 3-32; Nevins, *Ordeal of the Union*, I, 205-208; Dix, *Memoirs*, I, 240; Smith, *Blair Family*, I, 239-243; Prospectus of the Free Soil Democrat, August 30, 1848, in Political Papers, MoHS; St. Louis *Union*, September 25, 1848; *Missouri Republican*, October 19, 1848.

28. J. N. Bailey to Abiel Leonard, September 2, 1848, in Leonard Manuscripts, Missouri State Historical Society; St. Louis *Union*, 1848 — July 13; August 26; September 12; October 25 and 26; also *Missouri Republican*, October 10 and 20, 1848; and Benton to David L. Sayre, October 6 [7?], 1848, in Benton Letters, New York Historical Society.

29. Van Buren to Blair, December 11, 1848, cited in Smith, *Blair Family*, I, 243; Benton, *View*, II, 723.

30. Blair to Van Buren, December 30, 1848, in Van Buren Papers, LofC; Dyer, *Great Senators*, 191, 197, 198, 202-203, 205, 207; "Senator Benton's Egotism," in *Missouri Historical Review*, XXXI (July, 1937), 489-490.

31. Richardson, *Messages and Papers*, VI, 2479, 2489-2492; *CG*, 30/2, 33-37.

32. Blair to Van Buren, January 27, 1849, in Van Buren Papers, LofC; *CG*, 30/2, 470-474. Cf. Cotterill, "National Railroad Convention," *Missouri Historical Review*, XII (July, 1918), 203-207.

33. *Niles National Register*, LXXV (January 17, 24, February 7, 14, 1849), 45-46, 49, 84-88, 100-104; Benton, *View*, II, 733-736; Wiltse, *Calhoun: Sectionalist*, 378-388; Nevins, *Ordeal of the Union*, I, 221-225; McClure, *Opposition in Missouri*, 136-137.

34. *Senate Journal*, 14 Assembly, 1 Session, 64-66; *Missouri Republican*, January-March 1849; McClure, *Opposition in Missouri*, 138-143;

Merkel, *Anti-Slavery in Missouri*, 120, 121 ff.; Blair to Van Buren, January 27, 1849, Van Buren Papers, LofC.
35. Quaife, *Diary*, IV, 329-330; Benton, *View*, II, 737-738. Cf. Nevins, *Ordeal of the Union*, I, 7, 228.
36. St. Louis *Union*, March 2 and April 21, 1849.

CHAPTER 15

1. St. Louis *Union*, May 8 and 9, 1849.
2. Montgomery Blair to Van Buren, May 12, 1849, in Van Buren Papers, LofC; cf. also McClure, *Opposition in Missouri*, 166 ff.; Ray, "Retirement of Thomas H. Benton from the Senate," 4, 5, 13; Merkel, "The Slavery Issue and the Political Decline of Thomas Hart Benton, 1846-1855," in *Missouri Historical Review*, XXXVIII (July, 1944), 394-396; Merkel, *Anti-Slavery in Missouri*, 123 ff.
3. St. Louis *Union*, May 25 and 29, 1849; Benton, *Col. Benton's Great Speech! to the People of Missouri Delivered at the Capitol of the State*, 1-14.
4. St. Louis *Union*, 1849 — May 29; June 2, 4, 7, 12, 14, 16, 20, 27; July 4; also Van Buren to Blair, June 16, 1849, in Smith, *Blair Family*, I, 254; Foote and Henry Young to Calhoun, June 5 and 6, 1849, in Boucher, *Correspondence*, 506-507; Calhoun to Andrew Pickens Calhoun, June 23, 1849, in Jameson, *Correspondence*, 768.
5. St. Louis *Union*, 1849 — June 16, 18, 22, 28; July 17, 21, 23, 24; August 9, 10, 15, 28, 29; September 5; and *Missouri Republican*, July 4 and 7, 1849; also McClure, *Opposition in Missouri*, 175-179.
6. St. Louis *Union*, July 21, 23 and 24, 1849; Birch, *Speech in Reply to those of Hon. Thomas H. Benton, passim*, 3-5, 8-9, 22, 43-47, 48; cf. McClure, *Opposition in Missouri*, 146, 153-156, 163, 177-178; *Birch* vs. *Benton*, in *26 Missouri Reports 153;* Sworn Statement by Benton, July 17, 1850, in Benton Documents, Missouri State Historical Society; Boone, "A *Cause Célèbre — Birch* vs. *Benton*," in Stewart, *History of the Bench and Bar of Missouri*, 377-379.
7. St. Louis *Union*, 1849 — May 5, 19, 22, 25; June 20, 22; July 11 ff.; August 2, 4, 7, 9, 15, 18, 20; also Z. G. Draper to Abiel Leonard, July 26, 1849, in Leonard Manuscripts, Missouri State Historical Society.
8. *Letter from Hon. H. S. Foote, of Mississippi, to Hon. Henry A. Wise*, 1, 2, 7; Calhoun to Andrew Pickens Calhoun, July 24, 1849, in Jameson, *Correspondence*, 769; Calhoun to Samuel Treat, July 9, 1849, in Treat Papers, MoHS; Calhoun, *Address . . . to the People of the Southern States, passim*, 1, 19-20.
9. For the Fayette speech: Grissom, "Personal Recollections," 134-135; Benton, *Speech . . . Delivered at Fayette, Howard County, Missouri on Saturday the First of September, 1849*, 3-32; St. Louis *Union*, October 9, 10, and 11, 1849.
10. *Ibid.*, September 12, and October 6 and 15, 1849; *Missouri Republican*,

1849 — May 30; August 11; September 28; October 5; also McClure, *Opposition in Missouri,* 180-186, 192.

11. Adam Klippel to Chase, September 14, 1849, in Bourne, *Diary and Correspondence,* 471-474. (Emphasis added.)

12. Darby, *Personal Recollections,* 182-183; St. Louis *Union,* October 16-19, 1849; *Missouri Republican,* October 18, 1849; Cotterill, "National Railroad Convention," 207-215.

13. St. Louis *Union,* October 18, 19, 1849; *Missouri Republican,* October 19, 1849.

14. *Ibid.,* 1849 — October 24, 27, 31; November 1, 2, 3, 10, 14.

15. Seward, *Seward at Washington . . . with Selections from His Letters, 1846-1861,* 104, 105, 120.

16. Cf. Benton to O'Fallon, January 17, 1850, in O'Fallon Collection, MoHS.

17. First Annual Message, in Richardson, *Messages and Papers,* V, 9-24; Hamilton, *Zachary Taylor: Soldier in the White House,* 256-259; Benton, *View,* II, 740-742.

18. Seward, *Seward at Washington,* 116; *CG,* 31/1, 97-98, 165-168.

19. *Ibid.,* 244-247, 293, 323 ff., Appendix 100, 115-127; cf. Benton, *View,* II, 742.

20. Wiltse, *Calhoun: Sectionalist,* 473-478; Webster to Fletcher Webster, March 31, 1850, in McIntyre, *Writings and Speeches,* XVIII, 363; Wentworth, *Congressional Reminiscences,* 23-24.

21. *CG,* 21/1, 430-432, 656-660 ff., Appendix 446-450; Benton to [?], April 5, 1850, Benton Letters, PHS; Hamilton, *Zachary Taylor,* 300-301, 316, 319.

22. Cf. Washington *Union,* March 16, 1850; Hamilton, *Zachary Taylor,* 284-286, 298-301, 334 ff., 330; Poage, *Henry Clay and the Whig Party,* 216, 220-221, 233; William H. Haywood to Van Buren, May 7, 1850, in Van Buren Papers, LofC.

23. *CG,* 31/1, 762, 769, 1153-1154, 1479-1481; letter of July 1, 1850, in Bremer, *The Homes of the New World,* I, 438-439; Dyer, *Great Senators,* 279; Sargent, *Public Men and Events,* II, 361; Wentworth, *Congressional Reminiscences,* 48; Foote, *Casket of Reminiscences,* 337, 338-339; Benton to Pearce, April 22, 23 and July 27, 1850, Pearce Papers, Maryland Historical Society; Benton to Tindall, April 18, 1850, and to Colonel Force, n. d., Benton Papers, Personal Miscellany, and Blair to Van Buren, April 27, 1850, Van Buren Papers, and Broadsides Collection, LofC.

24. *CG,* 31/1, 769-775, 780-781, 944-948.

25. Hamilton, *Zachary Taylor,* 332-337, 339, 343-344, 377-380, 382-384; Nevins, *Ordeal of the Union,* I, 320; letter of July 9, 1850, in Seward, *Seward at Washington,* 138.

26. *CG,* 31/1, 1173, Appendix 676-684; Benton, *Anti-Compromise Speech, in the Senate, passim;* letters of June 10, 19, in Seward, *Seward at Washington,* 139, 140. Cf. Nevins, *Ordeal of the Union,* I, 338.

27. Benton, *View,* II, 765-766; Hamilton, *Zachary Taylor,* 401-404.

28. Letters of July 10, 20, 1850, in Bremer, *Homes of the New World,* I, 465-466, 481-483.
29. *CG,* 31/1, 1432-1830; Van Deusen, *Henry Clay,* 409-413; Hamilton, *Zachary Taylor,* 402-404.
30. *CG,* 31/1, 1490-1491, 1504, 1555, 1573, 1589, 1647, 1660, 1829, 1830, Appendix 1484-1485, 1589, 1590, 1624, 1625, 1630; Benton, *View,* II, 779-780.
31. Benton to Clayton, December 8, 1850, Clayton Papers, LofC.
32. For the Missouri political situation: *Missouri Republican,* December 5, 1849; *St. Louis Union,* 1850 — March 11, 13, 25, 29; April 2. Also McClure, *Opposition in Missouri,* 197-200, 205; Smith, *Blair Family,* I, 264-265.
33. *Old Bullion,* 1850 — July 29, 30, 31; August 1, 2, 3, 5; St. Louis *Union,* 1850 — July 29; August 1, 3, 5; October 24; and *Missouri Republican,* August 29, 1850. Also Benton to [?], August 29, 1850 [?], in Miscellaneous Papers, New York Library.
34. S. T. Glover to Abiel Leonard, St. Louis, August 3, 1850, in Leonard Manuscripts, Missouri State Historical Society; McClure, *Opposition in Missouri,* 213-214.
35. St. Louis *Union,* 1850 — October 15; November 5, 9, 11; *Missouri Republican,* 1850 — October 16; November 1, 4, 5, 11. Also Benton to R. D. Van Nostrand, October 23, 1850, Miscellaneous Manuscripts, Mercantile Library, St. Louis.
36. *Missouri Republican,* November 11, 12, 13, 15, 16, and 19, 1850; Alex F. Denny to Chauncey Wyman, November 26, 1850, in Denny Letters, MoHS; Bremer, *Homes of the New World,* I, 94.
37. St. Louis *Union,* November 13, 14, and 15, 1850; *Fifth Annual Report . . . Mercantile Library Association,* 15, 16; Benton, Lecture on the Progress of the Age (Manuscript) — in Mercantile Library, St. Louis.
38. *CG,* 31/2, 6-7, 56-58; Benton, *Highway to the Pacific: Grand National Central Highway, passim.*
39. *CG,* 31/2, 151, 541-544, Appendix 138-143, 173-179; Blair to Van Buren, February 25, 1851, in Van Buren Papers, LofC.
40. St. Louis *Union,* 1851, January 3, 6, 9; also A. M. Coffy to Smith, January 17, 1851, in Harding, *Life of George R. Smith,* 182.
41. *House Journal,* 16 Assembly, 1 Session, 88-93, 94-104, 107-111, 114-115, 123, 125, 128, 132-136, 137, 138, 139-143, 147; also *Missouri Republican,* January 9, 10, 15, 16, and 20, 1851; St. Louis *Union,* January 13, 18, 20, and 21, 1851.
42. *Missouri Republican,* January 24 and 25, 1851; St. Louis *Union,* January 24 and 25, 1851; also Samuel R. Ralston to D. W. Jordan, February 20, 1851, in Overdyke, "Southern Family on the Missouri Frontier," *Journal of Economic History,* XVII (May, 1951), 227; and McClure, *Opposition in Missouri,* 181, 214.
43. Chase to Hamlin, January 15, 1851, in Bourne, *Diary and Correspondence,* 229; Blair to Van Buren, January 26, 1851, in Van Buren Papers, LofC; also Washington *Union,* January 25 and February 2, 1851.

CHAPTER 16

1. *Missouri Republican,* 1851 — March 3, 12, 24, 26; April 6-9; also Benton Speech, quoted in McClure, *Opposition in Missouri,* 218; Grissom, "Personal Recollections," 129-130; Benton to [?], March 21, 1851, in Benton Letters, New York Historical Society; and Bowlin to A. J. Donelson, May 5, 1851, in "Selected Letters from the Donelson Papers," in *Tennessee Historical Magazine,* III (December, 1917), 271-274.

2. Blair to Van Buren, January 26 and February 6, 1851, Preston King to John Van Buren, February 25, 1851, and Benton to Dix, November 4, 1851, in Van Buren Papers; and Welles to [?], May, 1851, in Gideon Welles Papers — both LofC; also Chase to Hamlin, August 14 and December 21, 1850, in Bourne, *Diary and Correspondence,* 217, 227. Cf. Smith, *Blair Family,* I, 272-274.

3. For the political "war" in Missouri: *Missouri Republican,* November 1851-August 1852, *passim;* Van Buren to Blair, August 16, 1852, in Bedford Brown Papers, Duke; Blair to Van Buren, August 16, 1852, in Van Buren Papers, LofC; Washington *Union,* August 6 and 10, 1852.

4. Benton to Sally McDowell, July 24, 1851, in McDowell Family Papers, UVa; and to Van Buren, September 11 and 20, 1851, in Van Buren Papers, LofC.

5. *Missouri Republican,* 1852 — March 18, 20; May 16; August 1, 13; also Benton to Jessie Benton Frémont, March ?, 1852, in Nevins, *Frémont,* 405; and to Father deSmet, "½ after 11," March 16, 1852, copy, in Benton Papers, MoHS; and Blair to Van Buren, April 3, 1852, in Van Buren Papers, LofC.

6. Blair to Van Buren, September 30, 1852, and Benton to Van Buren, January 16, 1853, in Van Buren Papers, LofC; also Benton to "My Dear Old Friend" [?], February 3, 1853, in Benton Papers, MoHS.

7. For the gestation and development of the *Thirty Years' View:* Benton to Dix, May 15, 1851; Benton to Van Buren, June 16, 30, July 14, September 11, 20, 25, 28, October 13, 22, 1851, and January 11 and 16, 1853; Van Buren to Benton, July 17, 1851; and Blair to Van Buren, November 27, 1853 — all in Van Buren Papers, LofC; Benton to [Montgomery Blair], August 29, 1851, in Blair Papers, and Benton to Clayton, June 11, 16, August 28 [1852], in Clayton Papers — LofC. Also Benton to B. F. Butler, May 25, 1851, in Benton Papers, and to Alexander Kayser, October 27, 1853, in Glasgow Collection, MoHS; and to Hamlin, June 16, 1851, in Meigs, *Benton,* 423; Washington *Union,* July 24, and September 25, 1851, and July 12, 1853; New York *Evening Post,* July 1853-April 1854; Bryant & Company to Benton, July 16, 1853, in Bryant-Godwin Papers, New York Public Library.

8. Washington *Union,* April 27, 1854; *Missouri Democrat,* May-July, 1854 — esp. May 9, July 24 and September 12; also Buttre, "Thomas Hart Benton," in *American Portrait Gallery* (1877), n.p.; "Extracts from the Diary of Edmund Ruffin," *William and Mary College Quarterly His-*

torical Magazine, XXIII (July, 1914), 31-45; New York *Post,* quoted in *Missouri Democrat,* July 18, 1854; "Literary Notice," *Harper's Magazine,* IX (July, 1854), 276; Benton to ?, May 29, 1854, Benton Letters, New York Historical Society; and Benton, *View,* I, iii, iv, 122, 205-208.

9. *Missouri Democrat,* 1853 — April 7, 13, 15, 16, 22, 23, 26, 27; May 2, 4, 13, 17; *Missouri Republican* — 1853, April 15, 16, 22, 23, 27; May 2, 4, 17, 27; also Benton to [Montgomery Blair?] April 30, 1853, in Blair Papers, LofC; and cf. Nichols, *Franklin Pierce,* 216 ff., 221, 229, 247, 248, and Nevins, *Ordeal of the Union,* I, 45-51.

10. *Missouri Democrat,* 1853 — April 27; May 3, 11, 12, 13, 14, 16, 17, 18; *Missouri Republican,* 1853 — May 4, 17, 21; also Benton, *Letter . . . Central National Highway* (1853), *passim;* letters from Benton, in *Missouri Democrat,* May 16, 1853, and *National Intelligencer,* September 6, 1853, in Nevins, *Frémont,* 409-410; Atchison to Treat, May 29, 1853, copy, Reynolds Papers, MoHS, and Atchison, *Address . . . to the People of Missouri,* 1-3; John D. Stevenson to George R. Smith, June 5, 1853, Harding, *Life of George R. Smith,* 189-190.

11. *Congressional Directory* (1854), chart; Wentworth, *Congressional Reminiscences,* 50; Bungay, *Off-Hand Takings,* 345; letters of January 1 and 4, 1854, in Seward, *Seward at Washington,* 215, 217.

12. *CG,* 33/1, 44, 69, 181, 246, 323, 331, 348, 369, 918-919, 1467, 1640, 1732, 1752-1753, 1782-1784, 1803-1804, 1834.

13. Cf. Nevins, *Ordeal of the Union,* II, 78-80, 88-121; Nichols, *Franklin Pierce,* 319-324, 333-338; Washington *Union,* January 24, 1854; letter from Seward, January 8, 1854, in Seward, *Seward at Washington,* 217.

14. For the Kansas-Nebraska debate, Benton's speeches, and public reaction: *CG,* 33/1, 986-989, 1875, Appendix 557-561, 698-699, 728, 743-744, 749, 795, 1041, 1065, 1175, 1232-1233; Benton, *Kansas and Nebraska,* 1-8; Wentworth, *Congressional Reminiscences,* 51-55; letter from Seward, April 25, 1854, in Seward, *Seward at Washington,* 227; Washington *Union,* 1854 — April 26, 28, 30; May 7; July 7; *Missouri Democrat,* 1854 — April 29; May 1, 2, 8; Nevins, *Ordeal of the Union,* II, 122 ff.; Rayback, "American Working Man and the Anti-Slavery Crusade," 161.

15. *CG,* 33/1, 1519-1520, 1561-1563, Appendix 1031-1036.

16. Washington *Union,* April 25 and July 9, 1854; also letters of William Goodell, Horace Greeley, and Charles A. Davis, August 14, 19 and 29, 1854, in Dumond, *Letters of James Gillespie Birney,* II, 1164-1168; and cf. Benton to "Hon. Mr. Chase," July 26, 1854, in Benton Letters, PHS.

17. *Missouri Democrat,* May-June, 1854 — especially May 8; June 21, 24, 30; July 1; also Washington *Union,* May 27, 1854. Cf. *Missouri Republican,* 1853 — April 16, 20; May 3, 5.

18. [Benton], *To the Democratic Voters of the St. Louis Congressional District,* 1-4.

19. *Missouri Democrat,* 1854 — July 10, 11, 27; August 7-9, 11, 12, 14, 15, 25. Cf. Ryle, "Slavery and Party Realignment in Missouri in the State Election of 1856," *Missouri Historical Review,* XXXIX (April, 1945),

321, 323; John Daugherty to [?], August 8, 1854, in Benton Papers, MoHS.
20. *Missouri Democrat,* 1854 — November 17, 18, 21, 30; December 27.
21. *House Journal,* 18 Assembly, 1 Session, *passim,* 202, 214; cf. Rollins to Leonard, November 29, 1854, in Leonard Manuscripts, Missouri State Historical Society; Carr, *Speeches . . . January 27, 1855,* 4-6; Blair, *Remarks . . . Upon the Subject of the Senatorial Election,* 1-5, 7. Cf. Harding, *Life of George R. Smith,* 190 ff.
22. *Missouri Democrat,* December 21, 23, 25, 27, 28, and 30, 1854; Benton, *Discourse . . . Before the Maryland Institute,* 1-16; and *Discourse . . . Before the Boston Mercantile Library Association,* 3-24.
23. *CG,* 33/2, *passim,* 1190; Benton, *Speech . . . On the Pacific Railroad Bill* (1855), 3-18.
24. *Missouri Democrat,* 1854 — August 19; September 14, 18; Washington *Union,* September 13, 1854, and March 1, 1855; *Death and Obsequies of Mrs. Elizabeth McDowell Benton,* 1, 2, 4, 5.
25. Washington *Union,* 1855 — February 28; March 1, 15; also Frémont, "Senator Thomas H. Benton," 244; and Buttre, "Thomas H. Benton," n.p.
26. *Missouri Democrat,* 1855 — March 26, 27; April 4-6; May 22; also Leonard to Mrs. Abiel Leonard, March 26, 1855, in Leonard Manuscripts, Missouri State Historical Society; and Rice, *A Funeral Discourse on Mrs. Elizabeth Benton,* 5-17.
27. *Missouri Democrat,* June 14, 1855.

CHAPTER 17

1. *Missouri Democrat,* 1855 — April 6, 30; June 26; August 24; also May 16 and 28, 1856; Benton to Clayton, July 21, 1855, in Clayton Papers, LofC; to Asbury Dickens, December 27, 1855, in Miscellaneous Files, Chicago Historical Society; to [?], January 2, February 2, 1856, Houghton Library, Harvard University; to Van Buren, August 16 and September 1, 1855, in Van Buren Papers, LofC; to A. B. Merriam, August 10, 1855, in Benton Letters, New York Historical Society; to D. Appleton and Company, August 14, 1855, in Miscellaneous Papers, New York Public Library; also Washington *Union,* March 29, 1856; and Benton, *View,* II, 787-788.
2. Atchison to Corbin, March 16, 1856, in Corbin Papers, Rutgers College Collection, copies in MoHS; Benton to Clayton, July 29 and August 2, 1855, in Clayton Papers, LofC; Benton to Messers Bryant and Company, September 16, 1855, in Bryant-Godwin Papers, New York Public Library; Pierce, *Memoir and Letters of Charles Sumner,* III, 456, 466; Nevins, *Ordeal of the Union,* II, 380-450.
3. *Missouri Democrat,* April 30, 1855; also 1856 — January 14; June 3-7; August 14; and cf. letter from Benton, March 12, 1856, in Washington

Union, March 29, 1856; Smith, *Blair Family,* I, 341-343; Nevins, *Frémont,* 432-438.

4. *Missouri Democrat,* 1856 — April 8, 22, 24, 25, 30; May 16, 22; June 5, 10; also Green to Corbin, December 5, 1855, January 15, 1856, and Atchison to Corbin, March 16, 1856, in Corbin Papers, Rutgers College Collection, copies in MoHS; Smith, *Blair Family,* I, 336-337, 343-345, 375. Cf. Ryle, "Slavery and Party Realignment in Missouri," 327, 329-330.

5. For the St. Louis Speech and the "Forty Days' Campaign": *Missouri Democrat,* 1856 — June 16-20, 23-26, 28, 30; July 3, 7-11, 14, 15, 21, 24, 28-31; August 1-3; also Oliphant, "Recollections of Thomas H. Benton," 434.

6. *Missouri Democrat,* July 26, 1856; Corbin to Thomas C. Reynolds, July 27, 1856, in Reynolds Papers, MoHS; Washington *Union,* July 29, 1856; draft of a circular, written by John F. Snyder for George N. Williams, 1856, in Snyder Collection, MoHS.

7. *Missouri Democrat,* August 2, 3-5, 8, and 11, 1856; Washington *Union,* August 15 and September 13, 1856.

8. *Missouri Democrat,* August 14 and 15, 1856; Washington *Union,* August 23, 1856. Also Benton to Lyman Draper, September 1, 1856, in Draper Correspondence, Wisconsin Historical Society; and Poore, *Reminiscences,* I, 503.

9. Bancroft to Marcy, September 24, 1856, in Howe, *Life and Letters of George Bancroft,* II, 123-124; Douglas to Treat, December 20, 1856, in Treat Papers, MoHS.

10. *Missouri Democrat,* November 4 and 24, 1856; *Thirteenth Annual Report . . . Mercantile Library Association,* 16-17.

11. *House Journal,* 19 Assembly, 1 Session, 82, 83; *Missouri Democrat,* 1857 — January 16; February 24; April 3, 4, 6, 7, 11; May 19; December 4. Cf. Merkel, *Anti-Slavery in Missouri,* 237-247; and Smith, *Blair Family,* I, 399-401.

12. For Benton's New England circuit: *Missouri Democrat,* 1856 — November 7, December 2, 3, 8; Benton to Mr. Crowell, November 21, 1856, in Benton Letters, New York Historical Society, and to Mr. Calef, December 9, 1856, in Norcross Collection, Massachusetts Historical Society; Todd, "A Reminiscence of Benton," in *Atlantic Monthly,* XVI (September, 1870), 363-365, 367.

13. "Remarks of Thomas H. Benton at the New England Celebration in New York," in *National Intelligencer,* Washington, December 25, 1856.

14. Benton to Sparks, January 1, [14], 1857, Houghton Library, Harvard University; *Missouri Democrat,* 1857 — January 20, 29; February 17.

15. Benton to Van Buren, February 7, 1857, in Van Buren Papers, LofC.

16. *Missouri Democrat,* 1857 — February 28; March 4; May 1, 6, 15; June 4, 16; July 14, 29; also Wentworth, *Congressional Reminiscences,* 56.

17. *Missouri Democrat,* 1853 — March 13; October 26, 30; November 30; also Ehrlich, *History of the Dred Scott Case,* 51-378; Stenberg, "Some

Political Aspects of the Dred Scott Case," in *Mississippi Valley Historical Review,* XIX (March 1933), 571-573; Hopkins, *Dred Scott's Case,* 33-40, 47-50, 161-176; Smith, *Blair Family,* I, 382-397; Swisher, *Taney,* 495-523.

18. Benton, *Historical and Legal EXAMINATION of . . . the DRED SCOTT CASE,* 1, 3, 4, 5, 7, 8, 11, 26, 31-130, 193; especially 31, 32, 54, 75, 121, 129, 193.

19. *Missouri Democrat,* 1857 — September 17, 21, 28; October 3, 17, 26, 30; November 30; also Benton to Buchanan, September 10 [1857], in Benton Papers, PHS; and Will of Thomas H. Benton, September 13, 1857, Register of Wills, District of Columbia.

20. Benton to Blair, December 1, 1857, in Washington *Union,* July 28, 1858.

21. *Missouri Democrat,* October 26 and 30, 1857; January 5, 1858; also Benton to George Robertson, November 1, 1857, in *Missouri Democrat,* November 30, 1857; to [Jared Sparks?], January 3, 1858, Houghton Library, Harvard University, and to ?, January 29, 1858, in Benton Letters, PHS; and to Mr. Shillington, "Tuesday Evening" [March 30, 1858], in Charles A. Brown Autograph Collection, University of Rochester. Cf. Washington *Union,* March 28, 1858.

22. For Benton's illness and death: Washington *Union,* April 10, 11 and 13, 1858; *Missouri Democrat,* 1858 — March 24; April 8, 9, 10, 14; also Blair to Van Buren, April 2, 1858, in Van Buren Papers, LofC; Benton to Brant, March 30, April 1, 1858, Mercantile Library, St. Louis; Jones, *Colonel Benton and His Contemporaries,* 1, 3, 5, 6, 7, 25, 29; Nevins, *Frémont,* 459-460; New York *Tribune,* April 8, 1858, quoted in *Missouri Democrat,* April 12, 1858; Memorandum . . . "Interview with Col. Benton, When Upon His Death Bed," by L. C., in Lewis Cass Papers, University of Michigan; Letter of Richard Taylor Jacob, August 2, 1858, in Washington *Union,* September 2, 1858; Recollection of Jessie Benton Frémont, quoted in Meigs, *Benton,* 517.

23. New York *Tribune,* April 14, 1858; March 10, 1860 — quoted in Nevins, *Ordeal of the Union,* I, 170; Tyler to Robert Tyler, June 3, 1858, in Tyler, *Letters and Times,* II, 19; Washington *Union,* April 11, 1858; Leonard to Reeves Leonard, April 24, 1858, in Leonard Manuscripts, Missouri State Historical Society.

24. Cf. Washington *Union,* 1858 — May 18; June 18; July 28; August 10; Sepetmber 2; also F. P. Blair, Jr., and F. P. Blair, Sr., "Col. Benton's Opinion of the Administration," New York *Tribune,* May 25, 1858; Jones, *Colonel Benton and His Contemporaries, passim;* cf. Smith, *Blair Family,* I, 431-439; Benton to Blair, December 1, 1857, in Washington *Union,* July 28, 1858; and Benton to ?, January 29, 1858, in Benton Letters, PHS.

25. *Missouri Democrat,* April 15, 16 and 17, 1858; Oliphant, "Recollections of Thomas H. Benton," 435; Johnson, *Personal Recollections,* 7; Bay, *Bench and Bar,* 21.

Personal Acknowledgments

Over a period of nearly ten years, many people have assisted me in many different ways in preparing this book. My debt of gratitude to all of them is great, from those who have aided me anonymously as efficient archivists or librarians, to those with whom I have had more personal contact.

To my mother, LUCY MATTHEWS CHAMBERS, and to my wife, SUSAN ROSS CHAMBERS, I can only suggest the warmth of the gratitude I feel. Their encouragement, their willingness to bear the tribulations that go with a long piece of research and writing, and their close and fruitful criticism, make this most especially their book. Reading with a professional eye, my wife has made innumerable felicitous suggestions for improvements in narrative, characterization, and style.

Next, my colleagues and former colleagues at Washington University in St. Louis. In particular this story owes much to DR. GEORGE D. STOUT, of the Department of English, who helped me develop my conception of what a biography might be, and who read and criticized the manuscript in more than one draft. Much valuable assistance has also been given by PROFESSORS ARNOLD J. LIEN, THOMAS H. ELIOT, OLIVER E. NORTON, and CARL A. McCANDLESS, of the Department of Political Science; and by PROFESSORS ROLAND G. USHER, RALPH P. BIEBER, and FRANK VANDIVER, of the Department of History, and also by DR. RICHARD RUDNER, DR. WALTER EHRLICH, and FRED G. KETTLECAMP.

In addition, PROFESSOR ARTHUR SCHLESINGER, JR., of Harvard, to whose insight into the Jackson period and friendly encouragement I am much indebted, and PROFESSOR ARTHUR C. COLE of Brooklyn College, have read and criticized the entire manuscript, and I have enjoyed help in various forms from PROFESSORS BERNARD MAYO of the University of Virginia, HOLMAN HAMILTON of the University of Kentucky, and WILLIAM C. BINKLEY of Vanderbilt, DR. CHARLES M. WILTSE, and DR. FRONTIS W. JOHNSON.

Archivists and librarians everywhere have been patient, resourceful, and kind, including CHARLES VAN RAVENSWAAY, Director, MARJORY

DOUGLAS, and the staff of the Missouri Historical Society, St. Louis; EDNA GORDON, RUTH HARRY, ELIZABETH TINDALL, and other members of library staffs in St. Louis; FLOYD C. SHOEMAKER, Secretary, and SARAH GUITAR, Librarian, Missouri State Historical Society, and DR. FRANCIS W. ENGLISH, Western Historical Manuscripts Collection, Columbia, Missouri; DR. J. G. deROULHAC HAMILTON and DR. R. D. W. CONNOR, both of whom gave me particularly friendly personal aid at the University of North Carolina, and W. F. BURTON, MRS. MARY J. ROGERS, DR. B. E. POWELL, HELEN H. SALLS, and others at the North Carolina Department of Archives and History, and at Duke University; MRS. JOHN TROTWOOD MOORE and MR. ROBERT T. QUARLES, JR., at Nashville, Tennessee; JOHN WYLLIE, who gave me a friendly reception at the University of Virginia beyond the call of duty, and MRS. J. A. JOHNSTON, Virginia Historical Society, Richmond; and finally, but not least, the STAFF OF THE MANUSCRIPTS DIVISION, LIBRARY OF CONGRESS, Washington, and OTHER LIBRARIANS ACROSS THE COUNTRY who answered requests for materials.

To old friends who have helped me in various ways, I want to extend my thanks — in particular to BENJAMIN ROTH, DR. DAVID T. GRAHAM, MRS. NORMA TILLEY, and EUGENE H. BUDER, of St. Louis. Again, my thanks to IRVING DILLIARD, Chairman, Editorial Page, *St. Louis Post-Dispatch;* to CAPTAIN TOM HENDERSON, and JOHN H. HENDERSON and his son, who gave me not only information but a pleasant day at Franklin, Tennessee. In addition, I have received help or encouragement from THOMAS HART BENTON and from CLYDE H. PORTER, both of Kansas City, Missouri; and from DR. E. PENDLETON TOMPKINS, Lexington, Virginia; HILARY CROCKETT, JR., Franklin, Tennessee; and MR. EDWIN M. LYNCH, Hillsboro, North Carolina.

For cheerful and conscientious effort in typing and retyping manuscripts, I thank MRS. MARGARET SCHMIDT and MRS. JOAN ROZIER STEPHENS, formerly of St. Louis, and EARLINE INGRAM, of St. Louis.

Finally, I want to express my deepest appreciation to DUDLEY H. CLOUD and MRS. CLOUD, and to MRS. EDWIN R. HILLER, JR., of the Atlantic Monthly Press, Boston. All have been good friends and given me aid and encouragement in many ways; to the first I owe an immense debt which only an author who has received constant help and criticism from a fine editor can realize.

WILLIAM NISBET CHAMBERS

Sources

I. MANUSCRIPTS AND PAPERS

JESSE BENTON PAPERS — North Carolina Department of Archives and History, Raleigh, N.C.

FACULTY RECORDS, 1799-1814; MISCELLANEOUS PHILANTHROPIC SOCIETY PAPERS; YANCEY PAPERS; SOUTHERN HISTORICAL COLLECTION — University of North Carolina, Chapel Hill, N.C.

ACCOUNT OF A DUEL WITH GENERAL JACKSON (THB, Circular, 1813); and COFFEE PAPERS, DYAS COLLECTION — Tennessee Historical Society, Nashville, Tenn.

CORRESPONDENCE OF THE ADJUTANT GENERAL'S OFFICE — National Archives, Washington.

BENTON MANUSCRIPTS, in MISCELLANEOUS FILES and in EDWARDS PAPERS; JACKSON PAPERS — Chicago Historical Society, Chicago, Ill.

BENTON PAPERS; RUFUS EASTON PAPERS; LUCAS PAPERS; DUELS ENVELOPE; CORBIN PAPERS, RUTGERS COLLEGE COLLECTION, copies; Miscellaneous Documents in BLAIR PAPERS, CHOUTEAU and CHOUTEAU-PAPIN PAPERS, DENNY LETTERS, CARLOTA GLASGOW COLLECTION; LINN PAPERS, DEMUN PAPERS, MAFFIT COLLECTION, O'FALLON COLLECTION, POLITICAL PAPERS, REYNOLDS PAPERS, SCHOOLS COLLECTION, SNYDER COLLECTION, SUBLETTE PAPERS, TREAT PAPERS, and JULIUS S. WALSH COLLECTION; RECOLLECTIONS OF THB, by EDWARD DOBYNS, MANUSCRIPT — Missouri Historical Society, St. Louis, Mo.

BENTON DOCUMENTS, Miscellaneous Manuscript Files; THOMAS A. SMITH MANUSCRIPTS; and LEONARD MANUSCRIPTS — Missouri State Historical Society, Columbia, Mo.

PRESTON COLLECTION — Virginia Historical Society, Richmond, Va.

BENTON PAPERS, in PERSONAL MISCELLANY; JESSE BENTON PAPERS; BLAIR PAPERS; BROADSIDES COLLECTION; HENRY CLAY PAPERS; THOMAS J. CLAY PAPERS; JOHN M. CLAYTON PAPERS; JACKSON PAPERS (two series); POLK PAPERS; SCHOOLCRAFT PAPERS; VAN BUREN PAPERS; Miscellaneous Documents in BANCROFT PAPERS, J. S. BLACK PAPERS, and

CARRINGTON-McDOWELL PAPERS; GIDEON WELLES PAPERS — Library of Congress, Washington.

McDOWELL PAPERS; BEDFORD BROWN PAPERS — Duke University Library, Durham, N.C.

CARTOONS COLLECTION; McDOWELL FAMILY PAPERS (two series); Manuscripts in STUART PAPERS; WALKER FAMILY PAPERS — Alderman Library, University of Virginia, Charlottesville, Va.

BENTON LETTERS — Pennsylvania Historical Society, Philadelphia, Pa.

BENTON and RELATED DOCUMENTS — in MISCELLANEOUS MANUSCRIPT FILE, New York Historical Society, New York, N.Y.; in BRYANT-GODWIN and in MISCELLANEOUS PAPERS, New York Public Library, New York, N.Y.; in APPLETON, BANCROFT, NORCROSS, and MISCELLANEOUS COLLECTION, Massachusetts Historical Society, Boston, Mass.; in Houghton Library, Harvard University, Cambridge, Mass.; in JAMES A. PEARCE PAPERS, R. B. DALLAM PAPERS, and VERTICAL FILE, Maryland Historical Society, Baltimore, Md.; in MOSES DAWSON COLLECTION, Xavier University Library, Cincinnati, Ohio; in CURD PAPERS, WESTERN HISTORICAL COLLECTION, University of Missouri, Columbia, Mo.; in JOHN DAUGHERTY COLLECTION, Kansas State Historical Society; in DRAPER CORRESPONDENCE, Wisconsin Historical Society; in University of Texas Library, Austin, Texas; and in CHARLES A. BROWN AUTOGRAPH COLLECTION, University of Rochester, Rochester, N.Y.

LEWIS CASS PAPERS — William L. Clements Library, University of Michigan, Ann Arbor, Mich.

MISCELLANEOUS MANUSCRIPTS, and LECTURE ON THE PROGRESS OF THE AGE (THB, Manuscript, 1850) — Mercantile Library, St. Louis, Mo.

II. CONTEMPORANEOUS NEWSPAPERS AND MAGAZINES

Evening Post (1853-1854) — New York, N.Y.
Fayetteville Gazette — Fayetteville, N.C., January 10, 1791.
Globe and *Daily Union* — Washington, D.C.
Harper's New Monthly Magazine (July, 1854) — New York, N.Y.
Impartial Review and Cumberland Repository (1806-1808); *Democratic Clarion and Tennessee Gazette* (1810-1813); *Clarion* (1813-1814) — Nashville, Tenn.
Missouri Gazette (1815-1822); *Enquirer* (1819-1820); *Missouri Republican, Missouri Advocate* (1824-1826); *St. Louis Beacon* (1829-1832); *Missouri Argus* (1835-1841); *Missouri Reporter* (1843-1845); *Missourian* (1843-1846); *Union* (1846-1851); *Old Bullion* (1850); *Missouri Democrat* (1853-1858) — St. Louis, Mo.

Niles Weekly Register — Baltimore, Md.
United States Magazine and Democratic Review (1837-1845, 1858) — New York, N.Y.

III. PUBLIC DOCUMENTS

American State Papers: Documents, Legislative and Executive, of the Congress of the United States: on Finance — five volumes (Washington, D.C., 1832-1859).

Annals of the Congress of the United States; Register of Debates in Congress; Congressional Globe; Congressional Directory (Washington, D.C.).

BURIAL RECORDS, Bellefontaine Cemetery (St. Louis, Mo.).

CARTER, CLARENCE E., Ed.: *The Territorial Papers of the United States . . . Louisiana-Missouri 1815-1821* (Washington, D.C., 1951).

COMMISSION BOOK, 1807-1812, manuscript, Tennessee State Archives (Nashville, Tenn.).

DEED BOOKS, and RECORD OF MARRIAGES 1782-1830, Rockbridge County, Virginia (Court House, Lexington, Va.).

1 District of Columbia Circuit Court Reports (Washington, D.C.).

DOCKET, SUPREME COURT OF THE UNITED STATES, Bound Manuscript Volumes, 1806-1858 (Washington, D.C.).

Journal of the Senate of the State of Missouri, and . . . *of the House of Representatives*, 1820-1856 (Washington, D.C.).

Journal of the Senate of the State of Tennessee, and *Acts Passed* . . . , 8 Assembly, 1 Session, 1809 (Washington, D.C.).

Land Claims in Missouri, 24 Congress, 1 Session, House Document 270 (Washington, D.C., 1836).

LISTS OF TAXABLE PROPERTY, Orange County Records (State Department of Archives and History, Raleigh, N.C.).

MINUTE BOOKS, County Court of Maury County, 1808-1809; Circuit Court, Maury County, 1810-1815; County Court of Williamson County, 1800-1815; Superior Court, District of Mero, 1797-1809 (Tennessee State Archives, Nashville, Tenn.).

MINUTES OF THE CIRCUIT COURT OF THE COUNTY OF ST. LOUIS, 1816-1821 (St. Louis, Mo.).

Missouri Reports, 1821-1850 (St. Louis, Mo.).

ORIGINAL AND GENERAL RECORDS, St. Louis and St. Louis County, 1815-1858, Recorder of Deeds Office (St. Louis, Mo.).

Proceedings in Congress Upon the Acceptance of the Statutes of Thomas H. Benton and Francis P. Blair Presented by the State of Missouri (Washington, D.C., 1900).

RICHARDSON, JAMES D., Ed.: *A Compilation of the Messages and Papers of the Presidents,* twenty volumes (New York, N.Y., 1897-1922).

ROLL OF ATTORNEYS TAKEN FROM THE RECORDS FOR THE YEAR 1815 TO 1849, Bound Manuscript Volume, Circuit Court for the City of St. Louis (St. Louis, Mo.).

SAUNDERS, WILLIAM L., AND CLARK, WALTER, Eds.: *The Colonial and State Records of North Carolina, 1622-1790,* thirty volumes (Raleigh, N.C., 1886-1910).

TAX BOOKS, Williamson County, and WILLS AND INVENTORIES, Williamson County (County Court House, Franklin, Tennessee).

WILL OF THOMAS H. BENTON, Register of Wills, District of Columbia (Washington, D.C.).

WILLS, GRANVILLE COUNTY, 1746-1771, and Orange County, 1753-1819 (State Department of Archives and History, Raleigh, North Carolina).

Yerger's Tennessee Reports, 1823.

IV. PRINTED CORRESPONDENCE, DIARIES, AND CONTEMPORANEOUS PUBLICATIONS

ADAMS, CHARLES FRANCIS, Ed.: *Memoirs of John Quincy Adams, Comprising Parts of His Diary from 1795 to 1848* — twelve volumes (Philadelphia, Pa., 1874-1877).

AMBLER, CHARLES HENRY, Ed.: *Correspondence of Robert M. T. Hunter, 1826-1876,* in Annual Report, American Historical Association, 1916 (Washington, D.C., 1918).

Annexation of Texas, Opinions of Messrs. Clay, Polk, Benton, and Van Buren . . . (n.p., n.d.).

ATCHISON, D. R.: *Address of Senator Atchison to the People of Missouri* (Washington, D.C., 1854).

BARKER, EUGENE C., Ed.: *Austin Papers,* Annual Report, American Historical Association, 1919 (Washington, D.C., 1924).

BASSETT, JOHN SPENCER, Ed.: *Correspondence of Andrew Jackson,* six volumes (Washington, D.C., 1926-1933).

[BATES, EDWARD]: *Edward Bates Against Thomas H. Benton* (St. Louis, Mo., 1828).

BECK, LEWIS C.: *A Gazetteer of the States of Illinois and Missouri* . . . (Albany, N.Y., 1823).

BENTON, THOMAS H.: *Thirty Years' View; or, A History of the Working of the American Government for Thirty Years, from 1820 to 1850,* two volumes (New York, 1854-1856).

BENTON, THOMAS H., Ed.: *Abridgment of the Debates of Congress from*

1789 to 1856 [1850], sixteen volumes (New York, N.Y., 1857-1863).

BENTON, THOMAS H.: "Auto-Biographical Sketch," in *Thirty Years' View*, Edition of 1883 (New York, N.Y., 1883).

BENTON, THOMAS H.: *Historical and Legal EXAMINATION of that Part of the Decision of the Supreme Court of the United States in the DRED SCOTT CASE, Which Declares the Unconstitutionality of the Missouri Compromise Act, and the Self-Extension of the Constitution to Territories, Carrying Slavery Along with It* (New York, N.Y., 1858).

BENTON, THOMAS H.: MISCELLANEOUS ARTICLES AND PAMPHLETS — "Sir John Oldcastle's Remarks on the Judiciary of the State of Tennessee," and articles signed OLDCASTLE, *Impartial Review and Cumberland Repository*, Nashville, Tenn., February-July and May-August, 1808; "JOURNAL of a Voyage from Nashville, Ten. to New Orleans in the winter of the year 1813," in the *Clarion*, Nashville, Tenn., January-February, 1813; "A Memoir of Edward Hempstead, Written in 1818," in Washburne, E. B., *Historical Sketch of Charles S. Hempstead* (Galena, Illinois, 1875); *Selections of Editorial Articles from the St. Louis Enquirer, on the Subject of Oregon and Texas, as Originally Published in that Paper, in the Years 1818-19* (St. Louis, Mo., 1844); Letter to Jonathan Russell, Senate Chamber, March 29, 1822, in *Proceedings of the Massachusetts Historical Society, XLVII* (Boston, Mass., 1914), 309-310; Letter . . . August 28 [1822], in *Missouri Republican*, January 9, 1870; *The Substance of Colonel Benton's Argument, Before the Supreme Court at Nashville, in the Suit of John Smith T, ads. Nicholas Wilson* (n.p., n.d.); *Speech . . . on the Amendment of the Constitution of the United States, January 30, 1824* (Washington, D.C., 1824); *Speech . . . on the Mission to Panama, March 13, 1826* (Washington, D.C., 1826); *Speech on the Bill to Graduate the Price of the Public Lands . . . May 16, 1826* (Washington, D.C., 1826); *Mr. Benton's Speeches, on the Public Lands, Delivered in the Senate of the United States at the First Session of the Twentieth Congress* (Washington, D.C., 1828); *Speech of Mr. Benton of Missouri, in Reply to Mr. Webster . . . 1830* (Washington, D.C., 1830); *Speech . . . on the Introduction of a Resolution on the State of the Currency . . . January 20, 1832* (Washington, D.C., Globe Office, 1832); *Speech . . . on the Reduction of Revenue and Regulation of Commerce . . . March 15, 1832* (n.p., n.d.); *Speech . . . January 24th, 1833 [On Distributing the Proceeds of the Public Lands]* (n.p., n.d.); *Speech . . . On the Expunging Resolution . . . January 12, 1837* (n.p., n.d.); *Speech . . . on the Bill to Separate the Government from the Banks, the Independent Treasury Bill . . . March 14, 1838* (n.p., n.d.); *Speech . . . on the Bill Providing for the Reduction and Graduation of the Price of the Public Lands* (Washington, D.C., 1838); *Letters of Senator Benton to His Constituents in 1839* (St. Louis, Mo., 1840); *The Missouri Delegation to their Constituents, Signed by Thomas Hart Benton, Lewis F. Linn, John Miller, John Jameson*, (n.p., 1840); *Three Speeches . . . on the Annexation of Texas to the United States . . .* (New York, N.Y.,

1844); *Substance of . . . Speech delivered at Saint Louis, Saturday, October 19, 1844* (St. Louis, Mo., 1844); *Speech on the Oregon Question; delivered in the Senate of the United States May 22, 25 and 28, 1846* (Washington, D.C., 1846); *Col. Benton's Great Speech! to the People of Missouri: Delivered at the Capitol of the State* (n.p., 1849); *Speech . . . Delivered at Fayette, Howard County, Missouri, on Saturday the First of September, 1849* (Jefferson City, Mo., 1849); *Anti-Compromise Speech . . . June 10, 1850* (n.p., n.d.); *Highway to the Pacific, Grand National Central Highway, Speech . . . December 16, 1850* (n.p., n.d.); *Letter to the People of Missouri, Central National Highway to the Pacific* (St. Louis, Mo., 1853); *Nebraska and Kansas, Speech . . . April 25, 1854* (Washington, D.C., n.d.); *To the Democratic Voters of the St. Louis Congressional District* (Washington, D.C., 1854); *Discourse . . . Before the Maryland Institute, on the Physical Geography of the Country Between Missouri and California, with a view to show its adaption to settlement, and the construction of a Railroad; Delivered at Baltimore, Tuesday evening, December 5, 1854* (n.p., n.d.); *Discourse . . . Before the Boston Mercantile Library Association . . . Wednesday Evening, December 20, 1854* (Washington, D.C., 1854); *Speech . . . on the Pacific Railroad Bill . . . in the House of Representatives, January 16, 1855* (Washington, D.C., 1855).

[BENTON, THOMAS H., and others] *Addresses on the Presentation of the Sword of Gen. Andrew Jackson to the Congress of the United States* (Washington, D.C., 1855).

BIRCH, JAMES H.: *Speech in Reply to those of Hon. Thomas H. Benton . . . July 16, 1849* (Jefferson City, Mo., 1849).

BLAIR, FRANCIS P., JR.: *The Address, Resolutions and Proceedings of the Democracy of St. Louis* (St. Louis, Mo., 1848).

————: *Remarks . . . in the Joint Session of the General Assembly of Missouri, Upon the Subject of the Senatorial Election* (n.p., n.d.).

————, and BLAIR, F. P. Sr.: "Col. Benton's Opinion of the Administration," New York *Tribune*, May 25, 1858.

BOGY, LEWIS V.: *Speech of . . . the Democratic Nominee for Congress, in the First District* (St. Louis, Mo., 1852).

BOUCHER, CHAUNCEY S., and BROOKS, ROBERT P., Eds.: *Correspondence Addressed to John C. Calhoun, 1837-1849,* in Annual Report, American Historical Association, 1929 (Washington, D.C., 1930).

[BOURNE, EDWARD G., Ed.]: *Diary and Correspondence of Salmon P. Chase,* in Annual Report, American Historical Association, 1902 (Washington, D.C., 1903).

BREMER, FREDERIKA: *The Homes of the New World; Impressions of America,* two volumes (New York, N.Y., 1853).

BROWN, EVERETT S., Ed.: *The Missouri Compromises and Presidential Politics, 1820-1825, from the Letters of William Plumer, Junior . . .* (St. Louis, Mo., 1926).

BUNGAY, GEORGE W.: *Off-Hand Takings; or, Crayon Sketches of the Noticeable Men of Our Age* (New York, N.Y., 1854).

CALHOUN, JOHN C.: *Address . . . to the People of the Southern States, and Letter of Gen. Lewis Cass, to Mr. Ritchie* (St. Louis, Mo., n.d.).

CARR, PETER: *Speeches . . . Delivered in Joint Session of the Legislature of Missouri, January 27, 1855* (St. Louis, Mo., 1855).

Charless' Missouri and Illinois Magazine Almanac, for 1818 (St. Louis, Mo., n.d.).

COLTON, CALVIN, Ed.: *The Private Correspondence of Henry Clay* (New York, N.Y., 1856).

Complete Regular Army Register of the United States . . . 1779 to 1879 (Washington, D.C., 1881).

"CORRESPONDENCE OF JUDGE TUCKER," *William and Mary College Quarterly Historical Magazine*, Series I, XII (October, 1903), 84-95.

[CURTIUS]: *Torch Light — An Examination of the Origin, Policy and Principles of the Opposition to the Administration, and an Exposition of the Official Conduct of THOMAS H. BENTON . . .* (St. Louis, Mo., 1826).

Death and Obsequies of Mrs. Elizabeth McDowell Benton (n.p., n.d.): Pamphlet, Missouri State Historical Society (Columbia, Mo.).

DEWITT, CHARLES G.: "The Great Webster-Hayne Debate," *Ulster Sentinel*, February 17, 1830, in *Olde Ulster*, IX (November, 1913), 332-337.

DUMOND, DWIGHT L., Ed.: *Letters of James Gillespie Birney, 1831-1857*, two volumes (New York, N.Y., 1938).

DYER, OLIVER: *Phonographic Report of the Proceedings of the National Free Soil Convention* (Buffalo, N.Y., 1848).

EDWARDS, NINIAN W., *History of Illinois, from 1778 to 1833; and Life and Times of Ninian Edwards* (Springfield, Ill., 1870).

"EXTRACTS FROM THE DIARY OF EDMUND RUFFIN," *William and Mary College Quarterly Historical Magazine*, XXIII (July, 1914), 31-45.

Fifth Annual Report, and *Thirteenth Annual Report of the Directors of the St. Louis Mercantile Library Association* (St. Louis, Mo., 1851 and 1859).

FLINT, TIMOTHY, *Recollections of the Last Ten Years, Passed in Occasional Residences and Journeyings in the Valley of the Mississippi, . . . in a Series of Letters to the Rev. James Flint* (Boston, Mass., 1826).

GRIMSLEY, THORNTON, to JOHN BELL, April 16, 1841, in *Oregon Historical Society Quarterly*, XXIV (December, 1923), 434-437.

HARDING, SAMUEL BANNISTER: *Life of George R. Smith, Founder of Sedalia, Missouri* (Sedalia, Mo., 1904).

HOWE, M. A. DE WOLFE: *The Life and Letters of George Bancroft*, two volumes (New York, N.Y., 1908).

HUNT, GAILLARD, Ed.: *The First Forty Years of Washington Society, Portrayed by the Family Letters of Margaret Bayard Smith* (New York, N.Y., 1906).

JAMESON, J. FRANKLIN, Ed.: *Correspondence of John C. Calhoun*, in Annual Report, American Historical Association, 1899 (Washington, D.C., 1900).

[JONES, WILLIAM CAREY]: *Colonel Benton and His Contemporaries* (Washington, D.C., 1858).

[KENNEY, LUCY]: *History of the Present Cabinet, Benton in Ambush for the Next Presidency* . . . (Washington, D.C., 1840).

Letter from Hon. H. S. Foote, of Mississippi, to Hon. Henry A. Wise (n.p., n.d.).

Letters of Messrs Clay, Benton, and Barrow, on the Subject of the Annexation of Texas to the United States (n.p., n.d.).

"LETTERS OF AMOS ADAMS LAWRENCE," in *Proceedings of the Massachusetts Historical Society, LIII* (Boston, Mass., 1920), 48-57.

"LETTERS OF JAMES K. POLK TO CAVE JOHNSON," and ". . . TO ANDREW J. DONELSON," *Tennessee Historical Magazine*, I (September, 1915), 209-256; III (March, 1917), 51-73.

"A LOOKER ON HERE IN VERONA," *Sketches of United States Senators, of the Session of 1837-'8* (Washington, D.C., 1839).

LUCAS, J. B. C., Ed.: *Letters of Hon. John B. C. Lucas from 1815 to 1836* (St. Louis, Mo., 1905).

McGRANE, REGINALD C., Ed.: *The Correspondence of Nicholas Biddle Dealing with National Affairs, 1807-1844* (Boston, Mass., 1919).

McINTYRE, J. W., Ed.: *The Writings and Speeches of Daniel Webster*, eighteen volumes, National Edition (Boston, Mass., 1903).

MAGOON, E. L.: *Living Orators in America* (Dublin, Ireland, 1849).

[MALLORY, DANIEL, Ed.] *The Life and Speeches of Henry Clay*, two volumes (New York, N.Y., 1844).

MAURY, SARAH MYTTON: *The Statesmen of America in 1846* (London, England, 1847).

MISSOURI HISTORICAL SOCIETY, "Letters of William Carr Lane, 1819-1831," in *Glimpses of the Past*, VII (St. Louis, Mo., 1940).

MOORE, JOHN BASSETT, Ed.: *The Works of James Buchanan, Comprising His Speeches, State Papers and Private Correspondence*, twelve volumes (Philadelphia, Pa., 1908-1911).

Morrison's St. Louis Directory, for 1852 (St. Louis, Mo., 1852).

NEVINS, ALLEN, Ed.: *The Diary of Philip Hone, 1828-1851*, two volumes (New York, N.Y., 1927).

NEWSOME, A. R., Ed.: "Letters of Romulus M. Saunders to Bartlett Yancey, 1821-1828," *North Carolina Historical Review*, VIII (October, 1931), 427-462.

OVERDYKE, W. DARRELL: "A Southern Family on the Missouri Frontier: Letters from Independence, 1843-1855," *Journal of Southern History*, XVII (May, 1951), 216-237.

PAXTON, JOHN A.: *The St. Louis Directory and Register* (St. Louis, Mo., 1821).

PENN, SHADRACH, JR.: *Letters to Col. Thomas H. Benton* (St. Louis, Mo., 1843).

QUAIFE, MILO M., Ed.: *The Diary of James K. Polk, During His Presidency,* four volumes (Chicago, Ill., 1910).

REEVES, J. S., Ed.: "Letters of Gideon J. Pillow to James K. Polk, 1844," *American Historical Review,* XI (July, 1906), 832-843.

"REMARKS OF THOMAS H. BENTON AT THE NEW ENGLAND CELEBRATION IN NEW YORK," *National Intelligencer* (Washington, D.C., December 25, 1856).

RICE, THE REV. N. L.: *A Funeral Discourse on Mrs. Elizabeth Benton . . . Monday, March 26, 1855* (St. Louis, Mo., 1855).

[SAMPSON, WILLIAM H., Ed.]: *Letters of Zachary Taylor from the Battlefields of the Mexican War* (Rochester, N.Y., 1908).

SCOTT, NANCY M.: *A Memoir of Hugh Lawson White . . . With Selections from His Speeches and Correspondence* (Philadelphia, Pa., 1856).

"SELECTED LETTERS FROM THE DONELSON PAPERS," *Tennessee Historical Magazine,* III (June, December, 1917), 136-162, 271-274.

SEWARD, FREDERICK W.: *Autobiography of William H. Seward . . . with . . . Selections from His Letters from 1831 to 1846* (New York, 1877), and *Seward at Washington . . . with Selections from His Letters, 1846-1861* (New York, N.Y., 1891).

SIMS, GEORGE: "An Address to the People of Granville County," June 6, 1765, *North Carolina Historical Review,* III (January, 1926), 57-67.

STAPLES, ARTHUR G., Ed.: *The Letters of John Fairfield* (Lewiston, Me., 1922).

STEINER, BERNARD C., Ed.: "Taney's Correspondence with Van Buren," *Maryland Historical Magazine,* VIII (December, 1913), 305-326.

[THOMAS, FRANCIS]: *Statement of Francis Thomas* (n.p., 1845).

"TO PROMISE YET NOT PAY," *Missouri Historical Review,* XXXV (January, 1941), 265.

TYLER, LYON G.: *The Letters and Times of the Tylers,* two volumes (Richmond, Va., 1884).

"VAN BUREN-BANCROFT CORRESPONDENCE," *Massachusetts Historical Society Proceedings,* XLII (Boston, Mass., 1909).

WASHBURNE, E. B., Ed.: "The Edwards Papers," *Chicago Historical Society Collections* (Chicago, Ill., 1884).

WEBSTER, FLETCHER, Ed.: *The Private Correspondence of Daniel Webster,* two volumes (Boston, Mass., 1857).

WETMORE, ALPHONSO: *Gazetteer of the State of Missouri* (St. Louis, Mo., 1837).

WHEAT, FRANCIS M., Ed.: "Senator Benton Lays His Plans — Some Newly-discovered Material on the Frémont Court-Martial," *California Historical Society Quarterly*, XIII (June, 1934), 150-154.

WILLIS, N. PARKER: *Hurry-Graphs, or, Sketches of Scenery, Celebrities, and Society, Taken from Life* (New York, N.Y., 1851).

V. MEMOIRS AND PERSONAL RECOLLECTIONS

ADDRESS BY THOMAS T. GANTT, March 14, 1882, newspaper clipping, Missouri Historical Society (St. Louis, Mo.).

"ADÉLE DE P. GRATIOT'S NARRATIVE," *Collections of the State Historical Society of Wisconsin*, X (Madison, Wis., 1888), 261-275.

BAY, W. V. N.: *Reminiscences of the Bench and Bar of Missouri* (St. Louis, Mo., 1878).

COLLIER, L. T.: "Recollections of Thomas H. Benton," *Missouri Historical Review*, VIII (April, 1914), 136-141.

DARBY, JOHN F.: *Personal Recollections of Many Prominent People Whom I Have Known, and of Events* (St. Louis, Mo., 1880).

DAVIS, JAMES D.: *The History of the City of Memphis . . . Also, The "Old Times Papers"* (Memphis, Tenn., 1873).

[DAVIS, VARINA HOWELL]: *Jefferson Davis: A Memoir*, two volumes (New York, N.Y., 1890).

DIX, MORGAN, COMP.: *Memoirs of John Adams Dix*, two volumes (New York, N.Y., 1883).

DYER, OLIVER: *Great Senators of the United States Forty Years Ago, 1848 and 1849* (New York, N.Y., 1889).

FAGG, THOMAS J. C.: "Thomas Hart Benton," *Missouri Historical Review*, I (October, 1906), 22-37.

FITZPATRICK, JOHN C., Ed.: *The Autobiography of Martin Van Buren*, Annual Report, American Historical Association, 1918 (Washington, D.C., 1920).

FOOTE, HENRY STUART: *Casket of Reminiscences* (Washington, D.C., 1874).

FORNEY, JOHN W.: *Anecdotes of Public Men* (New York, N.Y., 1874).

FRÉMONT, JOHN CHARLES: *Memoirs of My Life*, two volumes (Chicago, Ill., 1887).

[FRÉMONT, JESSIE BENTON]: "Biographical Sketch of Senator Benton in Connection with Western Expansion," in Frémont, *Memoirs of My Life* (Chicago, Ill., 1887).

FRÉMONT, JESSIE BENTON: "Senator Thomas H. Benton," *Independent*, LV (January, 1903), 240-244.

FRÉMONT, JESSIE BENTON: *Souvenirs of My Time* (Boston, Mass., 1887).

GOODRICH, S. G.: *Recollections of a Lifetime, or Men and Things I Have Seen*, two volumes (New York, N.Y., 1857).

GRISSOM, DANIEL M., "Personal Recollections of Distinguished Missourians," *Missouri Historical Review*, XVIII (January, 1924), 129-145.

H———, "About Thomas H. Benton," *Charlotte Democrat,* October 1, 1880.

JOHNSON, CHARLES P.: *Personal Recollections of Some of Missouri's Eminent Statesmen and Lawyers* (St. Louis, Mo., 1903).

KEYES, E. D.: *Fifty Years' Observation of Men and Events* (New York, N.Y., 1884).

"MARK ALEXANDER AND HIS ANCESTRY, EXTRACTS FROM A LETTER . . . July 2, 1876," *William and Mary College Quarterly Historical Magazine,* XXV (January, 1917), 206-207.

MARTINEAU, HARRIET: *Retrospect of Western Travel,* two volumes (New York, N.Y., 1838).

MILLER, SALLY CAMPBELL PRESTON: "James McDowell," *Washington and Lee University Historical Papers* (Baltimore, Md., 1895), V, 37-202.

MOORE, ALFRED WADDELL: *Some Memories of My Life* (Raleigh, N.C., 1908).

OLIPHANT, JOHN R.: "Recollections of Thomas H. Benton," *Missouri Historical Review,* XIV (April-July, 1920), 433-435.

KOSSUTH R. PLUMMER TO FRANCIS PRESTON FRÉMONT, April 20, 1918, Manuscript in Frémont Papers, Bancroft Library, University of California (Berkeley, Cal.).

PERRY, BENJAMIN F.: *Reminiscence of Public Men* (Philadelphia, Pa., 1883), and *Reminiscences of Public Men, with Speeches and Addresses,* second series (Greenville, N.C., 1889).

POORE, BEN: PERLEY: *Perley's Reminiscences of Sixty Years in the National Metropolis,* two volumes (Philadelphia, Pa., 1886).

POWER, TYRONE: *Impressions of America, During the Years 1833, 1834 and 1835,* two volumes (London, England, 1836).

[PRESTON, WILLIAM C.]: "Personal Recollection of Eminent Men: Colonel Thomas H. Benton," *Land We Love,* V (June, 1868), 119-122.

QUAIFE, MILO M., Ed.: *Kit Carson's Autobiography* (Chicago, Ill., 1935).

SARGENT, NATHAN: *Public Men and Events, from . . . 1817, to . . . 1853,* two volumes (Philadelphia, Pa., 1875).

TODD, WILLIAM C.: "A Reminiscence of Benton," *Atlantic Monthly,* XXVI (September, 1870), 362-367.

WASHBURNE, E. B.: *Historical Sketch of Charles S. Hempstead* (Galena, Ill., 1875).

WENTWORTH, JOHN: *Congressional Reminiscences, Adams, Benton, Calhoun, Clay and Webster* (Chicago, Ill., 1882).

WISE, HENRY A.: *Seven Decades of the Union* (Philadelphia, Pa., 1872).

VI. GENERAL HISTORIES AND SPECIAL STUDIES

ABERNETHY, THOMAS PERKINS: *From Frontier to Plantation in Tennessee, A Study in Frontier Democracy* (Chapel Hill, N.C., 1932).

AMBLER, CHARLES HENRY: *Thomas Ritchie: A Study in Virginia Politics* (Richmond, Va., 1913).

ANDERSON, HATTIE M.: "The Jackson Men in Missouri in 1828," *Missouri Historical Review,* XXXIV (April, 1940), 301-335.

BATTLE, KEMP P.: *History of the University of North Carolina,* two volumes (Raleigh, N.C., 1907).

BEMIS, SAMUEL FLAGG: *John Quincy Adams and the Foundations of American Foreign Policy* (New York, N.Y., 1949).

BILLON, FREDERICK L.: *Annals of St. Louis,* two volumes (St. Louis, Mo., 1886-1888).

BOGART, ERNEST L., and KEMMERER, DONALD L.: *Economic History of the American People* (New York, N.Y., 1947).

BOOSER, JAMES H.: "Origin of the Direct Primary," *National Municipal Review,* XXIV (April, 1935), 222-223.

BOWERS, CLAUDE G.: *The Party Battles of the Jackson Period* (Boston, Mass., 1922).

BOYD, WILLIAM K.: "Some North Carolina Tracts of the Eighteenth Century," *North Carolina Historical Review,* III (January, 1926), 52-55.

BROWN, KENNETH L.: "Stephen Girard, Promoter of the Second Bank of the United States," *Journal of Economic History,* II (November, 1942), 125-148.

BRUCE, WILLIAM CABELL: *John Randolph of Roanoke 1773-1833,* two volumes (New York, N.Y., 1922).

BUELL, AUGUSTUS C.: *History of Andrew Jackson,* two volumes (New York, N.Y., 1904).

BUTTRE, LILLIAN D.: "Thomas Hart Benton," in *American Portrait Gallery* New York, N.Y., 1877).

CABLE, JOHN RAY: *The Bank of the State of Missouri* (New York, N.Y., 1923).

CARROLL, EBER M.: "Politics During the Administration of John Quincy Adams," *South Atlantic Quarterly,* XXIII (April, 1924), 141-154.

CATTERALL, RALPH C. H.: *The Second Bank of the United States* (Chicago, Ill., 1903).

CHITWOOD, OLIVER PERRY: *John Tyler: Champion of the Old South* (New York, N.Y., 1939).

CLARK, VICTOR S.: "The Influence of Manufactures Upon Political Sentiment in the United States from 1820 to 1860," *American Historical Review,* XXII (October, 1916), 58-64.

CLEAVES, FREEMAN: *Old Tippecanoe: William Henry Harrison and His Times* (New York, N.Y., 1939).

COLE, ARTHUR C.: *The Whig Party in the South* (Washington, D.C., 1913).

COTTERILL, R. S.: "The National Railroad Convention in St. Louis, 1849," *Missouri Historical Review,* XII (July, 1918), 203-215.

DIDIER, EUGENE L.: "Thomas H. Benton as a Lawyer," *Green Bag,* XVIII (November, 1906), 585-587.

DORFMAN, JOSEPH: "The Jackson Wage-Earner Thesis," *American Historical Review,* LIV (January, 1949), 296-306.

DORSEY, DOROTHY B.: "The Panic of 1819 in Missouri," and "The Panic and Depression of 1837-1843 in Missouri," *Missouri Historical Review,* XXIX (January, 1935), 79-91; XXX (January, 1936), 132-161.

EHRHARDT, GEORGE: "Expelled from North Carolina University on Theft Charge, Boy Becomes U. S. Senator," *News and Observer,* February 5, 1928 (Raleigh, N.C.).

EHRLICH, WALTER: *History of the Dred Scott Case Through the Decision of 1857,* Unpublished Doctoral Dissertation, Washington University (St. Louis, Mo., 1950).

ERIKSSON, ERIK McKINLEY: "The Federal Civil Service Under President Jackson," *Mississippi Valley Historical Review,* XIII (March, 1927), 517-540.

FITZSIMONS, MATTHEW A.: "Calhoun's Bid for the Presidency, 1841-1844," *Mississippi Valley Historical Review,* XXXVIII (June, 1951), 39-60.

FOOTE, HENRY STUART: *The Bench and Bar of the South and Southwest* (St. Louis, Mo., 1876).

FUESS, CLAUDE MOORE: *Daniel Webster,* two volumes (Boston, Mass., 1930).

GARRAGHAN, THE REV. GILBERT J., S.J.: "The Beginnings of St. Louis University," *St. Louis Catholic Historical Review,* I (January, 1919), 85-102.

GARRATY, JOHN A.: *Silas Wright* (New York, N.Y., 1949).

GENTRY, WILLIAM RICHARD JR.: *"Full Justice": the Story of Richard Gentry and His Missouri Volunteers in the Seminole War* (St. Louis, Mo., 1937).

GOODRICH, CARTER: and DAVISON, SOL: "The Wage Earner in the Westward Movement," *Political Science Quarterly,* L (June, 1935), 161-185; LI (March, 1936), 61-146.

GRESHAM, L. PAUL: "Hugh Lawson White as a Tennessee Politician and Banker, 1807-1827," *East Tennessee Historical Society Publications,* 18 (1946), 25-46.

HAILPERIN, HERMAN: "Pro-Jackson Sentiment in Pennsylvania, 1820-1828," *Pennsylvania Magazine of History and Biography,* L (July, 1926), 193-240.

HAMILTON, HOLMAN: *Zachary Taylor: Soldier of the Republic* (Indianapolis, 1941), and *Zachary Taylor: Soldier in the White House* (Indianapolis, Ind., 1951).

HAMILTON, W. J.: "The Relief Movement in Missouri, 1820-1822," *Missouri Historical Review*, XXII (October, 1927), 51-92.

HAMMOND, BRAY: "Jackson, Biddle, and the Bank of the United States," and "Banking in the Early West: Monopoly, Prohibition, and Laissez-Faire," *Journal of Economic History*, VII (May, 1947), 1-23, and VIII (May, 1948), 1-25.

HENDERSON, ARCHIBALD: *North Carolina, the Old North State and the New*, two volumes (Chicago, Ill., 1941).

HIBBARD, BENJAMIN HORACE: *A History of the Public Land Policies* (New York, N.Y., 1924).

HOPKINS, VINCENT C., S.J.: *Dred Scott's Case* (New York, N.Y., 1951).

JAMES, MARQUIS: *The Life of Andrew Jackson*, one-volume edition (Garden City, L.I., 1940).

JORDAN, H. D.: "A Politician of Expansion: Robert J. Walker," *Mississippi Valley Historical Review*, XIX (1932-1933), 362-381.

KELSAY, ISABEL THOMPSON: "The Presidential Campaign of 1828," *East Tennessee Historical Society Publications*, 5 (1933), 67-80.

LAMB, JANIE P. B.: " 'Smithfield,' Home of the Prestons, in Montgomery County, Virginia," *Virginia Magazine of History and Biography*, XLVII (April, 1939), 109-125.

LEWIS, THOMAS R.: "Thomas H. Benton's Analysis of His Audience," *Quarterly Journal of Speech*, XXXV (December, 1949), 441-447.

LINN, ELIZABETH A., and SARGENT, NATHAN: *The Life and Public Services of Dr. Lewis F. Linn* (New York, N.Y., 1857).

LYNCH, DENIS TILDEN: *An Epoch and A Man: Martin Van Buren and His Times* (New York, N.Y., 1929).

MACCORMAC, EUGENE I.: *James K. Polk, a Political Biography* (Berkeley, Cal., 1922).

MCCANDLESS, PERRY G.: *Thomas H. Benton, His Source of Political Strength in Missouri from 1815 to 1838*, Unpublished Doctoral Dissertation, University of Missouri (Columbia, Mo., 1953).

MCCLURE, CLARENCE H.: *Opposition in Missouri to Thomas Hart Benton* (Warrensburg, Mo., 1926).

MCGRANE, REGINALD C.: *The Panic of 1837: Some Financial Problems of the Jacksonian Era* (Chicago, Ill., 1924).

MAGERS, ROY V.: "An Early Missouri Political Feud," *Missouri Historical Review*, XXIII (January, 1929), 261-269.

MEIGS, WILLIAM M.: *Life of Thomas Hart Benton* (Philadelphia, Pa., 1904).

MERKEL, BENJAMIN: *Anti-Slavery in Missouri, 1819-1865*, Unpublished Doctoral Dissertation, Washington University (St. Louis, Mo., 1939); and "The Slavery Issue and the Political Decline of Thomas Hart Benton, 1846-1856," *Missouri Historical Review*, XXXVIII (July, 1944), 388-407.

MIMS, EDWIN, JR.: *The Majority of the People* (New York, N.Y., 1941).
MISSOURI HISTORICAL SOCIETY: "Earliest Picture of St. Louis," in *Glimpses of the Past*, VIII (1941), 7-9.
MORTON, OREN F.: *A History of Rockbridge County, Virginia* (Staunton, Va., 1920).

NASH, FRANCIS: *Hillsboro: Colonial and Revolutionary* (Raleigh, N.C., 1903).
NATIONAL PARK SERVICE, Department of Interior: *Map of the Site of the Jefferson National Expansion Memorial, Showing the Location of Various Historic Sites and Buildings* (Typescript and Map, St. Louis, 1939).
NEVINS, ALLAN: *Frémont: Pathmarker of the West* (New York, N.Y., 1939).
————: *Ordeal of the Union*, two volumes (New York, N.Y., 1947).
NICHOLS, ROY FRANKLIN: *Franklin Pierce: Young Hickory of the Granite Hills*, (Philadelphia, Pa., 1931).
NOLEN, RUSSELL M.: "The Labor Movement in St. Louis Prior to the Civil War," *Missouri Historical Review*, XXXIV (October, 1939), 18-37.

OSTROGORSKI, M.: *Democracy and the Organization of Political Parties*, two volumes (New York, N.Y., 1902).

PARKS, JOSEPH HOWARD: *Felix Grundy: Champion of Democracy* (Louisiana State University Press, La., 1940).
PARTON, JAMES: *Life of Andrew Jackson*, three volumes (New York, N.Y., 1860).
PESSEN, EDWARD: "Did Labor Support Jackson? the Boston Story"; and "Note on 'Did Labor Support Jackson?'" *Political Science Quarterly*, LXIV (June, 1949), 262-274, and LXV (September, 1950), 441-444.
PIERCE, EDWARD L.: *Memoir and Letters of Charles Sumner*, four volumes (Boston, Mass., 1894).
POAGE, GEORGE RAWLINGS: *Henry Clay and the Whig Party* (Chapel Hill, N.C., 1936).
PORTER, KENNETH WIGGINS: *John Jacob Astor, Business Man*, two volumes (Cambridge, Mass., 1931).
PORTER, SARAH HARVEY: *The Life and Times of Anne Royall* (Cedar Rapids, Iowa, 1909).

RAMSEY, J. G. M.: *The Annals of Tennessee to the End of the Eighteenth Century* (Philadelphia, Pa., 1853).
RAY, P. O.: "The Retirement of Thomas H. Benton from the Senate and Its Significance," *Missouri Historical Review*, II (October, 1907, January, 1908), 1-14, 97-111.
RAYBACK, JOSEPH G.: "The American Workingman and the Antislavery Crusade," *Journal of Economic History*, III (November, 1943), 152-163.
REZNECK, SAMUEL: "The Depression of 1819-1822," and "The Social His-

tory of an American Depression, 1837-1843," *American Historical Review*, XXXIX (October, 1933), 28-47, and XL (July, 1935), 662-687.

RIEGEL, ROBERT E.: *Young America* (Norman, Okla., 1949).

ROBERTSON, JAMES R.: "A Pioneer Captain of Industry in Oregon," *Quarterly of the Oregon Historical Society*, IV (June, 1903), 150-167.

ROGERS, JOSEPH M.: *Thomas Hart Benton* (Philadelphia, Pa., 1905).

ROOSEVELT, THEODORE: *Thomas H. Benton*, American Statesman Series (Boston, Mass., and New York, N.Y., 1899).

RYLE, WALTER H.: "Slavery and Party Realignment in Missouri in the State Election of 1856," *Missouri Historical Review*, XXXIX (April, 1945), 320-332.

SCHARF, J. THOMAS: *History of St. Louis City and County*, two volumes (Philadelphia, Pa., 1883).

SCHLESINGER, ARTHUR M., JR.: *The Age of Jackson* (Boston, Mass., 1945).

SCHURZ, CARL: *Life of Henry Clay*, two volumes (Boston, Mass., 1888).

"SENATOR BENTON'S EGOTISM," *Missouri Historical Review*, XXXI (July, 1937), 489-490.

SHOEMAKER, FLOYD C.: *Missouri's Struggle for Statehood, 1804-1821* (Jefferson City, Mo., 1916); and *Missouri and Missourians: Land of Contrasts and People of Achievements*, five volumes (Chicago, Ill., 1943).

SMITH, JUSTIN H.: *The Annexation of Texas* (New York, N.Y., 1941), and *War With Mexico*, two volumes (New York, N.Y., 1919).

SMITH, WILLIAM ERNEST: *The Francis Preston Blair Family in Politics*, two volumes (New York, N.Y., 1933).

SOULARD, AMADÉE: "The Bloody Island Cross Mark," *St. Louis Globe Democrat*, June 25, 1899.

SPENCER, IVOR D.: "William L. Marcy Goes Conservative," *Mississippi Valley Historical Review*, XXXI (September, 1944), 205-224.

SQUIRES, MONAS N.: "A New View of the Election of Barton and Benton to the United States Senate in 1820," *Missouri Historical Review*, XXVII (October, 1932), 28-45.

STANWOOD, EDWARD: *A History of the Presidency from 1788 to 1897* (Boston, Mass., 1898).

STENBERG, RICHARD R.: "The Jefferson Birthday Dinner, 1830," *Journal of Southern History*, IV (August, 1938), 334-345.

————: "Some Political Aspects of the Dred Scott Case," *Mississippi Valley Historical Review*, XIX (March, 1933), 571-577.

STEPHENS, F. F.: "Banking and Finance in Missouri in the Thirties," *Proceedings of the Mississippi Valley Historical Association*, X (1920), 122-134.

STEWART, A. J. D., Ed.: *The History of the Bench and Bar of Missouri, with Reminiscences of the Prominent Lawyers of the Past . . .* (St. Louis, Mo., 1898).

SULLIVAN, WILLIAM A.: "Did Labor Support Andrew Jackson?" *Political Science Quarterly*, LXII (December, 1947), 569-580.

SWISHER, CARL BRENT: *Roger B. Taney* (New York, N.Y., 1935).

THOMAS, JAMES W., and WILLIAMS, T. J. C.: "Francis Thomas," in *History of Allegany County, Maryland*, two volumes (n.p., 1923).

THURMAN, FRANCIS LEE: "Red House, Rockbridge County, Virginia," *Virginia Magazine of History and Biography*, XLVII (July, 1939), 244-247.

TILLEY, NANNIE MAY: "Political Disturbances in Colonial Granville County," *North Carolina Historical Review*, XVIII (October, 1941), 339-359.

TOCQUEVILLE, ALEXIS DE: *Democracy in America*, Phillips Bradley, Ed., Vintage Books Edition, two volumes (New York, N.Y., 1954).

TURNER, FREDERICK JACKSON: *Rise of the New West, 1819-1829*, (New York, N.Y., 1906), and *The United States, 1830-1850, the Nation and Its Sections* (New York, N.Y., 1935).

VAN DEUSEN, GLYNDON G.: *The Life of Henry Clay*, (Boston, Mass., 1937).

VAN RAVENSWAAY, CHARLES: "The Tragedy of David Barton," *Bulletin of the Missouri Historical Society*, VII (October, 1950), 35-56.

VIOLETTE, EUGENE MORROW: "Spanish Land Claims in Missouri," *Washington University Studies, Humanistic Series*, VIII (St. Louis, Mo., 1921).

WADDELL, JAMES R.: "Thomas Hart Benton," *International Review*, XII (May, 1882), 480-496.

WALTERS, RAYMOND, JR.: "The Origins of the Second Bank of the United States," *Journal of Political Economy*, LIII (June, 1945), 115-131.

Washington and Lee University Historical Papers: I-V (Baltimore, Md., 1890-1895).

WELLINGTON, RAYNOR G.: "The Tariff and Public Lands from 1828 to 1833," American Historical Association, Annual Report for 1911 (Washington, D.C., 1913), 179-185.

WILTSE, CHARLES M.: *John C. Calhoun: Nationalist, 1782-1828; John C. Calhoun: Nullifier, 1829-1839;* and *John C. Calhoun: Sectionalist, 1840-1850* (Indianapolis, Ind., 1944, 1949, 1951).

WOODFORD, FRANK B.: *Lewis Cass: The Last Jeffersonian* (New Brunswick, N.J., 1950).

YOUNG, SARAH S.: *Genealogical Narrative of the Hart Family in the United States* (Memphis, Tenn., 1882).

Index